Advances in Computational Intelligence and its Applications

About the Conference

It is with great pleasure and enthusiasm that we welcome you to the International Conference on Advances in Computational Intelligence and its Applications (ICACIA-2023). In the ever-evolving landscape of technology, computational intelligence stands as a cornerstone, shaping the future of diverse fields and industries. This conference serves as a nexus for researchers, academicians, and industry experts to converge, exchange ideas, and explore the latest advancements in the realm of computational intelligence.

ICACIA-2023 emerges as a platform for fostering interdisciplinary collaboration and knowledge dissemination, bringing together experts from the fields of artificial intelligence, machine learning, data science, and related areas. The conference aims to unravel the latest breakthroughs, methodologies, and applications that leverage computational intelligence to address complex challenges and fuel innovation.

As we navigate the intricacies of the digital age, computational intelligence plays a pivotal role in transforming data into meaningful insights, automating decision-making processes, and enhancing the efficiency of various systems. ICACIA-2023 is designed to be a crucible for these transformative ideas, where researchers and practitioners can share their experiences, methodologies, and results, thereby contributing to the collective growth of the computational intelligence community.

The conference agenda encompasses a diverse array of topics, ranging from foundational theories to practical applications across various domains. Through keynote presentations, paper sessions, and interactive discussions, ICACIA-2023 endeavors to facilitate a rich intellectual exchange that transcends traditional boundaries.

We extend our sincere appreciation to the organizing committee, program chairs, and reviewers for their unwavering commitment and dedication in ensuring the quality and relevance of the conference. Special gratitude is also extended to the authors whose valuable contributions have enriched the conference program.

We hope that ICACIA-2023 serves as a catalyst for new collaborations, inspires innovative research directions, and provides a fertile ground for the growth of computational intelligence. Together, let us embark on a journey of exploration and discovery, shaping the future of computational intelligence and its transformative applications.

Welcome to ICACIA-2023!

Advances in Computational Intelligence and its Applications

Navigating the Frontiers of AI, Machine Learning, and Data Science in the Digital Era

International Conference on Advances in Computational Intelligence
and its Applications (ICACIA-2023)

Edited by
Dr. Sheikh Fahad Ahmad
Dr. Shadab Siddiqui
Dr. Rajib Debnath
Dr. Kakali Das
Dr. Figlu Mohanty
Dr. Sumit Hazra

CRC Press
Taylor & Francis Group
Boca Raton London New York

CRC Press is an imprint of the
Taylor & Francis Group, an **informa** business

First edition published 2024
by CRC Press
4 Park Square, Milton Park, Abingdon, Oxon, OX14 4RN

and by CRC Press
2385 NW Executive Center Drive, Suite 320, Boca Raton FL 33431

CRC Press is an imprint of Informa UK Limited

British Library Cataloguing-in-Publication Data
A catalogue record for this book is available from the British Library

ISBN: 978-1-032-78612-4 (pbk)
ISBN: 978-1-003-48868-2 (ebk)

DOI: 10.1201/9781003488682

Typeset in Times LT Std
by Aditiinfosystems
Printed and bound in India

Advances in Computational Intelligence and its Applications (ICACIA-2023) – Dr. Sheikh Fahad Ahmad et al. (eds)
© 2024 Taylor & Francis Group, London, ISBN 978-1-032-78612-4

Contents

Advances in Computational Intelligence and its Applications (ICACIA-2023) – Dr. Sheikh Fahad Ahmad et al. (eds)
© 2024 Taylor & Francis Group, London, ISBN 978-1-032-78612-4

List of Figures

Advances in Computational Intelligence and its Applications (ICACIA-2023) – Dr. Sheikh Fahad Ahmad et al. (eds)
© 2024 Taylor & Francis Group, London, ISBN 978-1-032-78612-4

List of Tables

Advances in Computational Intelligence and its Applications (ICACIA-2023) – Dr. Sheikh Fahad Ahmad et al. (eds)
© 2024 Taylor & Francis Group, London, ISBN 978-1-032-78612-4

About the Editors

Dr. Sheikh Fahad Ahmad received his Ph.D. degree in Computer Science and Engineering from Babu Banarasi Das University Lucknow, U.P. in the year 2020. He received his M. Tech and B.Tech in Computer Science & Engineering in the year 2013 and 2008 respectively from Integral University, Lucknow, U.P. India. He is currently working as an Associate Professor in the Department of Computer Science and Engineering, Koneru Lakshmaiah Education Foundation, Hyderabad. He has more than 13 years of teaching experience in reputed Universities. He is also the member of Editorial Boards, Program and Technical Committees of many International Journals as well as he is in the advisory committees of many International Journals. Currently he is supervising six candidates in PhD Program and he has around 30 International Publications and 3 Patents. His research areas include Sound analysis, Pattern Recognition, Machine Learning, and Data Science.

Dr. Shadab Siddiqui received his Ph.D. degree in Computer Science and Engineering from Babu Banarasi Das University Lucknow, U.P. in the year 2021. He received his M. Tech (Computer Science) 2014 Integral University, Lucknow, U.P. India. He is currently working as an Assistant Professor in Department of Computer Science and Engineering, Koneru Lakshmaiah Education Foundation, Hyderabad. Total Experience of 10 Years in Academics. His research interest includes Cloud Computing, Artificial Intelligence and Wireless Sensor Networks. Also, reviewer in various International Journals and Conferences.

Dr. Rajib Debnath received his Bachelor of Technology (Information Technology) degree from Bengal Institute of Technology and Management, Shantiniketan, West Bengal, India, in 2010. Masters in Technology (Computer Science and Engineering) and Doctor of Philosophy (Ph.D) under Computer Science and Engineering Department of Tripura University (A Central University), Suryamaninagar, Tripura, India in 2012 and 2022 respectively. Currently working as an Assistant Professor in Koneru Lakshmaiah Education Foundation (Deemed to be University) Hyderabad, India. His topics of interest are related to the field of Computer Vision, Object Detection, Machine Learning, Image and Video Processing etc.

Dr. Kakali Das received her Bachelor of Engineering (Computer Science and Engineering) degree from Tripura Institute of Technology, Tripura, India in 2012, Masters in Technology (Computer Science and Engineering) degree from Tripura University (A Central University), Suryamaninagar, Tripura, India in 2014, and Doctor of Philosophy (Ph.D) degree under Computer Science and Engineering Department of Tripura University (A Central University), Suryamaninagar, Tripura, India. Currently working as an Assistant Professor in Koneru Lakshmaiah Education Foundation (Deemed to be University) Hyderabad, India. Her topics of interest are related to the field of Medical Image Processing, Infrared Imaging, Machine Learning, Computer Vision etc.

Dr. Figlu Mohanty received her Ph.D. degree in Computer Science and Engineering from IIIT Bhubaneswar, Odisha in the year 2020. She received her M.Tech degree in Computer Science and Information Security from KIIT University, Bhubaneswar, Odisha, India. She is currently working as an Associate Professor in Department of Computer Science and Engineering, Koneru Lakshmaiah Education Foundation, Hyderabad. Her research interest includes Medical Imaging, Pattern Recognition, Machine Learning, Image Processing, and Data Science.

Dr. Sumit Hazra received his Ph.D. degree in Computer Science and Engineering from NIT Rourkela, Odisha in the year 2023. He received his M. Tech degree in Computer Science and Engineering from VIT University, Vellore, India. He is currently working as an Assistant Professor in Department of Computer Science and Engineering at Koneru Lakshmaiah Education Foundation, Hyderabad. His research interests include Gait Analysis, Cognitive Science, Artificial Intelligence, Pattern Recognition, Computer Vision and so on.

Advances in Computational Intelligence and its Applications (ICACIA-2023) – Dr. Sheikh Fahad Ahmad et al. (eds)
© 2024 Taylor & Francis Group, London, ISBN 978-1-032-78612-4

Preface

It is with great pleasure and enthusiasm that we welcome you to the International Conference on Advances in Computational Intelligence and its Applications (ICACIA-2023). In the ever-evolving landscape of technology, computational intelligence stands as a cornerstone, shaping the future of diverse fields and industries. This conference serves as a nexus for researchers, academicians, and industry experts to converge, exchange ideas, and explore the latest advancements in the realm of computational intelligence.

ICACIA-2023 emerges as a platform for fostering interdisciplinary collaboration and knowledge dissemination, bringing together experts from the fields of artificial intelligence, machine learning, data science, and related areas. The conference aims to unravel the latest breakthroughs, methodologies, and applications that leverage computational intelligence to address complex challenges and fuel innovation.

As we navigate the intricacies of the digital age, computational intelligence plays a pivotal role in transforming data into meaningful insights, automating decision-making processes, and enhancing the efficiency of various systems. ICACIA-2023 is designed to be a crucible for these transformative ideas, where researchers and practitioners can share their experiences, methodologies, and results, thereby contributing to the collective growth of the computational intelligence community.

The conference agenda encompasses a diverse array of topics, ranging from foundational theories to practical applications across various domains. Through keynote presentations, paper sessions, and interactive discussions, ICACIA-2023 endeavors to facilitate a rich intellectual exchange that transcends traditional boundaries.

We extend our sincere appreciation to the organizing committee, program chairs, and reviewers for their unwavering commitment and dedication in ensuring the quality and relevance of the conference. Special gratitude is also extended to the authors whose valuable contributions have enriched the conference program.

We hope that ICACIA-2023 serves as a catalyst for new collaborations, inspires innovative research directions, and provides a fertile ground for the growth of computational intelligence. Together, let us embark on a journey of exploration and discovery, shaping the future of computational intelligence and its transformative applications.

Welcome to ICACIA-2023!

Acknowledgements

We wholeheartedly extend our profound gratitude to the chief patrons, **K. Satyanarayana**, President of KL University, **K. L. Havish**, Vice-President, and **K. Raja Hareen**, Vice-President, for their unwavering support and indispensable guidance that shaped every facet of this conference.

Our deepest appreciation resonates with **Prof. A. Ramakrishna**, the esteemed Principal, and **Dr. Arpita Gupta**, Head of the Department, whose consistent encouragement and invaluable insights have been pivotal in crafting the essence of this conference.

A special acknowledgment is reserved for **Prof. L. Koteswara Rao**, whose unflagging support and expert guidance contributed immeasurably to the depth and quality of this work.

We extend our heartfelt gratitude to our esteemed keynote speakers: **Dr. Anup Nandy**, Assistant Professor at NIT Rourkela; **Dr. Haider Raza**, Senior Lecturer at the University of Essex, U.K.; and **Dr. Rafal Scher**er from Czestochowa University of Technology, Poland. Their illuminating perspectives and profound contributions have enriched and shaped the contours of this conference.

Our sincere thanks go to the esteemed session chairs: **Dr. P. C. Srinivas Rao, Dr. Halima Sadia, Dr. Mohd. Haleem, Dr. Shahid Hussain, Dr. Mrinal Kanti Bhowmik, Dr. Suvendu Rup**, and all the reviewers. Their insightful moderation and guidance during discussions have significantly elevated the calibre and impact of this conference.

We extend our heartfelt appreciation to our esteemed faculty colleagues, non-teaching staff members, and the dedicated student organizing committee whose unwavering support has been a cornerstone of this endeavour.

Their collective expertise and collaborative efforts have been instrumental in shaping every facet of this conference, and we are profoundly grateful for their unwavering support and invaluable contributions.

Advances in Computational Intelligence and its Applications (ICACIA-2023) – Dr. Sheikh Fahad Ahmad et al. (eds)
© 2024 Taylor & Francis Group, London, ISBN 978-1-032-78612-4

A Non Conventional Pre-Processing Method for Financial Risk Analysis Data

1

Vikram Kalvala[1]

Research Scholar, Department of Computer Science & Engineering,
Koneru Lakshmaiah Education Foundation, Hyderabad

Sheikh Fahad Ahmad[2]

Associate Professor, Department of Computer Science & Engineering,
Koneru Lakshmaiah Education Foundation, Hyderabad

ABSTRACT—In both business and personal financial planning, financial risk analysis is critical. Due to the rising volatility of the financial trend, many inverters employ risk prediction to create investment portfolios. Because financial trends are significantly influenced by both technical and non-technical factors, predicting risk is challenging. As a result, computer-aided risk prediction approaches are becoming increasingly common. Machine learning algorithms have recently improved risk prediction techniques. These algorithms divide the modelling procedure into two steps: training and forecasting. However, existing machine learning risk prediction algorithms have many flaws. This is because data is obtained from many sources, sometimes with the assistance of people, and then trimmed until it is insufficient and inaccurate. Data preparation is required in financial prediction frameworks or techniques. Henceforth, this work proposes a novel strategy for identification and replacement of missing values, using mean analysis method outliers, with a max – mean analysis method and noisy data treatment using the formatting and transformation method. This work demonstrates nearly 91% accuracy during the missing value treatment nearly 92% accuracy during the outlier analysis and nearly 80% accuracy during the noisy data treatment process. The overall time for this proposed method is 0.9012 ns.

KEYWORDS—Domain specific, Threshold, Missing value, Outlier treatment, Noisy data treatment, Data cleaning

1. Introduction

There is a huge quantity of investor sentiment, i.e., subjective appraisal and debate of financial instruments, in online financial textual information. It would be tremendously helpful if there was a way to automate the sentiment analysis of such a massive volume of online financial writings. An NLP-based technique to noise reduction from raw online financial texts is presented in this paper, as well as an improved format for extracting features from the data. In order to decrease the amount of noise in online informal text, we propose to use a six-step NLP processing pipeline that includes a newly built syntactic and semantic combined negation handling technique [1]. Each system implementation includes a new sentiment categorization system with three levels of classification. Tests reveal that the pre-processing technique developed by the researchers beats alternative approaches. A comparison is made between the combined negation handling method and three other approaches to negation handling.

Many software issues may be traced back to configuration errors. It's been shown in previous research that a software system's configuration problem may result in significant financial losses. To discover, diagnose, and remedy configuration issues has attracted a variety of research projects. A method for determining whether a defect is a configuration issue might save developers

[1]vikram.kalvala@gmail.com, [2]er.fahad@gmail.com

DOI: 10.1201/9781003488682-1

time in the debugging process. Configuration bug reports prediction is the technical term for this issue. To fix this issue, For the purpose of training an information gain multinomial using naive Bayes produces the best results [2].

A Bankruptcy Prediction Computational Model (BPCM model) is investigated in this paper, which uses a combination of semantic methodologies and machine learning analytic techniques to store, structure, and pre-process raw financial data in order to evaluate a company's bankruptcy level [3]. It's not uncommon for financial data to be intertwined, disparate, and susceptible to duplication. The primary objective of Data pre-processing strategies that use ontologies are the focus of this study.

2. Related Work

After setting the context of the research in the previous section of this work, in this section the parallel and recent research outcomes are analysed. An enterprise financial crisis early warning system based on BP neural networks is proposed in this study to address the issue of poor accuracy in the conventional financial crisis early warning system. To successfully handle financial crisis data, the system's hardware consists principally of the pre-processing module for early warning information and power circuit modules, as well as the financial crisis early warning module. The financial data is properly trained using a BP neural network [4]. There is no significant difference in experimental results between the designed and traditional early warning systems for financial crises, indicating that both systems are capable of accurately identifying companies' financial status and of providing technical assistance to help businesses thrive through times of financial crisis.

Data mining has become a crucial method for uncovering patterns and information buried in datasets. One of the most important aspects of a successful Data Mining model preparation is the pre-processing of the data. A microfinance institution's default clientele may be predicted using data mining techniques, and this research examines the impact of data pre-processing on the actual dataset used in the analysis. As a result, a variety of data pre-processing methods have been explored and tested on the dataset. The Credit Scoring model makes use of two types of Data Mining categorization algorithms: the Generalized Linear Model and the Decision Tree. The conclusion is that a well-prepared and pre-processed set of data makes the Credit Scoring Model far more accurate and efficient [5].

Big data applications in a variety of disciplines are centred on data mining. Getting started with data pre-processing is an important first step. The explosion of educational data and the use of databases has made the data on underprivileged kids more useful. Data on low-income students is collected via a student financial assistance management system, however this system is plagued by issues such as missing values, redundant characteristics, and noise. This paper presented a unique pre-processing approach called DPBP to address this issue. Preparing the data, defining characteristics, combining characteristics, and removing missing numbers are the four processes of DPBP. First, the dataset is prepared by extracting data. A feature selection technique is then used to narrow the range of possible characteristics. The feature decomposition sets are then obtained in the third step, which conducts feature combination. In the end, this approach came up with the most accurate and complete dataset. This work's suggested strategy considerably enhances data quality and stability, as shown by a series of studies [6].

When it comes to streamed data, machine learning methods are notoriously difficult to implement since they need the careful interaction of many technologies. For this reason, financial specialists need to be able to apply Complex Event Processing (CEP) and Machine Learning (ML) technologies via simple and easy-to-use interactive interfaces. CEP engines are used as a pre-processing function in this work's open architecture to train and forecast machine learning models. This method is shown in a few cases involving the processing of data streams from the financial markets [7].

There has been much research on the issue of class imbalance during the last two decades. Those working in the field of statistics have lately discovered that the uneven distribution issue extends outside the realm of classification tasks as well. Among these newly explored tasks, regression issues are among the most difficult to solve because of the problem of domain imbalances. A bias toward the target variable's values that are underrepresented in the available data occurs in an unbalanced regression. Approaches to pre-processing this data were discussed. These strategies alter the training set such that the learner is forced to concentrate on the rarest of the rare situations. For unbalanced regression tasks, as far as this study is aware, there has been no investigation into how data inherent properties affect performance. Using pre-processing approaches for unbalanced regression issues, this paper investigates the effects that particular data properties may have on the findings. Data features that may be relevant in regression issues are defined in this study in order to attain this purpose. then go ahead and do this task This research relies on a custom-built database for this purpose. According to this study, all features analysed have a distinct behaviour that is connected to the degree of data characteristics available, and the learning method used [8].

Content contributed by users has grown rapidly since the read-write network was restructured, resulting in a vast amount of unusable data. As online unstructured data has been analysed in the past several years, sentiment analysis and opinion mining have become the most popular tools for identifying user sentiment. This study will employ pre-processing processes such as normalisation and stop words removal approach [9], which are necessary in any sentiment analysis system due to the unstructured processed data.

"Identifying the stock-price dynamism signals in financial time series data is a basic and fascinating task when given a financial time series dataset. The pre-processing stage of understanding the marketing signal patterns in financial computing is frequently the representation of time series in line segments, which is a vital job. Based on segmented linear regression models, this study focuses on the optimization challenge of determining the best possible segmentation of such time series. Accordingly, this study defines the issue of Multi-Segment Linear Regression (MSLR) of determining the appropriate segmentation of an economic time series, designated as the MSLR problem, in order to minimise the global square error of segmented linear regression. A two-level dynamic programming (DP) method known as OMSLR is presented in this paper, which demonstrates the algorithm's optimality. It is possible to find the finest trading techniques in financial markets using OMSLR's two-level DP architecture. $O(n^2)$ time is required because of the large number of non-overlapping segments needed to cover all the data points [10] in the time series."

"In-Depth strengthening for financial trading, learning approaches have given effective tools for training successful agents [11]. Although the noisy and non-stationary nature of financial data typically necessitates input normalisation algorithms that are carefully built and tweaked, otherwise the agents are unable to consistently conduct successful trades. Deep adaptive input normalisation has been proposed in this study to circumvent this constraint and train DRL agents for financial trading without any further pre-processing. Adaptive normalisation, i.e., normalising the input observations after (implicitly) identifying the distribution that generated them, is the goal of the proposed technique, which comprises of two trainable neural layers. To better capture price patterns, the suggested technique uses group-based normalisation rather than a single-input normalisation, which provides for more accuracy. Experiments on two tough FOREX currency pairs have shown that a simple implementation and use of the suggested technique may lead to huge gains over current normalising methods."

3. Mathematical Foundation

After the detailed analysis of the parallel research outcomes in the previous section of this work, in this section, the proposed mathematical models are analyzed.

Assuming that the transaction data set, T, is a time dependent collection of data points T_t, then the relation between each element can be formulated as,

$$T[] \to \sum_{t=1}^{n} T_t \tag{1}$$

Here, each and every data point, T_t, is an attribute set comprising of multiple elements or attributes represented as a_i. Thus, this can be formulated as,

$$T_t \to |a_1, a_2, a_3, \dots a_n|_t \tag{2}$$

During the rigorous processing of the dataset, if any of the attribute values are found to be null or, Φ then that specific entity can be identified to contain missing value. This can be represented as,

$$\text{If } a_i(t) \Leftrightarrow \Phi \tag{3}$$

Further, the data cleaning process recommends that the missing value must be replaced with the identified and calculated value from the domain of the missing value attribute. The traditional method for missing value replacement depends on the mean value calculation or moving average value calculation, $a_i(t)_M$, of the attribute domain. This can be formulated as,

$$a_i(t)_M = \text{Mean}(a_i(1\dots t)) \tag{4}$$

Or for moving average,

$$a_i(t)_M = \frac{\displaystyle\sum_{t=1}^{n} a_i(t)}{\Delta \displaystyle\sum_{i=1}^{t} a_i(t)} \tag{5}$$

Finally, the $a_i(t)_M$ must be replaced with the missing value.

Assuming that the transaction data set, T, is a time dependent collection of data points T_t, then the relation between each element can be formulated as,

$$T[] \rightarrow \sum_{t=1}^{n} T_t \qquad (6)$$

Here, each and every data point, T_t, is an attribute set comprising of multiple elements or attributes represented as a_i. Thus, this can be formulated as,

$$T_t \rightarrow |a_1, a_2, a_3, \dots a_n|_t \qquad (7)$$

The life cycle term or the LCT and the outlier detector, θ, are interrelated and can be defied as following,

$$\int_{t=1}^{n} LCT[t] \cap \theta = 1 \qquad (8)$$

Here, the LCT can be defined and represented as,

$$LCT[t] = \frac{a_i[1 \dots t]}{\Delta t} \qquad (9)$$

Further, if any attribute instance is detected to contain the outlier as defined following, then the instance must be replaced with the outlier factor, θ.

$$\text{If } a_i(t) > \theta \qquad (10)$$

Finally, θ must be replaced with the outlier or noisy data instances.

Further, based on the proposed mathematical models, in this section of the work, in the next section, the proposed algorithm is furnished.

4. Proposed Methology

After the detailed analysis on the proposed mathematical model for this work, in this section the workable algorithm is furnished.

Algorithm: Domain Specific Threshold Based Data Cleaning (**DSTBDC**) Algorithm
Input: Dataset as D[]
Output: Pre-Processed Dataset as DS[]

Process:
 Step - 1. Initiate the Process by loading the Dataset as D[]
 Step - 2. For each attribute in D[] as D[i]
      a. Calculate the mean as M = sum(D[i])/Count(D[i])
      b. Calculate the upper limit as UL = Max(D[i])
      c. Calculate the lower limit as LL = Min(D[i])
      d. Identify the missing value as X[] = Call MVT(D[i])
      e. X[] = M
      f. Identify the outlier as Y[] = Call OT(D[i],UL, LL)
      g. Y[] = M
      h. Identify the Noisy Data as Z[] = Call NDT(D[i])
      i. Replace X[], Y[] and Z[] into DS[]
 Step - 3. End For
 Step - 4. Return DS[]

Sub Module - I: Missing Value Treatment
 MVT(D[i]) {
      For each value in the domain D[i] as D[i][j]
          If D[i][j] = null
              X[] = D[i][j];
      End For
      Return X[]
      }

```
Sub Module - II: Outlier Treatment
OT(D[i],UL,LL)  {
                For each value in the domain D[i] as D[i][j]
                        If D[i][j] > (UL - UL*5%) or D[i][j] < (LL - LL*5%)
                                Y[] = D[i][j];
                End For
                Return Y[]
                }
Sub Module - III: Noisy Data Treatment
NDT(D[i])  {
                For each value in the domain D[i] as D[i][j]
                        If D[i][j] Not Equals to Format(D[i])
                                Z[] = D[i][j]
                End For
                Transform(Z[]) = Format(D[i])
                Return Z[]
                }
```

The benefit of this proposed algorithm is discussed in detailed in the previous section of this work.

Further, in the next section of this work, the obtained results are discussed.

5. Results and Discussion

The obtained results are highly satisfactory and are furnished in this section of the work.

Firstly, the dataset description is furnished here [Table 1.1].

Table 1.1   Dataset analysis [12]

Properties	Values
"Number of Rows"	500
"Number of Attributes"	11
"Number of Unique Values"	309
"Number of Outliers"	947
"Number of Missing Values"	764
"Number of Noisy Data"	816

It is natural to realize that, the testing sample data [12] is highly diversified and can be utilized for any testing for pre-processing. Further, the initial dataset characteristics are visualized graphically here [Fig. 1.1].

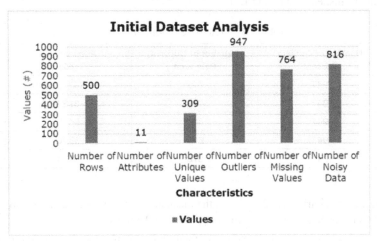

Fig. 1.1   Dataset analysis

Further, this algorithm is tested on a total of 5 iterations on the same dataset to identify the benefits over machine learning of this proposed algorithm. Firstly, the missing value analysis results are furnished here [Table 1.2].

Table 1.2 Missing value treatment analysis

Trial Seq (#)	Number of Missing Values Present	Number of Missing Values Removed	Accuracy (%) (A1)	Time (ns) (T1)
1	764	693	90.71	0.253
2	764	697	91.23	0.548
3	764	644	84.29	0.405
4	764	495	64.79	0.351
5	764	476	62.30	0.282

Source: Author

The best accuracy achieved during the trials is 91.23% and the mean accuracy achieved is the 78.66%. The same is visualized graphically here [Fig. 1.2] with a mean time to complete the process as 0.368 ns.

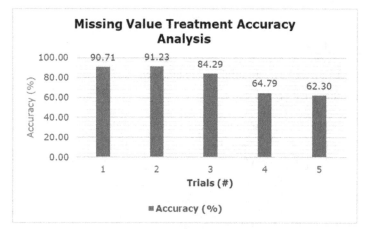

Fig. 1.2 Missing value treatment

Source: Author

After the missing values are replaced using the first part of the algorith, in the second phase, the outlier analysis treatments are carried out and the results are furnished here [Table 1.3].

Table 1.3 Outlier treatment analysis

Trial Seq (#)	Number of Outliers Present	Number of Outliers Removed	Accuracy (%) (A2)	Time (ns) (T2)
1	947	831	87.75	0.164
2	947	775	81.84	0.502
3	947	860	90.81	0.294
4	947	840	88.70	0.310
5	947	878	92.71	0.418

Source: Author

The best accuracy achieved during the trials is 92.71% and the mean accuracy achieved is the 88.36%. The same is visualized graphically here [Fig. 1.3] with a mean time to complete the process as 0.338 ns.

After the outliers are replaced with the mean value in the second phase of the algorithm, in the third phase, the noisy data treatments are carried out and the results are furnsihed here [Table 1.4].

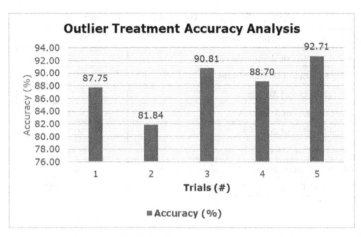

Fig. 1.3 Outlier treatment

Source: Author

Table 1.4 Noisy data treatment analysis

Trial Seq (#)	Number of Noisy Data Present	Number of Noisy Data Removed	Accuracy (%) (A3)	Time (ns) (T3)
1	816	597	73.16	0.506
2	816	646	79.17	0.354
3	816	582	71.32	0.493
4	816	618	75.74	0.506
5	816	656	80.39	0.366

Source: Author

The best accuracy achieved during the trials is 80.39% and the mean accuracy achieved is the 75.96%. The same is visualized graphically here [Fig. 1.4] with a mean time to complete the process as 0.445 ns.

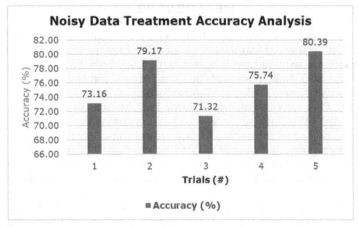

Fig. 1.4 Noisy Data Treatment

Source: Author

Further, the summary of the total process is furnished here [Table 1.5].

Henceforth, it is natural to realize that, the proposed work demonstrates tremendous outcomes with signficantly less time complexity.

Further in the next section of this work, the final research conclusions are furnsihed.

Table 1.5 Data Pre-processing summary

Characteristics	Values
Initial Number of Unique Values	309
Final Number of Unique Values	309
Initial Number of Attributes	11
Final Number of Attributes	11
Initial Number of Rows	500
Final Number of Rows	500
Mean Best Accuracy (%) (A1 + A2 + A3)/3	88.11
Total Best Time (ns) T1 + T2 + T3	0.9012

Source: Author

6. Conclusion

Financial risk analysis is crucial in the planning of both commercial and personal financial affairs. A growing number of inverters are using risk prediction to construct investment portfolios because of the increasing volatility of the financial trend. Because financial trends are substantially impacted by both technical and non-technical elements, it is difficult to foresee risk in the financial markets. Computer-aided risk prediction methodologies are becoming more popular because of this trend. Machine learning algorithms have lately made significant advances in the field of risk prediction. Both the training and forecasting phases of the modelling technique are divided into two stages by these algorithms. Existing machine learning risk prediction systems, on the other hand, have a number of shortcomings. This is due to the fact that data is gathered from several sources, sometimes with the aid of individuals, and then pruned until it is inadequate and erroneous. In order to use financial prediction frameworks or approaches, data preparation is necessary. As a result, this paper provides a unique approach for the detection and replacement of missing values using the mean analysis technique, the treatment of outliers using the max – mean analysis method, and the treatment of noisy data using the formatting and transformation method. During the missing value treatment phase, this study displays nearly 91 percent accuracy, nearly 92 percent accuracy during the outlier analysis process, and nearly 80 percent accuracy during the noisy data treatment process, among other results. It takes 0.9012 ns to complete the suggested procedure in its entirety.

REFERENCES

1. G. Eason, B. Noble, and I. N. Sneddon, "On certain integrals of F. Sun, A. Belatreche, S. Coleman, T. M. McGinnity and Y. Li, "Pre-processing online financial text for sentiment classification: A natural language processing approach," 2014 IEEE Conference on Computational Intelligence for Financial Engineering & Economics (CIFEr), London, UK, 2014, pp. 122–129.

2. X. Xia, D. Lo, W. Qiu, X. Wang and B. Zhou, "Automated Configuration Bug Report Prediction Using Text Mining," 2014 IEEE 38th Annual Computer Software and Applications Conference, Vasteras, Sweden, 2014, pp. 107–116.

3. N. Yerashenia, A. Bolotov, D. Chan and G. Pierantoni, "Semantic Data Pre-Processing for Machine Learning Based Bankruptcy Prediction Computational Model," 2020 IEEE 22nd Conference on Business Informatics (CBI), Antwerp, Belgium, 2020, pp. 66–75.

4. N. Li, "Design of enterprise financial crisis early warning system based on BP neural network," 2021 13th International Conference on Measuring Technology and Mechatronics Automation (ICMTMA), Beihai, China, 2021, pp. 33–36.

5. J. Nalić and A. Švraka, "Importance of data pre-processing in credit scoring models based on data mining approaches," 2018 41st International Convention on Information and Communication Technology, Electronics and Microelectronics (MIPRO), Opatija, Croatia, 2018, pp. 1046–1051.

6. H. Huang, B. Wei, J. Dai and W. Ke, "Data Preprocessing Method For The Analysis Of Incomplete Data On Students In Poverty," 2020 16th International Conference on Computational Intelligence and Security (CIS), Guangxi, China, 2020, pp. 248–252.

7. N. N. Tri Luong, Z. Milosevic, A. Berry and F. Rabhi, "A Visual Interactive Analytics Interface for Complex Event Processing and Machine Learning Processing of Financial Market Data," 2020 24th International Conference Information Visualisation (IV), Melbourne, Australia, 2020, pp. 189–194.

8. P. Branco and L. Torgo, "A Study on the Impact of Data Characteristics in Imbalanced Regression Tasks," 2019 IEEE International Conference on Data Science and Advanced Analytics (DSAA), Washington, DC, USA, 2019, pp. 193–202.

9. V. Kansal and R. Kumar, "A Hybrid Approach for Financial Sentiment Analysis Using Artificial Intelligence and Cuckoo Search," 2019 5th International Conference on Advanced Computing & Communication Systems (ICACCS), Coimbatore, India, 2019, pp. 523–528.

10. C. -J. Wu, W. -S. Zeng and J. -M. Ho, "Optimal Segmented Linear Regression for Financial Time Series Segmentation," 2021 International Conference on Data Mining Workshops (ICDMW), Auckland, New Zealand, 2021, pp. 623–630.

11. A. Nalmpantis, N. Passalis, A. Tsantekidis and A. Tefas, "Improving Deep Reinforcement Learning for Financial Trading Using Deep Adaptive Group-Based Normalization," 2021 IEEE 31st International Workshop on Machine Learning for Signal Processing (MLSP), Gold Coast, Australia, 2021, pp. 1–6.

12. Dua, D. and Graff, C. (2019). UCI Machine Learning Repository [http://archive.ics.uci.edu/ml]. Irvine, CA: University of California, School of Information and Computer Science.

Advances in Computational Intelligence and its Applications (ICACIA-2023) – Dr. Sheikh Fahad Ahmad et al. (eds)
© 2024 Taylor & Francis Group, London, ISBN 978-1-032-78612-4

An Analytical Study of Sentimental Analysis During COVID-19 Pandemic

2

Patlolla Mani Chandana[1], Sura Mythri[2]
Student, Koneru Lakshmaiah Education Foundation, Hyderabad

Sheikh Fahad Ahmad[3]
Associate Professor, Department of Computer Science & Engineering,
Koneru Lakshmaiah Education Foundation, Hyderabad

Shadab Siddiqui[4]
Assistant Professor, Department of Computer Science & Engineering,
Koneru Lakshmaiah Education Foundation, Hyderabad

ABSTRACT—Discovering information about undiscovered phenomena is fascinating. Similar to feelings, opinions, sentiments, and emotions. All of the terms mentioned above are related to sentimental analysis. The method of removing views or sentiments from data through analysis. Different methods exist, but they all center on sentiment extraction. But none of the methods produces precise findings. When summarizing the content of an online product review, sentiment analysis classifies a body of text as having either a favourable or negative impression. It is possible to perform sentiment analysis by counting the words from an emotional terms dictionary, by fitting conventional. Subjectivity includes objective and subjective, polarity includes negative, positive, and neutral, and emotions are used to elicit the author's feelings includes angry, happy, surprised, sad, jealous, and mixed. The theoretical underpinnings and application examples of sentiment analysis in libraries are thus covered in this paper. Our lives have been profoundly altered by COVID-19. The world we once knew has changed, and now we live in a new environment that is always changing reorganization, which has permanently changed how we interact with one another and live. When it comes to informing, disseminating, and directing the flow of information in society, risk communication is crucial in this context. Regarding the effect, readiness, response, and mitigation by governments, health organizations, non-governmental organizations (NGO), mass media, and stakeholders, COVID-19 has presented a significant pandemic risk management issue. In this manuscript we have listed out the sentiment analysis that will help us to interpret the real time data on Twitter, which shows the impact of COVID-19 in day to day lives of humans. Also, state-wise analysis in India is done to recognize the sentiments of people during COVID-19.

KEYWORDS—Sentimental analysis, Natural-language-processing (NLP), Lexicon-based methods, Term frequency inverse document frequency (TF-IDF), Bag of words (BOW), Artificial neural networks (ANN), Support vector machines (SVM)

1. Introduction

When conducting in-depth research or making daily decisions, we regularly seek the advice of others. We peruse political message boards, peruse appliance evaluations, and seek out restaurant suggestions when deciding which politician to back. Today, you may use the Internet to explore the opinions of millions of people on a range of subjects, such as the most recent

[1]chandanapatil2021@gmail.com, [2]mythrisura@gmail.com, [3]er.fahad@gmail.com, [4]cseshadabsiddiqui@gmail.com.

DOI: 10.1201/9781003488682-2

political theories and technological advancements. To determine the sentiment and categorize words into positive, negative, and neutral categories, businesses now use natural language processing, statistical analysis, and text analysis. The most successful businesses recognize the value of comprehending the thoughts and feelings of their clients, including what they are saying, what they mean, and how they are saying it.

2. Literature Review

Huang et al, 2020, suggested about Covid-19. A brand-new coronavirus is the infectious disease known as Coronavirus Disease (COVID-19). In December 2019 in Wuhan, China, the first reports of what would eventually be called the Corona Virus were made. The first cities to experience the disease's impacts were Wuhan and a few other South East Asian cities. The virus was found to be human-to-human transmissible on January 20, 2020, in Guangdong, China, after two medical professionals were accused. In addition, the US and South Korea reported the first cases. On January 30, 2020, Italy became the first nation in Europe to reveal incidents. In January, incidents were also reported from Germany, Finland, and Italy. As of May 10th, the COVID-19 epidemic in Somaliland has led to several establishments to close, causing a sudden halt in business throughout the majority of industry sectors.

A few of the pressing issues that retailers and brands face include the supply chain, the workforce, cash flow, consumer demand, sales, and marketing (Donthu & Gustafsson, 2020). The COVID-19 is likely to result in the collapse of several well-known businesses in a variety of sectors as consumers stay at home and economies contract (McKee & Tucker, 2020). In addition to its effects on public health, corona-virus illness significant economic shock was brought on by 2019. Approximately 25% of small businesses had temporarily closed their doors just a few weeks after the pandemic began, and COVID-19 was mostly to blame for all of these closures. Business proprietors have horrified by issues facing their companies, such as irregular business operations, labour practices, and financial limitations that may apply to companies with uncertain futures.

Since this impact not just the economy but everyone in society, but also business and consumer behaviour has undergone substantial changes. The number of company owners in the majority of important industries decreased significantly, with agriculture being the lone exception. The number of company owners in the sectors of construction, dining, lodging, and transportation all fell dramatically as a result of COVID-19. 2020 reports that the crisis has already changed into a shock to the economy and labour market, affecting demand as well as supply, consumption, and investment (ILO & OECD, 2020). Global economic activity has been hampered by the COVID-19 epidemic. The virus has harmed governments' financial capabilities in addition to affecting workers and businesses. The number of new corona-virus cases in India increased by 66 in a single day, reaching its highest level since March 26, 2020, while the number of active cases decreased to 1,755, according to data released by the Health ministry of the union on Tuesday. The total number of Covid-19 cases was 4.46 crore (4,46,82,785). The data updated at 8 am showed that there have been 5,30,740 fatalities. A weekly positivity rate of 0.07% was reported, while the daily positivity rate was 0.05 %. The national COVID-19 recovery rate has increased to 98.81%, and active cases now make up 0.1% of all infections. The case fatality rate has been recorded at 1.19%, and 4,41,50,289 people have recovered from the sickness. The primary technical method for examining user attitudes and opinions is sentiment analysis. The primary machine learning algorithms, deep learning models, and lexicon-based methodologies used in sentiment analysis today. The approaches based on a sentiment lexicon require to create or gather the lexicon first, then analyse the sentence's syntax or directly match the sentiment word, and then calculate the sentence's sentiment score by adding up the sentiment weights of the individual sentiment words. Despite being straightforward, this approach produces subpar outcomes. In spite of the fact that existing research techniques have begun to use the strategy of combining many models for sentimental analysis jobs, the present approaches are still mostly dependent on input phrases and a limited number of models also use emotional dictionaries as input.

3. What Is Sentimental Analysis?

This kind of text analysis employs both machine learning and Natural Language Processing. Other titles for sentiment analysis include opinion mining & emotion AI.

Analyzing the positive or negative sentiment of the reader in literature that contains their positive, neutral, or negative feelings is known as sentiment analysis. Businesses frequently utilise it to analyse customers, assess brand reputation, and detect sentiment in social data.

3.1 Sentimental Analysis Processing

"Machine learning and lexicon-based methods" are the two primary methodologies utilized in sentiment analysis. The machine learning technique called supervised learning since it trains the text classifier using information that has been labelled by humans.

The lexicon-based approach breaks a sentence up into words and uses a dictionary to rank the semantic orientation of each word. The results are then obtained by adding the scores collectively. For instance, you establish two lists of polarized terms, namely, positive and negative words (such as good, best, ugly, etc.). It is necessary to count both "positive+" and "negative-" phrases in the text. When there are more positive words than negative words in the text, and vice versa, the text will reflect a good emotion.

Fig. 2.1 Importance of sentimental analysis

Source: https://gottsteinpsy532.wordpress.com/unit-7-emotion-and-the-internet/

Due to the increased freedom with which individuals now communicate their thoughts and feelings, "sentiment analysis" is easily becoming into a vital method for tracking & understanding sentiments. Consumer sentiment analysis is important since it indicates what customers like and dislike about you, your business, your products and services, your brand, etc.

SENTIMENTAL ANALYSIS TECHNIQUES

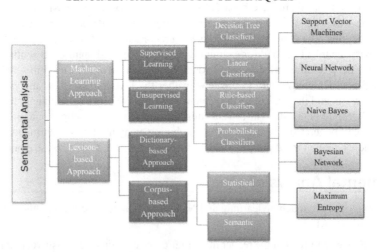

Fig. 2.2 Represents the sentimental analysis techniques

Source: https://devopedia.org/sentiment-analysis

One technique for examining customer feedback is sentiment analysis, which can help you identify the key issues and complaints people have with your product or service.

Sentiment analysis, often known as "opinion mining," can help you ascertain whether the public's opinion of any aspect of your business has changed. This tool for sentiment analysis assists in rating the opinions and provides you.

3.2 Methodology Used

Lexicon-based opinion mining use text mining techniques to analyse data and is the most straightforward method for analyzing text format data. This approach makes use of R libraries like tidy-text, tidy-verse, word-cloud, etc. We have access to a variety of predefined functions through these libraries, which we can immediately use on unstructured data. The sentences are sorted into positive and negative emotions, such as anger, fear, happiness, and trust, using this process. One of the two main techniques for conducting sentiment analysis is the use of a lexicon. It is necessary to deduce the sentiment from the semantic orientation of the text's words or sentences. In the lexicon-based method, a text message is represented as a collection of words. On the basis of this illustration of the message, sentiment values are then established.

3.3 Proposed Work

Sentiment analysis is a difficult machine learning task. It is not easy to analyse the sentiment of text because when people communicate their ideas or beliefs on a certain topic in writing, they may use sarcasm, have conflicting opinions, or utilize everyday language to do so. Methods for Machine learning & Natural Language Processing can be employed for sentimental analysis. Term Frequency Inverse Document Frequency & Bag-Of-Words are two helpful NLP techniques. Machine learning algorithms include Artificial Neural Networks (ANN), Support Vector Machines (SVM), Logistic-Regression, Random Forests, Deep Learning Techniques like LSTM and bi-directional LSTM, etc. Using NLP methods, the text data is pre-processed and vectorized. The data is used to train a variety of Machine-Learning models using a variety of methodologies after being vectorized. Deep learning analysis COVID-19 sentiments as new cases arise.

Understanding how individuals react to traumatic situations like natural disasters, politically unstable circumstances, and terrorism is of interest to social scientists and psychologists. Due to the profound social upheavals and unemployment brought on by the COVID-19 outbreak, many psychological problems, including depression, have surfaced. Deep learning language models have demonstrated promise when used with data from social networks like Twitter for sentiment analysis. A terrible occurrence, the worldwide coronavirus disease pandemic of 2019 (COVID-19) increased unemployment, psychological issues, and depression. It had a substantial impact on the global economy. Computational modelling and machine learning have played a significant role in research across a wide range of fields as a result of the abrupt changes in society, the economy, and transportation. The new coronavirus SARS-CoV-2 rapidly caused the COVID-19 epidemic in China in December 2019. According to worldwide health organization, more than 100,000 confirmed deaths and tens of millions of verified cases have been reported worldwide. On all social media sites, the spyware is generating headlines. As a result, these social media platforms are exposed to and presenting a variety of viewpoints, thoughts, and emotions throughout various outbreak-related events. Using big data, computer scientists and academics can analyse public sentiment about current events, particularly those related to the epidemic. Thus, an analysis of these emotions will yield fascinating results. Previous research in this field, to the best of our knowledge, has concentrated on a single infectious illness type.

3.4 Framework for Sentiment Analysis on Twitter for COVID-19

The approach to sentiment analysis using deep learning involves four key steps: tweet extraction, model building and training with LSTM, BD-LSTM, and BERT, and prediction using chosen COVID-19 data. In Table 2.1's framework diagram, the key elements are highlighted. We can see that the framework employs multi-label classification, which can produce a number of different results simultaneously, e.g., a tweet may be humorous and upbeat. The most effective model is selected for Indian tweets about COVID-19 prediction after training. Multi-label categorization is included in the framework, which allows multiple findings to be presented at once, allowing a tweet to be both uplifting and humorous.

Table 2.1 Overall sentiments with polarity in Maharashtra

Month	Positive	Neutral	Negative
Nov, 2019	0	0	2
Dec, 2019	0	0	0
Jan, 2020	20-25	25-30	15-20
Feb, 2020	155-160	140-145	115-120
Mar, 2020	>9000	>5500	>3800
Apr, 2020	>11500	>7000	>4000
May, 2020	>1150	>600	>500

Source : https://ieeexplore.ieee.org/abstract/document/9358301

Table 2.1 demonstrates that up until December, nobody in Maharashtra knew anything about the Corona Situation. In January and February, they began to get somewhat concerned about Corona, although they largely remained indifferent.

People began to understand the effects of the viral sickness in March, and this is reflected in the rise in the number of tweets. People began to understand the effects of the viral sickness in March, and this is reflected in the rise in the number of tweets.

4. Results Analysis

The words "corona" and "COVID" were used more than 50,000 times between November 2019 and May 2020, according to Fig. 3.3. There were fewer than 6000 uses of the phrases don, day, country, and government. Corona, COVID, 19, covid19, virus, India, people, amp, lockdown, and fight were the top 10 most often used words.

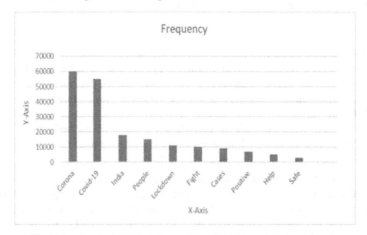

Fig. 2.3 Analysis of Tweet reactions in different states of India

Source: https://ieeexplore.ieee.org/abstract/document/9358301

Figure 3.4 displays the total number of tweets sent from all Indian states. Between December 2019 and May 2020, Madhya Pradesh had 44,252 more tweets than any other state in India. The state of Jammu and Kashmir came in second with 31,769 tweets. Third-placed Madhya Pradesh had 18,577 tweets. Rajasthan ranked fourth with 13,732 tweets between December and May 2019. There was only one tweet from Mizoram during this time.

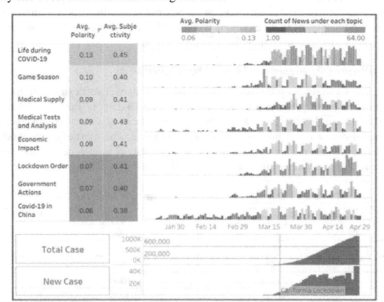

Fig. 2.4 Depicts that the Twitter-sentiment-analysis during Covid-19

Source: https://towardsdatascience.com/twitter-sentiment-analysis-based-on-news-topics-during-covid-19-c3d738005b55 Prior to March, there were very few topics, such as COVID-19, that were reported in corona virus-related news.

Following the release of COVID-19, especially for topics like medical tests, the amount of pertinent news pieces began to rise. One interesting conclusion was that the execution of the lockdown order, starting in mid-March, coincided with the peak of the majority of news stories during COVID-19. The news the life of COVID-19 participants is unquestionably the most unbiased and positive in terms of emotion, followed by the topics Game Season, Medical Supply, and Medical Tests and Analysis. Contrarily, COVID-19 garnered the most unfavourable and subjective criticism.

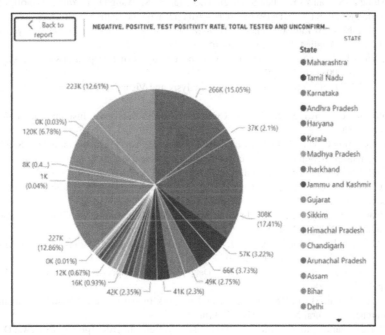

Fig. 2.5 Depicts that the number of negative cases; positive cases, test positivity rate, and total number of people tested, and unconfirmed cases in india during Covid-19.

Source: Google Image

5. Conclusion

By this we want to conclude that the Sentiment analysis is crucial since it aids in determining people's emotional and attitude states. There are numerous ways for people to communicate their positive or negative emotions. This paper helps us to know more about the Sentimental analysis. According to the analysis in this paper, people in India tended to communicate their ideas in a positive manner. The author has searched for the problem statement and collected all the information regarding the research. The members in team collected the graphs and related data from different resources and completed abstract along with the references

REFERENCES

1. Tiwari A, Gupta R, Chandra R. Delhi air quality prediction using LSTM deep learning models with a focus on COVID-19 lockdown. arXiv preprint arXiv:210210551. 2021.
2. Khan, R., Siddiqui, S., & Rastogi, A. (2021). Crime Detection Using Sentiment Analysis. ADCAIJ: Advances in Distributed Computing and Artificial Intelligence Journal, 10(3), 281–291. https://doi.org/10.14201/ADCAIJ2021103281291
3. A. D. J. A. a. S. Dubey, Twitter Sentiment Analysis during COVID19 Outbreak, 2020
4. Alamoodi, A., Zaidan, B., Zaidan, A., Albahri, O., Mohammed, K., Malik, R., & Hameed, H. (2020). Sentiment analysis and its applications in fighting COVID-19 and infectious diseases: A systematic review. Expert Systems with Applications, 114155. - PMC - PubMed
5. Caitlin Doogan, Wray Buntine, Henry Linger, and Samantha Brunt. 2020. Public perceptions and attitudes toward COVID-19 non-pharmaceutical interventions across six countries: a topic modelling analysis of twitter data. Journal of medical Internet research 22, 9 (2020), e21419

6. Cinelli M., Quattrociocchi W., Galeazzi A., Valensise C.M., Brugnoli E., Schmidt A.L., Zola P., Zollo F., Scala A. The COVID-19 social media infodemic. Sci. Rep. 2020

7. Chakraborty K., Bhatia S., Bhattacharyya S., Platos J., Bag R., Hassanien A.E. Sentiment Analysis of COVID-19 tweets by Deep Learning Classifiers—A study to show how popularity is affecting accuracy in social media. Appl. Soft Comput. 2020

8. C. Kaur and A. Sharma, "Twitter Sentiment Analysis on Coronavirus using Textblob", EasyChair, pp. 2516-2314, 2020

9. Guo Y.-R., Cao Q.-D., Hong Z.-S., Tan Y.-Y., Chen S.-D., Jin H.-J., Tan K.-S., Wang D.-Y., Yan Y. The origin, transmission and clinical therapies on coronavirus disease 2019 (COVID-19) outbreak—An update on the status

10. Kamaran H Manguri, Rebaz N Amin Ramadan and Pshko R Mo-hammed, "Twitter Sentiment Analysis on Worldwide COVID-19 Outbreaks", Kurdistan Journal of Applied Research, pp. 54-65, 2020

11. Kruspe A, Häberle M, Kuhn I, Zhu XX. Cross-language sentiment analysis of European Twitter messages during the COVID-19 pandemic. arXiv preprint arXiv:200812172. 2020

12. M. Ra, B. Ab and S. Kc, COVID-19 Outbreak: Tweet based Analysis and Visualization towards the Influence of Coronavirus in the World, 2020

13. Samuel J., Ali G., Rahman M., Esawi E., Samuel Y. COVID-19 Public Sentiment Insights and Machine Learning for Tweets Classification. Information. 2020

14. Twitter Sentiment Analysis during Covid-19 Outbreak in Nepal Pokharel Bishwo Prakash Available at SSRN 3624719, 2020

15. V. S. P. R. Guntaka, A. K. Gupta and S. Somisetty, Twitter sentiment analysis and visualization - In Proceedings: 16th Annual Symposium on Graduate Research and Scholarly Projects, Wichita, KS:Wichita State University, pp. 31, 2020

16. W.H.O. (2020, 04 17). Q&A on coronaviruses (COVID-19). Retrieved from World Health Organization: https://www.who.int/emergencies/diseases/novel-coronavirus

17. Yang Q, Alamro H, Albaradei S, Salhi A, Lv X, Ma C, et al. SenWave: Monitoring the Global Sentiments under the COVID-19 Pandemic. arXiv preprint arXiv:200610842. 2020

18. Shinde GR, Kalamkar AB, Mahalle PN, Dey N, Chaki J, Hassanien AE. Forecasting models for coronavirus disease (COVID-19): a survey of the state-of-the-art. SN Computer Science. 2020

19. Do, H. H., Prasad, P. W. C., Maag, A., & Alsadoon, A. (2019). Deep learning for aspect-based sentiment analysis: A comparative review. Expert Systems with Applications, 118, 272–299

20. Chen, S., Peng, C., Cai, L., & Guo, L. (2018). A deep neural network model for target-based sentiment analysis. In: 2018 IEEE International Joint Conference on Neural Networks (IJCNN) (pp. 1–7)

21. Zhang L, Wang S, Liu B. Deep learning for sentiment analysis: A survey. Wiley Interdisciplinary Reviews: Data Mining and Knowledge Discovery. 2018

22. Math Alrefai, Hossam Faris, Ibrahim Aljarah—Sentiment analysis for Arabic language: A brief survey of approaches and techniques. 2018.

Advances in Computational Intelligence and its Applications (ICACIA-2023) – Dr. Sheikh Fahad Ahmad et al. (eds)
© 2024 Taylor & Francis Group, London, ISBN 978-1-032-78612-4

SQL Injection Attacks: Exploiting Vulnerabilities in Database Systems

3

D. Usha Sree[1], P. Harshitha Reddy[2],
G. Vineel Kumar Reddy[3], M. Sumanth[4]

Department of Computer Science Engineering, Hyderabad,
Telangana, KL University

ABSTRACT—This document is a deep description of SQL Injections Attacks and the prevention methods used to prevent the attacks. SQL injection attacks remain a persistent threat to database systems and continue to cause significant harm to organizations worldwide. A detailed study of the types of attacks and their prevention methods is presented in this paper.

KEYWORDS—Exploitation, Malicious, Critical, Injection, Attack

1. Introduction

The paper presents a detailed study of what an SQL Injection attack is. and how can we classify them along with their preventive measures for each attack in order to reduce the exploitations.

1.1 What exactly is a SQL Injection?

An SQL Injection, often known as (SQLi), is a sort of cyberattack in which malicious code is injected into the input fields of an application to alter the SQL statements that the underlying database executes. As a result, attackers can get around authentication safeguards and access private information without authorization, change or delete records, and even take over the entire system. One of the most common and harmful types of web application assaults, SQL injection attacks represent a serious threat to businesses of all sizes and in all sectors. It is crucial for businesses to comprehend how SQL injection attacks operate and how to stop them from compromising the security of their databases and sensitive data. We will talk about the typical exploitation methods employed in SQL injection attacks in this paper.

2. Assert by SQL Injection: Impacts

Attacks using SQL injection may be extremely harmful to a company. Companies have access to confidential consumer and corporate information, and SQL injection attacks frequently target such information. A malicious user's successful completion of a SQL injection attack can have a variety of effects:

- *Unapproved access:* Attackers may be able to obtain sensitive data, such as personally identifiable information (PII), financial data, and other private data, using SQL injection attacks.
- *Data theft:* Attackers can steal sensitive data by extracting it from the database by injecting malicious SQL code.

[1]ushadsree1@gmail.com, 2010030315@klh.edu.in; [2]harshithareddy1p@gmail.com, 2010030284@klh.edu.in;
[3]vineel4446@gmail.com, 2010030053@klh.edu.in; [4]manthrigaliasumanth@gmail.com, 2010030237@klh.edu.in

DOI: 10.1201/9781003488682-3

- *Data manipulation:* Attackers have the ability to change or remove database entries, which might result in erroneous data, system problems, and significant legal ramifications.
- *System compromise:* SQL injection attacks can also be used to take control of the underlying system, potentially giving attackers complete control over the affected organization's network.
- *Financial loss:* Data breaches resulting from SQL injection attacks can lead to significant financial losses due to fines, legal fees, and loss of customer trust.
- *Reputation damage:* Organizations that experience a data breach due to an SQL injection attack may suffer significant damage to their reputation and loss of trust from customers, investors, and partners.
- *Give a potential attacker control of your system:* If a database user has administrator rights, an attacker using malicious code can get access to the system. Create a database user with the fewest rights feasible to protect yourself against this type of vulnerability.
- *Giving an attacker full access to your system:* If you check user names and passwords using flimsy SQL statements, an attacker might access your system without being aware of a user's credentials. When an attacker has full access to your system, they can obtain sensitive data and manipulate it to do more harm.
- *Data integrity compromise:* By using SQL injection, attackers can modify or remove data from your system.

Overall, a SQL injection attack may have serious and pervasive impacts, hence it is crucial for companies to take proactive measures to stop these attacks from happening.

2.1 Exactly how do SQL Injection Attacks Happen?

The computer language SQL was developed primarily for handling data in relational data stream management systems. Users are able to execute several operations, including those for retrieving, modifying, and deleting records, using SQL queries. Sadly, hackers are also able to take advantage of this language by including dangerous code into strings that are submitted to a SQL server for execution. Particularly vulnerable to SQL injection attacks are online apps and web pages with user-input fields, such as forms that take free text. SQL injection attacks may be carried out in a variety of ways by malevolent individuals. The usual flow of a SQL injection attack is shown in the stages below:

- *Reconnaissance:* The attacker identifies a vulnerable web application that accepts user input and submits SQL queries to a database.
- *Exploitation:* The attacker tricks the web application into executing both the malicious and valid SQL code by injecting it into the input fields.
- *Bypassing authentication:* If the malicious code is successfully injected, the attacker can exploit it to get around security measures and access sensitive information, change or delete records, or even take over the system.
- *Data retrieval:* The attacker is able to access the database and obtain private information by injecting SQL code. They might, for instance, retrieve sensitive data like credit card numbers, usernames, and passwords using the "SELECT" command.
- *Modifying or deleting data:* If the attacker is able to modify or delete records in the database, they can cause significant damage to the system. For example, they can modify user account details or delete entire databases, resulting in data loss or system failure.
- *Covering their tracks:* To avoid detection, the attacker may attempt to cover their tracks by deleting or modifying log files, clearing their browser history, or using encryption to hide their activities.

In addition to causing considerable monetary losses, legal risks, and reputational harm, SQL injection attacks may be disastrous for businesses. As a result, it is crucial for businesses to put in place robust security measures and to routinely audit their online apps for vulnerabilities in order to find and fix them before they can be exploited.

2.2 SQLi Symptoms

A good SQL injection attack could go undetected. But occasionally there are visible indicators, such as:

- Receiving too many inquiries in a short period of time. You could observe a lot of emails coming through your website's contact form, for instance.
- Advertisements that reroute to dubious websites.
- Message problems and odd pop-ups.

Example

Let's look at a fictional web application that enables customers to browse merchandise in an online shop. After receiving user input, the search function creates a SQL query to locate related goods in a database. A possible SQL query might be something like this:

SELECT FROM products WHERE name LIKE 'search term'; (1)

The search term part of the query is a placeholder that will be replaced with the user's search term. For example, if a user searches for "t-shirt", the query will be executed as:

SELECT * FROM products WHERE name LIKE 't-shirt';

Now, let's say an attacker wants to exploit this web application using an SQL injection attack. They could input a specially crafted string that includes malicious SQL code into the search field, such as:

'OR1 = 1; (2)

The final SQL query would seem as follows:

SELECT * FROM products WHERE name LIKE' (3)

Due to the fact that the criterion 1=1 is always true, this SQL query would always return all entries from the products table. By using the - symbol to comment out the remaining portion of the query, all rows are returned regardless of the original criteria.

By injecting this code, the attacker can bypass the authentication mechanism of the web application and gain access to sensitive information. For example, they could execute the following query to retrieve all usernames and passwords from the database:

SELECT username, password FROM users; (4)

The attacker can access sensitive data by inserting this code, which gets beyond the web application's authentication system. They may run the following query, for instance, to get every username and password stored in the database:

The attacker could then use this information to log in as a legitimate user, modify records, or even delete entire databases.

SQL injection attacks can be even more complex than this, involving multiple steps and techniques to bypass security measures and execute malicious code. However, this example should give you a basic understanding of how an SQL injection attack can be performed and its potential impact on a web application and its data.

2.3 Practices to Protect the Database from SQL Injection

Here are several best practices that organizations can implement to protect their databases from SQL injection attacks:

- *Use structured query language or prepared statements:* To keep user input and SQL code distinct, use structured query language or prepared statements rather than appending input from the user with SQL statements. By doing this, harmful code won't be introduced into the SQL query.
- Always verify user input to make sure it adheres to the desired format and type of data. For instance, verify that an input is in fact a number before utilising it in a SQL query if a user is supposed to submit a numeric value.
- *Implement input sanitization:* Use input sanitization techniques such as data filtering and data normalization to remove or escape special characters and prevent them from being used as part of an SQL injection attack.
- *Use least privilege:* To limit the harm that an attacker may cause if they are successful in exploiting a SQL injection vulnerability, restrict the rights and access privileges of database users.
- *Update software frequently:* To stop vulnerabilities from being exploited, keep software, especially online applications and database management systems, updated with the most recent security patches and upgrades.
- Regularly analyse your database and online apps for vulnerabilities to find and repair before attackers may take advantage of them.

Organizations may greatly lower the risk of a SQL injection attack and safeguard their databases and sensitive data from hostile actors by putting these best practises into effect.

2.4 Different Kinds of SQL Injection Attacks

Depending on the attack's approach and the tactics employed by the attacker, SQL injection assaults can be divided into a number of distinct categories. The most typical forms of Sql injections are listed below:

- *In-band SQL injection:* In this form of attack, the attacker launches the attack and retrieves the results using the same communications system (in-band).
- *Error-based SQL injection:* In order to learn more about the database's structure, contents, or execution environment, the attacker takes use of error messages that the database generates.
- *Union-based SQL injection:* In order to combine the output of two or more SQL searches and retrieve data, the attacker can inject a UNION statement.
- *Blind SQL injection:* In this type of attack, the attacker does not receive the results of the attack directly. Instead, the attacker sends a payload that changes the behavior of the query, and the resulting behavior can be inferred by observing changes in the application's behavior or timing.
- *Boolean-based SQL injection:* The attacker exploits Boolean logic to infer the results of the attack.
- *Time-based SQL injection:* The attacker exploits the delay caused by certain SQL In this kind of attack, the perpetrator is not given immediate access to the attack's outcomes. Instead, the attacker delivers a payload that modifies the query's behaviour, and the outcome may be deduced by tracking changes in the application's timing or behaviour.statements to infer the results of the attack.
- *Out-of-band SQL injection:* In this type of attack, the attacker uses a different communication channel (out-of-band) to launch the attack and retrieve the results.
- *DNS-based SQL injection:* A DNS query trigger is injected by the attacker onto a server that is under their control. In order to obtain the attack's outcomes, the intruder can then watch the DNS traffic.
- *HTTP-based SQL injection:* A payload that the attacker injects causes HTTP requests to be sent to a website under their control. The assailant can then see the This type of attack launches the attack and retrieves the findings over a different communication channel (out-of-band). HTTP protocol to retrieve the attack's outcomes.
- *Compounded SQL injection:* In this type of attack, the attacker uses a combination of different SQL injection techniques to launch a successful attack. For example, the attacker may use in-band SQL injection to identify vulnerabilities and then use out-of-band SQL injection to retrieve data.

It's worth noting that these types of SQL injection attacks are not mutually exclusive, To carry out a successful attack, the attacker in this kind of attack combines several SQL injection techniques. For instance, the attacker might employ SQL injection while in-band to find security holes before using SQL injection while out-of-band to retrieve data.and an attacker may use a combination of these techniques to achieve their goals. By understanding the different types of SQL injection attacks, organizations can better protect their databases and web applications from these types of threats.

2.5 Attack Using in-band SQL Injection

In-band SQL injection is a type of SQL injection attack where the attacker uses the same communication channel (inband) to launch the attack and retrieve the results. In this type of attack, the attacker sends an SQL query to the application that includes malicious code. This code is executed by the database server, which may result in unintended consequences, such as disclosing sensitive data, modifying or deleting data, or even taking over the entire database server. There are two subtypes of in-band SQL injection attacks: error-based and union-based. In an error-based attack, the attacker exploits error messages generated by the database to extract information about the database structure, data, or execution environment. For example, the attacker may inject an invalid SQL query that generates an error message revealing sensitive information. In a union-based attack, the attacker injects a UNION statement to join the results of two or more SQL queries to extract An SQL injection attack known as a "in-band" attack occurs when the attacker launches the assault and then retrieves the results using the same communication channel. A SQL query containing malicious code is sent to the programme by the attacker in this kind of attack. This code is performed by the database server, which could have unforeseen results like leaking private information, changing or deleting files, or even taking over the database server as a whole. Error-based and union-based attacks are two sorts of in-band SQL injection attacks. An attack that is based on errors makes use of the database's error messages to gather details about the data, the execution environment, or the database's structure. Using an incorrect SQL query as an illustration, the attacker couldinformation.

In-band SQL injection attacks are common and dangerous because they allow the attacker to directly retrieve the results of the attack through the same channel used to launch the attack. To prevent in-band SQL injection attacks, it is important to implement proper input validation, use parameterized queries or prepared statements, and limit the access privileges of database users. Additionally, regular security audits can help identify and patch vulnerabilities before they can be exploited by attackers.

2.6 Unannounced SQL Injection Attack

Out-of-band In a SQL injection attack, the attacker launches the attack and retrieves the results using an additional communication channel (out-of-band). In this kind of attack, the attacker can send a SQL query containing malicious code to the programme. The database server executes this code, which could have unforeseen repercussions including leaking private information, editing or removing files, or even take over the database server as a whole.

Out-of-band SQL injection attacks differ from in-band SQL injection attacks in that the attacker uses a different channel, such like DNS or HTTP requests, to obtain the attack's results. As an illustration, in a DNS-based SQL injection attack, the attacker can inject a payload that causes DNS queries to be sent to a server that is under their control. Once the DNS traffic has been observed, the attacker can get the attack's outcomes. When an attacker uses HTTP-based SQL injection, they inject a payload that causes HTTP requests to be sent to a server they control. The intruder can then review the Http to get the attack's outcomes.

Since out-of-band SQL injection attacks do not rely on direct connection with the application or database server, they might be more challenging to identify and stop than in-band attacks. Use parameterized queries or prepared statements, restrict database user access privileges, and provide sufficient input validation to protect against out-of-band SQL injection attacks. Out-of-band assaults can also be detected and prevented with the aid of network traffic monitoring, firewall configuration, and the installation of intrusion detection systems.

2.7 Blind SQL Injection Attack

Blind SQL injection is a kind of SQL injection attack in which the perpetrator is unable to access the attack's outcomes directly. In this kind of attack, the attacker can send a SQL query containing malicious code to the programme. The database server executes this code, which could have unforeseen repercussions including leaking private information, editing or removing files, or even taking over the database server as a whole.

Blind Attacks do not, however, give the attacker immediate feedback regarding the effectiveness of the assault or the outcomes of the query, in contrast to in-band SQL injection attacks. Instead, to determine the outcome of the attack, the attacker must use indirect techniques, including detecting changes in the application's behaviour or timing..

Blind SQL injection attacks have two subtypes: time-based and Boolean-based. A boolean-based attack uses the application's responses to boolean requests to allow the attacker to deduce the attack's outcome. An attacker might, for instance, insert a SQL query that asks a true-or-false question to see if the programme reacts differently based on the response. A time-based assault takes use of the application's reaction time to deduce the attack's outcome. In order to determine whether a SQL query was successful, the attacker can, for instance, inject a query that, if it is successful, delays the result. In contrast to in-band attacks, blind SQL injection attacks might be more challenging to identify and stop. This is because they do not

2.8 How to Recognise and Stop a SQL Injection Attack

A successful SQL injection attack could expose critical information and undermine customer trust, which could result in significant harm. It is crucial to quickly identify this kind of attack because of this. Several methods exist for identifying and preventing SQL injection attacks. Companies can adhere to the following guidelines to avoid a SQL injection attack:

- Employees should receive preventative training. To understand how SQLiattacks occur and how they may be avoided in online applications, it is crucial that IT personnel, including DevOps, system administrators, and software developers, acquire the right security training.
- Never rely on user input. The possibility of an effective SQL injection grows with every piece of user input included in a SQL query. The easiest method to reduce this kind of danger is to surround user input with security protections.
- Utilize an allowlist as opposed to a blocklist. It is advised to validate and filter user input using an allowlist as oppose to a blocklist because hackers can frequently get around a blocklist. This is due to the fact that a blocklist contains a list of every application or executable that can be harmful to the network. As a result, everything else on the internet can function aside from the things on the block list. A security breach is definitely feasible before the list is changed since administrators are unable to keep up with the thousands of additional malware and virus samples that are developed every day and update blocklists with the latest attack varieties and zero-day vulnerabilities.
- Update your route, and make use of the most recent applications. Outdated software is one of the most frequent causes of SQL injection vulnerabilities. Older technology is unlikely to have SQLi security built in, and unpatched software is frequently simpler to manipulate. This also applies to programming languages. Older syntax and languages are more open to attack. Use PHP Data Objects, for instance, in place of legacy MySQL.

- Make use of proven preventative measures. Written from scratch query strings don't provide enough defence against SQL injection. Input validation, prepared statements, and parameterized queries are the best ways to secure web applications.
- Conduct routine security scans. Regular web application scanning identifies potential vulnerabilities and fixes them before they cause significant harm.
- *Input validation:* Proper input validation is the first line of defense against SQL injection attacks. Input validation ensures that the data entered into web forms, user input fields, or other user inputs is in the correct format and doesn't include any nefarious code.
- *Queries using parameters or prepared statements:* These strategies can assist guard against SQL injection attacks. By separating the Query language logic from of the input from the user data, these techniques stop malicious code from running.
- *Least privilege:* Limiting the access privileges of database users can help prevent SQL injection attacks. Only grant the minimum necessary privileges to each user or application to perform their required functions.
- Use web application routers: By inspecting incoming requests and preventing shady behaviour, a WAF can assist in detecting and preventing SQL injection attacks.
- *Monitor database activity:* Monitoring the database activity for unusual or suspicious behavior can help detect SQL injection attacks. This can be done using auditing tools, log files, or other monitoring mechanisms.
- Maintaining software applications up to date with the most recent security patches and upgrades is important. This assists in preventing the exploitation of known vulnerabilities.

Some database administrators think that by limiting the sort of statements that can be submitted to its arguments, a stored procedure statements can frequently help minimize the risk of SQL injection attacks. The fact that there are several workarounds and fascinating statements that may still be sent to stored processes means that not all attacks are prevented by this.

2.9 SQL Injection Attacks' Effects

A business may suffer significant losses as a result of a good SQL injection attack. This is due to the fact that a SQL injection attack may

- Expose private information. Attackers have the ability to retrieve data, which puts the SQL server's sensitive data at risk of exposure.
- Alter the integrity of the data. Attackers have the ability to change or remove data from your system.
- Compromise the privacy of users. Depending on the information kept on the SQL server, a breach could reveal private user data such addresses, telephone number, and credit card details.
- Give an attacker system admin rights. If a databases user has administrative rights, malicious code from the attacker can be used to enter the system.
- Give an attacker full control over your system. Without knowing a user's credentials, an attacker could access your system if you use shoddy SQL statements to verify usernames and passwords. An attacker can then access and manipulate sensitive information to cause mayhem.

An SQL injection attack can be costly not only financially but also in terms of lost consumer trust and reputational harm if private data like identities, address, telephone number, and credit card details are taken. Once lost, client trust can be very challenging to restore.

3. Information About SQL Injections

Since 1998, when cybersecurity expert and attacker Jeff Forristal first described SQL injection attacks, they have been a common occurrence. They didn't seem to attract much attention, though, until 2002.

The fact that SQL injections are listed among the top 10 threats to the security of web applications by the Open Web Application Security indicates that they are among the most common security attacks. The existence of automation systems for performing SQL injections has increased both the possibility of Sql injections exploits and the harm they can do. Since attackers had to manually execute these exploits in the past, the probability of a company being attacked with a Cross - site scripting was somewhat reduced.

As a result of a string of high-profile attacks on significant organisations, including TalkTalk, in which an outdated dataset was the primary cause of the breach, these attacks have now established themselves as one of the most widespread and consistently rated highest security known vulnerabilities in database software history.

Good SQL injection attacks provide attackers access to sensitive information, the ability to modify records, to execute database administration tasks, and the ability to restore database files.

Two sorts of application assaults that can destroy a company are SQL injections and bridge scripting. Learn about the five most common application security risks and how to avoid them.

3. Conclusion

The SQL injection attack is a serious and prevalent threat to the security of databases and web applications. It can cause significant damage to an organization, including data loss, financial loss, and damage to reputation. In this research, we have explored the different types of SQL injection attacks, the methods and techniques used by attackers to exploit vulnerabilities, and the best practices for preventing and detecting such attacks. Through our analysis, we have identified that Input validation and parameterized queries are among the best practises for avoiding SQL injection attacks., least privilege, web application firewalls, and monitoring database activity. Organizations may greatly decrease the risk of Sql injections and safeguard their crucial data by putting these best practises into effect.. Overall, SQL injection attacks remain a serious threat to database security, and it is essential for organizations to remain vigilant and proactive in their approach to prevention and detection. Organizations may guarantee the integrity and protection of their data by keeping abreast of the most recent security measures and adopting a proactive security approach.

REFERENCES

1. Halfond, W. G.,Viegas, J., Orso, A.[2006]' A classification of SQL injection attacks and countermeasures. In Proceedings of the 2006 international workshop on Software Engineering for secure systems (pp. 1–7). ACM.
2. Rahayu, S., Indrayana, I. (2019). Detection of SQL injection attacks in web applications using machine learning techniques. Journal of Information Security and Applications, 49, 102384.
3. Kaur, P., Bala, S. (2019). Prevention and detection of SQL injection attacks: A survey. Computer Science Review, 33, 19–46.
4. Lin, F., Chen, Y. F., Lin, C. C. (2017). A hybrid approach for detecting SQL injection attacks in web applications. Journal of Network and Computer Applications, 78, 66–76.
5. Panda, P., Patra, M. R. (2018). Analysis of different types of SQL injection attacks and prevention techniques. Journal of Network and Computer Applications, 108, 46–63.
6. Ahmad, F., Nazir, B., Ali, M. (2020). A novel algorithm for SQL injection attack detection using machine learning. IEEE Access, 8, 184782-184791. Anwar, M. W., Imran, M., Khan, S. U., Sharif, M. (2019). An enhanced technique for prevention and detection of SQL injection attacks. International Journal of Network Security. 21(4): 636–648

Advances in Computational Intelligence and its Applications (ICACIA-2023) – Dr. Sheikh Fahad Ahmad et al. (eds)
© 2024 Taylor & Francis Group, London, ISBN 978-1-032-78612-4

Energy Efficient Clock Synchronization Method in IoT Applications

4

Saijshree Srivastava[1]

Assistant Professor, Department of Computer Science and Engineering,
GLBITM Greater Noida

Abhishek Sharna[2], Surendra Singh Chauhan[3]

Assistant Professor, Department of Computer Engineering & Applications,
GLA University, Mathura

Smiley Gandhi[4]

Assistant Professor, Department of Computer Engineering, BBDITM

ABSTRACT—IoT signifies a decentralized and self-arranging framework. In this framework, there is no bondage on the mobility of sensor devices. The sensor nodes are generally placed at remote location. Due to this reason, these networks face a major issue of power consumption. With this strategy, access to these locations is made easier and the results are more accurate. IoT uses both established and new technology to be implemented inside the many sensor, networking, and robotics applications. IoT makes use of the most recent technology developments in a number of areas. With the use of these developments, various changes have been achieved in the delivery of commodities, services, and products. A world can be assumed here in which numerous thinks are interlinked using IP protocols. Such that the information can be sensed, transmitted and shared using the IoT technology. There is a regular collection, analysis and processing of data by the interconnected objects in such a manner that planning, management and decision making can be provided effectively. Thus, a network of physical objects results is creating an IoT. Not only the networks of computers generate this system but there are different sizes of devices that are interlinked and thus can communicate amongst each other such that the important information can be shared. To make sure that proper control and real time monitoring is being performed within the devices and the information gathered is being forwarded to the control and administration, stipulated protocols are provided in these systems. The elastic time technique is efficient to prolong the network service time. This work will make improvement in elastic timer method for clock synchronization using time lay technique. The proposed improvement leads to improve network throughput, reduce delay and packet loss.

KEYWORDS—Clock synchronization, Internet of things, Energy harvesting, Energy efficiency

1. Introduction

WSN is a fundamental part of IoT. The sensors' nodes are deployed within the network sense the environmental conditions and collected all the required information. Further, the multi-hop communication has been utilized in order to transfer collected data to sink node. The correlation made between the gathered data got from conveyed sensor hubs with the sink hub in the WSN organize [3]. For moving all the gathered detected information to the sink hub for which hand-off hubs have been utilized. As compared to the end devices, the more processing capability is present in these nodes.

---

[1]swatisrivastava817@gmail.com, [2]abhi8001@gmail.com, [3]surendrahitesh1983@gmail.com, [4]smilegandhi@gmail.com

DOI: 10.1201/9781003488682-4

The unnecessary information from its child nodes has been received by the relay node in case of the IoT applications based on periodic monitoring. In order to increase the network resource and node's power consumption, there is impact of crowding related sensed data together on it. Therefore, only the required data is forwarded by the relay nodes to the BS instead of presence of redundant values that minimizes the energy dissipation. There is enhancement in the utilization of resources for the transmission of data therefore named as the data aggregation. It is the technique by means of which data is gathered and integrated collected by the sensor nodes using aggregation function in the WSN.

Therefore, removal of data redundant transmission is the prime focus of data aggregation that leads to improve in the service time of network. The defined correlated data packets must be aggregated together in order to make efficient data aggregation. The processing of sensor node is shown how data is collected by it using routing packets throughout the network.

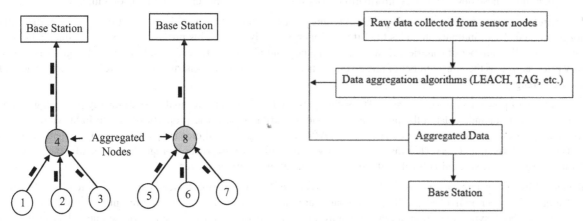

Fig. 4.1 Data models in the IoT without and with aggregation [2]   **Fig. 4.2** Data aggregation algorithm architecture [2]

The two models are shown in Fig. 4.2 in which one picture is with aggregation and other is without aggregation as shown above [2]. The data is gathered from the environment by the sensor nodes using periodic sensor nodes such as 1, 2, 3 and 5, 6, 7 in these models after which this sensed data is sent to higher ranking nodes 4 and 8. Therefore, these two nodes play the role of aggregators. These hubs total the information bundles assembled by the kids' hubs. Along these lines, in the non-information total model each of the three information bundles, for example, hubs 1, 2, 3 are gathered and sent by hub 4 to the base station. Be that as it may, on account of the subsequent model, the aggregator hub 8 transmitted just a single information bundle to the sink. Along these lines, there is a decrease in the quantity of information bundles before their conveyance to the sink utilizing the information total strategy in this system.

The architecture of data aggregation algorithm has shown in Fig. 4.2. A number of aggregation protocols, including LEACH, PEGASIS, TAG, and others, are utilised by the sensor node to deliver sensed data to the algorithm. Thereby, following the efficient path, the aggregated data is transferred to the sink. The data coming from different sensor nodes can be easily fused by in-network data aggregation. Therefore, in IoT applications, there are various aggregation functions that can be utilized for the processing. The aggregation function can be divided into further various parts given below:

(i) **Duplicate sensitive:** Due to correlation, multiple data packets have been received by the aggregated node. There is repetition of the same type of information multiple times at the time when aggregation takes place [18]. The duplicate sensitive function is the final result dependent on the counts of duplication. Therefore, the average value (Avg) is given by this function all the time it processes.

(ii) **Duplicate Insensitive:** The dependence on the ultimate outcomes of an aggregation task on a sole value is the reason it is called as a duplicate insensitive function. Therefore, the maximal or minimal value is given by the function is duplicate insensitive (Max, Min).

(iii) **Loss-less:** The preservation of original information after the data compression is the process followed in loss-less aggregation function. In this at the receiver side all the information is recovered from their aggregated value in an appropriate manner.

(iv) **Lossy:** The recovery of original information after integration is not possible in the lossy aggregation. Therefore, the original information is not preserved by compressed data.

The Internet of things in a broader way can be described as a network of Internet-linked vehicles, user devices and Smart phones. Generally, this approach includes simpler sensor nodes and wireless devices. These devices perform different tasks such as object detection, sensing, management and mechanization [4]. The least complex, inactive RF devices have comparatively small range. IoT makes use of these devices in huge number because of their low cost. Energy enabled RF devices with somewhat small range facilitates high-quality performance in terms of sense and automation. IoT alludes not just to PCs and Smartphone slinked over the Internet but also provide wireless connectivity to the greater part of the large number of "things" and gadgets connected to the broadband or LANs [6][7]. The main aim here is the efficient resource utilization. These huge numbers of things also provide batteries with the same number. The proper purchase, maintenance and disposal of these batteries are essential. Energy harvesting is a competent approach by means of which distant can be energized with clean energy [9]. Internets of things are generally deployed with Wireless sensor devices. These devices are linked to the network via wireless medium. These devices collect information about the physical parameters of their surroundings.

In IoT, wireless sensor devices are deployed at different places for the purpose of data collection. However, there may be a major hindrance. This hindrance includes the fitting of energy supply wires. This provision does not produce a big challenge in case of a smaller number of batteries. However, when a large number of batteries is used, some challenges arise due to large battery price as well as the large number of preservation charges. In this way, the distribution of wireless sensor devices presents a major challenge.

The harvesting of power can solve this issue. The techniques used to harvest power make use of energy producing components. These components include solar cells, piezoelectric devices, and thermoelectric properties that the light, vibration, and heat energy can be converted into electric power [10][11]. After that, the generated electric power is used efficient manner. In any case, the level of generated harvested may be limited which results in less power storage. Subsequently, the techniques that generate energy require a solution for the effective management of generated power.

Embedded wireless systems and networks heavily rely on time. Every network device keeps a separate clock. Because there are differences between individual oscillators and hardware inherent diversity, the clocks present in many devices locally are asynchronous. Clock synchronization, a crucial feature in those networks, is used to synchronize many devices to a common global time [12]. If sensor readings from several sources are not synchronized in the temporal dimension, there is a risk of incorrect identification and even mismatching in the condition. This is true for event-driven applications like environmental monitoring and protection. Therefore, clock synchronization plays a key role in obtaining correct data regarding network management and protocols.

The growth of IoT applications has led to the deployment of several million wireless devices in the environment. In IoT systems, heterogeneous devices are present together with several wireless standards including WiFi, ZigBee, and Bluetooth. The synchronization of the clocks among various devices is crucial for enabling cooperation and interoperation. In an industrial IoT system, it is necessary to control the pipeline with precise timing when there are many manufacturing units and sensors. Without synchronizing the clocks of those units and sensors, there are several flaws and inconsistencies in the pipeline that produce ineffective outputs [13][14]. The Cross-technology clock synchronization (CTCS) method has been used to synchronize the clocks of heterogeneous wireless devices, although it is regarded as a significant issue. It enables direct connection between devices using various wireless technologies. As a result, the shared gateway uses the above-mentioned approach to forward timestamps. Additional synchronization errors can be noticed as a result of a hazy end-to-end timestamp transmission delay when using a gateway.

Direct data transmission between technologies has several benefits, as demonstrated by the development of cross-technology communication (CTC) [15]. Time and energy modulation are being developed in order to modulate data from WiFi to ZigBee. Even when CTC is present, normal synchronization techniques cannot be used in the enhanced CTCS method. This occurs for the reasons listed below, including low CTC throughput and increased channel noise during CTC transmission. As many wireless packets must be used to modulate the timestamp, the channel is used for a longer amount of time [16][17]. Due to this, local processing and network propagation are delayed and uncertain. The CTCS signal is impacted by noise, which causes erroneous clock calibration findings. Thus, this signal's noise is still a big problem.

2. Problem Formulation and Methodolgy

In order to improve security in IoT, there is a need to come up with a solution which will provide efficient communication between IoT devices. The method of ELASTIC TIMER is carried out in sensing the channel. The data is encrypted and decrypted using symmetric encryption algorithm. The key utilized for this purpose requires renovation from time to time. The maintenance of time synchronization is performed between source and destination with the help of ELASTIC TIMER. The GPS is implemented in the ELASTIC TIMER protocol for synchronizing the clock in which network bandwidth is consumed. In this way, the bandwidth consumption of the network is maximized.

So, to provide enhanced clock synchronization and secure channel access for both unidirectional and bidirectional communication, we have come up with a solution where we will use RSA algorithm to establish secure channel between source and target. This will produce increased security for the network. For efficient clock synchronization, the technique of time lay will be designed for IoT devices. The WSN is the decentralized network in which no central controller is present and sensor nodes keep on joining the network any time. The cluster head takes initiative for clocks' synchronization related to the sensor nodes which are in their cluster. An IoT network' architecture is different from wireless sensor networks due to which the gateways take an initial step for the clock synchronization. The gateway passes the clock synchronization message to the IoT devices.

3. Methodology

The sensor network is carried out in the infinite sensor nodes at first. The combination of all the sensor nodes is performed in a cluster. These clusters are established based on the sensor nodes. There is a cluster head which is available in every cluster. These cluster heads are chosen by the means of election algorithm. For the cluster head, the node which includes more resources and energy is elected in the cluster. The data of all the nodes is transmitted to cluster heads. Afterward, the cluster head transfers this data further to their destinations. The route of transmitting the data is investigated and the path is created from a source to destination using AODV routing protocol. This protocol assisted in determining the virtual as well as dynamic paths.

The synchronization of sensor nodes is very essential with cluster head to keep the minimization of packet collision in the network. The presence of a sink can be seen at the network. Subsequently, the clusters which include cluster head and node are available in it. At first, one cluster has transmitted the message to the sink. When the sink is received this message, it will reduce the transmission delay from the message and its current time will be computed. Finally, the sink sends the message to the similar cluster head. At this time, the cluster head will minus its delay during transmission from the message and its time will be computed also. Finally, the final delay is obtained, which is the transmission delay of a sink-transmission delay of the cluster head.

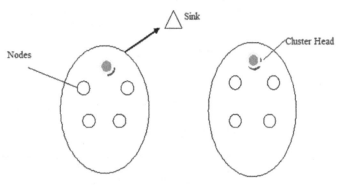

Fig. 4.3 the cluster head delivers a message to the sink

Source: Made by Author.

At last, the clock of the cluster head will set on the basis of present timing after delay. This procedure will be performed till the similar clock is obtained by all the cluster heads. The same procedure is carried out at synchronizing of the clock from cluster head and node in a cluster. The Fig. 4.10 represents that the clock message is transmitted to sink from the cluster head to perform synchronization. The Fig. 4.11 signifies that the message is sent to cluster head by the sink. The cluster head will reduce the delay from the message when it receives the message from the sink. The computation of final delay is done in the cluster head for the final clock timing. At last, its deduction is performed from the timing. The time which will remain is considered as the final time for a clock setting. The setting of the clock of all the other nodes is performed after

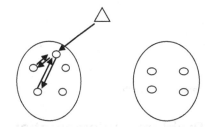

Fig. 4.4 Messages are sent from the sink to the cluster head and other nodes

Source: Made by Author

transmitting a message to the cluster head initially. The deduction of transmission delay and transmission of the message back to node will help cluster time in computation of time. The calculation of time is performed by the node when it deduces the transmission delay from the message. The final delay computed again and it will minus from the present time. The remaining time will be considered as the final time and the setting of node's clock is depending upon it. The Fig. 4.11 represents that there are two stages included for the synchronization of an entire network.

In the first stage, the cluster head is synchronized. The synchronization of the sensor nodes is performed within the cluster in the second stage. The cluster head transmits the RTS packets to all cluster heads in the network at the primary phase. The cluster heads expose the clocks after receiving the RTS packets. After that, the cluster head transmits the CTS packets to sink. The cluster head adjusts the clocks when CTS packets are sent to the sink node. The clocks of sensor nodes will be adjusted in accordance with time by the sensor nodes in case of receiving PING messages which are sent from the cluster heads. The synchronization of the whole network is completed in this way when it consumes less energy and there is not any occurrence of packet loss.

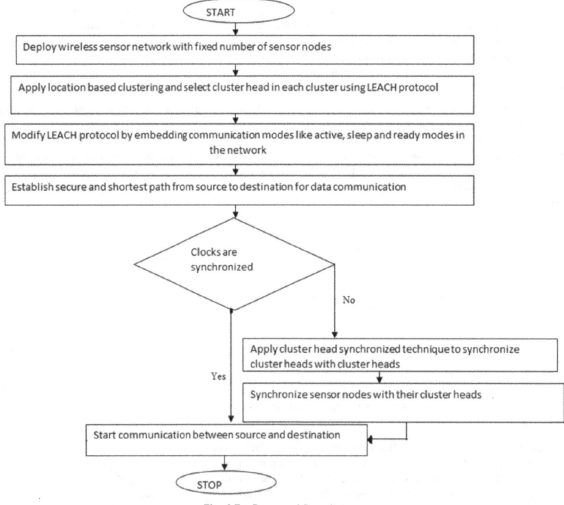

Fig. 4.5 Proposed flow diagram

Source: Drawn by Author

3. Problem Implementation

The NS2 referred as the network simulator version 2. The simulator NS2 is carried out for performing simulations of network. The tree like structure is pursued by network simulator version 2 in which the simulation of wired and wireless networks is performed. There are a variety of inbuilt properties of NS2 and antenna type, channel type, standard, area, protocol is some of these properties. The MAC layer, physical and link layer type etc. are employed these properties to discover paths. The wireless networks utilize the header files which are earlier described. The wired simulations are performed using network simulator version 2. There are numerous ARP queues which are inbuilt and include RED, BLUE, and SQF etc. The simulation based on text as well as on animation is presented by the simulator NS2. The network animator is employed to represent the simulation based on the animation and the .tr files are employed to signify the simulation based on text. The C++ is utilized in the backend of NS2 and TCL is utilized at the front end to perform simulation. The NS2 tool is based on Linux and Ubuntu 12.04 is carried out as the platform.

Table 4.1 simulation parameters used for the solution implementation

Parameter	Description
Channel	Wireless
Number of nodes	100
Area	200*200(m)
Initial Energy	(100 joules)
Network Interface Type	Phy/WirelessPhy
Interface Queue type	Droptail/PriQueue
Routing Protocol	AODV
Antenna Type	Omni
Topology	Random

Source: Made by Author

3.1 Network Deployment

The utilization of nodes is done in the system at random. There are only finite numbers of sensor nodes. This system has employed 100 nodes to perform simulation. There are a number of things which can be sensed by sensor nodes. The communication is performed between the nodes and the sink node. The communication between the sink node and end users is done with the help of internet.

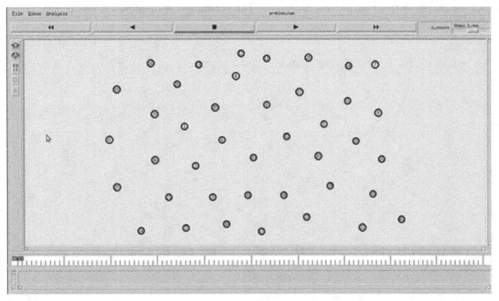

Fig. 4.6 Network deployment

Source: Made by Author

3.2 Cluster Formation

The cluster is established by exchanging resources of nodes with each other or among the nodes of neighbors. The multi-hop communication is selected in the system to communicate effectively. The nodes are selected for generating a single cluster under this procedure.

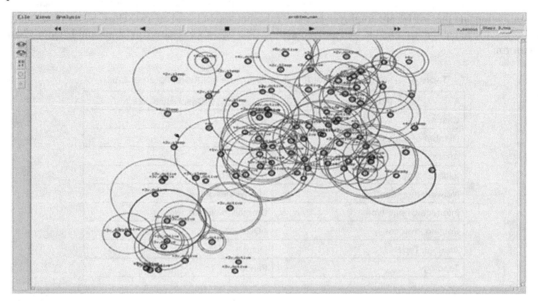

Fig. 4.7 Cluster formation

Source: Made by Author

3.3 Sink Deployment and Cluster Formation

The sensor nodes are utilized to construct a cluster. There are 11 clusters generated from 100 sensor nodes due to which the communication among each other become possible in those clusters for the transformation of information to the base station. The size of the cluster is fixed during this procedure. The consumption of energy is reduced by selecting multi-hop communication.

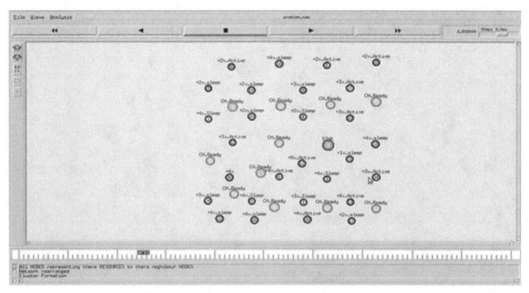

Fig. 4.8 Sink deployment and cluster formation

Source: Made by Author

3.4 Cluster Head Selection

After the formation of fixed size clusters, one cluster head is selected from each cluster. For this selection, the LEACH protocol is utilized which select the cluster head on the basis of remaining energy on nodes. The resources of nodes are exposed to the neighboring nodes by them. The communication among the Cluster head is done for transmitting the data to the sink node. There is one sink node which is selected on the basis of the highest energy.

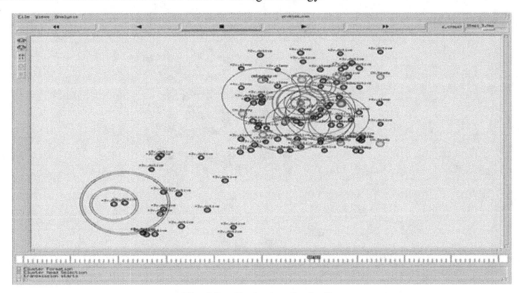

Fig. 4.9   Cluster head selection

Source: Made by Author

3.5 Intra-cluster Communication Starts from Source

Any node can sense the channel when it wants. After gathering the data, the nodes transmit that data to its cluster head. After that this data is sent to the base station by the cluster head. The transmission of data is done from source to cluster head. Furthermore, one cluster head is communicated with another cluster head.

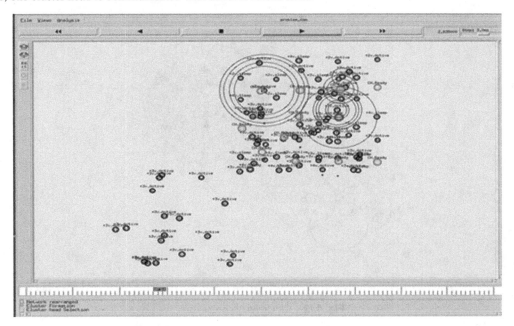

Fig. 4.10   Intra-cluster communication from source

Source: Made by Author

3.6 Collision of Packets

The AODV protocol is employed to determine the path for routing packets because there is a fixed path established among the cluster heads. Thus, the issue is generated due to this fixed path and it resulted in packet loss. In case of mismatching of nodes' clock, the packet may loss in the system under the transmission process. The RFID is utilized for channel sensing. As a result, the maximum energy is consumed and the network lifetime is decreased.

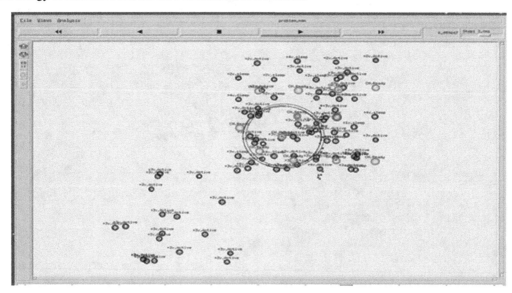

Fig. 4.11 Packet collision

Source: Made by Author

3.7 Clock Synchronization

A time lay method is carried out for the synchronization of all the clocks in this system due to which no mismatch will occur in timings. First of all, the synchronization of cluster heads is completed after that node are synchronized in the cluster.

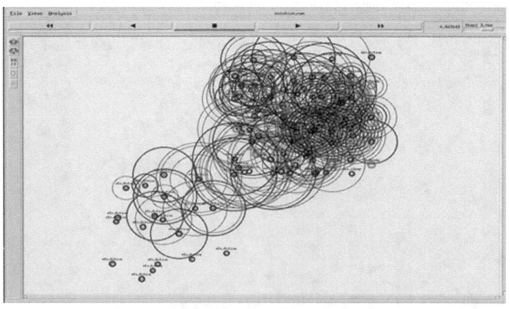

Fig. 4.12 Clock synchronization

Source: Made by Author

3.8 Virtual Path Establishment

The cluster heads are useful for investigating the path from a source to the base station. The path is formed with the help of AODV routing protocol I. The cluster heads receive the outer request packets by source. The cluster heads include the route to the destination, and they also broadcast reply packets to the source.

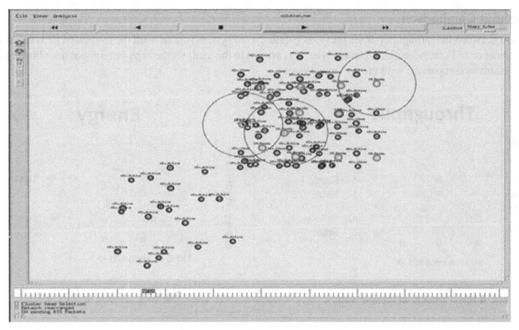

Fig. 4.13   Virtual path establishment

Source: Made by Author

4. Comparison and Analysis

4.1 Delay Comparison

The comparison between the previous method based on Elastic Timer and suggested E Elastic timer-based system for analyzing the performance in terms of delay. It is demonstrated that the less delay is achieved using suggested E Elastic Timer based system than previous system.

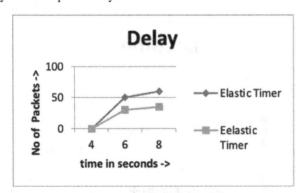

Fig. 4.14   Delay comparison

Source: Made by Author

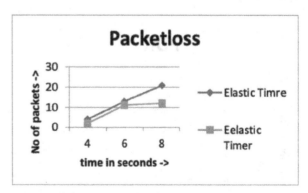

Fig. 4.15   Packetloss comparison

Source: Made by Author

4.2 Packetloss Comparison

The previous Elastic based method and the suggested EElastic timer method are compared to analyze their performance on the basis of packet loss. The analysis represents that less packets loss is observed with the use of suggested technique than the previous method.

4.3 Throughput Comparison

The comparison between the throughput of the previous Elastic based system is done with the suggested EElastic timer scheme so as the performance of both the methods can analyze. It is proved in the analysis the high throughput has obtained in EElastic Timer based system in comparison with the previous system.

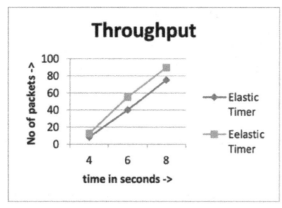

Fig. 4.16 Throughput comparison

Source: Made by Author

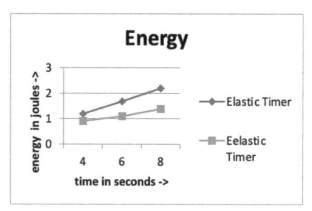

Fig. 4.17 Energy comparison

Source: Made by Author

4.4 Energy Comparison

The energy of previous Elastic based system and the suggested EElastic timer system is compared for analyzing the performance. It is demonstrated in the analysis that the suggested system has a smaller amount of energy than the previous Elastic Timer Scheme.

4.5 PDR Comparison

The comparison between the previous Elastic based system and the suggested EElastic timer system is performed on the basis of PDR and their performance is analyzed. It is observed that a superior PDR is obtained in suggested system in comparison with previous system.

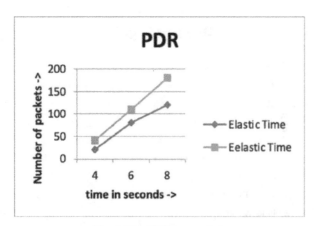

Fig. 4.18 PDR comparison

Source: Made by Author

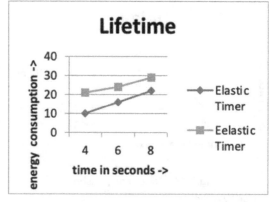

Fig. 4.19 Lifetime comparison

Source: Made by Author

4.6 Lifetime Comparison

The lifetime of the previous Elastic based system and the suggested EElastic timer system is compared to analyze the performance. It is observed that the higher lifetime is included in suggested system than earlier system.

4.7 Table of Comparison

Table 4.2 Delay comparison

Time	Elastic Time	EElastic Time
4	0	0
6	50	30
8	62	32

Source: Made by Author

The Table 4.2 illustrates that the comparison is performed among elastic time method and the Eelastic time method on the basis of delay. It is observed that that Eelastic timer method has less delay in comparison with elastic timer method

Table 4.3 Packet loss comparison

Time	Elastic Time	EElastic Time
4	5	3
6	14	11
8	21	12

Source: Made by Author

The Table 4.3 represents that the packet loss of the proposed algorithm is compared with the previous algorithm to analyze their performance. It is examined that the EElastic timer algorithm has less packet loss than the previous algorithm.

Table 4.4 Throughput Comparison

Time	Elastic Time	EElastic Time
4	11	8
6	40	55
8	75	90

Source: Made by Author

The Table 4.4 signifies that the comparison of the elastic timer system is performed with EElastic timer method for analyzing the performance in terms of throughput. The higher throughput is obtained from EElastic timer method in comparison with the previous method.

Table 4.5 Energy comparison

Time	Elastic Time	EElastic Time
4	1.1	8
6	1.7	55
8	2.3	90

Source: Made by Author

The Table 4.5 represents that the comparison of energy consumption of previous elastic is performed with the suggested EElastic timer method to analyze the performance. The analysis indicated that the EElastic timer method is consumed less energy than the previous method.

Table 4.6 PDR comparison

Time	Elastic Time	EElastic Time
4	1.1	0.9
6	1.7	1
8	2.3	1.5

Source: Made by Author

The Table 4.6 illustrates that the elastic timer method and the suggested EElastic timer method are compared with respect to the PDR. It is evaluated that suggested method has obtained superior PDR in comparison with the previous method.

Table 4.7 Lifetime comparison

Time	Elastic Time	EElastic Time
4	20	40
6	80	110
8	120	180

Source: Made by Author

The Table 4.7 represents that the comparison of lifetime of previous timer method with the suggested EElastic timer method. The Eelastic timer method has acquired higher lifetime in comparison with the previous method.

5. Conclusion

The Internet of things is self-configured and decentralized kind of network. The sensor nodes detect information and transmit it to the network's server. Data is transferred from the sensor node via wireless channels. The elastic time method is implemented for the allocation of these channels to every sensor node. The synchronization of sensor nodes' clocks is not completed in well manner. Thus, the elastic time does not work well. The enhancement of the elastic timer method will be suggested in this research work to sense the channel. The clocks of the sensor nodes are synchronized by implementing time lay method along with the elastic timer method. This suggested method has potential for synchronizing the sensor nodes' clock, maximizing the lifetime of the networks and decreasing the delay as well as loss of packet.

REFERENCES

1. A. Ray and D. De, "Data Aggregation Techniques in Wireless Sensor Network: A Survey," International Journal of Engineering Innovation and Research, vol. I, no. 2, pp. 81–92, 2012.
2. V. Pandey, "A Review on Data Aggregation Techniques in Wireless Sensor Network,". Journal of Electronic and Electrical Engineering, vol. I, no. 2, 2010
3. J. Bhatti and S. Waraich, "Trends towards Optimistic Data Aggregation Techniques," in International Conference on Innovations in Information Embedded and Communication Systems (ICIIECS), pp. 1–7, Mar 2015.
4. M. Dagar and S. Mahajan, "Data Aggregation in Wireless Sensor Network:a Survey;' International Journal of Information and Computation Technology., pp. 0974–2239, 2013.
5. N. S. Patil and P. Patil, "Data Aggregation in Wireless Sensor Network;' in IEEE International Conference on Computational Intelligence and Computing Research (ICCIC), 2010.
6. RuinianLi1 , Carl Sturtivant2 , Jiguo Yu3,∗ , and Xiuzhen Cheng, "A Novel Secure and Efficient Data Aggregation Scheme for IoT", IEEE, 2018
7. Zhijing Qin, Di Wu Member, IEEE, Zhu Xiao Member, IEEE, Bin Fu, and Zhijin Qin Member, IEEE, "Modeling and Analysis of Data Aggregation from Converge cast in Mobile Sensor Networks for Industrial IoT", IEEE, 2018
8. Tianqi Yu, Student Member, IEEE, Xianbin Wang, Fellow, IEEE, and Abdallah Shami, Senior Member, IEEE, "Recursive Principal Component Analysis based Data Outlier Detection and Sensor Data Aggregation in IoT Systems", IEEE, 2017
9. Sabin Bhandari, Shree Krishna Sharma, Xianbin Wang, "Latency Minimization in Wireless IoT Using Prioritized Channel Access and Data Aggregation", IEEE, 2017
10. YulongShen, Tao Zhang, Yongzhi Wang, Hua Wang, and Xiaohong Jiang, "MicroThings: A Generic IoT Architecture for Flexible Data Aggregation and Scalable Service Cooperation", IEEE, 2017

11. Asim Zeb, Sonia Wakeel, Taj Rahman, Inayat Khan, M. Irfan Uddin, Badam Niazi, "Energy-Efficient Cluster Formation in IoT-Enabled Wireless Body Area Network", Computational Intelligence and Neuroscience, vol. 2022, Article ID 2558590, 11 pages, 2022. https://doi.org/10.1155/2022/2558590

12. Niu, Y., Yang, T., Hou, Y. *et al.* Consensus tracking-based clock synchronization for the Internet of Things. *Soft Comput* **26,** 6415–6428 (2022). https://doi.org/10.1007/s00500-022-07165-x

13. S. Srivastava, S. Prakash, Review on enhanced energy efficient routing protocol of WSN and use of IoT, in *International Conference on Recent Trends in Science & Technology* (Mysuru, India, 2020)

14. Praveen, K.V., Prathap, P.M.J. Energy Efficient Congestion Aware Resource Allocation and Routing Protocol for IoT Network using Hybrid Optimization Techniques. *Wireless Pers Commun* **117,** 1187–1207 (2021). https://doi.org/10.1007/s11277-020-07917-8

15. S. Zhu, X. Zheng, L. Liu and H. Ma, "AirSync: Time Synchronization for Large-scale IoT Networks Using Aircraft Signals," in *IEEE Transactions on Mobile Computing*, doi: 10.1109/TMC.2021.3070644.

16. Rana, B., Singh, Y. (2022). Duty-Cycling Techniques in IoT: Energy-Efficiency Perspective. In: Singh, P.K., Singh, Y., Kolekar, M.H., Kar, A.K., Gonçalves, P.J.S. (eds) Recent Innovations in Computing. Lecture Notes in Electrical Engineering, vol 832. Springer, Singapore. https://doi.org/10.1007/978-981-16-8248-3_42

17. Almudayni, Z., Soh, B., Li, A. (2022). A Comprehensive Study on the Energy Efficiency of IoT from Four Angles: Clustering and Routing in WSNs, Smart Grid, Fog Computing and MQTT & CoAP Application Protocols. In: Hussain, W., Jan, M.A. (eds) IoT as a Service. IoTaaS 2021. Lecture Notes of the Institute for Computer Sciences, Social Informatics and Telecommunications Engineering, vol 421. Springer, Cham. https://doi.org/10.1007/978-3-030-95987-6_4

18. N. M. Pradhan, B. S. Chaudhari and M. Zennaro, "6TiSCH Low Latency Autonomous Scheduling for Industrial Internet of Things," in *IEEE Access*, vol. 10, pp. 71566–71575, 2022, doi: 10.1109/ACCESS.2022.3188862.

Advances in Computational Intelligence and its Applications (ICACIA-2023) – Dr. Sheikh Fahad Ahmad et al. (eds)
© 2024 Taylor & Francis Group, London, ISBN 978-1-032-78612-4

Farm to Home: An e-commerce Application for Farmers and Consumers

5

N. Anusha[1]

Associate Professor, Department of Computer science and Engineering,
Vidya Jyothi Institute of Technology, Hyderabad, Telangana, India

**Pyata Sai Keerthi*[2], Manyam Ramakrishna Reddy[3],
A. Ramesh*[4] and M. RishithIgnatious[5]**

UG student, Department of Computer science and Engineering,
Vidya Jyothi Institute of Technology, Hyderabad, Telangana, India

ABSTRACT—E-commerce is one the most extensively used platforms for the application of information technology that is booming as an important component of information construction. Farmers in India are not so familiar with the technologies that can help them increase their production as well as sales which acquire them with more profits. Selling the yield in the weekly market for the price fixed by the government or to the agent to the price fixed by the agent in a farming market are the traditional ways that have been followed from ancient times in India by the farmers. Marketing through these traditional methods are leading to loss for both farmers and consumers. In order to overcome the challenges faced by the farmers as well as consumers, farm to home, an e-commerce web application is proposed and developed in this research. This application gives a freedom to farmers to sell their product directly to customers for a better price without any middle-man-ship or agents. Through this application, the farmers can sell their product at a better price and consumers can buy fresh fruits and vegetables at market price. The proposed system ensures a stable market as well as a better return to the farmers. This application protects the interest of both consumers and producers. The main motive of this application is to remove the agents and provide direct connection between the farmers and consumers.

KEYWORDS—Application, Consumers, E-commerce, Farmers, Farming

1. Introduction

Farming is the art and science of cultivating land for growing the crop (or yield or harvest or product) (Wang, 2020). According to food and agriculture organization (FAO), in the year 2020,the share of the farming population around the globe is 67 percent of the total population (Top,2020).Farming recorded 39.4% of the GDP in India upon agronomic commodities in October, 2022. Farming provides around 58 % of livelihood to Indians (Top, 2022).In recent years (2017-2022), agronomy has become the primary source of income for half of the population in India, contributing 20 to 21 % of the country's GDP (Top,2020, Top, 2022). India is one of the largest producers of fruits, vegetables and spices. Bananas, guava, mango, papaya are a variety of fruits mostly cultivated in the states of Andhra Pradesh, Maharashtra, Karnataka, Assam in India. Gusto, pepper, and chilies are the spices mostly cultivated in Kerala and Tamil Nādu states of India (Top, 2022).

[1]anusha.nallapareddy@gmail.com,*[2]keerthireddy1125@gmail.com, [3]sunderreddy55@gmail.com,*[4]ramesh29122000@gmail.com, [5]rishithignatious.02@gmail.com.

DOI: 10.1201/9781003488682-5

Selling the yield in the weekly market or to the agent are the traditional ways that have been followed from ancient times in India by the farmers. Farmers sell their yield in the weekly market at value that is fixed by the government. And the farmers who got more yield sell their production to the agents in the farming market for the price fixed by the agents (Top,2020). These agents quote very less and purchase the yield from the farmers and sell the same to consumers at a higher rate and earn more profits. This leads to loss for both farmers and consumers.

In order to overcome these challenges faced by the farmers as well as consumers, farm to home, an e-commerce web application is proposed and developed in this research. E- commerce is one the most widely used platforms (Wen, 2010, Chen *et al* 2008) for the application of information technology that is booming as an important component of information construction. It is also considered as a crucial factor in the new commercial world (Wen, 2010, Chen *et al* 2008), as it began to be adopted in many countries and lend them to the implementation of their development plans. It is estimated that e-commerce activities will be a vital source of foreign exchange and an indicator of national development (Chen *et al* 2008). Agriculture is also one of the growing platforms in the e- commerce world (Wen, 2010).

Through the farm to home e-commerce application proposed in this research, farmers can sell their produce for a better price, earning profits and consumers can buy fresh fruits and vegetables at market price. This application gives a freedom to farmers to sell their product directly to customers. The proposed system ensures a stable market as well as a better return to the farmers. This application protects the interest of both consumers and producers. The main motive of this application is to remove the agents and provide direct connection between the farmers and consumers.

The proposed farm to home application might even help the government to check with the daily price fluctuations in the market, since there is no proper established platform where they can compare prices to address the high prices that are affecting farmers and consumers (Top,2020, Pani and Mishra 2015). To stay current with changing requirements, it is necessary for a system with modern technologies that will assist farmers' in selling their yield at a good price (Yan *et al* 2010).

2. Methodology

The farm to home e-commerce application is a platform for farmers and consumers, where the farmers can sell their yield directly to customers and food processing industries by eliminating dealerships. This e-commerce application developed with J2EE, HTML, CSS in front end and Java, JSP, MySQl in back end.

The farmers in India have traditionally marketed their harvests in the weekly market or to an agent since from the ancient days. In the weekly market, farmers sell their harvest for a price fixed by the government. The farmers that received a higher yield sell their produce to the agents in the agricultural market for the price fixed by the agents (Top,2020). These agents offer very low prices, buy the crop from the farmer, sell it to the consumer at a higher price, and make more money. To help farmers, farm to home, an e-commerce web application is developed in this research. This application is for farmers as well as for consumers.

The architecture of the proposed farm to home (F2H) e-commerce application is given in Fig. 5.1. This application is an interface between farmer and buyer. The farmers and buyers can initially register in this application by giving the required details. Admin will then verify the details given by them and approve or reject their registration to the application. Once after the successful registration, the farmers and users can login to this application by using their credentials. To this application, the registered farmers can add the yield details such as quantity available, price and its images on the farmers' page. Farmers can also update this information in the application when required. Admin helps the farmers by notifying if there is any bug found regarding the adding and managing of the details of the commodities in the application. The registered buyer can log into the application using his/her credentials and can shop the items that are available from the customer page. Through this application admin helps both farmers and customers by suggesting the range market prices of each product per kilogram (kg) in their location. In addition, admin also checks the details updated by the farmers in the farmer page and suggests farmers for corrections if needed. This application creates transparency between buyer and seller thus increasing assurance on the application by both farmers and consumer.

While shopping, buyers can compare the pricing given by farmers with market price in that location then can order the items required through the application. This application creates an environment where consumers and farmers do not lead any kind of loss. Buyer can choose items and quantity required from any farmer in the application, add to the cart. The consumer after paying for the products he selected can then proceed to checkout after completion of the shopping. Then the farmer gets the notification of the order, accepts the order and sends the delivery agent to the warehouse and collects specified products and delivers them to consumers on time.

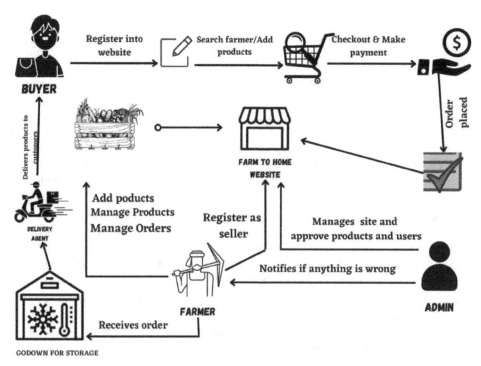

Fig. 5.1 Architecture of the farm to home e-commerce application

3. Results and Discussions

The home page of the farm to home application is depicted in Fig. 5.2. This application provides an interface for sellers, buyers and admin in individual pages in one stop platform. Through this home page (refer Figure 2) admin, farmers and buyers can register to the application by selecting the respective option. The farm to home application allows farmers and buyers to register and then login to their individual pages using their own credentials.

Fig. 5.2 Home page of farm to home application.

Farmers can register by giving necessary details (refer Fig. 5.3) such as first name, last name, government identification (ID), E-mail ID, etc.,. Later, the admin verifies the details provided by the seller during registration and adds these details to the application database. Incomplete or any false details provided by the farmer, leads to rejection of the registration of the farmer in the application.

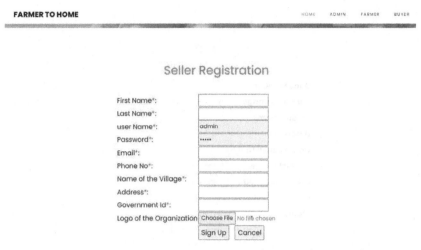

Fig. 5.3 Farmer's registration page

Farmer can register in the application (refer Fig. 5.3) by using any government issued ID such as Aadhar, ration card, etc., The admin will do approval of the farmer registration, once the farmer provides necessary details while registering to the application (refer Fig. 5.4).

FARMER TO HOME

Seller Name	Email	Mobile	
farmer	farmer@gmail.com	+916301836606	Approved
keerthi	keerthireddy1125@gmail.com	+916301836608	Approved
keerthi	sunderreddy55@gmail.com	1236544569	Rejected

Fig. 5.4 Approval or rejection of the seller profile

Once the admin verifies and approves the request, the farmers can then login to the application using his/her own credentials (refer Fig. 5.5). After successful login it will open the farmer's page.

Fig. 5.5 Farmer login page

A farmer can then add his/her own product details to the application (refer Fig. 5.6) by providing all the required details of the product. Later when required, farmers can also manage/update the products and product details (refer Fig. 5.7).

HOME   ADD PRODUCTS   MANAGE PR

Add PRODUCTS

Code Number:

Bar-Code Image: Choose File | No file chosen

Product Name:

Description:

Organisation Logo: Choose File | No file chosen

Product Image: Choose File | No file chosen

Large ImagePath: Choose File | No file chosen

Price:

Status: Select Status ✓

Insert   Cancel

Fig. 5.6   Addition of commodity details in the farmer's page

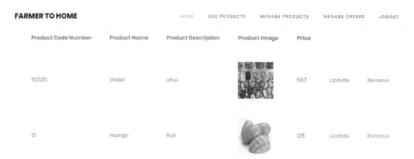

FARMER TO HOME   HOME   ADD PRODUCTS   MANAGE PRODUCTS   MANAGE ORDERS   LOGOUT

Product Code Number	Product Name	Product Description	Product Image	Price		
112333	Shoes	uhui		567	Update	Remove
12	mango	fruit		128	Update	Remove

Fig. 5.7   Managing the product details in the farmer page

The buyers can register to the application by providing necessary informationsuch as name, password, e-mail, phone number, Country, Zip code (refer Fig. 5.8).

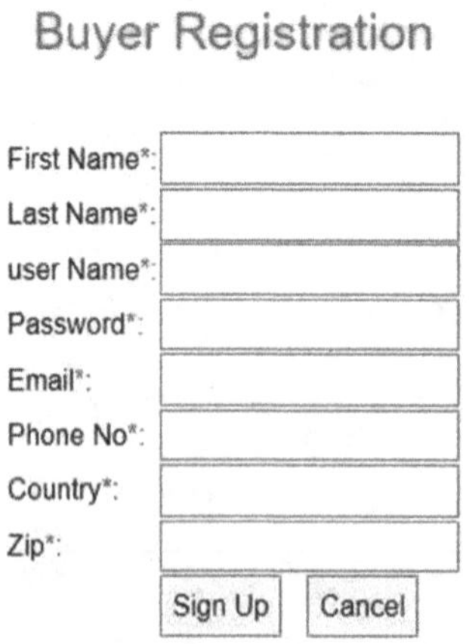

Buyer Registration

First Name*:

Last Name*:

user Name*:

Password*:

Email*:

Phone No*:

Country*:

Zip*:

Sign Up   Cancel

Fig. 5.8   Buyer registration page

The registered buyers to the application can login to the farm to homeapplication using the credentials. Buyer can select a farmer from the list (refer Fig. 5.9) and can shop the products of his/her choice by selecting and adding them to the cart (refer Fig. 5.10).

List of Farmers	Farmer Poducts
farmer	Shop
keerthi	Shop
karthik12	Shop
ram	Shop
ramesh	Shop
ajay	Shop
karthik12	Shop
akshu	Shop

Fig. 5.9   List of farmers view in the consumer page

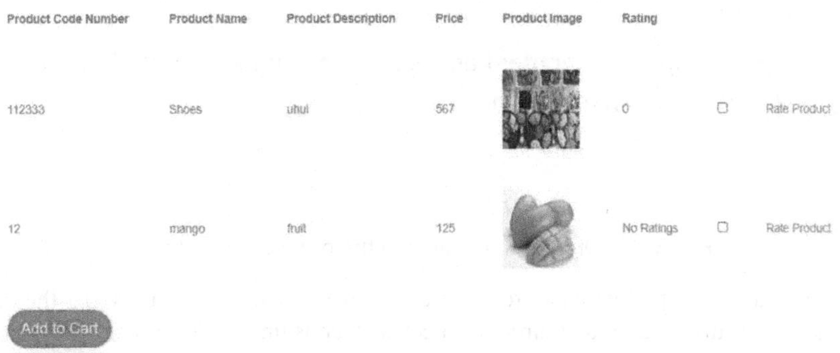

Product Code Number	Product Name	Product Description	Price	Product Image	Rating		
112333	Shoes	uhui	567		0	☐	Rate Product
12	mango	fruit	125		No Ratings	☐	Rate Product

Add to Cart

Fig. 5.10   View of the cart of selected products and quantity by buyer

Buyer can also view the items list and quantities added to the cart, can modify the order if needed (refer Fig. 5.11). Then the payment can be made for the products shopped by choosing a payment gateway and confirming the order (refer Fig. 5.12). Once after successfully placing the order and completion of shopping (refer Fig. 5.13) the buyers can logout from the application.

Your Cart Items

Product Name	Image	Price	
Shoes		567	Remove

Total($):567.0

Continue Shopping | Procees To Checkout

Fig. 5.11   View the products in the carts by buyer

After successful completion of shopping by the buyer, the order details will benotified to the respective farmers.

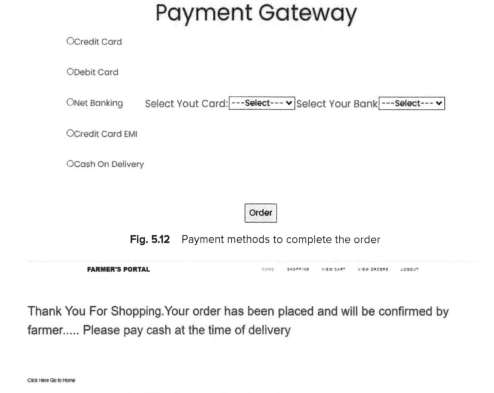

Fig. 5.12 Payment methods to complete the order

FARMER'S PORTAL   HOME   SHOPPING   VIEW CART   VIEW ORDERS   LOGOUT

Thank You For Shopping.Your order has been placed and will be confirmed by farmer..... Please pay cash at the time of delivery

Click Here Go to Home

Fig. 5.13 Order confirmation of the order to the buyer

Thus, the farm to home e-commerce application is for farmers as well as for consumers. To the registered farmers, this application gives pricing power of the product and direct connect with consumers. Consumers will get fresh organic products with a reasonable price directly from farmers avoiding the agents.

4. Conclusion

The E-commerce application proposed and developed in this research is a solution for both farmers and customers. It gives power of updating product price and yield details to farmers. Both farmers and consumers can benefit through this application. Farmers earn marginal profits and customers get fresh fruits and vegetables at better prices. This application will help farmers to sell their production according to the cost given by the government with some marginal profits without any middle-man-ship or agents. The application admin authenticates the farmer by verifying the government identification provided while registration. This research can be enhanced by adding soil testing and crop recommendation pages, where the farmer can enter the soil details and get the crop recommendation. This application can also be enhanced to help farmers in buying good quality seeds. Furthermore, this research can be further enhanced to help farmers globally.

REFERENCES

1. Baourakis, G., Daian, G. (2002). E-Commerce in the Agribusiness Sector: Present Situation and Future Trends. In: Pardalos, P.M., Tsitsiringos, V.K. (eds) Financial Engineering, E-commerce and Supply Chain. Applied Optimization, Springer, Boston, MA. 70(3): 213–230.
2. Boddie W and Kun L. 2008. Health care, public health, and the food and agriculture critical infrastructures. IEEE Engineering in Medicine and Biology Magazine, 27(6): 54–58.
3. Carlos E. Carpio, Olga Isengildina-Massa, R. David Lamie and Samuel D. Zapata. 2013. Does E-Commerce Help Agricultural Markets? The Case of MarketMaker. Choices, 28(4): 1–7.

4. Dalali S, Adarsh C. J, Abhishek B. K and Akshay K. 2023. Organic Mart: E Commerce Web Site for Agriculture. In: Kumar, A., Senatore, S., Gunjan, V.K. (eds) ICDSMLA 2021. Lecture Notes in Electrical Engineering, 846: 593–602.

5. Deng-Neng Chen, Jeng B, Wei-Po Lee and Cheng-Hung Chuang. 2008. An agent-based model for consumer-to-business electronic commerce. 34 (1): 469–481.

6. Dong M. 2016. International comparisons on business model of agriculture e-commerce between India and China. 2016 International Conference on Industrial Economics System and Industrial Security Engineering (IEIS).

7. Heng Wang, Lan Fang and Shaojian Chen. Can e-commerce alleviate agricultural non- point source pollution?—A quasi-natural experiment based on a China's E- Commerce Demonstration CityEnvironment Heng Wan, 846.

8. Top 10 Agricultural Producing Countries in The World. 2020. https://www.tractorjunction.com/blog/top-10-agricultural-producing-countries-in-the- world/ <Accessed on 17th August 2022>

9. Top 10 Agricultural Producing Countries in The World. 2022. https://plantila.in/top-10-agricultural-producing-countries-in-the-world <Accessed on 21st August 2022>

10. https://ieeexplore.ieee.org/document/8697615<Accessed on 7th September 2022>

11. Kong, and Sherry Tao. 2019. E-Commerce Development in Rural China. In The Chinese Economic Transformation: Views from Young Economists, edited by LIGANG SONG, YIXIAO ZHOU, and LUKE HURST, ANU Press.,12(1): 129–142.

12. Kiruthika U, Raja S. K. S, Balaji V and Raman, C. J. 2020. E-Agriculture for Direct Marketing of Food Crops Using Chatbots. 2020 International Conference on Power, Energy, Control and Transmission Systems (ICPECTS).

13. Nan L. 2021. RETRACTED ARTICLE: Agricultural climate change and design of agricultural product e-commerce   trading platform based on remote sensing technology. Arab J Geosci, 14: 443.

14. Pani S and Mishra J. 2015. Building semantics of E-agriculture in India: Semantics in e- agriculture. 2015 International Conference on Man and Machine Interfacing (MAMI).

15. Patel, A.N., Ahmed, A., Rohini, B.R. (2022). An Approach Towards E-Commerce for Agriculture with Modern Technologies. In: Kumar, A., Senatore, S., Gunjan, V.K. (eds) ICDSMLA 2020. Lecture Notes in Electrical Engineering, 783: 985–99.

16. Rolf A. E. Mueller. 2001. E-Commerce and Entrepreneurship in Agricultural Markets." American Journal of Agricultural Economics, JSTOR, 83(5): 1243–49.

17. Henderson, Jason, Frank Dooley, and Jay Akridge. 2004. Internet and E-Commerce Adoption by Agricultural Input Firms." Review of Agricultural Economics, 26(4): 505– 20.

18. Sugiarti Y, Maman U, Mintarsih F, Anwas E. O. M and Syarifah E. 2019. Design and Build Mango E-Commerce Information System. 2019 7th International Conference on Cyber and IT Service Management (CITSM). doi:10.1109/citsm47753.2019.8965402 Telminova N. V, Kosorukova I. V, Kosorukova O. D and Kalinkina K. E. 2023. Systems Perspectives on the Development of E-commerce Companies in Agriculture. In: Trukhachev, V.I. (eds) Unlocking Digital Transformation of Agricultural Enterprises. Innovation, Technology, and Knowledge Management. 213–222.

19. Wang Y and LanHongjie. 2015. Fresh agricultural products supply chain in the e- commerce environment vulnerability model. 2015 International Conference on Logistics, Informatics and Service Sciences (LISS).

20. Wang Y. 2020. Construction of E-commerce Platform System for Targeted Poverty Alleviation. 2020 International Conference on Computer Engineering and Application (ICCEA). doi:10.1109/iccea50009.2020.00028

21. Wen W. 2010. Agricultural e-commerce application mode in China. 2010 2nd IEEE International Conference on Information Management and Engineering.

22. Yan W, Shuanggen H, Qi C and Yuan P. 2010. Opinions about the Development of Agricultural e-Commerce in the New Socialism Countryside Construction. 2010 International Conference on E-Business and E-Government.

23. Yangeng, W., Yuena, K., Weihua, Z. (2012). The Study on Chinese Agricultural E- Commerce Development. In: Wu, Y. (eds) Software Engineering and Knowledge Engineering: Theory and Practice. Advances in Intelligent and Soft Computing, 114: 207– 213.

24. Yi, M and Deng, W. 2009. A Utility-Based Recommendation Approach for E- Commerce Websites Based on Bayesian Networks. 2009 International Conference on Business Intelligence and Financial Engineering.

25. Ying S. and Lei Y. 2021. Research on E-commerce Data Mining and Managing Model in The Process of Farmers' Welfare Growth. 2021 13thInternational Conference on Measuring Technology and Mechatronics Automation (ICMTMA).

26. Zhang M, Zhou Y and Li L. 2022.Manufacturing firms' E-commerce adoption and performance: evidence from a large survey in Jiaxing, China. Inf Technol Manag. 23(4): 233–243.

27. Zhao Z and Tian Y. 2014. Discussion about agricultural e-commerce situation and optimization. 2014 International Conference on Management Science & Engineering 21th Annual Conference Proceedings.

28. Zhihao Qin, Bin Xu, Xiaoping Xin, Qingbo Zhou, Hong'ou Zhang and Jia Liu. 2004. Integration of remote sensing and GIS technology to evaluate grassland ecosystem health in north China. IEEE International IEEE International IEEE International Geoscience and Remote Sensing Symposium, 2004. IGARSS '04. Proceedings.

29. Zikang H, Yong Y, Guofeng Y and Xinyu Z. 2020. Sentiment analysis of agricultural product ecommerce review data based on deep learning. 2020 International Conference on Internet of Things and Intelligent Applications (ITIA).

Note: All the figures in this chapter were made by the authors.

Advances in Computational Intelligence and its Applications (ICACIA-2023) – Dr. Sheikh Fahad Ahmad et al. (eds)
© 2024 Taylor & Francis Group, London, ISBN 978-1-032-78612-4

Smart Farming:
The Future of Agriculture

6

**Manjunadha Mallina*, Sakinala Sri Sai Pawan,
Narra Manas, Anuradha Nandula, Subhranginee Das**
Department of Computer Science and Engineering,
Koneru Lakshmaiah Education Foundation, Hyderabad, India

ABSTRACT—AI use in agriculture is one of the most effective ways to control food scarcity and adapt to the needs of a growing population. This article offers a summary of AI's use in agronomic fields and developments in study facilities. The assessment begins by highlighting two areas where AI may have a significant impact the control of weeds and soil, followed by "Internet of Things (IoT)" a Technology that has a lot of promise for use in the future is mentioned three issues that require Unevenness needs to be solved in "AI-based technology" to become more widely used in markets, dispersion of automation, accurate processing of enormous data sets via algorithms swiftly, with security, and privacy of data and device privacy. Robotic tractors targeted at various sectors of the agricultural economy have been considerably enhanced and then despite highlighting the difficulty of using machines and algorithms that have been validated in recent years The review indicates a thriving experimental environment compared to real surroundings growth and a promising future for application.

KEYWORDS—Artificial intelligence (AI), Plantix, Prospera, One-soil, Internet of thing's (IOT)

1. Introduction

John McCarthy first proposed a study based on the notion that "any facet of learning or any other feature of intelligence can, in principle, be so clearly characterised that a machine can be constructed" at the 1955 Dartmouth Conference, which is where the term "Artificial Intelligence" was first used [1]. Due to its ability to address issues that people find challenging to effectively solve, artificial intelligence (AI), one of the main branches of computer science, has recently made inroads into a number of industries, including manufacturing, healthcare, finance, and education [2]. Still, humans are astonished by what AI is capable of Garry Kasparov's defeat by IBM's Deep Blue in the 1997 chess world championship and Lee Sedol's defeat by AlphaGo in the 2016 go world championship are two historical examples of this. AI can outperform the majority of human brainpower thanks to deep learning, which is at the heart of AlphaGo [3].

Agriculture, a crucial sector for every nation, continues to be one of the biggest issues. There are 820 million hungry people on the planet right now [4]. Additionally, it is anticipated that by 2050, there will be 9.1 billion people on the planet, requiring a 70 percent increase in food production. More investment will be required in addition to the anticipated agriculture investments; otherwise, some 370 million In 2050, there would be famine [5]. Water shortages will also exist by 2025 as a result of the gap between the world's population of more than three billion and the water supply's planned use [6]. The agriculture sector is protected by AI from a number of problems, including food safety, population increase, climate change, and a lack of skilled labour [7].

---

*Corresponding author: manjunadha949@gmail.com

DOI: 10.1201/9781003488682-6

2. Literature Survey

Precision farming and glasshouse farming, as well as other significant applications of agriculture, were examined by Juan Jess Roldán, et al. Along with planting and harvesting, they studied field environmental monitoring, plant assessment, and plant care. They also talk about the future usage of manipulators, ground vehicles, and aerial robots to do these tasks. The authors described the investigations and related steps mixes precision farming and glasshouse farming [8].

B. Ragavi et al. created "AGROBOT" on the foundation of IoT and AI for the seed-sowing mechanism. It keeps an eye on the weather, water needs, and fertiliser and pesticide requirements. Farmers receive information for real-time field monitoring via cloud services. lowers labour expenses and enhances the harvest to production cycle. [9]

The topic of disruptive technologies, which includes agriculture, has experienced a sharp rise in interest in recent years. The fourth industrial revolution has altered the setting of agricultural technology by utilising artificial intelligence (AI) technologies and placing a strong emphasis on data-driven analytical approaches [10].

Over the past few decades, agricultural robots have been the subject of much research and development, and they are currently being examined by numerous organisations around the world. Robert Bogue plans to offer a synopsis of some key and recent agricultural robotics research and advancements. He also provides a list of the robots that have been produced so far, including the ladybug and RIPPA robots [11].

Redmond Agricultural robotics were the subject of an informative review by Ramin Shamshiri and colleagues. It presents difficulties, and multirobot and swarm approaches are given particular consideration [12].

By managing weeds effectively and precisely, modern AI techniques help to reduce the need for herbicides. Reverse propagation machine vision was employed by Burks and associates [13] to train a neural network to recognise weeds of five different species. Shi et al. took a different technique, and [14] was created utilising neural networks and image analysis.robot used for harvesting.

Paddy Arif et al. [15] used artificial neural network systems to assess soil moisture. Other well-known systems that use artificial neurone networks for irrigation and soil include those developed by Junior et al. [16], Hinnell et al. [17], and patriol et al. [18].

3. AI Applications in Agriculture

Farmers would have additional challenges, just as there were with previous agricultural methods. In order to solve these issues, AI is widely used in this sector. In agriculture, artificial intelligence has developed into a revolutionary technology. It helps farmers in numerous ways, such as increased agricultural yields, pest control, soil monitoring, and many other things. Following are some significant applications of artificial intelligence in the agricultural sector:

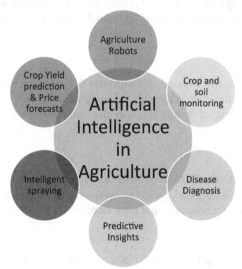

Fig. 6.1 The above diagram describes about the AI uses in agriculture

3.1 Forecasting of Weather and Prices

Farmers find it difficult to choose the best options for harvesting, sowing seeds, and solitary preparation due to climate change, as we indicated in challenges. Using AI weather forecasting, which offers information on weather analysis, farmers may plan the sort of crop to produce, the seeds to plant, and the crop harvesting process. Farmers may have a better idea of crop prices in the coming weeks thanks to price forecasting, which can help them maximise their profits.

3.2 Crop Health Surveillance

Crop quality is greatly influenced by the kind of soil and its nutrient concentration. Although it is difficult to evaluate, the soil's quality is declining because of the rapid deforestation.

AI has created a new software tool called Plantix to deal with this issue. PEAT developed this technique to identify soil deficiencies, including plant pests and diseases. Farmers can use this application to better their use of superior fertiliser to boost the quality of their crop. Farmers can use this programme to take images of their plants and use AI's image recognition capabilities to learn more about their quality.

3.3 Farming Robotics

Robotics are frequently used in various industries, mostly in manufacturing, to do challenging tasks. Numerous AI businesses are now building robots for the agricultural sector. These AI robots are made to be capable of managing a range of farming tasks.

AI robots are also taught to harvest crops more quickly than humans, identify and remove weeds, and evaluate crops for quality.

3.4 Spraying with Intelligence

Robotics are commonly utilised to complete difficult jobs in a variety of industries, mostly in manufacturing. Today, many AI-based companies are producing agricultural robots. These AI robots are designed to do a variety of farming jobs.

Additionally, AI robots are taught to find and eliminate weeds, harvest crops more quickly than humans, and assess the quality of harvested products.

4. Agricultural AI Start-Ups

4.1 Prospera

It was established in 2014 by an Israeli startup. This business develops sophisticated farming solutions. It creates cloud-based solutions that gather all field data, including soil/water, aerial photos, etc., and combine that data with a device that is used in the field. This gadget, called the Prospera device, draws conclusions from the data. A variety of sensors and technologies, including computer vision, power the device.

4.2 Blue River Technology

Blue-River Technology is a start-up company situated in California that was founded in 2011. It uses robotics, artificial intelligence, and computer vision to create the latest in agricultural equipment. This apparatus uses computer vision to recognise individual plants, ML determines the course of action, and robotics carry out the activity. This enables farmers to reduce expenses and use of pesticides in farming.

4.3 One Soil

One soil is a programme created to assist farmers in making wiser decisions. For precision farming, this app employs computer vision and a machine-learning algorithm. It keeps an eye on the crops from a distance, spots issues in the fields, checks the weather, and figures out how much nitrogen, phosphate, and potassium fertiliser to use, among other things.

4.4 Fasal

In numerous locations around the world, the application of AI in the agriculture industry is growing daily. However, compared to the richer region, agricultural holdings per farmer in the poorer region are lower, which is advantageous for automated monitoring because it only needs a smaller number of low-bandwidth and small-sized devices to collect all of the necessary agricultural data. Fasal, an Indian start-up, is active in this sector. To give farmers real-time data and insights, it makes use of inexpensive sensors and AI. With this, farmers can gain access to real-time, useful information pertinent to daily activities on the farm. Devices from the company are simple to use in compact spaces. In order to provide precision farming that is accessible to all farmers, they are building AI-enabled machines.

5. IoT Applications in Agriculture

By integrating the newest sensors and IoT systems with agricultural procedures, a fundamental transformation in every element of farming activities is feasible. Smart farming has the potential to revolutionise agriculture by integrating wireless sensors and the Internet of Things seamlessly. The internet may assist in enhancing solutions to many common agricultural issues, including as crop yield optimisation, drought response, soil aptitude, irrigation, and insect management, by using smart farming techniques

5.1 Soil Sampling and Mapping

To obtain field-specific information that is helpful when making decisions at various phases, soil analysis is absolutely essential. The primary goal of soil analysis is to determine the farmland's nutritional state, and depending on the field's nutritional deficit, different actions are done. The kind of soil, crop history, fertilisers, irrigation level, etc. are some aspects that aid in our analysis of the nutrients in the soil. Many firms provide sensors and instruments for soil testing, and these kits help farmers understand the condition of the soil. The crop's growth can be improved depending on the data given.

5.2 Irrigation

Numerous irrigation techniques, including drip irrigation and sprinkler irrigation, can address problems with water waste that already existed in more conventional techniques like flood irrigation and furrow irrigation. A lack of water can harm plants by reducing the quality and quantity of the crops, depleting the soil's nutrients, and causing diseases. Considering aspects like irrigation technique, crop type, soil type, and soil moisture content makes it difficult to estimate the amount of water required for crops. With this in mind, the soil and moisture control system use wireless sensors. This aids in the crop's efficient use of water and improves crop health. Agricultural water stress index irrigation management is one of the IoT approaches used to increase crop productivity. To monitor the environment and provide data, wireless field sensors have been deployed. Crop water stress index (CWSI) calculations also make use of additional data, such as meteorological data and satellite imagery, which improves water consumption effectiveness.

5.3 Fertilizers

Fertilization is used in smart farming because it aids in estimating the dose of nutrients needed, reducing any adverse environmental effects. The projected nutrient dose used in smart agriculture eventually lessens the detrimental effects of those nutrients on the environment. The kind of soil, crop variety and absorption capacity, yield, nutrient type, weather, etc. are prerequisites for fertilisation. We can quickly assess the amount of soil nutrients using satellite photos, which can further improve the fertilizer's effectiveness in determining the state of crop nutrients. Smart fertilising benefits from GPS accuracy and autonomous vehicles. To find the pests and kill them with insecticides, IoT-based gadgets, intelligent robots, and drones are deployed.

6. Hardware Components of IoT

6.1 Soil Moisture Sensor

It can identify soil moisture. The sensor uses the open short circuit operating principle and includes both analogue and digital output input. The output in this system is roughly indicated by the LED output. Dry ground causes the electricity to cease moving and become an open circuit. If the ground is wet, the circuit is closed and the output is zero while the current is flowing. Levels are used to indicate sensor information. Since it resists corrosion, the sensor can manage the cost of the farmer for a very long period at a low cost.

6.2 Temperature and Humidity Sensor

Both humidity and temperature may be measured with it. Information regarding this system's performance is displayed. In the event that the threshold is surpassed, the LED begins to flash and the numbers are immediately posted on the website so the farmer may inspect them.

6.3 The Arduino Uno

A microcontroller card that works with the ATmega328 is called the Arduino Uno. The Arduino Uno has all sensors. For the Arduino Uno, these sensors offer data about the surrounding environment. To notify farmers about sensor readings and essential steps, Arduino Uno employs cloud computing and makes the necessary judgements and takes the necessary measures. Additionally, use GSM to send them a message.

7. Adopted Approach

When farmers consider the benefits of AI and IOT for sustainable farming, using this technology may seem like a natural next step. Everyone is aware that there are still a number of significant, including the following:

7.1 AI improves Decision-making

For the agriculture sector, predictive analytics has been a genuine windfall. It assists farmers in overcoming some of the industry's most difficult problems, including analysing market demands, projecting prices, and determining the best window of time to plant and harvest a crop. AI-powered equipment can also assess the health of the soil and the crops, suggest fertiliser applications, track the weather, and assess crop quality. These and other advantages of artificial intelligence in agriculture help farmers make wiser choices and operate their operations effectively.

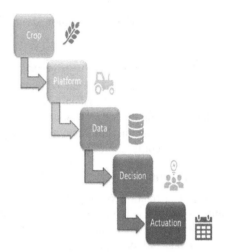

Fig. 6.2 The above diagram describes about AI decision making

7.2 AI Reduces Expenses

Farmers may grow more crops with less resources and costs by using precision farming techniques and AI-enabled machinery. Farmers can make the right decisions at each stage of farming thanks to real-time insights provided by AI. With this wise choice, there will be less product and chemical loss, and time and resources will be used more effectively. Additionally, it enables the farmers to pinpoint the precise regions that require pesticide application, fertilisation, and irrigation, reducing the amount of chemicals that are applied to the crop. All of these factors add up to less herbicide use, higher crop quality, and increased profit with less resources.

7.3 AI Helps with the Labour Shortage

The agriculture sector has long struggled with a labour deficit. This problem of farming automation can be resolved by AI. Farmers can complete tasks without adding more workers thanks to AI and automation. Some examples include driverless tractors, intelligent irrigation and fertilising systems, smart spraying, vertical farming software, and AI-based harvesting robots. When compared to human farm workers, AI-powered machinery and equipment are much faster and more accurate.

8. Conclusion

We can simply cut back on labour, investments, and farming tools and equipment in agriculture by employing the AI farming system. In comparison to previous operating methods, the automated system will require fewer farmers and less time. Since AI maximises the usage and power of resources, it can be acceptable and useful in agriculture. It eliminates resource shortages and excess labour. AI's introduction has some application in agriculture. This report evaluated a number of studies and found that agricultural activities could benefit from beneficial use of AI and IOT.

REFERENCES

1. Marvin L. Minsky, Nathaniel Rochester, Claude E. Shannon, and John McCarthy. "A proposal for the Dartmouth summer artificial intelligence research project, August 31, 1955." (2006). AI journal 27, no. 4: 12–12.
2. I. Ghosh, S. Das, G. Banerjee, and U. Sarkar. A review of the literature on artificial intelligence in agriculture[J]. 2018, Volume 7(3), Pages 1–6, International Journal of Scientific Research in Computer Science Applications and Management Studies

3. Mike, C., Fu, etc. AlphaGo by Google DeepMind, Or/ms Today, 2016.

4. Food insecurity and hunger. www.fao.org/hunger/en/ is the website of the Food and Agriculture Organization of the United Nations, which was established in 2020.

5. A third more mouths to feed by the year 2050. UN Food and Agriculture Organization, UN Food and Agriculture Organization, 2020, www.fao.org/news/story/en/item/35571/icode/.

6. Adoption of Artificial Intelligence in Agriculture, Popa, Cosmin. University of Agricultural Sciences & Veterinary Bulletin, 2011.

7. java t point of view https://www.javatpoint.com/artificial-intelligence-in-agriculture.

8. J.J. Rodrguez, J. del Cerro, D. Garzón-Ramos, P. Garcia-Aunon, M. Garzón, J. de León, and A. Barrientos. Agricultural Robots: State of the Art and Real-World Experiences. robots in service. Technology, 2018.

9. Impact Factor: 7.429, Volume 9, Issue 8, August 2021, International Journal of All Research Education and Scientific Methods (IJARESM), ISSN: 2455-6211 Visit www.ijaresm.com to access it online. Indian publication IJARESM www.ijaresm.com Page 510 Agriculture and Artificial Intelligence: A Literature Review.

10. https://doi.org/10.1007/s10479-020-03922-z Annals of Operations Research.

11. Robots are set to revolutionise agriculture, according to Bogue R. 2016; Ind. Rob., 43(5): 450–456.

12. Int J Agric & Biol Eng, vol. 11, no. 4, pp. 1–14, 2018. Redmond Shamshiri, et al., "Research and development in agricultural robotics: A perspective on digital farming."

13. Backpropagation neural network design and assessment for categorising weed species using colour picture texture. T. F. Burks et al., Transactions of the ASAE, vol. 43 no. 4, pp. 1029–1037, 2000.

14. Weed Real-time Identification Based on Neural Network Analysis and Testing, In Proc. International Conference on Computer and Computing Technologies in Agriculture, Y. Shi, H. Yuan, A. Liang, and C. Zhang (pp. 1095- 1101). 2007 Springer, Boston, Massachusetts

15. "Estimation of soil moisture in paddy fields using artificial neural networks," arXiv preprint arXiv: 1303.1868, C. Arif, M. Mizoguchi, and B. I. Setiawan, 2013.

16. Web-based expert system for diagnosing micronutrient deficiency in crops, S. S. Patil et al., Proceedings of the World Congress on Engineering and Computer Science, Vol. 1, 2009.

17. Irrigation science, vol. 28 no. 6, pp. 535–544, 2010. A. C. Hinnell et al., "Neuro-Drip: estimate of subsurface wetting patterns for drip irrigation using neural networks."

18. African Journal of Agricultural Research, vol.11 no.43, pp. 4413–4424, 2016, J. da Silva et al., "Comparison of mapping soybean regions in Brazil with perceptron neural networks and vegetation indicators."

Note: All the figures in this chapter were made by the author.

Advances in Computational Intelligence and its Applications (ICACIA-2023) – Dr. Sheikh Fahad Ahmad et al. (eds)
© 2024 Taylor & Francis Group, London, ISBN 978-1-032-78612-4

Literature Review Energy Efficient i Street Lighting System

7

Sumeet Sharma[1], Jaina Vamshi[2], P. Prithish Sai Reddy[3]

Koneru Lakshmaiah Education Foundation, Hyderabad, India

ABSTRACT—The goal of the smart city effort is to provide better, more specialized services that can raise inhabitants' standards of living while fostering sustainability. Services need to be more independent and continuously adapt to changes in their environment and information from other services if they are to succeed in achieving both of these seemingly conflicting goals. The main concept we wish to achieve is "energy on demand," which refers to providing energy, in this case light, just when required. According to the study, saving energy can result in energy savings of up to 65% and a 35% improvement in lamp lifetime. When compared to the typical ON-OFF switching method, this revolutionary technique results in significant financial and energy savings.

KEYWORDS— Intelligent street lighting, Street light controller (SLC), Sensor-based energy management, SSL implementation, Web-based software, Energy and cost savings

1. Introduction

The conventional street lighting method makes use of extremely straightforward methods that enable or disable the lights in accordance with the control of light intensity. The procedures required a wide range of tools, including timers, nightfall sensors, and astronomical clocks, among others. These systems were created with the capacity to turn on and off in a predetermined amount of time. There are numerous further systems that were created using

- utilising "light sensitive photocells" to turn on the lights at dusk and turn them off at morning,
- Street lights equipped with GPRS are meant to turn on and off in accordance with information received based on location-specific characteristics (Sun set, latitude, sun set and the longitude)
- A more advanced control system that is equipped with LED lighting and enhanced with the capacity to lower the lights, schedule the on/off times, and further adjust the light intensities.
- The current traditional street light system has problems with:
- An absence of knowledge on the current state of the lighting and the environmen.
- An inadequate system for monitoring and setting the ON/OFF timing of lights.

Fig. 7.1 Intelligent street lightning system
Source: http://istockphoto.com

[1]2110030031@klh.edu.in, [2]2110030153@klh.edu.in, [3]2110030115@klh.edu.in

DOI: 10.1201/9781003488682-7

- There is no strategy in place to maximise the effectiveness of the street lighting system.
- Controlling the independent street light unit, including switching it ON/OFF, identifying faults, and replacing it, among other things. [6]

2. Problem Statement

Currently, a manual system is in place in which the light is manually turned on and off, frequently in the evening and morning. As a result, significant energy is lost between ON and OFF.

3. Objective

On testing the i Street Light on road of width 4.0 m at a stretch of 1 K.M, we have concluded that angle of 88 degree and at an height of 12m is suitable to cover more area with high intensity of light. Hardware Component used in this project are Arduino Board, Led Lights, Proximity Sensor, Wi-Fi Module, Current Regulator.

For Cloud Services we are opting for our own server, AWS (Amazon Web Services) or any other company.[7]

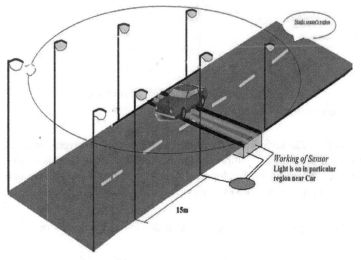

Fig. 7.2

Source: https://contest.techbriefs.com/2015/entries/electronics/5895(Techbriefs)

4. Methodology

The proposed Street Light is far better in comparison of old-style Street lights.

As per old style street lights Halogen bulbs are consuming more energy and producing a lot of heat energy which also leads to Global Warming, as per our i Street lights we are using Led bulbs to reduce the consumption of energy and reducing the chances of Global Warming.

As recent reports say that there is about 50% difference in energy consumption of Led lights and Halogen bulbs and the expected lifespan of LED lights ranges from 35 000 to 502 000 hours. This is significantly more time than any other HPS bulb, whose maximum expected life is only 24 000 hours. Clearly, the minimum lifespan of an LED light is greater than the maximum durability of an HPS bulb.

As we can observe that there is 35% of less energy consumption through our i Street Lights than old style Street Lights.

5. Implementation and Result

The idea of intelligent street lighting is spreading quickly and is a widely used model in industrialized cities. Using motion detection sensors, increasing the main goals of SSL implementation in Nagpur were to improve the energy efficiency of street

Fig. 7.3 Location of Nagpur's street lighting

Source: https://ieeexplore.ieee.org/document/9144848 (IEEE)

lights and reduce power consumption. The technical features of the project will be covered in this section, as well as a contrast between the energy use before and after the SSL implementation. A Place of Study This study will focus on a roadway in Nagpur that is part of a 6-kilometer "Smart Strip" development. Starting at Japanese Garden Square and ending at Orange City Hospital Square, this street runs straight for almost 6 kilometers. Figure 7.3 depicts the locations of the street's lighting points. [5]

Location of Nagpur's lighting points [3]. B-Technologies The following technologies or components are necessary for a successful SSL implementation:

1. *Smart LED luminaire:* Acon LED 'Smart Street Lamp' from Suveg Electronics, with an optical system based on IP 67, has been used by the city as their smart LED luminaire. An external control node for motion detection is attached to the 120 W LED.

2. *Street Light Controller (SLC):* The street lights are integrated with this device, which also stores all of the vital lighting system logs and parameters. It provides remote control dimming and intelligent ON/OFF switching, and health status is continuously being monitored. Cimcon Lighting Inc. provides the SLC utilized in this city. [9].

3. *Wireless Gateway:* This device uses a communication network for backhaul, such as 3G or 4G, or Ethernet, to synchronize data between the SLC and the lighting control software. It is made up of a radio module for setting up, commissioning, and maintaining wireless mesh networks. Using open protocols, the wireless mesh devices' I/O is mapped, making it simple to integrate them with one another between systems.

4. *Web Based software:* This program is a web-based management tool that enables control over the lighting infrastructure as well as real-time usage data.

The SSL system flow diagram utilized in Nagpur is shown in Fig. 7.3. All of the streetlights across the street have SLC and motion detection sensors installed. These use the ZigBee protocol to interact with the wireless gateway. There are eight wireless gateways in all, eight of which are found at intersections and are assigned a group of bulbs. The data center's web servers, which deliver data through wired medium, are connected to the wireless gateways.[5]

It is clear that these technologies will result in significant energy and cost savings. The value of smart lighting systems is demonstrated by the evaluation of energy use and operating costs of various LED- Street Lighting Systems. Future development will benefit from a comparison of the suggested methodology with different street lighting systems, as shown in the following sections.[5]

Table 7.1 Comparative advantages: Power consumption and cost analysis of conventional vs. smart street lighting systems

Advantage	Analysis
Power consumption analysis	The research of traditional and smart street lighting systems included a 100-Watt LED bulb installed in 36 streetlights implemented to improve cost-effectiveness and reduce energy usage.
Cost analysis	For a better understanding of the suggested methodology, a comparison of economic analysis with various street lighting systems is computed. Consumption information for various lighting schemes is taken from Fig. 7.4 to examine LED and smart lighting systems based on their operating cost consumption.

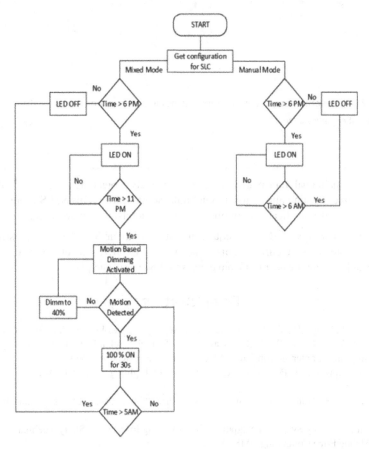

Fig. 7.4 Smart street lights in Nagpur: A process flow diagram

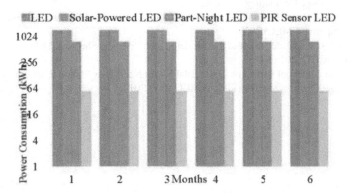

Fig. 7.5 Usage of energy by different smart lighting systems for 6 months

Source: http://link.springer.com (Springer)

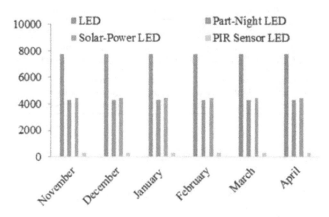

Fig. 7.6 Present energy cost of various street lights schemes during 2019–2020

Source: http://semanticscholar.org (Semantics Scholar)

6. Conclusion

Saving the current is this paper's main goal. It primarily serves to effectively protect the electricity. Utilizing sensors to conserve energy without wastage. Safe street lighting allows for tranquil automobile traffic. This SSLS is appropriate for highway roads and small streets. This approach is also applicable to public spaces like hotels, workplaces, etc.

It regulates the current overflow. This system doesn't require any human labour. This SSLS is mostly utilized on roads and in cities to cut down on energy waste and save current. This smart lighting improves the effectiveness of street lights while also fostering a safe atmosphere and making it easier to manage costs and power usage.[7]

REFERENCES

1. Y. Wu, C. Shi, X. Zhang and W. Yang, "Design of new intelligent street light control system", IEEE ICCA 2010, pp. 1423-1427, 2010.
2. H. S. H. Chung, N. M. Ho, S. Y. R. Hui and W. Z. Mai, "Case study of a highly-reliable dimmable road lighting system with intelligent remote control", 2005 European 5 Conference on Power Electronics and Applications, 2005.
3. J. Higuera, W. Hertog, M. Perálvarez, J. Polo and J. Carreras, "Smart Lighting System ISO/IEC/IEEE 21451 Compatible", IEEE Sensors Journal, vol. 15, no. 5.
4. Deepak K Srivatsa, B Preethi, R Parinita, G Sumana and A Kumar, "Smart Street Lights", Texas Instruments India Educators' Conference, 2013.
5. Energy Efficient Smart Street Lighting System in Nagpur Smart City using IoT-A Case Study Ruchika Prasad 2020 Fifth International Conference on Fog and Mobile Edge Computing(FMEC),2020.
6. Eergy_Efficient Smart Street Lighting System in Nagpur Smart City using IoT-A Case Study Ruchika Prasad 2020 Fifth International Conference on Fog and Mobile Edge Computing(FMEC),2020.
7. Energy and Economic Analysis of Smart Technologies on Street Ligt System Arshad Mohammad 2020 Fifth International Conference on Fog and Mobile Edge Computing(FMEC),2020.
8. Smart Street Light Lamps Rishikesh Lohote ;TejalBhogle; Vaidehi Patel; Vishakha Shelke 2018 International Conference on Smart City and Emerging Technology(ICSCET), 2019.
9. Intelligent street light system in context of smart grid Hafiz Bilal Khalil;Naee Abas;Shoaib Rauf 2017 8th International Conference on Computing, Communication and Networking Technologies (ICCCNT),2017.

Advances in Computational Intelligence and its Applications (ICACIA-2023) – Dr. Sheikh Fahad Ahmad et al. (eds)
© *2024 Taylor & Francis Group, London, ISBN 978-1-032-78612-4*

Robotics in Medical and Health Care: A Critical Review

8

Narra Manas*, Sakinala Sri Sai Pawan,
Manjunadha Mallina, Dasari Anantha Reddy[1]
Department of Computer Science and Engineering,
Koneru Lakshmaiah Education Foundation, Hyderabad, India

ABSTRACT—Due of the demand for collaborative robots, robotic technology advancements have historically been concentrated on the industrial sector. However, the service industries, particularly the healthcare industry, do not operate in this manner. The healthcare industry has not received enough attention, which has created new opportunities for the development of service robots that assist people with impairments, illnesses, and cognitive difficulties. In an effort to combat the challenges and adversities brought on by this epidemic, the COVID-19 epidemic has also functioned as a spur for the creation of service robots in the healthcare industry. The employment of service robots is lucrative because they not only slow the transmission of disease and lower the risk of fatal mistake, but they also enable front-line employees to avoid direct contact with patients while focusing on higher priority duties and avoiding exposure to infectious agents. This paper provides an overview of several robotic technology kinds and applications in the medical and healthcare fields. The use of robotics is formerly there in healthcare, but it's not main-aqueduct yet and it would take some time for that to come a reality Pay attention to the necessity of robotics in the healthcare industry, as well as their added benefits to healthcare quality and cost savings over the long term. With this, telemedicine, the future of healthcare, would become a reality, making it much simpler and less expensive for patients to obtain high-quality treatment anywhere in the world without physically going to the hospital, the sanitorium.

KEYWORDS—Cognitive, Rehabilitation, Adaptable, Ameliorate, Orthopedic, Surgical

1. Introduction

The federated regions with distinctive enterprises associated to the management and control of the new coronavirus complaint in 2019 and the expanding role of robots in healthcare (COVID- 19). Comparable robots are mostly used in hospitals and other similar situations that operate as a counterblockade to provide cleanliness, sterility, and aid while minimizing human-to-human interaction. This will help to lessen the risk to the lives of medical personnel and other participants in the COVID-19 epidemic. In order for sanitarium operations to optimise the use of medical robots for exciting medical procedures, the current study aims to underline the importance of medical robotics in general and connect its application with the viewpoint of COVID-19 operations.

This is true even though telemedicine is frequently employed and useful in cases like these. In essence, cutting-edge medical technology was necessary for the recent success of the health sectors in China and Korea in carrying out active containment of the COVID-19 epidemic.

Automation and robotics are being used more and more in healthcare and related fields[1][2]. The International Federation of Robots (IFR), which forecasts a 9.1 billion USD industry by 2022, predicts that demand for medical robots would rise

*Corresponding author: manasn2003@gmail.com
[1]anantha.d@klh.edu.in

DOI: 10.1201/9781003488682-8

significantly over the upcoming several years. Robots help physicians and other medical professionals carry out complex and precise tasks while also reducing their burden and improving the efficiency of healthcare institutions as a whole[3].

Medical robots utilise contemporary technology to carry out a range of tasks required for cleaning, sterilising, transport, nursing, rehabilitation, and surgical applications [4].Such complex and agile robots often employ adaptive, reliable embedded controllers for navigation and control. Because they must be free of germs and other impurities that might spread infectious illnesses to other patients, robots used in healthcare and medicine must conform to high hygiene requirements. Most surgical end effectors have just one purpose in mind. It is occasionally necessary to sanitize service robots to stop the spread of illness.

Cleaning procedures for cooking robots are different because they may be washed after usage. The majority of hospital care robots are mobile robots with limited degrees of freedom and a large payload capacity (DOF). On the other hand, multi-DOF surgical robots are adaptable, accurate, and reliable equipment that provide performance comparable to that of a skilled human surgeon with a minimum error margin, usually within millimetres[5][6]. The "Delta" robot, also known as FlexPicker (ABB, Zurich, Switzerland), is an illustration of a parallel kinematic manipulator (PKM). It was first created for surgical applications but is now widely employed in the food processing industry.

The use of a robot in a hospital should be safe enough not to put the patient, the operator, the medical staff, the attending doctor, or the surgeon at risk. Surgical robots must adhere to the safety standards outlined in standard IEC 80601-2-77[7]. IEC 80601-2-78 provides the fundamental performance and safety requirements for rehabilitation robots. The designers of such equipment must always provide straightforward architecture, simple handling, and rapid maintenance. Maintenance is simple for medical service robots that assist patients with prostheses, orthoses, hearing aids, and visual prosthesis[8]. Medical robots must always have access to AC/DC power for this vital machinery to function continually.

Medical facilities need reliable power solutions and the use of a variety of renewable energy sources, from large, centrally situated city hospitals to purpose-built field hospitals[9]. For mobile robots in hospitals, wireless power transfer is also being developed to lessen the need for frequent charging. Since there is a huge need for healthcare robotic solutions, those solutions must be affordable in order to be widely available and simple to install everywhere in the world, including in poor countries.

The many needs for robots in healthcare are as follows:

- Dynamics and Kinematics
- Refinement and dexterity
- Sterilization
- User Security
- Simple handling and upkeep
- Power Requirements
- Cost

2. Literature Review

Robots are primarily categorised according to the many uses they have in healthcare and related industries. These robots are best used at the hospital's front desk to tell patients and visitors about the hospital's many departments and units. They can deal with a lot of guests without being worn out and point them in the direction of the doctor of their choice. Additionally, they captivate hospitalized kids by creating enjoyable experiences for them, which lessens their symptoms of illness.[10]

Similar to how human nurses assist doctors in the hospital, these robots are designed to do so. Given that Japan has the highest percentage of elderly people (those over 75 years old) among OCED countries, nurse robots are often deployed in Japanese hospitals. The medical institutes around the country are becoming concerned about this. Because there is a shortage of qualified candidates for senior care, more Japanese individuals feel obligated to care for elderly family members at home rather than at their places of employment[11]. Additionally, because of the heavy patient load, nursing and healthcare professionals experience high levels of stress and tiredness. The Japanese government is seeking for technical answers to provide for the nation's elderly patients. Several nursing robots are being utilized to aid elderly patients in Japan, including Paro (AIST, Toyama, Japan), Pepper (Softbank Robotics, Paris, France), and Dinsow (CT Asia Robotics, Bangkok, Thailand). These robots provide lifting assistance as well as therapeutic support. Each of these robots is essential to the Japanese healthcare system in some way. For instance, Dinsow includes unique characteristics for those with Alzheimer's. The acceptability of service robots varies from nation to nation, nevertheless.

Approximately 800,000 persons in the European Union (EU) experience cardiac arrest each year, and only 8% of these patients survive [12]. Because emergency services normally take 10 minutes to respond, a major portion of these casualties are the result of brainstem death, which begins just 4-6 minutes after acute cardiac arrest.

After an accident, receiving qzuick medical attention is essential to preventing trauma from getting worse. As a result of quick recovery, more lives can be saved by accelerating emergency response. In the circumstances of drowning, cardiac arrest, shocks, and respiratory problems, this is particularly true. It is possible to create lightweight, transportable disaster medical supplies, CPR tools, and Automated External Defibrillator (AED) devices that may all be transported to the emergency site by a drone. These robots are useful for delivering emergency care to a patient who is on the go or in a remote location as quickly as feasible. The Ambulance Drone (TU Delft, Netherlands) has created a lightweight micro payload that includes vital medical equipment for life support. An Automated Defibrillator is what the early prototype is supposed to give (AED)[13].

Material pushing and pulling is necessary for numerous jobs in hospitals. Serving robots can be used to complete these labor-intensive chores with ease. Additionally, robots are used to deliver food to a variety of hospital patients. As seen in they are employed to convey ordinary and contaminated garbage, dispense medications, remove dirty laundry, deliver fresh bed linen, and serve meals and beverages inside the hospital.

Robots are employed to mop and/or dry vacuum in hospitals to clean them[14]. Hospital cleaning robots appear to be able to deliver the innovation that non-industrial robot systems' designers had long anticipated. To remove chemicals and bacteria from hospitals, these robots are essential. Peanut Robot (San Francisco, USA) uses a highly dynamic robotic gripper and sensor system to clean hospital bathrooms. Hospital floors are cleaned by the self-sufficient Swingobot 2000 (TASKI, South Carolina, USA) cleaning robot.

In radiology, where there are risks to human operators and high radiation levels, robots are increasingly in demand as one of the primary technologies. The Siemens Twin Robotic X-ray (Siemens Healthineers, Henkestr, Germany) is a medical breakthrough that provides 3D imaging, fluoroscopy, and angiography[15]. The doctor may view 3D images in real time while the robot takes the place of the patient and completes a large number of X-rays in only one room. Small hairline fractures in the bone are frequently missed by conventional 2D X-rays, needing a computed tomography (CT) 3D scan to confirm the diagnosis. A CT system is not necessary with the Multitom Rax Twin Robotic X-ray system since a 3D image may be simply acquired on the same system.

MIS is now expanding across a wide range of surgical methods because to fourth-generation Da Vinci surgical systems from Intuitive Surgical in California, USA. For surgeons utilising Da Vinci systems, this provides an interface that is dependable, has an upgradeable design, and allows for variable configurations. The management of inventory and increased efficiency are

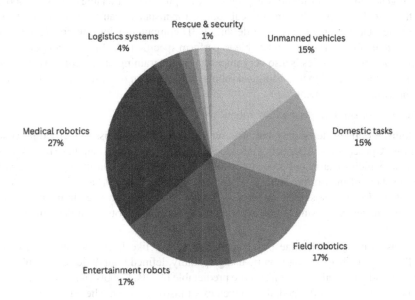

Fig. 8.1 The vitality of robotics in the healthcare industry

two benefits of standardising equipment and parts in hospitals[16]. A sensitive, seven-axis, lightweight robot that can carry out a range of surgical operations is called the LBR Med. It is very adaptable and simple to integrate into medical devices. It is perfect for use in medical technology because of its sensitive sensors, all-encompassing safety measures, sanitary surfaces, and a controller designed for direct human operator interface. Additional sorts of specialised surgical robots are used for biopsies, general endoscopic, cranial, and spine surgery. The Korean equivalent of Revo-I is known as the Da Vinci surgical system. To carry out challenging surgical procedures, KUKA (Augsburg, Germany) uses its high-performance serial KUKA LBR Med surgical robot.

3. Health Care Robotics Benefits

3.1 Exemplary Patient Care

Intelligent curatives, frequent and individualised monitoring for cases with habitual conditions, minimally invasive operations, and social commerce for senior cases are all made possible by medical robots. also, when robots reduce workloads, nurses and other healthcare providers can communicate with cases more tête-à-tête and show further compassion, both of which can ameliorate cases' long- term good[17].

3.2 Effortless Clinical Workflows

The use of independent mobile robots(AMRs) streamlines regular tasks, eases the physical burden on mortal workers, and promotes more dependable operations. By keeping track of supplies and timely ordering, these robots can help insure that inventories, outfit, and specifics are available where they're needed, addressing staffing dearths and issues. cleaning and sanitising AMRs make it possible for sanitarium apartments to be instantly gutted and prepared for new cases, freeing up staff members to concentrate on case- centered, value- driven work[17].

3.3 Safe Working Conditions

In hospitals where there's a possibility of complaint exposure, AMRs are used to convey inventories and linens to help keep healthcare staff safe. Hospital acquired infections(HAIs) can be dropped by planting cleaning and disinfection robots, which are formerly being used by hundreds of healthcare facilities1. AMRs, similar as social robots, help with heavy lifting by moving beds or cases, easing the physical burden on healthcare professionals[17].

3.4 Robotic Surgical Assistants

The use of artificial intelligence in surgical robotics is growing. Computer vision enables surgical robots to discern between diverse tissue types in their field of view. Modern surgical robots, for instance, can help surgeons steer clear of nerves and muscles while doing surgeries. During operations, high-definition 3D computer vision can give surgeons detailed information and improve performance. In the future, robots will be able to perform specific tasks like suturing or other little subprocedures while the surgeon watches carefully. Robotics is also very important in the training of surgeons. Artificial intelligence (AI) and virtual reality simulation systems are used to teach surgical robots. Surgeons can practise treatments and hone abilities utilising robotic controls within the virtual environment.

There are two major categories of surgeries assisted by robotics:

1. Robotic prostatectomy, robotic hysterectomy, bariatric surgery, and other soft tissue-focused procedures are examples of torso minimally invasive procedures. After being introduced through a tiny incision, these robots lock into place, offering a stable platform from which to carry out procedures under remote control. During open surgery, large incisions were utilised to perform the bulk of interior procedures. There was a larger chance of infection and other issues, and recovery times were much longer. Even for a skilled surgeon, it is quite challenging to operate manually through a button-sized incision. These treatments are made simple and accurate using surgical robots, with the aim of lowering infections and other problems.

2. Orthopedic operations to carry out routine orthopaedic procedures like knee and hip replacements, devices can be preprogrammed. These robots help the surgeon by using spatially defined boundaries and combining intelligent robotic arms with 3D imaging and data analytics to offer more predictable results. Robots can be programmed to execute specific orthopaedic surgery with the help of AI modelling, given exact instructions on where to go and what to do.

4. Adopted Approaches

One of the most well-known uses of medical robotics in the modern world is the employment of robots, computers, and software to accurately operate surgical equipment via one or more tiny incisions for various surgical operations. Small robots that can be driven to particular locations to do activities like obtaining a sample or cauterising a leaking blood artery may soon replace traditional endoscopy. Microrobots may be used to administer therapy, such as radiation or medication, to a particular spot while moving through blood arteries. Robotic endoscopic capsules can be consumed to track the gastrointestinal tract, gather information, and relay diagnostic findings to the user.

The following list includes five robots that are now being deployed in hospitals and other healthcare institutions to improve patient outcomes and care standards.

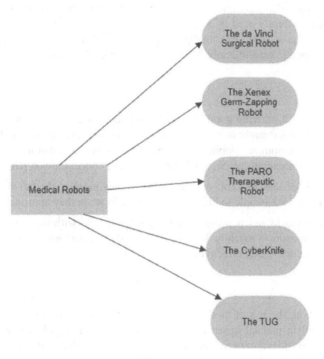

Fig. 8.2 Types of medical robot's

4.1 The da Vinci Surgical Robot

Although it seems impossible, more than 250,000 people in the United States pass away every year due to medical mistakes, some of which were probably avoidable.

Although this is a large area including a variety of issues, it is unquestionably true that the more control surgeons have over their procedures, the better. The da Vinci Surgical System is a multi-armed wonderbot that is being used to reduce surgical mistakes and make treatments less invasive for thousands of patients. The da Vinci Surgical System gives surgeons more precise control during a range of operations. The da Vinci System uses magnified 3D high-definition vision and controls that strap to a surgeon's wrists and hands to make tiny, precise incisions that human hands would not otherwise be able to do. Because the process is less invasive than traditional surgery, patients recover more rapidly and this provides surgeons better control.

4.2 The Xenex Germ-Zapping Robot

Another prevalent problem in healthcare, hospital-acquired infections (HAIs), might be reduced with the use of robots in addition to minimising medical and surgical mistakes.

In order to solve this basic problem, the Xenex, an automated and transportable robot, is used to disinfect whole hospital rooms in minutes using pulsed, full-spectrum UV rays that kill a range of infectious microorganisms. It aims to reduce HAIs by removing the bacteria that cause them, which are known to cause infections like Methicillin-resistant Staphylococcus aureus and can be particularly difficult to cure (MRSA). The robot is also sort of cute; it looks like an R2-D2 made for saving lives.

4.3 The PARO Therapeutic Robot

The PARO Therapeutic Robot was developed to simulate the therapeutic benefits of animals without employing actual animals. It is an interactive device that looks like a newborn harbour seal. Although trained animals are frequently made available to meet the needs of the moment, animal therapy is frequently used to reduce patient stress. The ideal candidate is the amiable, canine PARO. It has been demonstrated that PARO can ease patients' anxiety and reduce tension in elderly people with dementia[18].

4.4 The CyberKnife

With sub-millimeter accuracy, the Cyberknife robotic surgery system applies radiation therapy to malignancies. The CyberKnife system, developed in the 1990s, is currently used in hospitals and cancer treatment facilities across the United States to treat cancer. The CyberKnife has made it possible to treat malignancies in parts of the body like the prostate, head, neck, and liver that were previously difficult to operate on surgically. Because this "surgery" is non-invasive, less radiation is absorbed by healthy organs and tissues[19].

4.5 The TUG

Even though you might not consider it, moving goods like food, supplies, and other items around the hospital slows down operations. A typical 200-bed hospital is thought to carry food, linens, lab samples, garbage, and other commodities at a rate of 53 miles per day. 7 Enter TUG, an autonomous mobile robot created by Aethon Inc. that transports supplies to the appropriate locations, relieving staff members of strenuous physical labour so they can concentrate on patient care[20].

They are equipped with a multitude of sensors to prevent collisions as they move to the lab and have the hospital's floor plan recorded into them. Additionally, they ask people to kindly step to the side when they approach packed halls.

Medical robotics will develop to do tasks independently, more effectively, and with more accuracy. Robots of all types will continue to advance as new developments in machine learning, data analytics, computer vision, and other technologies enable them to do tasks autonomously, accurately, and effectively.

5. Conclusion

As a result of healthcare digitization, the use of medical robots has considerably improved the safety and quality of health management systems as compared to manual approaches. Medical robots are largely categorised using application-based categories to meet every component of hospital services, ranging from highly advanced surgical robots to cleaning robots. A cyber-physical system (CPS), power management using optimised algorithms and renewable sources, fault tolerant control, and reliable designs are some of the choices available in the design and operation of medical robots for dependable and secure functioning inside healthcare facilities. In the Colombian context, 82.9% of participants expressed a favourable opinion on the advancement and application of robotics in healthcare settings. Finally, participants generally showed a favourable attitude toward using robots and suggested their implementation in the current environment.

REFERENCES

1. Iqbal J., Khan Z., Khalid A. Prospects of robotics in food industry. *Food Sci. Technol.* 2017;**37**:159–165. doi: 10.1590/1678-457x.14616. [CrossRef] [Google Scholar] [Ref list]
2. Khan Z.H., Khalid A., Iqbal J. Towards realizing robotic potential in future intelligent food manufacturing systems. *Innov. Food Sci. Emerg. Technol.* 2018;**48**:11–24. doi: 10.1016/j.ifset.2018.05.011. [CrossRef] [Google Scholar] [Ref list]
3. Taylor R.H., Menciassi A., Fichtinger G., Fiorini P., Dario P., Siciliano B., Khatib O. *Medical Robotics and Computer-Integrated Surgery.* Springer; Berlin, Germany: 2016. pp. 1657–1684.
4. Bouteraa Y., Ben Abdallah I., Ghommam J. Task-space region-reaching control for medical robot manipulator. *Comput. Electr. Eng.* 2018;**67**:629–645. doi: 10.1016/j.compeleceng.2017.02.004.
5. Balasubramanian S., Chenniah J., Balasubramanian G., Vellaipandi V. The era of robotics: Dexterity for surgery and medical care: Narrative review. *Int. Surg.*
6. Bai L., Yang J., Chen X., Sun Y., Li X. Medical Robotics in Bone Fracture Reduction Surgery: A Review. *Sensors.* 2019;**19**:3593. doi: 10.3390/s19163593. *J.* 2020;**7**:1317. doi: 10.18203/2349-2902.isj20201057.

7. Chinzei K. Safety of surgical robots and IEC 80601-2-77: The First International Standard for Surgical Robots. *Acta Polytech. Hung.*

8. Petrescu R.V. Medical service of robots. *J. Mechatron. Robot.* 2019;**3**:60–81. doi: 10.3844/jmrsp.2019.60.81.

9. Iqbal J., Khan Z.H. The potential role of renewable energy sources in robot's power system: A case study of Pakistan. *Renew. Sustain. Energy Rev.* 2017;**75**:106–122. doi: 10.1016/j.rser.2016.10.055.

10. Karabegović I., Doleček V. The Role of Service Robots and Robotic Systems in the Treatment of Patients in Medical Institutions. *Micro Electron. Telecommun. Eng.* 2016;**3**:9–25. doi: 10.1007/978-3-319-47295-9_2.

11. Kumar B., Sharma L., Wu S.-L. Job Allocation schemes for Mobile Service Robots in Hospitals; Proceedings of the 2018 IEEE International Conference on Bioinformatics and Biomedicine (BIBM) (IEEE); Madrid, Spain. 3–6 December 2018; pp. 1323–1326.

12. Samani H., Zhu R. Robotic Automated External Defibrillator Ambulance for Emergency Medical Service in Smart Cities. *IEEE Access.* 2016;**4**:268–283. doi: 10.1109/ACCESS.2016.2514263.

13. Momont A. Ambulance drone. [(accessed on 20 March 2020)]; Available online: https://www.tudelft.nl/en/ide/research/research-labs/applied-labs/ambulance-drone/

14. Prassler E., Ritter A., Schaeffer C., Fiorini P. A Short History of Cleaning Robots. *Auton. Robot.* 2000;**9**:211–226. doi: 10.1023/A:1008974515925.

15. Twin Robotic X-Ray. Siemens. [(accessed on 19 March 2020)]; Available online: https://www.siemens-healthineers.com/robotic-x-ray/twin-robotic-x-ray [Ref list]

16. Da Vinci Surgical Robots. [(accessed on 18 March 2020)]; Available online: https://www.intuitive.com/en-us/products-and-services/davinci [Ref list]

17. This review is taken from intel products page https://www.intel.in/content/www/in/en/healthcare-it/robotics-in-healthcare.html#:~:text=Robots%20in%20the%20medical%20field,with%20and%20caring%20for%20patients

18. Locsin R.C., Ito H., Tanioka T., Yasuhara Y., Osaka K., Schoenhofer S.O. Humanoid Nurse Robots as Caring Entities: A Revolutionary Probability? *Int. J. Stud. Nurs.* 2018;**3**:146. doi: 10.20849/ijsn.v3i2.456.

19. Cyberknife—Precise Robotic Treatment as Individual as Every Patient. [(accessed on 19 March 2020)]; Available online: https://www.accuray.com/cyberknife/[Ref list]

20. TUG-Change Healthcare. Aethon. [(accessed on 18 March2020)]; Availableonline: https://aethon.com/mobile-robots-for-healthcare/

Note: All the figures in this chapter were made by the author

Advances in Computational Intelligence and its Applications (ICACIA-2023) – Dr. Sheikh Fahad Ahmad et al. (eds)
© *2024 Taylor & Francis Group, London, ISBN 978-1-032-78612-4*

Automatic Speed Control of Vehicles at Accident Zone

9

**Hanumanthu Manasa[1], Ega Sri Harsha[2],
Teepireddy Nikitha Reddy[3]**

Department of Computer Science and Engineering,
Koneru Lakshmaiah Education Foundation, Hyderabad, India

ABSTRACT—This project's goal is to automatically regulate the speed of vehicles in zones with speed limits, such as school and hospital zones, U-turns, etc. Special types of transmitters that are set to the 433 MHZ frequency are mounted in a specific area. These transmitters emit an RF signal constantly. The vehicle's receiver is triggered when it comes into contact with this radiation. Every time the car enters the zone, the speed is regulated by receiving the signal; that is, every time the speed is reduced to a cutoff and maintained until the vehicle exits the zone, at which point the vehicle can accelerate on its own.

KEYWORDS— RF transmitter and receiver, Intelligent speed adaptation (ISA), Active accelerator pedal (AAP), Ecological driving operation, Speed verification and adaptation, Speed limit regulation, Electric car routing

1. Introduction

At the moment, reckless driving and excessive speed are the main causes of accidents. No one does the concept of human lives. Because there are more automobiles on the road, accident rates are rising year over year. The government has taken far too many measures to stop this kind of conduct, but they are insufficient. A laser-based control system has been created by the majority of manufacturers, however, it is too expensive. However, when a person crosses the road, it cannot be detected adequately, thus we tried to create a method to easily control these things. The vehicle's receiver and RF transmitter are both located in the areas around the road. After that, it sends the data to the controller. The controller will receive input from an ultrasonic sensor or a separate module that monitors the current speed. The driver does not slow down. When the driver exceeds the set speed limit, the control is automatically transferred but the information is sent to the closest police station. The data includes the vehicle's registration number and current speed. The GSM module assists the controller in transmitting data. After that, the owner pays the fine amount.

2. Literature Review

Mary Spichkova and others Proposed smart formal models of speed verification and adaptation. The author of this work describes the ISA (Intelligent Speed Adaptation) algorithm. Fully autonomous driving refers to a situation where the car is the only intelligent object on the road. It requires a formal modeling method for the relevant intelligent vehicle units to improve road safety and enable constraint units that represent variations in speed limits in different countries.

Magnus HJALMDAHL et al., Speed control by means of an active accelerator pedal in a car The AAP algorithm is described by the author of this article (Active Accelerator Pedal).

[1]manasahanumanthu01@gmail.com, [2]sriharsha.eaga@yahoo.in, [3]2110030352@klh.edu.in

DOI: 10.1201/9781003488682-9

Rafael Basso and other Published Electric car routing that considers traffic. The author of this research put up a methodology for route optimization for electric commercial vehicles. Acceleration, weather, and distance minimization are all impacted by this strategy. Qingfeng Lin et al. the proposed ecological driving operation based on communication between the vehicle and the infrastructure at multiple signalized intersections. The author uses the Legendre pseudo spectral (LPS) approach in this paper. It is based on the substantial fuel benefit of road travel. To reduce fuel usage, an optimal control problem (OCP) is created. It has been discovered that the two-stage or three-stage style of operation makes for the best driving performance. With this technique, the vehicle's speed remains constant but the fuel usage is only decreased.

3. Controller Unit

3.1 RF Transmitter and RF Receiver

A 433 MHz RF transceiver module is a set of two tiny radio frequency (RF) electrical modules that are used to send and receive radio alerts between any two devices. The receiver module receives information from the receiver stop and the transmitter module transmits information from the transmitter stop to the receiver stop.

Fig. 9.1   RF transmitter and RF receiver [6]

Specifications of RF transmitter

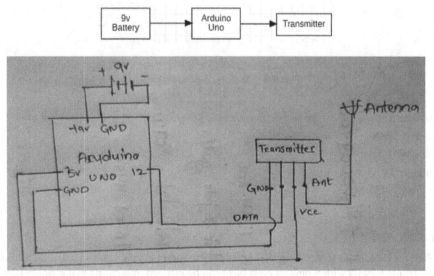

Fig. 9.2   Sketch of connections for arduino to RF trasmitter

Source: Author

- The maximum range of the antenna under typical circumstances is 100 meters.
- TX 433 MHz is the frequency of the receiver and its typical sensitivity is 105 Dbm. Frequency range: 433.92 MHz
- RX supply current: 3.5 mA
- RX IF frequency: 1MHz
- RX operating voltage: 5V
- 3 to 6 volts for TX power
- 412 Dbm TX output power

Specifications of RF receiver

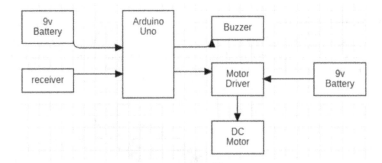

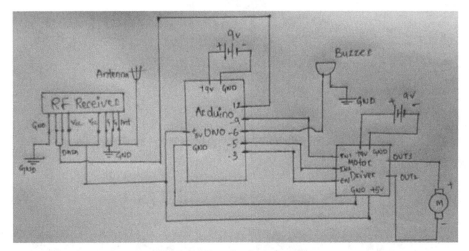

Fig. 9.3 Sketch of connections

Source: Author

- The antenna's maximum range under typical circumstances is 100 meters.
- RX Supply Current: 3.5 mA
- RX IF Frequency: 1MHz
- RX Operating Voltage: 5V
- RX Receiver Frequency: 433 MHz
- RX Typical Sensitivity: 105 Dbm

3.2 Motor Driver

A basic motor controller, the L293D integrated chip (IC) enables us to direct the path and speed of a DC motor while driving it. To control the motor, a 16-pin L293D with 8 pins on each facet can be utilized, indicating that a single L293D can power up to two DC vehicles. There are two H-bridge circuits in the L293D. The H-bridge is the most straightforward circuit for changing the polarity of a load.

Fig. 9.4 Motor driver [7]

Motor Driver Specifications

A wide supply voltage range of 4.5 to 36 volts is available. Separate logic supply for input Internal ESD Defense Inputs with high noise immunity

- Inductive transient suppression using output clamp diodes
- 600 mA output modern-day in line with channel
- 1.2 A height output cutting-edge according to channel
- Operational Temperature variety: 0 to 70 °C
- There is an automatic thermal shutdown option.

3.3 DC Motor

The outside frame dimensions of the 180 dc motors are 31.5x20.2x15.4mm as a rule. It is indicated by the number 180. The number is the same as the 775 motors. Almost all manufacturers use the conventional and common 2 mm shaft size. The shaft's length can range from 6 mm to 15 mm depending on the application, although a 9 mm shaft is the most typical. The motor's rotational speed (rpm) and operating voltage are directly proportional, and the rpm must be calibrated to meet the project's requirements. Its 3 to 8 volt nominal operational voltage range.

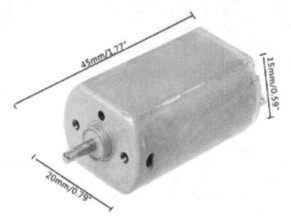

Fig. 9.5 DC motor [8]

3.4 Bread Board

An alternative to soldering, a soldering iron can be used to build temporary electrical prototypes and test circuit designs. Most electronic components in digital circuits can be connected to one another by inserting their wires or terminals into the appropriate holes and, if necessary, making a reference to the wires. Under the cutting board, metal strips connect the holes inside the cutting board's pinnacle. The placement of the metal strips is depicted below. Be careful that the pinnacle and bottom rows of holes are connected horizontally and separated in half while the remaining holes are linked vertically.

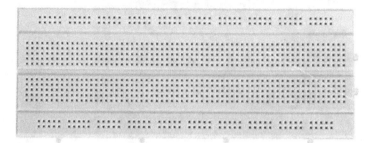

Fig. 9.6 Bread board [9]

3.5 Arduino Uno

A microcontroller board called Arduino UNO is based on the ATmega328 (datasheet). It contains a USB port, a power jack, an ICSP header, a reset button, a 16 MHz ceramic resonator, 6 analog inputs, 14 virtual enter/output pins, 6 of which can be used as PWM outputs contains everything needed to support the microcontroller; to use it, connect a USB cable, AC-to-DC adapter, or battery.

Fig. 9.7 Arduino UNO [10]

Fig. 9.8 Buzzer [11]

3.6 Buzzer

This buzzer is an active buzzer, which means that even if you only supply steady DC power, it will chirp at a set frequency (2300–300 Hz) on its own. If you're looking for a buzzer that can produce a variety of tones from an oscillating entrance signal, take a peek at our passive buzzer. Given that they can produce a variety of tones while an oscillating signal is applied and can be operated with stable DC current, some people prefer to buy active buzzers.

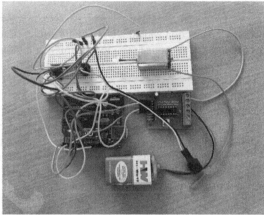

Fig. 9.9 The final connections made

Source: Author

4. Proposed Procedure

- Arduino UNO is an ATmega328p microcontroller that accepts analog input and outputs it through digital pins.
- Consider an Arduino UNO and supply it with a 9-volt power source.
- Use the Arduino Droid app to transfer the RF transmitter code from the Arduino to the Arduino UNO.
- Use jumper wires to connect the Arduino's output power supply to the Vcc and GND pins of the RF transmitter.
- The Arduino's 5v output power source is sufficient to operate the transmitter.
- To connect the RF Transmitter data terminal, disconnect the jumper connection from digital PIN 12. (DATA).
- Provide the Arduino UNO with the motor driver and RF receiver Arduino code.
- Give the Arduino a 9-volt battery supply and disconnect the jumper from analogue PIN 5v & GND.
- An additional 9 volt battery supply is added to the motor driver because the jumper connection provided to connect the power supplies for the RF receiver and motor driver is insufficient for the operation of a 9 volt DC motor.
- PIN 12 is linked to the data terminal for the RF Receiver (DATA).
- PIN 9,5,3 is attached to the motor driver as input signals for the terminals (IN1, IN2, EN).
- PIN 6 is connected to the buzzer; when the receiver is in an accident zone, the buzzer will ring.
- The motor driver is then linked to the 9-volt DC motor through the output terminals (OUT1, OUT2).
- The transmitter and receiver have the ability to regulate the motor's speed.
- The motor speed is reduced when the receiver receives a message from the transmitter. Later, when the receiver is not in the transmission route, the speed can increase to its maximum level.
- Buzzer will emit a sound to let you know when the receiver has successfully received a message from the transmitter.

5. Advantages

- A low power transmitter is sufficient for use.
- Many accidents that could happen are prevented.
- Compatible with all car safety systems.
- Less labour is needed
- There are edges that are steep.
- Driver attentiveness will increase.
- The automatic regulation of the headlights' high and low beams.
- Managing the horns of the vehicles in and around hospitals, schools, etc.

6. Disadvantages

RF Transmitter connection should always be turned on. Every vehicle should be required to connect the RF receiver module since the buzzer will emit sound even in transmission regions located distant from the receiver.

7. Conclusion

This project's work has taught us that installing RF technology in automobiles can help us reduce the number of traffic accidents. People moving through school zones, hospital zones, and curves on the road can benefit from this project. RF Modules are used to automatically reduce the speed of moving vehicles at high speeds. To make the project function, we laboured arduously throughout the semester. Despite numerous challenges and frustrating moments, we managed to finish the project on schedule. The project presented us with a number of challenges. But if we take a stride toward creating a safer road for a better future, all of our efforts will have been fruitful.

REFERENCE

1. Silvia Magdici and Matthias Althoff, "Adaptive cruise control with safety guarantees for autonomous vehicles", Science Direct, 2017.
2. Shigeharu Miyata, Takashi Nagakami, Sei Kobayashi, Tomoji Izumi, Hisayoshi Naito, Akira Yanou, et al., "Improvement of Adaptive Cruise Control Performance", Journal of Advances in Signal Processing, 2010.
3. Vignesh H Sai, Mohammed Shimil, M Nagaraj, B Sharmila and Pandian M Nagaraj, "RF based Automatic Vehicle Speed limiter by controlling Throttle Valve", International Journal of Innovative Research in Science & Technology, vol. 4, no. 1, 2015.
4. Y Yamamura, Y Seto, H Nishira and T Kawabe, "An ACC design method for achieving both string stability and ride comfort", Journal of Systems Design and Dynamics, vol. 2, no. 4, pp. 979–990, 2008.
5. M. Persson, F. Botling, E. Hesslow and R. Johansson, "Stop and Go Controller for Adaptive Cruise Control", Proceedings of the 1999 IEEE International Control Applications Conference, vol. 2, pp. 1692–1697, 1999.
6. https://www.google.com/imgres?imgurl=https%3A%2F%2Fwww.electronicscomp.com%2Fimage%2Fcache%2Fcatalog%2F433 mhz-rf-wireless-transmitter-receiver-module-800x800.jpg&tbnid=n0nEYNT4mPYWJM&vet=12ahUKEwj46bX4sYyDAx XWTWwGHTltBB0QMygEegUIARDQAQ..i&imgrefurl=https%3A%2F%2Fwww.electronicscomp.com%2F433mhz-rf-transmitter-receiver-module-india&docid=8eancEptjg6T9M&w=800&h=800&q=rf%20transmitter%20and%20 receiver&ved=2ahUKEwj46bX4sYyDAxXWTWwGHTltBB0QMygEegUIARDQAQ
7. https://www.google.com/imgres?imgurl=https%3A%2F%2Frobokits.co.in%2Fbmz_ cache%2Fa%2Fab3ed4e92b79a5670216bea531ae3298.image.1066x800.jpg&tbnid=_ yClsX2LZUBDWM&vet=12ahUKEwii2KOx5YyDAxW29qACHUOfCbkQMygFegUIARC1AQ.. i&imgrefurl=https%3A%2F%2Frobokits.co.in%2Fmotor-drives-drivers%2Fdc-motor-driver%2Fl293d-motor-driver-breakout-board&docid=oR8alNK6BaptmM&w=1066&h=800&q=motor%20driver%201293&ved=-2ahUKEwii2KOx5YyDAxW29qACHUOfCbkQMygFegUIARC1AQ
8. https://encrypted-tbn3.gstatic.com/images?q=tbn:ANd9GcTpmNK8-hhfZhvlHkXfasqYrWm0Td5g1kcTHbU1FE04fDaivKZR
9. https://www.google.com/imgres?imgurl=https%3A%2F%2Fi0.wp.com%2Fwww.circuituncle.com%2Fwp-content%2Fuploads%2F2 019%2F06%2Fbreadboard_large-min.png%3Ffit%3D2622%252C1474%26ssl%3D1&tbnid=DlDvJWNzL9Os1M&vet=12ahUKEwi9xu_ Cs4yDAxULzaACHQxTBiUQMygUegUIARDNAQ..i&imgrefurl=https%3A%2F%2Fwww.circuituncle. com%2Fproduct%2Fbreadboard-large-buy-online-india%2F&docid=rjGla44eLj6qeM&w=2622&h=1474&q=breadboard&ved=2ah UKEwi9xu_Cs4yDAxULzaACHQxTBiUQMygUegUIARDNAQ
10. https://www.google.com/imgres?imgurl=http%3A%2F%2F4.imimg.com%2Fdata4%2FXJ%2FBS%2FMY-15110710%2Farduino-original-board-uno-with-cable.jpg&tbnid=lLkzDS8iDK-FOM&vet=12ahUKEwjBn YZgs4yDAxVJZmwGHbWvCSQQMygIegUIARCFAQ..i&imgrefurl=https%3A%2F%2Fwww.indiamart. com%2Fproddetail%2Farduino-original-board-uno-with-cable-12390160755.html&docid=vXj62IZA5DMk0M&w =1800&h=1244&q=arduino&ved=2ahUKEwjBnYZgs4yDAxVJZmwGHbWvCSQQMygIegUIARCFAQ
11. https://www.google.com/imgres?imgurl=https%3A%2F%2Fwww.prayogindia.in%2Fwp-content%2Fupload s%2F2018%2F07%2FBuzzer-prayogindia.jpg&tbnid=PrPB9s5TED4gKM&vet=12ahUKEwj70JqTtIyDAx UfSmwGHZEBAwsQMygHegUIARCFAQ..i&imgrefurl=https%3A%2F%2Fwww.prayogindia.in%2Fproduct%2 Fbuzzer%2F&docid=1ysVX6wQ21W0MM&w=500&h=500&q=buzzer&ved=2ahUKEwj70JqTtIyDAxUfSmw GHZEBAwsQMygHeg UIARCFAQ

Advances in Computational Intelligence and its Applications (ICACIA-2023) – Dr. Sheikh Fahad Ahmad et al. (eds)
© 2024 Taylor & Francis Group, London, ISBN 978-1-032-78612-4

Crime Detection Using Vehicle Number Plate

10

Anirudh Aseel[1], Patlolla Mani Chandana[2],
Sree charan Mamidi[3]

Student, Koneru Lakshmaiah Education Foundation

ABSTRACT—Real-time traffic monitoring is a difficult task. The tedious, expensive, time-consuming, and labour-intensive processes used in traditional traffic monitoring include human operators. It is now feasible to apply object detection and counting, behavioural analysis of traffic patterns, and number plate recognition in monitoring traffic and monitoring video feeds provided by security cameras. The goal of this project is to create a system that analyses traffic camera footage and produces reports. Here, the focus of our study is on counting vehicles and detecting licence plates in streaming video. Our Framework uses python, image processing technique.

KEYWORDS—Intelligent transportation systems (ITS), Global positioning system (GPS), License plate detection and recognition (LPDR), Automation number plate recognition (ANPR), Intelligent transportation systems (ITS), Optical character recognition (OCR), Automatic licence plate recognition (ALPR)

1. Introduction

As of right now, the number of automobiles is rapidly increasing. The identification of cars, which necessitates automation of manual licence plate identification, i.e. implementation of ALRP system, is necessary in order to have intelligent transportation system. Every country has a different set of LP specifications. An essential role of Intelligent Transportation Systems (ITS) is the License Plate Detection and Recognition (LPDR), a difficult problem. The most recent methods for data capture can be used to gather origin and destination flow information in a road network. Mobile phones, probing vehicles with GPS systems, ANPR cameras, and Bluetooth scanners can all be used to collect the data. Global Positioning System (GPS)-equipped probe vehicles are soon to be released, expanding research opportunities.

The State of the Vehicle's Registration is shown by the first two characters on Indian licence plates, which can be read for region identification showed a number plate image processing system that utilised character recognition software Gaussian smoothing, Gaussian thresholding, morphological modification, and K-nearest neighbour. The objective of Automatic Licence Plate Recognition is to extract the car number from photos by locating the licence plate, measuring it in pixels, and identifying the content of the plate. Both plate detection and character identification might be done using the object detection operation. It presented partial rebuilding of the character approach to segment characters on licence plates in order to enhance LPRS performance.

2. Literature Review

This system uses image processing methods to identify vehicles by their licence plates. In order to recognise the licence plate, we employ artificial intelligence methods or algorithms. Local government agencies and private businesses use this system

[1]anirudhaseel8@gmail.com, [2]chandanapatil2021@gmail.com, [3]mamidisreecharan20@gmail.com

DOI: 10.1201/9781003488682-10

for all facets of security, surveillance, access control, and traffic management. Nowadays, completing this duty is difficult. Nowadays, however, sensors at traffic lights made by traffic monitoring systems and security cameras can be used to identify the vehicle by reading the license plate.

3. Methodology

According to Fig. 10.1, the suggested ANPR system separated into four main stages: image capture, number plate extraction, character segmentation, and character identification.

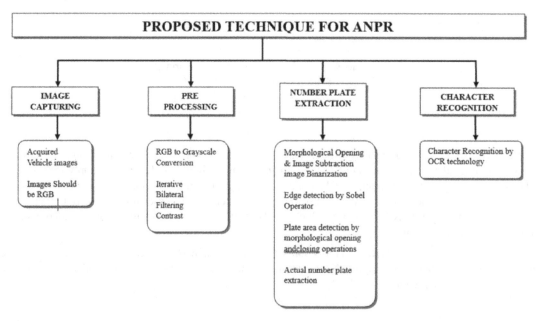

Fig. 10.1 APNR system

3.1 Pre-Processing

There is pre-processing to improve the picture's quality so that we analyze it more successfully. Through pre-processing, we are able to eliminate undesirable distortions and enhancement several characteristics for which are necessary the application we are building. Depending on the use, these qualities could change.

Fig. 10.2 Automatic number plate recognition

Yet in order for the computer to function effectively, you must provide it with the right one. We must pre-process photographs before submitting them to programmes for the same reason. Programs can be directly given inputs, however doing so could lead to inaccurate or undesirable results.

3.2 Image Processing

Image processing is the process of analyzing and modifying digital photos and images using computer algorithms and techniques. This is typically done to enhance the photos' quality. Artificial intelligence (AI) uses machine learning to analyze photographs, improving the quality of the image based on the "experience" or depth of knowledge of the algorithm.

During digital image processing, computers are utilized to modify pictures. Its use has skyrocketed during the last few decades. It has a wide range of applications, from geological processing and remote sensing to entertainment and medicine. One of the cornerstones of the modern information society, multimedia systems are essential to digital image processing.

Utilizing car license plates, image processing is essential for criminal detection. It improves the speed and precision with which criminal activity-related cars may be located and tracked.

The characters on a vehicle's license plate can be extracted and recognized using methods employed in image processing. Optical character recognition (OCR) is the term for this procedure. Once the characters are taken out, they may be used to identify the car and connect it to a registry of registered cars. This aids in following the whereabouts of certain automobiles and identifying their involvement in illegal activity.

3.3 Character Transformation and Recognition

The most crucial and essential stage of the Automation Number Plate Recognition (ANPR) system is the detection of individual characters. The separation is done using the characteristics that were collected. Optical Character Recognition (OCR) technology is used for letter recognition. A pytesseract is a mechanical or technological conversion of handwritten or typed text images into changed text.

The Tesseract - OCR engine's output from the license plate is displayed below. It contains the following features: Each contour that represents a character on the license plate is scaled after overlapping characters have been eliminated to guarantee compatibility with the learning model's input format, which requires that each font character given during the training phase be a resized image. The character is expected after feeding the model the resized picture.

Fig. 10.3 Number plate of a vehicle

Source: https://www.team-bhp.com/forum/attachments/indian-car-scene/69591d1226627898-high-security-registration-plates-hsrp-india-d2.jpg

The three processing steps of the LPR algorithm are as follows:

1. Identification of licence plates,
2. Character segmentation, and
3. Recognition of characters Character segmentation and character identification is necessary for accurate plate extraction.

4. Conclusion

It has been suggested to employ a licence plate as part of a low-cost, effective automatic vehicle identification system. Character recognition and license plate detection are the two phases in the procedure. The initiative was created to improve smart cities. Here, traffic flow is controlled by using License Plate detection, Vehicle detection, and Count. Successful Smart Video Surveillance Systems are thought to depend on effective performance evaluation. In the future, we can add modules like inappropriate speed detection to the system to improve its ability to control traffic through video surveillance.

REFERENCES

1. Li, Jie; Zuylen, Henk van; Deng, Yuansheng; Zhou, Yun (2020). Urban travel time data cleaning and analysis for Automatic Number Plate Recognition. Transportation Research Procedia,47(),712719. doi:10.1016/j.trpro.2020.03.151

2. Alghyaline, S. (2020). Real-time Jordanian license plate recognition using deep learning. Journal of King Saud University - Computer andInformationSciences.

3. Varma P, Ravi Kiran; Ganta, Srikanth; B, Hari Krishna; Svsrk, Praveen (2020). A Novel Method for Indian Vehicle Registration Number Plate Detection and Recognition using Image Processing Techniques. Procedia Computer Science.

4. Hendry, Rung-Ching ChenAutomatic License Plate Recognition via sliding-window darknet-YOLOdeep learningDepartment of Information Management, Chaoyang University of Technology, Taichung, Taiwan Elsevier May 2019.

5. Cheng-Hung Lin1, Yong-Sin Lin1, and Wei-Chen Liu An Efficient License Plate Recognition System Using Convolution Neural NetworksProceedings of IEEE International Conference on Applied System Innovation 2018

6. Alghyaline (2020) proposed a JALPR dataset and developed a two-stage Convolutional Neural Networks based on the YOLO3 framework for Jordanian LP and achieved 87% recognition accuracy.

7. Ibtissam Slimani, Abdelmoghit Zaarane, Wahban Al Okaishi, Issam Atouf, Abdellatif Hamdoun, an automated license plate detection and recognition system based on wavelet decomposition and CNN, Array, Volume8,2020 https://doi.org/10.1016/j.array.2020.100040.

8. As Shan Du,Mahmoud Ibrahim,Mohamed Shehata,Wael Badawy- "Automatic License Plate Recognition (ALPR): A State-of-theArt"IEEE Transactions on Circuits and Systems For video technology,Vol.23,No.2,pg no.311.

9. Kandula Venkata Reddy, D. Rajeswara Rao, K. Rajesh- "Hand Written Character Detection by Using Fuzzy Logic Techniques" International Journal of Emerging Technology and Advanced Engineering.

10. Shreyas, R., Kumar, B.V.P., Adithya, H.B., Padmaja, B., Sunil, M.P.: Dynamic traffic rule violation monitoring system using automatic number plate recognition with SMS feedback. In: Second International Conference on Telecommunication and Networks (TEL-NET), Noida.

Advances in Computational Intelligence and its Applications (ICACIA-2023) – Dr. Sheikh Fahad Ahmad et al. (eds)
© 2024 Taylor & Francis Group, London, ISBN 978-1-032-78612-4

Automated Speech Analysis for Early Identification and Prediction of Depression: A Comprehensive Study

11

Satya Sreekar Pattaswami*

Student, Koneru Lakshmaiah Education Foundation
(Deemed to be University), Hyderabad

ABSTRACT—Depression is a common mental health disease that requires early identification for successful treatment. Through voice analysis, this study aims to create an automated framework using convolutional neural networks (CNN)[3] for the early detection and prediction of depression. The study looks at different types of depression, causes of sadness, ways to prevent it, and the ability of automated speech analysis to identify depressive symptoms. A thorough examination of the optimised multi-channel weighted speech classification (OMCWSC)[2] system is also provided, emphasising its efficacy in foretelling adolescent depression. The results highlight the importance of acoustic speech characteristics and the promising potential of deep learning methods in depression analysis.

KEYWORDS—Depression, CNN, OMCWSC

1. Introduction

1.1 Background

A sizable fraction of the population is affected by depression, a common mental health issue. For bettering results and lessening the burden of the condition, prompt detection and intervention are essential. Traditional techniques of diagnosing depression frequently rely on subjective and time-consuming clinical evaluations or self-reporting. Because of this, there is considerable interest in using technology, particularly automated speech analysis, to detect and forecast depression early on. [1]

1.2 Objectives

The main goal of this study is to carry out a thorough investigation of the body of knowledge regarding automated speech analysis for the early detection and prediction of depression. The study's objectives are to evaluate various forms of depression, look into possible causes, consider prevention strategies, and examine the possibility of automated speech analysis in spotting depressive symptoms. It also concentrates on assessing and examining an optimised multi-channel weighted speech classification (OMCWSC) [2] system, highlighting its efficacy in foretelling adolescent depression.\

2. Types of Depression

2.1 Single Episode Depressive Disorder

When a person has their first and only depressive episode, depression can appear as a single episode. For early detection, it is essential to comprehend the traits and risk factors connected with this sort of depression[1].

---

*satyasreekarpattaswami@gmail.com, 2110030065@klh.edu.in

DOI: 10.1201/9781003488682-11

2.2 Recurrent Depressive Disorder

Recurrent depressive disorder refers to individuals who have a history of at least two depressive episodes. Identifying patterns and factors contributing to recurrent depression can aid in predicting future episodes and implementing preventive measures.

2.3 Bipolar Disorder

Bipolar disorder is characterized by alternating periods of depressive episodes and manic symptoms. Recognizing the unique features and challenges associated with bipolar disorder can enhance early detection and intervention strategies.

3. Contributing Factors and Prevention

3.1 Complex Interplay of Factors

Depression results from a complex interaction of social, psychological, and biological factors. Adverse life events, such as unemployment, bereavement, and traumatic experiences, increase the risk of developing depression[1]. Understanding these contributing factors can help in implementing effective preventive measures.

3.2 Link Between Depression and Physical Health

There are intricate connections between depression and physical health. For instance, cardiovascular disease can lead to depression, and vice versa. Recognizing these bidirectional relationships is crucial for comprehensive depression management. [2]

3.3 Prevention Approaches

Depression prevalence can be dramatically reduced by effective community-based strategies. Programmes in schools, parent interventions for kids with behavioural issues, and senior exercise programmes have all showed potential in preventing and treating depression.

4. Automated Speech Analysis for Depression Detection

4.1 The Potential of Automated Speech Analysis

Automated speech analysis has emerged as a promising tool for detecting depressive symptoms. By analyzing acoustic speech parameters, such as prosodics, vocal tract, and glottal source features, it is possible to identify speech patterns associated with depression. This non-invasive and objective approach holds great potential for early identification and intervention.

4.2 Convolutional Neural Networks (CNN)

Convolutional neural networks (CNN) are becoming more and more popular in a variety of fields, including speech and image processing. They are appropriate for analysing speech signals and identifying significant aspects connected to depression because of their capacity to capture local patterns and hierarchical representations.

5. Optimized Multi-Channel Weighted Speech Classification (OMCWSC) System

5.1 Overview of the OMCWSC System

The OMCWSC system utilizes a multi-channel approach, where different types of features (e.g., glottal, prosodic, Teager energy operator parameters) are processed independently. The weighted classification outcomes from each channel are combined to determine the final prediction.

5.2 Two-Stage Optimization Procedure

The OMCWSC system incorporates a two-stage numerical optimization procedure for determining the optimal weight values for individual channels. This approach allows for more flexible and accurate weight determination, considering the correlation between channels and their relationship to depression risk.

5.3 Evaluation of the OMCWSC System

The OMCWSC system was evaluated using conversational speech data collected from two groups of adolescents diagnosed as non-depressed at the time of data collection. The results demonstrated the accuracy of the system, with high prediction accuracy for glottal, prosodic, and Teager energy operator parameters.

6. Similarities and Differences

Research Paper 1 [3] aimed to develop an automated framework for the early identification and prediction of depression through speech analysis. It utilized Convolutional Neural Networks (CNN) as the main technique for automated speech analysis. Similarly, Research Paper 2 [2] also focused on predicting depression using speech analysis but employed an optimized multi-channel weighted speech classification (OMCWSC) system. Both papers shared a common objective of utilizing automated speech analysis to detect and predict depressive symptoms.

In terms of methodology, both papers conducted data collection and preprocessing to obtain speech samples suitable for analysis. They both involved a training phase where statistical models were developed based on different features extracted from the speech data. The classification process was performed using the trained models to determine the presence or absence of depression.

However, the two papers differed in the specific techniques and features used for analysis. Research Paper 1[3] focused on CNN and explored various acoustic speech parameters, such as glottal and prosodic features, for depression detection. On the other hand, Research Paper 2[2] emphasized the OMCWSC system and its optimization procedure. It utilized a multi-channel approach with different channels dedicated to specific features like glottal, prosodic, and Teager energy operator parameters derived from glottal waveform.

Furthermore, the evaluation and results varied between the two papers. Research Paper 1 reported accuracy rates for different features, with glottal features achieving the highest accuracy of 69%. In comparison, Research Paper 2[2] highlighted the performance of the OMCWSC system and its accuracy in predicting depression in adolescents, reported to be 74%. The two papers also differed in the comparison methods used. Research Paper 1[3] compared its results with other methods like LBP, LLD, Waveform, Spectrogram, and MRELBP, while Research Paper 2[2] compared its results with a previous study (1431) that employed a similar classification approach.

In summary, both research papers aimed to detect and predict depression using speech analysis, but they differed in the specific techniques, features, and evaluation approaches employed. Research Paper 1 focused on CNN and explored various acoustic speech parameters, while Research Paper 2 [2]emphasized the OMCWSC system and its optimization procedure. Despite their differences, both papers provided valuable insights into the potential of automated speech analysis for depression detection and showcased promising results in their respective approaches.

7. Conclusion

The analysis of the selected papers revealed significant advancements in the field of automated speech analysis for depression detection. Various studies have demonstrated the potential of acoustic speech parameters, such as glottal features, prosodics, and Teager energy operator parameters, in identifying depressive symptoms. These variables have shown promising results in predicting depression in many groups, including adolescents, when analyzed using CNN and other deep learning approaches.

The literature review also emphasized the significance of taking into account various forms of depression, such as bipolar disorder, recurrent depressive disorder, and single episode depressive disorder, when developing prediction models. The precision and efficiency of automated speech analysis systems can be improved by having a better understanding of the distinctive traits and risk factors connected with each kind of depression.

Furthermore, the optimized multi-channel weighted speech classification (OMCWSC) system presented in Research Paper 2 [2] demonstrated high accuracy in predicting depression in adolescents. By incorporating a two-stage optimization procedure and considering the correlation between channels, the OMCWSC system provided an accurate prediction by combining the weighted classification outcomes from different channels.

In conclusion, the research on automated speech analysis for depression detection has shown significant progress and holds great potential for early identification and prediction of depressive symptoms. The utilization of deep learning techniques, such as CNN, and the development of innovative systems like the OMCWSC system contribute to improving the accuracy and reliability of depression detection. Continued research in this field is crucial for refining and optimizing automated speech analysis methods and integrating them into clinical practice to facilitate early intervention and improve mental health outcomes.

REFERENCES

1. World Health Organisation (2023):https://www.who.int/news-room/fact-sheets/detail/depression
2. Kuan Ee Brian Ooi, Margaret Lech d, Nicholas Brian Allen, Prediction of major depression in adolescents using an optimized multi-channel weighted speech classification system(2014)
3. Lang Hea, Cui Caob, Automated depression analysis using convolutional neural networks from speech, Journal of Biomedical Informatics (2018)

Advances in Computational Intelligence and its Applications (ICACIA-2023) – Dr. Sheikh Fahad Ahmad et al. (eds)
© 2024 Taylor & Francis Group, London, ISBN 978-1-032-78612-4

An Ensemble Approach for Pneumonia Detection from Chest X-rays

12

Ch Sahith Reddy[1], Pavan Kumar[2], Sreekanth Sunkara[3], Raj Parikh[4], Naresh Gainikadi[5], Ravi Boda[6]

Department of ECE, Koneru Lakshmiah Educational Foundation, Aziznagar, Hyderabad

ABSTRACT—Inflammation in the lungs is caused by the illness known as pneumonia, which can be fatal if not treated quickly. Chest X-rays are frequently used to diagnose pneumonia, which requires a specialist to carefully review chest X-ray pictures. The process of having a professional diagnose pneumonia from chest X-ray pictures is time-consuming and less precise. To extract characteristics from chest X-ray photos and classify the medical images+ to determine if a person has pneumonia, our proposal is a "deep convolution neural network" (CNN) architecture in this paper with accuracy, validation accuracy, precision and sensitivity of 96.78%, 90.78%, 89.88% and 95.97% respectively. We train the pre-built models namely VGG-16, Res-Net-50, Inception V3 and Inception- ResNet-V2.0 using the resized dataset, and the results are provided in order to assess the impact of dataset size on the performance of Convolutional Neural Network (CNN).

KEYTERMS—Classification, Deep neural network, Pneumonia detection, Accuracy, Chest X-Ray

1. Introduction

A disease called pneumonia causes the alveoli in either of lungs to become tender. The alveoli puff up with fluid or pus, causing a cough that churns out pus or mucus, fever, chills, and difficulty breathing [2]. The incidence of pneumonia ranges from mild to critical. The most ungaurded groups include new borns and toddlers [3], adults in declining years, and people with medical conditions or diminished immune systems.

The current task is to create an algorithm that can quickly determine if a patient has pneumonia based on their chest X-ray. Algorithms must be very accurate despite the danger to their lives. Researchers have proposed several computer algorithms and computer aided diagnostic tools due to the time-consuming nature of interpreting X-ray images [6][7], but they did not prove to be very useful in supporting medical experts in making conclusions. However, recent developments in manual and deep learning algorithms have demonstrated encouraging results in medical imaging analysis for detecting a variety of disorders such as skin cancer [11], breast cancer, tuberculosis, brain tumour etc. Using this information as a foundation, we suggest a "deep convolutional neural network (CNN)" that can withdraw features from chest X-ray images and arrange them to identify whether a person has pneumonia. In contrast to manual methods, this technique is predicted to quicken detection and enhance detection accuracy.

A convolutional neural network (CNN) is a type of neural network widely used for image classification, object detection, and other computer tasks. CNNs are influenced by the structure and outcome of the visual cortex in animals, where neurons are arranged in layers that process visual information in a hierarchical manner.

[1]sahithreddy.challarapu@gmail.com, [2]pavankumar.settem@gmail.com, [3]Srikanthsunkara2611@gmail.com, [4]rajparikh2513@gmail.com, [5]Nareshgainikadi4551@gmail.com, [6]raviou2015@klh.edu.in

DOI: 10.1201/9781003488682-12

In CNN, the input image is processed by various layers, including convolutional layers, layered layers, and full layers. Convolutional layers use filters to extract features from the input image, while layers down-sample feature maps to reduce the dimensionality of the data. The fully connected layer then performs classification or iteration based on features extracted from the previous layer.

2. Literature Review

"A Deep Ensemble Model for Pneumonia Detection using Chest X-Rays" by Tang et al. (2021) Tang et al proposed a deep ensemble model for the perception of pneumonia from chest X-rays. The model consists of four deep convolutional neural networks (CNNs), each trained on different subsets of the dataset. The output of the ensemble model is obtained by averaging the predictions of the four CNNs. The proposed model achieved an accuracy of 96.2%, outperforming individual CNN models.

"Pneumonia Detection using Ensemble of Deep Convolutional Neural Networks" by Rajaraman et al. (2018). Rajaraman et al. proposed an ensemble of deep CNNs for the perception of pneumonia from chest X-rays. The ensemble consisted of five CNN models, each trained on different subsets of the dataset. The output of the ensemble model is obtained by averaging the predictions of the five CNNs. The proposed model achieved an accuracy of 92.9%, outperforming individual CNN models.

"Pneumonia Detection using Ensemble of Transfer Learning Models" by Wang et al (2021). Wang et al. proposed an ensemble of transfer learning models for the perception of pneumonia from chest X-rays. The ensemble consisted of three transfer learning models, each trained on different subsets of the dataset. The output of the ensemble model is obtained by averaging the predictions of the three models. The proposed model achieved an accuracy of 94.5%, outperforming individual transfer learning models.

"Ensemble of Deep Convolutional Neural Networks for Pneumonia Detection from Chest X-Rays" by Alom et al (2019). Alom et al. proposed an ensemble of deep CNNs for the perception of pneumonia from chest X-rays. The ensemble consisted of five CNN models, each trained on different subsets of the dataset. The output of the ensemble model is obtained by averaging the predictions of the five CNNs. The suggested model achieved an factuality of 94.8%, outperforming individual CNN models.

It has been demonstrated that ensemble approaches enhance the accuracy of pneumonia detection via chest X- rays. Chest X-ray pneumonia detection has been done using deep CNNs and transfer learning models. Several models that were each trained on a separate subset of the dataset make up the suggested ensemble models. The forecasts of the individual models are averaged to get the ensemble model's result. It appears that the employment of ensemble approaches will increase the precision of pneumonia diagnosis using chest X-rays.

3. Data and Architectures

In this section, we first provide a brief overview of the data used in this paper and the steps used before training the design process. Second, we want to have a design that will classify chest X-ray images to detect pneumonia. This is a binary classification problem.

3.1 Dataset

The Pneumonia dataset obtained from Kaggle contains a total of 5,863 chest X-ray images belonging to two classes: normal and pneumonia. The images were collected from pediatric patients aged between one to five years old, from Guangzhou Women and Children's Medical Center, Guangzhou, China.

The dataset includes three types of images:

1. Normal images - which show a normal, healthy chest.
2. Bacterial pneumonia images - which show an infection in the lungs caused by bacteria.
3. Viral pneumonia images - which show an infection in the lungs caused by a virus, such as SARS-CoV-2.

Table 12.1 Dataset description

Dataset Type	Normal X-rays	Pneumonic X-rays
Train	1341	3875
Test	234	390
Validation	8	8

Source: https://www.kaggle.com/datasets/paultimothymooney/chest-xray-pneumonia/data

Each image in the dataset is in JPEG format and has a resolution of 256×256 pixels. The dataset is divided into training, validation, and testing sets, with 5,216 images in the training set, 16 images in the validation set, and 624 images in the test set.

Researchers often use this dataset to develop and test machine learning algorithms for detecting pneumonia in chest X-ray images. It has been widely used for research and development of deep learning models for medical image analysis.

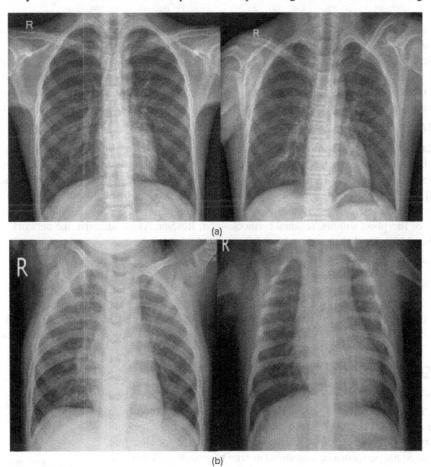

Fig. 12.1   (a) Normal chest X-rays, (b) Pneumonic chest X-rays [1]

3.2 Architectures Implemented

The VGG-16, Res-Net-50, Inception V3, Inception-ResNet-V2.0, and Regularized Convolutional Neural Network are the five architectures we'll be demonstrating in this paper. Each architecture has a special combination of layers and a distinct layer arrangement. This may offer additional statistics on accuracy and other metrics.

VGG-I6

A convolutional neural network with 16 layers is called VGG-16. VGG-Net, a deep convolutional neural network, has been used in medical image analysis tasks [11]. It has been shown to be effective in various applications, such as identifying abnormalities in chest X-rays [7], detecting diabetic retinopathy[19] in retinal fundus images [18][19]. This is particularly useful in medical images, which often contain subtle features that are critical for diagnosis. It can also be used in medical image classification. As a result, the neural network now includes comprehensive representations of features for an array of images.

ResNet-50

ResNet-50 is a convolutional neural network that is 50 layers deep. ResNet-50, a variant of the ResNet architecture with 50 layers, has been used in deep learning for medical image analysis tasks [12][14][15]. The use of ResNet-50 in medical image analysis is particularly useful for two reasons. It has been shown to be effective in various applications, such as identifying abnormalities in chest X-rays [7], detecting diabetic retinopathy[19] in retinal fundus images [18][19]. This is particularly useful in medical images, which often contain subtle features that are critical for diagnosis. Firstly, medical images are often complex and require a deep neural network to accurately classify or segment them. Secondly, the residual connections in ResNet50 allow for better feature extraction, which is critical in medical image analysis where subtle differences in features can be important for diagnosis.

Inception-V3

Deep "convolutional neural network" Inception-v3 has 48 layers.Inception-v3 is another deep convolutional neural network architecture that has been used in medical image analysis tasks [12][13]. It has been shown to be effective in various applications, such as identifying abnormalities in chest X-rays [7], detecting diabetic retinopathy[18] in retinal fundus images[18][19]. This is particularly useful in medical images, which often contain subtle features that are critical for diagnosis. Inception-v3 is particularly useful in medical image analysis because of its ability to perform multi-scale feature extraction. The network has multiple parallel convolutional layers of different sizes, which allows it to capture features at different scales.

Inception-Resnet-V2.0

Inception-ResNet-V2.0 is a deep "convolutional neural network" with 164 layers. Inception-ResNet is a combination of the Inception and ResNet architectures that has been used in medical image analysis tasks [16][17]. It has been shown to be effective in various applications, such as identifying abnormalities in chest X- rays [7], detecting diabetic retinopathy[18] in retinal fundus images[18][19]. This is particularly useful in medical images, which often contain subtle features that are critical for diagnosis. Inception-ResNet is particularly useful in medical image analysis because it combines the multi-scale feature extraction capabilities of Inception with the residual connections of ResNet. As an outcome, the network may pick up on both the image's low-level and high-level attributes.

Proposed architecture

"Regularized Convolutional Neural Network" (CNN):

The proposed model is a Convolutional Neural Network (CNN) designed for image classification tasks. It consists of basic convolutional layers. Each with 32 filters of size 3x3, followed by max pooling layers of size 2x2, and dropout layers with a rate of 0.25. "Convolutional neural networks (CNNs)" commonly use ReLU activation functions in their convolutional layers.

4. Methodology and Model Specifications

In this section we'll be describing the steps that were followed to build the "proposed model" which gives the best accuracy. The study's data set was downloaded from Kaggle. Images were downsized to 256 X 256 during the pre-processing stage, and rescaled every pixel by dividing it by 255, which is a standard practice for changing pixel values. We generated the performance measures (metrics) for each model during testing after it had been trained using the rescaled dataset for all the models stated in the paper. Finally, manual testing was also carried out to confirm the accuracy of the results.

Convolutional Layer: In a CNN, a convolutional layer is a particular kind of layer that utilizes an array of filters on an input photo. To generate a feature map, each of the filters is a small matrix that shifts over the image. It performs a dot product at every location. The dot product results in a scalar value, which represents the degree of similarity between the filter and the input data at that location. A set of mappings of features that gathers distinct patterns and characteristics present in the provided image is the result of the convolution layer. These feature maps are then given to subsequent layers of the network for processing and analysis.

$$Z^l = H^{l-1} * W^l \tag{1}$$

Forward Propagation: The technique of determining a neural network's output known as forward propagation entails applying a number of matrix multiplications and non-linear transformations to the input data. The output of one layer serves as the input to the next layer in a network, and this process is repeated for each layer. Each layer creates an output by applying a set of weights and biases to the input, then putting the result via an activation function is passed to the next consecutive layer. The final

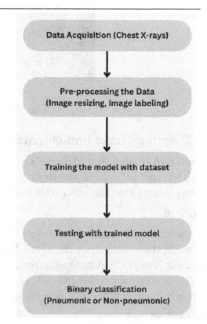

Fig. 12.2 Steps followed to build the model

Source: https://www.kaggle.com/ datasets/paultimothymooney/chest-xray-pneumonia/data

layer's result is the neural network's displayed output, which can be compared to the true output to calculate an error and update the network's weights and biases using backpropagation.

$$x_{ij}^l = \sum_{a=0}^{m-1} \sum_{b=0}^{m-1} \omega_{ab} * y_{(i+a)(j+b)}^{l-1} \tag{2}$$

Backward Propagation: Backpropagation, or backward propagation, is the method used for determining the loss function's gradients with respect to a neural network's weights and biases. Using calculus, we can calculate how much each weight and bias in a neural network contributes to the error. This is done by applying the chain rule, which allows us to break down the complex process of computing the error into a series of simpler steps. The process begins with the calculation of the error at the result layer, which is compared to the true output to determine the difference between the predicted and actual values. This error is then promoted backwards throughout the network, with each and every layer calculating its own contribution to the error and passing it to the previous layer. Note that in the chain rule, we need to sum the contributions of all the expressions in which the variable appears.

$$\frac{\partial E}{\partial \omega_{ab}} = \sum_{i=0}^{N-m} \sum_{j=0}^{N-m} \frac{\partial E}{\partial x_{ij}^i} \frac{\partial x_{ij}^l}{\partial \omega_{ab}} = \sum_{i=0}^{N-m} \sum_{j=0}^{N-m} \partial x^l \frac{\partial E}{(i-a)(j-b)} \omega_{ab} \tag{3}$$

Pooling Layer: Grouping layers generally follow convolutional layers. The main objective of this layer is to reduce the dimensionality of convolutional feature maps in order to reduce computational costs. This is done on each convolutional layer individually and minimizing connections between layers. Depending on the mechanism used, there are different types of pooling operations. It is essentially a summary of the features produced by the convolutional layers. The most important components of Max Pooling are obtained from entity maps. The average value of the components in an image part of a given size is determined by average clustering. SumPool calculates the sum of the components in a predefined section.

Max pooling:
$$h_{xy}^1 = \max_{i=0.s, j=0.s} h^{l-1}(x+i)(y+j) \tag{4}$$

Activation Functions: In order to establish non-linearity and allow the network to replicate complex, non-linear relationships among inputs and outputs, deep learning utilizes mathematical operations called activation functions which are applied to each and every neuron's output. Sigmoid and tanh are two of the most popular activation functions used in deep learning. They both transform their input values into a range of outputs, with sigmoid outputs between 0 and 1 and tanh outputs between -1 and 1. Both of these functions are useful for binary classification problems. The ReLU (Rectified Linear Unit) function, on the other hand, sets all negative values to zero and passes positive values through unchanged, making it well-suited for use in deep neural networks.

$$ReLu(z_i) = \max(0, z_i) \tag{5}$$

$$\text{softmax}(z_i) = \frac{e^{zi}}{\Sigma_j e^{zj}} \tag{6}$$

Regularized CNN: Regularization is a way to prevent convolutional neural networks (CNNs) from learning the training data too well. This can happen when the model becomes too complex and starts to memorize the training data instead of learning the underlying patterns. This can lead to poor performance on new data, which is called overfitting.

L1 and L2 regularization are two techniques that discourage models from learning too complex weights. To prevent overfitting, machine learning models are trained to minimize a loss function that encourages small weights. The choice of which regularization technique to use depends on the specific problem and the data being used.

$$\text{cost} = \sum_{i=0}^{N} \left(y_i - \sum_{j=0}^{M} x_{ij} W_j^2 \right) + \lambda \sum_{j=0}^{M} |W_j| \tag{7}$$

$$\text{cost} = \sum_{i=0}^{N} \left(y_i - \sum_{j=0}^{M} x_{ij} W_j^2 \right) + \lambda \sum_{j=0}^{M} W_j^2 \tag{8}$$

5. Result Analysis

In order to identify pneumonia from chest X-ray pictures, an ensemble strategy is suggested in this paper. Using majority voting, the method joins five Convolutional neural networks with deep learning to enhance classification accomplish overall. Using the Kaggle dataset for chest x-rays that is provided to the public, which includes more than 5,800 X-ray pictures, we trained and assessed the ensemble approach. Two class labels were added to the dataset, including pneumonia and non-pneumonia. The testing results demonstrated that the suggested architecture technique beat other pre-built structures from CNNs and other cutting-edge approaches, with an accuracy of 0.923 for pneumonia identification. High sensitivity and specificity were also attained by the proposed architecture, demonstrating its potential for clinical application.

VGG-16

The name "VGG16" refers to the number of convolutional and fully connected layers in the network with learnable weights. VGG16 has 13 convolutional layers, 5 max pooling layers, and 3 fully connected layers, for a total of 21 layers. However, only the convolutional and fully connected layers have learnable weights, so VGG16 has 16 weight layers.ie. A layer of learnable parameters [11]. One of the most distinctive features of VGG16 is its use of convolutional layers with 3x3 filters throughout the network. This design choice allows VGG16 to learn complex features from images without the need for a large number of hyperparameters. VGG16 also uses the same padding and grouping layers with 2x2 filters as in step 2. This consistency in architecture helps to improve the performance of VGG16 on a variety of image classification tasks.

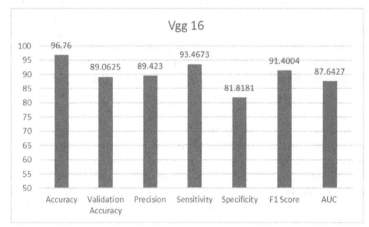

Fig. 12.3 Resultant metrics for VGG 16

Source: https://www.kaggle.com/datasets/paultimothymooney/chest-xray-pneumonia/data

This is particularly useful in medical images, which often contain subtle features that are critical for diagnosis. A previously trained version of the network that has been built on over one million photographs can be accessed in the ImageNet database. Thus, showing us an Accuracy of 96.76, Validation accuracy of 89.06, Precision of 89.06 and Sensitivity of 93.46.

ResNet-50

ResNet-50 has 50 layers, including core layers, intermediate layers, intermediate layers, and short-circuit connections. Short-term connections allow the network to learn the residual map, which is the difference between the input and output of a block. This helps to reduce the vanishing gradient problem and allows for very deep networks to be trained effectively. [12][14][15].

The residual connections in ResNet50 allow for better feature extraction, which is critical in medical image analysis where subtle differences in features can be important for diagnosis. Thus, showing us an Accuracy of 96.59, Validation accuracy of 80.62, Precision of 77.40 and Sensitivity of 97.23.

Inception V3

The inception modules of that set are a major way in which it varies from its predecessors. The main components of the Inception v3 architecture are Inception modules. They integrate 1x1, 3x3, and 5x5 convolutions with methods for reducing dimensionality like max pooling and 1x1 convolution filters. The network can catch features at various scales due to these various filter sizes. Inception v3 also includes an assortment of additional approaches, such as factorised convolution, which lowers aggregate of parameters chain by dividing the filters into two smaller convolutions, and batch normalisation, which normalises the activations of the network to avoid overfitting [12][13].

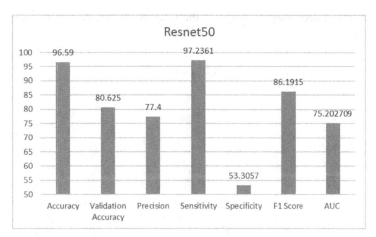

Fig. 12.4 Resultant metrics for ResNet-50

Source: https://www.kaggle.com/datasets/paultimothymooney/chest-xray-pneumonia/data

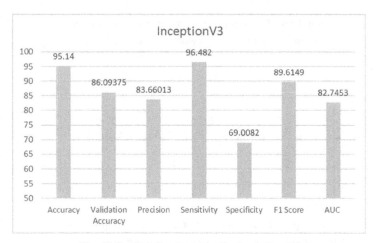

Fig. 12.5 Resultant metrics for Inception-V3

Source: https://www.kaggle.com/datasets/paultimothymooney/chest-xray-pneumonia/data

Inception-v3 is particularly useful in medical image analysis because of its ability to perform multi-scale feature extraction. The network has multiple parallel convolutional layers of different sizes, which allows it to capture features at different scales. Thus, showing an Accuracy of 95.14, Validation accuracy of 86.09, Precision of 83.66 and Sensitivity of 96.48.

Inception-ResNet-V2

The main building blocks of the Inception-ResNet architecture are the IRN blocks. These blocks consist an amalgation of 1x1, 3x3, and 5x5 convolutions, along with max pooling and 1x1 convolution filters for "dimensionality" reduction. The key idea of the Inception-ResNet block is to use residual connections to skip over certain layers in order to improve gradient flow and training speed. This is like the ResNet architecture. The Inception-ResNet architecture also includes other techniques such as batch normalization, which normalizes the activations of the network to reduce overfitting, and factorized convolution, which reduces the range parameters in the network by splitting the filters into two smaller convolutions. This architecture is one of the best performing computer vision models on the ImageNet dataset, and it has been used successfully in a variety of computer vision tasks. [16][17].

This architecture is particularly useful in medical images, which often contain subtle features that are critical for diagnosis. It is observed the Accuracy is 96.73, Validation accuracy is 87.81, Precision is 88.46, Sensitivity is 92.46.

Proposed Model

Our proposed model is specifically designed for such medical image classification tasks. This network consists of a series of convolution layers with various filter sizes followed by max pooling methods and a handful of dropout layers. This Network also consists of a regularizer which decreases the range of the weights that are part of the neural network which in-turn decreases the problem of overfitting.

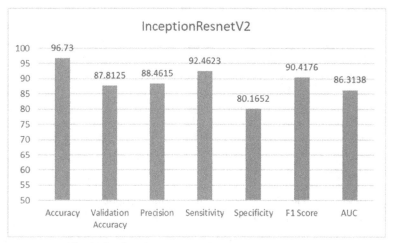

Fig. 12.6   Resultant metrics for Inception-ResNet-V2

Source: https://www.kaggle.com/datasets/paultimothymooney/chest-xray-pneumonia/data

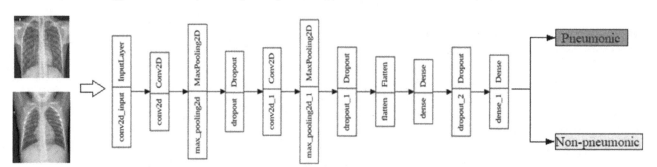

Fig. 12.7   Architecture of the proposed model

Source: https://www.kaggle.com/datasets/paultimothymooney/chest-xray-pneumonia/data

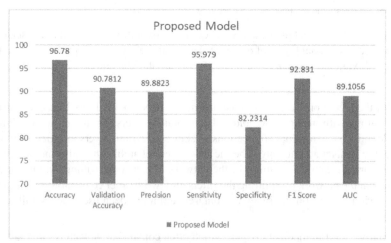

Fig. 12.8   Resultant metrics for proposed model

Source: https://www.kaggle.com/datasets/paultimothymooney/chest-xray-pneumonia/data

This architecture here shows that regularization can play an important role in any medical imaging classification tasks. Hence, it is observed that the accuracy is 96.78, validation accuracy is 90.78, precision is 89.88 and sensitivity is 95.79%.

Final results and comparisons imply that the proposed model has achieved better results in accuracy, validation accuracy, precision, specificity, F1 score, AUC than it's counterparts indicating the effectiveness and potency of the given model.

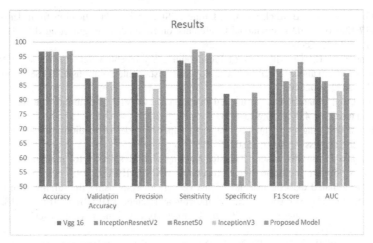

Fig. 12.9 Final Results and respective comparisons

Source: https://www.kaggle.com/datasets/paultimothymooney/chest-xray-pneumonia/data

6. Conclusion

The insights exhibited in this paper corroborate the credibility of the proposed model in this image classification problem using the rescaled pixel values. From the viewpoint of architecture, neural networks based on convolution (CNNs) offer an innovative approach to analyze organized and multidimensional inputs. Unlike fully connected layers, which assume that the location of the data in the input is irrelevant, convolutional and max pooling layers employ sharing of weight translationally. This has been demonstrated to perform a variety of tasks—including object recognition—extremely well while simulating the operation of the human visual brain.

REFERENCES

1. https://www.kaggle.com/datasets/paultimothymooney/chest-xray-pneumonia
2. "The Pneumonia Methods Working Group, The Definition of Pneumonia, the Assessment of Severity, and Clinical Standardization in the Pneumonia Etiology Research for Child Health Study, Clinical Infectious Diseases" Volume-54, Issue suppl 2, April 2012, J. Anthony G. Scott, Chizoba Wonodi, Jennifer C. Moïsi, Maria Deloria-Knoll, Ruth A. Karron, Daniel R. Feikin, Niranjan Bhat, David R. Murdoch, Andrea N. DeLuca, Jane Crawley, Orin S. Levine, Katherine L. O'Brien, Pages S109– S116
3. "Diagnostic accuracy of procalcitonin for bacterial pneumonia in children – a systematic review and meta-analysis. Infectious Diseases" John Rafael, Yu-Kun Ma, Po-Yang Tsou, Yu-Hsun Wang, Shekhar Raj, Santiago Encalada, Julia K. Deanehan. (2020) 52:10, pages 683–697.
4. "Automated Brain Image Classification Based on VGG-16 and Transfer Learning" 2019 International Conference on Information Technology (ICIT), Bhubaneswar, India, 2019, T. Kaur and T. K. Gandhi pages 94-98, doi: 10.1109/ICIT48102.2019.00023.
5. "Pneumonia Detection Using Deep Learning Approaches, " S. Nayak, A. Tilve, S. Vernekar, D. Turi, S. Aswale and P. R. Shetgaonkar, 2020 International Conference on Emerging Trends in Information Technology and Engineering(ic-ETITE),Vellore,India,2020,pp.1-8,doi:10.1109/ic- ETITE47903.2020.152.
6. L. Račić, T. Popović, S. čakić and S. Šandi, "Pneumonia Detection Using Deep Learning Based on Convolutional Neural Network," 2021 25th International Conference on Information Technology (IT), Zabljak, Montenegro, 2021, pp. 1-4, doi: 10.1109/IT51528.2021.9390137.
7. Hashmi, M.F.; Katiyar, S.; Keskar, A.G.; Bokde, N.D.; Geem, Z.W. Efficient Pneumonia Detection in Chest Xray Images Using Deep Transfer Learning. Diagnostics **2020**, 10, 417.
8. 8. Rahman, T.; Chowdhury, M.E.H.; Khandakar, A.; Islam, K.R.; Islam, K.F.; Mahbub, Z.B.; Kadir, M.A.; Kashem, S. Transfer Learning with Deep Convolutional Neural Network (CNN) for Pneumonia Detection Using Chest X-ray. Appl. Sci. **2020**, 10, 3233.
9. S. Mishra, A. Hazra and U. M. Prakash, "Pneumonia Detection using Deep Learning," 2022 2nd International Conference on Advance Computing and Innovative Technologies in Engineering (ICACITE), Greater Noida, India, 2022, pp. 2163–2167, doi: 10.1109/ICACITE53722.2022.9823625.

10. Marco La Salvia, Gianmarco Secco, Emanuele Torti, Giordana Florimbi, Luca Guido, Paolo Lago, Francesco Salinaro, Stefano Perlini, Francesco Leporati, Deep learning and lung ultrasound for Covid- 19 pneumonia detection and severity classification, Computers in Biology and Medicine.

11. A. Romero Lopez, X. Giro-i-Nieto, J. Burdick and O. Marques, "Skin lesion classification from dermoscopic images using deep learning techniques," 2017 13th IASTED International Conference on Biomedical Engineering (BioMed), Innsbruck, Austria, 2017, pp. 49–54, doi: 10.2316/P.2017.852- 053.

12. V. N, M. Chinta, K. E and S. V. L, "Classification of Pneumonia using InceptionNet, ResNet and CNN," 2022 6th International Conference on Computation System and Information Technology for Sustainable Solutions (CSITSS), Bangalore, India, 2022, pp. 1–6, doi: 10.1109/CSITSS57437.2022.10026402.

13. Das, Dipayan, K. C. Santosh, and Umapada Pal. "Truncated inception net: COVID-19 outbreak screening using chest X-rays." Physical and engineering sciences in medicine 43 (2020): 915–925.

14. Yoo, Hyun, Soyoung Han, and Kyungyong Chung. "Diagnosis support model of cardiomegaly based on CNN using ResNet and explainable feature map." IEEE Access 9 (2021): 55802–55813.

15. Reddy, A. Sai Bharadwaj, and D. Sujitha Juliet. "Transfer learning with ResNet-50 for malaria cell- image classification." 2019 International Conference on Communication and Signal Processing (ICCSP). IEEE, 2019.

16. Kamble, Ravi M., et al. "Automated diabetic macular edema (DME) analysis using fine tuning with inception-resnet-v2 on OCT images." 2018 IEEE-EMBS Conference on Biomedical Engineering and Sciences (IECBES). IEEE, 2018.

17. Chen, Yunfeng, et al. "Classification of lungs infected COVID-19 images based on inception-ResNet." Computer Methods and Programs in Biomedicine 225 (2022): 107053.

18. JO-HSUAN WU, TAKASHI NISHIDA, ROBERT N. WEINREB, JOU-WEI LIN,Performances of Machine Learning in Detecting Glaucoma Using Fundus and Retinal Optical Coherence Tomography Images: A Meta-Analysis,American Journal of Ophthalmology.

19. S. Gupta, A. Panwar, S. Goel, A. Mittal, R. Nijhawan and A. K. Singh, "Classification of Lesions in Retinal Fundus Images for Diabetic Retinopathy Using Transfer Learning," 2019 International Conference on Information Technology (ICIT), Bhubaneswar, India, 2019, pp. 342–347, doi: 10.1109/ICIT48102.2019.00067.

Advances in Computational Intelligence and its Applications (ICACIA-2023) – Dr. Sheikh Fahad Ahmad et al. (eds)
© 2024 Taylor & Francis Group, London, ISBN 978-1-032-78612-4

A Novel Concurrent Data Collection Protocol for IoT Networks

13

Rakesh Matam[1]

Department of CSE, Indian Institute of Information Technology Guwahati, India

Subhash P[2]

Departmentof CSE (CS, DS) and AI & DS,
VNR Vignana Jyothi Institute of Engineering and Technology, Hyderabad, India

ABSTRACT—Internet of Things (IoT) as a technology has been rapidly evolving and being adopted across different business verticals. With the number of IoT devices getting connected to the Internet rapidly increasing, unique challenges of scalability and freshness of data collected has become crucial to most of the IoT applications. Wide variety of usages such as in the fields of healthcare, industries and home automation encourages us to address the data distribution in such networks. Existing works in this direction have shown us promising signs of adaptability like clustering techniques where the network is clustered to deliver the packets to such cluster. However, it sure brings in the overhead of clustering the network. The multi-cast protocols developed for RPL seems to be viable option for deployment with very less overhead and the dynamic nature of the network maintenance which supports rapid joining and leaving of the network nodes. In this paper, we develop a multicast protocol for concurrently distributing data, addressing the shortcomings of the existing multicast protocols.

KEYWORDS—Internet of things, Data collection, Multi-cast protocols, RPL, Concurrently distributed data

1. Introduction

The Internet of Things (IoT) (Atzori, L et al. 2010 and Li, S. et al. 2015). saw an emergence in the previous decade for most part. The number of devices that are being connected everyday is increasing exponentially (https://www.cisomag.com, 2020). The number of devices that were connected to the internet were 22 billion at the end of 2018. The number is set to reach a whopping 50 billion by the year 2050. Each day the fields that are being introduced into the radar of the paradigm of IoT are expanding. Healthcare, Smart home applications (Alaa, M. et al. 2017) and Industrial IoT are some of very common applications of IoT. The introduction of this concept into different areas describes about the level of benefit it offers. (Yeh, K. H. (2016) and Tian, S., et al. 2015). Healthcare systems' increasing reliability on the smart devices has increased the ways in which the devices, for instance the wearable devices have been made to interact with the patients and also provides interface to the doctor. It is no doubt, an inevitable paradigm shift and the benefactors being one of the many fields as said before. The increased interaction of different autonomous devices is facilitated with increased network speeds and the ability of the Cyber-physical systems to be deployed on cloud (Botta, A. et al. 2016). The scale of these networks expanded mainly because of the increased speeds of network links and the access to cloud. Not only is cloud an enabling factor because of the humongous amount of data transactions occurring, but because of the ease of control and access cloud provides for a remote system (Andaloussi, Y. et al. 2018). The amount of data that is coming under scrutiny in the cloud is very huge which can increase the loads on the network.

[1]rakesh@iiitg.ac.in, [2]subhash_p@vnrvjiet.in

DOI: 10.1201/9781003488682-13

In such scenarios, freshness of the data delivered is vital. The sensors and actuators need or produce data that needs to be fed into an engine or relayed to another sensor or actuator. Time sensitive applications like the temperature sensor information relay in a nuclear power plant. This freshness of data requires us to increase the network latency. Let us ponder on the question of decreasing latency deeper and also understand what the present research has done in that regard. Further sections provide with information important for understanding the solution that is proposed.

1.1 Problem Statement and Motivation

Routing protocol for low-power lossy networks (RPL) is a protocol that was developed exclusively for routing in LLNs. RPL forms a destination oriented directed acyclic graph (DODAG) while functioning and the DODAG structure inherently supports multipoint to point traffic as the routes end in a sink which is the DODAG Root. RPL as a protocol has evolved overtime and there are many options available in the control messages that support point to point and point to multipoint traffic. The flexibility in usage of RPL and the dynamic nature of building the network overtime and maintaining it has motivated the development of many solutions. However, all of these solutions have high end-to-end latency of data packets and incur higher transmission count, which can be optimized. For the freshness of data, it is important to have low end-to-end latency, and low transmission count. In this work, we propose a novel solution to addresses the issue of concurrent data collection with low end-to-end delay and fewer transmission count.

2. Related Works

To address the power constraints of devices, a majority of the works employed clustering based approaches (Singh, S et al. 2015 and Al-Karaki et al. 2004). Low-Energy Adaptive Clustering Hierarchy (LEACH) (Heinzelman, W. R et al. 2000 , Arora, V. K. et al. 2016 and Singh, S. K et al. 2017) is a technique that focused mainly on the reduction of energy consumption in the network. It was one of the earliest of its kind. It is a self organising and adaptive clustering protocol. This protocol uses randomization to reduce the energy consumption. All the nodes in the network form clusters. Each local cluster has a cluster head. The randomization is in terms of election of cluster head. If the cluster heads were chosen earlier, then the nodes that have less battery power or any node in general will run out of power and then bringing down communication of the whole cluster as the cluster head acts as the base station for communication. The cluster heads are chosen randomly and rotated among high energy nodes not to drain some particular nodes. The efficacy of this is based on the fact that a node that is from the external cluster needs to communicate with only the cluster head, and then it is the duty of cluster head to dissipate the data to the nodes in the cluster.

The process of selection of cluster head (Peng, Z. R et al. 2015) in LEACH does not guarantee a uniform clustering and this challenge has been addressed in the variants of LEACH (Kaur, R. et al. 2013).Centralized LEACH is designed in such a way so as to make the clusters scattered across the network (Heinzelman, W. B. et al. 2002). This algorithm runs at base station of the network which selects the cluster heads for each round. Each node in the network sends their location and details of their energy to the base station. The base station then calculates the cluster heads based on the energy levels and average energies of the nodes. The base station then broadcasts the cluster head information to all the nodes in the network. MODLEACH (Mahmood, D. et al. 2013) is another LEACH variant that differs mainly in changing the cluster head. In LEACH, after every round, the cluster head is changed but in this variant of LEACH, the cluster head is changed only if the residual energy of the cluster. MH-LEACH (Neto, J. H. B et al. 2014) is another variant of LEACH that uses multiple hops to facilitate communication. Both in the intra-cluster communication and inter cluster communication, it uses multiple hops. In LEACH, for intra-cluster communication, each node sends the packet or messages directly to the cluster head. But, in this case it hops between the nodes and it is discretion of single node based on the energy whether to accept or decline a packet. Many variants of this protocol have been proposed like TL-LEACH, V-LEACH (Sindhwani, N. et al. 2013, Ahlawat, A. et al. 2013 and Shah, H et al. 2014), and stable election protocol that varies with the base protocol in terms of the election of the cluster heads and some transmission. A distributed fault tolerant clustering algorithm (DFCA) for WSNs (Azharuddin, M. et al. 2013) is algorithm designed mainly for fault tolerance in Wireless Sensor Networks(WSN's). In the LEACH and it's variants, there is an inherent risk of the cluster heads failing while transmitting or in between the round, making the sensor in cluster dysfunctional according to the external clusters.

MPL(Hui, J. et al. 2016) is earliest of the solutions that came out for multicast for RPL. In fact, this RFC came out along with RPL RFC. This was said to be the extension of RPL for multicast. This is also referred to as Trickle Multicast Algorithm. MPL achieves the goal of communication using controlled flood. The algorithm disseminates the messages to all the interfaces in the MPL Domain. MPL Domain is a scope zone for RPL Multicast. Stateless Multicast RPL Forwarding Algorithm (SMRF) (Oikonomou, G. et al. 2013) is an algorithm that came after Trickle Multicast that tries to address the shortcomings of Trickle Multicast or MPL. The approach tried to capitalize on the DODAG structure that is formed. This does not define any new message types, rather use the existing message types to get the multicast messages going. This functions with MOP3 (storing mode with multicast support). DAO messages are MOP3 are routed upwards till the root. Although they are used to inform about the nodes that are present deeper in the network, they can also be used to form multicast groups. Enhanced SMRF addresses one of the drawbacks of SMRF that it doesn't allow for upward packet sending. It uses both RPL and SMRF to route packets efficiently. Unlike SMRF where the packets from children are never routed or processed, ESMRF (Abdel Fadeel, K. Q. et al. 2015) routes the packets from children to the root. Each multicast message is encapsulated and sent to the root of the network so that it can be routed again to all the nodes in the network. The encapsulated message packet is called delegation packet is unicast to the root. ESMRF, since inherits methodologies from SMRF also avoids processing of duplicate packets.

3 Proposed Concurrent Data Collection Protocol

3.1 Network Structure and Assumptions

We assume that the network supports RPL as a protocol which means all the control messages should be actively supported by the network and the repair mechanism is in place to do a global repair. Once the nodes in the network fail, the network should be iterated to form another network to repair as said in the RFC of RPL. Mode of Operation 3 (MOP3) is supported by the network. The protocol operates in MOP3 and it is assumes that the network supports that. Hence both downward and upward route is present and an edge in the network means bidirectional in nature and can be used for both. The protocol stack implemented across all the devices is uniform and supports the implementation of Multicasting. The network is said to form a DODAG as specified in RPL. Special kind of nodes should be allowed to operate, called as border routers, which we will discuss about in further sections. All the properties of the nodes is inherited form RPL and hence the rank, Objective function and floating properties are inherently present for use. There is a multicast tree that is formed. We need to find a multicast head in the multicast nodes, which we will describe in the further sections. Multiple DODAGs should be able to operate in tandem and each DODAG functions independently. Support should be provided to have multiple roots in the network and each root has a network. Support for Link Layer unicast and link layer broadcast should be provided.

3.2 Properties of Border Router

A border router is a special router that can join two networks at the same time. It has higher processing power and battery power that normal nodes. It should be able to constitute two interfaces. Each interface should have the Physical Layer, Data Link Layer and Network Layer different. The two interfaces should be able to independently route packets. The two interfaces should be able to route across the interfaces. For example a packet received in interface 1 should be able to be sent on interface 2.

3.3 Selection and circulation of Multicast Head

The process of selecting a multicast head is important for the protocol. Each node knows the multicast address in which it is interested in . We use a special DAO message to elect the multicast head. This DAO message is special in the case that this message can originate only in the leaf nodes. i,e the nodes that have no incoming edges when we consider the DODAG structure.

1. The leaf nodes constitute the DAO message and it does not require an ACK message.
2. The node puts all the multicast addresses that it is interested in and mentions that the multicast head is itself by inserting it's address against the multicast address.
3. The flag for DAO ACK is set to false.
4. Once constituted, it sends the message in upward direction.
5. Each node takes the DAO messages and processes it if it came from one of its children.
6. For each of the multicast address that the node is interested in:
   (a) If there is an entry in the message, update the new cluster head to be the node's address.
   (b) Else make en entry in the for another multicast cluster head.
7. The root also processes the same way as other nodes. Once it has processed, it sends the information to all the nodes in the network.

8. Each node updates the multicast head information in their tables.
9. A border router sends the information available in both the interfaces to both the interfaces giving the global information of the cluster head

3.4 Process of New Node Joining

Initially the number of roots that are there in the network should be decided by the user according to the application. The newnode that wants to join broadcasts DODAG Information Solicitation Message and awaits a reply. The node that is already present in the network send out DIO, in reply to DIS sent. The new node collects the DIO and checks if it is eligible to be a border router. If it is eligible and is willing, it can join more than one network and it has to have two interfaces dedicated to both the networks. The eligibility is calculated using the state of each node and the information that is given through DIO and the willingness of each node to be a border router depends on the calculated probability(random probability). Once the border router sets up, it sends a packet notifying the root of the same and the root publishes the same via DIO. Figure 13.1 depicts the flow chart for the process.

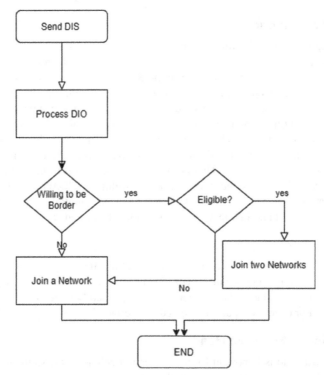

Fig. 13.1 New node joining the network

3.5 Reacting to a Query

When a node constitutes a multicast packet, it knows which node is the multicast head. It queries for the multicast head. The following depicts how each kind of node reacts to the query that the source of the multicast packet sends out.

Source: The source constitutes a special packet. This packet has information of source address, multicast head address, array of addresses denoting the addresses that it has traversed and a sequence number that is unique to each message. The source sends out the packet to root and all the border routers if the multicast head is not present in the children of the source node. Once it gets a reply, it stops, else waits for certain amount of time before sending out another query. If the node gets a reply from the root that the node is present in the same DODAG, the source floods the query across the network. The packet structure remains the same.

Intermediate Node (not Border Router): If the Intermediate node is the multicast head, the address is appended to the array of addresses and constitutes a reply-query packet with source and destination address and as the route is traced, it will be sent along the same. It registers the sequence number of the message. If the intermediate node is not multicast head, it appends the address to the array of addresses and sends to the intended next hop by looking at the destination. This is done only after checking the sequence number of the message. If the sequence number if already present in the node's list or the sequence number is lesser that the one that is present in the list, it discards the message as it is probably a duplicate message.

Border Router: If the message reaches a border router, it checks on the other side of the interface, for example if the query message comes on interface1, I will check in the network that pertains to interface2. If the address is there in the network, then it constitutes a message saying so. If there is no such node, it discards the message. The reply query message is same as that explained for the intermediate node.

Root: If the query message reaches the root, the root checks whether the multicast head the source is looking for is in the network. If it is present in the network, the root replies the same to the source. It creates a reply query message using the fields of thequery message. It traces the route that is formed in the network.

3.6 Functioning of the Protocol

The protocol assumes that the DODAG is already formed according the described methods. The following steps detail how each of the node types interact with the protocol.

Source:

1. Source wants to send the message to a multicast group.
2. Check in the list which node is the multicast head of the multicast group.
3. Constitute a packet to be sent to that multicast head. The packet has sequence number, RPLInstanceID, source address, destination address, the array of addresses, payload, the identification that this is a multicast message.
4. Copy the route that was replied back when the query was put out.
5. Send out the packet along the route.

Intermediate Node(Not Border Router): When a multicast message arrives, the node checks whether the sequence number is valid. Which means it the sequence number of the received packet is greater than that of in the table. It accepts the packet further for processing by registering the sequence number in the list. Check if the node is interested in the message. If it is interested in the message, send the message to the higher layers for processing. If the node has interested children in the multicast message, send the message downwards in the network. Send the message up the network. If it is a border router or a multicast head, process according to their specifications. If the message was a multicastmessage unicast from the preferred parent, process it and send the unicast message to the children. Figure 13.2 gives a flow of logic for deciding the fate of the packet.

Border Router: If the packet reaches a border router, shift the packet to the other side of the interface and then process it according to the intermediate node processing. One condition that should be checked here is whether the border router is a multicast head or interested in the message. These cases should be handled appropriately.

Multicast Head: If the message receives the multicast head, stop forwarding the message and process the packet. Constitute a unicast message that is a copy of the payload from the multicast message and send it to the children. This is how the processing of the data message is processed by different kind of nodes.

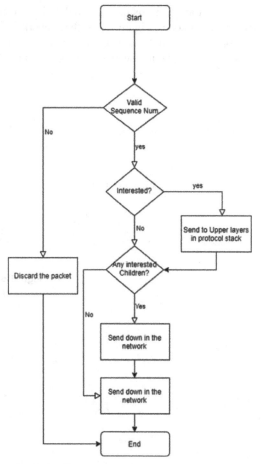

Fig. 13.2 Flow of logic for an intermediate node

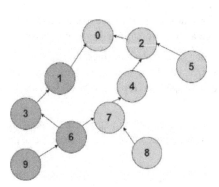

Fig. 13.3 BMRF algorithm for 10 nodes

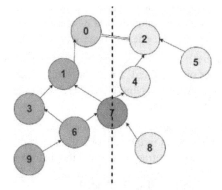

Fig. 13.4 The proposed algorithm for 10 nodes

4. Performance Analysis and Experimental Results

The proposed protocol is implemented on NetSim, a discrete event network simulator. The Simulations were carried out for varying number of nodes. Along with the proposed protocol, the BMRF routing technique was also to derive the metric of number of transmissions that occurred during the communication phase. Figure 13.3 is the network for simulating BMRF for 10 number of nodes. Figure 13.4 is the network for simulating the proposed algorithm for 10 number of nodes. Orange node is the border router in the network. Figure 13.5 is the network for simulating BMRF for 20 number of nodes. Figure 13.6 is the network for simulating the proposed algorithm for 20 number of nodes.

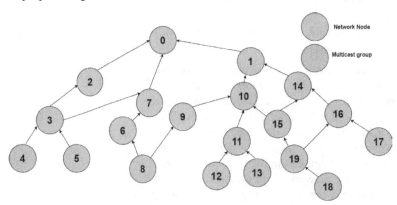

Fig. 13.5 BMRF algorithm for 20 nodes

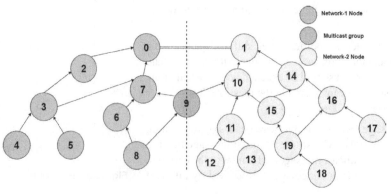

Fig. 13.6 Proposed algorithm for 20 nodes

Figure 13.8 is the network for simulating BMRF for 30 number of nodes. Figure 13.9 is the network for simulating the proposed algorithm for 30 number of nodes. Figure 13.10 is the network for simulating BMRF for 40 number of nodes. Figure 13.11 is the network for simulating the proposed algorithm for 40 number of nodes. To plot the graph for the metrics, a multicast message was sent from the leaf nodes in the network, except the leaves that are part of the multicast tree. All the networks feature a clustered Multicast tree. It is to show the improvement in the number of transmissions in the network. The improvement would also be there if the multicast groups are not clustered. The worst case performance that the proposed algorithm will show in terms of number of transmissions is the performance achieved by BMRF. Figure 13.7 features the number of nodes along x-axis and the number of messages that are transmitted along y axis. Number of edges were plotted in the graph to show that the proposed algorithm would work for a general case. Had the network been made to work like that, the number of edges wouldn't have made a near straight line in the graph.

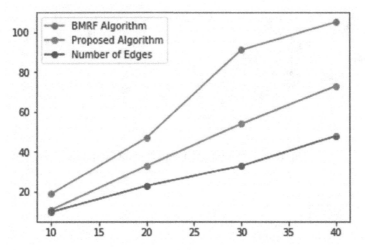

Fig. 13.7   Performance comparison in terms of transmission count

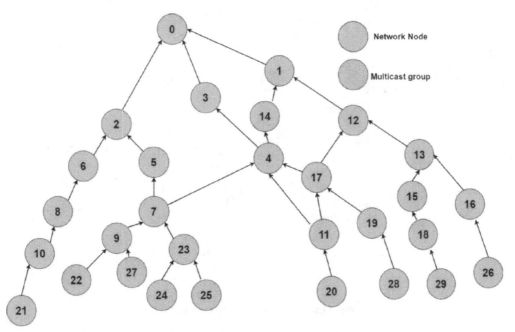

Fig. 13.8   BMRF algorithm for 30 nodes

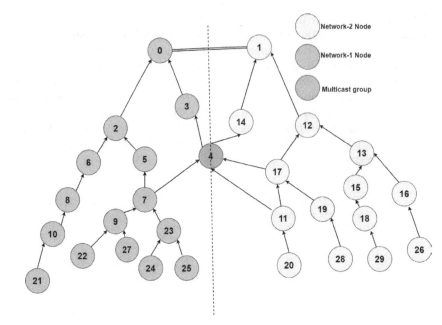

Fig. 13.9 The proposed algorithm for 30 nodes

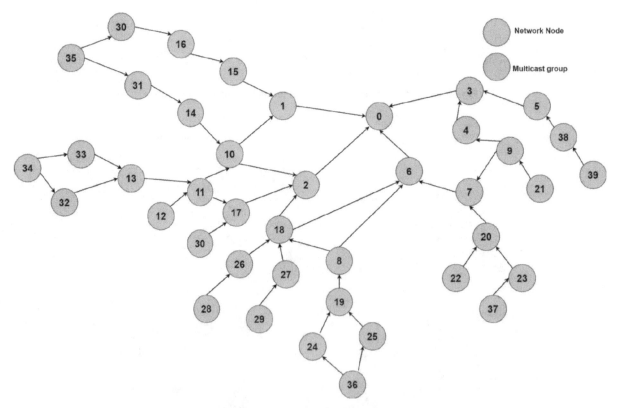

Fig. 13.10 40 Nodes BMRF algorithm

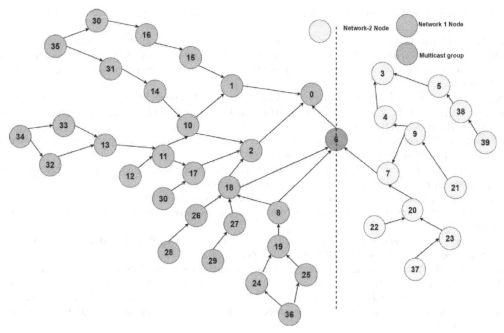

Fig. 13.11 The proposed algorithm for 40 Nodes

5. Conclusion

With IoT rapidly evolving and being adopted across different business verticals, there is tremendous growth in the number of smart devices getting connected to the Internet. This results in some unique challenges related to scalability and freshness of data collected. With variety applications, especially in smart healthcare, industries and home automation, there is a need to address the data distribution in such networks. Existing works in this direction employ different techniques to address the issues related to scalability, specifically techniques based on clustering. The multicast protocols developed for RPL seems to be viable option for deployment with very less overhead and the dynamic nature of the network maintenance which supports rapid joining and leaving of the network nodes. The proposed algorithm is shown to outperform BMRF and hence the successors in the number of transmissions. The proposed algorithm is an improvement over the BMRF algorithm. However, the requirement of higher processing power compared to BMRF is a limitation. The reduction in the processing would be a future research direction that needs to be explored.

REFERENCES

1. Atzori, L., Iera, A., & Morabito, G. (2010). The internet of things: A survey. Computer networks, 54(15), 2787–2805.
2. Li, S., Xu, L. D., & Zhao, S. (2015). The internet of things: a survey. *Information systems frontiers*, *17*, 243–259.
3. "https://www.cisomag.com/iot-devices-market-is-estimatedto-increase-between-2020-to-2025/," 2020.
4. Alaa, M., Zaidan, A. A., Zaidan, B. B., Talal, M., & Kiah, M. L. M. (2017). A review of smart home applications based on Internet of Things. *Journal of network and computer applications*, *97*, 48–65.
5. Yeh, K. H. (2016). A secure IoT-based healthcare system with body sensor networks. *IEEE access*, *4*, 10288–10299.
6. Tian, S., Yang, W., Le Grange, J. M., Wang, P., Huang, W., & Ye, Z. (2019). Smart healthcare: making medical care more intelligent. *Global Health Journal*, *3*(3), 62–65.
7. Botta, A., De Donato, W., Persico, V., & Pescapé, A. (2016). Integration of cloud computing and internet of things: a survey. *Future generation computer systems*, *56*, 684–700.
8. Andaloussi, Y., El Ouadghiri, M. D., Maurel, Y., Bonnin, J. M., & Chaoui, H. (2018). Access control in IoT environments: Feasible scenarios. Procedia computer science, 130, 1031–1036.
9. Singh, S. P., & Sharma, S. C. (2015). A survey on cluster based routing protocols in wireless sensor networks. *Procedia computer science*, *45*, 687–695.

10. Al-Karaki, J. N., & Kamal, A. E. (2004). Routing techniques in wireless sensor networks: a survey. *IEEE wireless communications, 11*(6), 6–28.
11. Heinzelman, W. R., Chandrakasan, A., & Balakrishnan, H. (2000, January). Energy-efficient communication protocol for wireless microsensor networks. In *Proceedings of the 33rd annual Hawaii international conference on system sciences* (pp. 10-pp). IEEE.
12. Arora, V. K., Sharma, V., & Sachdeva, M. (2016). A survey on LEACH and other's routing protocols in wireless sensor network. Optik, 127(16), 6590–6600.
13. Singh, S. K., Kumar, P., & Singh, J. P. (2017). A survey on successors of LEACH protocol. *Ieee Access, 5*, 4298–4328.
14. Peng, Z. R., Yin, H., Dong, H. T., & Li, H. (2015). LEACH protocol based two-level clustering algorithm. *International Journal of Hybrid Information Technology, 8*(10), 15–26.
15. Kaur, R., Sharma, D., & Kaur, N. (2013). Comparative analysis of leach and its descendant protocols in wireless sensor network. *International Journal of P2P Network Trends and Technology, 3*(1), 51–55.
16. Heinzelman, W. B., Chandrakasan, A. P., & Balakrishnan, H. (2002). An application-specific protocol architecture for wireless microsensor networks. *IEEE Transactions on wireless communications, 1*(4), 660–670.
17. Mahmood, D., Javaid, N., Mahmood, S., Qureshi, S., Memon, A. M., & Zaman, T. (2013, October). MODLEACH: a variant of LEACH for WSNs. In *2013 Eighth international conference on broadband and wireless computing, communication and applications* (pp. 158–163). IEEE.
18. Neto, J. H. B., Rego, A., Cardoso, A. R., & Celestino, J. (2014, February). MH-LEACH: A distributed algorithm for multi-hop communication in wireless sensor networks. In *ICN* (Vol. 2014, pp. 55–61).
19. Sindhwani, N., & Vaid, R. (2013). V LEACH: an energy efficient communication protocol for WSN. Mechanica Confab, 2(2), 79-84.
20. Ahlawat, A., & Malik, V. (2013, April). An extended vice-cluster selection approach to improve v leach protocol in WSN. In *2013 Third International Conference on Advanced Computing and Communication Technologies (ACCT)* (pp. 236–240). IEEE.
21. Shah, H., & Bhoyar, S. R. (2014). Improved V-Leach Protocol in Wireless Sensor Network with Data Security. *OSR J. Electron. Commun. Eng, 9*, 49–54.
22. Azharuddin, M., Kuila, P., & Jana, P. K. (2013, August). A distributed fault-tolerant clustering algorithm for wireless sensor networks. In *2013 International conference on advances in computing, communications and informatics (ICACCI)* (pp. 997–1002). IEEE.
23. Hui, J., & Kelsey, R. (2016). *Multicast protocol for low-power and lossy networks (MPL)* (No. rfc7731).
24. Oikonomou, G., Phillips, I., & Tryfonas, T. (2013). IPv6 multicast forwarding in RPL-based wireless sensor networks. *Wireless personal communications, 73*, 1089-1116.
25. Abdel Fadeel, K. Q., & El Sayed, K. (2015, May). ESMRF: enhanced stateless multicast RPL forwarding for IPv6-based low-power and lossy networks. In *Proceedings of the 2015 Workshop on IoT challenges in Mobile and Industrial Systems* (pp. 19–24).

Note: All the figures in this chapter were made by the author.

Advances in Computational Intelligence and its Applications (ICACIA-2023) – Dr. Sheikh Fahad Ahmad et al. (eds)
© 2024 Taylor & Francis Group, London, ISBN 978-1-032-78612-4

Implementation of Converting Indian Sign Language into Indian Language Using IoT-based Machine Learning Algorithms

14

D. Sivabalaselvamani*

Associate Professor, Kongu Engineering College,
Perundurai, Erode, Tamil Nadu, India

D. Selvakarthi

Assistant Professor, Kongu Engineering College,
Perundurai, Erode, Tamil Nadu, India

L. Rahunathan

Associate Professor, Kongu Engineering College,
Perundurai, Erode, Tamil Nadu, India

S. Gokulprasath, D. Jagane, S. Logeshwar

PG Scholar, Kongu Engineering College,
Perundurai, Erode, Tamil Nadu, India

ABSTRACT—A language is a basic tool used to share information, ideas, and feelings with people. Communication plays a major role in people's life. To communicate with more people, common languages like Tamil, English, etc., are used by people. However, sign language was utilized by the dumb and deaf to communicate. Deaf and dumb people can find it difficult to communicate with normal people because they don't know the sign language they use to communicate. This is becoming a barrier between normal people and deaf and dumb people. To solve this problem can create a machine learning model to detect sign language and translate it into normal language. This helps disabled people to communicate with normal people without any difficulties. The available solutions are either not real-time or only moderately accurate. On both metrics, this system produces good performance. It can recognize some ISL motions and hand poses. A camera is used to collect sign language, which is then analyzed using a machine learning model to predict the sign and translate it into text. The sign images are collected by using a camera and the images are labeled by their sign. After that, images are used to train and test the model. Using this method can reduce the difficulties. Because no additional hardware, like gloves or the Microsoft Kinect sensor, is needed, it is user-friendly. Only a camera is used to capture and detect sign language. With a small amount of data, this approach predicts sign language effectively.

KEYWORDS—TensorFlow, Indian sign language, Deaf community

1. Introduction

The Deaf community in India uses Indian Sign Language, a visual language, for communication. With its grammar, vocabulary, and syntax that are different from spoken languages, it is a rich and complicated language. The use of machine learning techniques to recognize and translate ISL into spoken languages has gained popularity in recent years. This can be particularly

*Corresponding Author: sivabalaselvamani@gmail.com

DOI: 10.1201/9781003488682-14

useful for Deaf individuals who rely on ISL as their primary mode of communication, as it can allow them to better interact with the hearing population and access information and services. There are numerous ways to construct a machine learning-based ISL recognition system. Convolutional neural networks are frequently used to identify images of hand motions, which can be recorded using a camera or another visual sensor.

2. Literature Survey

Kinjal Mistree et al. [1], Deaf people utilize sign language, a visual and comprehensive natural language, to communicate with hearing people and with one another. This article presents a method that uses an ISL picture as an input and outputs the associated class. Sharvani Srivastava et al. [2], Communication is the act of conveying or sharing thoughts, sentiments, or information. Both parties must be able to speak and comprehend the same language for two people to create communication. Deaf and dumb people, however, use various communication methods. S.Rajarajeswari et al. [3], the most common form of communication for those who have trouble hearing and speaking in sign language. Keerthi Reddy Velmula et al. [4], an important part of daily living is communication. It can be challenging for those who have communication issues to interact with others. Sign language is used to help the deaf and dumb communicate with others. Numerous sign languages exist. Indian sign language was used in the writing of this study. S. Sharma et al. [5], to facilitate communication between the signer and non-signer communities, an effective sign language recognition system (SLRS) can identify sign language motions. This research proposes a deep learning-based SLRS that is computer vision-based. C.Aparna et al. [6], with the use of convolutional neural networks (CNNs) and large short-term memories, we suggest a deep learning method for recognizing sign language in this research (LSTM). Khushbu Sinha et al. [7], People who don't know sign language may use the trained model to understand sign language and get an accurate text output for the same by comparing it to the input supplied to identify the signs. A camera will be used to feed the sign language in real time. Soumen Das et al. [8], the trained model may be used by people who don't know sign language to comprehend sign language and produce correct text by comparing the output to the input provided to identify the signs. Ashish Sharma et al. [9], three models—a pre-trained VGG16 with fine-tuning, a VGG16 with transfer learning, and a hierarchical neural network—were investigated based on a range of trainable parameters. Purkayastha et al. [10], Computer vision and machine learning researchers are increasingly focusing on the recognition of sign language. The alphabet of Indian sign language will be recognized in this study using deep learning and machine learning.

3. Methodology

3.1 Data Collection

Collecting data for the model plays a major role in getting good results after the whole process. To collect the data here one can use a camera with help of OpenCV and python pictures are taken. For saving the images with different names UUID model in python is used. Real-time computer vision is the primary focus of OpenCV's functions. Using a camera and python, OpenCV reduces the difficulties in collecting the data. Here augmentation or any other complex methods are not used to collect the data. Collecting data difficulties are reduced by this method as shown in Fig. 14.1.

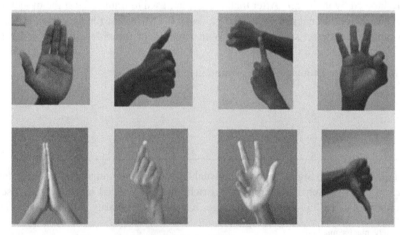

Fig. 14.1 Data set language

3.2 Data Pre-processing

Unclean data can be converted into clean data collection via a process known as data preparation. To put it another way, data is typically obtained from various sources in raw form, making analysis impractical. For this reason, pre-processing the data is necessary. In this case, to use TensorFlow object detection images must be labelled by their sign. It helps the object detection model recognize the sign in the image.

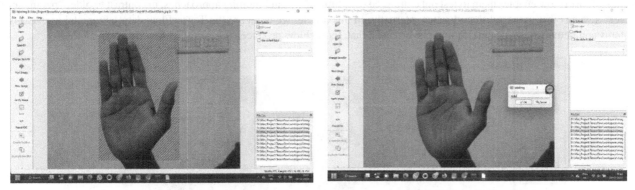

Fig. 14.2 Data collection   **Fig. 14.3** Labeling image

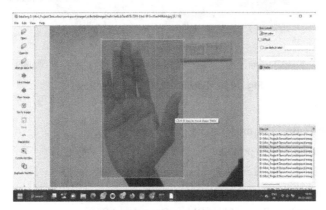

Fig. 14.4 Marking sign

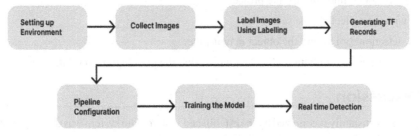

Fig. 14.5 Labeling image

3.3 Algorithms

Object Detection

The problem of object detection in computer vision is locating and identifying things in pictures and videos. It is an important and widely used application of machine learning, with a wide range of applications including self-driving cars, security systems, and robotics. In object detection, the goal is to identify and locate objects of interest within an image or video. This is typically done by training a machine learning model on a large dataset of images that contain the objects of interest, along with annotations that indicate the location of the objects within the images. The model is then able to use this training data to make predictions on new images, identifying and localizing the objects of interest within the image.

TensorFlow

The machine learning system TensorFlow performs at scale and under various conditions. TensorFlow uses dataflow graphs to explain computation, shared state, and the operations that change it. This design gives the application developer flexibility because TensorFlow enables them to test out cutting-edge optimizations and training approaches, in contrast to older "parameter server" systems that managed shared states internally. In this article, we compare the TensorFlow dataflow model to existing systems and demonstrate the outstanding performance that TensorFlow produces in several real-world applications.

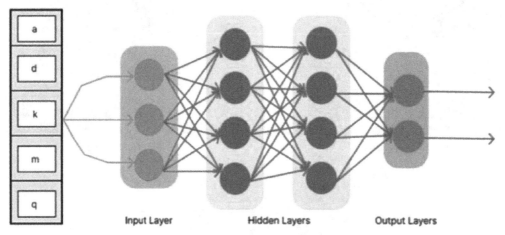

Fig. 14.6 Formulation of tension flow

Algorithm related to a dataset

Step 1: Download and extract the TensorFlow model zoo.

Step 2: Download and install and compile the protobuf.

Step 3: Install the Object detection API to detect the hand sign inside the images

Step 4: Prepare the data to feed the TensorFlow zoo model.

Step 5: To connect labels to integer values, TensorFlow Object Detection API.

Step 6: Select the suitable model architecture for the project.

Step 7: Train the model with the collected data set.

Step 8: Utilize an object detection tool to find the object in real-time.

Step 10: The detected class is translated into the Indian language using the google trans module.

4. Result and Discussion

Indian Sign Language poses are instantly recognized by the established system. The system was developed utilizing TensorFlow's object detection API. The pre-trained model, SSD Mobile Net v2 320x320, was acquired from the TensorFlow model zoo. The recently created dataset, which has been trained via transfer learning, comprises 15 photos for each symbol. There was an overall loss of 0.08 during the final 20,000 training steps; localization loss was 0.002; classification loss was 0.016; and regularization loss was 0.06. As can be seen in the graphic below, the step 17600 loss was the least, coming in at 0.08 as shown in Fig. 14.9.

The system's output depends on the confidence level, which is now 95% on average as shown in Fig. 14.7 and 8. The confidence rate for each sign is noted and summarized in the outcome by expanding the dataset, the system's confidence level may be raised, which will improve the system's identification capabilities. Consequently, the system's performance is enhanced and improved. In addition, the recognized classes of signs are translated into a given Indian language, which helps various regions of Indian utilize the Indian sign language recognition system.

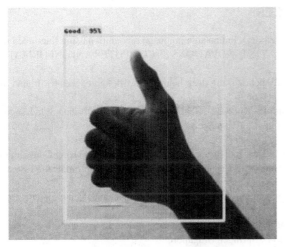

Fig. 14.7 Real-time detection

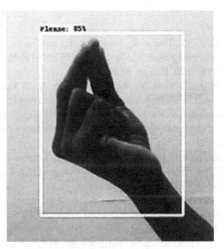

Fig. 14.8 Real-time detection

```
INFO:tensorflow:Step 17400 per-step time 1.873s
I1225 19:56:30.591351 140699338602368 model_lib_v2.py:705] Step 17400 per-step time 1.873s
INFO:tensorflow:{'Loss/classification_loss': 0.019253742,
 'Loss/localization_loss': 0.0026312857,
 'Loss/regularization_loss': 0.06875377,
 'Loss/total_loss': 0.0906388,
 'learning_rate': 0.05985175}
I1225 19:56:30.591747 140699338602368 model_lib_v2.py:708] {'Loss/classification_loss': 0.019253742,
 'Loss/localization_loss': 0.0026312857,
 'Loss/regularization_loss': 0.06875377,
 'Loss/total_loss': 0.0906388,
 'learning_rate': 0.05985175}
INFO:tensorflow:Step 17500 per-step time 1.829s
I1225 19:59:33.451373 140699338602368 model_lib_v2.py:705] Step 17500 per-step time 1.829s
INFO:tensorflow:{'Loss/classification_loss': 0.015910752,
 'Loss/localization_loss': 0.0051227845,
 'Loss/regularization_loss': 0.06847169,
 'Loss/total_loss': 0.08950523,
 'learning_rate': 0.0596287}
I1225 19:59:33.451754 140699338602368 model_lib_v2.py:708] {'Loss/classification_loss': 0.015910752,
 'Loss/localization_loss': 0.0051227845,
 'Loss/regularization_loss': 0.06847169,
 'Loss/total_loss': 0.08950523,
 'learning_rate': 0.0596287}
INFO:tensorflow:Step 17600 per-step time 1.841s
I1225 20:02:37.573128 140699338602368 model_lib_v2.py:705] Step 17600 per-step time 1.841s
INFO:tensorflow:{'Loss/classification_loss': 0.01615333,
 'Loss/localization_loss': 0.002677649,
 'Loss/regularization_loss': 0.068178706,
 'Loss/total_loss': 0.08700968,
 'learning_rate': 0.05940484}
I1225 20:02:37.573523 140699338602368 model_lib_v2.py:708] {'Loss/classification_loss': 0.01615333,
 'Loss/localization_loss': 0.002677649,
 'Loss/regularization_loss': 0.068178706,
 'Loss/total_loss': 0.08700968,
 'learning_rate': 0.05940484}
```

Fig. 14.9 Loss rate

5. Conclusion and Future Works

In India, deaf and dumb people have many problems because of the communication gap with normal people. They use sign language and hand signs to communicate with others, but normal people don't know about that. Because of that, they can't share their thoughts, feelings, and expressions with normal people. An automated Indian sign language detection system can solve this problem. It helps translate to sign language Signs of the normal Indian language. By using TensorFlow Object detection API we achieve this solution for this problem. This model is trained with the signs of deaf and dumb people, so it can detect the signs in real time with a good accuracy rate. To create the data collection, webcam Python and OpenCV are used to reduce the cost. The created model gives 88.20% of the average score in detection in real-time. With less number of datasets, this model has achieved good accuracy. In the future, more signs can be detected by giving more datasets with a good amount of accuracy. This system can be used in various sign languages with the appropriate dataset.

REFERENCES

1. Sharma, C. M., Tomar, K., Mishra, R. K., & Chariar, V. M. (2021, September). Indian sign language recognition using fine-tuned deep transfer learning model. In Procc. of INTERNATIONAL CONFERENCE ON INNOVATIONS IN COMPUTER AND INFORMATION SCIENCE (ICICIS) (pp. 62–67).
2. Sharma, A., Sharma, N., Saxena, Y., Singh, A., & Sadhya, D. (2021). Benchmarking deep neural network approaches for Indian Sign Language recognition. Neural Computing and Applications, 33(12), 6685–6696.
3. Rajarajeswari, S., Renji, N. M., Kumari, P., Keshavamurthy, M., & Kruthika, K. (2022). Real-Time Translation of Indian Sign Language to Assist the Hearing and Speech Impaired. In Innovations in Computational Intelligence and Computer Vision (pp. 303–322). Springer, Singapore.
4. Velmula, K. R., Linginani, I., Reddy, K. B., Meghana, P., & Aruna, A. (2021). Indian Sign Language Recognition Using Convolutional Neural Networks. In Proceedings of International Conference on Advances in Computer Engineering and Communication Systems (pp. 393–400). Springer, Singapore.
5. Sharma, S., Gupta, R., & Kumar, A. (2021). Continuous sign language recognition using isolated signs data and deep transfer learning. Journal of Ambient Intelligence and Humanized Computing, 1–12.
6. Aparna, C., & Geetha, M. (2020). CNN and stacked LSTM model for Indian Sign Language recognition. In Symposium on Machine Learning and Metaheuristics Algorithms, and Applications (pp. 126–134). Springer, Singapore.
7. Sinha, K., Miranda, A. O., & Mishra, S. (2022). Real-Time Sign Language Translator. In Cognitive Informatics and Soft Computing (pp. 477–489). Springer, Singapore.
8. Das, S., Biswas, S. K., & Purkayastha, B. (2022). A deep sign language recognition system for Indian sign language. Neural Computing and Applications, 1–13.
9. Sharma, A., Sharma, N., Saxena, Y., Singh, A., & Sadhya, D. (2021). Benchmarking deep neural network approaches for Indian Sign Language recognition. Neural Computing and Applications, 33(12), 6685–6696.
10. Uchil, A. P., Jha, S., & Sudha, B. G. (2020). Vision based deep learning approach for dynamic Indian sign language recognition in healthcare. In International conference on computational vision and bio inspired computing (pp. 371–383). Springer, Cham.

Note: All the figures in this chapter were made by the authors.

Advances in Computational Intelligence and its Applications (ICACIA-2023) – Dr. Sheikh Fahad Ahmad et al. (eds)
© 2024 Taylor & Francis Group, London, ISBN 978-1-032-78612-4

A Comprehensive Survey on Deep Fake Object Creation and Detection: Challenges, and Future Directions

15

Mainak Saha[1], Sourav Dey Roy[2], Santanu Das[3]

Department of Computer Science and Engineering,
Tripura University (A Central University), Suryamaninagar, Tripura (W), India

Mrinal Kanti Bhowmik[4]

Department of Computer Science and Engineering,
Tripura University (A Central University), Suryamaninagar, Tripura (W), India

Department of Computer Science and Engineering, Tandon School of Engineering,
New York University, New York City, NY 11201, USA

ABSTRACT—Recently, there has been a lot of public concern over fake images and videos created by computer manipulation, particularly with Deep Fake technologies. Deep Fake technologies are basically a synthetic generative deep learning algorithm which produces or modifies features of digital content in a way that makes it difficult to differentiate between real and fake features. This technology has substantially evolved and encourages a wide variety of applications in the media, video gaming business, and film industries. Surveys on deep fake-based methods (i.e., for both creation and detection) in the past have predominantly examined facial deep fake images and videos. Moreover, survey on the deep fake-based objects creation and detection techniques are less understood in the literature. In this paper, we provide a comprehensive survey and analysis of the various vision based deep fake object generation techniques and deep learning-based approaches for fake objects detection. The paper also reviews publicly available object based deep fake datasets. In this paper, the performance of published papers is also compared. To help future researchers for better understanding the problems, we also presented various open difficulties and potential future paths that need to be solved to enhance the production and detection of deep fake objects generation and detection.

KEYWORDS—Deep fake, Deep fake objects, Generation, Creation, Detection

1. Introduction

Over the past several years, fake multimedia has emerged as a major issue, especially with the development of so-called "Deep Fake", which are fake media that have been altered using robust and user-friendly deep learning methods, such as autoencoders (AE) or generative adversarial networks (GAN). The term "Deep Fake" gained its popularity after a Reddit user claimed to have created a machine learning algorithm that enabled him to insert famous faces of celebrities into pornographic movies in late 2017 (Verdoliva, 2020). Virtual reality, video games, photography, and movie-making are just a few examples of deep fake applications (Nguyen et al., 2022). Moreover, it is possible to use deep fakes to sow political and religious division among nations, spread false information, and mislead voters (Nguyen et al., 2022). Also, the Earth's satellite photos can even be manipulated to create fictitious items, such as a bridge over a river, to mislead military analysts (Nguyen et al., 2022). On social

[1]mainak.skms@gmail.com, [2]souravdeyroy49@gmail.com, [3]santanud803@gmail.com, [4]mrinalkantibhowmik@tripurauniv.ac.in

DOI: 10.1201/9781003488682-15

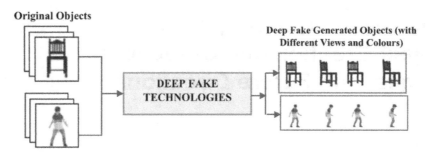

Fig. 15.1 Deep fake objects

Source: Author

media, numerous fake videos featuring actors and politicians were widely shared and garnered a lot of attention. A threat to global security arises when deep fake techniques can be used to produce fake speeches of international leaders.

Since the invention of photography, image alteration has been practiced, and sophisticated image/video editing programs have been around for a long-time. Multimedia forensics research has been ongoing for at least 15 years and is getting more and more attention from the academic community as well as large IT corporations and various organizations (Verdoliva, 2020). There are several categories of deep fakes like face-swap, lip-sync, and puppet-master (Nguyen et al., 2022). Those are basically altered and manipulated facial images, audio recordings, and videos. Among several categories of deep fakes, very little attention has been given till date for deep fake-based objects generation in the indoor and outdoor scenes and its effective detection. Deep Fake based objects are the fake objects which are created using various well-known deep learning methods (for example GAN) so as to generate various fake objects (i.e., in various orientations, shapes, colours, and scales). These fake objects are further incorporated in real world outdoor scenarios so as to make them more realistic in appearance as compared to the other objects present in the scenes. Some examples of deep fake objects are shown in Figure 1. The deep fake-based object generation and its effective detection has various real-world applications. Generally, surveillance cameras are installed in various public places including border areas for continuous monitoring. And there may be a chance for the forgers to use deep fake technologies for creating a false content that a suspected drone has been seen in the border area which is suspected to be implemented by the neighbouring country for monitoring of the foreign land. Thereafter uploading these fake contents in social media, may create negative sentiments among people and may arise in reducing the peace and harmony of the country. Therefore, significant attention must be given by the forensics communities for effective generation of deep fake-based objects in the scenes and consequently develop deep learning based techniques for effective localization of the forgeries done in the media contents so as to maintain the peace and harmony of the country. During the past few years, several surveys are conducted for facial deep fakes (Nguyen et al., 2022), (Malik et al., 2022), (Masood et al., 2022), (Mirsky et al., 2021). But till date, no surveys have been conducted that provides a thorough analysis thereby specially focusing on the vision-based techniques for deep fake object creation and detection and their effective challenges towards technique development.

Depending upon this phenomenon, our contributions are:

1. The paper provides the elaborate illustration of various challenges faced by the research communities for dealing with deep fake-based object generation and detection.

2. The paper provides a review on vision-based techniques for deep fake based object generation and also reviews the techniques for detection (in terms of localization) of the fake objects in the scenes. Due to the non-availability of techniques for detection of deep fake-based objects, the paper provides a review on deep learning-based techniques for fake objects localization.

3. The paper also describes various deep fake object dataset publicly available for the research community.

4. The paper also compares the published results for deep fake-based objects generation and the deep learning fake objects detection techniques on the used datasets by the research community.

The main goal of this survey is to provide the reader an understanding of how emerging deep fake object are produced and identified. Also, the paper will inform the reader of recent advancements, trends, and challenges in deep fake object research.

2. Related Work

2.1 Challenges for Deep Fake Object Generation and Detection

With the blooming interest in deep fake-based techniques for creation and detection of fake objects, there are several challenges that need to be tackled by the research community while designing a model/ algorithm for deep fake-based object creation and detection shown in Fig. 15.2. In this section, various challenges for deep fake object creation and detection are described.

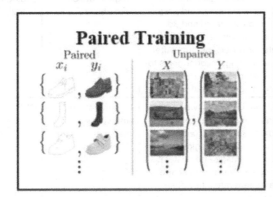

Fig. 15.2 Various challenges of deep fake represented as paired training, illumination conditions, occlusions, and spatio-temporal coherence

Source: Author

Challenges for Deep Fake based Object Creation

It has been a significant effort to enhance the visual quality of the deep fake objects so as to make them more realistic in appearances. But there are few issues that remains challenging for the deep fake-based object generation techniques so as mentioned below:

- **Paired Training**: High-quality output may be produced by a trained supervised model, but data pairing is sacrificed. The goal of data pairing is to find comparable input instances from the training data in order to produce the desired output (Zhu et al., 2017). In situations, when many objects and several identities are present throughout the training stage, this procedure is time taken and inappropriate.
- **Illumination Conditions**: Modern fake object generation techniques generate false information in controlled settings with constant illumination (Xiao et al., 2020). However, if the lighting suddenly changes, as it does in indoor/outdoor scenarios, the resulting multimedia (i.e., images or videos) will have weird glitches and inconsistent colours.
- **Occlusions**: Occlusion, which occurs when the object region is covered by objects like glasses or other objects, is one of the key problems with deep fake object creation (Pepikj et al., 2013).
- **Spatio-Temporal Coherence**: The appearance of obvious artefacts like flickering and jitter between frames is another challenge of created deep fake objects (Bengar et Al., 2019). These impacts happen as a result of the deep fake object creation frameworks' failure to account for temporal consistency as they operate on each frame.

Table 15.1 Survey on deep fake object generation methods

Authors/ Year	Used Methods	Object's Type	Working Principle	Purpose	Performance
T. Kaneko et al., 2018 [11]	Classifier's posterior GAN	Fake Objects in same class	The proposed method is extended version of AC-GAN (Auxiliary Classifier GAN)	To generate fake objects of the class to which the input image belongs	Accuracy: 99:7%
K. Olszewski et al., 2019 [19]	Transformable Bottleneck Network	3D Objects (Chair, Human, Car, etc.)	The encoder takes input in form of 2D image and pass it through the 2d and 3d Conv. layers and resample the encoder's outputs. After resampling decoder helps to transformed the outputs into an image of a fake objects.	To generate 3d fake objects.	L1:0.083 SSIM: 0.9425
R. Arandjelović et al., 2019 [3]	Copy-Pasting GAN	Fake Real time Scenarios	Generator takes two input images source and destination. The generator copies a small region of the source image and pastes it into the destination image and generate a new fake image.	To generate real time spliced images using GAN.	ODP: 98.3%
T. Kramberger et al., 2020 [12]	Fine-Tuned StyleGA	Fake Car Images	The method generates fake car images using fine-tuned Style GAN. The proposed Architecture has been trained on 46 million car images.	To create a fake car image dataset (LSUN-Stanford car datasets).	FID: 3.7%
SSIM: Structural Similarity Index Measure; ODP: Object Discovery Performance; FID: Fréchet Inception Distance					

Challenges for Deep Fake based Object Detection

Consequently, there are several challenges for deep fake-based object identification methods so as to effectively localize the deep fake objects and are discussed below:

- **Quality of Deep Fake Datasets**: A key element in the development of deep fake object detection systems is the availability of sizable databases of deep fake objects. However, comparing the quality of movies from these datasets to genuine modified content distributed on the internet exposes significant discrepancies.

- **Performance Evaluation**: Since each sample might either be real or fake, deep fake object detection algorithms are currently stated as a binary classification issue. Such classification is simpler to construct in a controlled setting, where we produce and validate deep fake object recognition methods using either authentic or false audio-visual input. Videos can be changed in real world situations in ways other than deep fakes, therefore the presence of edited content does not guarantee that the video is authentic.

- **Temporal Aggregation**: Deep fake object detection techniques now in use examine the likelihood that each video frame is genuine or altered by using binary classification at the frame level. These methods, however, do not take into account the consistency of time between frames and are susceptible to two possible issues: (i) deep fake object material exhibits temporal abnormalities, and (ii) genuine or fake frames may occur at regular intervals. Additionally, these approaches need to integrate the scores from each frame to provide a final value, which adds an extra step to the process of computing.

Survey on Deep Fake Object Generation

Due to the high ability of manipulated multimedia (i.e., images or videos) and the ease-of-use of its applications for a wide variety of users (i.e., from experts to beginners), deep fakes have grown in popularity. Most of these applications were created using deep learning methods. In this section, the review on various vision-based methods for deep fake-based objects generation are described. The analysis of deep fake-based methods for object generation are shown in Table 15.1. T. Kaneko et al. (2018) proposed Classifier's posterior GAN to generate class distinct and class mutual fake objects. They have modified the generator input of the AC-GAN for class overlapping data to generate various types of objects in different orientations and view. Transformable Bottleneck Network proposed by K. Olszewski et al. (2019) to generate 3D transformation of 2D images. The encoder takes input in the form of 2D image and passes it through the 2d and 3d Convolution layers and resample the encoder's outputs. After resampling, the decoder helps to transform the outputs into a 3D image of a 2D object which is fake. R. Arandjelović et al. (2019) proposed Copy-Pasting GAN to generate spliced images. Here, Generator takes two input images source and destination. The generator copies a small region of the source image and pastes it into the destination image and generates a new spliced (fake) image. T. Kramberger et al. (2020) has fine-tuned the StyleGAN architecture and trained on 46 million original car images taken from the Stanford dataset and the LSUN dataset. Then, to optimize zoom levels and lower picture noise, to create a fake car image dataset (LSUN-Stanford car dataset).

2.2 Survey on Deep Learning based Fake Object Detection

In response to increasingly sophisticated and realistic manipulated content, large efforts are being carried out by the forensic community to design improved methods for fake multimedia content detection. Deep learning based algorithms/models are being used to detect the manipulate data. Depending on the huge body of existing literature, this section of the manuscript provides a survey on deep learning based techniques/ algorithms for fake objects detection in the real-world scenes. Table 15.2 considers the diverse goals of the deep learning based techniques for fake objects detection. Through a multi scale guided learning strategy, Z., Li, et al. (2022) proposed a deep learning model for localizing image splicing using not only local image features but also global information. They have evaluated their proposed methods on CASIA v1.0, Columbia Uncompressed, and DSO-1 datasets. S. S. Ali, et al. (2022) proposed a deep learning architecture to detect double compression image forgery detection. Y Wei et al. (2022) proposed Synthetic Adversarial Networks (SANs) and Hybrid Dense U-Net (HDU-Net) for tampered region localization. They have evaluated their proposed method on SF-Data. The method has achieved 0.547 F1 score and accuracy of 0.747 on average. X Jin et al. (2021) proposed a dual stream deep learning network for feature extraction from a video to detect object based video forgery. Further they will integrate the CRF layer to fine-tune the segmentation results. The proposed model has evaluated on four state of the art object based video forgery dataset (i.e., SULFA,

Table 15.2 Survey on deep learning based fake object detection methods

Authors/ Year	Method Used	Type of Localization	Dealing with	Purpose	Performance Evaluation
Z. Li et al., 2022 [13]	Multi-scale guided learning	Binary mask	Images	For Image Splicing Localization	**F1:** 0.64; 0.53; 0.51
X. Jin et al., 2022 [9]	Multi-level deep feature fusion	Semantic Mask	Videos	For Splicing Detection in Videos	**F1:** 0.595
S. S. Ali et al., 2022 [2]	Traditional Blocks of CNN	Binary mask	Images	For identifying image forgeries	**Accuracy:** 92.23
Y. Wei et al., 2022 [22]	Synthetic Adversarial Networks (SANs) and Hybrid Dense U-Net(HDU-Net)	Binary mask	Images	For Image splicing forgery detection	**F1:** 0.547 **Accuracy:** 0.747
X. Jin et al., 2021 [8]	Dual-stream networks and depthinformation embedding	Binary mask	Videos	Object-based video forgery detection	**F1:** 0.442; 0.250; 0.403; 0.088
B. Ahmed et al., 2020 [1]	Mask-RCNN	Binary mask	Images	Image splicing detection	**AUC:** 0.967
J.H. Bappy et al., 2019 [4]	LSTM and Encoder-Decoder	Binary mask	Images	For Detection of Image Forgeries	**AUC:** 0.7936
Y. Liu et al., 2019 [14]	Deep Matching Network based on Atrous (DMAC)	Binary Mask	Images	Image splicing detection	**AUC:** 0.9511; 0.7739
M. Huh et al., 2018 [10]	Learned Self-Consistency (LSM)	Semantic Mask	Images	Image splicing detection	**F1:** 0.88; 0.52
CNN- Convolutional Neural Network; F1- F-Measure; AUC- Area Under the Curve					

REWIND, GRIP and VTD) and achieved the f1 scores 0.442, 0.250, 0.403, 0.088 respectively. B. Ahmed et al. (2020) proposed a deep neural architecture by replacing the feature pyramid network layers in ResNet-FPN. The architecture is designed for feature extraction from forged images after that the features will be trained by Mask RCNN to generate the mask for the forged region. The proposed model has achieved AUC value of 0.967. J.H Bappy et al. (2019) proposed a LSTM and encoder decoder network to segment the forged region. The proposed model captured the JPEG quality loss, up sampling, down sampling, rotation, and shearing, based on these perimeter segments of the forged regions. The model has trained on three publicly available well-known dataset and achieved AUC of 0.7936. X. Jin et al. (2022) proposed a method based on designing a novel framework for splicing localization based on discontinuous noise distribution and object contours. The proposed model is trained on publicly available spliced video datasets and achieved an F1 score of 0.595. M. Huh et al. (2018) proposed a method based on the discrepancy of the metadata tags between the authentic and spliced regions of the spliced images. The method has been evaluated on the Columbia and Carvalho dataset and achieved F1 scores of 0.88 and 0.52 respectively. Y. Liu et al. (2019) proposed a deep matching network based on atrous convolution (DMAC) based on designing an adversarial learning network to learn a deep matching network for splicing detection in images. DMAC method has been evaluated on CASIA and MFC2018 datasets and achieved AUC of 0.9511 and 0.7739 respectively.

2.3 Review on Deep Fake Object Based Datasets

The development of robust and efficient techniques for deep fake-based objects identification and localization are advanced from the available benchmark datasets that provides a balanced coverage of real-world challenges of forensics applications. In this section, the various deep fake-based objects publicly available for the research community are described. The main publicly accessible deep fake-based object datasets for studies on the detection of manipulation carried out depending on whole object synthesis are included in Table 15.3. From the huge body of existing datasets, only two datasets are relevance here and each of the datasets are created based on the GAN architecture. One of the datasets is ShapeNet (Chang et al., 2015). ShapeNet is a large-scale repository for 3D computer aided design (CAD) models developed by researchers from Stanford University, Princeton University and the Toyota Technological Institute at Chicago, USA. The repository contains over 300M models with 220,000 classified into 3,135 classes. ShapeNet Parts subset contains 31,693 meshes categorized into 16 common object classes (i.e., table, chair, plane etc.). Each shapes ground truth contains 2-5 parts (with a total of 50-part classes). Another dataset is LSUN-Stanford Car Dataset (Kramberger et al., (2020). The Stanford car dataset and the LSUN vehicle dataset is used to enhance the GAN's performance. Then, to adjust zoom levels and lower picture noise, a new, combined dataset was pruned. The number of photos that could be utilized for training decreased as a result of this approach, but the quality rose. By instructing the StyleGAN with the default parameters, this trimmed dataset was assessed. 2,067,710 automobile photos with more customized zoom settings and reduced noise were produced by pruning the combined LSUN and Stanford datasets.

Table 15.3 Review of deep fake object datasets

Year	Dataset	Types of objects	No of Images	Availability
2020	ShapeNet [19]	Table, chair, plane etc.	220,000	Public
2020	LSUN-Stanford Car Dataset [20]	Car	2,067,710	Public

3. Conclusion and Future Directions

This paper presents a first survey and thorough analysis on deep fake-based object generation techniques and also surveys various vision based deep learning methods for fake object detection. From extensive surveys it can be concluded that there are few papers on detecting and generating deep fake objects. In contrast, the forensic community is not that active in the particular problem space discussed in this paper. Therefore, there are several scopes for the forensics community to advance the proposed area. These are:

- **Deep Fake based Forged Object Generation in Real-World Outdoor Scenarios**. As reviewed in Table 15.1 and Table 15.3, it can be observed that almost all the techniques proposed in the literature are designed for single deep fake objects generation (such as car, table, chair, bird, etc.). But these techniques do not focus on generation of forged objects based on the deep fake technologies in real-world outdoor scenarios where several other candidate objects are present in the scene. Moreover, no such dataset is available for the forensics community. Therefore, there is a need for designing a technique for fake object generation using deep fake technologies in real-world outdoor scenarios thereby providing various representative challenges of the real world.

- **Deep Fake based Forged Object Detection Technique**. As reviewed in Table 15.2 of the manuscript, it can be observed that although there are many techniques developed by the forensics community for fake object detection, novel models/ algorithms for detection of the forged objects generated through deep fake technologies are still not explored. Therefore, instead of advancing the techniques for forged object detection, the forensics community needs to explore developing a new model/ algorithm for detection of the forged objects generated through deep fake technologies.

4. Acknowledgment

The work is supported by SERB International Research Experience (SIRE) Fellowship awarded to Mrinal Kanti Bhowmik for the year 2022-2023 under the Grant No. SIR/2022/000387, Dated: 12/05/2022 from Science and Engineering Research Board (SERB), Department of Science and Technology, Government of India. The authors would also like to thank Prof. Nasir Memon, Department of Computer Science and Engineering, New York University, NY 11201, USA for his kind support to carry out this work.

REFERENCES

1. Ahmed, B., Gulliver, T. A., and alZahir, S. (2020). Image splicing detection using mask-RCNN. Signal, image and video processing. 14: 1035–1042.
2. Ali, S. S., Ganapathi, I. I., Vu, N. S., Ali, S. D., Saxena, N., and Werghi, N. (2022). Image forgery detection using deep learning by recompressing images, Electronics. 11(3): 403.
3. Arandjelović, R., and Zisserman, A. (2019). Object discovery with a copy-pasting gan, arXiv preprint arXiv:1905.11369.
4. Bappy, J. H., Simons, C., Nataraj, L., Manjunath, B. S., and Roy-Chowdhury, A. K. (2019). Hybrid lstm and encoder–decoder architecture for detection of image forgeries, IEEE Transactions on Image Processing, 28(7): 3286–3300.
5. Bengar, J. Z., Gonzalez-Garcia, A., Villalonga, G., Raducanu, B., Aghdam, H. H., Mozerov, M., and Van de Weijer, J. (2019). Temporal coherence for active learning in videos, In 2019 IEEE/CVF International Conference on Computer Vision Workshop (ICCVW), 914–923.
6. Chang, A. X., Funkhouser, T., Guibas, L., Hanrahan, P., Huang, Q., Li, Z., Savarese, S., Savva, M., Song, S., Su, H., Xiao, J., Yi, L., and Yu, F. (2015). Shapenet: An information-rich 3d model repository, arXiv preprint arXiv:1512.03012.
7. D'Avino, D., Cozzolino, D., Poggi, G., and Verdoliva, L. (2017). Autoencoder with recurrent neural networks for video forgery detection, arXiv preprint arXiv:1708.08754.
8. Jin, X., He, Z., Xu, J., Wang, Y., and Su, Y. (2021). Object-based video forgery detection via dual-stream networks, In 2021 IEEE International Conference on Multimedia and Expo (ICME) 1–6.
9. Jin, X., He, Z., Xu, J., Wang, Y., and Su, Y. (2022). Video splicing detection and localization based on multi-level deep feature fusion and reinforcement learning, Multimedia Tools and Applications, 81(28): 40993–41011.
10. Huh, M., Liu, A., Owens, A., and Efros, A. A. (2018). Fighting fake news: Image splice detection via learned self-consistency. In Proceedings of the European conference on computer vision (ECCV), 101–117.
11. Kaneko, T., Ushiku, Y., and Harada, T. (2018). Class-distinct and class-mutual image generation with GANs, arXiv preprint arXiv:1811.11163.
12. Kramberger, T., and Potočnik, B. (2020). LSUN-stanford car dataset: Enhancing large-scale car image datasets using deep learning for usage in GAN training, Applied Sciences. 10(14): 4913.
13. Li, Z., You, Q., and Sun, J. (2022). A Novel Deep Learning Architecture with Multi-Scale Guided Learning for Image Splicing Localization. Electronics, 11(10): 1607.
14. Liu, Y., Zhu, X., Zhao, X., and Cao, Y. (2019). Adversarial learning for constrained image splicing detection and localization based on atrous convolution, IEEE Transactions on Information Forensics and Security, 14(10): 2551–2566.
15. Malik, A., Kuribayashi, M., Abdullahi, S. M., and Khan, A. N. (2022). DeepFake detection for human face images and videos: A survey. IEEE Access, 10: 18757–18775.
16. Masood, M., Nawaz, M., Malik, K. M., Javed, A., Irtaza, A., and Malik, H. (2022). Deepfakes Generation and Detection: State-of-the-art, open challenges, countermeasures, and way forward. Applied Intelligence. 1–53.
17. Mirsky, Y., and Lee, W. (2021). The creation and detection of deepfakes: A survey, ACM Computing Surveys. 54(1): 1–41.
18. Nguyen, T. T., Nguyen, Q. V. H., Nguyen, D. T., Nguyen, D. T., Huynh-The, T., Nahavandi, S., Nguyen, T. T., Pham, Q. V., and Nguyen, C. M. (2022). Deep learning for deepfakes creation and detection: A survey. Computer Vision and Image Understanding, 223: 103525.
19. Olszewski, K., Tulyakov, S., Woodford, O., Li, H., and Luo, L. (2019). Transformable bottleneck networks, In Proceedings of the IEEE/CVF International Conference on Computer Vision, 7648–7657.
20. Pepikj, B., Stark, M., Gehler, P., and Schiele, B. (2013). Occlusion patterns for object class detection, In Proceedings of the IEEE Conference on Computer Vision and Pattern Recognition, 3286–3293.

21. Verdoliva, L. (2020). Media forensics and deepfakes: an overview. IEEE Journal of Selected Topics in Signal Processing, 14(5): 910–932.

22. Wei, Y., Ma, J., Wang, Z., Xiao, B., and Zheng, W. (2022). Image splicing forgery detection by combining synthetic adversarial networks and hybrid dense U-net based on multiple spaces. International Journal of Intelligent Systems. 37(11): 8291–8308.

23. Xiao, Y., Jiang, A., Ye, J., and Wang, M. W. (2020). Making of night vision: Object detection under low-illumination. IEEE Access, 8: 123075–123086.

24. Yang, C., Li, H., Lin, F., Jiang, B., and Zhao, H. (2020). Constrained R-CNN: A general image manipulation detection model, In IEEE International conference on multimedia and expo (ICME), 1–6. IEEE.

25. Zhu, J. Y., Park, T., Isola, P., and Efros, A. A. (2017). Unpaired image-to-image translation using cycle-consistent adversarial networks, In Proceedings of the IEEE international conference on computer vision, 2223–2232

Advances in Computational Intelligence and its Applications (ICACIA-2023) – Dr. Sheikh Fahad Ahmad et al. (eds)
© 2024 Taylor & Francis Group, London, ISBN 978-1-032-78612-4

Development of Renal Tumor Accuracy Prediction Model Using Machine Learning Algorithms

16

D. Sivabalaselvamani*

Associate Professor, Kongu Engineering College,
Perundurai, Erode, Tamil Nadu, India

D. Selvakarthi, K. Nanthini

Assistant Professor, Kongu Engineering College,
Perundurai, Erode, Tamil Nadu, India

K. Iswarya, M. Maheshwari

PG Scholar, Kongu Engineering College,
Perundurai, Erode, Tamil Nadu, India

ABSTRACT—Kidney cancer can develop from renal tumors, just like many other malignancies. Your kidneys may be harmed by kidney tumors, which will lessen their capacity to keep you healthy. A serum creatinine blood test can be used to assess the creatinine in your blood. By doing so, the tumor can be located, and cancer can be stopped in its tracks. We will now use machine learning methods in supervised learning to predict the tumor's accuracy. The supervised learning approach aims to "supervise" or "train" algorithms to correctly identify data or predict outcomes. The most successful supervised learning algorithms for classification and prediction include Logistic Regression, XG Boost, and K-Nearest Neighbour. Using the aforementioned machine learning technique, we will forecast the accuracy of renal tumors in this work.

KEYWORDS—Renal tumor, Accuracy prediction, Serum creatinine, Supervised learning-KNN, XG Boost

1. Introduction

With more than 76,000 new cases reported each year, renal cancer is among the top 10 most prevalent cancers in the US. Like many other tumors, renal tumor can result in renal cancer. Tumors are defined as abnormal bodily growths. An unnatural growth in the kidney is known as a renal tumor. There are both benign (non-cancerous) and malignant renal tumors (cancerous). While some cancers grow slowly, others quickly spread. Aggressive tumors that are developing and spreading quickly. Renal tumors are illnesses that harm your kidneys and lessen their capacity to keep you healthy. However, the precise cause of a person's renal tumor may not be understood. Issues created when DNA in cells in one or both kidneys mutate, which may result in uncontrolled cell proliferation and growth Complications such as high blood pressure, an excess of calcium in the blood, a high red blood cell count, and the spread of malignancy are possible. Predicting renal tumors accurately can ensure that patients receive the best possible care and recover quickly, thereby preventing the condition from getting worse. Rather than utilizing express programming, AI, a use of man-made consciousness, empowers the framework to consequently gain for a fact. Every aspect of the economy, including healthcare, education, transportation, food, entertainment, and other assembly lines, is being transformed by machine learning. Machine learning applications can help healthcare professionals make new treatments,

*Corresponding author: sivabalaselvamani@gmail.com

DOI: 10.1201/9781003488682-16

improve patient care, and improve diagnostics. Managed learning and solo learning are the two classifications of AI. A specific set of algorithms is required for each learning task. This study makes use of the supervised learning algorithms KNN, LR, and XG Boost. We find that default values generated using machine learning methods (logistic regression, k-nearest neighbour, and xgboost) are much more accurate than default values generated by other models. This study's goal is to develop a novel decision-support system that can forecast renal tumor disease. This study compares the accuracy, precision, and execution time of the XG classifier, Logistic Regression (LR), and K-Nearest Neighbour (KNN) classifiers for predicting renal tumors. The above algorithms used can vary greatly depending on the classification domain of the application.

2. Literature Survey

Siddheshwar Tekale et al. [1] this study suggests using machine learning algorithms like decision trees and support vector machines to predict chronic kidney disease. They achieved a 99.99% accuracy rate. This study concludes that the supervised learning algorithm predicts accuracy with the highest degree of accuracy. Parul Sinha et al. [2] KNN and SVM are contrasted in this work for the purpose of predicting chronic kidney disease. As a result of the analysis, we discovered that the KNN classifier outperformed the SVM classifier. To improve the objective function's solutions in next work, new classifiers can be applied, and their performance can be assessed. Selvarathi C et al. [3] this study examines the detection and diagnosis of kidney stones, cystic kidney disease, and likely renal cancer by utilizing machine learning and convolutional neural networks (CNN). They also attained an accuracy of 85.2%.

Fernandez et al. [4] the primary objective of this study is to use an analysis of the Chronic Kidney Disease dataset to classify CKD cases and non-CKD cases. Marwa Almasoud and others 5] this study examines the accuracy with which machine learning algorithms can predict chronic kidney disease using the smallest possible collection of data. [] Morshedul Bari Antor and Co. 6] this quality is one of the main signs of chronic kidney disease, and we use it to see how well our analysis of the condition is working. Logistic Regression, Naive Bayes, Multilayer Perceptron, Stochastic Gradient Descent, Adaptive Boosting, Bagging, Decision Tree, and Random Forest classifier are among the eight machine languages used to measure analysis using tools. Serek Azamat et al. [7] investigate how clinical factors and the support vector machine method affect how people with chronic renal disease are classified.

Mirza Muntasir Nishat et al. [8] this research provides a thorough analysis of machine learning algorithms' accuracy, precision, sensitivity, and F1 score in detecting chronic kidney disease. By comparing several performance metrics across four machine learning models, a comparative analysis is shown. They obtained a 99.75% accuracy score from this analysis. Vijendra Singh et al. [9] in this work, the classifiers Support Vector Machine (SVM), K-Nearest Neighbor (KNN), Logistic Regression (LR), Random Forest (RF), and Naive Bayes (NB) are used. Nephrologists may find the recommended method beneficial in the early diagnosis of chronic kidney disease. The proposed strategy may be a useful tool.

Poonia, Ramesh Chandra, and others 10] this article proposes fake brain organizations, support vector machines (SVM), guileless Bayes, and the k-nearest Neighbor technique (KNN) for use in astute symptomatic expectation and arrangement models for the recognition of kidney sickness (NB). This study offers a brilliant element-based expectation model with a 93% exactness rate for recognizing kidney sickness. Paola Romagnan and others [11] Most CKD patients risk kicking the bucket or encountering sped-up cardiovascular sickness. It can be difficult to get renal replacement therapy for people with end-stage renal disease. This study predicts how anemia, metabolic acidosis, and secondary hyperparathyroidism will affect cardiovascular health and quality of life, as well as the necessary diagnostic and therapeutic approaches.

LeileiZhou, ZuohengZhang et al. [12] This study examines the impact of transfer learning on computed tomography (CT) images for the categorization of benign and malignant kidney tumors, with the goal of enhancing classification accuracy by developing patient-level data. Adeola Ogunleye et al. [13] the models using individual feature selection techniques perform better than the reduced model using only about half of the entire set of characteristics. Due to its excellent performance, the extreme gradient boosting (XGBoost) is chosen as our fundamental model for this paper's examination of various popular and contemporary AI algorithms in the context of CKD. Shang-Feng Tsai et al. [14] the first study to use machine learning to forecast IR in people with chronic renal disease was this one. In our study, the Random Forest machine learning method produced the greatest SHapley Additive exPlanations value discrimination and receiver operating characteristic curve accuracy. Mirza Muntasir Nishat, Fahim Faisal et al. [15] This study provides a mechanism for analyzing how well different boosting machine learning methods work to improve the accuracy of forecasting chronic kidney disease (CKD).

3. Methodology

3.1 Data Collection

Data collections a crucial component in the creation of any data-related tasks. It is the procedure of compiling and analysing data on targeted adjustments to an existing system in order to deliver precise responses to pressing questions and evaluate results. All data gathering aims to obtain trustworthy data that motivates analysis and yields truthful but deceptive responses to the queries posed. The dataset gathered is composed of csv files with numerical data. Patient information is presented in 1140 rows and 26 columns. The columns are listed below.

Id	Pus Cell	Potassium	Coronary Artery Disease
Age	Pus Cell Clumps	Hemoglobin	Appetite
Blood Pressure	Bacteria	Packet Cell Volume	Pedal Edema
Specific Gravity	Blood Glucose Random	White Blood Cell Count	Anemia
Albumin	Blood Urea	Red Blood Cell Count	Class
Sugar	Serum Creatinine	Hypertension	
Red Blood Cell	Sodium	Diabetes Mellitus	

Fig. 16.1   List of column

Source: Author

3.2 Data Pre-processing

Pre-handling alludes to the adjustments done to our information before we give it to the calculation. Data preparation is one method for making clean data sets out of dirty data. In machine learning projects, the data format needs to be accurate in order to get better results from the used model.

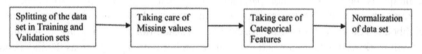

Fig. 16.2   Pre-processing

Source: Author

The preparation of data involves four key critical processes as shown in Fig. 16.2. Data set division into Training and Validation sets: Your model must be tested before being deployed. This stage is crucial. Because all incoming data is unseen when it is distributed, the evaluation must be performed on that data as well. The primary goal of the train test split is to divide the original data set into two distinct parts: train, which consists of training data and labels, and test, which consists of testing data and labels.

```
[ ]    1 from sklearn.model_selection import train_test_split

[ ]    1 x_train,x_test,y_train,y_test=train_test_split(x,y,test_size=0.25,random_state=0)
```

Fig. 16.3   Splitting dataset coding

Source: Author

X and y were sent as parameters to the function train test split, which correctly splits X and y into four subsets: X train, X test, y train, and y test yielding 25% testing data and 75% training data.

Addressing missing values: If the data set is filled with NaNs and other undesirable numbers, your model will undoubtedly perform similarly. Therefore, it's crucial to take care of these missing data.

Preserving categorical features: By converting categorical traits into integers, we can handle them. There are two typical methods for doing this. We are going to use one of the methods.

Label coding: We can translate categorical values into numerical labels using Label Encoder. Here, we've created a Label Encoder object, fitted it to our categorical column using the fit method, and then applied it using the transform method.

```
[ ]  from sklearn.preprocessing import LabelEncoder

[ ]  label_encode_x=LabelEncoder()

[ ]  label=label_encode_x.fit_transform(dataset["red blood cell"])

[ ]  label
     array([2, 2, 1, ..., 2, 2, 2])

[ ]  dataset.drop("red blood cell",axis=1,inplace=True)
     dataset["red blood cell"]=label
     dataset
```

Fig. 16.4   Label encoder coding

Source: Author

Norming of the data set: This gets us to the dataset normalization stage, the last step in the data pretreatment procedure. According to certain experiments, a normalized data collection outperforms a non-normalized data set on machine learning and deep learning models by a large margin. The goal of normalization is to translate values into a common scale without distorting the differences between the range of values. Here, a dataset was normalized using a Standard Scaler. By using this technique, our dataset's mean and standard deviation will both be 0. In either case, we can simply mix them using the various NumPy routines

3.3 Algorithms

K-Nearest Neighbour

A machine-learning technique is the supervised non-parametric K-nearest neighbours' classifier. The term "non-parametric" refers to the model's training phase without any parameter adjustments. It is based on distance and divides things into classes based on their close neighbours. The k-closest neighbours calculation is additionally non-straight. In contrast to simpler models like linear regression, it will work well with data when the connection between the x point as the independent variable and the y point as the dependent variable is not straight.

Find k-closest neighbours: To determine which records share the most characteristics with the target record, one must first determine its k-nearest neighbours. This procedure is also referred to as similarity search or distance calculation.

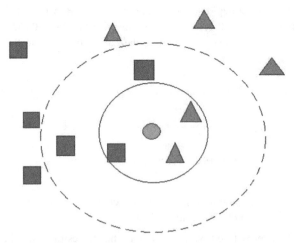

Fig. 16.5   K-Nearest neighbour

Source: https://www.analyticsvidhya.com/blog/2018/03/introduction-k-neighbours-algorithm-clustering/

The k value of the k-neighbors classifier must be determined: Using the ideal k value, you can make the model as accurate as possible. The easiest solution is to find the k value that gives the best results on the testing set. The following are our stages:

1. Pick a random k value. k is typically chosen at random from 3 to 10, but there are no established guidelines. Even though improved metrics aren't usually the result, decision boundaries are frequently smoothed when k is big, and decision boundaries become unstable at low k values. Thus, it's dependably a question of falling flat.
2. Test out a few k qualities and see how precise they are on the testing set.
3. Use the model with the lowest error rate and k.

The calculated k-distance: K-distance is the distance between data of interest and a given question point. We must select one of the four distance metrics in order to compute it: the distances of the Euclidean plane, the Manhattan plane, the Minkowski plane, and the Hamming plane.

Result of KNN algorithm

By using the KNN method, we were able to achieve testing accuracy of 96.55% and training accuracy of 97.31%.

Logistic Regression

A classification method called supervised logistic regression, also known as supervised machine learning, uses some dependent variables to predict the likelihood of a particular class. After calculating the sum of the input features, the logistic of the outcome is basically generated by the logistic regression model. The result of logistic regression is always between 0 and 1, which is appropriate for a binary classification problem. A twofold (yes/no) occasion's not entirely settled or anticipated utilizing double grouping. The probability that the current sample will be placed in class 1 and vice versa increases with the value.

Working of logistic regression

Machine learning often works by predicting a numerical result or a qualitative class. The prediction is a numerical value in a linear regression situation, and the input is a continuous variable. The errand is seen as a characterization challenge while expecting a subjective result (class). This simple dichotomy does not apply to all algorithms.

Logistic regression is a member of the regression family because it predicts outcomes using quantifiable correlations between variables. It acknowledges both persistent and discrete factors as contributions, rather than direct relapse, and its result is subjective.

The logistic regression algorithm investigates the connections between variables. It assigns probabilities to discrete outcomes by utilizing the Sigmoid function, which converts numerical data into an expression of probability between 0 and 1.0. Contingent upon whether the occasion happens, the likelihood goes from 0 to 1. With a cut-off of 0.5, you can partition the populace into two gatherings for parallel expectations. Bunch An incorporates all that is more noteworthy than 0.5, and bunch B incorporates all that is under 0.5.

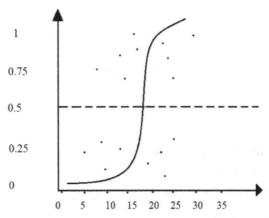

Fig. 16.6 Logistic regression curve

Source: https://machinelearningmastery.com/logistic-regression-for-machine-learning/

After data points are classified using the sigmoid function, a hyper plane is employed as a decision line to divide two categories (as much as possible). The decision boundary can then be used to forecast the kind of upcoming data points.

Algorithm Related to a Dataset

Step 1: Pre-processing of the collected dataset.

Step 2: Logistic regression is being used to fit the training set.

Step 3: Estimating a test's results

Step 4: Correctness of the test result (Creation of Confusion matrix)

Step 5: Visual representation of the test set results.

Result of logistic regression algorithm:

By using the logistic regression method, we were able to achieve testing accuracy of 98.08% and training accuracy of 99.36%.

XG Boost Algorithm

The ensemble machine learning approach based on trees a scalable machine learning system for tree boosting is called XGBoost. "Extreme gradient boosting" is the definition of "XGBoost". The optimal tree model is chosen by using closer approximations. For each supervised machine learning problem that satisfies the following criteria, take into account utilizing XGBoost: Large number of training observations; few features in comparison to the number of training observations; strong performance when data contains both category and numerical features; examination of model performance metrics.

$$\text{obj}(\theta) = \text{L}(\theta) + \Omega(\theta) \tag{1}$$

L(θ) – How well a model fits training data is determined by training loss.

Predictive models are encouraged by optimizing training loss

While you perform well when fitting training data, you at least approach training data, which is ideally near to the underlying distribution.

$\Omega(\theta)$ – Model complexity is measured via regularization.

Regularization optimization promotes straightforward models

Future forecasts from simpler models typically have less volatility, which stabilizes prediction.

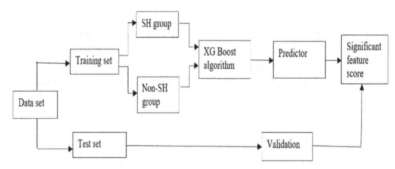

Fig. 16.7 XG Boost flow chart

Source: Authors

Algorithm related to a dataset

Step 1: Import the libraries that XG Boost needs.

Step 2: Prepare our dataset's training data (as x_train, y_train) for classification.

Step 3: Get the model and its Score for train data.

Step 4: Prepare our dataset's testing data (as y_train, y_train) for regression.

Step 5: Retrieve the model and its test data score

Result of XG boost algorithm

By using the XG Boost method, we were able to achieve testing accuracy of 100% and training accuracy of 98.47%

4. Result and Discussion

Estimating a machine learning model's performance is one of the most important steps in developing an efficient one. The dataset is acquired and put to use in a machine learning technique using the Python computer language. We have looked for the condition known as a renal tumor. The analysed findings are contrasted based on accurately identified instances, accuracy, TP Rate, and FP Rate. The efficiency or quality of the model is evaluated using a variety of measures, often known as performance metrics or evaluation metrics. The proportion of accurate predictions to all other guesses is how accuracy is measured.

1. True positives (TP) and true negatives (TN) make up accurate predictions (TN).
2. The whole set of positive (P) and negative (N) instances make up each forecast.
3. False positives (FP) and false negatives (TN) make up P
4. While FP and TN make up N.

Now let us discuss the result one by one which we got by our work using the mentioned algorithm.

KNN – In this we predict both train and test data and getting accuracy by using prediction and parameter. We got 97.31% for training and 96.55% for testing.

```
#Knn algorithm
from sklearn.neighbors import KNeighborsClassifier
knc = KNeighborsClassifier()
knc_model = knc.fit(x_train,y_train)
tr_pred_knc = knc_model.predict(x_train)
ts_pred_knc = knc_model.predict(x_test)
from sklearn.metrics import accuracy_score,classification_report,plot_confusion_matrix
tr_acc_knc = round(accuracy_score(y_train,tr_pred_knc),4)
ts_acc_knc = round(accuracy_score(y_test,ts_pred_knc),4)
print("Training Accuracy is:-",round(tr_acc_knc*100,2),"%")
print("Testing Accuracy is:-",round(ts_acc_knc*100,2),"%")
print("Classification report for xtest data:-\n\n",classification_report(y_test,ts_pred_knc),"\n")
print("Confusin Matrix for xtest data:-\n\n",plot_confusion_matrix(knc_model,x_test,y_test))


Training Accuracy is:- 97.31 %
Testing Accuracy is:- 96.55 %
Classification report for xtest data:-

            precision    recall  f1-score   support

        0        0.97      1.00      0.98       147
        1        0.96      0.95      0.96       110
        2        0.00      0.00      0.00         4
```

Fig. 16.8 Accuracy of KNN

Source: Authors

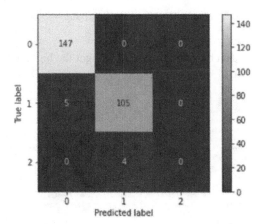

Fig. 16.9 KNN-confusion matrix

Source: Authors

Logistic Regression: Logistic regression was imported from sklearn. linear_model and predicted the test and train data then we got 99.36% for training and 98.08% for testing.

```
from sklearn.linear_model import LogisticRegression
lr = LogisticRegression(random_state=101)
lr_model = lr.fit(x_train,y_train)
tr_pred_lr = lr_model.predict(x_train)
ts_pred_lr = lr_model.predict(x_test)
from sklearn.metrics import accuracy_score,classification_report,plot_confusion_matrix
tr_acc_lr = round(accuracy_score(y_train,tr_pred_lr),4)
ts_acc_lr = round(accuracy_score(y_test,ts_pred_lr),4)
print("Training Accuracy is:-",round(tr_acc_lr*100,4),"%")
print("Testing Accuracy is:-",round(ts_acc_lr*100,4),"%")
print("Classification report for xtest data:-\n\n",classification_report(y_test,ts_pred_lr),"\n")
print("Confusin Matrix for xtest data:-\n\n",plot_confusion_matrix(lr_model,x_test,y_test))

Training Accuracy is:- 99.36 %
Testing Accuracy is:- 98.08 %
Classification report for xtest data:-

            precision   recall  f1-score   support

        0      0.99      1.00     1.00       147
        1      0.96      0.99     0.98       110
        2      0.00      0.00     0.00         4
```

Fig. 16.10 Accuracy of LR

Source: Authors

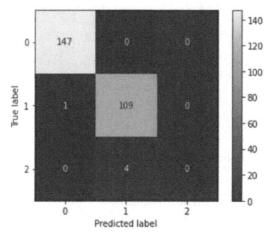

Fig. 16.11 LR-confusion matrix

Source: Authors

XG Boost: We predicted the train and test data by using parameter and got the highest accuracy of training data is 100% and testing data is 98.47%.

```
import xgboost as xgb
xgb_model=xgb.XGBClassifier(objective="binary:logistic",random_state=42)
xgb_model.fit(x_train,y_train)
tr_pred_xgb = xgb_model.predict(x_train)
ts_pred_xgb = xgb_model.predict(x_test)
from sklearn.metrics import accuracy_score,classification_report,plot_confusion_matrix
tr_acc_xgb = round(accuracy_score(y_train,tr_pred_xgb),5)
ts_acc_xgb = round(accuracy_score(y_test,ts_pred_xgb),5)
print("Training Accuracy is:-",round(tr_acc_xgb*100,4),"%")
print("Testing Accuracy is:-",round(ts_acc_xgb*100,4),"%")
print("Classification report for xtest data:-\n\n",classification_report(y_test,ts_pred_xgb),"\n")
print("Confusin Matrix for xtest data:-\n\n",plot_confusion_matrix(xgb_model,x_test,y_test))

Training Accuracy is:- 100.0 %
Testing Accuracy is:- 98.467 %
Classification report for xtest data:-

            precision   recall  f1-score   support

        0      1.00      1.00     1.00       147
        1      0.96      1.00     0.98       110
        2      0.00      0.00     0.00         4
```

Fig. 16.12 Accuracy of XGB

Source: Authors

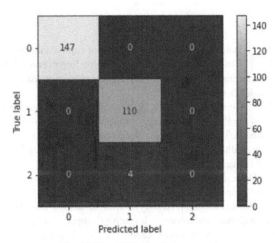

Fig. 16.13   XGB-confusion matrix

Source: Authors

To hypothesize that this approach could be used to more complicated circumstances. In order to create models when processing more complicated data, numerous algorithms are used. The more effective algorithms that result in various misjudgements are retrieved as component models following misjudgement analysis. The performance of the classifier is then enhanced by the development of an integrated model. Additionally, we enhanced the effectiveness and accuracy of the machine learning algorithms by pre-processing them with the aid of the Python library tool. The below table represents the respected algorithm with accuracy.

Table 16.1   Accuracy

Model	Accuracy Score
KNN	96.55
Logistic Regression	98.08
XG Boost	98.47

Source: Authors

This research presents a machine learning-based method for selecting the best methodology for accuracy prediction. The feature extraction and models used to the dataset enhanced the performance accuracy of the models and made it easier to identify clients who were qualified. Among the machine learning algorithm's other algorithms, XG Boost has the highest accuracy. The best result is shown by XG Boost, which has an accuracy of 98.47%.

5. Conclusion and Future Enhancements

We used a renal tumor dataset from the Kaggle website for this study. To assess the precision of the renal tumor, using three supervised machine learning algorithms - K-Nearest Neighbor, XG Boost, and Logistic Regression-we developed a disease prediction model for it. Categorical and non-categorical variables from the chronic kidney disease dataset were used to train the created chronic kidney disease prediction. After using the algorithm, we determine that XG Boost, which has a 98.47% accuracy rating, has the most accuracy compared to the other two techniques. This can aid patients and medical professionals in the early detection of renal tumors in order to save lives.

The project has a wide future potential. The renal disease patient care system will be built on the results of this investigation. The use of deep learning or picture datasets to compute the precise accuracy for renal disorders is a further development of this work because these offer stronger performance than those three machine learning algorithms and enable future feature selection strategies to improve prediction accuracy.

REFERENCES

1. Tekale, S., Shingavi, P., Wandhekar, S., & Chatorikar, A. (2018). Prediction of chronic kidney disease using machine learning algorithm. International Journal of Advanced Research in Computer and Communication Engineering, 7(10), 92–96.

2. Sinha, P., & Sinha, P. (2015). Comparative study of chronic kidney disease prediction using KNN and SVM. International Journal of Engineering Research and Technology, 4(12), 608–12.

3. Selvarathi C., Devipriya P., Indumathi R., Kavipriya K. (2021) "A survey on detection and classification of chronic kidney disease with a machine learning algorithm" Annals of the Romanian Society for Cell Biology 2021: Volume 25: Issue 4.

4. Gudeti, B., Mishra, S., Malik, S., Fernandez, T. F., Tyagi, A. K., & Kumari, S. (2020, November). A novel approach to predict chronic kidney disease using machine learning algorithms. In 2020 4th International Conference on Electronics, Communication and Aerospace Technology (ICECA) (pp. 1630–1635). IEEE.

5. Almasoud, M., & Ward, T. E. (2019). Detection of chronic kidney disease using machine learning algorithms with least number of predictors. International Journal of Soft Computing and Its Applications, 10(8).

6. Emon, M. U., Islam, R., Keya, M. S., & Zannat, R. (2021, January). Performance Analysis of Chronic Kidney Disease through Machine Learning Approaches. In 2021 6th International Conference on Inventive Computation Technologies (ICICT) (pp. 713–719). IEEE.

7. Amirgaliyev, Y., Shamiluulu, S., & Serek, A. (2018, October). Analysis of chronic kidney disease dataset by applying machine learning methods. In 2018 IEEE 12th International Conference on Application of Information and Communication Technologies (AICT) (pp. 1–4). IEEE.

8. Nishat, M. M., Faisal, F., Dip, R. R., Nasrullah, S. M., Ahsan, R., Shikder, F., ... & Hoque, M. A. (2021). A comprehensive analysis on detecting chronic kidney disease by employing machine learning algorithms. EAI Endorsed Transactions on Pervasive Health and Technology, 7(29), e1-e1.

9. Singh, V., Asari, V. K., & Rajasekaran, R. (2022). A Deep Neural Network for Early Detection and Prediction of Chronic Kidney Disease. Diagnostics, 12(1), 116.

10. Poonia, R. C., Gupta, M. K., Abunadi, I., Albraikan, A. A., Al-Wesabi, F. N., & Hamza, M. A. (2022, February). Intelligent Diagnostic Prediction and Classification Models for Detection of Kidney Disease. In Healthcare (Vol. 10, No. 2, p. 371). MDPI.

11. Romagnani, P., Remuzzi, G., Glassock, R., Levin, A., Jager, K. J., Tonelli, M., ... & Anders, H. J. (2017). Chronic kidney disease. Nature reviews Disease primers, 3(1), 1–24.

12. Zhou, L., Zhang, Z., Chen, Y. C., Zhao, Z. Y., Yin, X. D., & Jiang, H. B. (2019). A deep learning-based radiomics model for differentiating benign and malignant renal tumors. Translational oncology, 12(2), 292–300.

13. Ogunleye, A., & Wang, Q. G. (2019). XGBoost model for chronic kidney disease diagnosis. IEEE/ACM transactions on computational biology and bioinformatics, 17(6), 2131–2140.

14. Lee, C. L., Liu, W. J., & Tsai, S. F. (2022). Development and validation of an insulin resistance model for a population with chronic kidney disease using a machine learning approach. Nutrients, 14(14), 2832.

15. Nishat, M. M., Faisal, F., Dip, R. R., Shikder, M. F., Ahsan, R., Asif, M. A. A. R., & Udoy, M. H. (2020, December). Performance investigation of different boosting algorithms in predicting chronic kidney disease. In 2020 2nd International Conference on Sustainable Technologies for Industry 4.0 (STI) (pp. 1–5). IEEE.

Advances in Computational Intelligence and its Applications (ICACIA-2023) – Dr. Sheikh Fahad Ahmad et al. (eds)
© 2024 Taylor & Francis Group, London, ISBN 978-1-032-78612-4

Attendence System based on Viola-Jones Algorithm and PCA

17

**Kotrangi Sagar*, N. Kalyan Yadhav,
R. Venkatesh, P. Anvesh, C.N.Sujatha**

Electronics and Communication Engineering, SNIST

ABSTRACT—Face detection is one of many biometric strategies that can be applied with smart and automatic attendance management systems. An individual's facial structure can be used to uniquely identify them, and unlike other forms of identity, this kind of identity cannot be misplaced, stolen, or faked. This work encourages us to suggest a facial recognition-based system for class participation. The chance of system hacking is considerably reduced when facial recognition is used with passwords, admission cards, and Identification numbers, for example, to prevent theft and fraud. In the proposed work, a USB (universal serial bus) camera was first turned on using the graphical user interface (GUI) software application. Each student's detected face is captured by the USB camera and saved in a record. The dataset is then split into training and testing halves. The Viola-Jones methodology is used during the identification phase to recognize and separate the student's facial picture from the video image. To avoid information loss during the classification process, the number of pixels is then scaled. The Classification Technique (PCA) is then used in the identification mode to extract features from face images.

KEYWORDS—Biometric recognition, Data set, Graphical user interface, Image scaling, Training set, Viola Jones algorithm

1. Introduction

A face recognition-based attendance system is a method of identifying the faces of students taking part using biometrics of the face based on high-definition monitor footage and other information technology. My facial recognition project will enable computer systems to identify and recognise human faces in images and videos captured by surveillance cameras in real time. To improve the performance of face recognition, numerous algorithms and techniques have been developed. Converting video frames to images makes it easier for students' faces to recognize their presence and automatically mirrors the attendance database. Face recognition allows the system to recognize a person or any object by facial comparison. A facial recognition device is a device that takes an image or video and compares it with other devices in a database. The face recognition step compares all necessary parts such as composition, shape and proportions. During verification and identification, subjects stand in front of the video unit for a few seconds, after which they are compared with previously recorded images. The use of facial recognition in society has many advantages, including: Improve security and prevent crime.

Match detection detects a face if the image of the subject and the previously recorded image match, and does not detect a face if they do not match. Facial recognition systems are very useful tools for security purposes. Facial recognition is very useful for military and police to identify suspects, criminals and terrorists. If these people cannot be identified, they will undoubtedly have a lot to do with society. Identifying those who are damaging public property can also be very helpful during civil unrest. It also helps stop illegal immigration across borders. Face recognition is used to identify missing persons. For example, someone in

*Corresponding author: sagarkotrangi123@gmail.com

DOI: 10.1201/9781003488682-17

our family disappeared months or years later. I don't know if that person is our family. This missing person also has amnesia and cannot identify us. Facial recognition can be used in this scenario. The biggest problem with traditional attendance management systems was the accuracy of the data collected. This is because attendance may not have been recorded. This is due to the possibility that some people's presence could be inferred from the data without our knowledge by outside parties. For instance, the system disregarded the fact that Student A was forced to attend class even though he was too lethargic to do so, and Student B assisted him in signing his attendance. Assuming authorities enforce it, a lot of manpower and time may have to be wasted, which is also totally unrealistic. Therefore, all attendances recorded by previous systems are unreliable for analytical purposes. A second problem with traditional systems is that they take too long. Let's say it takes about a minute for the student to sign her 3-4 page list of names. In an hour, only roughly 60 pupils can sign attendance. This is plainly time-consuming and inefficient. The ability of legitimate data subjects to access this information is a third problem. As an illustration, the majority of parents are keenly interested in monitoring their child's whereabouts to make sure they truly attend college or school. However, parents had no access to such information in earlier systems. Previous systems must therefore be updated in order to increase productivity, assure data accuracy, and guarantee that information is available to these authorized parties. Nowadays, computer programs called facial recognition systems are utilized to automatically recognize or validate a person. For this purpose, facial features selected from the images are compared to a face database. Facial recognition systems focus on contactless human-machine interfaces.

2. Literature Survey

The following individuals' research and their published articles provided inspiration for our project:

1. Mathew Turk and Alex Pentland's "Eigenfaces for Recognition" program has developed a computer system that can track and locate a subject's head and then identify the subject by matching facial features to those of well-known people. The simulation method used in this system draws inspiration from information theory, biology, and the practical demands of accuracy and performance in close to real time. This method, instead of involving the healing of three-dimensional geometry, treats the identification of facial features problem as a deeply two-dimensional recognition problem, taking advantage of the fact that these faces are typically straight and can therefore be defined by a constrained set of two-dimensional characteristic views.

2. Face recognition is referred to as a two-dimensional problem in "Fast Recognition of Faces with Eigenfaces" by Arun Vyas and Rajbala Tokas. Using PCA, surface reorganization is accomplished. Face photos are positioned in a region that encodes the most notable variations between existing photographs.

   A group of faces without common facial features like eyes, noses, and lips are used in the Eigenface approach to create face space. The Eigenface method uses PCA to identify pictures. The method operates by contrasting previously extracted face photos with a collection of face spaces that clearly show notable variations among known face images. Faces are labeled in the present database as known or unknown after being imitated.

3. Vinay Hiremath and Ashwini Mayakar's paper, "Face Identification Using the Eigenface Approach," is a step toward creating a face recognition system that can identify static photos. It may be changed to function with moving images.

   In this instance, we can perform the same process after changing the dynamic photos the camera sent us to static ones. The foundation of this strategy is an information-theoretic method that reduces facial images to a limited number of eigenfaces, or distinct feature images. These make up the majority of the face photos in the initial training collection. Recognition is accomplished by categorizing the face through contrasting its location in the face space to the positions of known people when a fresh image is projected into a subspace termed "face space" that spans the eigenfaces. This low-dimensional space can be easily found using the Eigenface approach. An eigensurface, which can be thought of as a characteristic of other surfaces, is a surface with an eigenvector for each dimension of its surface space. The individual vectors of the set, which are the eigenvectors of the covariance matrix, can be combined linearly to represent each face. His Eigenface method of facial recognition works well in confined settings and is quick and easy to use. One of the more workable answers to the facial recognition issue is this. Low error rates are sufficient for many facial recognition applications, rather than flawless identification. It is preferable to present a small set of potential matches rather than exploring a huge database of faces. The Eigenface method makes it simple to get this limited selection of possible matches for a given image.

4. "Face Identification Using the Eigenfaces and Artificial Neural Networks," by Himanshu Agrawal, Mr. Manish Kumar, Nikunj Jain, and Mayank Agarwal. We start off by outlining the process. Her two methods—feature extraction using the

primary component evaluation and identification using a feed-forward-back propagating neural network—are combined in the suggested methodology. On 400 images divided into 40 classes, the methodology was evaluated. When determining recognition values for test batches, nearly all feature extraction variations are taken into account. On the Olivetti face system and the Oracle Research Laboratory (ORL), the proposed method was tested. The test yielded a detection rate of 97.018%.

5. One of the most popular biometric technologies for identifying people is facial recognition. It is utilized in a number of industries, such as transportation, electronic payments, and identification systems.

6. One of the various biometric techniques that artificially intelligent and automated presence management systems can use is facial recognition. Facial recognition has also been demonstrated to be effective in preventing fraud, crimes, ensuring public safety, and increasing consumer happiness. Using this identity, several access control systems can be built. The growing acceptance of biometric authentication solutions is being fueled by these developments in image processing and computational capacity.

7. A person's identity can be established using the distinctive depiction of each individual face's facial structure. This is so because each face conveys details about a person's characteristics, emotions, and even potential behavior.

8. It cannot be stolen, lost, or reproduced, in contrast to other types of identity. The likelihood of system hacking is considerably decreased by the use of modern techniques like facial recognition, identifying numbers, passwords, and access cards, which can also be used to prevent theft and fraud.

9. Facial recognition systems recognize a person's face image and identify allowed users rather than only establishing if an authorized account is being used or if a user's personal password is required. provides you.

3. Propose Methodology

The current system of manually rating faculty attendance has done an excellent job of accomplishing its goal. The old way of keeping track of attendance could not work anymore with the entrance of new technology into the classroom, such virtual classrooms. Even though institutions are offering more study programs, manually processing attendance might be time-consuming. So that we can efficiently register them in our project, we want to deploy facial recognition technology in schools to establish an attendance registration system.

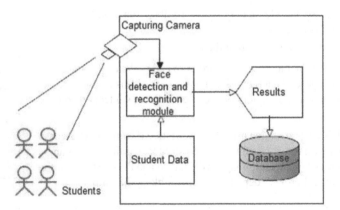

Fig. 17.1 Proposed system

A block diagram of the suggested system for a face recognition-based class registration system is shown in Fig. 17.1. The system requires the installation of a recording device in the classroom that can efficiently record the photos of every student enrolled in the class. To get the intended result, this photograph has been processed. The surgery is briefly explained below.

To take pictures: Cameras are set up in classrooms to capture images of the pupils' faces. Cameras should be placed so that the faces of every pupil can be captured. This camera requires a wireless or wired connection to a computer system for additional processing. We employ the computer's built-in camera in our prototype.

Image processing: The facial recognition algorithm is used to process the obtained image. Cropped photos are preserved so they can be processed. The name and ID number of the student were manually entered into the database along with the face image recognition module. We use PYTHON for all picture gathering and processing processes. The following steps are required for the full process:

(a) **Create a database:** To start, we took photos of the enrolled pupils' faces. In our systems, we each captured three images. The facial recognition algorithm then processes this data. The image acquisition toolbox in PYTHON is used to achieve this. To 240 X 300 pixels, the face's clipped image has been resized.

(b) **Image cropping and face detection**: The taken screenshot of the classroom is initially checked for faces. By running the view through the Computer view Toolbox, this is achieved the CascadeObjectDetector() function. The Viola-Jones algorithm is the foundation of this function. The priority of this algorithm is dependability and speed. Faces are located, cropped, and scaled into 240 X 300 photos that match the train database exactly.

(c) **Face recognition:** For face recognition, fixed-position eye and months were used to normalize faces and refine feature placements. The three primary eigenvectors are preserved, and the front eigenspace is created using the face tracking image. A single space is all that is needed since the face images have been warped into face-to-face projections. Then, face recognition with additional temporal information was carried out using the Eigen face approach. Each person's projection coefficients were modeled as a distribution that is Gaussian, and the faces were ranked according to how likely they were to match.

(d) **Sign up to attend:** For an intuitive output format that is also familiar to the majority of the organization's personnel, we keep recorded attendance in Excel spreadsheets. The Spreadsheet Link EX toolbox is used for this. If a student is found, the relevant cell is updated with a '1'; otherwise, it is updated with a '0'. Information formatted in Excel can be retrieved more rapidly.

3.1 System Installation

The creation of a database of registered students is the first stage in putting the system in place. In actuality, this phase ought to be a component of the admissions procedure that collects the relevant data from the applicant. The training database for the algorithm is this set of pictures. Then, using eigenface methods, the face recognition algorithm calculates eigenfaces for face recognition using the database. I made a function in this project called "training.m" just for this purpose. This function works as follows:

- Take photographs of students
- To detect faces in images, use the Computer Vision Toolbox function visionCascadeObjectdetector. The Viola-Jones algorithm is used to power this function.
- Cropped versions of detected faces are stored in the database.

This function must be in the same folder as your main program code. The train database is likewise located in the "TrainDatabase" folder. For the greatest results, this is also saved in the same folder. The system is then set up to monitor the attendance of students who have registered.

In this project, photos of people's faces are taken using an external USB camera. A database was then searched for and filled with categories for the discovered face traits. Faces can be recognized using database information. A result image is displayed and the existence of the identified student is acknowledged. Fig. 17.2 depicts the study's block diagram.

Graphical user interface

A graphical user interface (GUI) is used in your application's user interface. By providing a basic and clean design, as well as straightforward and intuitive controls like buttons, list boxes, sliders, and menus, a strong user interface makes a software simple to operate. The GUI works in an understandable and predictable manner, letting the user know what to expect while completing an action, allowing them to concentrate solely on using the application without thinking about the mechanics. By selecting and organizing GUI components with the aid of GUIDE tools, programmers can create and modify the characteristics of MATLAB GUIs.

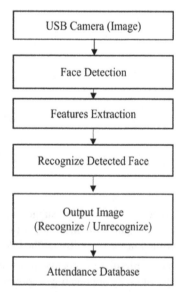

Fig. 17.2 Flow chart

Image input

An interface built on the MATLAB GUI is used to enroll in courses. Students must provide personal information during registration, including their name, and a camera photographs their face in real time. Because biometric-based systems demanded that each person be registered, this action was performed. Using the MATLAB R2020a program and training photos from the database, face recognition was performed.

Recognition of faces

The Viola-Jones method is used in the GUI's detection phase to identify faces from video camera frames. The Viola-Jones method was the first object recognition system to provide real-time object tracking.

The method also produces images with a high detection rate fast and flexibly, making it appropriate for application in real-time.

In order to create an efficient face detector for real-time applications including picture integration, extraction of features, attention cascade classifiers, and AdaBoost, the Viola-Jones face detector is founded on three key concepts.

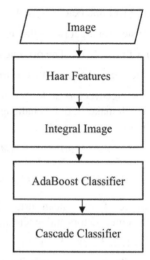

Fig. 17.3   Flow of Viola Jones algorithm

3.2 Feature Extraction

An important part of face recognition or shape analysis is methods for feature extraction, which have been used to extract characteristics from images using worldwide or structural approaches. A real-time detection technique that utilizes PCA (principal component analysis) and the Viola-Jones algorithm was proposed in this paper. Using these techniques, we construct "eigenfaces" and compare the data we've gathered for every picture using Euclidean distance classification techniques. Apply the PCA approach to real images created from scaled and cropped facial photographs to extract attributes. It's also among the finest ways to spot patterns.

This method also reduces the dimensionality of the data and chooses the most appropriate basis for the representation of image vectors. The non-zero an eigenvalue of the picture's covariance matrix are expanded into an eigenspace to produce this image vector. This approach for linear unsupervised reduction of dimensionality is also the most popular. This PCA approach for obtaining picture features consists of multiple phasesImage scale parameters like length (N) and height (M) have no bearing on PCA. This is because PCA processes n total photos, whereas MN only processes one. The following are the steps for computing eigen surfaces:

Step 1: Set up your training area.

Obtain pictures of the training faces I1, I2, I3, I4,..., In. Faces should make proportionate, centered expressions.

Step 2: Keep a record of it.

The database's face images are all vectorized before being included to the training set. S. \sS = {Γ1, Γ2, Γ3, ... C n }

$$
\begin{matrix}
\Gamma_1 & \Gamma_2 & \Gamma_3 & & \Gamma_N \\
\begin{bmatrix} a11 \\ a12 \\ a13 \\ \vdots \\ aMN \end{bmatrix} &
\begin{bmatrix} a11 \\ a12 \\ a13 \\ \vdots \\ aMN \end{bmatrix} &
\begin{bmatrix} a11 \\ a12 \\ a13 \\ \vdots \\ aMN \end{bmatrix} & \cdots &
\begin{bmatrix} a11 \\ a12 \\ a13 \\ \vdots \\ aMN \end{bmatrix}
\end{matrix}
$$

Dimension Reduced Matrix

$$
\begin{matrix}
\Gamma_1 & \Gamma_2 & & \Gamma_N \\
=\begin{bmatrix} a11 & a12 & \dots & a1n \\ a21 & a22 & \dots & a2n \\ a31 & a32 & \cdots & a3n \\ \vdots & \vdots & \vdots & \vdots \\ aMN1 & aMN2 & \cdots & aMNn \end{bmatrix}
\end{matrix}
$$

Step 3: Determine the face's mean vector.

$$\varphi = \frac{1}{n}\sum_{i=1}^{N} \Gamma_i$$

$$
\begin{bmatrix}
\frac{a11+a12+\cdots+a1n}{n} \\
\frac{a21+a22+\cdots+a2n}{n} \\
\vdots
\end{bmatrix}
$$

The formula below is used to determine the average face vector ():

In step four, get rid of the mean/mean face vector.

i = i i = 1.2,..., n The original face is subtracted from the average face vector, and the difference is recorded in variable i.

Step 5: generation of a covariance matrix.

The eigenvectors and eigenvalues are computed using the covariance matrix. AAT, on the other hand, is MNMN dimensional, which makes it quite challenging to compute. AAT and A T A have identical eigenvalues, and their eigenvectors are connected by ui = Avi.

$$C = \frac{1}{n} \sum_{i=1}^{N} \Phi i \Phi i T = AA^T \ , (MN \times MN)$$

$$A = [\Phi 1 \, \Phi 2 \, \cdots \Phi n] \quad , (MN \times n)$$

where, after the mean surface has been eliminated, A is the matrix created by joining the column vectors. 2.4.6. In step 6, obtain the eigenvectors and eigenvalues.

I = 1, 2, 3,..., n - 1, and ui = avi.

AAT's eigenvectors are ui, while AT A's eigenvectors are vi. The eigenvalues of AT A are calculated and arranged. The total number of nonzero eigenvectors can be fewer than one (n-1) since eigenvalues less than one are discarded. Eigenfaces are principal component distributions for face images.

Project a picture of your own face on your own face in step seven.

I = UT(i), I = 1.2,...,n - 1, etc.

I created the projection image i by using the algorithm to project several smiles onto my face, using I as the central vector and removing the average area.

3.3 Photo Editing

Given that it is built on the idea of image processing itself, this component of the system is crucial. The procedure is explained in the flowchart's sequence of appearance under the image processing heading.

3.4 Snap a Photo

The condition of the classroom is captured on camera to effectively capture each student's face. Our algorithms use this image to be processed further. Since the prototype just needs a resolution of 1366x768, I utilized a laptop camera with that resolution. A higher resolution camera should be employed to process big classes more precisely

3.5 Face Recognition and Cropping

Python receives the taken image and loads it. A matrix of numbers relating to the values of individual pixels makes up an image. The algorithm's input face is somewhere in this collection of numbers that the software is unaware of. This work is taken over by face recognition. Use the Computer Vision Toolbox's "vision.CascadeObjectDetector()" function to accomplish this. This function uses the Viola-Jones algorithm to identify faces. In the appendix, a description of it is provided. This algorithm's steps go in the following order:

- Review the photo that was taken in the preceding action.
- As previously said, the photograph above reveals faces.
- Crop the image so that the face is clearly visible, and save the result as separate JPEG image files in a folder.

The algorithm recognizes every aspect that may be seen in the photographs taken in the classroom. They must all be sat properly and upright to avoid the system locking out a student.

3.6 Eigenfaces' Face Recognition Software

For face detection in this project, the Eigenfaces algorithm was employed. It has a reasonable level of accuracy and is a quick and affordable facial recognition solution.

In the training dataset, her 2D photos are converted into 1D vectors.

These vectors combine to create a training image matrix.

- Create a vector to represent the mean values, and then take that vector and subtraction each image vector.
- Arrange these mean vectors to create the training matrix.
- To determine the eigenvalues and eigenvectors, compute the covariance matrix.
- Since the eigenvector associated with the highest eigenvalue shows the largest variance, the vectors should be stored by eigenvalues in a way that the first vector corresponds to the highest eigenvalue. Normalization is applied to vectors.
- The training set's retrieved person images are converted into vectors, mean-reduced, then forecast using an eigenvector grid.
- The Euclidean distance between the woman's two vectors in the image from the training dataset and the test image is calculated for classification.
- When there is a smaller than threshold difference between the practice and test areas.

It is regarded as known and held by a specific person in the database. It is considered as unknown if not.

The system logs a person's presence in her MS Excel database after a successful recognition. The section that follows will go over this.

3.8 Keep in Mind Acknowledged Entries

The Excel worksheet's field for that person is updated with a '1' when the algorithm discovers a match for that particular date. The default setting is '0' in all other cases. This suggests that the person isn't there. MS Excel offers a very effective way to store data. The section that follows will go over this.

3.9 Update the Attendance list in Excel

The MS Excel Sheet and the PYTHON IDE are linked using the Spreadsheet Link Ex toolbox. The value in that particular Excel spreadsheet is updated when a recognized face resembles a person in the dataset. This is handled by the xlswrite() function.

Candidate identification is determined by the image index.

The face that was found is accurate.

- A prepared table in the appropriate format is required (attendance.xls on our system).
- The classroom date and time are added to the corresponding cell in the spreadsheet using the index value.

4. Results

On a known test picture as well as in real time, we evaluated the result using all of the features we created. The output of several tasks is displayed in the screenshots in the paragraph that follows. With the aid of four volunteers, we put the whole thing through its paces.

4.1 Work

- Install the necessary libraries, facial recognition system software requirements.
- Create a project in PyCharm IDLE.
- Create a database and store all student/person images in the database.
- Enter and run the correct source code.
- Error-free code runs and the system or laptop camera opens and starts working.
- Recognize the faces of students and people in front of the camera and from previously stored images of people in the database.
- Attendance is also saved in his CSV file.

Gather the training data set

Make a database of students enrolled using the TrainDatabase function and save it to a folder.

Each candidate's pictures of herself are kept in a database with help of four volunteers. To increase accuracy while increasing computation time, we may boost the amount of training photos. Variations in the computation period are not a problem with the us application because the teaching time is normally at least an hour, which is far longer than the computation time of the method.

At this point, it's important to bear in mind that ambient light will help you clearly view the front of the item when taking the picture. The student's position and attitude should vary a little bit for each photograph to get the best outcomes.

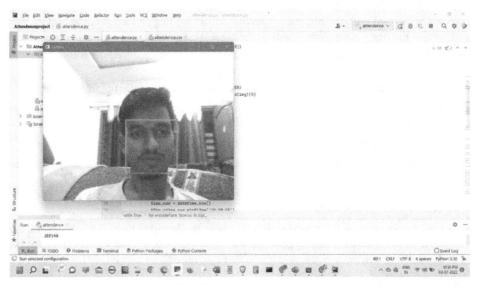

Fig. 17.4 Image capture

Image capture, face detection, cropping:

Fig. 17.5 Capture and face identification in the classroom

There is also a photo of the associated classroom. All kids' faces should be able to be seen clearly on the cameras. Based on typical lighting and appropriate student posture, faces are caught effectively. Effective classroom lighting must be maintained. The organization of suitable alternatives should also occur in the event of a power loss. Figure 17.5's discovered faces will all be clipped and saved in the Test File folder. The following techniques then read the image and carry out further processing.

The folder's path must be precise. Additionally, a number is automatically issued to each face's identification. This makes it simpler to read photos from directories.

Face recognition

To obtain a result, a cropped facial expression image is input into an algorithm that recognizes faces. The images are subjected to the Eigenface algorithm and especially in comparison to the database. This will result in the outcome shown in Fig. 17.6.

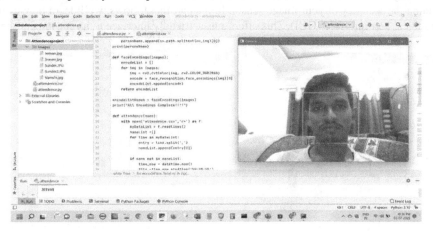

Fig. 17.6 Students are identified and relevant messages are displayed.

If a person's photo does not exist inside the database, it is simply ignored. To avoid false alarms, proper illumination should be maintained.

4.2 Output in MS Excel

You will get output like this:

Several functions within the table can be utilized to derive the result in an appropriate format, as shown in Fig. 17.7. You can acquire this format's output in this way: The following parameters should be utilized, as shown in the figure.

PYTHON's Worksheet Link Ex toolbox is used to perform this functionality.

If a student is the sole participant in each subject, she receives a 'A.' The sheet is also given the date and time. You can use a better system to collect as much student information as you need with reliability of your image sensor as long as you have a good platform. We will gain knowledge how to integrate all of these characteristics using a graphical user interface in the following section (GUI). This provides its users with a user-friendly interface.

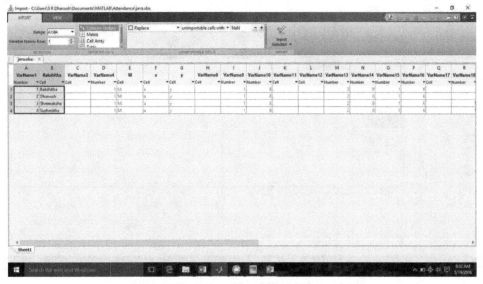

Fig. 17.7 Excel format output (.xlsx)

4.3 Graphical User interface

Following the completion of the codeA student earns a "A" if she is the only participant in each topic. The time and date are also written on the sheet. As long as you have a solid platform, you can employ a superior method to gather all the student data you require while maintaining the accuracy of your image sensor. In the part that follows, we'll learn how to combine all of these features utilizing a graphical user interface (GUI). This offers a user-friendly interface to its consumers shown in Fig. 17.8.

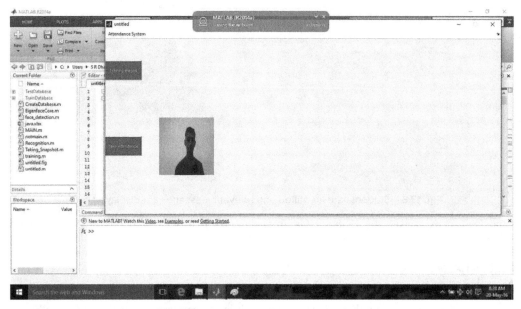

Fig. 17.8 System graphical user interface

The GUI is shown in the following picture. The following features are part of the GUI:

At the touch of a button, you can collect training photographs. The axis displays the captured image, the face that was recognised, and the cropped image.

The classroom has streaming video from Axis. The screenshot below illustrates the operation of the GUI.

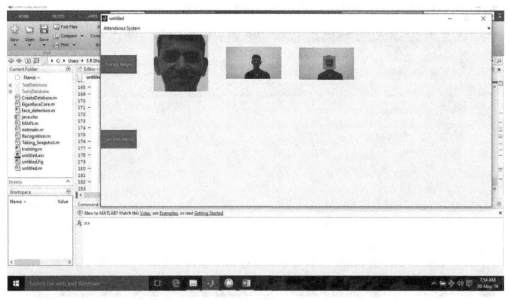

Fig. 17.9 Acquisition of training images by GUI

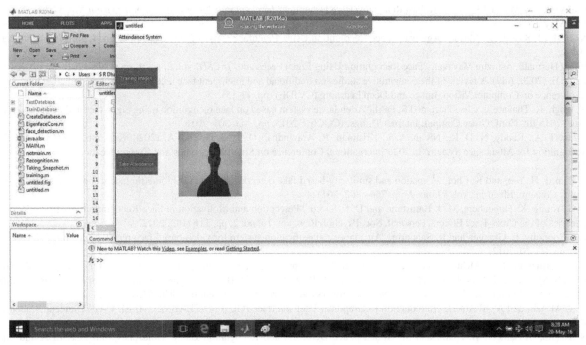

Fig. 17.10   Attendance registration via GUI

5. Conclusion

Face recognition software has made considerable strides during the past 20 years. For secure payments, monitoring and protection operations, creating access control, and other uses, machines may now automatically authenticate identification information. These applications are often employed in organized environments, and high detection accuracy can be achieved using detection approaches that make use of the current environment. On the other hand, advanced facial recognition technologies will be widely applied in smart gadgets.

In this environment, computers and machines can be helpful. To accomplish this, machines must be capable of consistently recognise neighbours in a way that is consistent with regular human interaction patterns. It should take into account human intuition when it is likely to be noticed without needing any special action. While these goals currently appear achievable, there are many challenges for personal recognition technologies to work reliably under a variety of conditions and using information from one or more modalities need to research. This is a new technology that can offer many advantages. Facial recognition saves resources and time, and can even create new revenue streams for businesses that use it properly. By capturing images from cameras and CCTV and applying technologies such as facial recognition and recognition, Reduce human intervention and increase security. Many applications can be implemented based on face detection and recognition like Employee Attendance Systems, Security and Police Applications, Criminal Investigations.

Acknowledgements

We would like to express our immense gratitude to our college Sreenidhi Institute of Science and Technology for allowing us to work on this project. We would like to thank Dr. Asha Devi's mam for your expert advice and constant encouragement throughout this project. We are fortunate to work under your guidance. Providing all the resources and sharing your knowledge, and constantly reviewing our work, enabled us to finish this project.

REFERENCES

1. M. T. a. A. Pentland, "Eigenfaces For Recognition," *Journal of Cognitive Neuroscience,* vol. 3, no. 1, 1991.
2. A. V. a. R. Tokas, "Fast Face Recognition Using Eigen Faces," *IJRITCC,* vol. 2, no. 11, pp. 3615-3618, November 2014.

3. Paul Viola and Michael J. Jones, "Robust Real-Time Face Detection," *International Journal of Computer Vision,* vol. 57, no. 2, pp. 137-154, May 2004.

4. N. J. M. M. K. a. H. A. Mayank Agarwal, "Face Recognition Using Eigenface aproach," *IRCSE,* vol. 2, no. 4, pp. 1793-8201, August 2010.

5. Vinay Hermath, Ashwini Mayakar, "Face Recognition Using Eigen Faces and,"*IACSIT,* vol. 2, no. 4, pp. 1793-8201, August 2010.

6. Jiang, E. (2020, July). A review of the comparative studies on traditional and intelligent face recognition methods. In 2020 International Conference on Computer Vision, Image and Deep Learning (CVIDL) (pp. 11-15).

7. P. Wagh, R. Thakare, J. Chaudhari, and S. Patil, "Attendance system based on face recognition using eigen face and PCA algorithms," Proc. 2015 Int. Conf. Green Comput. Internet Things, ICGCIoT 2015, pp. 303–308, 2016.

8. Kiran, T. A., Reddy, N. D. K., Ninan, A. I., Krishnan, P., Aravindhar, D. J., & Geetha, A. (2020, September). PCA based Facial Recognition for Attendance System. In 2020 International Conference on Smart Electronics and Communication (ICOSEC) (pp. 248-252).

9. Y. Kim, J. H. Yoo, and K. Choi, "A motion and similarity-based fake detection method for biometric face recognition systems," IEEE Trans. Consum. Electron., vol. 57, no. 2, pp. 756– 762, 2011.

10. S. G. Young, K. Hugenberg, M. J. Bernstein, and D. F. Sacco, "Perception and Motivation in Face Recognition: A Critical Review of Theories of the Cross-Race Effect," Personal. Soc. Psychol. Rev., vol. 16, no. 2, pp. 116–142, 2012.

11. J. F. Connolly, E. Granger, and R. Sabourin, "An adaptive classification system for video-based face recognition," Inf. Sci. (Ny)., vol. 192, pp. 50–70, 2012.

12. D. N. Parmar and B. B. Mehta, "Face Recognition Methods & Applications," Comput. Technol. Appl., vol. 4, no. 1, pp. 84–86, 2014.

13. Wafi, N. M., Sabri, N., Yaakob, S. N., Nasir, A. S., Nazren, A. R., & Hisham, M. B. (2017). Classification of Characters Using Multilayer Perceptron and Simplified Fuzzy ARTMAP Neural Networks. Advanced Science Letters, 23(6), 5151–5155.

14. R. Y. Al Ashi and A. Al Ameri, "Introduction to Graphical User Interface (GUI) MATLAB 6.5," IEEE UAEU Student Branch UAE Univ., pp. 1–35, 2004.

15. N. Hazim, S. Sameer, W. Esam, and M. Abdul, "Face Detection and Recognition Using ViolaJones with PCA-LDA and Square Euclidean Distance," Int. J. Adv. Comput. Sci. Appl., vol. 7.

16. A. M. Devan, M. Venkateshan, A. Vignesh, and S. R. M. Karthikraj, "Smart Attendance Recognition System Using Face," Adv. Nat. Appl. Sci., vol. 11, no. 7, pp. 139–144, 2017.

17. Nasrudin, M. W., Yaakob, S. N., Othman, R. R., Ismail, I., Jais, M. I., & Nasir, A. S. A. (2014, January). Analysis of geometric, Zernike and united moment invariants techniques based on intra-class evaluation. In 2014 5th International Conference on Intelligent Systems, Modelling and Simulation (pp. 7–11). IEEE.

18. Yadav, M., Koul, R., & Suneja, K. (2020, February). FPGA Based Hardware Design of PCA for Face Recognition. In 2020 7th International Conference on Signal Processing and Integrated Networks (SPIN) (pp. 642-646).

19. N. T. Deshpande and S. Ravishankar, "Face Detection and Recognition using Viola-Jones algorithm and fusion of LDA and ANN," IOSR J. Comput. Eng., vol. 18, no. 6, pp. 1–6, 2016.

20. M. C. Kirana, Y. R. Putra, and F. W. Sari, "Comparison of Facial Feature Extraction on Stress and Normal Using Principal Component Analysis(PCA) Method," Proc. 2017 5th Int. Conf. Instrumentation, Commun. Inf. Technol. Biomed. Eng. ICICI-BME 2017, no. November, pp.

Note: All the figures in this chapter were made by the authors.

Advances in Computational Intelligence and its Applications (ICACIA-2023) – Dr. Sheikh Fahad Ahmad et al. (eds)
© *2024 Taylor & Francis Group, London, ISBN 978-1-032-78612-4*

Encipher Image Transmission Through MIMO System with Rayleigh Fading Environment Using AES Encryption Algorithm

18

Krishna Dharavathu, Jammula Lakshmi Narayana
Professor, Dept. of ECE, PSCMR College of Engineering and
Technology, Vijayawada, India

T Anand Babu
Assistant Professor, Dept. of ECE,
Gudlavalleru Engineering College, Gudlavalleru, India

**Itta Asha Latha, Marella Lakshmi Srujitha,
Narisetty Geethika, Challapalli Sai Sri Ram**
Students, Dept. of ECE, PSCMR College of Engineering and
Technology, Vijayawada, India

ABSTRACT—It is renowned that the rendition of wireless communication systems is rapidly expanding, this can be ameliorated by using multiple transmit and multiple receive antennas, which is generally associated with the MIMO technique. The habitue of electronic gadgets is rapidly growing by every individual. Most of the information transmitted now is in the form of digital. During dissemination, the information can be deceived by an illicit person which leads to precariousness for the sender. For this, the circumspection of the data must be preserved when required to communicate the data. Maintaining a high trustworthiness and more secure data from source to destination is a brag requirement in modern days. This paper accentuates data security for the secure transmission of images. Here, a (Multiple Input and Multiple Output) MIMO system is designed using AES algorithms under a MATLAB environment. The numerical results make known that the MIMO system with the AES algorithm shows elite performance.

KEYWORDS—LTE, MIMO, AES, 5G, 6G, Encryption

1. Introduction

With the rapid evolution of technology, information is being distributed digitally at a blistering speed. Data should be consecrated from sleuths. Different technologies and virtuosities are designed to subvert the data with an utmost spike in cyber-attacks occurring in the universe to guarantee the clandestinity and entirety of the data. To sustain confidentiality and integrity between the source and destination, different methods and technologies, including data hiding, stenography, and encryption, have been developed to cushion the data.

Nowadays Cyber-attacks are increasing in frequency around the globe, so cyber security is now a concern for individuals as well as governments. A security certificate plays a crucial role when it comes to protecting data from unauthorized access in fields such as telemedicine, the military, financial transactions, and mobile applications. Historically, wars have been fought

[1]krishnadharavath4u@gmail.com, [2]principal@pscmr.ac.in, [3]anand.digital07@gmail.com

DOI: 10.1201/9781003488682-18

through weapons between countries, but now they are fought through cyber-attacks. Here, the MIMO (Multiple Input Multiple Output) systems have been designed to overcome all these problems in security aspects. In this, the image encryption and decryption method are used to transmit the data by increasing the data rates and efficiency through Multiple Input and Multiple Output (MIMO) systems. MIMO has been adapted to 4G, 5G as well as 6G LTE systems, and MIMO is used in most modern applications. [1-10]

Part II of the study describes the MIMO system and Advanced Encryption Standard that were employed, while part III of the paper offers the simulation findings. In the concluding portion, the conclusions are drawn.

2. MIMO System and Advanced Encryption Standard (AES)

Multiple antennas are utilized at both the source (transmitter) and the destination (receiver) in wireless communications using MIMO (Multiple Input, Multiple Output). If the encryption block is used on the transmitter side and the decryption block is utilized on the receiver side as shown in Fig 1., the system is referred to as a crypto MIMO system.

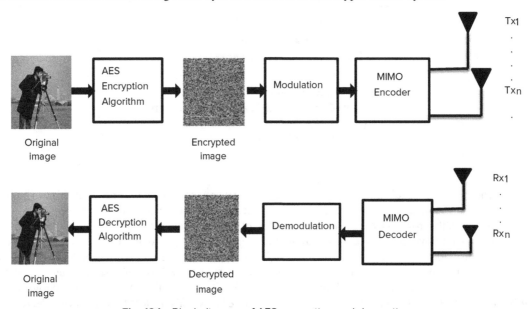

Fig. 18.1   Block diagram of AES encryption and decryption

The AES algorithm, also known as Rijndael, is a powerful and secure symmetric block cipher that transforms a block of a 128-bit message into cipher text using keys of 128, 192, or 256 bits. Compared to the DES algorithm, which uses a 56-bit key, AES is exponentially stronger. Because the sub-processes are performed in reverse order in each round, AES encryption and decryption algorithms must be implemented independently[2-3]. Among the four AES encryption operations, only the Add Round Key operation is its inverse, since it is an exclusive-or operation. It is necessary to define inverse operations for the three other operations, Shift Rows, Sub Bytes, and Mix Columns, to carry out the decryption process[11-13]. As part of the reverse operation of Add Round Key, the entire AES key schedule must be expanded in the same manner as it was during e-encryption. Whenever an exclusive operation is performed, the appropriate key should be used. In this paper, we present the reverse proof of AES encryption. More information about AES is provided in [14-20].

3. Simulation Results and Discussions

For effective transmission of the encrypted image, 1 x 2 and 2 x 2 crypto MIMO systems with the AES encryption method are taken into consideration in this part. Rayleigh models the relevant MIMO system in the MATLAB simulation environment. With a BPSK modulation technique, the channel between the transmitter and receiver is fading. The cameraman test picture, a common benchmark MATLAB database image, is acknowledged for this study and is accessible in.tiff file as shown in Fig. 18.2.

Fig. 18.2 Cameraman

For the cameraman test image, the performance of BER and the number of faults for 1 x 2 and 2 x 2 MIMO systems with appropriate SNRs are provided in Table 18.1, respectively. According to the preceding table, an increase in SNR results in a commensurate drop in BER and an increase in the number of mistakes in the recovered decrypted image.

Table 18.1 Comparisons of the cameraman image's BER and number of mistakes with SNR

SNR	BER				Number of Errors			
	1x2 MIMO		2x2 MIMO		1x2 MIMO		2x2 MIMO	
	Original System	AES	Original System	AES	Original System	AES	Original System	AES
0	0.1152	0.1154	0.0406	0.0400	60408	60509	21290	20970
2	0.0755	0.0745	0.0182	0.0180	39574	39408	9518	9431
4	0.0443	0.0445	0.0065	0.0067	23244	23348	3432	3496
6	0.0236	0.0238	0.0020	0.0021	12370	12502	1054	1075
8	0.0119	0.0117	$4.7e^{-04}$	$4.5e^{-04}$	6234	6160	250	241
10	0.0056	0.0054	$1.1e^{-04}$	$1.2e^{-04}$	2933	2853	59	64
12	0.0025	0.0024	$2.6e^{-05}$	$1.9e^{-05}$	1307	1249	14	10
14	0.0010	$9.8e^{-04}$	$7.6e^{-06}$	$5.7e^{-06}$	543	518	4	3
16	$4.4e^{-04}$	$5.1e^{-04}$	$1.9e^{-06}$	0	235	268	1	0
18	$1.9e^{-04}$	$1.5e^{-04}$	0	0	103	83	0	0
20	$5.9e^{-05}$	$8.2e^{-05}$	0	0	31	43	0	0
22	$4.5e^{-05}$	$3.0e^{-05}$	0	0	24	16	0	0
24	$5.7e^{-06}$	$1.5e^{-05}$	0	0	3	8	0	0

For the cameraman image taken into consideration for this work, Fig. 18.3 arbitrates the fluctuations of the BER against SNR plots of the MIMO system. It is believed that when SNR increases, the bit error rate drops. When compared to 1 x 2 MIMO systems, the 2 x 2 MIMO system performs very well, according to the observation regarding the typical MIMO system. The recovered image from the 2 x 2 MIMO system has higher PSNR values at both low and high BERs.

For the cameraman picture taken into consideration for this work, Fig. 18.4 arbitrates the variations of the PSNR with BER plots of the MIMO systems. When compared to 1 x 2 MIMO systems, the 2 x 2 MIMO system performs very well, according to the observation regarding the typical MIMO system. The recovered image from the 2 x 2 MIMO system has higher PSNR values at both low and high BERs. When compared to the original system, the performance of a 2 x 2 crypto MIMO system using the AES encryption technique is the best. It also produces good PSNR values even when there is mistake.

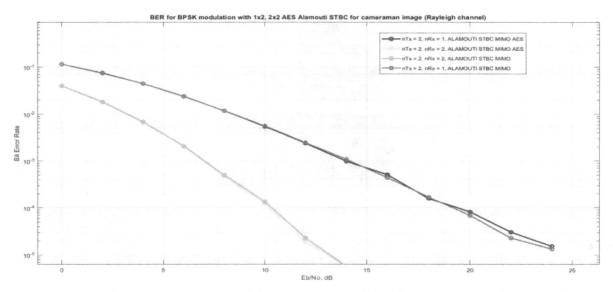

Fig. 18.3 BER curves of cameraman image for a 1 × 2 and 2 × 2 MIMO system (Conventional system & AES)

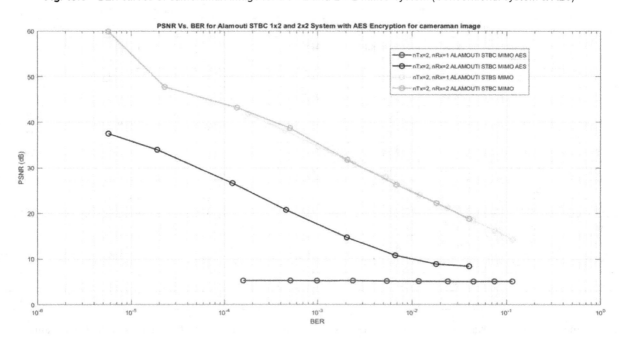

Fig. 18.4 For a 1 x 2 and 2 x 2 MIMO system (conventional system & AES), the PSNR against BER curves of the Cameraman picture

Table 18.2 compares the PSNR values for the 1 x 2 and 2 x 2 MIMO systems with the correlate with SNRs for cameraman pictures. As SNR grew, the PSNR values in the recovered original and decrypted image increased, as can be seen in the table. Its PSNR value will be infinite if the original signal and the signal received at the receiver are identical.

Figure 18.5 arbitrates the abnormality of the PSNR contrast SNR curves of the MIMO systems for the cameraman appearance considered for this work. It is perceived that the PSNR increases with increasing in SNR. The observation about the conventional MIMO structure is that the 2 x 2 MIMO structure has excellent performance compared with the 1 x 2 MIMO systems. The 2 x 2 MIMO system redeemed image accomplished high PSNR values even at little SNRs.

Table 18.2 Comparisons of PSNR with SNR for cameraman Image

SNR	PSNR			
	1x2 MIMO		2x2 MIMO	
	Original System	AES	Original System	AES
0	14.33371	5.0912	18.8293	8.3838
2	16.1794	5.1051	22.2333	8.9048
4	18.4369	5.0656	26.2543	10.8526
6	21.1443	5.0969	31.7612	14.7967
8	24.3077	5.1355	38.6988	20.3256
10	27.4483	5.1723	43.2019	27.2466
12	31.2486	5.2655	47.7720	34.0748
14	33.7147	5.2249	59.8928	37.8928
16	39.5883	5.2658	Inf	45.3713
18	42.7757	5.2723	Inf	Inf
20	Inf	Inf	Inf	Inf
22	Inf	Inf	Inf	Inf
24	Inf	Inf	Inf	Inf

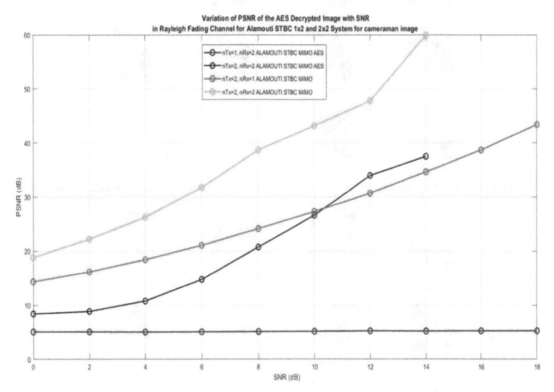

Fig. 18.5 PSNR against SNR curves for the cameraman's image in a 1x2 and 2x2 MIMO system (conventional system and AES)

To more clearly comprehend the receiver of the MIMO (conventional and Crypto) system corresponding to different SNRs, respectively, optical analysis of the recovered and decrypted images can be used. Images taken by the original videographer and recovered from the original MIMO system are shown in Figs 18.6 and 18.7. Similar to this, Figs. 18.8 and 18.9 show the decrypted cameraman photos that were recovered at the receiver after using AES encryption techniques.

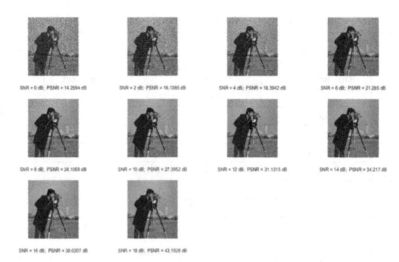

Fig. 18.6 Optical examination of the original picture at the receptacle of the 1x2 MIMO Systems

Fig. 18.7 Optical examination of the original picture at the receptacle of the 2x2 MIMO Systems

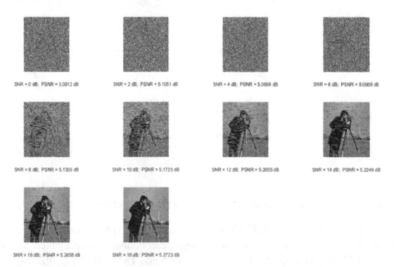

Fig. 18.8 Optical examination of the original picture at the receptacle of 1x2 MIMO System with AES

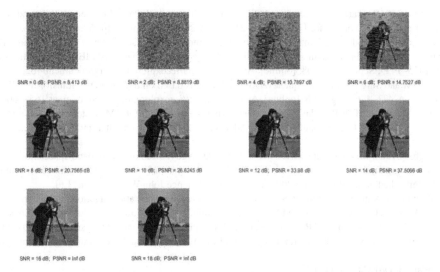

Fig. 18.9 Optical examination of the original picture at the receptacle of 2x2 MIMO System with AES

When compared to 1 x 2 MIMO systems, the 2 x 2 MIMO system obtained images from these that are more noise-resistant. Images that have been decrypted using the AES cryptosystem are more resistant to noise than they were using the original system. The quality of the recovered images from the original MIMO systems at the receiver is not significantly deteriorated at very low SNRs, according to the final analysis of all the MIMO systems taken into account in this work. The original MIMO system had better optical inspection at low SNR. Because the bits are adjusted before being converted into block data, if a mistake occurs in a single pixel's bit, it may spread to the following block of data.

4. Conclusion

Images in this study are encrypted using a variety of encryption techniques, which are modulated using a crypto MIMO system over a Rayleigh Fading channel using BPSK modulation. The AES encryption technique with the MIMO system for transmitting encrypted images is superior to the original system, according to the findings of MATLAB simulations and optical analysis. Due to the avalanche effect in the block, cryptographic systems offer good security but are also more vulnerable to bit mistakes. Security and image quality are trade-offs that never come without consequences. The findings collected show that the AES encryption technique offers superb security. The AES crypto MIMO system is therefore seen as being more sophisticated than the original MIMO system.

REFERENCES

1. Dharavathu, K., and Anuradha, D. M. (2017). Image Transmission and Hiding through OFDM system with different Encrypted schemes. International Journal on Future Revolution in Computer Science and Communication Engineering, 3(9).
2. Dharavathu, K., and Anuradha, M. S. (2021). Secure Image Parameters Comparison for DES, AES, and Rubik's Cube Encryption Algorithms. In Cloud Security (pp. 188–202). CRC Press.
3. Dharavathu, K., and Mosa, S. A. (2020). Efficient transmission of an encrypted image through a mimo–ofdm system with different encryption schemes. Sensing and Imaging, 21(1), 13.
4. Krishna, D., and Anuradha, M. S. (2017, August). Image transmission through the OFDM system under the AWGN channel. In IOP Conference series: materials science and engineering (Vol. 225, No. 1, p. 012217). IOP Publishing.
5. D. Krishna, Dr. M. Satya Anuradha, "Image Transmission Through OFDM System Under the Influence of AWGN channel," IOP Conference Series: Materials Science and Engineering 225 (ICMAEM-2017) 012217. Available: http://doi.org/10.1088/1757/-899X/225/1/012217.
6. Salwa M. Serag Eldin, "Optimized OFDM Transmission of Encrypted Image over Fading Channel," Springer, sense Imaging, 2014. Available: http://doi.org/10.1007/s11220-014- 0099-3/
7. N.S. Sai Srinivas, "OFDM System Implementation, Channel Estimation and Performance comparison of OFDM Signal", in IEEE International Conference on Electro Magnetic Interference compatibility (INCEMIC), Visakhapatnam, India, Jul 2015, pp.461-466

8. P. Tan and N.C. Beaulieu, "A Comparison of DCT-Based OFDM and DFT-Based OFDM in Frequency Offset and Fading Channels", IEEE Transactions on communications, vol.54, no. 11, pp. 2113–2125, Nov 2006. Available: http://ieeexplore.ieee.org/document/4012512/.

9. F. Gao, T. Cui, A.. Nallanthan, and C. Tellambura, "Maximum likelihood-based Estimation of Frequency and Phase Offset in DCT-OFDM Systems under Non-Circular Transmission: Algorithms, Analysis and Comparisons", IEEE Transactions on Communications, vol. 56, no. 9, pp. 1425–1429, September 2008. [online]. Available: http://ieeexplore.ieee.org/document/4623796/

10. R. Merched. On OFDM and Single-Carrier Frequency-Domain Systems based on trigonometric transforms", IEEE Signal Processing Letters, vol. 13, no. 8, pp. 473–476, Aug 2006. [online]. Available: http://ieeexplore.ieee.org/document/1658060/

11. Nisha Achar, Garima Mathur, Prof. R.P. Yadav, "Performance Analysis of MIMO OFDM System for Different Modulation Schemes Under Various Fading Channels", International Journal of Advanced Research in Computer and Communication Engineering, Vol. 2, Issue 5, May 2013.

12. Haixia Zhang, Dongfeng Yuan, Matthias Patzold, Yi Wu and Van Duc Nguye, "A novel wideband space-time channel simulator based on the geometrical one-ring model with applications in MIMO-OFDM systems", Wireless Communications and Mobile Computing. 2010, 11: 108–120. Published online 4 February 2009 in Wiley Inter Science John Wiley & Sons, Ltd.

13. Dalin Zhu, BalasubramaniamNatarajan and Justin S. Dyer, "Peak-to-average power ratio reduction in space–time coded MIMO-OFDM via pre-processing", Wireless Communications and Mobile Computing. 2011, 10: 758–771. John Wiley & Sons, Ltd.

14. Md. Mejbaul Haquel, Mohammad Shaifur Rahmani and Ki-Doo Kim, "Performance Analysis of MIMO-OFDM for 4G Wireless Systems under Rayleigh Fading Channel", International Journal of Multimedia and Ubiquitous Engineering, Vol. 8, No. 1. January, 2013.

15. IEEE 802.11a standard. ISO/IEC 8802-11, 1999.

16. Draft IEEE 802.11g standard. Further higher speed physical layer extension in the 2.4GHz band, 2001.

17. Flevina Jonese D'Souza, Dakshata Panchal, "Advanced Encryption Standard AES) Security using Hybrid Approach," 2017 International Conference on Computing, Communication, and Automation (ICCCA), IEEE, 2017.

18. Ako Muhammad Abdullah, "Advanced Encryption Standard (AES) algorithm to Encrypt and Decrypt Data," June 2017.

19. Dalia Yehya, Mohamad Joudi, "AES Encryption: Study & Evaluation," November 2020.

20. J. Daemen and V. Rijmen, The Design of Rijnadael. Secaucus, NJ, USA: Spriger-Verlag New York, Inc., 2002.

Note: All the figures and tables in this chapter were adapted by the authors from MATLAB and its simulation results.

Advances in Computational Intelligence and its Applications (ICACIA-2023) – Dr. Sheikh Fahad Ahmad et al. (eds)
© 2024 Taylor & Francis Group, London, ISBN 978-1-032-78612-4

A Comparative Study of Stock Return's Analysis and Prediction with the Impact of Macroeconomic Variables Using SVM and LSTM

19

Kallol Chandra[1], Gopinath K.[2]
Student, Christ (Deemed To Be University), Pune, Lavasa Campus

K. T. Thomas[3]
Assistant Professor, Christ (Deemed To Be University), Pune, Lavasa Campus

Kedar Shankarrao Vishnu[4]
Assistant Professor, Kirit P.Mehta School of Law,
Narsee Monjee Institute of Management Studies(Deemed To be University)

ABSTRACT—The stock market is untidy, uncertain, and volatile. It is a challenging and rigorous task to forecast and predict stock prices or returns accurately. Due to a significant surge in the importance of stock markets in recent decades for both a country's economy and the investors who are investing an amount in the stocks, it is very essential to understand the behavior and underlying patterns in the stock prices. Now, with the introduction of artificial Intelligence and computation, it has become a lot more simpler and efficient to predict stock prices in a programmatic way. Over time we have seen stock markets are affected by various factors ranging from companies' finances to changes in macroeconomic factors and even unprecedented political shifts. In this study, we try to predict the stock returns with the influence of both internal stock market factors and external macroeconomic factors using one machine learning model – Support Vector Machine(SVM) and one deep learning model- Long Short term Memory(LSTM). We try to comparing the performance of the two models with some key standard indicators of RMSE, MAPE, and MBE. For our analysis, we use the stock data of the top three pharmaceutical companies listed in the National Stock Exchange(NSE) India.

KEYWORDS—Macroeconomic factors, SVM, LSTM, Stock returns prediction

1. Introduction

In the modern world today, understanding the performance of the stock market is very essential for the growth, development, and economic stability of a country. Stock markets are susceptible to variations of macroeconomic factors in a country and are also sensitive to various uncertain events. Stock markets are a blend of dynamic, non-linear, and unpredictable in character. As a result, analyzing and predicting stock prices accurately has always been a challenge for researchers and investors. This prediction depends on a vast array of reasons from international and national economic stability, political conditions, the company's financial conditions, etc. For decades economists, financial experts, and investors tried to analyze stock market volatility considering changes in different macroeconomic indicators and have come up with numerous reasons for the non-linearity in the stock market. For example, a positive GDP growth rate of a country has a positive impact on its stock market whereas unstable government or political disruptions have a very volatile and negative impact on stock prices. The nature of the stock markets is inducing more and more researchers to explore the undiscovered indicators behind the volatility.

[1]kallol.chandra@msea.christuniversity.in, [2]gopinath.k@msea.christuniversity.in, [3]Thomas.kt@msea.christuniversity.in, [4]Vishnu.kedar@nmims.edu

DOI: 10.1201/9781003488682-19

With time various measures have been used by researchers and investors to predict stock prices. Traditionally two main techniques are followed while forecasting, technical analysis, and qualitative analysis. Technical analysis uses the historical data of internal factors like opening and closing prices to predict the stock price. Whereas qualitative analysis involves considering various external stock market indicators for prediction. In modern days numerous methods have developed with a base of the two traditional ways. Time series analysis of historical data, Machine learning, and most recently deep learning algorithms have been employed for forecasting stock prices. Each technique has its advantage and disadvantage but new machine learning and deep learning algorithms have proven to be more accurate in predictions in case of large data sizes due to the advanced intelligence and computation installed in them. For a close, to accurate prediction, the most important function of a model is to trace the hidden patterns and complex relations in the non-linear stock price dataset. Machine learning techniques can predict close to 60-86 percent more accurately than its past time series models whereas deep learning models are achieving better accuracy than machine learning ones. So progress in artificial intelligence has a huge impact on stock market predictions. However, the predictions and forecasting vary with different datasets and other factors mentioned above. In this study, the most important reason for choosing the pharmaceutical industry for analysis and prediction is because of the variations and sudden uprising in the healthcare industry post covid 19.

2. Literature Review

2.1 Stock Price Analysis and Predictions Using Traditional Time Series Models

Sheikh Mohammad et al. forecasted closing prices with ARIMA and implemented it through the Box Jenkins method which assumed past prices of stocks affect their future prices. They collected historical data on the Indian stock market from Sensex and Nifty Indexes from January 2016 to December 2018[1]. Similarly scrutinizing the literature on stock price prediction and analysis, Rui Shan et al. came up with a comparative analysis of two-time series forecasting models. They authenticated their study on the SSE composite index historical data and fitted the data set on two forecasting models involving ARIMA and ARCH and tried to come up with a forecast model with fewer errors in the short run.[2]

2.2 Stock Market Analysis Using Machine Learning Algorithms

Mehr Vijh et al. proposed a pair of machine learning techniques, Artificial Neural Networks, and Random Forest to accurately predict the coming day closing price. They used data from five companies belonging to five different industries. The paper suggested the comparison between the two machine learning models that evaluated the stocks based on the factors of RMSE and MAPE[3]. Likewise, Bruno Miranda et al. through their study tried to predict stock prices in both daily and up-to-date frequencies. Even though according to Efficient Market Hypothesis, it is not possible to forecast stock price changes constantly, this study proposed an intensive computational technique of Support vector regression and also compared it with Random forest. The data was collected over a span of fifteen years ranging from January 2002 to May 2017 of three blue chip and three small-cap stocks of USA, Brazil, and China totaling 18 stocks[4]. Ranjan Kumar Das et al. proposed a new machine-learning technique of fine-tuned support vector regression in which a grid search technique was applied for time series forecasting of stock prices. They tried to predict up to daily, up to monthly, and accumulating monthly stock prices and increased the accuracy through parameter validation. The study considered stocks of eight different companies and along with prediction gave an analysis of the volatility and risk involved through the machine learning model[5]. Another inquiry by Yuxuan Hang et al. proposed stock prediction by machine learning algorithms based on fundamental analysis. They collected stock data for 22 years which was converted into quarterly data and analysed with three machine learning algorithms, Feed Forward Neural Network(FNN), Random Forest, and Adaptive Neural Fuzzy Inference System(ANFS). They improvised Random Forest with feature selection and bootstrap aggregation which helped in increasing the accuracy of the model[6].

2.3 Stock market Analysis Using Deep Learning Models

Deep Learning models are introduced by researchers as an update to all the machine learning models in stock market prediction. Deep learning was inspired by human brains. They require a lot less human intervention as compared to machine learning models. They work well with unstructured and large datasets and predict stock market volatility with a touch of human thinking. Hiransha et al. with historical data tried to predict the stock market with four different types of deep learning models, Multilayer perception(MLP), Recurrent Neural Networks(RNN), Long-Short-Term Memory(LSTM), and Convolutional neural networks(CNN). The data was collected from a couple of stock exchanges, the National Stock Exchange of India (NSE) and the New York stock exchange[7]. Similarly, Kazuhiro et al. tried to predict stock prices with nonnumerical components such as political conditions and global occasions. The primary goal was to consider previous information regarding stock predictions and newspaper information in prediction. These then were extracted and inserted into neural networks for prediction. The experiment with non-numeric factors and the use of neural networks achieved a smaller error percentage than multiple regression analysis at a level of significance of 5%[8]. On the other hand, Nikou et al. undertook research comparing the efficiency of machine learning and deep learning techniques to anticipate the stock prices. They used the daily closing price data of the iShares MSCI United Kingdom exchange-traded(ET) fund. The research by its study concluded that deep learning algorithms were more efficient and advantageous than machine learning algorithms for prediction[9]. A study by Daniel Stifanic et al. which was conducted during the covid 19 tried to predict the impact of the pandemic on the movement of crude oil prices and three use stocks DJK, S&P 500, and NASDAQ. As the paper tries to forecast both the stock prices and the crude oil price it aimed to integrate the stationary wavelet transform (SWT) and bidirectional long short-term memory(BDLSTM). Through the analysis, they gained up-to-the-mark results[10]

2.4 Stock Price Analysis with the Influence of Macro-Economic Variables

Many researchers have come up with various macroeconomic factors like Gross Domestic Product(GDP), Inflation, Exchange rate, gold prices, interest rates, and oil prices which have proved as key macroeconomic indicators affecting stock market volatility. The exchange rate of the stock market has a positive correlation with these indicators but they change depending on the markets and periods. Joseph Tagna Talla investigated the impact of interest rates and money supply on stock prices of the Stockholm Stock Exchange using Multivariate Regression Model based on ordinary least squares, and the Granger causality test. Monthly data of the stocks were used ranging for the period of 1993-2012. They found interest rate is inversely related to price variations, and has a notable negative influence on stock prices. The supply of money had a direct relationship although it was not significant[11]. Similarly, Omodero and Mlanga analyzed the effect of macroeconomic variables on Nigeria's stock market and found out interest and exchange rates don't have a considerable influence on stock prices. Although the effect of inflation was significant[12]. Celebi and Honig studied the influence of macroeconomic factors on the German Stock Exchange. They used data from 27 years and found out many indicators impacted the stock prices during pre and post-war times.

3. Data and Variables

3.1 Data Collection

To analyse the performance of stock returns specifically in the pharma industry we collected historical data top 3 pharmaceutical companies listed in the National Stock exchange(NSE) from the Yahoo Finance website. We analysed the monthly stock returns of Cipla, Sun Pharma and Dr. Reddy's ranging for a period of 25 years, from January 1996 to December 2021. The most important reason for selecting these three particular stocks is because of their volatile returns through out. We used log returns of stock as the dependent variable in our models over normal returns as it is symmetric. We induce both internal and external factors which affect stock returns. Closing price, volatility, previous month's returns, and volume are our internal stock market factors, and along with that, we employ the macroeconomic indicators- the exchange rate of India and inflation which is represented by the Consumer Price Index(CPI).

3.2 Dependent Variable

Logarithmic Stock return: This is one of the most commonly used valuation techniques to measure the profitability of a stock and has a significant impact on investor sentiment.

3.3 Independent Variable

This study considers a combination of both internal as well external factors which affect the stock market. Closing price, stock price volatility, previous month's stock returns, and volume of stocks traded in a month are our internal stock market factors, and along with that, we employ the macroeconomic indicators- the exchange rate of India and inflation which is represented by the Consumer Price Index(CPI).

4. Methodology and Model Specifications

In our study, we employ three models for the analysis and forecasting of stock returns and try to compare the results. We use one machine-learning model-SVM, and one deep learning model-LSTM. The study aims to compare traditional and modern forecasting algorithms with both internal and external factors. We use a multivariate analysis in the models. In this section, we try to give a brief understanding of the models used in our analysis.

4.1 Model Specifications

Support Vector Machine(SVM)

Support Vector Machine(SVM) is a machine learning model which can be used for predicting stock prices. SVM is advantageous because it applies a function that comprises the errors and regularized term which is derived from the structural risk minimization principle.

A linear model is used by SVM to apply nonlinear class boundaries with the help of nonlinear mapping. The data points existing on either side due to the creation of a boundary are labeled differently. This boundary in the multidisciplinary case is known as a hyperplane. The training examples which are most closely associated with the hyperplane are known as support vectors. In the case of linearly separable, the boundary splitting the binary decision classes in the three-character case can be described as:

$$y = a_0 + a_1 x1 + a_2 x2 + a_3 x$$

Here, y is the output, xi is the character values and ai are the weights. The four weights designated in the above equation are parameters determining the hyperplane. The maximum margin hyperplane can be represented with the help of support vectors:

$$y = b + \sum \alpha_i y_i x(i). \, x$$

In the equation y_i is the class value of training example $x(i)$. The vector x describes a test example and the support vectors are $x(i)$. Here, b and α_i are parameters determining hyperplane.

$$y = b + \sum \alpha_i y_i K(x(i), x)$$

Here the kernel function is represented by $K(x(i), x)$

Different Kernels are used in generating inner products to develop machines with nonlinear decision surfaces of different types. We have to choose a model that minimizes estimates among the different kernels.

Long Short Term Memory (LSTM)

Long Short-Term Memory (LSTM) is a kind of Recurrent Neural Network(RNN) which is suitable for extracting historical data and applying it for the purpose of future predictions. RNN is not sufficient to store long time memory, as a result, LSTM is used on the basis of the memory line. This use of memory line proves to be impactful for prediction with historical data of a long time. This particular memorization in LSTM of prior stages can be undertaken by trough gates with the employment of a memory line.

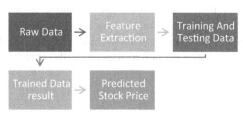

Fig. 19.1 Prediction process of LSTM model

Referring to Fig. 19.1. we can observe, in an LSTM model initially, the data is extracted followed by a feature extraction. Then the data is divided into training and testing sets accordingly and the stock price is predicted. Generally, an LSTM unit comprises a cell, an information door, an entry door, and a view door. The cell gathers values of collective time intervals and the three inputs control how data flows inward and outward of the cell. The key advantage of the LSTM is its capacity to learn contextually dependent time dependencies. Without the explicit application of the activation function under recurrent components, the LSTM units collect data over either a long or short period of time (hence the name). The capability of memorizing sequence data makes LSTM a unique kind of RNN.

5. Empirical Results

In this section, we will discuss the results and findings from our three models used for analysing and prediction purposes for three different stocks.

5.1 Analysis of Descriptive Statistics

Since we are considering both internal historical stock-related factors and external macroeconomic indicators it is essential to have a look at the descriptive statistical analysis of all. The independent variables in the study are closing price, the previous month's returns, volatility, the volume of shares traded, CPI, and exchange rates. The following table gives us an overview of the descriptive statistics:

Table 19.1 Descriptive statistics of Cipla

Observations	Closing Price	Previous Month Return	Volatility	Volume	Exchange Rate	CPI
Mean	303.622	0.015	0.079	3.44e+07	52.319	69.009
Median	289.456	0.027	0.095	3.46e+07	46.872	65.963
SD	243.697	0.095	0.008	3,303e+07	11.647	33.331
Count	309	309	309	309	309	309

Referring to Table 19.1 we can observe the mean, median, standard deviation, and the number of observations of all the independent variables determining the log returns of CIPLA.

Table 19.2 Descriptive statistics of Sun Pharma

Observations	Closing Price	Previous Month Return	Volatility	Volume	Exchange Rate	CPI
Mean	270.058	0.019	0.084	6.230e+07	52.319	69.009
Median	263.076	0.052	0.112	6.237e+07	46.872	65.963
SD	288.143	0.107	0.010	6.191e+07	11.701	33.508
Count	310	310	310	310	310	310

Referring to Table 19.2. we can observe the mean, median, standard deviation, and the number of observations of all the independent variables determining the log returns of SUN PHARMA.

Table 19.3 Descriptive statistics of Dr. Reddy's

Observations	Closing Price	Previous Month Return	Volatility	Volume	Exchange Rate	CPI
Mean	1503.407	0.014	0.082	1.057e+07	52.319	69.009
Median	1505.102	0.043	0.109	1.085e+07	46.872	65.963
SD	1385.370	0.099	0.009	8.322e+06	11.701	33.508

From Table 19.3. we can observe the mean, median, standard deviation, and the number of observations of all the independent variables determining the log returns of DR REDDY'S.

Accordingly, the standard deviation is highest for the closing price of all the stocks among the internal stock market factors which indicates greater fluctuations. And between the external macroeconomic factors CPI has a more standard deviation.

5.2 Model Evaluation

The main motive of the research was to compare the performance of machine learning and deep learning in stock price prediction using both the internal stock market and external factors. For that, we used Support Vector Machine(SVM) and Long Short Term Memory(LSTM).

In order to quantify the productiveness and the comparison of the models, we employ the three different stock historical data of CIPLA, SUN PHARMA, and DR. REDDY's into the two techniques. In the study, we predicted monthly log returns which are based on Root Mean Square Error(RMSE), Mean Absolute Percentage Error(MAPE), and Mean Bias Error(MBE) in order to get minimal errors for prediction purposes. RMSE is evaluated using Eq. 1.

$$\text{RMSE} = \sqrt{\sum_{i=1} n(Ri - fi)^2 / n} \qquad (1)$$

Here, 'Ri' refers to the actual log returns and 'Fi' refers to the predicted log returns, and 'n' refers to the data size. MAPE is used to assess the productiveness of the model and is represented in Eq. 2.

$$\text{MAPE} = \frac{1}{n} \sum_{i=1} n \frac{(Ri - Fi)}{Oi} * 100 \qquad (2)$$

Here, 'Ri' refers to the actual log returns and 'Fi' refers to the predicted log returns, and 'n' refers to the data size. MBE is used to assess the productiveness of the model and is represented in Eq. 3.

$$\text{MBE} = \frac{1}{n} \sum_{i=1} n (Ri - Fi) \qquad (3)$$

Here, 'Ri' refers to the actual log returns and 'Fi' refers to the predicted log returns and 'n' refers to the data size. For computational convenience, we converted the date column of the three stock market data into digits before training them in machine learning and deep learning models. The following diagrams show a comparison between the predicted and trained original data of log returns of three different pharmaceutical stock.

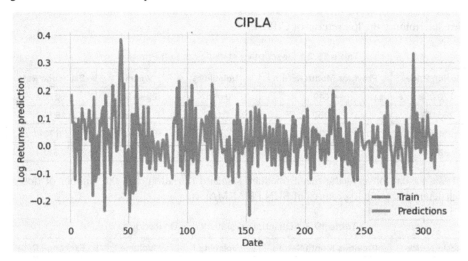

Fig. 19.2 Predicted V/S trained original log returns of Cipla

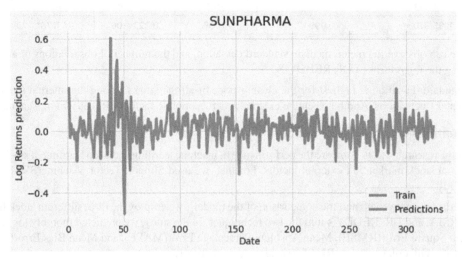

Fig. 19.3 Predicted V/S trained original log returns of Sun Pharma

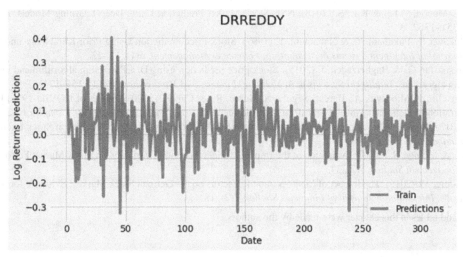

Fig. 19.4   Predicted V/S trained original log returns of Dr. Reddy's

SVM   LSTM

Table 19.4   Comparison of SVM and LSTM

Company	RMSE	MAPE	MBE	RMSE	MAPE	MBE
CIPLA	1.12	1.07%	-0.0522	0.45	0.30%	0.062
SUN PHARMA	1.30	1.09%	0.0762	0.46	0.19%	0.055
DR. REDDY'S	1.28	0.89%	-0.0310	0.47	0.25%	0.005

Referring to Table 19.4. we can infer that LSTM proves to be a better technique than SVM, having lower and better RMSE and MAPE values.

6. Conclusion

The study predicted the Log Returns with the influence of stock internal and external macroeconomic factors of the top three pharmaceutical companies of the National Stock Exchange(NSE). We used monthly stock market data and employed monthly CPI and exchange rates with that. The historical data included closing price, opening price, high price, and low price as variables, but detailed research has found these internal factors are not much significant in prediction. We tried to obtain higher accuracy in return instead of the closing price. We used SVM and LSTM to predict the next month's return and found that LSTM proves to be more accurate and specific than SVM based on the better values of the indicators of RMSE, MAPE, and MBE. However future research can be done in more detailed way with daily stock returns with the influence of macroeconomic factors but accurate data should be available from authenticated sources.

REFERENCES

1. Idrees, S. M., Alam, M. A., & Agarwal, P. (2019) Prediction Approach for Stock Market Volatility Based on Time Series Data. *IEEE Access*, 7, 17287–17298.
2. Zhang, J., Shan, R., & Su, W. (2009). Applying Time Series Analysis Builds Stock Price Forecast Model. *Modern Applied Science*, 3(5).
3. Vijh, M., Chandola, D., Tikkiwal, V. A., & Kumar, A. (2020). Stock Closing Price Prediction using Machine Learning Techniques. *Procedia Computer Science*, 167, 599–606.
4. Henrique, B. M., Sobreiro, V. A., & Kimura, H. (2018). Stock price prediction using support vector regression on daily and up to the minute prices. *The Journal of Finance and Data Science*, 4(3), 183–201.
5. Dash, R. K., Nguyen, T. N., Cengiz, K., & Sharma, A. (2021). Fine-tuned support vector regression model for stock predictions. *Neural Computing and Applications*.
6. Huang, Y., Capretz, L. F., & Ho, D. (2021). Machine Learning for Stock Prediction Based on Fundamental Analysis. *2021 IEEE Symposium Series on Computational Intelligence (SSCI)*.

7. M, H., E.A., G., Menon, V. K., & K.P., S. (2018). NSE Stock Market Prediction Using Deep-Learning Models. *Procedia Computer Science*, *132*, 1351–1362.

8. Kohara, K., Ishikawa, T., Fukuhara, Y., & Nakamura, Y. (1997). Stock Price Prediction Using Prior Knowledge and Neural Networks. *International Journal of Intelligent Systems in Accounting, Finance & Management*, *6*(1), 11–22.

9. Nikou, M., Mansourfar, G., & Bagherzadeh, J. (2019). Stock price prediction using DEEP learning algorithm and its comparison with machine learning algorithms. *Intelligent Systems in Accounting, Finance and Management*, *26*(4), 164–174.

10. Štifanić, D., Musulin, J., Miočević, A., Baressi Šegota, S., Šubić, R., & Car, Z. (2020). Impact of COVID-19 on Forecasting Stock Prices: An Integration of Stationary Wavelet Transform and Bidirectional Long Short-Term Memory. *Complexity*, *2020*, 1–12.

11. Joseph, T. T. (2013). Impact of Macroeconomic Variables on the Stock Market Prices of the Stockholm Stock Exchange (OMXS30). *International Finance*.

12. Omodero, C. O., & Mlanga, S. (2019). Evaluation of the Impact of Macroeconomic Variables on Stock Market Performance in Nigeria. *Business and Management Studies*, *5*(2), 34.

13. Celebi, K., & Hönig, M. (2019). The Impact of Macroeconomic Factors on the German Stock Market: Evidence for the Crisis, Pre- and Post-Crisis Periods. *International Journal of Financial Studies*, *7*(2), 18.

Note: All the figures and tables in this chapter were made by the authors.

Advances in Computational Intelligence and its Applications (ICACIA-2023) – Dr. Sheikh Fahad Ahmad et al. (eds)
© 2024 Taylor & Francis Group, London, ISBN 978-1-032-78612-4

Machine Learning Model for Improving the Overall Equipment Effectiveness in Industrial Manufacturing Sites

20

Biswaranjan Senapati[1]

Associate Professor, Computer Science Department,
Parker Hannifin Corp, USA

Awad Bin Naeem[2]

Ph.D Student, Computer Science Department,
National College of Business Administration & Economics, Multan, Pakistan

Renato R. Maaliw III[3]

Associate Professor, College of Engineering, Southern Luzon State University,
Lucban, Quezon, Philippines

ABSTRACT—Manufacturers have always pursued greater speed, scale, qualitative products and services, and simplicity across operations to optimize production while enhancing efficiency and reducing costs. With technologies like artificial intelligence (AI), industrial internet of things (IIoT), machine learning (ML), and analytics, companies can create hyper-connected ecosystem leveraging data to constantly optimize critical efficiency related key performance indicators (KPI) such as overall equipment effectiveness (OEE) score. The metrics can help accurately identify, predict, and prevent unplanned equipment failures and downtimes, including quality issues. This paper discussed the best possible ML model to predict the OEE score in order to improve the quality of production and the end production goals in order to fulfil customer orders based on availability, performance, and quality within manufacturing sites. Our results shows that ML with the advancement of quantum machine learning models could potentially gain the productivity, performance, and quality factors that are the key ingredients to gain maximum OEE score that could be the most effective manufacturing production solutions worldwide.

KEYWORDS—Artificial intelligence, Industry 4.0, Machine learning, Smart factory, Supervised learning, Unsupervised learning

1. Introduction

Due to the high demand for productions and customer-centric businesses, manufacturers are highly focused on digitalization, the adoption of intelligent equipment, and highly focused process integration and management (e.g., ERP & SAP) software to support and fulfil the customer's demands. They are capable of processing the order, and sales and operational planning as per schedule (e.g., sales orders, make-to-order (MTO), and make-to-stock (MTS)), which are significantly challenging, and fulfilling these customer demands is highly critical (Cabanillas, 2013). Most industrial production sites heavily utilize industrial automation, digitalization, and changes to industrial IOTs, sensors, machines, and equipment, which need a better OEE score and production optimization. Even in Industry 4.0, the most suitable digitally integrated technological innovation revolves around machines, equipment, and industrial sensors (Riesbeck). These elements collect, process, and optimize enterprise data per the manufacturing business process flows to gain production and OEE performance scores (Kao, 2017). Manufacturers

[1]bsenapati@ualr.edu, [2]awadbinnaeem@gmail.com, [3]rmaaliw@slsu.edu.ph

DOI: 10.1201/9781003488682-20

are adopting the best practices and applications of novel technologies such as machine learning (ML) and the industrial application of quantum computing (QC) and artificial intelligence (AI) to gain absolute results while considering production efficiencies (Puvanasvaran, 2010). OEE is the most standard and optimized global manufacturing practice (GMP) to support global compliance and enhance competitiveness in manufacturing industries. Based on global manufacturing best practices, the overall equipment effectiveness (OEE) is measured in percentage in a competitive manufacturing environment. Moreover, time invested in manufacturing a product that is truly productive and result-oriented in a specific production unit is the surest source of truth in the measurement of the OEE score (Kim, 2018). Based on the OEE score, manufacturers can easily understand the production scorecard, losses, and profit on a specific industrial production, the rate of production parameter, and the TCO and ROI of smart factories. The current OEE score for a particular manufacturing practice is 85% or above, which is "exceptional".

Based on literature, the following are the best benefits for OEE score in industrial manufacturing and smart factory production sites: (a) Ability to understand the equipment capacity that has been used at production sites; (b) Better visibility of the manufacturing and production processes in smart industrial sites; (c) Ability to understand the production factory's capabilities, turnover, and quality score; (d) Global compliance and international standards as per the new products and new markets; (e) Global competitiveness and international market shares; (f) Industrial automation and smart factories in Industry 4.0; (g) High profitable and low-cost of ownership in longer run and (h) Improve the highest level of production score and less defects or scraps.

In terms of manufacturing execution system and overall equipment effectiveness, we have stated that the most current trends of manufacturing effectiveness and the scorecard of OEE apply to industrial manufacturing practices and are the trends in industry 4.0/5.0. Manufacturers have a little higher in competitive, dynamic markets where production efficiencies must be higher than expected. Customer expectations are much higher than previous trends, and the industrial production score, quality score, and overall equipment effectiveness (OEE) are ideally under the normal range of 85%, which is the most competitive score for manufacturers in high-end productions (Acosta, 2020). In industrial manufacturing, the key performance indicators (KPIs) are based on the quality of productions, the availability of production scores, improving changeover setup times for machines or equipment, reducing production scrap, or changing the capacity to produce the best quality of products or services free of defects. Adopting the best technological innovations could quickly achieve production qualities and overall equipment effectiveness. These include new trends in the use of smart factories and smart industries; quantum computing's industrial revolutions, and AI and ML models to support the industrial innovations of Industry 4.0 (Rabie, 2000; Ulutas, 2011). Occurrence is impossible to achieve through traditional approaches or legacy systems that cannot manage the OEE score in production factories. Essential to the overall equipment effectiveness in manufacturing factories are the key indicators of production score, which conveys how well the equipment and machines are used to attain overall equipment efficacy in a manufacturing site (El Hassani, 2021; Abajo, 2004; Shi, 2007). There are a few key considerations and dependencies on the score of OEE, as stated below:

(a) *The availability factors*. It is the percentage of time that a piece of equipment can easily operate without the need for routine or planned maintenance.

(b) *The quality factors*. It is the proportion of qualitative factors that may have an impact on the goods, services, or manufactured parts.

(c) *The performance factors*. It is the percentage of a machine's maximum operation speed that is used by the machine or other equipment in a manufacturing site.

The core of the automation pyramid is depicted in Fig. 20.1, explaining the components of manufacturing execution systems and the flow of information across enterprises. The enterprise manufacturing execution systems are backed by back-office solid systems (ERP-SAP HANA S/4), which could save time, money, and manual efforts across the enterprise levels (Rostami, 2015). Enterprise manufacturing execution systems are backed by back-office solid systems (ERP-SAP HANA S/4), which could save time, money, and manual efforts across the enterprise levels. In industrial manufacturing, facilities require robust back-office systems (ERP-S/4HANA), which could save manual tasks and actions and integrate the complex business process within the manufacturing business process. Most of the complex production, operation, supply chain, warehouse, and shop floor activities could be controlled and managed by the HANA Manufacturing Execution System (MES) and deliver the most tangible benefits of the machine and operations in industrial activities.

The manufacturing execution systems and solutions could help the manufacturing business process, tasks, production orders, shop floor activities, and production status. It also involves updating the new or old material per customer order demands, order fulfillment per customer demand (MTO or MTS), updating the batch information, and managing the preventive and predictive maintenance as per the business needs in manufacturing and supply chain management (Singh, 2013; Wollschlaeger, 2017). The best practices of any manufacturing execution system also perform the required manufacturing activities. They can

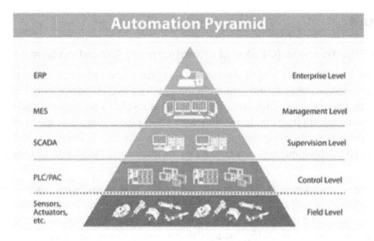

Fig. 20.1 MES automation pyramid and smart factory

manage work orders, production orders scheduling, warehouse management, tracking and trading, and work center and shop-floor activities management to support order fulfillment processing (sales orders, make-to-order, and make-to-stock) within the financial, supply chain, operational, and production planning lines of business (Nguyen, 2020; Nurpihan, 2019, Afefy, 2013). All these activities depend on the OEE score, production performance, and quality index in shop floor units (Corrales, 2020). Below are the core components of MES-manufacturing execution and optimization (Rathi, 2022). Production site key performance indicators:

(a) Production order management (MTS, MTO, and customer order) and supplier contracts.
(b) Work orders or manufacturing orders.
(c) Production scheduling and shop floor activities at production sites.
(d) Downtime tracking and overall equipment and device efficiencies.
(e) Integration with the WMS system and tracking and trading.

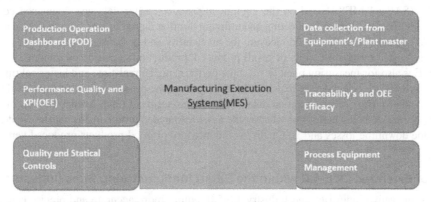

Fig. 20.2 Manufacturing execution systems and core components

Recent advancement in production is reaching its full potential and transforming the way goods are manufactured using AI. It includes predictive maintenance, quality control, supply chain and process optimization, and personalized manufacturing. Overall, the utilization of intelligent algorithms in manufacturing is astronomically increasing product quality and cost efficiency in general and provides an exciting future for timely and uninterrupted deliveries. In this paper, we have discussed the best possible machine learning model to predict the overall equipment effectiveness score, and an optimized solution to cover industrial manufacturing sites. The goal of the OEE score is to reduce downtime, unpredictable losses due to equipment breakdown, setup, minor stoppage, reduced speed, or even scrap production, and improve the quality of production and the end production goals while continuing to fulfil customer orders in the manufacturing objectives (Sales Order, Make to Order, and Make to Stock)

2. Related Literature

2.1 Overall Equipment Effectiveness (OEE) and Manufacturing Execution Systems

Researchers in manufacturing industries said that if we can get our efficiency measured in quality parameters, observe our performance, and understand our availability factors, we are improving our overall equipment effectiveness (OEE) score. It is the continuous measurement that needs to be followed throughout the lifecycle - a measurement to manage the effectiveness of the equipment level in the manufacturing industry. In manufacturing and production sites, the overall equipment effectiveness management (OEE score) could allow measuring the most key parameters and KPIs in the production sites. These include the analytical components of machines, equipment, plants/production facilities, and the site performance in either way (e.g., real-time and historical values).

Most of the time, the OEE score is also dependent on the equipment parts, device attributes, sensors, and IIOTs, which are used to manage the manufacturing business and optimize production planning activities. Some of the manufacturing key metrics are measured based on the capacity of the machine, devices, and industrial equipment, which may come from the various data sources within the production sites (Purr, 2015), the availability and performance of equipment, and the quality of goods produced by that equipment. In OEE systems, the following building blocks and critical KPIs could be measured per the equipment's performance and planned maintenance at production sites. Below are the critical functional building blocks in the OEE:

(a) Master data and its attributes in core ERP SAP applications.

(b) Shop floor integration frameworks and ERP dashboard for SFC.

(c) Dashboards used for the OEE configuration and access management.

(d) For the automated data collections within the SAP OEE systems.

(e) Capabilities on collecting reporting and analytical measurements.

2.2 SAP Manufacturing Execution Systems and SAP OEE for Large Industrial Manufacturing Sites

In manufacturing sites, the overall equipment effectiveness (OEE) of any equipment or machine is a widely utilized metric for measuring manufacturing performance and the efficiencies and effectiveness of the associated devices across the production units (Hugget, 2018). Actual equipment effectiveness OEE functionality could be easily captured and monitored within the back-office application (SAP S4 MES) based on the equipment/product master data and connected equipment across the production units. In SAP OEE, functions are collecting and utilizing familiar data sources (manufacturing and operational data) from various sources to obtain metrics that could measure the availability and performance of machines connected to factory production sites. It will also determine the quality of goods produced, production rates, and production efficiencies determined by that equipment. OEE is also for measuring plant or machine performance in real-time and historical time from various data points. While most OEE KPIs are calculated in real-time as displayed on the production order dashboard (PoD), OEE and its constituent KPIs are calculated using order-operation data converted into terms of time. Availability is a measure of the uptime of the resources: A) Performance is the metrics of whether the asset/resource is producing as per the rated capacity or nominal sped. It does not include downtime losses and B) Quality is the measure of good products produced versus the total quantity generated.

2.3 Applicability of Extended OEE 4.0 within the Smart Manufacturing Sites (Industries 4.0/5.0)

Manufacturing sites in innovative industries and Industry 4.0/5.0 require more accurate and precise calculative OEE scores, which can only be calculated by applying the best practices of extended overall equipment effectiveness (EOEE) and the assistance of digital applications (ML, AI, Quantum AI, ML). Industries 4.0 and the industrial application revolution in 5.0 well manage the extended overall equipment efficiencies. In total production planning and total predictive maintenance (TPM), the OEE4.0 plays a vital role concerning the overall equipment lifecycle and measures to identify, monitor, and optimize the availability, performance, and quality key performance indicators of the manufacturing process in manufacturing sites. Some ERP applications, like SAP S/4 Hana OEE, can predict measurable KPIs, obtain the best production services, manufacture additional value-added services within the machine and equipment, and manage the equipment master data with the equipment registered in the whole life maintenance plans.

Any profitability or losses can be calculated as per the existing master data, equipment classes, and their various critical attributes effectively and quickly as needed by industrial manufacturing sites. The OEE prediction score is an innovation from smart manufacturing best practices. It is derived from the "Japan Institute of Plant Maintenance," which is an integral part of good manufacturing practices and is the best philosophy of total productive maintenance in manufacturing sites. More than 98 million connected equipment, devices, and IIOTs were used and connected to industrial manufacturing facilities in the digital smart factory and shop floor center to perform the best production outcomes. The number of devices and equipment is still growing. According to a 2019 survey, manufacturers and researchers expect this number to exceed 160 million connections by 2025. A vast amount of operational data and manufacturing intelligence information could be used to gain more successful practices, which is the best way to calculate OEE scores.

2.4 Benefits of Extended OEE 4.0 in Manufacturing Businesses

The extended OEE 4.0 creates more effectiveness in production units and shop floor activities in manufacturing facilities and offers tremendous benefits to production sites which could quickly fulfil customer orders (MTO/MTS). A few of the benefits are listed below:

(a) On the go monitored and perform checks on overall system availability in sites.
(b) Capable to provide detailed reports on quality, availability, and performance of the equipment.
(c) Data acquisition and assignment automation and utilizations.
(d) Capable to read the actual machine utilization times.
(e) Update as per the TPM.
(f) Service and support management of the predictive and preventive and corrective maintenance and service.
(g) Review of effectiveness of measures taken along with preventive maintenance planning.
(h) Maintenance of the key major losses due to production losses and OEE (KPI).
(i) Related to production data such as downtimes, quantities, reason codes, and preventive maintenance per units.
(j) Out of box integration within the back-office (SAP ERP), MII, and analytical tools from SAP S/4 HANA in-memory computing.

3. Decision Making System to Improve the OEE Score at Manufacturing Production Sites

In this paper, we would like to highlight the best AI and ML models that could improve overall equipment efficiency and utilization of the smart industrial revolution. We determine the score of the OEE in a manufacturing production unit and compare it with another similar unit where smart manufacturing is not in the scope of implementation. A focus on and check the implications of various machine learning models with real-time production data variables, which could hamper the OEE score in real-time scenarios. There are few viewpoints on machine learning models and how the OEE score can be impactful in response to industrial manufacturing processing units. Here are a few novel research key characteristics:

(a) How the machine learning and AI models can impact the OEE score and manufacturing process in real-time.
(b) Effective management of OEE factors in real analytical tools (availabilities, quality, and performance)

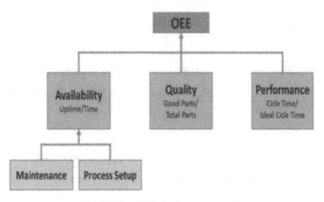

Fig. 20.3 OEE and components

The concepts of overall equipment effectiveness (OEE) were developed in the 1980s at the Japan Institute for Plant Maintenance (JIPM). They are still the best philosophy in the manufacturing space to control manufacturing production issues (Fig. 20.3).

In the Industry 4.0/5.0 revolution, OEE plays a vital role while considering good manufacturing practices and an optimized performance rate for the units producing materials and services on any shop floor. Typically, a good OEE score depends on the core combination of the performance of machines and equipment, quality, and the availability of industrial resources and machinery or equipment objects. The overall equipment effectiveness score makes a factory or production unit much more profitable and economically manageable for sustainability in business. The OEE calculation is depicted in the Equations below:

$$\text{Availability } (Av) = \left[\frac{\text{Running Time}}{\text{Available Time}} \right]$$

$$\text{Throughput } (Th) = \left[\frac{\text{Total Units} * \text{Ideal Cycle Time}}{\text{Running Time}} \right]$$

$$\text{Quality } (Qu) = \left[\frac{\text{Good Units}}{\text{Total Units}} \right]$$

$$\text{OEE} = \text{Availability} * \text{Performance} * \text{Quality Factor}$$

$$(\text{Availability}) = \left[\frac{\text{Actual Production Time}}{\text{Planned Production Time}} \right]$$

$$P(\text{Performance}) = \left[\frac{\text{Current Run Rate}}{\text{Ideal Run Rate}} \right]$$

$$Q(\text{Quality}) = \left[\frac{\text{Good Product}}{\text{Total Product}} \right]$$

where:

The Availability (A) for a particular part can be calculated as per the formula below:

$$\text{Availability } (A) = \left[\frac{\text{Available Time-Unplanned Downtime}}{\text{Available Time}} \right]$$

The planned downtime at a production or manufacturing facility may be caused by "excess capacity, planned breaks, planned maintenance, communication breaks, and team meetings," whereas "availability time = total available time-planned downtime." Unplanned downtime in production and manufacturing facilities is caused by a variety of factors, including breakdowns, setup and adjustment issues, delayed material delivery, and operator availability on-site. Unplanned downtime in production and manufacturing facilities is caused by a variety of factors, including breakdowns, setup and adjustment issues, delayed material delivery, and operator availability on-site. To calculate the quality rate in manufacturing sites, it can be derived by the formula:

$$\text{Quality Rate } (Q) = \left[\frac{(\text{Total Produced Parts-Defective Parts})}{\text{Total Produced Parts}} \right]$$

To calculate the Performance (P) or KPI of the production sites, use the following formula:

$$\text{Performance } (P) = \left[\frac{(\text{Total Production Parts})/(\text{Operating Time})}{\text{Idle Run Rate}} \right]$$

where:

$$\text{Operating Time} = \text{Available Time} - \text{Unplanned Downtime}$$

$$\text{Idle Run Rate} = \text{Number of Parts per Minute}$$

A good machine learning tool can be helpful to consider the optimal percentage of availability, percentage of quality or qualitative time, and percentage of the performance of the production sites, and we can expect the best percentage of overall equipment effectiveness of the production or manufacturing sites.

4. Implementation of Machine Learning to Gain Better OEE Score in Manufacturing Sites

To improve OEE in manufacturing sites, we must consider the key points below and gain greater visibility when it comes to implementing machine learning models for real-time prediction scores in manufacturing sites. Three types of machine learning algorithms are used to classify these techniques and provide the best prediction score for achieving OEE in manufacturing sites: supervised learning (Thakre, 2009), unsupervised learning (Ulutas, 2011) and reinforcement learning (Prasad, 2006). In the case of supervised learning, the issue is described by a vector X of input variables and a vector Finding a mapping function that connects X and Y, where $Y = f$, is the objective (X). The issue becomes an unsupervised learning situation if the only input variables are X and there are no target variables. Finally, reinforcement learning is a particular kind of machine learning in which an agent learns how to operate and make decisions in an environment by doing actions and receiving rewards. Since we are dealing with labeled data in the current study, we will explore a number of supervised machine learning algorithms (Biswaranjan, 2022).

4.1 Machine Learning Model for Availability (A)

A high availability score of 100% indicates that the process is always running planned production time over unplanned and planned stops or any breakdown maintenance of machines or equipment. We must consider the changeover time, which is the setup and adjustment time, and determine the opportunity for improvement. Through the help of virtual sensors (VS) and IIOT devices, ML can understand the real-production environment; simulate accurate sensor outputs, and any failure events on equipment or machines. Along with planned maintenance, ML can improve the availability score of the complex manufacturing site and help increase the overall OEE score. Our machine learning (ML) model can certainly help to manage the critical challenges while considering a good availability score, as described below:

(a) *Process Complexity:* Considered the most appropriate technologies and tools to support the process optimization of manufacturing sites and implement business process management (BPM) and BPML tools to manage them.

(b) *Response Delayed:* Considered the critical process management while handling the production of end products, materials, or the end products, which could be slow due to unavoidable delays in production or shopfloor constraints, or there could be issues due to failures or breakdowns in the maintenance of the sites.

(c) *Quality of signals to the devices:* Most of the time, the sensor from the device or equipment could be delayed due to poor connectivity or signal issues as industrial sites are connected with multiple devices, sensors, and IoT and IIoT equipment with another apparatus, which could have low signal flows.

In our research paper, we examined various ML algorithms and compared the best-suited models for use in industrial manufacturing facilities. Listed are the best machine learning models and their scores: A) XGBoost; B) KNN (K-Nearest Neighbors) and C) Random Forests.

4.2 Machine Learning Model for Quality (Q)

The quality score in industrial manufacturing sites should ideally be 100%, as expected in each production. There would be no compromise regarding the quality factor. This will enhance the overall equipment effectiveness score (OEE). In intelligent factories (Ritika, 2020), machine learning and AI could bring the most relevant qualitative factors as high as expected. It also considers data from business processes, smart meters, in-line sensors, IIOTs, IOTs, feedback from shop floor workers, manufacturing reporting, and quality control parameters from production sites. There are numerous advantages to using ML and AI tools, which will undoubtedly improve the capacity of smart factories (Gabahne, 2014). A few machine learning models could increase production capabilities and reduce the quality issue while supporting early fault prediction in connected devices and equipment. Visual anomaly detection detects defects and replaces manual efforts and process optimization by reducing the cycle times by 30%.

4.3 Machine Learning Model for Performance (Q)

Performance indicators and factors in production sites are critical when considering a better OEE score (Singh, 2013). It is the most effective method of monitoring the manufacturing process by observing the performance of equipment and devices in the field. Operating and idle time are the most important factors when considering the performance of the machines and equipment in production factories. We can improve the cycle time reduction in factories with the help of machine learning tools. In that case, the equipment's performance could quickly improve, and OEE can undoubtedly be better.

4.4 SAP OEE Supports in Manufacturing Sites

The SAP S/4 Digital solutions automate the manufacturing process effectiveness procedure, which is crucial in industrial manufacturing sites. The most well-known industrial indicator of total productive maintenance is OEE, which aids in measuring the vital elements in achieving availability, performance, and quality concerning the manufacturing process for specific goods and services. Inventory optimization is maintaining the proper amount of inventory to satisfy demand, function as a safety net in case of unforeseen disruption and prevent an unnecessary surplus. Inventory optimization is an agile approach that, at its finest, can anticipate and plan for risk and opportunity in addition to responding promptly to it. According to the SAP HANA solution, OEE (overall equipment effectiveness) evaluates equipment availability, production performance, and product quality elements to determine manufacturing productivity. By isolating and determining the root cause, OEE measurement and reporting are essential for attributing equipment-based losses to their source (s). Real-time and historical plant performance measurement and analysis are made possible by this component, which is part of the SAP MII core solution package. Utilizing popular manufacturing data sources, SAP OEE generates metrics that let you assess the equipment's performance and availability and the caliber of the commodities it produces.

5. Application of IOT and 6G for the Improvement of Production and OEE

Table 20.1 show the overall equipment effectiveness (OEE) is the benchmarking and baseline method to measure OEE and understand the utilization of a manufacturing operation or piece of equipment used in production factories. OEE is the most accurate way to understand the performance, capacity, and qualitative attributes of production units and calculate manufacturing productivity.

Table 20.1 Benchmarked OEE scores with applications of ML, QML and Digital Twins [4] [17]

OEE Scores	Benchmarks	Recommendations
100%	Perfect Production	Recommended to make a best practice
85%	World Class Scores	Absolutely recommended for long term goals
60%	Fair Discrete Manufacturing Agency	Highly recommended and best for industrial innovations
40%	Poor Score	Need serious improvements for digital solutions and AI, ML and Quantum Information sciences

Through instrumentation and analytics, the Internet of Things (IoT) assists manufacturing industry agencies in improving their OEE evaluation by providing a detailed understanding of equipment performance. Several of the critical factors of IoT-based industrial automation improve the OEE score:

(a) Capable of understanding and analyzing historical data related to maintenance planning, scheduling, and resource allocations in real-time.

(b) Advance notification of the predictive maintenance, failure notices, and downtime-related events at equipment and machines.

(c) Ability to lower the cost of labor, raw materials, and supplier costs and increase equipment availability to greater extents.

(d) Monitored and managed the production quality, availability, and performance of equipment in shop floor activities.

(e) Manage and monitor the industrial equipment, which helps the production process, calibration, temperature, speed, and production time of the machines.

(f) Better management of supply chain processes and the planning and operational activities of industrial manufacturing.

(g) Increase the OEE score effectively and in real-time.

6. Proposed Advanced Architecture in Digital Manufacturing Sites

Figure 20.4 depicts an advanced OEE architecture in smart factories that can be scaled up and deployed across manufacturing sites and are well-integrated with SAP Digital manufacturing cloud solutions. It also provides real-time integration with back-office functions (SAP S/4 HANA or legacy solutions). This will aid in managing innovative factory applications and shop floor activities, as well as providing a wide range of digital automation services in manufacturing facilities.

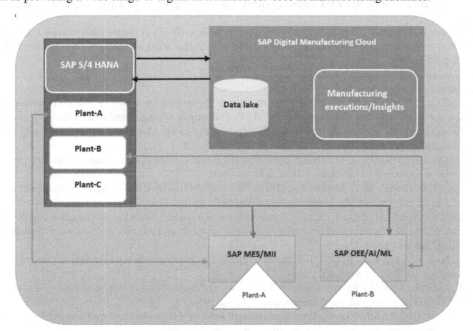

Fig. 20.4 SAP OEE advanced architecture diagram in industrial manufacturing sites

7. Conclusions

In the industrial revolution and smart manufacturing facilities, high-end enterprise resource planning systems like SAP S/4 Hana MES play a vital role and can manage the production efficiencies along with the high rate of OEE in industrial manufacturing sites. OEE score can be easily achieved with the help of the best machine learning tools and modeling them to gain the highest prediction score in real-time. The machine learning-based model could be the most effective, predictive, and more effective solution to support complex manufacturing problems and support the industry 4.0 revolutions and the decision-support processing in enterprise businesses in the production and supply chain industries. Our paper focuses more on the digital trends applicability to manufacturing and industrial solutions that could potentially save costs achieve the scope and understand the need for real-time effectiveness of OEE, qualitative factors, and production losses, as well as support to prevent breakdowns and preventive maintenance downtimes for the industrial equipment that is engaged in the production sites. We have also explained various ways to focus on and leverage the vital critical availabilities of manufacturing process sets and optimize the application of AI, ML, and quantum computing in production sites to gain the highest score of the OEE. It is demonstrated that using virtual sensor solutions and AI, ML-based IIOTs, and VS can reduce predictive maintenance, preventive maintenance, and machine downtime due to the goodness of a machine learning model (Djezeri, 2020; Kuo, 2011). ML can also help mitigate unfavorable production breakdowns by increasing equipment availability and effectiveness and predicting the best qualitative score most reliable for the production units.

REFERENCES

1. Abajo, N., Diez, A. Lobato, V. and Cuesta, S. (2004). ANN quality diagnostic models for packaging manufacturing: An industrial data mining case study. Proceedings of the 10th ACM SIGKDD International Conference on Knowledge Discovery and Data Mining, pp. 799–804.

2. Acosta, C., Héctor, P., Terán, C., Arteaga, O. and Terán, M. B. (2020). Machine learning in intelligent manufacturing system for optimization of production cost and overall effectiveness of equipment in fabrication models. J. Phys. Conf. Ser.

3. Afefy, I. H. (2013). Implementation of total productive maintenance and overall equipment effectiveness evaluation. Int. J. Mech. Mechatron. Eng. 13, pp. 69–75.

4. Senapati, B., Rawal, B.S. (2023). Adopting a Deep Learning Split-Protocol Based Predictive Maintenance Management System for Industrial Manufacturing Operations. In: Hsu, CH., Xu, M., Cao, H., Baghban, H., Shawkat Ali, A.B.M. (eds) Big Data Intelligence and Computing. DataCom 2022. Lecture Notes in Computer Science, vol 13864. Springer, Singapore. https://doi.org/10.1007/978-981-99-2233-8_2

5. Cabanillas D., Bonada F., Ventura R., Toni F., Evripidou V., Cartens L., et al (2013). A combination of knowledge and argumentation-based system for supporting injection mould design. In: Proceedings of 16th Catalan Congress of Artificial Intelligence (CCIA). Vic, Spain: IOS Press. pp. 293–296.

6. Corrales, L. C., Lambán, M. P., Korner, M. E. H. and Royo, J. (2020). Overall equipment effectiveness: Systematic literature review and overview of different approaches. Appl. Sci. 10, 6469.

7. Djeziri M. A., Benmoussa S. and Zio E. (2020). Artificial Intelligence Techniques for a Scalable Energy Transition. Review on Health Indices Extraction and Trend Modeling for Remaining Useful Life Estimation. Springer; Berlin/Heidelberg, Germany. pp. 183–223.

8. El Hassani, I., El Mazgualdi, C., Masrour, T. (2019). Artificial intelligence and machine learning to predict and improve efficiency in manufacturing industry. arXiv:1901.02256.

9. Gabahne L., Gupta M. and Zanwar D. (2014). Overall equipment effectiveness improvement: A case of injection molding machine. The International Journal of Engineering and Science (IJES). 3(8), pp. 1–10.

10. Huggett D. J. , Liao T. W., Wahab, M. A. and Okeil A. (2018). Prediction of friction stir weld quality without and with signal features. The International Journal of Advanced Manufacturing Technology. 95.

11. Kao, H. A., Hsieh, Y. S., Chen, C. H. and Lee, J. (2017). Quality prediction modeling for multistage manufacturing based on classification and association rule mining. In Proceedings of the 2nd International Conference on Precision Machinery and Manufacturing Technology (ICPMMT), Kenting, Taiwan, pp. 19–21.

12. Kim, A., Oh, K., Jung, J. Y. and Kim, B. (2018). Imbalanced classification of manufacturing quality conditions using cost-sensitive decision tree ensembles. Int. J. Comput. Integr. Manuf.

13. Kuo C., Chien C. and Chen J. (2011). Manufacturing intelligence to exploit the value of production and tool data to reduce cycle time. IEEE Transactions on Automation Science and Engineering. 8(1). pp. 103–111.

14. Nguyen, X. T. and Luu, Q. K. (2020). Factors affecting adoption of industry 4.0 by small and medium-sized enterprises: A case in Ho Chi Minh City, Vietnam. J. Asian Finance, Econ. Bus., vol. 7, no. 6, pp. 255–264.

15. Nurprihatin, F., Angely, M., Tannady, H. (2019). Total productive maintenance policy to increase effectiveness and maintenance performance using overall equipment effectiveness. J. Appl. Res. Ind. Eng. pp. 184–199.

16. Prasad A.M., Iverson L. R. and Liaw A. (2006). Newer classification and regression tree techniques: Bagging and random forests for ecological prediction. Ecosystems. 9: 181–199. DOI: 10.1007/s10021- 005-0054-1.

17. Biswaranjan Senapati, Bharat S. Rawal, Quantum Communication with RLP Quantum Resistant Cryptography in Industrial Manufacturing, Cyber Security and Applications, 2023, 100019, ISSN 2772-9184, https://doi.org/10.1016/j.csa.2023.100019

18. Purr S., Meinhard, J., Lipp, A., Werner, A., Ostermair, M. and Gluck, B. (2015). Stamping plant 4.0—Basics for the application of data mining methods in manufacturing car body parts. Key Engineering Materials. vol. 639, pp. 21–30.

19. Puvanasvaran A. P., Megat, H., Tang, S. H., Razali, M. M. and H. A. Magid (2010). Lean process management implementation through enhanced problem-solving capabilities. Journal of Industrial Engineering and Management. 3(3). pp. 447–493.

20. Rabie, A. (2000). A case study: Application of BasicMOST in a Lock's assembly. James Madison University Harrisonburg.

21. Rathi, R., Singh, M., Sabique, M., Al Amin, M., Saha, S. and Krishnaa, M. H. (2022). Identification of total productive maintenance barriers in Indian manufacturing industries. Mater. Today Proc. 2022, 50, pp. 736–742.

22. Riesbeck C. K., Schank R. C. Inside Case-Based Reasoning. Hillsdale, USA. Lawrence Erlbaum Associates.

23. A. M. Soomro et al., "Constructor Development: Predicting Object Communication Errors," *2023 IEEE International Conference on Emerging Trends in Engineering, Sciences and Technology (ICES&T)*, Bahawalpur, Pakistan, 2023, pp. 1–7, doi: 10.1109/ICEST56843.2023.10138846

24. B. Senapati, J. R. Talburt, A. Bin Naeem and V. J. R. Batthula, "Transfer Learning Based Models for Food Detection Using ResNet-50," *2023 IEEE International Conference on Electro Information Technology (eIT)*, Romeoville, IL, USA, 2023, pp. 224–229, doi: 10.1109/eIT57321.2023.10187288.

25. Naeem, A. B. ., Senapati, B. ., Chauhan, A. S. ., Makhija, M. ., Singh, A. ., Gupta, M. ., Tiwari, P. K. ., & Abdel-Rehim, W. M. F. . (2023). Hypothyroidism Disease Diagnosis by Using Machine Learning Algorithms. International Journal of Intelligent Systems and Applications in Engineering, 11(3), 368–373. Retrieved from https://ijisae.org/index.php/IJISAE/article/view/3178

26. Ritika, Farooqui, N. A. and Tyagi A. (2020). Data Mining and Fusion Techniques for Wireless Intelligent Sensor Networks. Handbook of Wireless Sensor Networks: Issues and Challenges in Current Scenario's. Advances in Intelligent Systems and Computing, vol 1132. Springer, Cham.

27. Rostami, H Dantan J. Y. and Homri L. (2015). Review of data mining applications for quality assessment in manufacturing industry: Support vector machines. Int. J. Metrol. Qual. Eng., vol. 6. no. 1. 401.

28. Shi, X., Schillings, P. and Boyd D. (2007). Applying artificial neural networks and virtual experimental design to quality improvement of two processes. International Journal of Production Research. vol. 42. no. 1.

29. Naeem, Awad Bin, Biswaranjan Senapati, Md. Sakiul Islam Sudman, Kashif Bashir, and Ayman E. M. Ahmed. 2023. "Intelligent Road Management System for Autonomous, Non-Autonomous, and VIP Vehicles" *World Electric Vehicle Journal* 14, no. 9: 238. https://doi.org/10.3390/wevj14090238

30. A. M. Soomro et al., "In MANET: An Improved Hybrid Routing Approach for Disaster Management," *2023 IEEE International Conference on Emerging Trends in Engineering, Sciences and Technology (ICES&T)*, Bahawalpur, Pakistan, 2023, pp. 1–6, doi: 10.1109/ICEST56843.2023.10138831

31. Singh R., Shah D. B., Gohil A. M. and Shah M. H. (2013). Overall equipment effectiveness (OEE) calculation—automation through hardware & software development. Procedia Engineering. 51: 579–584. DOI: 10.1016/j.proeng.2013.01.082.

32. Thakre, A. R., Jolhe, D. A. and Gawande, A.C. (2009). Minimization of engine assembly time by elimination of unproductive activities through 'MOST'. Second International Conference on Emerging Trends in Engineering and Technology (ICETET).

33. Ulutas, B. (2011). An application of SMED methodology. World Academy of Science, Engineering and Technology.

34. Wollschlaeger, M., Sauter, T. and Jasperneite, J. (2017). 'The future of industrial communication: Automation networks in the era of the Internet of Things and industry 4.0. IEEE Ind. Electron. Mag., vol. 11, no. 1, pp. 17–27.

Note: All the figures in this chapter were made by the author.

Advances in Computational Intelligence and its Applications (ICACIA-2023) – Dr. Sheikh Fahad Ahmad et al. (eds)
© 2024 Taylor & Francis Group, London, ISBN 978-1-032-78612-4

Hashgraph and Fog Computing Based Novel Framework for Online Teaching-Learning and Content Delivery

21

Naveen Tewari[1], Sandeep Budhani[2], Mukesh Joshi[3]
School of Computing, Graphic Era Hill University,
Bhimtal, Uttarakhand, India

Arun kumar Rai[4]
Department of CSE, Graphic Era Hill University,
Bhimtal, Uttarakhand, India

Pankaj Kumar[5]
Graphic Era Deemed to be University,
Dehradun, Uttarakhand, India

ABSTRACT—Disclosed are a Hashgraph & Fog based secured Online Learning & Content Delivery System and method for School Teaching. The system consists of numerous schools, numerous fog node devices with networking and processing capabilities, and a fog server. The fog nodes are set up to be connected to classrooms, teachers, and students in order to produce and receive online lesson materials. The fog node devices are connected to a fog layer and used to process and store data through a hashgraph network after receiving instructional materials from teachers. To ensure that all students may access the data, the fog node devices process it at the fog layer using fog computing before distributing it over the Hashgraph network. The numerous fog node devices transmit their processed data through the hashgraph network to the fog server and cloud data centres.

KEYWORDS—Fog computing, Hashgraph, E-Learning, Online teaching, Local area network, Wi-Fi

1. Introduction

A secure online learning and content delivery system based on hashgraphs and fog, as well as a method for school teaching, are disclosed. The system consists of a number of schools, a number of fog node devices with processing and networking capabilities, and a fog server. The fog nodes are set up to be connected to schools/teachers and students in order to generate and receive online teaching content. The fog node devices collect teaching materials from instructors and transfer them across a hashgraph network for processing and storage using a fog layer. The fog node devices fog compute on the data at the fog layer before disseminating it over the hashgraph network so that all students can access it. The hashgraph network is used by the various fog node devices to transmit processed data to the fog server and cloud data centres. The current invention broadly pertains to the field of hashgraph network and fog computing technology, and more specifically to online learning and content delivery systems for school teaching based on hashgraph and fog computing technology.

The Indian Patent Office has sought this evaluation in a similar manner for the patent with application number 202111032281.

[1]navtewari@gmail.com, [2]sandeepbudhani13@gmail.com, [3]mukul.san@gmail.com, [4]arunrai.dei@gmail.com, [5]Pankaj465@gmail.com

DOI: 10.1201/9781003488682-21

2. Literature Review

Roger P. Karrer, Antonio Pescapé, and Thomas Huehn's article "Challenges in Second-Generation Wireless Mesh Networks" [1] is published in the EURASIP Journal on Wireless Communications and Networking and predicts how a mesh WiFi network will be utilised to obtain data from the internet. They show that the WiFi network can be used to cover large areas such as an entire city. But they arise an issue of security in that network concerning the privacy of the user.

In a paper titled "A Novel Fog Computing Based Architecture to Improve the Performance in Content Delivery Networks" [2] that was published in Wireless Communications and Mobile Computing, Fatimah Alghamdi et al. provide an architecture for using fog in content delivery networks (CDN). They describe a routing strategy based on ICN (Information-centric Networking). For content delivery, they also examine the Mesh network.

"Methods and apparatus for packetized content delivery via a content delivery network" [3] are described in U.S. patent application US20190312915A1 submitted by Michael L. LaJoie et al. Methods and equipment for packetized content distribution over a content delivery network, such as video, audio, and data. According to one implementation, the content is packetized using the Internet Protocol (IP) and sent by a service provider to its subscribers through both managed and unmanaged networks. This allows for delivery of the content at any time, in any location, and via any chosen user device. The content that is delivered may come from a variety of sources, such as the Internet, the service provider, outside content providers (such as networks or studios), the subscriber(s), or other sources. By utilising common control and service functions within the network, the ability to integrate or combine services is made feasible, giving the service provider and subscriber more service and commercial opportunities. It is possible to move content delivery sessions from one device to another. A client-side architecture based on gateways and an infrastructure for network-based user interfaces are also provided.

Christopher Edward Struttmann submitted U.S. patent application US10121019B2 [4] that details a method for storing file differentials in a distributed blockchain. It describes a process that involves receiving a request to write a new version of a document to a tamper-evident, immutable data repository, determining that the new version of the document differs from the previous version of the document, and then responding by storing the difference between the old and new versions of the document in the tamper-evident, immutable data repository.

The above publication and patents are published showing that WiFi can be used as a medium of communication in the City wise network. Fog computing has the capability of delivering content more speedily, accurately and with low latency via a wifi network. But they all show their concern for securing content and user privacy.

In this regard, our invention shows a way of securing users with the help of the Hashgraph network. This algorithm can process almost 2.5 lack transactions per second, which makes it a fast content delivery solution. Hashgraph employs a consensus protocol that builds a directed graph using rumour history. Security is provided by Hashgraph using the asynchronous Byzantine Fault Tolerance (aBFT) consensus process [5]. This algorithm effectively handles and blocks many attacks, including DDoS (Distributed Denial of Service) and Man-in-the-Middle attacks, ensuring secure communication. If a user may submit a transaction to the network at all, a fair consensus method ensures that the transaction will be accepted by the network and that the order in which it was received will be fair. Hashgraph ensures that the consensus order accurately reflects the real order transactions that are received by the network. In other words, hashgraph guarantees both fair ordering and fair access [6].

3. Problem Definition

Many school students from rural and remote places and from low-income homes still face significant barriers to taking online courses, including inadequate or no internet access and expensive mobile data. Some of the major issues are-

- *Poor Connectivity:* This is the main issue in internet-based learning. Poor and slow connectivity in rural and urban areas creating trouble in providing online teaching.
- *The expensive price of Internet data:* Expensive cost of Internet data is one of the main issues that is to be addressed by the system providing education. As most of the peoples in India are from a lower middle class, they cannot afford the high cost of internet data. Therefore these students are not able to take part in online education.
- *Data size:* Due to high data cost, students are forced to limit their data size to lower possibility, due to which they are not able to attend all of the classes/video lectures, and also not able to download lecture content. Data gets over within 1-2 classes. They have to use internet optimally.

4. Proposed Architecture

Our system provides the solution to all the problems stated above. Our system is based on the City level municipal Wi-Fi network, that works without the internet.

- *Connectivity:* This local network provides better connectivity than the internet with fast data transfer rates.
- *Cost:* This system is based on the Hadera Hashgraph network over Fog nodes & server, which provides a low-cost network. All the students and teachers are connected with the network with the help of Wi-Fi, so do not have to pay for that. The initial setup cost can be bear by the school authorities and government jointly.
- *Data size:* There is no issue of data size in our system as it only provides the network and data is freely available to all connected students without any limit.

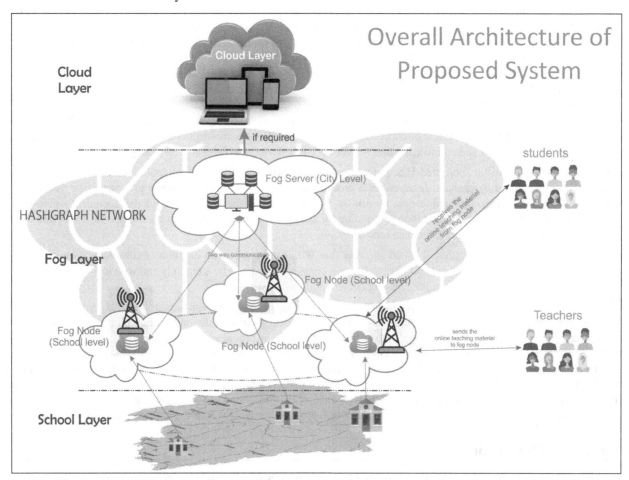

Fig. 21.1 Overall architecture

Apart from the above advantages, there are many other benefits of our system as discussed earlier - High speed, high security, low maintenance better connectivity, low cost, etc.

4.1 The System Architecture

1. *School Layer:* All the Schools in a city are connected to their Fog node individually. They can be connected via cable or Wi-Fi; it depends on the distance between the Fog node and the School.
2. *Fog Layer:* Fog Layer consists of different Fog nodes and a Fog Server.
   (a) The fog node is a small server (equipped with gateways & routers) with processing, storage & networking capability. This will also act as a small virtual data storage device. It will connect to all students and teachers and provide a non-wired (Wi-Fi) communication medium between them.

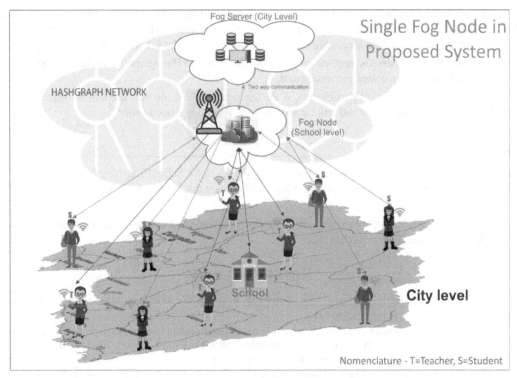

Fig. 21.2 Single Fog node architecture

- There is a single Fog node available for each school. The system is comprised of many fog nodes connected via a fog server. These fog nodes can be inhabited at the school level.
- It is a virtualized system.

(b) All the fog nodes are connected to the Fog server.

- The Fog server is used for load balancing and providing additional functionalities to the fog node.
- Secured network communication via Hashgraph will be applied and monitored by the Fog server.
- Fog server can also act as a long time storage device. The data that can be further used in the future by fog node/ students/ teachers can be stored in the Fog server.

3. *Cloud Layer:* The system has a communication link to the cloud server. This possibility (cloud server) is optional in our framework. This system is only responsible to provide communication in a private network at the city level, so it will work without the internet [7]. If required the fog server can be connected to the cloud server for storage purposes (for example if a school has a branch in another city and they want to share their content with that branch also then the cloud layer will be helpful to share and store content). This layer will be accessed via the internet [9].

4. *Hashgraph Network:* The Hashgraph is a distributed information structure that keeps up a developing list of information among a lot of network peers. It includes a consensus algorithm that is very fast, stable, & secure with low latency. Hashgraph is useful in this architecture because of its distributed nature. The network created with the Hashgraph is inexpensive, with 100% efficiency and fast throughput.

4.2 Working Flow

1. Schools, Teachers, and students are connected with a private Hashgraph & Fog computing based network for their Teaching & Learning purposes.

- Teachers/School provides the learning material via WiFi/ wired medium to a Fog Node which is responsible for creating the network (All the resources are shared with the help of this Fog Node).
- Students will be connected to their School's Fog node via WiFi and then retrieve the information shared with them by their Teachers/School.

- There are numbers of applications that can be installed and used for online teaching like Microsoft Teams/ Google Meet/ Cicso Webex/ Zoom etc. For the purposes of online communication and teaching, these programmes are placed on the fog server and are accessible to teachers, students, and the school via the fog node [8].
- Data shared between the persons/ applications is communicated via Hashgraph's Gossip protocol. The information is well secured, fast, and two way communicated.

2. After sharing of data among different participants, if the teacher/ school wants to store that information for further use, then it can be stored in the Fog server and will be accessed via Fog node when needed.

5. Conclusion

The proposed architecture "Online Learning and Content Delivery System for School Teaching based on Hash graph and Fog Computing Technology" is a proposing unique concept with the advantage that it provides better connectivity than the internet with fast data transfer rates.

Suggestion turns out to be a low-cost network where all the students and teachers can be connected with the network with the help of Wi-Fi and therefore do not have to pay for that

REFERENCES

1. Karrer, R.P., Pescapé, A. & Huehn, T. Challenges in Second-Generation Wireless Mesh Networks. J Wireless Com Network 2008, 274790 (2008). https://doi.org/10.1155/2008/274790
2. Alghamdi, F., Mahfoudh, S., & Barnawi, A. (2019). A novel fog computing-based architecture to improve the performance in content delivery networks. Wireless Communications and Mobile Computing, 2019, 1–13. https://doi.org/10.1155/2019/7864094
3. US20190312915A1 - Methods and apparatus for packetized content delivery over a content delivery network - Google patents. (2019, October 10). Google Patents. https://patents.google.com/patent/US20190312915A1/en?oq=US20190312915A1+
4. US10121019B2 - Storing differentials of files in a distributed blockchain - Google patents. (2018, November 6). Google Patents. https://patents.google.com/patent/US10121019B2/en?oq=US10121019B2+
5. N. Tewari and Dr. M. K. Sharma "Conceptual Framework for cloud supported E-Governance Services" IOSR Journal of Computer Engineering vol. 16 no. 1 pp. 134–145 2014.
6. N. Tewari and G. Datt, "Towards FoT (Fog-of-Things) enabled Architecture in Governance: Transforming e-Governance to Smart Governance," 2020 International Conference on Intelligent Engineering and Management (ICIEM), London, UK, 2020, pp. 223–227, doi: 10.1109/ICIEM48762.2020.9160037.
7. R. S. Bisht, S. Jain and N. Tewari, "Study of Wearable IoT devices in 2021: Analysis & Future Prospects," 2021 2nd International Conference on Intelligent Engineering and Management (ICIEM), London, United Kingdom, 2021, pp. 577–581, doi: 10.1109/ICIEM51511.2021.9445334.
8. M. Joshi, N. Tewari and S. K. Budhani, "Security Challenges in Implementing a Secured Hybrid Cloud Model for e-Health Services," 2020 9th International Conference System Modeling and Advancement in Research Trends (SMART), Moradabad, India, 2020, pp. 3–7, doi: 10.1109/SMART50582.2020.9337096.
9. N. Tewari and G. Datt, "A Systematic Review of Security Issues and challenges with Futuristic Wearable Internet of Things (IoTs)," 2021 International Conference on Technological Advancements and Innovations (ICTAI), Tashkent, Uzbekistan, 2021, pp. 319–323, doi: 10.1109/ICTAI53825.2021.9673353.

Note: All the figures in this table were made by the author.

Advances in Computational Intelligence and its Applications (ICACIA-2023) – Dr. Sheikh Fahad Ahmad et al. (eds)
© *2024 Taylor & Francis Group, London, ISBN 978-1-032-78612-4*

A Review of Churn Prediction in Telecommunication Industry

22

Aditi Chaudhary[1], Ali Rizvi[2],
Navneet Kumar[3], Ashish Kumar Mishra[4]
Department of I, T., REC Ambedkar Nagar, Uttar Pradesh, India

ABSTRACT—In today's scenario, the business environment has become very competitive. Business opportunities are decreasing day by day and becoming highly saturated. One such field is the telecommunication. There are enormous challenges in this field. These challenges are very complex because of high availability of service providers in a very competitive environment. Therefore, retaining customers has become extremely difficult. In general, the acquisition cost of customers exceeds the retention cost of pre-existing customers by five to ten folds [32]. Hence, the telecom industries have common consensus of taking essential steps to stop the customers from discontinuing the services. This will stabilize their growth and increase their overall market value. Various data mining methodologies have been proposed and utilized by several researchers for predicting the churned customers using record of heterogenous customers. In this paper, a review of the various types of existing customer data which is available in data sets that are openly available, the various predictive models and performance metrics which are used in the prediction of customer churn in telecom industry has been conducted. A real time survey of approximately 500 users has also been conducted to identify the major factors affecting customer churn in telecom industry.

KEYWORDS—Survey Churn prediction, Churn prediction, Telecom Churn, Churn prediction model

I. Introduction

The telecommunication industry suffers from multiple drawbacks which cause a lot of inconvenience to customers. Customer churn is a major problem that is occurring in the telecommunications sector in real time. Customer churn occurs when the user/customer is unsatisfied with the services offered to them. This dissatisfaction leads them to quit their current telecom subscription and switch to another one. The customers know what they want from their telecom service. If telecom companies know what the customer wants, the churn rate can be reduced greatly. The telecommunications industry experiences the highest churn rate so, it becomes very crucial to focus on retaining existing customers. A lot of attention is required to retain existing customers. It is because the acquisition cost of a new customer is five to ten times more than the retention of an old customer [32]. The churn rate mostly depends on the age and occupation of the customer. The telecom industry can be benefitted if they customize their services according to customers' age and occupation. Therefore, the motivation behind the review was to recognize the shortcomings of telecom companies. So that they can take necessary steps to remove these shortcomings to optimize their profit. A process called Customer Churn Prediction is used to determine whether a customer will churn (discontinue the services in the near future) or not. This prediction helps in finding the reasons of customer dissatisfaction so that the companies can take necessary steps to prevent the customer from leaving. With the help of churn prediction companies can avert decrease in profits that occur due to customer churn.

---

[1]aditi.it19-23@recabn.ac.in, [2]ali.it19-23@recabn.ac.in, [3]navneet.it19-23@recabn.ac.in, [4]akmishra@recabn.ac.in

DOI: 10.1201/9781003488682-22

Machine Learning algorithms can be used for predicting customer churn. These algorithms can be considered a powerful tool for identifying customers that are most inclined to leave. The first step towards building an accurate predictor algorithm is to establish a valid source of customer data. Then, in the next step feature extraction is performed on data to build a predictor model.

Factors that impact customer churn are determined using the latest customer data. This data has been collected by performing a real-time survey. From the survey, it has been found that the major factor affecting churn is Internet Facilities. These factors depend greatly on the age and occupation of customers. The relationship between age group and churn factors has also been established in the survey. A review of existing works on customer churn prediction considering three different factors has also been done. The considered factors are Datasets, Methods, and Metrics. Different existing algorithms have been analysed and ranked according to their accuracy. The accuracy of the SVM-Poly model has been found the highest among over 20 methods.

Hierarchy for customer churn prediction has been shown in Fig. 22.1.

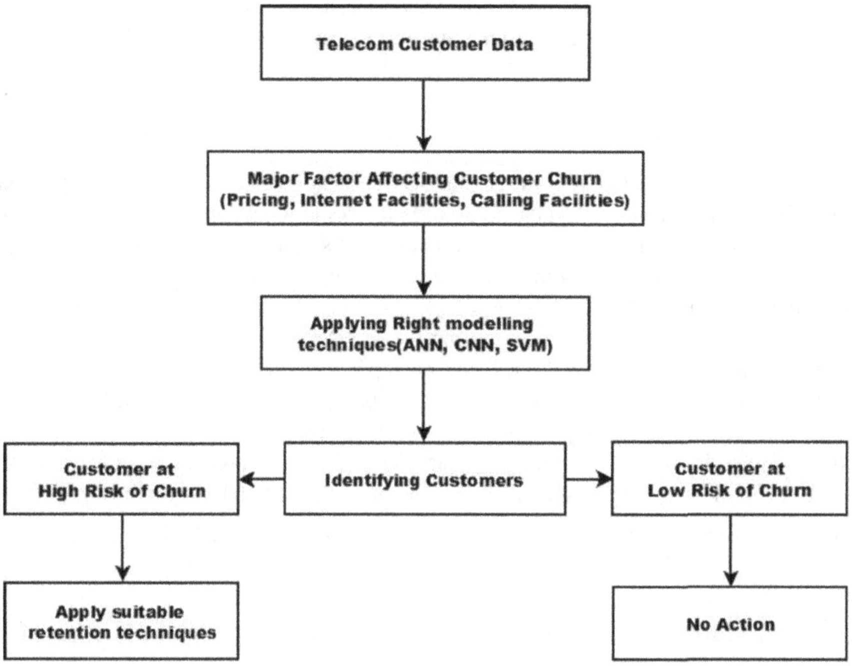

Fig. 22.1 Churn prediction hierarchy

The rest of the paper is organized as follows. In Section 2, a review of pre-existing techniques has conducted and their accuracy have been compared. Section 3 contains the details of a real time survey for factors affecting churn. Different research issues and challenges have been identified in Section 4. Finally, Section 5 concludes the paper.

2. Literature Review

In this segment, past works on customer attrition and its prediction are surveyed to compare their performances on the basis of accuracy. In subsection A, detail of datasets used is provided while in subsection B, the detail of existing algorithms along with their comparison is presented.

2.1 Datasets

The In the literature, various categories of data sets have been used. First category is the Cell2Cell dataset that is available on Kaggle [2] and also on website "Centre for Customer Relationship Management Duke University's". This dataset is widely used by several researchers [1][2][3][4][5]. The Cell2Cell dataset is comprised of 70,831 instances and 75 attributes. The second category dataset is the IBM Telco dataset. This data set is comprised of 21 attributes and 7043 rows. It can also be found easily on Kaggle. It is widely used in finding an accurate relationship between the churn and actions of the customer. It is also being used by numerous researchers [30], [31]. The third category of dataset is the PAKDD 2006 dataset. The PAKDD dataset was provided as part of the PAKDD 2006 data mining competition. An Asian company that successfully launched a 3G mobile telecommunication network released this dataset. It consists of 24,000 customers. Each customer is described by 250 attributes and a class label that is 2G or 3G. The training set consists of 18000 records and the test set consists of records of 6,000 customers. Among this, 3150 customers were churners and the remaining 20,850 were non-churners, in both the training and test set [26]. The fourth category is the KDD Cup dataset. The KDD Cup dataset was provided as part of the KDD Cup 2009 data mining competition2. Orange Labs, a European telecom company released this dataset. Orange Labs developed its own prediction models as part of its CRM system for identifying customers which have churned. The small version of this dataset consists a total of 50,000 records including training and test sets. Both the small and large versions of the dataset have both numerical and categorical variables. But, due to privacy reasons, the actual names of variables are not revealed in this dataset. For the large dataset, the first 14,740 variables are numerical in nature and the last 260 are categorical. In the small dataset, the first 190 variables are numerical and the last 40 are categorical. 3,672 customers are churners and the remaining 46,328 are non-churners [26]. Lastly, the CrowdAnalytix dataset has also been used. The CrowdAnalytix dataset is a public dataset provided by the CrowdAnalytix community. This dataset was a part of the churn prediction competition. The real name of the telecom company is kept anonymous. There are 20 predictor variables mostly about the customer usage patterns. There are 3333 records in the dataset, out of all the records, 483 are churners and the remaining 2850 are non-churners. Thus, the ratio of churners to non-churners in this dataset is 14% [26].

The IBM dataset and the Cell2Cell dataset have a dependent variable called churn. This variable signifies whether the customer has churned or not. The attributes in both the datasets have been divided into two forms. These forms are the categorial features in object class and the continuous features in numeric class [6]. The characteristics of datasets is presented in Table 22.1.

Table 22.1 Telecom datasets and their properties

Dataset	Total Count of Consumers	Total Count of Features	Count of Non-Churners	Count of Churners	Percentage of Non-Churners	Percentage of Churners	Region
PAKDD 2006 [26], [27], [28]	24,000	250	20,850	3,150	83	13	Asian
KDD Cup 2009 small [8], [26], [29]	50,000	15,000	46,328	3,672	92.5	7.5	Europe
Cell2Cell [1], [2], [3], [4], [5], [26]	70,831	75	50,326	20,505	71	29	USA
Crowd Analytix [26]	3,333	20	2,850	483	86	14	NA
Crowd Analytix [26]	7,043	21	5,177	1,866	73.5	26.5	California, USA

2.2 Algorithms Used

In this subsection several existing algorithms have been compared as presented in Table 22.2.

Support Vector Machine (SVM)

SVMs are generally referred to as Support Vector Networks, and were proposed by Boser, Vapnik and Guyon [11]. These are supervised learning models. Associated learning algorithms are used in SVMs. These algorithms recognize patterns by analysing the data and they are often used in regression analysis and classification. The concept of structural risk minimization (SRM) is utilized in SVM. Whenever there are data items of higher dimension, kernel functions are used by SVM. How to find the best kernel function is still a problem of research? In the problem of customer churn prediction, SVM outdoes Decision Tree (DT). In some cases, SVM performs better than Artificial Neural Networks (ANN). The performance of SVM is primarily driven by the type of data and its transformation [7].

Stacking-Based Ensemble Model

Stacking-based ensemble model is the merging of several models. The merging technique can improve the performance of the network by using the combination of various clustering methods. These clustering methods can be k medoids, k-means, and some random clustering. These methods are used with some other clustering techniques like Random Forest (RF), Decision Tree (DT), Gradient Boosted Tree, Deep Learning classifier and Naive Bayes classifier. These methods can be integrated with some of the ensemble ML algorithms such as boosting, bagging, stacking and voting [8].

Table 22.2 Previously used algorithms with their accuracy

Serial Number	Algorithm	Accuracy (%)
1	SVM-POLY [7]	96.85
2	SVM-RBF [7]	96.05
3	Stacking-Based Ensemble Model [8]	96
4	DT-C5.0 [7]	95.09
5	BPN [7]	95.09
6	LMT [15]	94.75
7	FT [15]	94.42
8	PSO-FSSA [8]	94.08
9	XG BOOST [20]	93.01
10	SVM Confusion Matrix [17]	91.56
11	Random Forest [15]	90.97
12	LR Confusion Matrix [17]	90.66
13	NB [15]	88.24
14	DS [15]	86.56
15	Hybrid Firefly Algorithm [8]	86.38
16	Logistic Regression [20]	85.34
17	Logit Boost [20]	85.19
18	FW-ECP [8]	84.9
19	AdaBoost [20]	84
20	Decision Tree [16]	80.14
21	KNN [15]	83.38
22	Cat Boost [16]	81.8
23	CNN [20]	75.4
24	LSTM [15]	72.7
25	GP AdaBoost	68.19

Decision Trees (DT)

Decision Trees are structures which are tree-shaped that represent sets of decisions capable of producing classification rules associated with a particular data set [9]. As Linoff and Berry noted "a structure that can be used to divide up a large collection of records into successively smaller sets of records by applying a sequence of simple decision rules" [10]. More sophisticated names given for these types of tree-based models are Regression Trees or Classification Trees. In a DT, class labels are represented by trees and combination of features. The trees and combination of features generate those class labels which are represented by branches. Decision trees are not very effective at obtaining non-linear relationships among attributes that are complex. However, in the dilemma of prediction of customer churn, a DT's accuracy can be pretty high, according to the form of the data [7].

Artificial Neural Networks

The Artificial Neural Network derives its name from the human brain. The brain consists of multiple neurons connected to each other. In a similar fashion, the ANN also has multiple neurons that are connected on various different layers. The ANN is a branch of artificial intelligence and aims to arrive at decisions like the human brain. An ANN is first trained and then it can make predictions. One of the best qualities of ANN is that it can work on any kind of data and is not restricted to a specific type, unlike other machine learning algorithms, Authors in paper [13] have shown that ANNs exceed Decision Trees in terms of performance. An ANN with multiple layers is known as a Multi-Layered Perceptron (MLP). The MLP makes use of the Back Propagation Algorithm to generate the output. It monitors how much our generated output differs from the desired output and adjusts the weights accordingly. Moreover, it was illustrated experimentally that the Neural Networks model outperforms Logistic Regression (LR) and also the C5.0 for predicting customer churn [12], [7].

Logistic Model Tree (LMT)

The LMT is an algorithm that uses the supervised learning technique. It is used for the classification of data. This Logistic Model Tree is a combination of Logistic Regression (LR) and Decision Tree (DT). This resultant algorithm provides outstanding predictions while maintaining an interpretable structure [14]. Logistic Regression is an unrivalled algorithm when it comes to establishing a relationship or dependency between the independent and dependent variables. But it's inefficient in resolving nonlinear data. Thus, it is combined with a decision tree as decision trees are excellent at finding a nonlinear relationship between dependent and independent variables. The output received at the leaf node of the decision tree is transformed into categorial form and then that data is deployed in logistic regression. The LMT structure has a collection of leaf nodes T and a set or collection of non-leaf nodes N [15]. The Logistic Model Tree can perform better and provides more accuracy than logistic regression and decision trees.

Functional Tree Algorithm

Functional Trees (FT) are a combination of multivariate Decision Trees and discriminant functions. These are combined using the concept of constructive induction. Functional Trees can also be defined as the generalized version of multivariate trees that have their features at leaves and decision nodes. The Functional Tree algorithm forms a classification tree by combining the node and leaf of a tree. As the dataset moves across the tree from root to leaf, the dataset's assortment of features keeps getting expanded at every decision node. This is achieved with the use of inbuilt functions. The direction/path of the dataset is determined with the use of the decision test of the node. In the end, the dataset is labelled as a leaf node with the help of a function or leaf-related constant. Functional Trees are used in tasks that involve the prediction of class labels of the provided dataset. What makes a Decision Tree different from a Functional Tree is that the Decision Tree divides the dataset into nodes by differentiating that value with a constant. On the other hand, a Functional Tree utilizes LR for the division of nodes (also called oblique split) and leaf prediction [15]. Thus, it can be used in the customer attrition problem.

CatBoost Classifier

CatBoost, commonly referred to as Categorial Boosting, is extensively used for classification and regression analysis. It was developed by Yandex and apart from classification and regression, it is also used in forecasting and recommendation systems. It applies gradient boost on Decision Trees. CatBoost provides quick predictions in comparison to Decision Trees. CatBoost can handle all kinds of available data but it works exceptionally well for categorical data. It can produce accurate results even after training on less amount of data. In other algorithms, the data needs to be pre-processed and then converted into numerical form so that a particular algorithm can be deployed. When it comes to CatBoost, we are not required to execute this conversion. It doesn't incorporate all of the statistical estimations for pre-processing of data [16].

Logistic Regression

LR is a supervised learning algorithm that is used to predict the value of the dependent variable. This is done by utilizing the independent values. The output produced by LR is probabilistic in nature. LR maps the output in the form of probability with the help of the sigmoid function. This sigmoid function converts the real value into a different value which is between 0 and 1.

The equation given below is the equation for Logistic Regression. The LHS is known as the odds ratio which is the probability of an event taking place divided by the probability of the event not taking place. It is shown in Eq. (1).

$$\log[w/(1-w)] = \gamma_0 + \gamma_1 x \tag{1}$$

In general, the values which are calculated by the sigmoid function are classified as category 1 if they are greater than or equal to 0.5 or category 0 if they are less than 0.5. The main issue with logistic regression is that result may often be subjected to overfitting. When it comes to churn prediction LR is an excellent tool as it accurately predicts which person or customer is likely to leave the organization. Other than that, it is actively utilized in medical field as a means of predicting diseases. Logistic Regression is advantageous because the results are easily interpreted and can be applied to both continuous and categorical variables [17].

XGBoost

It is a machine learning algorithm that is developed on the basis of a decision tree combined with the concept of gradient boosting. It was developed at the University of Washington. It is an optimal machine learning algorithm that offers extensive flexibility as it can utilize multiple cores of the CPU simultaneously. It is quite capable of managing unknown values and it has the function of cross-validating models while in development mode. This feature minimizes the case of overfitting. Gradient descent is deployed to locate the minima and to bring down the value of the loss function [16].

Logit Boost

It is a machine learning algorithm that is developed on the basis of a decision tree combined with the concept of gradient boosting. It was developed at the University of Washington. It is an optimal machine learning algorithm that offers extensive flexibility as it can utilize multiple cores of the CPU simultaneously. It is quite capable of managing unknown values and it has the function of cross-validating models while in development mode. This feature minimizes the case of overfitting. Gradient descent is deployed to locate the minima and to bring down the value of the loss function [16].

AdaBoost

AdaBoost is also referred to as an adaptive boosting algorithm. It is an ensemble method used in machine learning. It transforms weak classifiers into a single robust classifier. This algorithm works by assigning equal weights to all points and then it assigns a higher value of weight to misclassified points. In this way, higher emphasis is placed on wrongly classified items. AdaBoost is mostly used with decision trees with only one level [19]. It is used in classification problems.

Convolutional Neural Network (CNN)

It is a special kind of Artificial Neural Network (ANN) that is used for the analysis of data using a supervised learning algorithm. CNN is extensively used in analysing images and used to recognize objects in an image. Other than that it is used in pattern recognition and video auditing as well. It is also used to classify data that is one-dimensional. Stacked auto-encoders is a deep learning method that is unsupervised. This method is developed by taking multiple auto-encoders and stacking them together including one input layer, one hidden layer, and one output layer [20].

Random Forest (RF)

Random Forest works with an approach called divide and conquer. It uses the random subspace as a methodology. In this approach, a number of trees are created and each DT is trained by the selection of any random sample of attributes from the predictor attribute set. All the decision trees mature to their maximum length based on the parameters or attributes that are present. The dataset used for each decision tree is a subset of a single dataset. The final decision is made by taking the average of all the outputs from the decision trees. This increases the accuracy and overcomes the issue of overfitting. It is able to handle a lot of input data set with numerous data values (thousands) with no deletion. Moreover, it is can handle any values that are absent inside the data set which is used for training the model [16].

Naïve Bayes Classifier (NB Classifier)

NB Classifier uses an approach that is probabilistic. In this approach, none of the vector features are considered dependent on any other vector feature. Bayesian-type classifiers consider that each feature's value has some influence on the class that is independent [21]. NB Classifier is supervised and applies Bayes theorem. This Naïve feature simplifies computation. In simpler terms, it means that customer churn, which is a feature, is independent of all the other features present in the class. It is in no way influenced by other features of the class. The NB fails when it comes to computing large data sets [16].

Hybrid Firefly

A large number of comparisons leads to increased computation. This leads to inefficiency. To solve this problem Hybrid Firefly framework was devised. Hybrid Firefly takes the best features of the Firefly Algorithm and Differential Evolution. We can begin the classification process by building the search space. The firefly population which was originally generated is equally partitioned in the search space. The distribution of fireflies is performed arbitrarily. Each firefly's position is recorded and their initial intensities are identified based on their cartesian distance from test data [22].

PSO-FSSA

PSO and neighbourhood cleaning rule-based technique used to carry out customer churn prediction is proposed in [24]. Another technique that is similar to using Random Forest and PSO was proposed in [25]. These techniques have proved to be very costly and time inefficient. The cost and efficiency are significantly impacted when they were used to analyse churn by performing operations on telecom churn data which is massive in size. y, PSO incorporates with feature selection as its basic pre-processing mechanism (PSO-FS), PSO embedded with simulated annealing (PSO-SA) and also, PSO with Feature Selection combined with Simulated Annealing (PSO-FSSA) [23].

3. Real-time Survey for Factors Affecting Customer Churn

The most important problem in telecommunication sector is finding out the factors that cause the customers to churn. A real time survey has been conducted from 02/09/22 till 10/09/22 to find the root cause of churn in telecommunication industry. This section consists of 3 sub sections. In Sub-Section A, the objectives of the survey have been presented. Sub-section B describes the procedure that was used to conduct the survey. Data Analysis from the survey has been done in Sub-Section C.

3.1 Objectives of the Survey

Following are the major objectives of the survey conducted:

(i) To find the major factors impacting the customer churn.

(ii) To inquire about the needs of the customers and what they are expecting from their service provider.

(iii) To identify the necessary steps for the service providers to reduce customer churn.

3.2 Procedure

The instrument of survey is Google forms. It was circulated among 4 categories of customers. These categories are Student, Working Professional, Business Owner and Senior Citizen. It consisted of 6 questions to determine what factors contribute towards telecom churn.

The questions in the survey are:

(i) Which group/ category do you belong to?

(ii) Gender

(iii) What is your current service provider?

(iv) Which type of plan do you prefer?

(v) Are you satisfied with your current telecom services?

(vi) What is the most important factor for you to decide your sim card?

Approximately 500 responses have been received.

3.3 Data Analysis

From the responses received, factors affecting customer churn have been analysed.

These four factors are:

1. Internet Facilities
2. Pricing
3. Call facilities
4. Customer service

These four user categories which is given in the form -

1. Student
2. Senior Citizen
3. Working Professional
4. Business Owner

After analysis, it is found that the most affecting factor is the internet facilities as presented in Fig. 22.4.

The designed google form used for real time survey can be found on the link below: "https://docs.google.com/forms/d/e/1FAI pQLSdf06xd7wN5ZbIbZyKr1Jm65rbZv0n7pQSLml6eSlcNdR_9KQ/viewform" [34].

Category wise distribution of responses are shown in Fig. 22.3. The sample size comprises majorly of people belonging to the 'Student' category.

Major factor for people while deciding their service provider on the basis of their category:

- Student – Internet Facilities
- Senior Citizen – Call Facilities

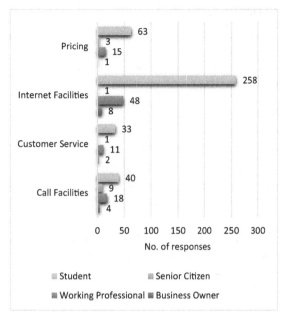

Fig. 22.2 Responses based on user preferences

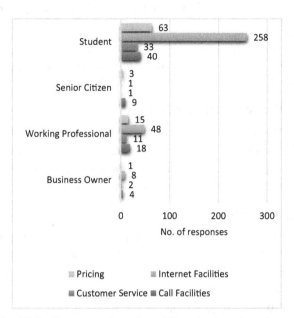

Fig. 22.3 Responses based on different categories of users

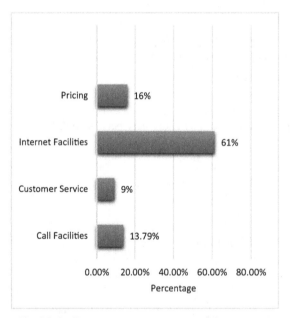

Fig. 22.4 Percentage representation of responses

- Working Professional – Internet Facilities
- Business Owner – Internet Facilities

Responses of the customers were in accordance to the graph in Fig. 22.4.

As presented in Fig. 22.4, Internet Facilities are the most impacting factor influencing telecommunication churn. The customers want better internet facilities at affordable price. According to this real time survey, the service providers can decide the require steps so that they can focus on the factor shown in Fig. 22.4 to reduce customer churn.

As presented in Fig. 22.4, Percentage of factors contributing towards churn:

- Internet Facilities – 61.1%
- Pricing – 16%
- Call Facilities – 13.79%
- Customer Services – 9%

4. Different Research Issues and Challenges

Customer churn is a major problem that is occurring in the telecommunications sector in real-time. The churn occurs when the user/customer is unsatisfied with the services offered to them. It is a problem that still has room for further improvements because there are some factors which remain unanalysed. Certain existing models discussed in this paper have a scope of improvement. Few possible research directions are pointed out as below:

- The performance of these models can be improved by changing the features, alteration of data cleaning process, using a combination of models, etc.
- To the best of our knowledge there is need of training with a large volume of dataset. The pre-existing models will perform better when applied on more telecom datasets which contain millions of records.
- Datasets prepared and released by companies operating in multiple countries will help in improved performance of churn prediction models. This will be specifically beneficial to the country or region that the company operates from.
- In the CNN model, the limitation is platform dependence and parameter setting. This can be improved by making the model platform independent [20].
- In SVM-POLY, SVM-RBF model, the limitation is Parameter setting and runtime overhead of SVM. It can be resolved by reducing the run time overhead [7].

5. Conclusion

In the paper, a review of different techniques used in the literature for reducing customer churn in telecommunication industry been presented. Various prediction models have been analysed and their performances have been compared. The accuracy of SVM-Poly model has been found the highest among over 20 methods. A real time survey is also conducted to find the factors affecting customer churn in telecommunication industry. It is found that the internet facilities are the most important factor, Hence, it can be concluded that there is still need of efficient churn prediction method with high accuracy and precession to avoid the challenge of customer churn in telecommunication industry.

In future, a model can be developed to ascertain the most crucial attribute that contributes to customer attrition. Feature selection can be done by using the benefit information along with the qualification rating filter. By recognizing churn values which are key from the customer data, CRM increases productivity. It can also suggest appropriate promotions to a group of users who can potentially become new customers. The company's marketing strategy will significantly improve upon the analysis of customers with same behavioural patterns. The result of the model will provide relevant information that will be crucial for companies in the telecom sector.

REFERENCES

1. Umayaparvathi, V., & Iyakutti, K. (2017). Automated feature selection and churn prediction using deep learning models. International Research Journal of Engineering and Technology (IRJET), 4(3), 1846–1854.
2. Ahmed, U., Khan, A., Khan, S. H., Basit, A., Haq, I. U., & Lee, Y. S. (2019). Transfer learning and meta classification based deep churn prediction system for telecom industry. arXiv preprint arXiv:1901.06091.
3. De Caigny, A., Coussement, K., & De Bock, K. W. (2018). A new hybrid classification algorithm for customer churn prediction based on logistic regression and decision trees. European Journal of Operational Research, 269(2), 760–772.
4. Idris, A., Khan, A., & Lee, Y. S. (2013). Intelligent churn prediction in telecom: employing mRMR feature selection and RotBoost based ensemble classification. Applied intelligence, 39, 659–672.
5. Idris, A., Khan, A., & Lee, Y. S. (2012, October). Genetic programming and adaboosting based churn prediction for telecom. In 2012 IEEE international conference on Systems, Man, and Cybernetics (SMC) (pp. 1328–1332). IEEE.

6. Fujo, S. W., Subramanian, S., & Khder, M. A. (2022). Customer churn prediction in telecommunication industry using deep learning. Information Sciences Letters, 11(1), 24.

7. Vafeiadis, T., Diamantaras, K. I., Sarigiannidis, G., & Chatzisavvas, K. C. (2015). A comparison of machine learning techniques for customer churn prediction. Simulation Modelling Practice and Theory, 55, 1–9.

8. Liu, R., Ali, S., Bilal, S. F., Sakhawat, Z., Imran, A., Almuhaimeed, A., ... & Sun, G. (2022). An Intelligent Hybrid Scheme for Customer Churn Prediction Integrating Clustering and Classification Algorithms. Applied Sciences, 12(18), 9355.

9. Jun Lee, S., & Siau, K. (2001). A review of data mining techniques. Industrial Management & Data Systems, 101(1), 41–46.

10. Linoff, G. S., & Berry, M. J. (2011). Data mining techniques: for marketing, sales, and customer relationship management. John Wiley & Sons.

11. Boser, B. E., Guyon, I. M., & Vapnik, V. N. (1992, July). A training algorithm for optimal margin classifiers. In Proceedings of the fifth annual workshop on Computational learning theory (pp. 144–152). Yorozu, T., Hirano, M., Oka, K., & Tagawa, Y. (1987). Electron spectroscopy studies on magneto-optical media and plastic substrate interface. IEEE translation journal on magnetics in Japan, 2(8), 740–741.

12. Au, W. H., Chan, K. C., & Yao, X. (2003). A novel evolutionary data mining algorithm with applications to churn prediction. IEEE transactions on evolutionary computation, 7(6), 532–545.

13. Au, W. H., Chan, K. C., & Yao, X. (2003). A novel evolutionary data mining algorithm with applications to churn prediction. IEEE transactions on evolutionary computation, 7(6), 532–545.

14. Landwehr, N., Hall, M., & Frank, E. (2005). Logistic model trees. Machine learning, 59, 161–205.

15. Usman-Hamza, F. E., Balogun, A. O., Capretz, L. F., Mojeed, H. A., Mahamad, S., Salihu, S. A., ... & Salahdeen, N. K. (2022). Intelligent Decision Forest Models for Customer Churn Prediction. Applied Sciences, 12(16), 8270.

16. Lalwani, P., Mishra, M. K., Chadha, J. S., & Sethi, P. (2022). Customer churn prediction system: a machine learning approach. Computing, 1–24.

17. Xiahou, X., & Harada, Y. (2022). B2C E-commerce customer churn prediction based on K-means and SVM. Journal of Theoretical and Applied Electronic Commerce Research, 17(2), 458–475.

18. Jain, H., Khunteta, A., & Srivastava, S. (2020). Churn prediction in telecommunication using logistic regression and logit boost. Procedia Computer Science, 167, 101–112.

19. Sina Mirabdolbaghi, S. M., & Amiri, B. (2022). Model Optimization Analysis of Customer Churn Prediction Using Machine Learning Algorithms with Focus on Feature Reductions. Discrete Dynamics in Nature and Society, 2022.

20. Mahalekshmi, A., & Chellam, G. H. Analysis of customer churn prediction using machine learning and deep learning algorithms.

21. Dong, T., Shang, W., & Zhu, H. (2011). Naive bayesian classifier based on the improved feature weighting algorithm. In Advanced Research on Computer Science and Information Engineering: International Conference, CSIE 2011, Zhengzhou, China, May 21-22, 2011. Proceedings, Part I (pp. 142–147). Springer Berlin Heidelberg.

22. Ahmed, A. A., & Maheswari, D. (2017). Churn prediction on huge telecom data using hybrid firefly based classification. Egyptian Informatics Journal, 18(3), 215–220.

23. Vijaya, J., & Sivasankar, E. (2019). An efficient system for customer churn prediction through particle swarm optimization based feature selection model with simulated annealing. Cluster Computing, 22, 10757–10768.

24. Faris, H. (2014). Neighborhood cleaning rules and particle swarm optimization for predicting customer churn behavior in telecom industry. International Journal of Advanced Science and Technology, 68, 11–22.

25. Idris, A., Rizwan, M., & Khan, A. (2012). Churn prediction in telecom using Random Forest and PSO based data balancing in combination with various feature selection strategies. Computers & Electrical Engineering, 38(6), 1808–1819.

26. Umayaparvathi, V., & Iyakutti, K. (2016). A survey on customer churn prediction in telecom industry: Datasets, methods and metrics. International Research Journal of Engineering and Technology (IRJET), 3(04).

27. Kaur, S. (2017). Literature Review of data mining techniques in customer churn prediction for telecommunications industry. Journal of Applied Technology and Innovation, 1(2), 28–40.

28. Ravichandran, S., & Ramasamy, C. (2016). Customer Retention of MCDR using 3SCDM Approaches. Databases (KDD), 5(8).

29. Doetsch, P., Buck, C., Golik, P., Hoppe, N., Kramp, M., Laudenberg, J., ... & Mauser, A. (2009, December). Logistic model trees with auc split criterion for the kdd cup 2009 small challenge. In KDD-Cup 2009 Competition (pp. 77–88). PMLR.

30. Fujo, S. W., Subramanian, S., & Khder, M. A. (2022). Customer churn prediction in telecommunication industry using deep learning. Information Sciences Letters, 11(1), 24.

31. Momin, S., Bohra, T., & Raut, P. (2020). Prediction of customer churn using machine learning. In EAI International Conference on Big Data Innovation for Sustainable Cognitive Computing: BDCC 2018 (pp. 203-212). Springer International Publishing.

32. Premkumar, G., & Rajan, J. (2013). Customer retention in mobile telecom service market in India: opportunities and challenges. Ushus Journal of Business Management, 12(2), 17–29.

Note: All the figures and tables in this chapter were made by the authors.

Advances in Computational Intelligence and its Applications (ICACIA-2023) – Dr. Sheikh Fahad Ahmad et al. (eds)

Speech Emotion Recognition (SER) on Live Calls While Creating Events

23

Rampelly SaiSree[1], Battula Pranavi[2], Chandhu Pullannagari[3], N. Srinivasa Reddy[4], C.N Sujatha[5]

Sreenidhi Institute of Science and Technology,
Department of Electronics and Communication Engineering

ABSTRACT—To enhance human-machine interaction, this study has examined speech emotion recognition is a field, a current focal point in research. Presently, researchers commonly categorize emotions into various groups by identifying distinguishing features. Contemporary investigations primarily concentrate on linguistic expressions, utilizing lexical analysis and emotion recognition as their central focus. In our project, we have chosen to classify emotions into five categories: anger, tranquility, fear, happiness, and sadness. Our project utilizes a system known as speech emotion recognition (SER), which capitalizes on the fact that the tone and pitch of speech often provide clues about the underlying emotions. The primary aim of this thesis is to detect emotions by developing a system capable of extracting, categorizing, and identifying data while also discerning the emotional content of the speaker. Each aspect of speech can be categorized into one of three groups: vocabulary (used words), visual characteristics (facial expressions of the speaker), and acoustic features (sound characteristics, including pitch, tone, jitter, etc.). To analyze human emotions using speech input, we have designed a Speech Emotion Recognition (SER) system. Differing from the current approach, which employs the CNN algorithm and the RAVDESS dataset, our proposed technology processes, defines, and recognizes emotional information for both male and female speakers, while also identifying emotions using the Librosa package for audio data.

KEYWORDS—Visual studio code, MFCC Classifier, Librosa, Feature extraction, Spectrograms, MLP Classifier

1. Introduction

One of the swiftest and simplest means for individuals to convey messages is through spoken signals. When it comes to linking a human with a machine, the speediest and most dependable approach is via speech signals. Humans naturally employ all their senses to the fullest extent possible. Although this is an innate ability for humans, machines face a formidable challenge in recognizing emotions. Consequently, an emotion recognition system utilizes emotional data to enhance communication between machines and humans. To detect emotions conveyed through speech by both male and female speakers is the objective of speech emotion recognition (SER). The aim of SER is to identify emotions in speech, regardless of the actual words spoken. However, as emotions can be idiosyncratic, capturing them in everyday speech, even for humans, can prove to be a daunting task. Several speech metrics under scrutiny include the Mel+ frequency cepstral coefficient (MFCC), linear predictive cepstral coefficient(LPCC), and fundamental frequencies.

Figure 23.1 depicts an illustration of the working of the speech emotion recognition model, initially the input file is taken as the sample for test data and the template is checked to process the data, the Librosa is an imported python package which is used

[1]sreesai821@gmail.com, [2]pranavi@170503@gmail.com, [3]chandup.kpl@gmail.com, [4]srinivasareddyn@sreenidhi.edu.in, [5]cnsujatha@gmail.com

DOI: 10.1201/9781003488682-23

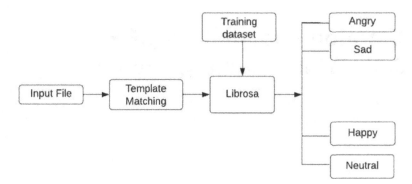

Fig. 23.1 Block diagram of (SER) speech emotion recognition

Source: Author

here and then feature extraction mechanism takes place here when the training data is given for the model which is to be trained initially to enhance the feature extraction mechanism and the output results of emotions can be obtained.

Librosa is a Python module or library which is used to recognise audio and musical sound signals. It standardises interfaces and names, provides a flatter package layout, backwards compatibility, modular functions, and understandable code. The final step to getting Librosa as a package is installing the pip file, which immediately updates as a use a package in PyCharm, Jupyter Notebook, or any other other source code content platform. Mel frequency cepstral coefficients (MFCC) are used to extract the data from the audio signal file in order to extract the features. The pitch level and amplitude of the signal can even be managed and hence the feature extraction mechanism takes place here using MFCC.MLP Classifier is also used as a base for feature extraction mechanism because it consists of different layers in feature extraction mechanism hence it is termed as Multilayer Perceptron classifier. By virtue of its name, the multi-layer Perceptron classifier, or MLP classifier, is associated with a neural network. MLP Classifier uses an underlying Neural Network to execute the task of classification, unlike other classification techniques like Naive Bayes Classifier or Support Vector Machine. Spectrograms are used in the recognition of spoken emotions. A spectrogram is a graphic depiction of a sound signal's amplitude that plots the frequencies that make up the signal against time or another variable.

2. Literature Survey

In June 2018, there was a notable surge in research aimed at discerning emotions through speech data. Cao et al. [10] introduced an innovative approach to address binary classification challenges. They treated each speaker's information as distinct queries and amalgamated the outputs from various rankers to enable multi-class predictions. To make the ranking Support Vector Machine (SVM) applicable for speaker-independent applications, they collected speaker-specific data for both training and testing phases. They also accounted for the possibility that each speaker might express various emotions, aiming to identify the dominant one. This method outperformed conventional SVM techniques in detecting emotional expressions, achieving an unweighted average (UA) or balanced accuracy of 44.4%.Chen et al. devised a three-tier speech emotion recognition system with the goal of enhancing speaker-independent recognition. They initially categorized emotions into coarse, medium, and fine distinctions before employing the Fisher rate to select the most relevant features. The output of the Fisher rate served is a component of the input data for their multi-level SVM-based classifier.

Furthermore, four comparative experiments were conducted in 2003 to reduce dimensionality PCA and ANN, or principal component analysis and artificial neural networks. While PCA proved to be less effective than Fisher for dimension reduction, SVM demonstrated better scalability than ANN for classification purposes.

New et al. [12] introduced an innovative method for classifying speech signals based on emotional content. Their system utilized discrete Hidden Markov Models (HMM) to describe the classifier and short-time log-frequency power coefficients (LPFC) to represent audio or speech signals. Initially, they categorized emotions into six groups and employed personal datasets, requiring both testing and training phases. The proposed technique, LPFC, was compared against Typical features are linear predictive cepstral coefficients (LPCC) and Mel-frequency cepstral coefficients (MFCC). The results demonstrated that LPFC outperformed the traditional features, achieving categorization accuracies of 78% (best) and 96% (average). These findings highlight the superiority of LPFC as a feature for emotion classification compared to traditional approaches.

In 2015, Wu et al. presented a study on the identification of human speech emotions using a unique feature called modulation spectral feature (MSF). This feature was extracted from a long-term spectro-temporal representation inspired by auditory processing, utilizing the concept of modulation frequency (mf) for speech decomposition. It aimed to convey essential information not captured by conventional short-term spectral features by including temporal modulation frequency components and acoustic frequency components. Classification used Radial Basis Function (RBF) to conduct and Support Vector Machine (SVM), and Visual Analogue Measures (VAM) were employed to assess MSFs. The experimental results demonstrated that MSFs outperformed MFCC and PLPC. Additionally, the inclusion of MSFs alongside prosodic features significantly improved recognition performance, achieving a classification recognition rate of 91.6%.In 2018 Ensemble's Random Forest to Trees (ERFTrees) by Rong et al technique showed a large number of characteristics for recognising emotions without requiring either language or linguistic knowledge. Small data sets with lots of features can use this strategy.

According to test results on a dataset of emotional speech from Chinese speakers, it can be concluded that the suggested approach increased the rate of emotion identification. The semantic labels technique employs the (Max Ent) The maximum entropy model. For the reason of emotion recognition, Max Ent modelled the relationship contrasting emotion states with emotion association rules (EARs).

In 2019, the performance metrics were determined based on different types of archives: MDT archives were utilized 80 percent of the time, SL-based recognition archives were employed combined AP and SL archives in 80.92 percent of the cases were utilized 83.55% of the time. These figures were derived from experimental results obtained from a private dataset.

Back in 2003, Narayanan [18] conducted research focused on recognizing emotions within a specific domain using speech samples from a call center application. The primary Finding both negative and pleasant feelings was the study's primary goal, such as anger and happiness. Various forms of information, including auditory, lexical, and discourse cues, were leveraged to discern emotions. Additionally, the study provided information on emotional salience from an information-theoretic perspective, aiming to gather data on the language-based aspects of emotional information. To work with these different types classifiers using both k-NN and linear discriminant analysis were applied. The study's results supported the notion that combining linguistic and auditory data yielded the most favorable outcomes. According to the findings, incorporating three sources of information as opposed to just one led to a 40.7% improvement in categorization accuracy for men and a 36.4% improvement for women. Specifically, for males, the accuracy enhancement ranged from 1.47% to 6.75%, while for females, it varied from 0.755% to 3.96%.

3. Methodology of Proposed Work

Loading and modifying audio: Extract the audio portion Resample Change the sample rate of audio from a file or URL. Transform audio between several formats (such as WAV, Mp3, and OGG).

Feature extraction for audio: Calculate an audio signal's MFCCs (Mel-Frequency Cepstral Coefficients). Identify and extract spectrum properties such the spectrogram, spectral centroid, and spectral roll off. Calculate chroma energy and other chroma characteristics.

Tracking the rhythm and tempo: Calculate the tempo of an audio signal in beats per minute. Recognize the beat in an audio source.

Adjusting the pitch and the time: Adjust the pitch of an audio transmission. altering an audio signal's length without altering its pitch. To hear sounds, plot the waveform of an audio signal. An audio signal's spectrogram should be shown. Create a graphic representation of the tempo and beat.

Segmenting audio: Recognize separate audio signal parts, such as choruses and verses. Add semantic tags to audio signals (such as "speech" and "music") to identify them.

Define the To extract the mfcc, chroma, and mel features from an audio file, use the function extract feature. The four parameters needed by this function are the file name, three Boolean arguments, and three qualities Mel Frequency, Mfcc Pitch categorization and the cepstral coefficient both represent the short-term power spectrum of the sound chroma. There are 12 categories altogether. It is free to access the Ryerson Audio Visual Data collection's Emotional Speech and Song dataset. In this dataset, 7356 files were evaluated 10 times by 247 individuals for emotional intensity, sincerity, and authenticity. To create the 24.8GB total dataset, 24 actors contributed. The speech signal's bandwidth was constrained in traditional narrow-band data transmission technologies to lower bit rates. For instance, in conventional telephony, the speech frequency range was constrained to 300 Hz to 3.4 kHz. It was sufficient to guarantee at least a basic level of speech understanding at the expense of excellent voice quality.

As a result, when bandwidth was severely constricted, speakers obviously found it challenging to communicate as much emotional information. The SER system was trained with two distinct sample frequencies to test this theory: To start, keep aliasing to a minimum. Second, by eliminating every other sample, the speech was down sampled by a factor of 2.

This study looked into how the -law algorithm, a voice companding technique, affected SER. In the USA, Japan, and Europe, variations of the mu-law companding were employed in pulse code modulation (PCM) transmission systems. The technique prioritises high-amplitude voice components while lowering low-amplitude speech components at the transmitter end using a logarithmic amplitude compression. The speech is transported via the communication channel after being compressed, where it picks up noise on the way. While maintaining the same signal-to-noise ratio (SNR) for both the high and low frequencies amplifying elements, the voice signal is re-expanded at the receiver end. In a transmission, high amplitude signal components would have low SNR values whereas high amplitude signal components would have high SNR values if there was no companding mechanism. The Librosa audio detection program is used throughout the described techniques for setup. The complete setting of audio feature extraction and path setup is done using Visual Studio Code program. In this study, we use the RAVDESS Dataset, Multilayer Perception Classifier, and Librosa to build a model to identify speech-based emotions. This will be able to detect feelings in audio files. After the dataset has been loaded and its characteristics have been retrieved, training and testing sets will be created. The model will then be trained before an MLP Classifier is created. Next, the model's precision will be evaluated. To extract characteristics from sound and music files, use the Librosa package. Mfcc, chroma, and mel characteristics were extracted. Mel Frequency (mfcc): The cepstral coefficient, which contains the 12 separate pitch categories, symbolises the sound chroma's short-term power spectrum. Mel: The frequency of a Mel Spectrogram. The flowchart in Fig. 23.2 shows how the model is divided into different emotion predictions and output is obtained. It also shows how the test and training datasets are combined with the feature selection process, which includes a feature extraction mechanism.

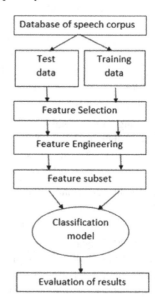

Fig. 23.2 Flowchart specifying the classification of test and training data sets

Source: Adapted from Sundarprasad, Neethu, "Speech Emotion Detection Using Machine Learning Techniques"

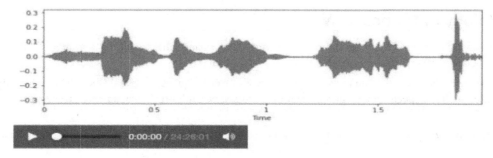

Fig. 23.3 Wave plot audio with surprise emotion

Source: Adpated from Vijayarajan Rajangam, Palani Thanaraj Krishnan, Joseph Raj Alex Noel,"Emotion classification from speech signal based on empiricalmode decomposition and non-linear features"

Figure 23.3 shows the wave plot is obtained based on the pitch variations of the extracted audio file and hence the graph entirely states the nature i.e., its amplitude and pitch. The emotional variation is observed with the following parameters too i.e., the pitch and amplitude variations of the audio file. Hence with observed parameters the feature extraction mechanism in the training data finally delivers the output to be a surprise emotion.

Figure 23.4 shows an emotion-filled Spectrogram for an audio recording. A spectrogram is a graphic depiction of the amplitude of a sound signal that is plotted with regard to the frequencies that make up the signal as well as time or another variable.

Figure 23.5 shows the wave plot is obtained based on the pitch variations of the extracted audio file and hence the graph entirely states the nature i.e., its amplitude and pitch. The emotional variation is observed with the following parameters too i.e., the pitch and amplitude variations of the audio file, hence with observed parameters the feature extraction mechanism in the training data finally delivers the output to be a neutral emotion. Because as in surprise is not that high here in neutral state of emotion.

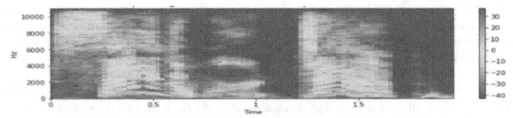

Fig. 23.4 Spectrogram for audio with surprise emotion

Source: Adapted from https://python-catalin.blogspot.com/2018/12/using-librosa-python-module.html?m=1

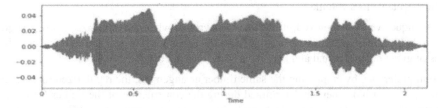

Fig. 23.5 Wave plot for audio with neutral emotion

Source: Adapted from Vijayarajan Rajangam,Palani Thanaraj Krishnan,Joseph Raj Alex Noel,"Emotion classification from speech signal based on empiricalmode decomposition and non-linear features"

Figure 23.6 shows the spectrogram for audio file of neutral emotion can be seen here. As seen here the shade of spectrogram level is comparatively high here in this spectrogram.

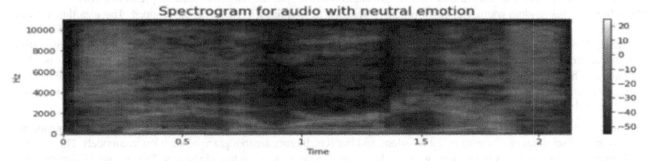

Fig. 23.6 Spectrogram for audio with neutral emotion

Source: Adapted from https://stackoverflow.com/questions/67451239/log-mel-spectrogram-using-librosa

3.1 For Calculating Accuracy the Following Algorithms are Used

This design emphasises the Zero Crossing Rate, Chroma Shift, Root Mean Square Value, Mel Spectrogram, and MFCC (Mel Frequency Cepstral coefficients). They are among the most often used audio features for emotional audio content, auditory identification, and information retrieval in the order of the music and value the content of the given audio. The zero crossing rate happens when there is a significant movement from ve to 0 to ve or from ve to 0 to ve. The Mel Spectrogram, as opposed to frequency sphere spectrograms, use the Mel scale to depict sound. A signal's frequency must undergo a logarithmic change in the Mel Scale. Diagram 3 displays the plates for the Surprise Emotion Wave plot and Spectrogram.

3.2 Different Algorithms Used for Training Model

Multilayer Perceptron Classifier (MLPC): A collection of artificial neural networks (ANNs) is known as a multilayer perceptron (MLP). MLP is rarely strictly associated with systems made up of repetitive layers of perceptron's (with threshold activation), rarely in close proximity to each feedforward ANN. Even though they only have a single retired subcaste, multilayer perceptron networks are rarely referred to as "vanilla" neural networks. A supervised bracket method for multi-band unrestricted optic remote viewing data is provided by multilayer perceptron. Multilayer perceptron (MLP) provide robust classifiers that may perform better than fresh classifiers; however, MLP Classifiers are constantly checked for the plethora of parameters that are unconstrained. Additionally, problems with MLPs include initial minima and extended training intervals.

Light Gradient Boosting Machine (LGBM): The grade boosting algorithm is implemented by the free and open-source Python package known as Light Gradient Boosting Machine, or simply Light GBM. By combining colorful automatic point selections, Light GBM extends the grade boosting algorithm and includes boosting examples and additional strong slants. As a result, Light GBM has the potential to accelerate training and improve prophetic performance. To distinguish the perspectives used to calculate the division, Light GBM uses grade- grounded one-side slice (GOSS). GOSS retains scenarios with big slants and only desultorily discards situations with minor slants in order to maintain the effectiveness of information gain estimation.

When there are more variables than samples in high-dimensional data, the Gradient Boosting Classifier (GB) is used as an ensemble classifier. However, no predictions have been made for the vaticination of specific occurrences. By categorizing a small sample size of samples from odd species, it is shown that grade-enhancing biases from uncommon important events occur. Only for a specific number of boosting iterations and a binomial loss function can the bias be eliminated by subsampling in conjunction with an acceptable loss volume.

When the bias against unique events is removed, it has been shown that when the data size is bity, the quantum of boosting duplications cannot be reliably anticipated from the training data. As a result, to suggest and estimate colorful developments for the special events bias of grade raising, actual and fake large-scale data are used.

In order to achieve point preference by employing the same timber arrangement, the regularized total reduction in the logical norms espoused in the split point judgement is determined during the construction of the timber for each point. This feature determines the Gini value of the point. The stoner selects the fashionable k characteristics based on personal desire after ranking each point according to its Gini Value for the relinquishment of features. Bracket goods are displayed by the ensemble learning technique classifier. Fundamentally, the performance of the timber. The Extra Trees Classifier (ET) separates itself from random wood while analysing the de-correlated decision trees (DTs) included therein by combining the results of numerous de-correlated decision trees (DTs) contained within a "tree". Based on the primary training set, that DT is actually classified in Extra Trees Forest. Based on the point set surrounding each testing knot, a random set of k- attributes is assigned to each tree.Each DT must decide which attributes are significant in order to split the statistics based on preset numerical parameters (Gini Index). This random approach, which produces separate de-correlated DTs, has been dropped. The idea that a set of classifiers can produce more trustworthy groups than a single classifier is the cornerstone of classifier ensembles, according to the Random Forest Classifier (RF). This is the foundation of the classifier ensembles' gospel. Breiman invented the innovative and safe arbitrary timber classifier in 2001. The potential for visually appealing decision trees to produce predictions is taken advantage of by a machine learning system called Random Forest. decision trees produced by random number generator. Each knot in the decision tree employs a random subset of characteristics to gauge the circumstance. The final thing is created when a number of distinct decision trees are combined by the random timber.$

Decision Tree Classifier (DT): Due to their harmonic delicacy and relatively cheap estimation cost, The most advantageous models in the disciplines of data mining, data wisdom, and machine literacy are thought to be decision tree models. The Benefits of Planting and Pruning Trees In brackets, we provide the most extreme decision tree classifiers. To generate the decision tree model in the tree structure phase, the training data set is repeatedly partitioned using a sectionally optimal pattern. Until all or the majority of workshops for various difficulties maintain the same class marking, this process is repeated. Tree trimming is used to reduce the leaves and branches that analyze single or very minor data vectors in order to improve the notion of a choice. An excellent illustration of how multistage judgment trees should be employed is the DTC, or decision tree classifier. A number of multistage techniques start by breaking down a complex judgment into a collection of unique, more straightforward judgments in order to anticipate the final result.

Decision Tree Classifier (DT) and Random Forest Classifier (RF) differences Since they both have the words "Tree" and "Forest" in their names, it is implied that a Random Forest is made up of several Decision Trees. The difference between a decision tree and an arbitrary tree is that a decision tree uses the complete dataset, parses the findings, and uses every point of interest, whereas an arbitrary tree randomly picks rows and features to create visually appealing decision trees. Applying a decision tree model to a specific training dataset reveals that the delicateness increases with the number of divisions. Whether someone has overfit the data or not cannot be determined without cross-validation (on the training data set). However, because a simple decision tree model is so straightforward, anyone using it needs to be familiar with the variables and their values in order to resolve the data and interpret the results. Random Forest necessitates a longer training period than a single decision tree. It would be wonderful if this were accepted because the amount of time it takes to train a variety of trees improves as we expand the forest. Despite their dependence and vulnerability on a particular variety of features.

3.3 Evaluation through MI Algorithms Only for Accuracy

We are all aware of how difficult it is to predict the speaker's emotions in real time. Numerous tests were carried out following the models' training in order to estimate their delicateness and performance. Table 23.1 below shows the model accuracy.

Table 23.1 Model performance of different classifiers

Model	Light gradient boosting machine	Random forest classifier	Extra trees classifier	Gradient boosting classifier	Multilayer perception classifier	Decision tree classifier
ACCURACY	0.9714	0.9585	0.9479	0.9448	0.924844	0.8831
F1 SCORE	0.9714	0.9585	0.9478	0.9449	0.925	0.883
KAPPA	0.9666	0.9516	0.9392	0.9355	0.92259	0.8636
MCC	0.9667	0.9517	0.9393	0.9357	0.912966	0.8638

Source: Author

4. Results and Discussions

Numerous observations and conclusions are possible based on the implementation's results. With reasonable accuracy of 75.97%, our model tests. We were able to more clearly distinguish between the emotions in speech thanks to our design and research. An MLP Classifier was used to extract features after the librosa library had read the sound file using the sound file library. As you can see, the model's accuracy rate was 72.4%. But for us, that's plenty. The project's final output, with a 72.4% accuracy rate, is shown here. This statistic is a rough percentage since, as shown by the present models, all accuracy models give us a range of estimations of percentages around 72%.

Scores for overall performance increase across all methods. The first strategy, which used the SVM method, was successfully implemented, scoring 83 percent; the second strategy, which used the KNN algorithm, was effective, scoring 80 percent; and the third strategy, which used the SVM algorithm, was the best of the three, scoring 90 percent. The results allow for the following conclusions to be drawn:

Observation 1: The SVM and KNN algorithms have steadily received high performance metric scores when comparing the results of the first and third approaches. However, the Gradient Boosting Trees, Random Forest, and Decision Trees each had their own scores that were decreasing. Between these approaches, the Bayesian Algorithm performed consistently. The SVM and KNN algorithms scored higher because to the third method's usage of dimensionality reduction. The dataset's size increases in proportion to the number of dimensions as the dimensionality of the data decreases. In the end, this lessens the classifier's bias towards any certain class. On the other hand, tree-based algorithms perform better when given a wider feature set. This occurs as a result of the decision tree becoming deeper as more features are added, enabling better results.

Observation 2: Overall, The second strategy performed less well than the first and second. This is due to the fact that the majority of the information is not present in the selected information of the audio signal. Furthermore, It is possible to draw the conclusion that MFCC values alone accurately classify an audio signal's emotional content.

Observation 3: The first approach's classification report reveals that the feelings of happiness and surprise are more frequently misclassified. The similarities between the features in these two categories account for this contradiction. Comparing the third approach's dimensionality reduction step to Chen et al.'s baseline system, this contradiction has been greatly reduced.

Figure 23.7 shows that, When file audio frequency is in the range of sad training list then the output is given sad.

Figure 23.8 shows that, When file audio frequency is in the range of disgust training list then the output is given disqust.

Figure 23.9 shows that, When file audio frequency is in the range of happy training list then the output is given happy.

Figure 23.10 shows that, When file audio frequency is in the range of calm training list then the output is given calm. The audio files are hence tested as samples for testing data by creating paths for each file and the audio file documents are tested here. This entire operation is hence performed in the visual studio code platform.

Fig. 23.7 Output 1

Fig. 23.8 Output 2

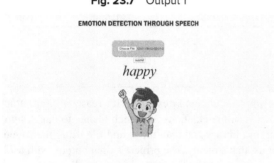

Fig. 23.9 Output 3

Fig. 23.10 Output 4

Source: Author

5. Conclusion

A new era of automation has begun as a result of the development of artificial intelligence and machine learning. The majority of these automated devices follow user voice commands. In addition to word recognition, robots might be able to comprehend the speaker's emotions, which would provide them various advantages over existing approaches (user). Automatic translation systems, computerised educational programmes, therapeutic diagnostic instruments, and automated contact centre dialogues all use automation to some extent, voice emotion detection systems can be used. This thesis provided a comprehensive explanation of the steps involved in developing a speech emotion detection system, and multiple tests were conducted to evaluate the effect of each move. The absence of publicly accessible speech materials at first made it difficult to create a trained model. After many experiments, the tactic that performed the best was selected. There have also been many novel feature extraction techniques proposed in prior studies. Learning how effectively each classifying algorithm can identify emotions is the last phase in the classifier selection process. The experiment's findings suggest that an integrated feature space may increase recognition rates more than a single feature would. The suggested project could be improved to make it more efficient, accurate, and valuable for upgrades in the future. The model might be improved to recognize additional types of events, such as depression and mood swings, in addition to feelings. These tools let therapists keep track of their patients' mood changes. Making computers emotional has the difficult side effect of incorporating a sarcasm detection mechanism. Sarcasm is more difficult to recognize as an emotion because it cannot be derived from the speaker's words or tone alone. Combining voice emotion recognition with language-based sentiment analysis can help identify potential sarcasm. Therefore, a speech-based emotion recognition system may have a variety of applications in the future.

6. Acknowledgement

We would like to express our immense gratitude to our college Sreenidhi Institute of Science and Technology for allowing us to work on this project. We would like to thank Mr. N. Srinivasa Reddy Sir for your expert advice and constant encouragement throughout this project. We are fortunate to work under your guidance. Providing all the resources and sharing your knowledge, and constantly reviewing our work, enabled us to finish this project.

REFERENCES

1. Soegaard, M. and Friis Dam, R. (2013). The Encyclopedia of Human-Computer Interaction. 2nd edition.
2. A. Georgogiannis and V. Digalakis, "Speech Emotion Recognition using non-linear Teager energybased features in noisy environments," 2012 Proceedings of the 20th European Signal Processing Conference (EUSIPCO), 2012, pp. 2045–2049.
3. H. Cao, R. Verma, and A. Nenkova, "Speaker-sensitive emotion recognition via ranking: Studies on acted and spontaneous speech," Computer. Speech Lang., vol. 28, no. 1, pp. 186–202, Jan. 2015.
4. L. Chen, X. Mao, Y. Xue, and L. L. Cheng, "Speech emotion recognition: Features and classification models," Digit. Signal Process., vol. 22, no. 6, pp. 1154–1160, Dec. 2012.
5. T. L. Nwe, S. W. Foo, and L. C. De Silva, "Speech emotion recognition using hidden Markov models," Speech Communication., vol. 41, no. 4, pp. 603–623, Nov. 2003.
6. J. Rong, G. Li, and Y.-P. P. Chen, "Acoustic feature selection for automatic emotion recognition from speech," Inf. Process. Manag., vol. 45, no. 3, pp. 315–328, May 2009.
7. S. S. Narayanan, "Toward detecting emotions in spoken dialogs," IEEE Trans. Speech Audio Process., vol. 13, no. 2, pp. 293–303, Mar. 2005.
8. B. Yang and M. Lugger, "Emotion recognition from speech signals using new harmony features," Signal Processing, vol. 90, no. 5, pp. 1415–1423, May 2010.
9. C.-C. Lee, E. Mower, C. Busso, S. Lee, and S. Narayanan, "Emotion recognition using a hierarchical binary decision tree approach," Inter speech, vol. 53, pp. 320–323, 2009.
10. S. Bjorn, S. Steidl, and A. Batliner, "The INTERSPEECH 2009 Emotion Challenge," 2009.
11. J. P. Arias, C. Busso, and N. B. Yoma, "Shape-based modelling of the fundamental frequency contour for emotion detection in speech," Computer. Speech Lang., vol. 28, no. 1, pp. 278–294, Jan. 2014.
12. M. Grimm, K. Kroschel, E. Mower, and S. Narayanan, "Primitives-based evaluation and estimation of emotions in speech," Speech Communication., vol. 49, no. 10–11, pp. 787–800, Oct. 2007.
13. K. H. Hyun, E. H. Kim and Y. K. Kwak, "Emotional Feature Extraction Based On Phoneme Information for Speech Emotion Recognition," RO-MAN 2007 - The 16th IEEE International Symposium on Robot and Human Interactive Communication, 2007, pp. 802–806, doi: 10.1109/ROMAN.2007.4415195.
14. F. Zalkow and M. Müller, "CTC-Based Learning of Chroma Features for Score–Audio Music Retrieval," in IEEE/ACM Transactions on Audio, Speech, and Language Processing, vol. 29, pp. 2957–2971, 2021, doi: 10.1109/TASLP.2021.3110137.

Advances in Computational Intelligence and its Applications (ICACIA-2023) – Dr. Sheikh Fahad Ahmad et al. (eds)
© *2024 Taylor & Francis Group, London, ISBN 978-1-032-78612-4*

Predicting Malignancy from Breast Histopathological Images Using Deep Neural Networks and Baseline Classifiers

24

Anindita Mohanta[1], Sourav Dey Roy[2]
Research Scholar, Computer Science and Engineering Department,
Tripura University (A Central University)

Niharika Nath[3]
Professor, Biological and Chemical Sciences Department,
New York Institute of Technology

Mrinal Kanti Bhowmik[4]
Assistant Professor, Computer Science and Engineering Department,
Tripura University (A Central University)

ABSTRACT—Cancer is one of the most deadly diseases around the world. Approximately, 38% of the entire population is suffering from cancer. Among various cancers, breast cancer is one of the most prevalent and deadly cancers in women, making it a hot research topic in the field of medicine. The majority of the time, a biopsy approach is used, in which tissue is taken and examined under a microscope. A histopathologist's lack of training could result in a misdiagnosis. Therefore, computer-aided automatic breast cancer diagnosis systems can help medical experts and pathologists for early diagnosis. From various vision based techniques, Convolutional neural networks (CNNs) have recently emerged as the preferred deep learning techniques for the classification and detection in the medical domain. In this paper, we measured the perception capability of CNNs for classification of histopathological images for breast abnormality detection. We adopted the standard CNNs models as different aspects of transfer learning module, fine-tuning module, and feature extraction module with the support vector machine (SVM) classifier for benign and malignant classification. For effective analysis, separate training and performance assessment is done on the used CNN models at four different image magnifying factors. This study can help to understand the usability of different deep learning approaches in the medical domain.

KEYWORDS—Breast cancer, Histopathological images, Convolutional neural networks, Classification, Performance evaluation

1. Introduction

In human body, cells divide and grow in a controlled way to produce more cells to maintain human health. But for different reasons like excessive consumption of alcohol, smoking cells divide more often in an uncontrolled manner, which increases the chance of cancer. Cancer affects the human body when cells grow abnormally in an uncontrolled way that is able to damage other body organs. That's why cancer research is one of the most important research areas in the medical field (Liu et al., 2007). The diagnosis of cancer is based on the analysis of cell's deformation using microscopic slides or images. Currently, most of the researchers focus on automatic computer-aided microscopic image analysis for cancer early diagnosis. Histopathological microscopic imaging is considered as a "gold standard" for diagnosis almost all types of cancer (Rubin et al., 2008). However,

[1]aninditamohanta01@gmail.com, [2]souravdeyroy49@gmail.com, [3]nnath@nyit.edu, [4]mrinalkantibhowmik@tripurauni.ac.in

DOI: 10.1201/9781003488682-24

histopathological image analysis is the only way to detect breast cancer with confidence (Yang et al., 2019). Histopathology is the study of disease symptoms by microscopic inspection of a processed and fixed biopsy on glass slides. In advancement of whole slide digital scanners, histopathology slides can be digitized and stored in digital image form (Gurcan et al., 2009). Moreover, histopathological slide or image understanding is a very time-consuming specialized task that depends on the pathologist's knowledge and experience. In addition, the diagnosis is frequently not agreed upon by the professionals. Considering these facts, there is an urgent need for an automatic computer aided cancer diagnosis system which can be able to recognize cancer accurately and more confidentially. For that, a significant amount of time and effort has been invested by numerous researchers. But majority of these works use handcrafted features like colour or texture descriptors (Yang et al., 2019) which are not generalizable. In recent years, deep learning architectures, particularly CNNs, have been used for automatic perform tasks like detection and classification in medical image analysis.

Depending upon this fact, in this paper, we assessed the prediction performance and capability of different CNN models for classification of histopathological images at four different magnifying factors of BreakHis dataset for breast abnormality prediction. For effective analysis, in our work, we compared the prediction performance of the well-known CNN models using four different approaches i.e., full training; transfer learning (TL) and last layer fine-tuning; TL and all layers fine-tuning; and CNNs with SVM classifier (with four different linear and non-linear kernels) at the same settings. The experimental findings of this study provided a better understanding of CNNs in the medical domain for breast abnormality prediction.

2. Related Work

There are a number of deep learning based models that are developed to improve healthcare systems, decrease time and cost of treatment, and to reach the medical facilities in rural and undeveloped areas. Janghel et al. (Janghel et al., 2010) conducted implementation and performance measurement of four different Artificial Neural Network (ANN) models for classification of benign and malignant cases for breast cancer diagnosis. Ubaidillah et al. (Ubaidillah et al., 2013) performed a comparative study on ANN and SVM for benign and malignant tumors classification. Spanhol et al. (Spanhol et al., 2017) developed a CNN based model for deep features extraction for more accurately breast cancer classification. Wei et al. (Wei et al., 2017) proposed a CNN based model for binary histopathological image classification. Motlagh et al. (Jannesari et al., 2018) conducted a comparative study on several Inception and ResNet classifiers for four types of cancer classification including breast cancer. Nazeri et al. (Nazeri et al., 2018) proposed a patch based method for histopathological image classification which consists of two CNNs. Matos et al. (de Matos et al., 2019) proposed a compact model based on texture filters that had less parameters than conventional CNN models for binary histopathological image classification. Zhu et al. (Zhu et al., 2019) proposed a histopathological image classification model by assembling multiple compact CNNs. Yang et al. (Yang et al., 2019) proposed a soft attention guided CNN for histopathological image classification. In their work, they were trying to transparent the network's decision making process to match or agreement the network generated image's features with a human expert. Kandel et al. (Kandel et al., 2020) conducted a comparative study on first order optimizers for histopathological image classification using CNNs. Gour et al. (Gour et al., 2020) proposed a residual learning-based CNN model for histopathological image classification. To sum up from our extensive survey, we found that there are no researches works are conducted so far based on comparative analysis in different CNN models with different deep learning approaches for histopathological images classification. Therefore, in our present work, we have predicted the capability of CNNs for histopathological image classification for breast abnormality detection.

3. Methodology: Convolutional Neural Networks for Histopathological Image Classification

In recent years, the uses of Convolutional Neural Networks (CNNs) have grown exponentially in the medical domain because of its speed, high accuracy, low cost and easy to implement nature. However, most of the computer-aided automatic diagnosis systems are based on CNN architecture which helps pathologists and doctors for disease diagnosis tasks. Although, CNN is derived from convolution algorithm which was inspired by the primary visual cortex (Suzuki, 2017). It is able to extract features or complex patterns automatically from a set of medical microscopic images without human expert or human interaction. Nowadays in the medical domain most of the deep learning based models are based on CNN pipelines for its good performance. CNN was first proposed by K. Fukushima in his paper on the "Neocognitron" in the year 1980. Later, Waibel et al. (Waibel et al., 1989) proposed weights and back-propagation training on CNN architecture. CNN model mainly consists of four types of layers namely convolutional layer, activation layer, pooling layer, and fully connected layer (FCL). The first three layers are called feature extraction layers and the last layer i.e. FCL is called as classification layer. The purpose of this layer is to predict test images based on the train data. Moreover, convolution, pooling, and FCL are meant for feature detection, feature selection, and classification, respectively. A complete CNN model forms when all these layers are stacked (O'Shea and Nash, 2015). In this study, we evaluated the prediction performance of different CNN models for classification of benign and malignant histopathological images at four different magnifying factors. We also compared the performance of the CNN models using four different approaches i.e. full training; transfer learning (TL) and last layer fine-tuning; TL and all layers fine-tuning; and CNNs with SVM classifier at the same settings to understand the usability of the CNN models in the medical domain. Overall diagram of our proposed work is illustrated in Figure 24.1.

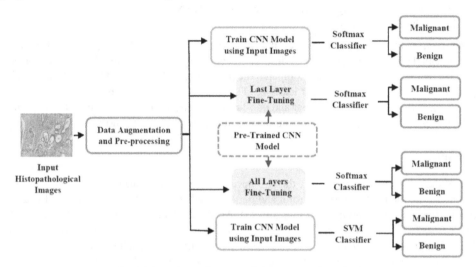

Fig. 24.1 Flow Diagram of the proposed analysis

Source: Auhtor

3.1 CNN as a Full-training Model for Breast Abnormality Prediction

In the first approach, we use CNN as a full-training model, where all the weights are initialized randomly before the beginning of the training phase, then all the weights are updated iteratively using forward and backward propagation, in result we find a local minimum for the cost function. In this approach, classification is based on the extracted features during the training phase. For that, CNNs require a large amount of label dataset which is difficult to fulfil in the medical field. To overcome over-fitting and convergence problems, we increase dataset size by using data augmentation and adjust learning parameters of the network. Therefore, CNNs with full training models are very tedious and time consuming. CNNs extract the input images features by using convolutional layers. To enable the search of the local features throughout the images, the connected weights are shared between the nodes in the convolutional layers. Thus, a convolutional layer with n kernels (each set of weights) learns to recognize n local features.

3.2 CNN with TL and Last Layer Fine-tuning for Breast Abnormality Prediction

In the second approach, we use CNNs with TL and last layer fine-tuning to understand the usability of pre-trained weights on medical image analysis. Because of the insufficient number of image datasets in the medical domain, learning from original images is often not the practical approach. In this study, we use TL that allows us to pre-training of CNN models (Bahadori et al., 2014) (Gui et al., 2018) using large scale natural image datasets (ImageNet). It can also help to eliminate over-fitting problems and improve network performance. In this study, we initialize weight of different layers of our models by using pre-trained models with last layer (FCL) fine-tuning means in the last layer of our models fine-tuning is applied on cancer dataset. Therefore, pre-trained weights are preserved while the FCL is updated continuously.

3.3 CNN with TL and All Layers Fine-tuning for Breast Abnormality Prediction

In the third approach, we use CNNs with TL and all layers fine-tuning where we update the weights of all layers of the pre-trained CNN models. Since, BreakHis breast cancer dataset is highly dissimilar from ImageNet dataset for that full layer fine-tuning is applied for accurate classification of benign and malignant classes. Therefore, we updated the pre-trained weights of each layer on BreakHis dataset.

3.4 CNN as a Feature Extractor with SVM Classifier for Breast Abnormality Prediction

In the last approach, we extract the features of benign and malignant classes using CNN models and then classify the extracted features using Support Vector Machine (SVM). In our present study, we classified extracted features of benign and malignant classes using the SVM classifier with four types of widely used kernels (i.e. linear kernel, Gaussian kernel, polynomial kernel and Gaussian radial basis function). In our comparative study, we show that the linear kernel gives better results as compared to other kernels for benign and malignant classification using the SVM classifier. Given the beverity of space, in our present study we only consider SVM classifiers with linear kernels (i.e., best performed kernel) for classification of benign and malignant histopathological images.

4. Experiment Results and Discussions

4.1 Used Dataset

For comparative study we used BreakHis dataset (Spanhol et al., 2015) which is a publicly available breast cancer dataset. The dataset consist of total 7909 histopathological images which mainly belongs into 2 classes namely benign (2480 images) and malignant (5429 images) with 4 different magnifying factors in PNG format with 700x460 resolutions and RGB color format. The images were collected in collaboration with the P&D Laboratory Pathological Anatomy and Cytopathology, Parana, Brazil. The breast tumor tissues were collected from a total 82 patients, which were processed and stained using H&E staining.

4.2 Data Augmentation and Pre-processing

In this paper, we used BreakHis dataset to classify benign and malignant histopathological images at four different magnifying factors (i.e. 4x2 = 8 classes). Hence this dataset is unbalanced and also contains insufficient data (7909 images) for network training. To solve these problems we used data augmentation techniques (Hussain et al., 2017). We utilize three different augmentation techniques i.e. flipping (vertical and horizontal flipping), rotating ($45°$, $90°$, $135°$) and scaling to generate new training images. After the data augmentation process we generated 47,454 new images. For data balancing we select smallest class volume i.e. 4,116 images from each classes (total $(4,116 \times 8) = 32,928$ images), where 90 percent images are selected for training (3,704 images per class) and 10 percent images are selected for testing and validation of the network (412 images per class). After data augmentation, we resized each image from $700 \times 460 \times 3$ dimensions to $224 \times 224 \times 3$ for further processing. After pre-processing, our dataset is ready for training and testing of the CNN models with different approaches.

4.3 Parameter Configuration

For experimental purposes, we take BreakHis dataset into two groups benign and malignant at four different magnifying factors. Although in the medical domain, most of the datasets are insufficient including BreakHis because of the availability of patients. To overcome this problem, we used batch normalization (Ioffe and Szegedy, 2015) and dropout 0.5 for regularization with batch sizes 32 and epochs 500 in training. Furthermore, the learning rate was applied with the start 0.001 setting. The training accuracy and validation accuracy are evaluated using stochastic gradient-descent optimizer (Sutskever et al., 2013) and binary cross entropy (Rusiecki, 2019) for 2 class (benign and malignant) classifications. For performance measurement we used standard parameters such as accuracy, recall or sensitivity, precision, F1-measure for testing performance and for training performance we used training accuracy and validation accuracy. The implementation and testing of every CNN model was done by a single computing system with following specifications: Model: DELL Precision Tower 5810, RAM: 64 GB, Processor: Intel Xenon (R), OS: Ubantu 18.04, and Anaconda 3.

5. Results and Discussions

In the first approach, we used CNN as a full-training model where models are learn during the training phases (shown in Table 24.1). The results of full training CNN models shows that Xception model classified benign and malignant histopathological images more accurately than all other models with 94% accuracy (at 100x magnification). In the second approach, we used CNNs with TL and last layer fine-tuning to overcome insufficient cancer dataset problems by using prior knowledge. The last layer fine-tuning allows us to update the last layer (FCL) on the cancer dataset. Therefore, pre-trained weights are preserved while the FCL is continuously updated (shown in Table 24.2). The results show that DenseNet121 classified histopathological images more accurately than all other models with 89% accuracy (at 400x magnification). In the third approach, we used CNNs with TL and all layers fine-tuning. Since, BreakHis breast cancer dataset is very different from ImageNet dataset for that all

Table 24.1   Performance evaluation of different neural network models using full training.

Model	Image Magnification Factor	Training Performance			Testing Performance		
		Training Accuracy	Validation Accuracy	Accuracy	Recall	Precision	F1-Measure
VGG16	40X	0.50	0.51	0.49	0.50	0.25	0.33
	100X	0.74	0.69	0.70	0.72	0.73	0.71
	200X	0.49	0.50	0.51	0.50	0.25	0.33
	400X	0.50	0.52	0.50	0.49	0.25	0.33
VGG19	40X	0.49	0.50	0.50	0.53	0.25	0.33
	100X	0.50	0.47	0.48	0.52	0.27	0.32
	200X	0.49	0.50	0.51	0.53	0.25	0.33
	400X	0.50	0.49	0.50	0.48	0.25	0.33
ResNet 101	40X	0.77	0.81	0.83	0.81	0.82	0.80
	100X	0.81	0.82	0.80	0.83	0.82	0.83
	200X	0.84	0.86	0.86	0.84	0.85	0.86
	400X	0.75	0.78	0.79	0.79	0.80	0.79
InceptionV3	40X	0.86	0.81	0.81	0.81	0.82	0.81
	100X	0.91	0.73	0.74	0.74	0.76	0.41
	200X	0.81	0.84	0.84	0.84	0.87	0.84
	400X	0.85	0.85	0.86	0.86	0.87	0.85
Xception	40X	**0.94**	**0.90**	**0.91**	**0.91**	**0.90**	**0.91**
	100X	**0.96**	**0.96**	**0.94**	**0.92**	**0.95**	**0.96**
	200X	**0.93**	**0.88**	**0.87**	**0.88**	**0.89**	**0.88**
	400X	**0.95**	**0.96**	**0.93**	**0.95**	**0.94**	**0.96**
DenseNet121	40X	0.83	0.77	0.76	0.77	0.80	0.77
	100X	0.74	0.76	0.77	0.78	0.79	0.76
	200X	0.85	0.86	0.86	0.87	0.88	0.87
	400X	0.87	0.88	0.87	0.88	0.90	0.88
NASNetLarge	40X	0.88	0.79	0.80	0.80	0.81	0.79
	100X	0.90	0.72	0.73	0.73	0.74	0.73
	200X	0.86	0.80	0.81	0.80	0.79	0.80
	400X	0.94	0.81	0.78	0.80	0.85	0.73
EfficientNetB7	40X	0.48	0.50	0.46	0.50	0.25	0.37
	100X	0.50	0.53	0.51	0.46	0.32	0.35
	200X	0.49	0.48	0.46	0.49	0.27	0.45
	400X	0.73	0.50	0.50	0.50	0.25	0.33

Source: Authors evaluated experimental results.

Table 24.2   Performance evaluation of different neural network models using TL and last layer fine-tuning

Model	Image Magnification Factor	Training Performance			Testing Performance		
		Training Accuracy	Validation Accuracy	Accuracy	Recall	Precision	F1-Measure
VGG16	40X	0.85	0.83	0.82	0.86	0.84	0.85
	100X	0.89	0.88	0.87	0.86	0.89	0.88
	200X	0.85	0.87	0.88	0.89	0.87	0.88
	400X	0.84	0.81	0.82	0.83	0.86	0.81

Model	Image Magnification Factor	Training Performance			Testing Performance		
		Training Accuracy	Validation Accuracy	Accuracy	Recall	Precision	F1-Measure
VGG19	40X	0.83	0.85	0.87	0.84	0.86	0.85
	100X	0.85	0.81	0.80	0.81	0.83	0.82
	200X	0.82	0.84	0.85	0.83	0.87	0.85
	400X	0.81	0.82	0.83	0.81	0.84	0.82
ResNet 101	40X	0.64	0.65	0.66	0.65	0.67	0.64
	100X	0.67	0.60	0.61	0.59	0.72	0.54
	200X	0.61	0.54	0.55	0.54	0.76	0.42
	400X	0.64	0.55	0.54	0.56	0.76	0.50
InceptionV3	40X	0.89	0.88	0.87	0.89	0.87	0.88
	100X	0.85	0.81	0.82	0.84	0.83	0.81
	200X	0.81	0.77	0.76	0.79	0.78	0.77
	400X	0.83	0.82	0.81	0.83	0.84	0.82
Xception	40X	0.86	0.82	0.83	0.83	0.84	0.85
	100X	0.88	0.83	0.84	0.81	0.80	0.83
	200X	0.87	0.82	0.84	0.82	0.83	0.81
	400X	0.86	0.82	0.81	0.82	0.80	0.83
DenseNet121	40X	**0.86**	**0.87**	**0.86**	**0.87**	**0.88**	**0.85**
	100X	**0.89**	**0.86**	**0.87**	**0.88**	**0.89**	**0.87**
	200X	**0.87**	**0.91**	**0.88**	**0.87**	**0.89**	**0.91**
	400X	**0.88**	**0.88**	**0.89**	**0.87**	**0.88**	**0.89**
NASNetLarge	40X	0.85	0.84	0.85	0.86	0.83	0.85
	100X	0.87	0.77	0.78	0.79	0.78	0.80
	200X	0.86	0.77	0.78	0.74	0.79	0.77
	400X	0.84	0.78	0.79	0.77	0.80	0.81
EfficientNetB7	40X	0.49	0.50	0.52	0.46	0.51	0.51
	100X	0.52	0.47	0.47	0.51	0.50	0.53
	200X	0.53	0.52	0.49	0.50	0.52	0.47
	400X	0.50	0.49	0.50	0.48	0.47	0.52

Source: Authors evaluated experimental results.

layers fine-tuning is applied for more accurate classification (shown in Table 24.3). In this experimental study, DenseNet121 with TL and all layers fine-tuning showed 89% accuracy at 40x magnification factor at best. The overall performance of this network is increased by the used of TL. In TL, DenseNet121 shows better accuracy compared to all other transfer learning CNN models. Moreover, VGG16 showed significantly increasing results by the used of TL. But Xception model's performance is decreased to accuracy (maximum) 94% to 86% by using TL. InceptionV3, NASNetLarge and EfficientNetB7 are not show any significant changes, whereas ResNet101 showed decreasing performance by the used of TL. In the last approach, we extract the features of benign and malignant classes using CNN models and then classify the extracted features using the SVM classifier (shown in Table 24.4). Overall, all the eight models give better performance using CNN as a feature extractor with SVM classifier. However, ResNet101 and EfficientNetB7 give their best performances using CNN as a feature extractor with SVM classifier with 93% classification accuracy at 40X and 100X magnification factor, respectively. At last we conclude that, Xception model gives overall best performance for medical image analysis in all these four approaches. As compared to all other approaches, the last approach i.e. CNN as a feature extractor with SVM classifier gives overall best results in all the eight models. Although, image magnifying factors (40x, 100x, 200x and 400x) don't showed any significant impact in histopathological image classification tasks.

Table 24.3 Performance evaluation of different neural network models using TL and all layers fine-tuning

Model	Image Magnification Factor	Training Performance			Testing Performance		
		Training Accuracy	Validation Accuracy	Accuracy	Recall	Precision	F1-Measure
VGG16	40X	0.82	0.87	0.84	0.86	0.88	0.85
	100X	0.89	0.84	0.85	0.85	0.85	0.85
	200X	0.85	0.86	0.86	0.86	0.86	0.86
	400X	0.83	0.85	0.84	0.85	0.83	0.86
VGG19	40X	0.50	0.50	0.54	0.51	0.35	0.33
	100X	0.51	0.49	0.53	0.50	0.25	0.30
	200X	0.49	0.50	0.51	0.50	0.25	0.33
	400X	0.48	0.47	0.47	0.53	0.28	0.35
ResNet 101	40X	0.59	0.57	0.58	0.58	0.64	0.52
	100X	0.64	0.73	0.74	0.74	0.74	0.73
	200X	0.59	0.56	0.56	0.56	0.70	0.47
	400X	0.61	0.62	0.62	0.62	0.71	0.58
InceptionV3	40X	0.86	0.85	0.85	0.85	0.85	0.85
	100X	0.86	0.84	0.84	0.84	0.85	0.84
	200X	0.81	0.77	0.77	0.77	0.80	0.77
	400X	0.82	0.78	0.78	0.78	0.79	0.78
Xception	40X	0.86	0.83	0.84	0.84	0.84	0.84
	100X	0.87	0.80	0.81	0.81	0.81	0.81
	200X	0.84	0.86	0.86	0.85	0.86	0.86
	400X	0.83	0.82	0.82	0.81	0.82	0.82
DenseNet121	40X	**0.89**	**0.88**	**0.89**	**0.89**	**0.90**	**0.89**
	100X	**0.88**	**0.84**	**0.84**	**0.84**	**0.86**	**0.84**
	200X	**0.90**	**0.86**	**0.85**	**0.86**	**0.88**	**0.86**
	400X	**0.86**	**0.85**	**0.86**	**0.84**	**0.84**	**0.86**
NASNetLarge	40X	0.87	0.80	0.81	0.84	0.82	0.81
	100X	0.88	0.83	0.84	0.82	0.80	0.83
	200X	0.86	0.81	0.80	0.81	0.82	0.84
	400X	0.87	0.75	0.74	0.75	0.73	0.75
EfficientNetB7	40X	0.50	0.50	0.51	0.49	0.25	0.36
	100X	0.48	0.47	0.48	0.50	0.28	0.33
	200X	0.49	0.52	0.52	0.48	0.26	0.35
	400X	0.47	0.49	0.50	0.52	0.24	0.32

Source: Authors evaluated experimental results.

6. Conclusion and Future Work

In this paper, various CNN models using different approaches for two-stage classification of histopathological images on BreakHis dataset for breast abnormality prediction are presented. Also, implemented transfer learning with fine-tuning using CNN architectures for comparative analysis and the use of these concepts are defined. The experimental findings of this study provided a better understanding of CNNs in breast abnormality prediction. Based on our study, we conclude that for histopathological image classification using the Xception model with specific settings is a reliable and effective strategy compared to the other CNN models. However, the computer-aided automatic diagnosis framework could extend in the field of

Table 24.4   Performance evaluation of CNNs as a feature extractor with SVM classifier

Model	Image Magnification Factor	Testing Performance			
		Accuracy	Recall	Precision	F1-Measure
VGG16	40X	0.88	0.89	0.87	0.88
	100X	0.87	0.86	0.89	0.86
	200X	0.86	0.85	0.86	0.87
	400X	0.85	0.84	0.85	0.86
VGG19	40X	0.86	0.87	0.85	0.86
	100X	0.86	0.85	0.86	0.87
	200X	0.85	0.84	0.85	0.86
	400X	0.84	0.83	0.84	0.82
ResNet101	40X	**0.93**	**0.89**	**0.91**	**0.92**
	100X	**0.91**	**0.90**	**0.92**	**0.90**
	200X	**0.90**	**0.92**	**0.91**	**0.92**
	400X	**0.88**	**0.87**	**0.89**	**0.88**
InceptionV3	40X	0.88	0.89	0.86	0.87
	100X	0.87	0.86	0.88	0.87
	200X	0.81	0.82	0.80	0.81
	400X	0.83	0.82	0.84	0.83
Xception	40X	0.88	0.89	0.87	0.88
	100X	0.89	0.88	0.89	0.87
	200X	0.87	0.86	0.85	0.84
	400X	0.85	0.86	0.87	0.85
DenseNet121	40X	0.92	0.93	0.90	0.92
	100X	0.89	0.88	0.91	0.89
	200X	0.90	0.92	0.90	0.89
	400X	0.86	0.85	0.86	0.84
NASNetLarge	40X	0.86	0.88	0.85	0.87
	100X	0.83	0.82	0.84	0.83
	200X	0.82	0.80	0.81	0.83
	400X	0.80	0.79	0.82	0.80
EfficientNetB7	40X	**0.92**	**0.90**	**0.91**	**0.89**
	100X	**0.93**	**0.91**	**0.93**	**0.92**
	200X	**0.89**	**0.87**	**0.90**	**0.89**
	400X	**0.90**	**0.88**	**0.91**	**0.91**

Source: Authors evaluated experimental results.

medical diagnosis as a supporting tool of a doctor or pathologist for early disease diagnosis. Based on this study in future cancer grading or subtype classification using CNN models may be carried out which may be more beneficial for cancer treatment and prevention.

7. Acknowledgment

The work of Anindita Mohanta was supported by AICTE Doctoral Fellowship (ADF) Programme (Application Number: 1638385211866).

REFERENCES

1. Bahadori, M. T., Liu, Y., & Zhang, D. (2014). A general framework for scalable transductive transfer learning. Knowledge and information systems, 38, 61–83.
2. de Matos, J., de Souza Britto, A., de Oliveira, L. E., & Koerich, A. L. (2019). Texture CNN for histopathological image classification. In 2019 IEEE 32nd international symposium on computer-based medical systems (CBMS) (pp. 580–583). IEEE.
3. Gour, M., Jain, S., & Sunil Kumar, T. (2020). Residual learning based CNN for breast cancer histopathological image classification. International Journal of Imaging Systems and Technology, 30(3), 621–635.
4. Gui, L., Xu, R., Lu, Q., Du, J., & Zhou, Y. (2018). Negative transfer detection in transductive transfer learning. International Journal of Machine Learning and Cybernetics, 9, 185–197.
5. Gurcan, M. N., Boucheron, L. E., Can, A., Madabhushi, A., Rajpoot, N. M., & Yener, B. (2009). Histopathological image analysis: A review. IEEE reviews in biomedical engineering, 2, 147–171.
6. Hussain, Z., Gimenez, F., Yi, D., & Rubin, D. (2017). Differential data augmentation techniques for medical imaging classification tasks. In AMIA annual symposium proceedings (Vol. 2017, p. 979). American Medical Informatics Association.
7. Ioffe, S., & Szegedy, C. (2015). Batch normalization: Accelerating deep network training by reducing internal covariate shift. In International conference on machine learning (pp. 448–456). pmlr.
8. Janghel, R. R., Shukla, A., Tiwari, R., & Kala, R. (2010). Breast cancer diagnosis using artificial neural network models. In The 3rd International Conference on Information Sciences and Interaction Sciences (pp. 89–94). IEEE.
9. Jannesari, M., Habibzadeh, M., Aboulkheyr, H., Khosravi, P., Elemento, O., Totonchi, M., & Hajirasouliha, I. (2018). Breast cancer histopathological image classification: a deep learning approach. In 2018 IEEE international conference on bioinformatics and biomedicine (BIBM) (pp. 2405–2412). IEEE.
10. Kandel, I., Castelli, M., & Popovič, A. (2020). Comparative study of first order optimizers for image classification using convolutional neural networks on histopathology images. Journal of imaging, 6(9), 92.
11. Liu, B., Yin, C., Liu, Z., Zhang, Z., Gao, J., Zhu, M., ... & Xu, K. (2007). Microscopic image analysis and recognition on pathological cells. In 2007 Canadian Conference on Electrical and Computer Engineering (pp. 1022–1025). IEEE.
12. Nazeri, K., Aminpour, A., & Ebrahimi, M. (2018). Two-stage convolutional neural network for breast cancer histology image classification. In Image Analysis and Recognition: 15th International Conference, ICIAR 2018, Póvoa de Varzim, Portugal, June 27–29, 2018, Proceedings 15 (pp. 717–726). Springer International Publishing.
13. O'Shea, K., & Nash, R. (2015). An introduction to convolutional neural networks. arXiv preprint arXiv:1511.08458.
14. Rubin, R., Strayer, D. S., & Rubin, E. (Eds.). (2008). Rubin's pathology: clinicopathologic foundations of medicine. Lippincott Williams & Wilkins.
15. Rusiecki, A. (2019). Trimmed categorical cross-entropy for deep learning with label noise. Electronics Letters, 55(6), 319–320.
16. Spanhol, F. A., Oliveira, L. S., Cavalin, P. R., Petitjean, C., & Heutte, L. (2017). Deep features for breast cancer histopathological image classification. In 2017 IEEE International Conference on Systems, Man, and Cybernetics (pp. 1868–1873). IEEE.
17. Spanhol, F. A., Oliveira, L. S., Petitjean, C., & Heutte, L. (2015). A dataset for breast cancer histopathological image classification. Ieee transactions on biomedical engineering, 63(7), 1455–1462.
18. Sutskever, I., Martens, J., Dahl, G., & Hinton, G. (2013). On the importance of initialization and momentum in deep learning. In International conference on machine learning (pp. 1139–1147). PMLR.
19. Suzuki, K. (2017). Overview of deep learning in medical imaging. Radiological physics and technology, 10(3), 257-273.
20. Ubaidillah, S. H. S. A., Sallehuddin, R., & Ali, N. A. (2013). Cancer detection using aritifical neural network and support vector machine: a comparative study. Jurnal Teknologi, 65(1), 73–81.
21. Waibel, A., Hanazawa, T., Hinton, G., Shikano, K., & Lang, K. J. (1989). Phoneme recognition using time-delay neural networks. IEEE transactions on acoustics, speech, and signal processing, 37(3), 328–339.
22. Wei, B., Han, Z., He, X., & Yin, Y. (2017). Deep learning model based breast cancer histopathological image classification. In 2017 IEEE 2nd international conference on cloud computing and big data analysis (ICCCBDA) (pp. 348–353). IEEE.
23. Yang, H., Kim, J. Y., Kim, H., & Adhikari, S. P. (2019). Guided soft attention network for classification of breast cancer histopathology images. IEEE transactions on medical imaging, 39(5), 1306–1315.
24. Zhu, C., Song, F., Wang, Y., Dong, H., Guo, Y., & Liu, J. (2019). Breast cancer histopathology image classification through assembling multiple compact CNNs. BMC medical informatics and decision making, 19(1), 1–17.

Advances in Computational Intelligence and its Applications (ICACIA-2023) – Dr. Sheikh Fahad Ahmad et al. (eds)
© 2024 Taylor & Francis Group, London, ISBN 978-1-032-78612-4

Framework for Home Layout Design by Semantic Parsing of Text

25

**Rushab Prakash Kulkarni[1], Shambhavi M. Puttane[2],
Sai Mihir J.[3], Jayashree R.[4], Shane Hansel Mendon[5]**

Computer Science and Engineering, PES University,
Bangalore, Karnataka

ABSTRACT—Home design is a complicated procedure that is frequently handled by licensed architects who are experts in the sector. We investigate many generating and validation approaches for semantic search-based retrieval results supplied by a user-based input for architectural design help, especially to design layout for their house, in this work. We've tried to develop a way that enables anyone with a strong command of the English language to express their desires through text. Additionally, the outcome of this procedure might not be what the customer had in mind or might differ from their conclusion. By using concise, clear English, our approach will enable both the average user and the interior designer to convey their imaginative ideas, and our project will be able to visualize the picture that they described. This approach can accurately construct a 3-D layout of the house, based on the text description while saving time and resources. This is mostly because software is objective, in contrast to humans.

KEYWORDS—3-D, Floor plan, Generation, Semantic text parsing, Natural language processing, Layout generation

1. Introduction

Everyone wishes to build a house as they desire, but is unable to do so due to communication issues with the designer or other constraints, it can be beneficial for a layperson who lacks the years of experience of a certified interior architect to envision their home beforehand. The user can avoid spending time orally describing their needs to the qualified architect. By using concise, clear English, our approach will enable both the average user and the interior designer to convey their imaginative ideas, and our project will be able to visualize the picture that they described. This approach can accurately construct a 3-D layout based on the text description while saving time and resources.

We provide a unique architecture-based framework for generating a 3-D layout that is graph-constrained. We encode the layout's characteristics into a graph structure of its relational networks based on the user's restrictions. We've added the option for the user to enter the number of rooms, room types, and room locations to make it easier to use. With the help of various techniques, such as sentence embedding, graphconstrained networks, and rendering tools, we'll then show users the near optimal 3-D layout or floor plan for their input. This study looks at how well each technique performs in various situations and at different times, as well as how well potential explanations and their confirmation may be predicted generally. In order to analyse these issues, we examine the overall performance, or the average rate of valid explanations, as well as how the rate of validation evolves as time passes.

---

[1]rushabpk31@gmail.com, [2]pshambhavi2@gmail.com, [3]saimihir.j@gmail.com, [4]jayashree@pes.edu, [5]shanemendon@gmail.com

DOI: 10.1201/9781003488682-25

2. Review of Literature

A House Plan Generative Model (HPGM) that translates the language input into a structural graph representation, predicts room layout using a Graph Conditioned Layout Prediction Network (GC-LPN), and produces interior texture using a Language Conditioned Texture GAN (LCT-GAN). After considerable post-processing, the final result of this job is a 3-D home model. In order to train and evaluate our model, the authors developed the first dataset for the Text-to-3-D House Model.[1]

Sentence-BERT (SBERT) is a BERT network-based siamese and triplet network that may construct semantically meaningful sentence embeddings. As a result, BERT may be used for a variety of new tasks that it could not previously accomplish. Some of the applications include large-scale semantic similarity comparison, and information retrieval via semantic search, etc.[2]

The authors provide sentence encoding models that are designed to be transferable to various NLP tasks. These models are effective and accurate at a variety of transfer activities. The encoding models include two variants that allow for a trade-off between precision and computational capacity. The authors analyse and discuss the relationship between model complexity, resource utilisation, transfer task training data availability, and performance for both kinds. They compare these models to baselines that use transfer learning at the word level with pre-trained word embeddings, and to baselines without any transfer learning. The results show that transfer learning using sentence embeddings typically outperforms transfer learning at the word level.[3]

For a variety of transfer tasks, using universal phrase representations trained on supervised data from the Stanford Natural Language Inference datasets consistently outperforms unsupervised approaches. The authors' work generally implies that natural language inference is appropriate for transfer learning to other NLP tasks.[4]

This study investigates learning document embeddings with Doc2Vec, a Word2Vec extension. The neural network model's purpose is to maximise the cosine similarity of the sentence embeddings for the pair given a pair of paraphrases, word embeddings, and a mechanism to create the word embeddings for a sentence embedding. The best Doc2Vec hyper-parameter settings for general-purpose applications were determined empirically. Doc2vec worked well even when trained on huge external corpora when helped by pre-trained word embeddings.[12]

Creating 3-D data that meets specific requirements is the foundation of controllable scene synthesis. Therefore, these standards need to be abstract, providing an easy-to-use interface for the user while still allowing for intricate control. Scene graphs, which are visual representations of a scene made up of objects (nodes) and their interactions (edges), have shown to be particularly useful for this purpose since they provide users meaningful control over the created data. To solve this issue, we present a novel method for directly generating forms from an end-to-end scene graph. We train a variational Autoencoder on the object and edge categories, as well as 3-D forms and scene layouts, using Graph Convolutional Networks (GCN), allowing us to sample new sceneries and shapes in the future.[11]

Researchers have developed a framework for automated layout creation that combines generative modeling, deep neural networks, and user involvement. The system, called Graph2Plan, uses a layout graph to incorporate user-specified design restrictions, such as room count, into the floor plan creation process. The neural network transforms the building boundary and layout graph into a floor plan that meets the given constraints. Graph2Plan starts by creating a preliminary floor plan based on the input boundary and layout graph, and then refines the room representations. It was trained on a large dataset of 80,000 annotated floor plans called RPLAN. The network uses convolutional processing and a graph neural network to process the building boundary, raster floor plan, and layout graph. The system's ability to adapt to various user inputs is demonstrated through ablation studies, comparisons with other methods, and both qualitative and quantitative evaluations.[14]

Researchers provide a deep neural network architecture for automating floor plan-based home searches. The query's ability to be either an image (such as an existing floor plan) or a drawing via a sketch pad interface is one of the framework's primary features. The proposed framework instantaneously detects the query type (photo or sketch) and searches the database for associated floor plan pictures. The following are the main contributions of our proposed strategy: (1) a novel unified floor plan retrieval framework based on multi-modal query, i.e., an understandable and practical sketch query mode as well as a query by example mode; and (2) a combination of auto-encoder, CNN for domain mapping and floor plan picture retrieval, and Cyclic GAN.[13]

The goal of this article is to investigate the use of machine learning and neural network models to examine some of the strategies now used by designers to automatically construct building floor plans and other spatial arrangements. This is a relatively recent trend in computational design, reflecting a rising interest in advanced generative and optimisation models among architects and building engineers. The first half of the essay contextualises self-organizing floor plans within the framework of computational and architectural design, emphasising its importance and possible advantages for both designers and software developers. With concrete examples, the major body of the paper explores various well-known approaches, including Generative Adversarial Networks (GAN). The articles conclusion reflects on potential risks and future advancements, and speculates on the direction this trend is likely to take.[15]

This paper provides a method for creating several types of floor plans using computer assistance at the initial stages of conceptual design in architecture. The procedures of gathering inspiration and looking for contextual support to improve the current building design dominate the early design phases. The generation approach presented in this study creates potential evolutions of the current design based on the most comparable prior designs using unique as well as existing artificial intelligence methodologies, specifically generative adversarial networks and case-based reasoning. The major objective of this strategy is to tell the designer about potential future changes to the present floor plan, which will help guide the design process.(16)

3. Dataset

The dataset includes natural language descriptions for each of the 13,478 room views and the 2,000 home images. These descriptions are initially created using a few prede-termined templates, and then they are polished by personnel. There are 193 different words in the description, which has an average length of 173.73 words. In our research, we generate the building plan using 1,600 pairings for training and 400 pairs for testing. [1], [5]-[9], [19]

4. Proposed Methodology

A House Plan Generative Model (HPGM), which can create 3-D house plans from provided linguistic terms, is proposed by the existing design approach in (1). The HPGM executive summary is as follows: The textual structural representations V, X, and A were created by parsing the specified text input using the Stanford Scene Graph Parser. The fundamental building arrangement is created by the GC-LPN using a graph convolutional network based on X and A. The resulting floor plan is then improved by post-processing. V claims that LCT-GAN produces appropriate textures for individual rooms. An objective House Plan is then constructed in 3-D via the 3-D scene-generating method.

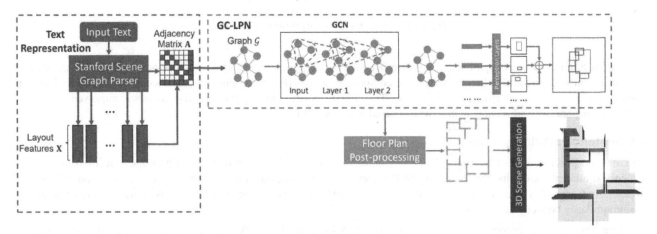

Fig. 25.1 Layout generation from text flowchart [1]

Our adopted strategy incorporates the previously mentioned design as a part of its structure. We provide a structure that separates sentence similarity and layout creation into two separate modules to simplify the visualization of a home plan for non-experts. The objective of determining sentence similarity is to compare two texts and evaluate their similarity. Sentence similarity models transform input texts into meaningful embeddings and evaluate their similarity. This process is extremely beneficial in this scenario as a regular user may not have the correct vocabulary to express their vision for building a house or may simply want to preview the outcome and make adjustments if needed.

Dealing with single words would be time-consuming, akin to dealing with enormous volumes of text, and we would be restricted by the information gleaned through word embeddings. We could deal with individual sentences instead. Sentence embedding techniques represent complete sentences as vectors that carry semantic data. This makes it simpler for the system to comprehend the context, purpose, and other nuances of the full text. The main five embedding methods currently in use are compared and contrasted in this module:

1. Doc2Vec [12]
2. SentenceBERT [2]
3. Infersent [3]
4. Universal Sentence Encoder [3]
5. Sentence Transformer (Hugging Face) [4]

Now that we have found our most identical sentence, first room count is listed, then connections between these rooms, finally design of these rooms. This is our most similar linguistic statement. Despite the weakly structured style, the direct usage of template-based language parser is difficult due to the wide range of language descriptions. [17], [18], [20]

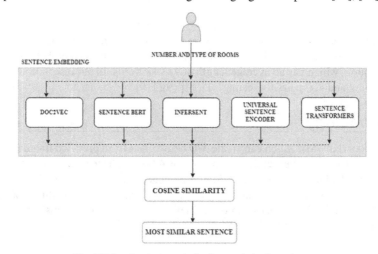

Fig. 25.2 Sentence similarity module flowchart

Source: Author

We employ Stanford Scene Graph Parser for post-processing and merging, to turn spoken inputs into graph structures. We use Graph Conditioned Layout Prediction Network, a component of the HPGM architecture described above, to create building layouts that adhere to the specifications (GC-LPN). The effectiveness of creating the objective layouts is improved by using a GCN to incorporate the adjacent data into the recovered features. [5]-[9].

4.1 Sentence Similarity

This module provides a brief overview of the five sentence encoders discussed before and how they are used to perform sentence similarity. We outline each necessary NLP library. We then define our corpus of language expressions, often known as phrases. Additionally, a tokenized version of these phrases will be preserved. Finally, a function is constructed to compute the cosine similarity between two vectors.

- **Doc2Vec**: This unsupervised method, introduced in 2014, extends the Word2Vec model by incorporating a second "paragraph vector." Furthermore, the paragraph vector may be incorporated into the model in two ways: distributed memory version of paragraph vector (PVDM) and distributed bag of words version of paragraph vector (PVDOBW). Before constructing a corpus of tagged sentences, we will utilise the Gensim model and other tools. Each phrase, represented as a TaggedDocument, complete with a tag, words list.[12]

- **SentenceBERT**: It is the current market leader, was first introduced in 2018, it immediately surpassed all competitors in terms of sentence embeddings. This BERT-based paradigm rests on four fundamental ideas: Attention, Transformers, BERT, and the Siamese Network. Sentence-BERT, which employs a Siamese network-like architecture, is fed two sentences. BERT models and a pooling layer use these two words to generate embeddings. The cosine similarity is then calculated using the embeddings of the two texts as inputs.[2]

- **InferSent**: InferSent, a supervised sentence embedding technology developed by Facebook AI Research, was unveiled in 2018. We encode a pair of sentences to yield real sentence embeddings, just like SentenceBERT. The following approaches can then be used to derive the relationships between these embeddings: The absolute difference between elements created by element-by-element concatenation. There are two versions of InferSent. Version 2 use fastText vectors, whereas Version 1 employs GLovE. Version 2 was utilised. We load our model and word embeddings, encrypt the test question, and give it an embedding. The cosine similarity between this query and each of our text's phrases is subsequently computed.[3]

- **Universal Sentence Encoder**: This BERT-based paradigm rests on four fundamental ideas: Attention, Transformers, BERT, and the Siamese Network. Sentence-BERT, which employs a Siamese network-like architecture, is fed two sentences. BERT models and a pooling layer use these two words to generate embeddings. The cosine similarity is then calculated using by taking input as the two text embeddings.[3]

- **Sentence Transformer**: The framework offers a substantial library of pre-trained models that have been optimised for a variety of tasks. It is constructed using Transformers and PyTorch. It's also easy to alter your own models. Numerous models are stored under this, including multi-qa-mpnet-base-dot-v1. Install the sentence transformer as this model is hosted under it. We need to define the user text and the existing corpus and keep them in separate arrays, Load the model, Encode the query and documents then compute the dot score between them accordingly then combine the doc and score and sort them in descending order based on the score.[4]

4.2 Graph Conditioned Layout Prediction Network (GC-LPN)

We utilized a Graph Conditioned Layout Prediction Network (GC-LPN) for proposing building plans that adhere to the specifications. We first run our dataset through the Stanford Scene Parser to convert the verbal descriptions into a structural graph. Each node in such a built graph is a room with certain characteristics (e.g., the room size, type, location). In feature matrix, where 1 denotes adjacent and 0 denotes not adjacent, the edges of the room serve as indicators of connection. The next step is to process the graph using the two-layer GCN model. [1]

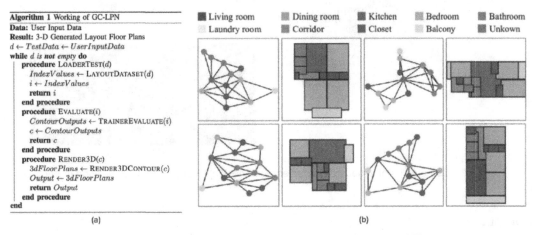

Fig. 25.3 Working of GC-LPN (a) Algorithm, (b) Illustration [17]

4.3 Metrics

Equations related to classification metrics taken for comparative analysis of different NLP Models and calculating similarity between semantically parsed text and giving similar queries to be sent to GC-LPN:

$$\text{Accuracy} = \frac{TP + TN}{TP + TN + FP + FN} \tag{1}$$

$$\text{Precision} = \frac{TP}{TP + FP} \tag{2}$$

$$\text{Recall} = \frac{TP}{TP + FN} \tag{3}$$

$$F1 = \frac{2 * \text{Precision} * \text{Recall}}{\text{Precision} + \text{Recall}} = \frac{2 * TP}{2 * TP + FP + FN} \tag{4}$$

$$\text{Consine}\,(x, y) = \frac{x \cdot y}{|x||y|} \tag{5}$$

5. Results and Discussion

5.1 Comparison of Sentence Embedding Models

The findings of our models, which compare the various NLP models used for text processing, are shown in the below figure. We noticed that clearly SentenceBert proved to be the best out of all the embeddings taken.

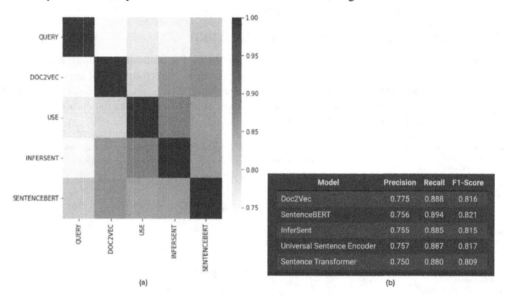

Model	Precision	Recall	F1-Score
Doc2Vec	0.775	0.888	0.816
SentenceBERT	0.756	0.894	0.821
InferSent	0.755	0.885	0.815
Universal Sentence Encoder	0.757	0.887	0.817
Sentence Transformer	0.750	0.880	0.809

(a)   (b)

Fig. 25.4 Comparison of various sentence embeddings, (a) Heatmap, (b) Classification metrics

Source: Authors

5.2 Final Output

See Fig. 25.5

6. Conclusion

This aim of this study was to enable the average user to visualise a 3-D design of the house they intended to construct in the future. Through this project, users without prior expertise will be able to understand some architectural concepts that may be difficult for them to do so. Sentence embeddings, Graph Convolution Networks, and Stanford Scene Parser are a few of the cutting-edge techniques that may be used to quickly and effectively visualise a user's description of a home by describing the number, kind, and location of the rooms. In our analysis, we find that LSTM outperforms RNN in terms of training and testing, delivering the best outcomes for users to view their floor plans. The most effective sentence embedding was SentenceBERT.

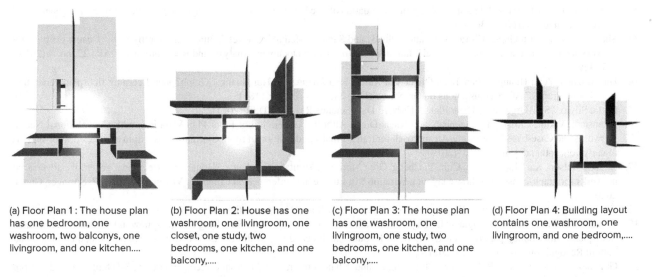

(a) Floor Plan 1 : The house plan has one bedroom, one washroom, two balconys, one livingroom, and one kitchen....

(b) Floor Plan 2: House has one washroom, one livingroom, one closet, one study, two bedrooms, one kitchen, and one balcony,....

(c) Floor Plan 3: The house plan has one washroom, one livingroom, one study, two bedrooms, one kitchen, and one balcony,....

(d) Floor Plan 4: Building layout contains one washroom, one livingroom, and one bedroom,....

Fig. 25.5 Similar 3-D generated floor plan outputs i.e., query: I want a building which has one bedroom, one kitchen, one living room

Source: Author

7. Future Works

We will be looking to integrate recommendations to be given regarding textures and colors based on input. The current model needs to be trained on more data and different types of data. Our current dataset describes single-story buildings, however it can be expanded to include multistory buildings. We can also attempt to incorporate Indian norms or Vasthu into the model in the future. We can implement real-time layout processing.

REFERENCES

1. Chen, Qi, Qi Wu, Rui Tang, Yuhan Wang, Shuai Wang, and Mingkui Tan. "Intelligent home 3-D: Automatic 3-D-house design from linguistic descriptions only." In Proceedings of the IEEE/CVF Conference on Computer Vision and Pattern Recognition, pp. 12625–12634. 2020.
2. Reimers, Nils, and Iryna Gurevych. "Sentence-bert: Sentence embeddings using siamese bert-networks." arXiv preprint arXiv:1908.10084 (2019).
3. Cer, Daniel, Yinfei Yang, Sheng-yi Kong, Nan Hua, Nicole Limtiaco, Rhomni St John, Noah Constant et al. "Universal sentence encoder." arXiv preprint arXiv:1803.11175 (2018).
4. Conneau, Alexis, Douwe Kiela, Holger Schwenk, Loic Barrault, and Antoine Bordes. "Supervised learning of universal sentence representations from natural language inference data." arXiv preprint arXiv:1705.02364 (2017).
5. Chang, Angel, Will Monroe, Manolis Savva, Christopher Potts, and Christopher D. Manning. "Text to 3-D scene generation with rich lexical grounding." arXiv preprint arXiv:1505.06289 (2015).
6. Chang, Angel, Manolis Savva, and Christopher D. Manning. "Semantic parsing for text to 3-D scene generation." In Proceedings of the ACL 2014 workshop on semantic parsing, pp. 17–21. 2014.
7. Chang, Angel, Manolis Savva, and Christopher D. Manning. "Learning spatial knowledge for text to 3-D scene generation." In Proceedings of the 2014 Conference on Empirical Methods in Natural Language Processing (EMNLP), pp. 2028–2038. 2014.
8. Schuster, Sebastian, Ranjay Krishna, Angel Chang, Li Fei-Fei, and Christopher D. Manning. "Generating semantically precise scene graphs from textual descriptions for improved image retrieval." In Proceedings of the fourth workshop on vision and language, pp. 70–80. 2015.
9. Zhang, Cheng, et al. "Holistic 3-D scene understanding from a single image with implicit representation." Proceedings of the IEEE/CVF Conference on Computer Vision and Pattern Recognition. 2021.
10. Yu, Chong, and Young Wang. "3-D-scene-GAN: Three-dimensional scene reconstruction with generative adversarial networks." (2018).
11. Dhamo, Helisa, et al. "Graph-to-3-D: End-to-end generation and manipulation of 3-D scenes using scene graphs." Proceedings of the IEEE/CVF International Conference on Computer Vision. 2021.

12. Lau, Jey Han, and Timothy Baldwin. "An empirical evaluation of doc2vec with practical insights into document embedding generation." arXiv preprint arXiv:1607.05368 (2016).
13. Sharma, Divya, Nitin Gupta, Chiranjoy Chattopadhyay, and Sameep Mehta. "A novel feature transform framework using deep neural network for multimodal floor plan retrieval." International Journal on Document Analysis and Recognition (IJDAR) 22, no. 4 (2019): 417–429.
14. Hu, Ruizhen, Zeyu Huang, Yuhan Tang, Oliver Van Kaick, Hao Zhang, and Hui Huang. "Graph2plan: Learning floorplan generation from layout graphs." ACM Transactions on Graphics (TOG) 39, no. 4 (2020): 118–1.
15. Carta, Silvio. "Self-Organizing Floor Plans." Harvard Data Science Review HDSR (2021).
16. Eisenstadt, Viktor, Christoph Langenhan, and Klaus-Dieter Althoff. "Generation of Floor Plan Variations with Convolutional Neural Networks and Case-based Reasoning-An approach for transformative adaptation of room configurations within a framework for support of early conceptual design phases." (2019).
17. Nauata, Nelson, Kai-Hung Chang, Chin-Yi Cheng, Greg Mori, and Yasutaka Furukawa. "House-gan: Relational generative adversarial networks for graph-constrained house layout generation." In European Conference on Computer Vision, pp. 162–177. Springer, Cham, 2020.
18. Zheng, Hao, Keyao An, Jingxuan Wei, and Yue Ren. "Apartment floor plans generation via generative adversarial networks." (2020).
19. Cruz, Steve, Will Hutchcroft, Yuguang Li, Naji Khosravan, Ivaylo Boyadzhiev, and Sing Bing Kang. "Zillow indoor dataset: Annotated floor plans with 360deg panoramas and 3-D room layouts." In Proceedings of the IEEE/CVF Conference on Computer Vision and Pattern Recognition, pp. 2133–2143. 2021.
20. Gimenez, Lucile, Sylvain Robert, Fr´ed´eric Suard, and Khaldoun Zreik. "Automatic reconstruction of 3-D building models from scanned 2D floor plans." Automation in Construction 63 (2016): 48–56.

URL Phishing Prediction with GUI Implementation Using Machine Learning

26

Ganditi Yoginath[1], Charian Sai Ganesh Reddy[2], Kalahastri V.N.S Revanth Kumar[3], C. N. Sujatha[4], V. Raghavendra[5]

Sreenidhi Institute of Science and Technology,
Department of Electronics and Communication Engineering

ABSTRACT—This study aims to showcase the utilization of an Extreme Learning Machine (ELM) to classify data obtained from phishing websites, which is available in the UC Irvine Machine Learning Repository database. Phishing stands as one of the most prevalent and perilous cybercrime tactics, targeting sensitive information used by both consumers and businesses for their transactions. Phishing websites employ various indicators within their content and adapt to different web browsers. When compared to alternative machine learning methods like Support Vector Machine and Naive Bayes for outcome assessment, the ELM was found to offer the highest accuracy. The implementation process takes place using the XAMPP Server for creating the database, while Django is employed to design the framework of the webpage. Online security faces significant threats from phishing attempts, which have persisted for a long time and continue to pose a substantial challenge. Phishing attacks are on the rise, with attackers employing innovative and diverse tactics. Hence, it becomes essential to comprehensively examine both traditional and emerging phishing techniques, and this paper delves into the strategies employed in phishing endeavors. The well-known Phishtank dataset, a standard in the realm of hacking websites, is accessible at https://phishtank.org/. It operates through a community-driven framework that monitors webpages for potential phishing sites. Users from various backgrounds report phishing locations, later validated by other users as "legitimate points." As a result, Phishtank maintains a real-time repository of phishing websites. Researchers utilize the Phishtank website to set up data collection for testing and uncovering phishing sites.

KEYWORDS—Phishing, ML, Extreme learning machine, SVM, NB

1. Introduction

The internet is now a need for us to conduct our daily lives due to how swiftly technology is evolving. As a result of fast technological innovation and widespread use of digital systems, data security in these systems has gained a critical role. The primary purpose of information system security is to ensure that the necessary precautions are taken in response to the hazards and threats that consumers are likely to experience while utilizing these technologies [15]. Phishing is the practice of impersonating a legitimate website so as to get sensitive data such as passwords, usernames, and identity numbers, which are frequently entered onto sites for a variety of reasons. In the content and web client information, phishing websites include a range of warning indications. While acting as the intended receiver, the fraudster(s) sends the phony website or email data. as a representative of a business, bank or another trustworthy provider that conducts trustworthy transactions. Links to websites that appear to be exact replicas of the relevant organizations' websites are provided in the text of the website or email, along with requests to submit or update personal information or reset password. phishing website characteristics Numerous papers [16-18]

[1]yoginathganditi@gmail.com, [2]chsaiganesh9000@gmail.com, [3]kalahastri13@gmail.com, [4]cnsujatha@gmail.com, [5]vraghavendray@gmail.com,

DOI: 10.1201/9781003488682-26

have discussed the use of artificial intelligence technologies to predict phishing websites. We examined phishing websites and noted their properties. The rules provided below are for the features of this database that were extracted. In the first section, we gave web feature equations and rules. These equations are required to comprehend phishing attacks. Characterization. Phishing is a well-known attack that tricks people into downloading risky content and divulging their personal information. The majority of phishing websites share the same URL and user experience as trustworthy websites. Blacklists, heuristics, and other strategies have all been advised for detecting phishing websites.

One class of techniques that has emerged as a powerful tool in enhancing data security is "machine learning." Machine learning empowers software developers to make highly accurate predictions without the need for explicit programming. The core principle of machine learning involves constructing algorithms that analyze input data through statistical analysis to predict output data. These algorithms continuously update their output as new input data becomes available. This concept is akin to data mining and predictive modeling, as both involve seeking specific patterns within data and adjusting software operations accordingly. Many individuals have become acquainted with machine learning through their online shopping experiences and the personalized marketing they encounter. This familiarity arises from recommendation engines that use machine learning to customize the advertisements they display in almost real-time. Machine learning has also found widespread use in various other domains, including fraud detection, spam filtering, network threat detection, predictive maintenance, and news content generation. One specific machine learning technique known as Elastic Learning Machine (ELM) is applied in categorizing data and comprises 30 distinct features. These features are further categorized into five subgroups, drawing from data extracted from websites in the UC Irvine Machine Learning Repository. These subgroups encompass Address bar-based features (Part 1 and Part 2), Abnormal-based features, HTML and JavaScript-based features, and Domain-based features.

The first subgroup comprises six address bar-based features. The first feature involves checking if the domain part includes an IP address; if it does, it's labelled as phishing, otherwise, it's considered legitimate. The second feature assesses URL length; if it's less than 54 characters, it's considered legitimate, between 54 and 75 characters is suspicious, and longer than 75 characters is phishing. The third feature examines the use of URL shortening services like "tinyurl"; if used, it's classified as phishing, otherwise, it's legitimate. The fourth feature looks for "@" symbols in URLs; if found and it's not a tinyurl, it's legitimate, otherwise, it's phishing. The fifth feature checks for the presence of "//" in the URL; if "//" appears after the 7th position in the URL, it's phishing, otherwise, it's legitimate. The sixth feature investigates the inclusion of prefixes or suffixes separated by "-" in the domain name; if "-" is present, it's considered phishing; otherwise, it's legitimate.

The second subgroup includes six more address bar-based features. The first feature evaluates subdomains and multi-subdomains by counting dots in the domain part; one dot is legitimate, two dots are suspicious, and more dots are phishing. The second feature assesses the use of HTTPS (Hypertext Transfer Protocol with Secure Sockets Layer) and the trustworthiness of the certificate issuer; if HTTPS is used with a trusted issuer and a certificate age of at least one year, it's legitimate. If HTTPS is used with an untrusted issuer, it's suspicious, and otherwise, it's phishing. The third feature examines the length of domain registration; if the domain expires in less than one year, it's phishing, otherwise, it's legitimate. The fourth feature checks for the source of favicons; if they are loaded from an external domain, it's phishing; otherwise, it's legitimate. The fifth feature investigates the use of non-standard ports; if the port is of preferred status, it's phishing; otherwise, it's legitimate. The sixth feature looks for the presence of "https" in the domain part of the URL; if "https" is found, it's legitimate; otherwise, it's phishing.

The third subgroup focuses on abnormal-based features and includes five input features. The first feature analyzes the percentage of the request URL; if it's less than 22%, it's legitimate; if it falls between 22% and 61%, it's suspicious, otherwise, it's phishing. The second feature examines the percentage of the URL of anchor tags; if it's less than 31%, it's legitimate; if it falls between 31% and 67%, it's suspicious, otherwise, it's phishing. The third feature looks at the percentage of links in "<meta>," "<script>," and "<link>" tags; if it's less than 17%, it's legitimate; if it falls between 17% and 81%, it's suspicious, otherwise, it's phishing. The fourth feature assesses server from handler (sfh); if sfh is "about: blank" or empty, it's phishing; if sfh refers to a different domain, it's suspicious; otherwise, it's legitimate. The fifth feature evaluates the submission of information to email; if the "mail()" function is used, it's phishing; otherwise, it's legitimate. The sixth feature examines abnormal URLs; if the hostname is missing from the URL, it's phishing; otherwise, it's legitimate.

The fourth subgroup covers HTML and JavaScript-based features, with five features in total. The first feature looks at website forwarding; if the number of redirect pages is less than or equal to 1, it's legitimate; if it's between 2 and 3, it's suspicious; otherwise, it's phishing. The second feature focuses on status bar customization; if hovering over a link changes the status bar, it's phishing; if it doesn't change, it's legitimate. The third feature checks for disabling right-click functionality; if right-click is disabled, it's phishing; otherwise, it's legitimate. The fourth feature assesses the use of pop-up windows with text fields; if pop-up windows contain text fields, it's phishing; otherwise, it's legitimate. The fifth feature examines iframe redirection; if iframe is used, it's phishing; otherwise, it's legitimate.

The final subgroup, in the Elm, includes domain-based features, divided into seven features. The first feature looks at the age of the domain; if it's over six months old, it's legitimate; otherwise, it's phishing. The second feature assesses DNS records; if there's no DNS record for the domain, it's phishing; otherwise, it's legitimate. The third feature considers website traffic ranking; if the website ranks below 100,000, it's legitimate; if it's above 100,000, it's suspicious; otherwise, it's phishing. The fourth feature evaluates PageRank; if PageRank is less than 0.2, it's phishing; otherwise, it's legitimate. The fifth feature checks Google indexing; if the webpage is indexed by Google, its legitimate; otherwise, it's phishing. The sixth feature examines the number of links pointing to the page; if there are no links pointing to the webpage, its phishing; if there are 1-2 links, it's suspicious; otherwise, it's legitimate. The final feature looks at statistical reports and identifies phishing if the host belongs to top phishing IPs or domains; otherwise, it's legitimate.

2. Literature Review

Identity theft has always been a major concern for thieves throughout history, even in the twenty-first century. By gaining access to another person's personal information and acting in their place, a criminal can almost completely remain anonymous while committing a crime. In the twenty-first century, digital identity theft has become more prevalent. The piles of electronic junk mail hide a new attack vector that can bypass many of the best anti-spam filters in use today, ready to steal critical personal data. Today, cunning criminals employ false communications to trick victims into falling into traps that are set up to steal their digital identities. What started as a malicious hobby that made use of several of the most popular Internet communication channels evolved into a prosperous business. Phishing is a term used to describe the practise of deceiving or manipulating a company's customer into divulging sensitive information for malicious purposes. Any online business may come against phishers trying to target their customers by impersonating them, ride the coattails of bulk mailings like spam, or using "bots" to systematically target victims. Criminals are focused on the accuracy of the private information they were able to collect through the attack, not the size of the firm.

In 2021, by using a variety of threat vectors, such as person attacks, key loggers, and other techniques, phishers can easily coerce customers into disclosing personal, economic, and password information. recreations in full of business websites. Spam was (and still is) an annoyance, a diversion, and an expense for everyone who got it, but phishing has already shown that it can be a serious threat, the capability to cause significant data losses and financial harm. Organizations may stop many of the most common and effective phishing attack routes by studying the tools and techniques employed by professional criminals as well as an analysis of the holes in their own perimeter defences or application. This paper addresses the security flaws and technologies that phishers employ and provides comprehensive, vendor-neutral advice on what organizations can do to prevent additional attacks. Security professionals may utilize this in-depth study, and customers could arm themselves to guard against the impending phishing scam that comes in their email. The volume and level of complexity of phishing schemes rise each month. Phishing attempts of today target a range of audience sizes, including bulk emails sent to millions of email addresses globally and extremely targeted consumer groups found through security holes in modest brick-and-mortar retail websites.

In 2004, a Gartner poll found that 57 million US Internet users had received phishing-related emails, with an estimated 1.7 million falling victim to these scams. The Anti Phishing Working Group (APWG) indicated that around 5% of email recipients were susceptible to phishing attacks. Some experts suggested that organizations might have to rely on third-party solutions to combat phishing due to security weaknesses in email protocols like SMTP. However, as cybercriminals continuously adapt, they could exploit alternative communication methods even if SMTP vulnerabilities were addressed. Despite efforts by some major financial and internet companies to raise awareness, many businesses had not taken proactive steps to combat phishing. Taking a proactive approach to security could provide organizations with tools to protect against phishers, increase customer confidence, and potentially win customer loyalty. This article examines research on detecting phishing attempts, which often target vulnerabilities in human behavior. As users are often the weakest link in the security chain, various tactics are employed to mitigate phishing attacks due to the complexity of the problem and the absence of a single solution. The study aims to review several recent phishing mitigation techniques, including detection, offensive defense, correction, and prevention, to provide an overview of where phishing detection fits into the broader mitigation process.

In 2013, phishing was described as a form of social engineering that exploits system weaknesses by manipulating users. Even systems theoretically secure against password theft could be compromised if users were tricked into changing their passwords over an insecure connection. Attackers could also exploit technological vulnerabilities to create convincing social engineering communications, like using authentic but spoofed domains. Consequently, countering cyber scams required a combination of technological and human solutions. Phishing attacks remained challenging to prevent because they targeted human vulnerabilities among system end users. Despite training with top user awareness software, users were unable to identify 29% of phishing attempts. Meanwhile, mass phishing attempts were scrutinized by phishing detection software, making it difficult to assess their performance against individual attacks. Even leading data security providers faced security breaches due to limitations in spoofing mitigation strategies. The study on phishing detection was conducted by researchers from Khalifa University in the United Arab Emirates due to the intricate nature of the problem. It also highlights the inconsistency in definitions of hacking found in the literature.

- Differentiating anti-phishing programmers based on the lifetime of a phishing effort. The many anti-phishing solution categories, including detection, are shown below. Before going into a specific technique, such as phishing detection methods, a general overview of the anti-phishing environment is required (What is the scope of this study?).
- Defining assessment metrics often used to assess the efficiency of phishing detection systems. This makes comparing different phishing detection algorithms easy.
- Outlining a literature assessment of anti-phishing detection strategies, including user awareness and software detection methods, to improve phishing attack detection.

A poorly organized neural network model could lead to underfitting, while overfitting can occur when the system is overly complex and fits every detail of the training dataset. To address overfitting, adjustments can be made to the neural network, such as adding more neurons to the hidden layer or introducing additional layers. It's important to set a realistic tolerated error rate to avoid getting stuck in minimum error values. Phishing attacks have a significant global economic impact, with a focus on webmail and financial/payment organizations, according to recent analyses from the Anti-Phishing Working Group. Cybercriminals create fake replicas of legitimate websites and emails, often from financial institutions, in an attempt to obtain sensitive information. These emails mimic the logos and slogans of real companies, and HTML allows them to replicate internet content, including images. This type of attack exploits the trust consumers have in company identifiers. Phishing attacks often involve sending deceptive emails to numerous recipients, redirecting them to fake websites, and posing a significant risk to user information [1-9]. Recent research on phishing has concentrated on various domain features such as website Uniform Resource Locators (URLs), website content, web page source code, and webpage snapshots. Organizations struggle to find effective anti-phishing software to identify harmful URLs and protect users, especially when malware is involved. Machine Learning (ML) methods are employed to swiftly identify malicious web pages and safeguard users. The conventional method for identifying malicious URLs relies on a blacklist, a list of harmful URLs compiled from user reports or expert judgment. However, the number of new malicious URLs not on the blacklist is increasing rapidly. Cybercriminals can create new malicious URLs using techniques like Domain Generation Algorithms to evade blacklists. Consequently, relying solely on a comprehensive blacklist to detect phishing websites is nearly impossible. To address these limitations, researchers have introduced machine learning-based approaches for identifying dangerous URLs through binary classification tasks, known as malicious URL detection. However, these methods have their drawbacks, including data collisions, potential loss of sensitive information, and system damage [10-14].

3. Proposed Methodology

In this project, by choosing the parameters of input and output for an ELM classifier, features in a database from a phishing website are categorised. Results provided by ELM Showcasing its superiority over alternative classification methods such as Support Vector Machine and Naïve Bayes, this research aims to establish its effectiveness in developing highly efficient automated processes for identifying online phishing activities. Additionally, when compared to existing literature, this study stands out as a high-performing one, achieving the highest test performance among published works in this field.

This section discusses the two key factors influencing the performance of a model and algorithm: firstly, the partitioning of the dataset into training and testing subsets, and secondly, the formulation of performance metrics. The first aspect leverages a three-phase data division method, following the K-Fold approach, which includes training, validation, and test data sets. Notably, the selection of the model and the assessment state are conducted in tandem.. A validation value is frequently used in the second measurement to assess how well the classifier model is performing. The three types of phishing assaults include searching engine phishing, spear phishing, and whaling attacks.

The loan approval procedure would be sped up. Because the entire method will be automated, deadly errors will be avoided. Those who qualify will obtain loans without restriction. We can find the attribute for bracketing requires by evaluating linguistic features. We begin by separating the host name and route of a URL, from which we gather a prize collection of keywords (strings separated by the letters "/," "?" "." "=," "-," AND "). We identified the lengthier URLs on phishing websites.

3.1 Dataset Collection

Information utilised in this collection of records. Selecting a subset of the whole amount of data that is accessible is the focus of this stage. For our model, we used a phishing dataset from vibrant online resources like Kaggle, along with some of our own data sets. Our model is tested using a 19-phishing dataset from Kaggle, while the other 81 datasets are used to train the model. The collection includes data from licit and phishing websites in 95812 rows and 11 columns.

3.2 Data Pre-processing

Sanctification, case selection, point birth, normalisation, metamorphosis, etc. are all examples of data pre-processing. The training dataset is the end product of data pre-processing. Pre-processing of the data may affect how the final processing's findings are understood. Data drawing might be a stage where missing data are filled in, noise is smoothed down, outliers are detected or removed, and incompatibilities are resolved. A system where specific databases or data sets are added is called data integration. To measure a specific set of data, gathering and standardisation are processes known as data transformation. By doing data reduction, we may obtain a dataset overview that is incredibly compact yet still contributes to the same analytical results. There are three common steps to follow: Data formatting: This is used for data formatting, Cleaning: This is used to replace missing data or remove it. Sampling: Because there may be more carefully chosen data, algorithms may execute more slowly. Before taking into account the entire set of data, we may choose a smaller sample of carefully chosen data that may be significantly faster for exploring and developing ideas.

3.3 Feature Extraction

Is an attribute addition from which we constructed additional columns. Finally, a classifier is used to train our modules. Some machine learning algorithms we used for reprised data. The chosen classifier is ELM as shown in Fig. 26.1.

3.4 Evaluation Model

It's a procedure for developing models. It assists us in selecting the appropriate model to represent data and comprehend its operation. Both approaches employ a test set to evaluate model performance and aid in avoiding overfitting. Based on their averages, each model's performance is calculated, and the impact is visualized. Correct predictions for test results are considered delicate.

3.5 Normal Dataset

A natural and secure website benchmark dataset is Alexa Rank. Alexa is a company with a commercial product that analyses online data. It gathers information on drug users' web surfing patterns from many sources and impartially analyses it for the purpose of reporting and bracketing internet-based URLs. Researchers gather a large number of high-calibre websites using the Alexa rankings as their standard dataset for testing and classifying websites. Each line in the graph represents the website's grade and domain name, and Alexa presents the dataset as a raw textbook train.

3.6 ELM Algorithm

In the context of feed-forward neural networks, when a single sub-layer or multiple layers of dormant nodes are employed for tasks like encapsulation, regression, clustering, sparse approximation, dimension reduction, and pattern recognition, the term "extreme learning machines" is employed when there is no requirement to adjust the parameters of these dormant nodes. These defunct bumps may be assigned at random and never simplified, or they could be passed on from the previous generation and never changed. Most of the time, retiring bump weights is taught in a single lesson, thereby creating a rapid literacy approach. According to the models' creators, they can produce good conception performance and literacy tens of thousands of times faster than back propagation networks. According to the investigation, these models can also perform better in bracket and retrogression procedures than support vector machines.

Figure 26.1(b) the above diagram shows the path of the URL phishing data set as it is extracted and pre-processed. sent to the ELM algorithm and analysed to find out if any malicious attacks are taking place or not. The output is shown in graphic form. Figure 26.1(a) and (c) the user gives the dataset, which is pre-processed by the system. Then algorithm is applied and to classify the datasets Hence, finds for malicious and malware if present.

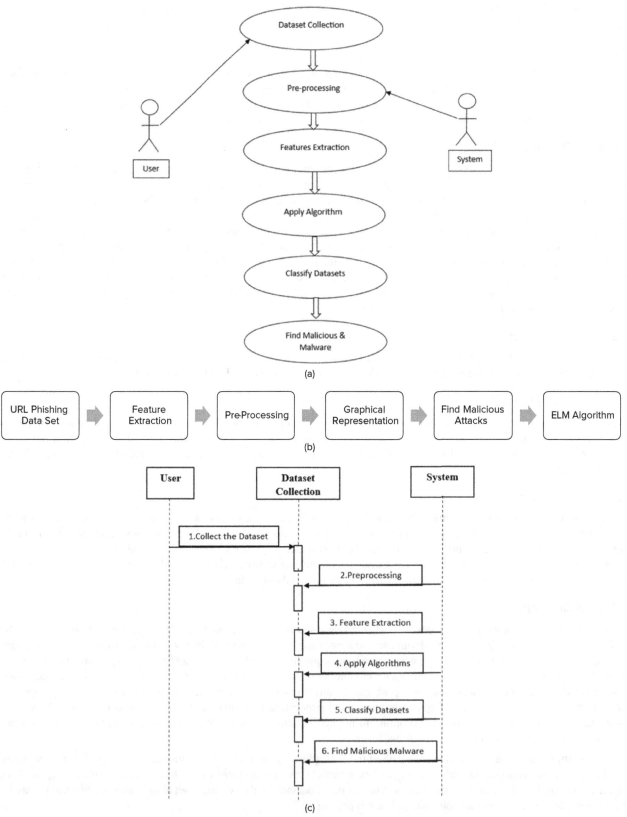

Fig. 26.1 (a) Use case diagram, (b) Block diagram (c) Sequence diagram

4. Results and Discussion

In this project, we utilize WAMP-server to establish the connection between the code and the web browser because a server is necessary for the linking of the framework with the code. The data set is imported into the Wamp server after being retrieved from Kaggle or any other sites that have.csv file extensions. The next step would be to run the command prompt, but you must do this from the precise spot where the code was saved on your computer or local network. Here, the files connected to the WAMP server are launched using the "run server" command. We receive the http link to the local host once this prompt has been successfully performed. Copying and pasting this link into the web server will cause the GUI to open in accordance with the Django framework's code. Syntax: python manage.py run server then open browser enters URL as http://127.0.0.1.8000 homepage will open as shown in Fig. 26.2.

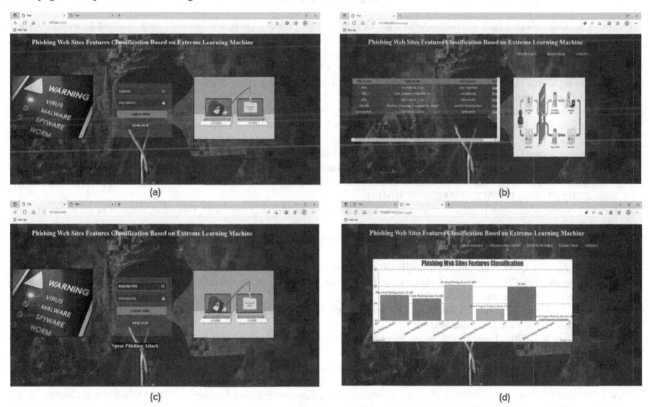

Fig. 26.2 (a) New user login, (b) User login page, (c) Spear phishing attack, (d) Result in bar graph

Figure 26.2(a) shows the project's GUI framework after pasting the http URL into the local browser. The New User must first register by selecting the New User option, and they must then input their login information using previously generated credentials. Figure 26.2(b) shows the user data that is stored on the website. Figure 26.2(c) In the above image, we will see a message displayed on the screen that shows the type of phishing attack being used. Figure 26.2(d) the output of attacks is featured and represented in the form of bar graphs.

5. Conclusion

This project aims to enhance the identification of phishing websites via the use of machine learning technology. We have greater accuracy of 89.34% and reduced false-positive rates when using the ELM algorithm. The outcomes also show that classifier performance improves with the amount of training data used. Future technologies will combine the blacklist method with the ELM algorithm of machine learning to more accurately detect phishing websites. The proposed study focused on the classification aspect of the phishing approach, where phishing websites are thought to automatically classify websites into a set range of class values using a variety of attributes and the class variable. ML-driven phishing strategies exploit website attributes to gather data that can aid in categorizing websites and detecting phishing sites. While complete eradication of phishing may not be achievable, it can be managed through the improvement of targeted anti-phishing methods and strategies, along with educating the public on recognizing and identifying fraudulent phishing websites. ML anti-phishing strategies are crucial to thwarting phishing attempts' constant evolution and complexity. The project's long-term objectives include identifying the most prevalent and dangerous phishing scams so that we can improve user security and stop people from falling for them. In addition, the study of this project can further go towards developing an unsupervised learning method for generating depth from a URL. With the assistance of new, very accurate machine learning-powered algorithms, other cybercrimes can also be prevented.

REFERENCES

1. Jain A.K., Gupta B.B. (2020) "PHISH-SAFE: URL Features-Based Phishing Detection System Using Machine Learning", Cyber Security. Advances in Intelligent Systems and Computing, vol.729, 2018, doi:10.1007/978-981-10-8536-9_44

2. Purbay M., Kumar D, (2021) "Split Behaviour of Supervised Machine Learning Algorithms for Phishing URL Detection", Lecture Notes in Electrical Engineering, vol. 683, 2021, doi:10.1007/978-981-15-6840-4_40

3. Gandotra E., Gupta D, (2021) "An Efficient Approach for Phishing Detection using Machine Learning", Algorithms for Intelligent Systems, Springer, Singapore, 2021, 10.1007/978-981-15-8711-5_12.

4. Hung Le, Quang Pham, Doyen Sahoo, and Steven C.H. Hoi, (2017) "URL Net: Learning a URL Representation with Deep Learning for Malicious URL Detection", Conference'17, Washington, DC, USA, arXiv:1802.03162, July 2017.

5. Hong J., Kim T., Liu J., Park N., Kim SW, (2020) "Phishing URL Detection with Lexical Features and Blacklisted Domains", Autonomous Secure Cyber Systems. Springer,10.1007/978-3-030-33432-1_12.

6. J.Kumar, A.Santhanavijayan, B.Janet, B.Rajendran and B.S. Bindhumadhava, (2020) "Phishing Website Classification and Detection Using Machine Learning," 2020 International Conference on Computer Communication and Informatics (ICCCI), Coimbatore, India,2020,pp.1–6, 10.1109/ICCCI48352.2020.9104161.

7. Hassan Y.A. and Abdelfettah B, (2017), "Using case- based reasoning for phishing detection", Procedia Computer Science;vol. 109, pp. 281–288.

8. Rao RS, Pais AR., (2019), Jail-Phish: "An improved search engine-based phishing detection system. Computers & Security"; 83:246–67.

9. Aljofey A, Jiang Q, Qu Q, Huang M, Niyigena JP, (2020),"An effective phishing detection model based on character level convolutional neural network from URL"; 9(9): 1514. Adversarial deep neural networks". In: Proceedings of the Sixth International Workshopon Security and Privacy Analytics; (pp. 53–60).

10. DATASET: Lichman, M. (2013). UCI Machine Learning Repository [http://archive.ics.uci.edu/ml]. Irvine, CA: University of California, School of Information and Computer Science

11. Gupta D, Rani R, (2020), "Improving malware detection using big data and ensemble learning", Computer Electronic Engineering; vol. 86, no.106729.

12. J.Anirudha and P.Tanuja, (2019)" Phishing Attack Detection using Feature Selection Techniques", Proceedings of International Conference on Communication and Information Processing 18 (ICCIP),10.2139/ssrn.3418542

13. Wu CY, Kuo CC, Yang CS, (2019)" A phishing detection system based on machine learning" In: 2019 International Conference on Intelligent Computing and its Emerging Applications (ICEA), pp28–32.

14. Chiew KL, Chang EH, Tiong WK, (2015)" Utilisation of website logo for phishing detection", Computer Security, pp. 16–26.

15. G. Canbek and S. Sagiroglu (2006), "A Review on Information, Information Security and Security Processes," Politek. Derg., vol. 9, no. 3, pp. 165–174, 2006.

16. L. McCluskey, F. Thabtah, and R. M. Mohammad (2014), "Intelligent rule based phishing websites classification," IET Inf. Secur., vol. 8, no. 3, pp. 153–160, 2014.

17. R. M. Mohammad, F. Thabtah, and L. McCluskey (2014), "Predicting phishing websites based on self-structuring neural network," Neural Comput. Appl., vol. 25, no. 2, pp. 443–458, 2014.

18. R. M. Mohammad, F. Thabtah, and L. McCluskey (2012), "An assessment of features related to phishing websites using an automated technique," Internet Technol. ..., pp. 492–497, 2012.

Note: All the figures in this chapter were made by the author.

Advances in Computational Intelligence and its Applications (ICACIA-2023) – Dr. Sheikh Fahad Ahmad et al. (eds)
© 2024 Taylor & Francis Group, London, ISBN 978-1-032-78612-4

Smart Farming with Fire Security System

27

**Kandula Hemanth Kumar[1], Ball Mukund Mani Tripathi[2],
Krishna Chaitanya Bodepudi[3] , Sri Vidya Punnamaraju[4],
Nedunuri Sai Vijaya Ramya[5]**

Velagapudi Ramakrishna Siddhartha Engineering College,Vijayawada

ABSTRACT—In this paper, a fire secured smart farming system is presented to reduce water waste and increasing the productivity by controlling the temperature, humidity, and soil moisture content of the field. The Microcontroller (ESP32) board, which manages the entire system, sends an interrupt signal to the valve, which receives it. The temperature sensor and soil moisture sensor are connected to the internal ports of the micro controller through a comparator, which detects changes in the ambient temperature. A signal to open the valve is sent when the system detects a drop in the soil's moisture level, which is continuously monitored by the system. The key advantages of the system is reducing water waste and fostering plant development.

KEYWORDS—ESP32, Flame detection, Cloud, Reference point, Moisture content

1. Introduction

The lack of water is a major issue that the world is facing at the moment, particularly in the agriculture sector. There are various ways to conserve water, and agriculture is one of the industries that relies on it. In addition to being dependent on water, agriculture also faces a serious issue with wastage. There are multiple ways that can help prevent agricultural water waste.

One of the most effective ways to reduce water wastage is by implementing automatic irrigation systems. These can be made to provide the correct amount of water at the right time. They can also be very cost-effective.

We decide which factors, such as water quantity and quality, soil characteristics, and weather, irrigation systems should track. The threshold will be decided upon taking into account the requirements of the crops and any changes to external factors such as temperature, soil quality, and humidity.

Horticulture is the cornerstone of our nation. A long time ago, agriculturalists made assumptions about the type of product to be produced based on the maturity of the soil. In the existing systems,they account for elements like moisture content, water level, and most crucially climate variables that would have made farming more challenging[1].

The goals of this paper are to assess the field's temperature, humidity, and soil moisture as well as to set up a fire detection security alarm system. The valve gets an interrupt signal from the ESP32 board, which controls the entire system. The physical parameters such as temperature and moisture sensing devices are connected with the internal ports of the microcontroller by a comparator, which monitors changes in ambient temperature.

---

[1]hemanthkumarkandula1@gmail.com, [2]ballmukund79@gmail.com, [3]krishnachaitanyakcb@gmail.com, [4]srividyapunnamaraju93@gmail.com, [5]saivijayaramya@gmail.com

DOI: 10.1201/9781003488682-27

2. Design of System

2.1 Soil Moisture Sensor

2.1 Soil Moisture Measurement:

Soil moisture sensor estimates dampness in the soil. It can be stationary or portable. The former one is fixed at specific place and the later can have different sites. The device works on the theory of dielectric permittivity. It has probes, which are planted into the soil. These inserted probes gauge the amount of moisture present in the soil; humid soil has a low resistance value, while dry soil has a high resistance value. Range of Soil Moisture Sensor is from 0 to1023.

2.2 DHT 11

The basic DHT11is a low cost measuring device that gives a signal on the data pin. It contains humidity measuring devices which are generally a capacitor and a thermistor.

The DHT11 can identify the presence of water vapour between two electrodes through variation in the resistance. The resistance varies due to presence of charge particles from the substrate because of water vapors. This decreases the resistance. The Operating voltage is 1.5V to 5.5V. Range of the sensor is 0-50°C Accuracy is +-2 degrees.

2.3 Flame Sensor

Flame sensor is sensitive to normal light. This Flame Sensor Module is used to identify flame or light sources with wavelengths between 760 and 1100 nm. This can detect the Infrared light because of its black epoxy coating. The sensitivity level can be changed by using a comparator built into the LM393 on-board op-amp. The sensor's sensitivity may be changed using the blue potentiometer, and it has both digital and analogue outputs.

2.4 Solenoid Valve

A solenoid valve is a valve that works electromechanically. It has wide range of operations from linear to different actuators. It switches and regulate the flow between ports of various structures. A manifold can accommodate several solenoid valves.

ZA two-port, two-way valve is an illustration of this. The connection or disconnection of the ports depend on the opening or closing the valves and thus controls the flow between them. In UN-powered condition, normally open valves (N.O.) remain open. Similarly, if a valve closes even when the solenoid is not engaged, it is considered to be typically closed (N.C.).

2.5 ESP32:

The ESP32-S is an ESP32-based wireless module with built-in 32Mbit Flash and compatibility for Wi-Fi and Bluetooth 4.2 in an SMD38 package. A metal shield and PCB antenna are also onboard. In a nutshell, it's a wireless module with a tiny form factor and a reasonable cost-effectiveness.

Since ESP32 can work as an independent self control unit as well as a dependent device to the host MCU, it decreases the stack overhead. The ESP32 has Wi-Fi and Bluetooth capabilities therefore, easily connects to different systems through proper interfaces.

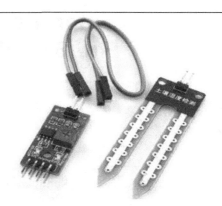

Fig. 27.1 Soil moisture sensor pinout
Source: https://images.app.goo.gl/ y3DPzUnZwLvcKgoj9

Fig. 27.2 DHT 11 sensor
Source: https://images.app.goo.gl/ YD2w5C1tsfJeCieXA

Fig. 27.3 Flame sensor
Source: https://projects.arduinocontent. cc/998f2ca3-c734-47ea-99f4-dbb57f85a490.jpg

Fig. 27.4 Solenoid valve
Source: https://images.app.goo.gl/ uWb42Jv3nYDafeSM6

Fig. 27.5 ESP32

Source: https://images.app.goo.gl/MUYSvAjUx1pafeZ19

3. Work Flow Chart

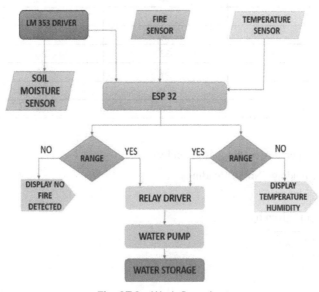

Fig. 27.6 Work flow chart

Source: Author

4. Implementation

This Irrigation system is Internet of Things (IoT) based, and it works with an ESP32 micro- controller, displays all of its operations. A threshold value is first established on a moisture sensor depending on the crop's needs. The sensor then continuously measures humidity and compares it to predetermined thresholds continuing watering is done even if the humidity reading is below the threshold. Pump is turned off automatically by sending signals using an ESP32 when the threshold value is achieved.

(i) Soil-immersed moisture sensors are reconnected to the main system. The sensors provide information on the soil's moisture content, which is shown on an LCD.

(ii) In the code, there are some parameters for the sensor output and their comparision.

(iii) The detection of the real amount of water presence .

(iv) This value is compared to threshold values

(v) If the real value is higher than a fixed quantity, a signal is generated that will open the valve automatically.

(vi) In opposite to previous case, the valve is closed for water flow.

(vii) User will get the status of temperature, humidity and soil moisture is displayed on LCD. Along with the display about irrigation-system, we are providing fire alarm system with the help of flame sensor which gives trigger to the buzzer and led. Flame detection is displayed on the lcd.

5. Result and Discussion

Table 27.1   Average temperatures

Months	Temperatures	
	High	Low
January	30	18
February	32	21
March	37	22
April	38	27
May	40	27
June	38	28
July	35	24
August	34	24
September	33	26
October	34	25
November	31	20
December	30	18

Source: Author

Average temperature for higher temperature readings is given by

$$\bar{X} = \text{Sum of readings/No. of Readings}$$

$$\bar{X} = 34.33$$

Standard Deviation of the readings is given by

$$\sigma = \frac{\sqrt{\sum (Xi - \bar{X})^2}}{\sqrt{N}}$$

$$\sigma = 3.199$$

The aforementioned equations for mean and standard deviation are used to identify a reference point of temperature and soil moisture content readings. In the code, these threshold values are employed.

Graphical Representation of Temperature Readings is shown on next page.

6. Conclusion

This paper is the overview of smart irrigation system will help in sensing and monitoring the moisture content of soil through soil moisture sensor ,and measure temperature ,humidity using DHT 11 sensor and implementing the fire security system using flame sensor and buzzer to alert the farmers, thereby sprinklers automatically do their work when there is ignition in the farm .Moreover,system is connected to cloud and the calculated standard deviation gives the precise value to the annual temperature.

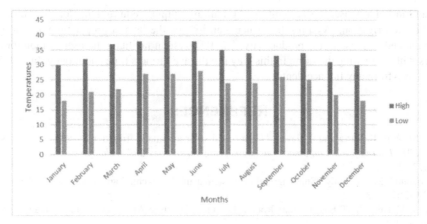

Fig. 27.7 Temperature graph

Source: Author

Fig. 27.8 An Image of cloud platform website monitoring the elements

Source: Author

Fig. 27.9 Output in serial monitor

Source: Author

The majority of the land in India is used for agriculture. Agriculture outputs require irrigation. The crop output is better and more suited when fields are irrigation. ,As a result, farmers can irrigate the land at proper time and in this way farmers can reduce the water wastage and increase in the productivity. The IOT system facilitate the user to monitor all these parameters from the remote places without visiting the farm. In this way it will save farmers time and money .In addition, the fire security system will protect the crop from any fire accidents.

REFERENCES

1. A. U. Rehman, R. M. Asif, R. Tariq and A. Javed, "Gsm based solar automatic irrigation system using moisture, temperature and humidity sensors," *2017 International Conference on Engineering Technology and Technopreneurship (ICE2T)*, 2017, pp. 1–4, doi: 10.1109/ICE2T.2017.8215945.
2. Naresh, Muthunoori, and P. Munaswamy. "Smart agriculture system using IOT technology." *International Journal of Recent Technology and Engineering* 7.5 (2019): 98–102.
3. Sowmika, T., and G. Malathi. "IOT Based Smart Rodent Detection and Fire Alert System in Farmland." *Int. Res. J. Multidiscip. Technovation* 2 (2020): 1–6.
4. Mannar Mannan, J., et al. "Smart scheduling on cloud for IoT-based sprinkler irrigation [J]." *International Journal of Pervasive Computing and Communications* 17.1 (2020): 3–19.
5. https://www.electronicscomp.com/12v-dc-1-2-inch-electric-solenoid-water-air-valve-switch-normally-closed?gclid=CjwKCAi Ap7GcBhA0EiwA9U0mti28 azJcx1RN2OitNb8CeAGc5hYe0imMMyDEllT_wwb7HzhR2NMG9BoCn6IQAvD_BwE https://lastminuteengineers.com/esp32-pinout- reference/
6. S. Salvi et al., "Cloud based data analysis and monitoring of smart multi-level irrigation system using IoT," 2017 International Conference on I- SMAC (IoT in Social, Mobile, Analytics and Cloud) (I-SMAC), 2017, pp. 752-757, doi: 10.1109/I- SMAC.2017.8058279.
7. D. Mishra, A. Khan, R. Tiwari and S. Upadhay, "Automated Irrigation System-IoT Based Approach," 2018 3rd International Conference On Internet of Things: Smart Innovation and Usages (IoT-SIU), 2018, pp. 1-4, doi: 10.1109/IoT-SIU.2018.8519886
8. Wu, Fan, et al. "Experimental study on fire extinguishing characteristics of automatic sprinkler system." *2015 Sixth International Conference on Intelligent Systems Design and Engineering Applications (ISDEA)*. IEEE, 2015.
9. Serdaroglu, Kemal Cagri, Cem Onel, and Sebnem Baydere. "IoT based smart plant irrigation system with enhanced learning." *2020 IEEE Computing, Communications and IoT Applications (ComComAp)*. IEEE, 2020.
10. K. Pernapati, "IoT Based Low Cost Smart Irrigation System," 2018 Second International Conference on Inventive Communication and Computational Technologies (ICICCT), 2018, pp. 1312-1315, doi: 10.1109/ICICCT.2018.8473292.
11. L. M. N. Rajkumar, S. Abinaya and V. V. Kumar, "Intelligent irrigation system — An IOT based approach," 2017 International Conference on Innovations in Green Energy and Healthcare Technologies (IGEHT), 2017, pp. 1-5, doi: 10.1109/IGEHT.2017.8094057.
12. Lal, Anish, and P. Prabu. "'Fire detection and prevention in agriculture field using IoT." *J. Xi'an Univ. Archit. Technol* 12.4 (2020): 3708–3719.
13. S. B. Saraf and D. H. Gawali, "IoT based smart irrigation monitoring and controlling system," *2017 2nd IEEE International Conference on Recent Trends in Electronics, Information & Communication Technology (RTEICT)*, 2017, pp. 815–819, doi: 10.1109/ RTEICT.2017.8256711.
14. García, L.; Parra, L.; Jimenez, J.M.; Lloret, J.; Lorenz, P. IoT-Based Smart Irrigation Systems: An Overview on the Recent Trends on Sensors and IoT Systems for Irrigation in Precision Agriculture. *Sensors* **2020**, *20*, 1042.
15. Pernapati, Kiranmai. "IoT based low cost smart irrigation system." 2018 Second International Conference on Inventive Communication and Computational Technologies (ICICCT). IEEE, 2018.
16. Shekhar, Yuthika, Ekta Dagur, Sourabh Mishra, and Suresh Sankaranarayanan. "Intelligent IoT based automated irrigation system." *International Journal of Applied Engineering Research* 12, no. 18 (2017): 7306–7320
17. P. Srivastava, M. Bajaj and A. S. Rana, "Overview of ESP8266 Wi-Fi module based Smart Irrigation System using IOT," *2018 Fourth International Conference on Advances inElectrical, Electronics, Information, Communication and Bio- Informatics (AEEICB)*, 2018, 1–5, doi: 10.1109/AEEICB.2018.8480949.
18. R. Togneri *et al.*, "Advancing IoT-Based Smart Irrigation," in *IEEE Internet of Things Magazine*, vol. 2, no. 4, pp. 20-25, December 2019, doi: 10.1109/IOTM.0001.190004 H. Benyezza, M. Bouhedda, K. Djellout and A. Saidi, "Smart Irrigation System Based Thingspeak and ESP32," *2018 International Conference on Applied Smart Systems (ICASS)*, 2018, pp. 1–4, doi: 10.1109/ICASS.2018.8651993.

Advances in Computational Intelligence and its Applications (ICACIA-2023) – Dr. Sheikh Fahad Ahmad et al. (eds)
© 2024 Taylor & Francis Group, London, ISBN 978-1-032-78612-4

Generation of 3D Images from Single View 2D Images Using Autoencoder

28

C. N. Sujatha[1], CH. Pranathi[2],
N. Hari Kumar Reddy[3], G. Sushma[4]

Sreenidhi institute of science and technology,
Department of Electronics and communication engineering

ABSTRACT—This paper delves into the intriguing realm of generating 3D images from 2D projections, employing a novel approach rooted in dimensionality reduction techniques, particularly focusing on Autoencoders. The pressing issue at hand is the inherent limitation of 2D images, which necessitates innovative solutions to manifest them in three dimensions. The challenge lies in training machines to decipher the intricate details of 2D images intelligently, ultimately leading to the creation of accurate 3D representations. In today's landscape, the majority of visual data comprises 2D images. However, comprehending real-world scenarios often demands a 3D perspective, making this pursuit invaluable to researchers and developers grappling with contemporary challenges. The process involves elevating the dimensionality from 2D to 3D while preserving the essential features of the original 2D image. The machine algorithm scrutinizes pixel values within the original image, allocating each pixel a specific coordinate within the third dimension. Additionally, a latent space representation is implemented to approximate noise reduction and filter out undesired anomalies. The reconstructed encoded image ultimately yields a coherent 3D model of the object, all within a single, two-dimensional space, with a keen focus on accentuating overlapping pixels. This paper methodically illustrates the expansion of deep learning techniques into the intricate task of single-image 3D reconstruction. This endeavor represents a pivotal challenge in the domain of computer graphics, as the human visual system inherently relies on interpreting 3D shapes from various viewpoints. Consequently, this approach promises to facilitate the inference of an object's 3D structure, even from a single perspective, thereby enriching our understanding of the visual world.

KEYWORDS—Autoencoding, Artificial neural network, Computer graphics, Deep learning, Dimensionality reduction, Feature extraction, Hidden layers, Latent space representation, Reconstruction

1. Introduction

To overcome the limitations of the 2D nature of the images by generating a 3D model of the same. Then approach deep learning algorithms for building the 3D models for the images. Among these autoencoding was the best- found solution for our problem statement. By utilizing the features of the autoencoders to build a model train and test them on real-life 2D images. Autoencoders represent a unique class of neural networks that operate in a fascinating manner. They essentially take the input data and work to recreate it as the output. What sets autoencoders apart is their ability to condense the input information into a simplified, lower-dimensional code or representation. From this compressed form, they then proceed to reconstruct the original output data. This intriguing process lies at the heart of autoencoders, making them a valuable tool in various applications. Figure 28.1 depicts a block diagram of the working of the autoencoder, initially, it pre-processes the image and makes it ready

[1]cnsujatha@gmail.com, [2]pranathichilukoti150@gmail.com, [3]harikumarreddy85@gmail.com, [4]gandusushma11@gmail.com

DOI: 10.1201/9781003488682-28

to be input, then it is given to the autoencoder to train and validate the model, and at the output end, it renders the 3D model in the form of a video file. Several autoencoders description follows.

Fig. 28.1 Block diagram of simple autoencoder

Source: Author

Figure 28.1 depicts a block diagram of the working of the autoencoder, initially, it pre-processes the image and makes it ready to be inputted, then it is given to the overcomplete autoencoder to train and validate the model, and at the output end, it renders the 3D model in the form of a video file.

A neural network (a specific example of an unsupervised learning model) that has been trained to breed its input picture within the output layer is referred to as a convolutional autoencoder. A picture is sent through an encoder, which could be a ConvNet, to create a low-dimensional illustration of the image. This encoder is skilled older more mature more experienced more responsible more established seasoned knowledgeable versed capable competent skillful full well-versed tried associate degree. The decoder takes this compressed image and reconstructs it using another sample ConvNet. Additionally, it is used in subject modelling, information reduction, and picture search. Because of the Python libraries, this project frequently employs NumPy, Keras, and Matplotlib for this project.

Encoded = dense (input_imag), Decoded = dense (N, activation=sigmoid), and Autoencoder = model (input_imag,decoded). Input_Image = Input (shape= (N)). The autoencoder comprises of an encoder that accepts input pictures as data, a latent space representation bottleneck, and a decoder that outputs rebuilt versions of the input images. This decoder will serve as the autoencoder's output, and the pictures it generates will contain more characteristics and requirements than the input images that are provided. In this project, the project typically victimize an overly thorough autoencoder. Due to the extra dimensions in the intermediate layer compared to the input and output layers, an over-complete autoencoder may be a type of autoencoder. This method gives us access to the entire picture. The greatest range of nodes, or having the largest dimensions in the middle layer in comparison to the other layers, is what distinguishes an under-complete autoencoder from an overcomplete autoencoder. Dimensionality reduction is a pivotal technique employed to address the challenge of generating 3D images from the projection views of 2D images. Within the realm of autoencoding, dimensionality reduction stands out as a potent and effective problem-solving approach. The process involves the machine's astute analysis of the 2D image, leveraging its intelligence to construct the perfect 3D image by comprehending the distinctive features encapsulated within the inputted 2D image.

While the majority of contemporary photographs are confined to the 2D realm, the need for 3D imagery becomes essential for researchers and developers grappling with the complex challenges of our world. When transitioning from 2D to 3D, the essential characteristics of the original 2D image are meticulously preserved. The computer system intelligently assesses each pixel's value in the original image, assigning it a specific coordinate within the newly expanded third dimension. Moreover, the process involves a latent space representation, effectively approximating noise reduction and eliminating any unwanted anomalies. By emphasizing the overlapping pixels, the encoded image undergoes a transformative reconstruction, resulting in a crystal-clear 3D representation of the subject within a singular, two-dimensional space. This intricate methodology relies on the prowess of an artificial neural network-equipped computer, which guides the input image through a series of hidden layers. Within these layers, the machine diligently analyzes the image's distinctive features, determining precisely which pixels require modification. Ultimately, this process yields a sharp 3D portrayal of the image at the receiving synapses. At its core, this approach is built upon the foundation of an autoencoder, a sophisticated mechanism that leverages deep learning algorithms to encode input images and subsequently generate output via the assistance of decoders. The primary utility of this autoencoder lies in its ability to automatically encode data and store it in a compressed format. The inherent advantage of effortlessly retrieving the original data from this encoded form is evident, particularly in terms of conserving valuable memory space. This technique holds significant promise, particularly for conveniently storing high-quality images of various visual spaces. Additionally, its potential extends to the realm of medical applications, where the clarity of MRI scans, especially in areas like the brain and certain skeletal components, often falls short of the precision required for accurate analysis and diagnosis of a patient's condition. Though in shape or appearance, items may never be totally isosceles, the researchers paid for this later in their research. For instance, because human hairstyles and expressions can change, it is impossible to constantly create the right half of the face using the left. Similar to how a cat's perception of its entire body may be problematic, the ratio is asymmetric. Even though each shape and ratio is isosceles, the appearance should fluctuate owing to lighting, which makes issues worse. The vast information philosophy of machine learning is carried through the intended strategies. They are absolute scenes-specific and don't require explicit explanation. Two different sorts of tactics will be used. The first one relies on a regression sorting strategy to learn to some extent a mapping from native image/attributes, such color, abstraction position, and motion at every picture element, to scene-depth at that picture element. The second method uses a nearest-neighbor regression sorting strategy to globally estimate the whole depth map of a test image from a collection of 3D images (images plus depth pairs or stereo pairs). It introduces indigenous methods and assesses each indigenous and global strategy's qualitative performance and, therefore, machine potency.

Additionally, it's evident that the global approach yields superior quality depth maps when compared to state-of-the-art techniques, while also significantly reducing computational effort and mitigating strategy flaws by up to four orders of magnitude. Now, let's delve into the concept of a simple autoencoder, which stands out as a unique neural network among its peers. Unlike other existing models, a simple autoencoder provides a distinct and explicit reconstruction mechanism for automatically encoded data. This is achieved through training a model using neural networks. Imagine a digital image with a missing pixel – the training model steps in to address this gap. It employs a clever technique by calculating the missing pixel's RGB value through an averaging process involving its neighboring pixels. This pivotal step is known as latent space representation, and it assumes a significant role in the encoding phase. What's truly remarkable is how this process yields a more coherent perspective when the compressed data is decoded back into its original form. This reconstruction process occurs once the entire region has been efficiently stored within a fundamental latent space representation. Unsupervised learning, where the computer learns with unlabeled input, includes simple autoencoders. Due to some reconstruction losses, an autoencoder's accuracy cannot be totally guaranteed. The majority of these rebuilding losses are caused by a particular. "Loss function" is a mathematical formula. An undercomplete autoencoder is typically trained using this loss function to minimize reconstruction and other losses. The input layer receives the raw data as input and, in the first half, passes through a few hidden layers. The encoding process begins here, and the nodes are subsequently translated via the code to get the completely encoded result. Reconstruction of the encoded data is done in the second half of the neural network, which is beneath the decoder, after this phase. Reconstruction is a vital component of the autoencoder, as the encoded data alone wouldn't serve a substantial purpose. Among all types of autoencoders, the basic autoencoder stands as the foundational building block. Each variation of autoencoder shares the fundamental characteristics mentioned. One of the remarkable advantages of these autoencoders is their ability to efficiently store the input data and subsequently reconstruct it. This approach optimizes RAM utilization and enhances hard disk storage efficiency. The fundamentals principles and techniques employed for creating 3D models from single-view or projection-view 2D images center around dimensionality reduction and feature extraction. Dimensionality reduction plays a crucial role in addressing the challenge of generating 3D images from 2D projection views. Within the domain of automatic encoding, dimensionality reduction emerges as a highly effective problem-solving method. Here, the machine leverages its intelligence to meticulously assess the 2D image, comprehending the unique characteristics embedded within it to craft an ideal 3D representation. While the majority of contemporary photographs are limited to 2D, the demand for 3D images is paramount for academics and developers seeking to understand and tackle the complexities of our world. Elevating the dimension from 2D to 3D ensures that the essential traits of the original 2D image remain intact. The computer system, during this transformation, evaluates the pixel values from the original image and assigns them coordinates within the newly introduced third dimension. Additionally, a latent space representation is implemented to approximate noise reduction and eliminate extraneous outliers. This intricate process involves an artificial neural network-equipped computer guiding the supplied image through a series of concealed layers. Within these hidden layers, the computer systematically evaluates the image's distinctive features, making informed decisions about which pixels require modification. The result is a clear and detailed 3D representation of the image at the receiving end of the neural network. The cornerstone of this method lies in the autoencoder, a deep learning technique that encodes input images and subsequently generates output by meticulously reconstructing them with the assistance of decoders. A key advantage of the autoencoder lies in its capacity to automatically encode input data and store it in a compressed format, alleviating the demands on memory storage. The encoded data can be readily converted back into its original form, making this approach an efficient means of preserving high-quality images within limited storage capacity. This strategy also finds valuable applications in the medical field, particularly in cases where MRI scans of the human body, including the brain and various skeletal components, lack the requisite clarity for thorough analysis and diagnostic purposes. When compared to ordinary autoencoders, variable autoencoders are more vibrant. The variable autoencoder, in contrast to the basic autoencoder, makes the statistical style of manifestation of the data encoding and reconstruction more similar to a mathematical manifestation. The variable encoder demonstrates how statistical and mathematical concepts like variance, mean, and standard deviation are utilized to represent the autoencoding process. Because the inputs pictures and the images that are produced as output images place a strong focus on the dimensional planes, such as the 2-dimensional and 3-dimensional planes, the variable auto encoder may render out the output more effectively than normal.

One of the explicit tools in the autoencoder neural networks renders a statistical status and parameters important to the encoding scheme of our first inputted data with the help of this tool. The maximum number of profiles views a three-dimensional object can have six to eight sides, or the standpoints, which are the top, bottom, sides (left-side view and right-side view), front and back views, as well as a few additional more detailed views. This type of methodology generates various forms of views very effectively. All other components in the model must be predicted and generated, hence a solid statistical tool is required. In order to operate the latent space representation, the statistical analysis can enable the machine to comprehend the depth of each pixel of the inputted picture. This information can be the pixel's RGB value or an assessment of its grayscale value. When compared variable autoencoders to other types like simple autoencoders, sparse autoencoders, denoising autoencoders, contractive autoencoders, and so on, the distinctive essence of variable autoencoders becomes apparent. In these other models, the process of representing the latent space lacks clarity and coherence. It often involves a simple approach of filling in missing parts by copying the pixel RGB values from neighboring areas. However, variable autoencoders take a different path. They tackle latent space representation explicitly and vividly. Here, the prediction of missing pixel RGB values is carried out through statistical estimation and calculations. This method results in predictions that harmoniously fit into the overall image, providing a coherent solution for image reconstruction. If you look at the various images, you'll see that each individual is grinning differently, indicating that either they aren't grinning too much or they are grinning a lot. Saying that a person is not smiling as much suggests that he is smiling to some level but is not exactly not smiling. For such a person, the latent smile characteristic is lower than it would be for someone who is fully smiling. You might more simply refer to the latent properties as a variable because they are one of the factors that can be anything. The aforementioned image demonstrates that the latent, the grin, skin tone, gender, beard, spectacles, and hair color are traits. Therefore, in the case of a variable autoencoder, these properties are checked while the latent space representation is being used. The project was originally intended to improve daily life by providing solutions to issues that arise in various real-world scenarios, such as the improvisation of medical MRI scans, aiding the police department, and creating 3D models for all of the 2D projection view photographs. The image processing stream was primarily significant to the scope for fixing the aforementioned issues. In which the deep learning idea of autoencoding is required for estimation and generation of 3D models from a single seen 2D picture. The closer details of the original 2D image are kept when the dimension is increased to 3D. The computer will take into account each pixel's value from the original image and work out which coordinate that particular pixel space belongs to in the third-dimension space. The latent space representation is also used to roughly remove noise and get rid of superfluous outliners. All of these latent features are taken into account and assessed on the basis of providing attention to these latent attributes when you provide a few images as the input to the autoencoder. The latent attribute, which is mostly utilized in 3D models for estimating poses and contains numerous characteristics at once for assessing the various stances in the photographs, determines the intensity of the graph. Watch out for how each image's latent characteristic has been determined numerically or mathematically, as well as how an intensity graph has been created for it. The smile latent characteristic is computed low and the intensity graph is similarly low for the first image, which features a kid who is not grinning and is displaying a sorrowful expression. The many inputs in the image above are compared using a single latent property. The smile has been selected as the latent attribute in this case. To determine the likelihood that each entered picture data has the grin, the smile's latent attribute is reviewed and estimated for each input. Each image's latent property is computed numerically or mathematically, and an intensity graph is created for it. The smile latent characteristic is computed low and the intensity graph is similarly low for the first image, which features a kid who is not grinning and is displaying a sorrowful expression.

And for the many images where a person is smiling differently, indicating that they are either not smiling at all or are smiling a lot. Let's say someone is not smiling as much, which implies they are smiling to some level but not absolutely not smiling. In this case, the latent smile attribute is lower than it would be for someone who is fully smiling. The latent attribute, which is mostly utilized in 3D models for estimating poses and contains numerous characteristics at once for assessing the various stances in the photographs, determines the intensity of the graph.

2. Literature Survey

In (1993) Avidehc Zakhore et al. proposed a novel technique for computer vision and pattern recognition to convert 2D to 3D They have proposed a new class of dithering algorithms for black and white (b/w) pictures based on various halftoning methods. The main goal of our method is to reduce distortion between the original continuous-tone image and its low-pass filtered halftone by dividing the image into tiny blocks. This equates to a quadratic programming issue with linear constraints that can be resolved using conventional optimisation methods. Examples of black-and-white halftone pictures created with our method are contrasted with halftones created using pre-existing dithering algorithms. With the availability of large 3D data sets like ShapeNet and improvements in machine learning techniques, several home-made attempts to rebuild 3D straight from 2nd images using learning-based techniques have been produced. Three fatal face datasets—CCelebi 3DFAW, BFM, and others—were used to test the experimenters' model. The model is used to accurately and precisely represent a person's emotions by calculating their facial expressions.

Another research by Sdren Forchhammer et al. (2000) In this study, They also used SUN Database for background and saved ground verify depth maps to estimate their generated 3D images. Complex geometrical information is needed for the 3D reconstruction of figure-grounded styles, and the majority of these styles rely heavily on the scene. Further, he implemented a technique for 3D mortal reconstruction based on geometric data has been presented. Other designs focused on enhancing the quality of 3D sensitive inputs, such as multi-view cameras and 3D scanners, as well as transforming this data into a 3D model. Even still, each of these approaches required more than one view of an item to gather enough data for 3D reconstruction. Further, the study of SQren Hein and Avideh Zakhor et al. (2011) proposed a method based on the halftoning technique. In this paper, he explained The viewpoint exceeds all other 3D shape reclamation styles on various common 3D markings by aligning its main axis to collect the global information and merging 2D Discrete Fourier transfigures and 2D Discrete Wavelet transfigures. While this was happening, then Lee et al. (2012) proposed the geometrical information for 3D reconstruction from a single 2D picture, making it delicate to develop a 3D model. In order to recreate the model in 3D, it is a must to additionally preserve the depth information of the scene or object. In the factual view using the prognosticated standpoint and comparing the ultimate to the ground-verity depth chart using the scale-steady depth error (SIDE)". Reconstruction methods based on literacy and data combine volumetric 3D models. In an emerging market, it is found from the analysis of P. Emmel et al. (1996) This paper investigates the Advances in deep literacy that have been misused by the exploration community to facilitate efficient modeling of a 2D picture into a 3D model. Because large-scale data sets like ShapeNet(5) are so sparse, most experimenters focus on creating a 3D voxelized model from a single 2D picture. Recently, bright strategies have been suggested to complete this job.

The study of Thrasyvoulos (1999) demonstrated a New Detection Method for Halftone Images Based on the Crisscross Checking Technique. The worrying issue of improved protection of digital data is important as the race for technological breakthroughs in the digital realm picks up speed. Without a doubt, information security and image processing are greatly hampered by the detection of data tampering. In this study, a crossing-checking method for halftone picture tamper detection is proposed. Jan Puzicha et al. (2000) In this study, A host picture is initially segmented into N blocks. A random integer will be used to jumble the separate blocks into code strings, which will then be concatenated into rows and columns of code. Hirobumi Nishida et al. (2001) used The MD5 and RSA algorithms will then be used with these code streams to create encrypted signed messages that will be concealed within the blocks. The row and column blocks will be examined for these extracted signed messages as part of the detection process. It is delicate to value geometrical information for 3D reconstruction from a single 2D picture, making it delicate to develop a 3D model. Plzuiisak Thieiuiviboon et al. (2001) In order to recreate the model in 3D, he additionally preserves the depth information of the scene or object. Reconstruction methods based on literacy and data combine volumetric 3D models. Rohan Tahir, et al. (2021) In this he used only variational autoencoders for the generation of a 3D view. This Literature indicates that several methods, such as creating a 3D model from point cloud data and a 3D model straight from 2D photos, have been used for 3D reconstruction throughout the course of many decades. For 3D reconstruction, the point-pall-grounded method uses configurations, morass, and Voronoi plates Although the experimenters cooked a new approach with their model, there are multitudinous failings.

Audrius Kulikajevas et al. (2021) tested various types of autoencoders for the generation of 3D view. In this paper, he proposed a technology based on Pixel Error Diffusion, especially with images of extreme facial expressions that needed to be fixed in order to homogenize the approach. According to this research, it is possible to create a 3D morphable form from a photograph of a human face, but this needs extensive constructed relationships and accurate 3D face scanning. Peter WM et al. (2002) In this paper, he introduced a balanced error to minimize the noise so that he built Some approaches recommend building a 3D form model using key points or lines. In certain experiments, the depth chart of a single picture is initially determined using machi machine literacy-based Furthermore employing RGB-D pictures, a 3D model is created. The use of an encoder-decoder-grounded convolutional neural network (CNN) to predict the future directly from a single picture has gained popularity. Nonetheless, the model is suitable to induce 3D images from a single-view image of objects without supervision. Johan phan et al. (2022) In this work, he proposes a size-invariant multi-step 3D generation workflow from a single 2D image using a combination of vector quantized variational encoder and he used the concept of size-invariant Generative Adversarial Networks (GAN) and he got a clear view of 3D representation.

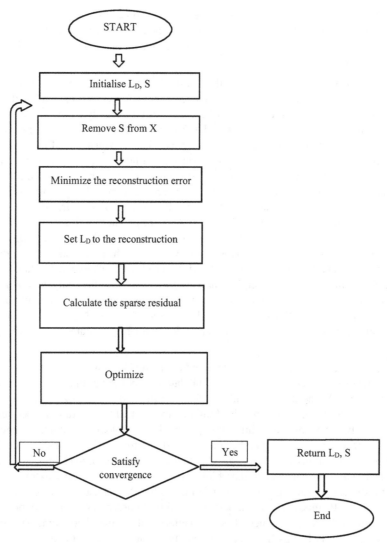

Fig. 28.2 Algorithm of a overcomplete autoencoder

Source: Author

3. Methodology of Proposed Work

In this proposed methodology, we are elaborating the steps involved in the implementation of proposed work as shown in the figure 2 as an algorithm. The overcomplete autoencoder was used to carry out the operation. The optimal approach for generating 3D models involves the utilization of overcomplete autoencoders. In this type of autoencoder, a single view or projection view serves as the input, and it possesses the capability to extrapolate and generate additional dimensions. The essence of overcomplete autoencoding lies in its ability to anticipate the missing perspectives by estimating from a single viewpoint. Contrastingly, there are undercomplete autoencoders that perform similarly to overcomplete ones but come with a built-in loss function. This distinction sets them apart. The presence of this loss function becomes apparent when dealing with numerous losses during the 3D model generation process. In undercomplete autoencoders, this loss function is eliminated in order to improve the output and get a better extinct.

Figure 28.2 shows the algorithm for the overcomplete autoencoder, where it computes two variables, L_D (low-rank public representation of auxiliary bearing data) and S(Degree of sparsity), as it transverses through the flow chart to optimize its values and satisfy the convergence. It will run into a loop if it does not satisfy the above conditions, and if it does satisfy them the algorithm will end.

The Undercomplete Autoencoder, which is the topic of this article, contains fewer nodes (dimensions) in the middle than the Input and Output layers do. In such designs, the intermediate layer is sometimes referred to as a "bottleneck." The center nodes (dimensions) of an overcomplete autoencoder are bigger than the input and output layers. Simply train our model using the reconstruction loss because an undercomplete autoencoder lacks an explicit regularization term. Therefore, ensuring that the number of nodes in the hidden layer is suitably restricted (s) is the only method to ensure that the model is not memorizing the input data. The most effective approach for crafting 3D models lies in harnessing the power of overcomplete autoencoders. In this specialized type of autoencoder, the input is derived from a single view or a projection view, endowed with the ability to predict and generate the supplementary dimensions. The generation of these extra dimensions stems from the process of estimating the content from a single perspective while speculating on potential alternative viewpoints. This particular class of autoencoders is aptly referred to as overcomplete autoencoding. In contrast, we have undercomplete autoencoders, which, while nearly as proficient as their overcomplete counterparts, introduce a distinctive feature—an embedded loss function. The presence of this loss function becomes more pronounced when multiple losses come into play during the construction of 3D models dimensions. These supplementary dimensions are generated by envisioning and estimating alternate viewpoints that complement the initial single perspective. This class of autoencoders is aptly referred to as overcomplete autoencoding. The basic autoencoder, variable autoencoder, and overcomplete autoencoder are the methods used to create 3D models from a single 2D projection picture. The project's ideation stage is closely related to the mathematical models and statistical analyses. Understanding the idea of autoencoding laid the groundwork for the achievement.

This technique worked really well for creating the 3D models. The Google CoLab platform was a fantastic resource for starting the project. Projects using deep learning and machine learning can be run on this platform. By default, this object file necessitates the use of third-party software, such as the freely available and open-source Blender program, to facilitate the creation, modeling, and visualization of 3D objects. To work with the obtained object file, you'll need to open it within the Blender program, typically by selecting the ".obj" file extension. It's important to note that the OpenCV packages alone lack the capability to generate a 3D model as an output. In Google Colab, representing the 3D model as the output involves running another code cell that requires the incorporation of packages like PyTorch. Furthermore, you can create a video file that is viewable within Google Colab or downloadable for external viewing, typically saving it as an ".mp4" file. You have the option to generate this video clip in either ".mp3" or ".mp4" format, but opting for the latter allows you to download the resulting 3D model. The video showcases a rotating view of the 3D model, providing a comprehensive display of the output derived from the 2D projection view. To enhance the accuracy of the output, one can employ a posture detector package. Moreover, refining the output for more precise results may involve introducing different 2D picture perspectives into the process.

4. Results and Discussion

This section presents various results obtained by the overcomplete autoencoder using the dimensionality reduction approach. As seen in figures 2 and 4, the model receives the original image of a person as input, and the results are displayed in figures 4 and 5. A person's original picture is sent to the model as input; the individual may be seen purportedly striking a stance. Four variables—albedo, depth, perspective, and illumination—are taken separately from the input photographs and are supposed to work together to reconstruct the image. Albedo, depth, perspective, and lighting may work together to approximate the original picture in three dimensions, although many things, such as human and feline faces, are asymmetrical. To compensate for the fact that they had previously assumed things were symmetrical even when they weren't, the researchers developed two measurements. Researchers claim that light, uneven albedo, and shape deformation are the causes of asymmetries. As a result, they explicitly accounted for asymmetric lighting in their models. Figure 28.2 shows the original image of a man posing which is used as an input image for our project. The picture contains no background it is so like that because the 3D model generation can be fuzzy in the presence of any background, and a proper 3D model of the above man image is fuzzy. The image is selected such that the deep learning model can identify the pose given by the human in the image.

Fig. 28.3 Image of a man

Figure 28.3 shows the original image of a man posing, which is used as an input image for our project. The picture contains no background; it is so like that because the 3D model generation can be fuzzy in the presence of any background, and a proper 3D model of the above man's image is sceptical. The image is selected such that the deep learning model can identify the pose given by the human in the image.

By enabling the creation of ground-breaking image processing-based applications, the capacity to convert 2D photos into 3D images has the potential to revolutionize the area of computer vision. Even though the researchers' model offered a unique approach, there are still a number of problems that must be handled before the approach can be applied to all face expressions, especially in the case of severe facial expressions. But from a single-view picture, the model can independently create 3D views of objects. To enlarge the model and create 3D. In future research endeavors, it will be crucial to expand the focus beyond representations of relatively simple objects, such as faces and symmetric shapes. The model's input and output pathways are constructed using the Google Colab libraries within their respective cells. Subsequently, the output path serves as the means to share the 3D model's object file. To work with this object file, you'll require additional software, such as the freely available and open-source 3D modeling and object visualization program Blender. To open the obtained object file, simply select the ".obj" file extension and utilize the Blender application. The process of depicting the 3D model as the output in Google Colab involves executing another code cell, which mandates the inclusion of packages like PyTorch. This step is necessary because the OpenCV packages alone lack the capability to generate the 3D model as an output. Furthermore, you have the option to create a video file through Google Colab, which can be saved in the ".mp4" format for viewing within the Colab environment or downloading for external viewing. Then download the 3D model that was produced in the.mp4 format as either the.mp3 or.mp4 format may be used to make this movie file. The movie illustrates the full output of the 2D projection view in the 3D model's rotation view. Use posture detection tools to understand and estimate the 3D model. Although the output is not precise, it might be made better to get more precise results. Entering many perspectives of a single 2D image is one method for doing this. The six photos below show the 3D versions of the provided 2D photographs. Blender, an open-source program for 3D graphics, is used to display the results, and the various viewpoints are displayed below.

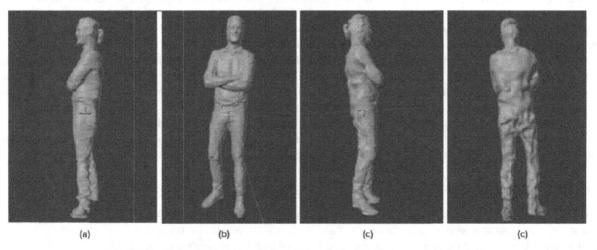

(a) (b) (c) (c)

Fig. 28.4 (a) Right side view, (b) Front view, (c) Left side view and (d) Back view

Source: Author

Figure 28.4(a) Shows the side view of the generated 3D model, this side is the input images left side view's and Fig. 28.4(b) shows the front view of the input image, which is the clear side of the total 3D model because the features of the front view, in the input image has more emphasis. Figure 28.4(c) shows the right-side view of the image, at this view the error particles are more clearly visible, and Figure 4(d) shows the back view, where most of the error percentage is residing due to the cluelessness of the back side of the input image.

To gain a comprehensive understanding of the visual model, all its elements are intricately woven together to form a composite spectrum image. This integrated view is instrumental in anticipating additional perspectives and assessing how the subject is positioned from various angles, including the rear, sides, and bottom. Moreover, the object file can serve as the foundation for creating a video file. This video clip can be conveniently viewed within Google Colab or saved in the ".mp4" format, allowing for playback that offers a more detailed examination of the subject. Figure 28.5 shows the generated video output in google colab residing in the results directory, followed by the recon (reconstruction) directory. The output is also obtained in the cell output block as a video with rotation of the 3D model which could intuitively depict the regeneration of the input image. A file created by the model can be stored in one of the folders within the google colab's own file system. The sample is located in the root directory. Go to a subdirectory called Results>sample folder>recon>result.mp4 through this sample directory. This method can only be used with photographs that have huma postures; it cannot be used with any other images. This is so that we may try

Fig. 28.5 PNG file of the obtained output

Source: Author

to detect various human stances from the inputted photographs using a pose estimator software. These libraries are imported using the pip package manager, which was used to obtain and install the aforementioned libraries. In certain cases, the libraries had to be installed during the runtime, which required restarting the runtime after each installation. This technique involves breaking down the entire image into distinct small segments using feature maps to gauge the depth of each pixel across various regions of the image. This process is initiated upon receiving input from the file system. The method employs a unique neural network architecture known as PiFuHD, an acronym for "multi-Level pixel aligned implicit function for high resolution." Typically, this design is harnessed for the transformation of 2D images into 3D representations. Upon receiving input from the file system, the approach dissects the entire image into discrete small components, utilizing feature maps to assess the depth of each pixel within different areas of the image. This assessment or prediction of the reverse side of the image presents a challenge, which can potentially be addressed by incorporating the same image from multiple angles.

Figure 28.5 the image file of the object files which is generated by using the platform of google colab, the above picture shows the front and back reconstruction of the input image of a man. The above figure depicts the spectrum of the portions of the front and back views of the inputted image. This is the figure of the object file opened as a .png file.

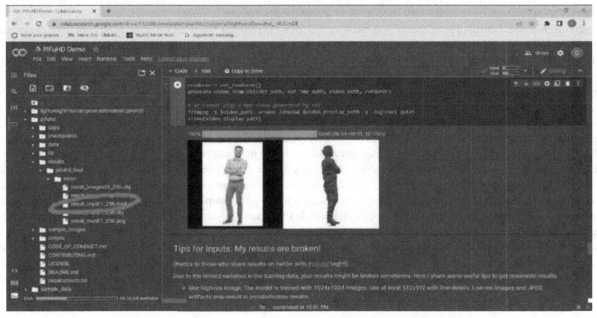

Fig. 28.6 Google colab work environment depicting the result directory

Source: Author

In Fig. 28.6, we can see the generated video output from google colab residing in the results directory, followed by the recon (reconstruction) directory. The output is also obtained in the cell output block as a video with rotation of the 3D model, which could depict the regeneration of the input image in an intutive way.

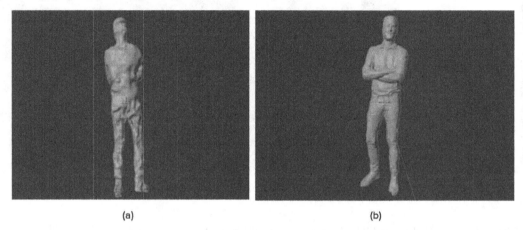

(a)   (b)

Fig. 28.7   (a) Back view of the 3D models and (b) Front view of the 3D model

Source: Author

Figure 28.7(a) shows the back view of the 3D models with apparent errors due to the lower number of hidden layers in the used algorithms; these anomalies can be rectified by enhancing and training the model more efficiently and Fig. 28.7(b) presents the front view of the 3D model with precision, this precision is obtained because the model has the least computation to do with the front view of the picture as the input image itself is of the front view.

5. Conclusion

According to the proposed study, the challenge of generating 3D images from the projection view of 2D photos finds its solution in the dimensionality reduction technique. This approach, known as dimensionality reduction, stands as an effective method within the realm of automated encoding for problem-solving. At the core of this methodology lies the autoencoder, a deep learning technique that encodes input images and subsequently generates output by decoding them with the assistance of decoders. The primary purpose of this autoencoder is to automatically compress input before automatically encoding it. This approach offers a dual benefit of both conserving memory space and facilitating the retrieval of original data from the encoded information. It presents an excellent method for conveniently preserving pristine images of various image spaces. Additionally, this technique holds potential applications in the field of medicine, particularly when dealing with MRI scans of the human body, including critical areas like the brain and various components of the skeletal system. In cases where these scans lack the necessary clarity for medical professionals to conduct thorough assessments of the patient's condition, this approach could prove invaluable. Furthermore, our human visual system naturally excels in interpreting three-dimensional shapes, making it possible to swiftly grasp the 3D form of an object by observing it from different angles. Looking ahead, the integration of 3D imaging into various aspects of everyday life, such as law enforcement, holds the promise of providing significant benefits and applications. These days, crimes are occurring frequently, and one of the most effective ways to catch criminals is to understand the CCTV footage that is recorded on-site. However, sometimes the images are difficult to understand, so by creating a clear 3D model, additional clues can be obtained that may help to solve the case as quickly as possible. In the medical field, 3D models may be utilized to comprehend MRI images in addition to the police department. Making a 3D model of the tumor, for instance, might help doctors comprehend the crucial condition if there is a brain tumor and they are unable to determine its severity or size. Sports industries may also utilize this technique by creating a 3D model of the players' stances since they use a third umpire to determine whether a cricket player is out or not. For the purpose of creating 3D models of the players and using them to improve estimates, the third umpire might be improvised. I think more explicit applications can be found in many other scopes for the use of 3D modeling in so many sectors. The most important tool for creating 3D models is the autoencoder.

REFERENCES

1. Avidehc Zakhor, Steve Lin, and Farokh Eskafi. A New Class of B/W Halftoning Algorithms. IEEE transactions On Image Processing, Vol. 2, No. 4, October 1993.

2. Sdren Forchhammer and Morten Forchhammer. Algorithms For Coding Scannedhalftone Pictures. Ch2614- 6/88/0000/02971988 IEEE, November 2000.

3. SQren Hein, and Avideh Zakhor. Halftone to Continuous-Tone Conversion of Error-Diffusion Coded Images.August 2011.

4. Lee, P.Huang, J. Lin, H. 3D model reconstruction based on multiple view image capture. In Proceedings of the 2012 International Symposium on Intelligent Signal Processing and Communications Systems, Tamsui, Taiwan, 4–7 November 2012; pp. 58–63.

5. P. Emmel, N. Rudaz, I.Amidrol; R.D. Hersch. Ditheringalgorithms For Variable Dot Sizeprinters. 0-7803-3258- X/1996 IEEE

6. Thrasyvoulos N. Pappas, David L. Neuhoff. Least-Squares Model-Based Halftoning, IEEE transactions On Image Processing, Vol. 8, No. 8, August 1999.

7. Jan Puzicha, Marcus Held, Jens Ketterer, JoachimM. Buhmann, and Dieter W. Fellner. On Spatial Quantization of Color Images. IEEE Transactions On Image Processing, Vol. 9, No. 4, April 2000.

8. Hirobumi Nishida. Model-Based Digital Halftoning with Adaptive Eye Filters. 0-7803-6725- 2001 IEEE. Plzuiisak Thieiuiviboon, Aiitoizio Ortega, aizdKeith M. Chuyg. Simplified Grid Messagepassingalgorithm With Application to Digital Image Halftoning. 0-7803-6725-2001 Ieee.

9. ChunghuiKuo, A. Ravishankar Rao and Gerhard Thompson. Wavelet-Based Halftone Segmentation And Descreening Filter Design. 0,-7803-7041-401/ 2001 IEEE.

10. Pingshan Li Jan P Allebach. Clusteredminority Pixel Error Diffusion. 0-7803-7622-2002 Ieee Icip 2002. Peter WM. Ilbery. Radially Balancederror Diffusion. 0-7803-7622- 2002 IEEE.

11. Tung-Shou Chen, Jeanne Chen, Yu-Mei Pan. A New Detection Method of Halftone Images Based on Crisscross Checking Technique. Proceedings of the IEEE Fifth International Symposium on Multimedia Software Engineering (ISMSE'03) 0-7695-2031 ©2003 IEEE.

12. C. Ahsew, A. G. Constantmidesf, L. Htisson. Colour Quantisation Through Dithering Techniques. 0-7803-77.50 Ieee2003

Advances in Computational Intelligence and its Applications (ICACIA-2023) – Dr. Sheikh Fahad Ahmad et al. (eds)
© *2024 Taylor & Francis Group, London, ISBN 978-1-032-78612-4*

Attention Based Bidirectional LSTM Model for Data-to-text Generation

29

Abhishek Kumar Pandey[1]

Research Scholar, School of Computer Science and Engineering,
Vellore Institute of Technology

Sanjiban Sekhar Roy*

Professor, School of Computer Science and Engineering,
Vellore Institute of Technology

ABSTRACT—Natural Language Processing (NLP) helps process human language computationally. Recently, automatic data-to-text generation, article generation, has received much popularity. Deep learning has already revolutionized the applicability of natural language processing, and attention mechanism has changed how we work with them. This paper uses the attention mechanism for Bidirectional Long-Term Short-Term Memory (Bi-LSTM) by automatically taking input as words and generating a sentence. The generated text is validated with the BLEU Score. Moreover, Bi-LSTM with attention model has shown good BLEU scores compared to other models such as LSTM, LSTM with attention, LSTM, and Bi-LSTM. Results are 0.67, 0.42, 0.21, and 0.24, respectively. The accuracy of Bi-LSTM with attention model is 92%

KEYWORDS—Natural language generation (NLG), Bi-directional LSTM, BLEU, Deep learning

1. Introduction

Recently researchers have found interest in data-to-text generation due to the applications of natural language processing and the availability of vast amounts of data. Data to an article generation has automatically converted the non-linguistic input into a new article in the natural language (REITER and DALE 1997; Gatt and Krahmer 2018)we give an overview of Natural Language Generation (NLG. It takes an article or story as input and generates the text as per the input context. The generation of text depends upon the input text, deep learning model takes the input text, and none of the words want to generate as an input and generates the whole sentence as per the given no of words as an output. The process of article generation uses structured data such as stories, news articles, Wiki bio, WebNLG, physical simulations, e-commerce reviews, spreadsheets, and expert system knowledge. In this paper, we generate some small stories based on Gutenberg stories. Two lakh sentences are used for the model training for article generation. Traditional methods for data to article generation implement the basic pipeline structure. Faille et al. proposed a pipeline structure based on three stages: document planner, micro planner, and surface realizer (Faille et al. 2020). Document Planner has two steps, such as content determination and document structuring. This process helps to decide the data domain and specify what and how the information will communicate. Micro planner work in two steps: text planner and sentence planner, which helps to determine the linguistic meaning of the sentence. The surface realizer is the last step, which allows setting every word in the proper order with grammatical rules. It uses morphology and orthography

*Corresponding author: s.roy@vit.ac.in
[1]abhishek.pandey2020@vitstudent.ac.in

DOI: 10.1201/9781003488682-29

to provide the correct order of the words. Recent neural network models have been free from these stages (Fan, Lewis, and Dauphin 2018). It is based on a training mechanism. Sequential generative models are used in the text generation process, where it first finds the features and sentence structure of the input text and trains the model according to the features. The neural network model generates the text based on features and sentence structure.

The recent neural generative models are Markov chain, Long Short Term Memory (LSTM), Recurrent Neural Network (RNN), Gated Recurrent Unit (GRU), Transformer, and attention-based neural network field (S. S. Roy et al. 2017; Hodges et al. 2019). These models provide end-to-end training and validation of results. The generative model can generate proficient texts but has problems capturing long-term dependencies and long paragraph generation. Basic LSTM and RNN models can generate articles and learn the relationship between two characters, but these models have challenges in avoiding redundancy and word selection. In this paper, the data-to-article generation task is accomplished by using the attention-based Bi-LSTM model, where we use Shakespeare stories as a dataset and will generate text based on the dataset.

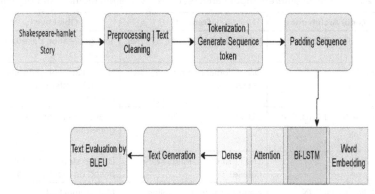

Fig. 29.1 Flow chart diagram of data for article generation

Figure 29.1 represents the flowchart diagram of a model implementation for data-to-article generation. This paper addresses redundancy and captures long-term dependencies, and we are interested in generating descriptive text such as small stories and articles. This paper combines the advantages of the LSTM model with the attention mechanism to generate text recurrently. This model is capable of focusing on sentence structure with less training resources. Attention is directly introduced inside the LSTM unit, which enriches the LSTM layers' hidden state (S. Roy and V. 2016)machine learning techniques are adopted for filtering email spams. This article examines the capabilities of the extreme learning machine (ELM. The result of the model shows an efficient result in the form of grammatical and short sentence generation. The BLEU mechanism is used to evaluate the result.

Therefore, this paper aims to achieve the following:

1. Applying the attention mechanism with LSTM and Bi-LSTM models.
2. We have conducted detailed experiments with contemporary and popular deep learning models such as LSTM, Bi-LSTM, Attention with LSTM, and Attention with Bi-LSTM for data to article generation.
3. We Evaluate the generated text with the help of different BLEU matrices, such as BLEU-1, BLEU-2, BLEU-3, BLEU-4, and BLEU-5.

The rest of the paper has been structured: Section 2 presents the survey structure, related surveys, and how reference works have been selected. Section 3 describes the modeling approach of LSTM, Bi-LSTM, and attention to the Bi-LSTM model; Section 4 presents experiments at different stages, such as dataset pre-processing, model fine-tuning, and results of the experiment. Section 5 states overall conclusions and future insights regarding the data-to-text generation experiments.

2. Literature Review

Data to an article generation literature provides exciting facts about traditional and recent generative models (Duboue and McKeown 2003). The conventional algorithm is designed with content selection for various domains, either manually hand-built (Kukich 1983; McKeown 1992) or by learning mechanism from the data. The text generation started with text summarizing and machine translation mechanisms (Konstas and Lapata 2012).

In recent years, neural network models have shown efficient results in sequence generation problems. The model adapts the end-to-end system for data to article generation instead of an individual component (van der Lee et al. 2022), such as generating a biography from the Wikipedia infobox (Bao et al. 2019; Chen et al. 2021), news headline generation by using DUC2003 and DUC2004 datasets (Ayana et al. 2020), research paper introduction generation from research paper collection(Wang, Hsiao, and Chang 2020) and Bengali text generation from Bengali text datasets (Abujar et al. 2019). Dethlefs et al. have followed the LSTM-based divide and conquer approach to generate input context text (Dethlefs, Schoene, and Cuayáhuitl 2021). The recent trends of research include table-to-text generation. Cao has proposed table-to-text generation from WEATHERGOV, WIKI BIO, WIKITABLE, and WIKIBIOCN datasets using RNN and LSTM models (Liu et al. 2018). We have also seen poetry generation in the literature proposed by Zhang and Lapata (Zhang and Lapata). Table 29.1 represents recent works in the data for article generation.

Table 29.1 Study of different model architectures, evaluation metrics, and objectives

References	Model Architecture	Dataset	Objective	Metrics
(Bao et al. 2019)	GRU based RNN	WIKIBIO, SIMPLE- QUESTIONS	Text generation based on Tables	BLEU-4 = 40.26
(Wei and Zhang 2019)	LSTM	Open-domain community QA dataset	Natural answer generation based on attention mechanism.	BLEU = 32.52 ROUGE = 40.42
(Ayana et al. 2018)	Bi-directional GRU, RNN	DUC2003, DUC2004	Cross-lingual headline generation	ROUGE-1 =14.44 ROUGE-2 = 3.04, ROUGE − L = 13.32
(Santhanam 2020)	LSTM	The Lord of the Rings story dataset	Data to stories generation based on input stories	Accuracy = 97%
(Abujar et al. 2019)	Bi-directional RNN	Bengali article from online resources	Multilingual text generation such as Bengali article generation.	Accuracy LSTM = 97% BI-LSTM = 98.766%
(Chakraborty et al. 2020)	LSTM	C programs with their comments,	Comment generation for the programming language	LSTM(256) Accuracy=82.67%

3. Modeling Approach

Many algorithms are used for the data to article generation, such as LSTM, RNN, Transformer, and CNN 1d. In this paper, we use the LSTM model as a base model, which is an attention-based model also known as the LSTM attention model. To begin with, the data for an article generation problem is as follows. We define the input as $m_t = \{k_o, k_1, \dots \dots \dots \dots \dots \dots, k_{t-1}, T\}$ at time t, Here α represents the structure latent variable and T shows the input text variable. The goal of data to article generation is to generate the sequence of words $X_{1:n} = (k_1, \dots, k_t, \dots, k_n)$, n represent the length of sequences. Every word in the sequence is generated by the following formulations

$$p_{(t)} = na\, m\{p(k_1, \dots, k_{t-1}, T, \alpha)\} \tag{1}$$

The next word is generated as a maximum probability at time t, and the final model will generate the whole sentence.

3.1 LSTM Model

LSTM is an advanced version of RNN unit and it was proposed in 1997(Chakraborty et al. 2020; Farooqui, Mishra, and Mehra 2022). The LSTM units contain the recurrent network unit, which remembers the values for the longer time duration. LSTM uses the three gates to control the flow of information, such as input gate, forget gate output gate, and a memory cell to remember the information. $x = \{x_1, x_2, \dots, x_T\}$ is a input sequence vector, and $h = \{h, h_2, \dots, h_T\}$ is hidden states for the LSTM units, Following equations represent the different gates (Tiwari, Shobhit, Sourav Khandelwal 2011; Wadhwa and Roy 2021). Equation (2) is input gate i_t, it decides the input information, the next gate controls the information as long as the information is present in the memory and it's equation(3) forgets gate f_t, The unit candidate status C_t is updated in the equation (4) and (5), and the final gate's output is gate o_t ;which is responsible for the result in equation(6). Equation(7) is responsible for the next hidden state of the LSTM.

$$f_t = \sigma(W_f[h_{t-1}, x_t] + b_f) \tag{2}$$

$$i_t = \sigma(W_i[h_{t-1}, x_t] + b_i) \tag{3}$$

$$c_t = \tanh \tanh (W_c[h_{t-1}, x_t] + b_c) \tag{4}$$

$$c_t = f_t * c_{t-1} + i_t * c_t \tag{5}$$

$$o_t = \sigma(W_o[h_{t-1}, x_t] + b_o) \tag{6}$$

$$h_t = o_t * \tanh(c_t) \tag{7}$$

In the equation (7), We represent the weight matrices and b represent the biases. The activation function is σ and here we used the sigmoid function.

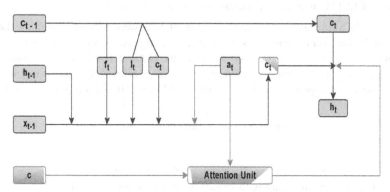

Fig. 29.2 Attention based LSTM unit

As shown in Fig. 29.2, the LSTM model directly inserts the information to the attention mechanism (S. S. Roy et al. 2022). The Blue marking in the graph is an attention mechanism. Here we take Shakespeare's-Hamlet story as an dataset, apply the pre-processing task on text data, build the model for training, and the finally we generate the new text as per model training.

3.2 Bi-LSTM Attention Mode

Bi- LSTM attention model is the combination of bidirectional LSTM model with attention mechanism, which makes good use of history information. Figure 29.1 represents the LSTM attention model for data to article generation.

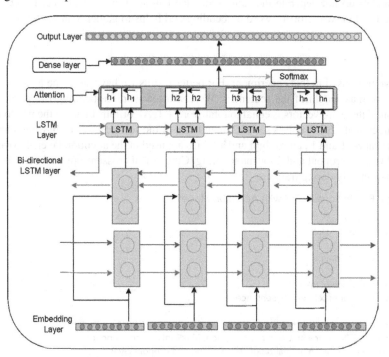

Fig. 29.3 Bi-LSTM with attention mechanism architecture

As shown in Figure 29.3, data is embedded as the input of LSTM cells and it generates the next word at time t. From time 0 to 1 LSTM gets the history of information in the sentence pattern (Lippi et al. 2019). Then the LSTM with attention unit calculates the result at time t and it is the input for the next LSTM cell at time $t + 1$.

At 0 time, expression for the initial input of LSTM unit is

$$x_0 = f(T, \alpha) \tag{8}$$

Equation for the Bi-LSTM output at time t

$$x_t = \text{Bi-LSTM}(\text{attention } (x_{t-1}, c)) \tag{9}$$

Here, c represents the result of LSTM attention with output word at time 0 to $t - 1$.

Algorithm of attention based LSTM model is represented in Table 29.2. As we see the algorithm the dataset is firstly converted into the token as per n gram. In the layer of model, firstly word embedding layer is introduced in the form of the dataset. After that, LSTM layers and attention layers were introduced to gather the features from the dataset such as a sentence structure (Pawade et al. 2018). On the basis of a sentence structure the article is generated. Generated text is updated as per attention mechanism, it helps to fix the length representing the form of LSTM unit. Attention mechanism is formulated in expression (10).

$$\text{attention } (x_{t-1}, c) = \tanh (x_{t-1}U, cV) \tag{10}$$

4. Experiments

In this section, the dataset and experiments result with validation matrices have been discussed. This experiment is based on LSTM, attention mechanisms, and Gutenberg stories taken as the dataset. This experiment is performed on Google colab for a better GPU system. The detailed experiment is discussed below.

4.1 Dataset

Data to article generation needs a high quality corpus. We have collected the dataset from the Gutenberg stories, which is an open source. "Shakespeare's-Hamlet" is the name of a story which is used in the experiments and it contains a story of 7 chapters and 3000 sentences. Data was collected as raw stories, then we performed pre-processing to clean the dataset such as ascii character removal, lowering the all sentences. After that tokenization processing had been performed, as per n-gram methodology. N-gram models do not generate the same sequence length of every sentence. Hereby, padding is introduced. Padding returns the same length text vector for word embedding and helps to gather features by word embedding and LSTM model.

4.2 Fine-Tuning

Tensorflow packages have been used in this experiment. For better results we have set some hyperparameters. We have taken the input length as equal to max length of the sentences. We also used word embedding(Liu et al. 2018) to train the word vectors and the dimension of the word vectors is equal to total word + 1. Algorithm 1 shown the psudo code for generating text. The hidden size of Bi-directional LSTM unit is set as 256 and 128 in the second layer of bi-directional LSTM unit. Shape of attention unit is set input shaper -1 and 1 . att_weigth and att_bias are used in the attention layer. To overcome the overfitting of the dataset we have used 0.25 in dropout and 2 for maxpooling. Categorical crossentropy and rmsprop is used to calculate the error and optimization respectively during training.

Algorithm 1   Algorithm for Bidirectional LSTM with Attention Model

Input	Shakespeare's-Hamlet Story
Output	Short text generation based on story
Step 1	Begin
Step 2	Import dataset and clean the data
Step 3	Data tokenization
Step 4	Convert into bi-gram sequence of token
Step 5	Pre-padding the token as per max length of sentence
Step 6	Model Building
	Step 6.1 Embedding Layer with dimension 16
	Step 6.2 Bidirectional LSTM layer with Batch normalization, MaxPooling and dropout layer
	Step 6.3 Attention layer with Batch normalization, MaxPooling and dropout layer

Step 6.4   Bidirectional LSTM layer with Batch normalization, MaxPooling and dropout layer
Step 6.5   LSTM layer with Batch normalization, MaxPooling and dropout layer
Step 6.6   Dense layer with softmax activation function
Step 7   Fitting of the network means adapting the weight on a training dataset
Step 8   Evaluation the network
Step 9   Make prediction of next word and generate the whole text
Step 10   End

Algorithm 1 shown the psudo code for the bidirectional LSTM with Attention model for generating text. Here we take story as an dataset, apply the pre-processing task on text data, build the model for training, and the finally we generate the new text as per model training.

4.3 Results

This section represents the results of the LSTM with attention model. We have provided the input text and the model generates the next 20 words on the basis of input words. The Table 29.3 shows the input words and the generated words. In this model we get 92.34% accuracy and 0.26 LOSS at 200 epoch and 64 batch size. Figure 29.4 shows the accuracy and loss.

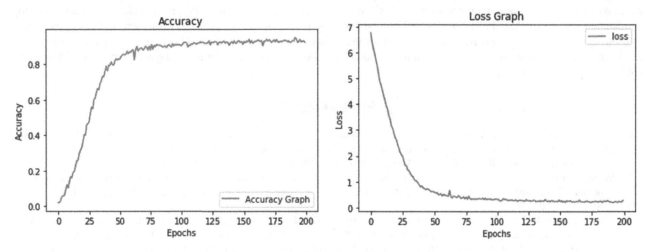

Fig. 29.4   Accuracy and Loss graph on Bi-directional LSTM with attention mechanism

We also used the BLEU matrices for the evaluation of generated text. BLEU is an algorithm for evaluating the quality of the text. It contains BLEU-1 , BLEU -2 , BLEU- 3 and BLEU -4. The output of BLEU always lies between 0 to 1. As shown in Table 29.2, Bidirectional LSTM with attention mechanism gives better results.

Table 29.2   Comparative study between different models

Model	BLEU -1	BLEU -2	BLEU -3	BLEU -4	BLEU -5
LSTM	0.24	0.31	0.27	0.32	0.51
Bi-LSTM	0.21	0.47	0.31	0.45	0.39
LSTM with Attention	0.42	0.51	0.39	0.54	0.44
Bi-LSTM with Attention	0.62	0.55	0.43	0.38	0.56

In Table 29.2 , we got the good result with Bidirectional LSTM with attention model. Here we get 0.62 score BLEU-1 matrix and the result of all BLEU matrix shown good result as comparatively LSTM, Bi-LSTM and LSTM with Attention model. Table 29.3 represent the some sample of the generated text on different models.

Table 29.3 represents the generated text sample by using deep learning models. Attention based Bi-LSTM models shown Comparatively good results.

Table 29.3 Sample of generated text by using deep learning models

Model	Input Text	Generated Text
LSTM	Dark house under	Dark house under ground ground ground and she was was sit under there all and
Bi-LSTM	Dark house under	Dark house under the ground and she was was sit there all and by day
LSTM with Attention	Dark house under	Dark house under and she was was sit there all and by day herself and it
Bi-LSTM with Attention	Dark house under	Dark house under the ground one day she was sit there all by and herself

5. Conclusion

This paper focuses on data-to-article generation using deep learning models. We analyzed some previous models and performed a comparative study with problems of the existing model and enhancement of the model.

In this paper, we proposed a Bi-LSTM-based attention model, combining the Bidirectional LSTM model with the Attention mechanism. This model has shown a good result compared to LSTM, Bi-LSTM, and LSTM with an attention mechanism. We have taken the Shakespeare's-Hamlet story from the Gutenberg stories, pre-processed the corpus, and cleaned the text with stop words and unnecessary ASCII characters to process these stories. It helps to gather the good features from the sentence, such as sentence structure. BLEU matrices are also used for the validation of text generation. This research has shown significant results in natural language generation. Although, we found some weaknesses in generating a long paragraph. These drawbacks could be resolved in future research.

REFERENCES

1. Abujar, Sheikh, Abu Kaisar Mohammad Masum, S. M.Mazharul Hoque Chowdhury, Mahmudul Hasan, and Syed Akhter Hossain. 2019. "Bengali Text Generation Using Bi-Directional RNN." 2019 10th International Conference on Computing, Communication and Networking Technologies, ICCCNT 2019, 1–5. https://doi.org/10.1109/ICCCNT45670.2019.8944784.

2. Ayana, Yun Chen, Cheng Yang, Zhiyuan Liu, and Maosong Sun. 2020. "Reinforced Zero-Shot Cross-Lingual Neural Headline Generation." IEEE/ACM Transactions on Audio Speech and Language Processing 28 (12): 2572–84. https://doi.org/10.1109/TASLP.2020.3009487.

3. Ayana, S Shen, Y Chen, C Yang, Z Liu, and M Sun. 2018. "Zero-Shot Cross-Lingual Neural Headline Generation." IEEE/ACM Transactions on Audio, Speech, and Language Processing 26 (12): 2319–27. https://doi.org/10.1109/TASLP.2018.2842432.

4. Bao, Junwei, Duyu Tang, Nan Duan, Zhao Yan, Ming Zhou, and Tiejun Zhao. 2019. "Text Generation from Tables." IEEE/ACM Transactions on Audio Speech and Language Processing 27 (2): 311–20. https://doi.org/10.1109/TASLP.2018.2878381.

5. Chakraborty, Shayak, Jayanta Banik, Shubham Addhya, and Debraj Chatterjee. 2020. "Study of Dependency on Number of LSTM Units for Character Based Text Generation Models." 2020 International Conference on Computer Science, Engineering and Applications, ICCSEA 2020. https://doi.org/10.1109/ICCSEA49143.2020.9132839.

6. Chen, Gang, Yang Liu, Huanbo Luan, Meng Zhang, Qun Liu, and Maosong Sun. 2021. "Learning to Generate Explainable Plots for Neural Story Generation." IEEE/ACM Transactions on Audio Speech and Language Processing 29: 585–93. https://doi.org/10.1109/TASLP.2020.3039606.

7. Dethlefs, Nina, Annika Schoene, and Heriberto Cuayáhuitl. 2021. "A Divide-and-Conquer Approach to Neural Natural Language Generation from Structured Data." Neurocomputing 433: 300–309. https://doi.org/10.1016/j.neucom.2020.12.083.

8. Duboue, Pablo A, and Kathleen McKeown. 2003. "Statistical Acquisition of Content Selection Rules for Natural Language Generation."

9. Faille, Juliette, Albert Gatt, Claire Gardent, Juliette Faille, Albert Gatt, Claire Gardent, The Natural, et al. 2020. "The Natural Language Generation Pipeline , Neural Text Generation and Explainability To Cite This Version: HAL Id: Hal-03046206 Explainability," no. December: 16–21.

10. Fan, Angela, Mike Lewis, and Yann Dauphin. 2018. "Hierarchical Neural Story Generation." ACL 2018 - 56th Annual Meeting of the Association for Computational Linguistics, Proceedings of the Conference (Long Papers) 1: 889–98. https://doi.org/10.18653/v1/p18-1082.

11. Farooqui, Nafees Akhter, Amit Kumar Mishra, and Ritika Mehra. 2022. "Concatenated Deep Features with Modified LSTM for Enhanced Crop Disease Classification." International Journal of Intelligent Robotics and Applications. https://doi.org/10.1007/s41315-022-00258-8.

12. Gatt, Albert, and Emiel Krahmer. 2018. "Survey of the State of the Art in Natural Language Generation: Core Tasks, Applications and Evaluation." Journal of Artificial Intelligence Research 61 (c): 1–64. https://doi.org/10.1613/jair.5714.

13. Hodges, Cameron, Senjian An, Hossein Rahmani, Mohammed Bennamoun, Valentina E. Balas, Sekhar R. Sanjiban, Dharmendra Sharma, and Pijush Samui. 2019. Handbook of Deep Learning Applications. Vol. 136. http://link.springer.com/10.1007/978-3-030-11479-4.

14. Konstas, Ioannis, and Mirella Lapata. 2012. "Unsupervised Concept-to-Text Generation with Hypergraphs." In Proceedings of the 2012 Conference of the North American Chapter of the Association for Computational Linguistics: Human Language Technologies, 752–61.

15. Kukich, Karen. 1983. "Design of a Knowledge-Based Report Generator." Annual Meeting of the Association for Computational Linguistics, Proceedings of the Conference, 145–50. https://doi.org/10.3115/981311.981340.

16. Lee, Chris van der, Thiago Castro Ferreira, Chris Emmery, Travis Wiltshire, and Emiel Krahmer. 2022. "Neural Data-to-Text Generation Based on Small Datasets: Comparing the Added Value of Two Semi-Supervised Learning Approaches on Top of a Large Language Model." http://arxiv.org/abs/2207.06839.

17. Lippi, Marco, Marcelo A Montemurro, Mirko Degli Esposti, and Giampaolo Cristadoro. 2019. "Of LSTM-Generated Texts" 30 (11): 3326–37.

18. Liu, Tianyu, Kexiang Wang, Lei Sha, Baobao Chang, and Zhifang Sui. 2018. "Table-to-Text Generation by Structure-Aware Seq2seq Learning." 32nd AAAI Conference on Artificial Intelligence, AAAI 2018, 4881–88.

19. McKeown, Kathleen. 1992. Text Generation. Cambridge University Press.

20. Pawade, Dipti, Avani Sakhapara, Mansi Jain, Neha Jain, and Krushi Gada. 2018. "Story Scrambler - Automatic Text Generation Using Word Level RNN-LSTM." International Journal of Information Technology and Computer Science 10 (6): 44–53. https://doi.org/10.5815/ijitcs.2018.06.05.

21. REITER, EHUD, and ROBERT DALE. 1997. "Building Applied Natural Language Generation Systems." Natural Language Engineering 3 (1): 57–87. https://doi.org/DOI: 10.1017/S1351324997001502.

22. Roy, Sanjiban Sekhar, Ali Ismail Awad, Lamesgen Adugnaw Amare, Mabrie Tesfaye Erkihun, and Mohd Anas. 2022. "Multimodel Phishing URL Detection Using LSTM, Bidirectional LSTM, and GRU Models." Future Internet 14 (11): 340.

23. Roy, Sanjiban Sekhar, Abhinav Mallik, Rishab Gulati, Mohammad S Obaidat, and P Venkata Krishna. 2017. "A Deep Learning Based Artificial Neural Network Approach for Intrusion Detection." In Mathematics and Computing: Third International Conference, ICMC 2017, Haldia, India, January 17-21, 2017, Proceedings 3, 44–53.

24. Roy, Sanjiban, and Dr.Madhu Viswanatham V. 2016. "Classifying Spam Emails Using Artificial Intelligent Techniques." International Journal of Engineering Research in Africa 22 (February): 152–61. https://doi.org/10.4028/www.scientific.net/JERA.22.152.

25. Santhanam, Sivasurya. 2020. "Context Based Text-Generation Using LSTM Networks." http://arxiv.org/abs/2005.00048.

26. Tiwari, Shobhit, Sourav Khandelwal, and Sanjiban Sekhar Roy. 2011. "E-Learning Tool for Japanese Language Learning through English , Hindi and Tamil," 52–55.

27. Wadhwa, Anmol, and Sanjiban Sekhar Roy. 2021. "Driver Drowsiness Detection Using Heart Rate and Behavior Methods: A Study." Data Analytics in Biomedical Engineering and Healthcare, 163–77.

28. Wang, Hei Chia, Wei Ching Hsiao, and Sheng Han Chang. 2020. "Automatic Paper Writing Based on a RNN and the TextRank Algorithm." Applied Soft Computing Journal 97: 106767. https://doi.org/10.1016/j.asoc.2020.106767.

29. Wei, Mengxi, and Yang Zhang. 2019. "Natural Answer Generation with Attention over Instances." IEEE Access 7: 61008–17. https://doi.org/10.1109/ACCESS.2019.2904337.

30. Zhang, Xingxing, and Mirella Lapata. "Chinese Poetry Generation with Recurrent Neural Networks." In Proceedings of the 2014 Conference on Empirical Methods in Natural Language Processing ({EMNLP}), 670–80. Doha, Qatar: Association for Computational Linguistics. https://doi.org/10.3115/v1/D14-1074.

Note: All the figures and tables in this chapter were made by the authors.

Advances in Computational Intelligence and its Applications (ICACIA-2023) – Dr. Sheikh Fahad Ahmad et al. (eds)
© 2024 Taylor & Francis Group, London, ISBN 978-1-032-78612-4

A Conceptualized Study on Blockchain Technological Algorithms, Cyber-Attacks and Application Perceptions

30

Vivek Khirasaria

Assistant Professor, Faculty of Engineering & Technology,
Sharda University, Uzbekistan

Suresh Kaswan

Professor, Faculty of Engineering & Technology,
Sharda University, Uzbekistan

Lisha Yugal, Akanksha Shangloo

Assistant Professor, School of Engineering & Technology,
Sharda University, India

ABSTRACT—The use of technology has increased in some ways revolutionized in many segments. Blockchain technology consists of increasing lists of record, known as blocks, that are safely connected to one another via encryption and decryption methodology known as Cryptography. Blockchain is an emerging technology that has the potential to revolutionize the global economy and establish a reliable connection in multi-party transactions. Blockchain has been deployed in a handful of actual use cases. Numerous blockchain applications exist, ranging from public and governmental services to cryptocurrencies, financial services, and risk management through the internet of things (IoT). There isn't a comprehensive assessment on the blockchain technology in terms of both technological and application perceptions, despite the fact that many research concentrate on implementing the technology in different application aspects. Therefore, efforts have been made to make an extensive review on the blockchain technology to narrow this gap. In the Present work taxonomy, blockchain consensus algorithms, its benefits, drawbacks, and various Blockchain applications are being discussed.

KEYWORDS—Blockchain, IoT, Consensus algorithms, Cyber attacks, Blockchain challenges

1. Introduction

Nakamoto originally discussed blockchain in 2008, and it was put into use in 2009. A series of blocks called a blockchain can be thought of as a public ledger where all committed transactions are kept. When more blocks are added to it, this chain keeps expanding. Blockchain is a relatively new database and data encryption system that verifies and transfers data using immutable ledgers, hash tables, and a decentralized network. Because immutable ledgers are used, a complete record of all data transactions completed between sender and receiver will always be available. This guarantees that the original data cannot be challenged or altered by attackers and provides total transparency to everyone utilizing the system. Blockchain facilitates information flow more quickly and practically for free because there is no third party to rely on. Third party validation is also eliminated by the decentralized network. Instead, before adding the data to the ledger, Blockchain technology verifies it via a system of nodes that communicate and agreed. Multiple nodes also increase the system's resilience compared to centralized

[1]vivek.khirasaria@shardauniversity.uz, [2]sureshkaswan@gmail.com, [3]lisha.yugai@sharda.ac.in, [4]akanksha.shangloo@sharda.ac.in

DOI: 10.1201/9781003488682-30

networks, where a single point of failure would bring the entire system to a halt. Due to these characteristics, Blockchain has gained a reputation for security in the financial sector and has begun to catch the attention of influential figures in other sectors.

2. Architecture of Blockchain

Blockchain is the chain of blocks, every block has mainly three elements. Data, Hash code and hash of previous block.

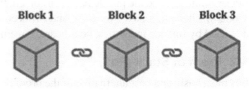

Data: The data is depending on the application of the blockchain. For example if the blockchain is related to financial transaction it contains information about transaction included sender, receiver, number of coin and other details about particular transaction.

Fig. 30.1 Blockchain architecture

Hash: A hash is a function that generates fixed length of the code for every input given to it. Since it makes it nearly impossible to guess the length of the hash if someone is trying to crack the hash code. The same data will always produce the same hashed value.

Hash of previous block: This element is most important part of blockchain. It makes blockchain. Every next block contains are information of the previous block which make the Blockchain a secure component.

3. Novel Blockchain Characteristics

The following are major characteristics of blockchain.

Distributed Ledgers: It is most important characteristic of blockchain technology. Blockchain ledger exists on the multiple nodes. Because each transaction in centralized transaction systems must be verified by a single trusted party, the central server has cost and performance limitations as a result.

Immutability: It means validated transactions cannot be reversible in any manners. It means any node is not able to modify data after adding it in blockchain or any data added by other node.

Enhanced Security: The blockchain uses only encrypted data. Within the block chains entire network, the process is further secured by encryption. The lack of a central authority does not allow for easy data modification on the network. Every piece of data on the blockchain is cryptographically hashed, giving each one a distinct identity on the network. Each block has its own distinct hash as well as the previous block's hash. The blocks are cryptographically linked to one another as

Fig. 30.2 Characteristics of blockchain

a result of this characteristic. Any attempt to update the data would require changing every hash ID, which is just not doable.

Consensus: Blockchain includes a consensus mechanism that enables the network to make choices quickly. Consensus is a decision-making technique that helps the network's active nodes rapidly arrive at a consensus and ensures the system runs smoothly. Although nodes might not have trust in one another, but the trust the algorithm that makes core decisions. There are numerous available consensus algorithms, each having advantages and disadvantages. A consensus algorithms is a must for any blockchain otherwise it will begin losing value.

Faster Settlement: Classical Banking system is working on the centralized settlement system and it has many loopholes and so many times it corrupted easily. Blockchain provides fast settlement compare to traditional system because no need of central node to approve any transactions.

Unanimous: Before records may be added to the chain, all blockchain nodes must validate the authenticity of the records. Any block that is being added to the chain must receive majority voting from all nodes in order to be added to the network. Nothing can be changed without the majority of the network's nodes' consent.

4. Blockchain Consensus Algorithms

Blockchain eliminates the requirement for a central node to oversee transactions and the addition of new blocks. Nodes are not required to have mutual trust. Consequently, some methods are required to guarantee the consistency of ledgers across different nodes.

4.1 Proof of Work (PoW)

The earliest kind of consensus in use in the blockchain industry is called Proof of Work. It is also referred to as mining, with miners denoting the participating nodes. With this technique, miners must use processing power to solve mathematical riddles or difficulties. They have access to a variety of equipment and techniques, including CPU mining, GPU mining, ASIC mining, and FPGA mining. Once the puzzle has been solved, the miner will receive a block. Numerous cryptocurrencies, including Bitcoin, Monero, Litecoin, ZCash, Vertcoin, and Primecoin, employ the Proof of Work technique. In terms of use and implementation it is used by finance industries, healthcare, governance, management and IoT.

4.2 Proof of Stack (PoS)

It is most basic and best alternative of the proof of work mechanism. In this method the miners are working as validator instead of miners. They will be granted the authority to create a block over anyone who conserves time and energy. They need to invest some capital into the blockchain stack in order to be recognized as a validator. Miners have privileged to take transaction fees in this method. Proof of stack is used by Ethereum 2.0 and it also supports Peercoin, PivX, Dash and Decred.

4.3 Delegated Proof of Stake (DPoS)

In DPoS, nodes stake their coins and cast their ballots for a certain number of parties; the more they stake, the higher their percentage of the vote. In this scenario, node X would spend 100 coins while node Y would spend 50 coins. X's vote is given more weight than Y's. DPoS is one of the fastest mechanisms as a result of this process. This technique is used by Bitshares, EOS, and Steem.

4.4 Leased Proof of Stake (LPoS)

The Waves platform utilises an enhanced PoS consensus technique called LPoS. Users can lease their balance to complete nodes in the blockchain using this approach. And the likelihood of the next block being created is higher for the one who leases the larger sum to the complete node.

4.5 Proof of Authority (POA)

It is an altered form of PoS. In this mechanism identities of validator is at stack. To verify the identity of validator is the resemblance between validators identity and documentation. In proof of authority validators are the only one who can produce new blocks and add to chain. In this mechanism number of validators are very small around 20 to 30.

4.6 Byzantine Fault Tolerance (BFT)

It is a feature of distributed network system but in block chain it works when need to reach on some agreement even when some of the nodes in the system fail to answer or giving wrong information.

4.7 Direct Acyclic Graph (DAG)

Every application development company needs to be familiar with this simple but effective algorithm. Every node in this method will constantly be ready to start mining. This method makes the validation fee and process free. Additionally, validating transactions between two nodes is fairly simple, which makes the process lightweight, quick, and safe.

4.8 Proof of Capacity (PoC)

In this mechanism the answers of the mathematical puzzles are stored in digital devices like hard disk. Nodes can use this stored date to produce blocks and add to chain. So those who are fastest in evaluation process they will get good chance to create blocks. Cryptocurrencies like burstcoin and spacemint works on this mechanism.

4.9 Proof of Burn (PoB)

This is alternative solution of PoS and PoW in terms of power consumptions. In this mechanism miners have to burn or ruin their cryptocurrency tokens which will provide them access to write in block according to coins they burn. This mechanism's best illustration is the slim coin.

4.10 Proof of Identity (PoI)

PoI is a system that relies on cryptography and user private key confirmation. Every recognized user has the ability to add, manage, and share a block of data with other network users. The block data's integrity and authenticity are guaranteed by this paradigm. And for that reason, smart cities use it.

4.11 Proof of Activity (PoA)

The Proof of Authority (PoA) technique combines the Proof of Work and Proof of Stack models. Similar to the PoW method, all miners will compete to solve mathematical and cryptographic riddles in this mechanism. And the block will only hold the information about the winner and rewards just like PoS. In this mechanism validator will validate every block data and they will also earn shares in it. The Espers and Decred coins are working on this.

4.12 Proof of Elapsed Time (PoET)

Intel created it to replace the puzzles needed for the proof of work. To determine when and how frequently the miner will generate blocks, it takes into account the CPU architecture and other mining hardware. On the basis of the right distribution and increasing the participation.

4.13 Proof of Importance (PoI)

It is modified version of the PoS. It considers shareholders and validators based reputation, balance, address, size of share and vote. This method makes networks expensive to break into and pays users for adding security to the blockchain.

5. Cyber Attacks on Blockchain

The blockchain is typically regarded as being both safe and scalable, although the security of a blockchain is strongly correlated with the amount of hash processing power it is supported by. There are only a few ways to attack a blockchain, but the four main types include consensus-based attacks, network-based attacks, attacks based on smart contracts, and wallet-based attacks.

5.1 Consensus Based Attacks

Consensus based attacks are the attacks done by the miner or pool of miners. They are using there hashing and computing power for dishonest mining of blocks. It has three major types.

Race Attack: On the blockchain network, two or more contradictory transactions can happen quickly one after the other. The wicked individual could send person A a Bitcoin in exchange for a service. He sends a conflicting transaction at the same time, spending the same bitcoin on himself. In this instance, the second conflicting transaction is mined into the block and is displayed by the other nodes as a legitimate transaction. This would be the harm caused by Person A, who provided services to the actor in exchange for Bitcoin. *51% Attack:* This attack is the major attack on the blockchain network. If one person have more than 51% control over blockchain network. He can spend double then the other users and he can generate blocks faster compare to other users.

Finney attack: If any payment is accepted with zero confirmation then this attack is possible. This attack is possible when one miner who already mined a block but not broadcasting information in network. He can use same block in the two different transactions. It is also known as double spending attack on blockchain network.

5.2 Network Based Attack

As the security of blockchain is dependent on the network of blockchain and P2P communication some major attacks on network can affect security of blockchain. Different four attacks are possible on the blockchain network.

(i) *DDoS Attack:* The assault known as a distributed denial of service causes the network to become unavailable to its actual users by flooding it with a high number of requests. All requests are made by a single node in DoS attacks, but requests are made by multiple nodes in DDoS attacks produced by several nodes That's why it is very much difficult to trace attackers in network. To prevent this attack need to introduce transactions fees so automatically malicious persons will decrease.

(ii) *Eclipse Attack:* This attack focus on the single node. Only attacking nodes will get the communication other nodes will not get any communication. Attacker will send transaction details and proof of payment to only target node and try to eclipsing it from entire network.

(iii) *Routing attack:* Routing attack is based on the blocking the messages travelling through the blockchain network before it will reach to destination node. Attacker will split network into two or more portions so that they cannot connect with one another. Routing attacks are further divided into two types. Partitioning Attack and Delay Attack are both attacks.

(iv) *Sybil Attack:* In Sybil attack, Attacker will create multiple id and pretending as different user. Attacker can control full network and manipulate it. This is the biggest issue in the P2P network because single user is managing all the communication with different identities.

5.3 Smart Contract Based Attack

In block chain technology, smart contract is the automated script or program used to run decentralized tools and applications. It will perform transactions between nodes as per the contracts. Once smart contract starts it will not stop until transactions are completed. After it will goes to immutable state. So if smart contract is not correct, currency is in risk. Decentralized autonomous organization attack is the one of the smart contract based attack. DAO is aims to write the code to reduce document work.

5.4 Wallet Based Attack

Wallets are the logic developed for user to regulate and to automate transactions. Each user in blockchain has its wallet to make transactions and payment. Attacker is targeting this wallet to perform malicious activity. One of the highest performed wallet based attack is parity multisig wallet attack. In this attack, attacker targeted ether wallet and used loopholes of ether network. Attacker added his account as joint account holder to victim's account and he freeze cryptocurrency of that user.

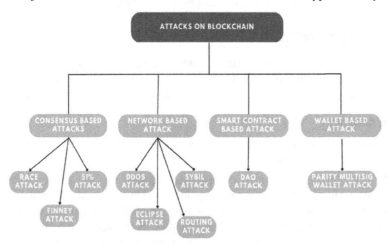

Fig. 30.3 Cyber attacks on blockchain

6. Conclusion

The paper starts with the technical details of blockchain and blockchain architecture. Architecture section provides brief information about elements of blockchain. In characteristics of blockchain section we discussed some of the major characteristics of blockchain which differentiate blockchain technology from centralized technology. Blockchain consensus algorithms section gives all the technical aspects of blockchain technology with application of each algorithm. In cyber-attacks on blockchain technology, we discussed latest and most affected attacks on the blockchain network.

REFERENCES

1. Mahmood, Zaigham. "Blockchain Technology." Advances in Data Mining and Database Management, 2021, pp. 1–16., https://doi.org/10.4018/978-1-7998-6650-3.ch001.

2. T. M. Hewa, Y. Hu, M. Liyanage, S. S. Kanhare and M. Ylianttila, "Survey on Blockchain-Based Smart Contracts: Technical Aspects and Future Research," in IEEE Access, vol. 9, pp. 87643-87662, 2021, doi: 10.1109/ACCESS.2021.3068178.

3. M. N. M. Bhutta et al., "A Survey on Blockchain Technology: Evolution, Architecture and Security," in IEEE Access, vol. 9, pp. 61048–61073, 2021, doi: 10.1109/ACCESS.2021.3072849.

4. Shubhani Aggarwal, Neeraj Kumar, Chapter Twenty - Attacks on blockchain Working model., Editor(s): Shubhani Aggarwal, Neeraj Kumar, Pethuru Raj, Advances in Computers, Elsevier, Volume 121, 2021, Pages 399–410.

5. S. Singh, A. S. M. S. Hosen and B. Yoon, "Blockchain Security Attacks, Challenges, and Solutions for the Future Distributed IoT Network," in IEEE Access, vol. 9, pp. 13938–13959, 2021, doi: 10.1109/ACCESS.2021.3051602.

6. S. Cohen, A. Rosenthal, and A. Zohar, "Reasoning about the future in blockchain databases," in Proc. IEEE 36th Int. Conf. Data Eng. (ICDE), Apr. 2020, pp. 19301933.

7. Maheshwari, S., Kumar, S., Trivedi, N.K., Rathore, V.S., Innovative Classroom Activity with Flipped Teaching for Programming in C Course—A Case Study, Advances in Intelligent Systems and Computing, 2021, 1183, (pp. 247–252).

8. Maheshwari, S., Kumar, S., Gill, R., Rathore, V.S., Analysis of Augmented Course Delivery and Assessment of Undergraduate Computer Engineering Programming Courses with the Use of ICT, Advances in Intelligent Systems and Computing, 2021, 1187, (pp. 481–488).

9. Sharma, Meenakshi, and Suresh Kaswan. "A Review on the Impacts of Social Media in Day To Day Life." Review of International Geographical Education Online 11.7 (2021).

10. Wang, Andy Ju An. "Security testing in software engineering courses." 34th Annual Frontiers in Education, 2004. FIE 2004.. IEEE, 2004.

11. Chaubey, Chitrangada, Swapnil Raj, and Suresh Kaswan. "Security and Privacy Issues in Location Dependent Services for Mobile Communication: A Synergistic Review." Materials Science and Engineering Conference Series. Vol. 1149. No. 1. 2021.

12. G. Srivastava, R. M. Parizi, and A. Dehghantanha, "The future of blockchain technology in healthcare Internet of Things security," in Blockchain Cybersecurity, Trust Privacy. Springer, 2020, pp. 161–184.

13. A. Bazarhanova, J. Magnusson, J. Lindman, E. Chou, and A. Nilsson, "Blockchain-based electronic identification: Cross-country comparison of six design choices," Tech. Rep., 2019.

Note: All the figures in this chapter were made by the author.

Advances in Computational Intelligence and its Applications (ICACIA-2023) – Dr. Sheikh Fahad Ahmad et al. (eds)
© 2024 Taylor & Francis Group, London, ISBN 978-1-032-78612-4

Computation of Environmental Deterioration by Observation of Annual NDVI Changes

31

Anubhava Srivastava

Department of Computer Science and Engineering,
School of Engineering and Technology, Sharda University, Greater Noida, India

Susham Biswas*

Department of Computer Science and Engineering, Rajiv Gandhi Institute of Petroleum Technology, Amethi, India

ABSTRACT—With the time, changes in the global environment occur by various factors like growth in population, deforestation, natural hazards earthquake, flood, and fire incident. Researchers always tried to calculate these factors by several mechanisms and all processing techniques face the same problem; they were wasting their maximum computation time in data collection. So in this research, we try to calculate the change in vegetation over satellite data on a planetary platform Google Earth Engine. We did our computation by calculating NDVI and EVI over the study area for an entire year and finding changes that happened in the study area. We have divided the vegetation index into five parts water, settlements and aquaculture, higher density crops, little vegetation, and forest on their NDVI values. In last we also calculated mean change over the study area and find change happen by which reason which part of the vegetation increased or decreased based on their value. The research outcome proves that Normalize Difference Vegetation Index is extremely useful in finding surface features of the visible area, which is highly useful for policy makers in making decisions. The analysis of vegetation can help in forecasting natural disasters, assessing damage, and devising new protection policies. According to the experimental study, forest or shrubland and barren land cover types decreased, while vegetation land, urban (built-up) areas, and water areas increased. We further calculated the change in land cover class from the year 2010 to the year 2022 to find the relevance of our computation, for calculating a change in land cover class we use classification and regression tree supervised machine learning algorithm that classified study areas with accuracy 89.27% in the year 2010 and 91.24 % in the year 2022.

KEYWORDS—Classification, Environmental change, Landsat, NDVI, Vegetation indices

1. Introduction

In a world characterized by rapidly evolving environmental challenges and a growing awareness of the critical need for sustainable practices, monitoring and comprehending the state of our ecosystems have become more crucial than ever before. Environmental deterioration, stemming from climate change, habitat loss, deforestation, and various human activities, poses significant threats to biodiversity, ecosystem stability, and the well-being of future generations. To effectively address these challenges, we must rely on advanced tools and methodologies that provide comprehensive insights into environmental changes. One such indispensable tool is the observation of annual Normalized Difference Vegetation Index (NDVI) changes.

The Normalized Difference Vegetation Index, or NDVI, stands as a cornerstone in the realm of remote sensing and environmental monitoring. It is a numeric indicator derived from satellite imagery and remote sensing technology, offering a means of quantifying the health and vitality of the Earth's vegetation cover. By assessing annual changes in NDVI, we gain valuable knowledge about the state of our ecosystems, can pinpoint land use dynamics, and evaluate the repercussions of climate change

*Corresponding Author: (Pgi18001, Susham)@rgipt.ac.in

DOI: 10.1201/9781003488682-31

and human activities on our environment. This comprehensive exploration aims to delve into the profound significance of utilizing annual NDVI changes in the computation of environmental deterioration. As we progress through this discourse, we will elucidate the principles behind NDVI, unveil the underlying science that makes it such a potent tool, and underscore its role in addressing critical ecological trends and challenges. Moreover, we will scrutinize case studies and practical applications, consider the limitations and future directions of NDVI analysis, and ultimately emphasize its pivotal role in our collective efforts to understand and mitigate environmental deterioration.

The essence of NDVI is rooted in the principle of reflectance. Living vegetation has a unique property of strongly reflecting near-infrared light while absorbing red light. In contrast, non-vegetated or stressed vegetation exhibits a different spectral response, leading to distinct NDVI values. This characteristic forms the basis for distinguishing between various types of land cover and assessing vegetation health.

Interpreting NDVI values is pivotal in understanding the health of vegetation and, by extension, the environment. A low or declining NDVI can indicate several conditions, including drought stress, deforestation, or land degradation. Conversely, a high and stable NDVI suggests robust and thriving vegetation.

2. Related Work

Different researchers have performed computation over machine learning algorithms using geospatial plateform GEE (Gorelick et al. 2017) for finding changes in land cover areas (Srivastava et al. 2022) computation of change in vegetation indices, (Yang et al. 2011) Computation of change in vegetation indices is a critical and crucial task for earth observation and machine learning makes it easier with the help of easy availability of data and computation on these data sets. (Ozyavuz, Bilgili, and Salici 2015) performed computation by NDVI and declare a change in vegetation over year 1987,2002, and 2012 by using Landsat 4 and Landsat 5 TM data sets. Another researcher, G. Meera (Gandhi et al. 2015) also computes changes in vegetation indices over the Vellore district using NDVI. Not over the change in forest and agriculture land, NDVI has the capability of computing change in other land cover areas like under the water also because its range between -1 to +1 where 0 stands for water indices. (Amani et al. 2020) performed change in water vegetation over an area of Iran. Normalize difference vegetation indices is not only used for computing change its also used for extracting different features of vegetation , (Bhandari, Kumar, and Singh 2012) performed computation for extracting feature of different vegetation indices(Srivastava, Umrao, and Biswas 2023)over Jabalpur and Ernakulam city (Srivastava, Umrao, Biswas, et al. 2023). Not only is the computation of vegetation indices or classification of land cover areas NDVI useful in monitoring crop cover (Ayyangar, Rao, and Rao 1980) drought monitoring (Nageswara Rao and Rao 1984) and agricultural drought assessment at national level (Kogan 1997) and global level (Thenkabail et al. 2021)

3. Study Area

Pauri, a district in the northern Indian state of Uttarakhand, is renowned for its stunning natural environment and diverse ecosystems. Pauri's diverse geography, which includes hills, forests, and valleys, supports a rich biodiversity. The region is home to a variety of flora and fauna. The forests of Pauri are primarily composed of oak, pine, and rhododendron trees, providing habitat for several wildlife species, including leopards, Himalayan black bears, and various bird species. Pauri is nestled in the foothills of the Himalayas, making it a part of the Himalayan ecosystem. The area's topography, altitude, and climate contribute to its unique environmental characteristics. The Himalayan region is crucial for regulating India's water resources, as many major rivers originate from the Himalayas. Pauri's contribution to this hydrological cycle is significant. Like many Himalayan regions, Pauri is vulnerable to the effects of climate change. Rising temperatures, erratic rainfall patterns, and glacial retreat pose challenges to the local environment and communities. Monitoring climate change impacts is crucial to ensure the resilience of Pauri's ecosystems and the well-being of its residents. Pauri faces environmental challenges common to hilly and forested regions, such as deforestation, soil erosion, and landslides. Balancing the needs of the growing population with environmental conservation is an ongoing challenge, requiring careful land-use planning and sustainable resource management.

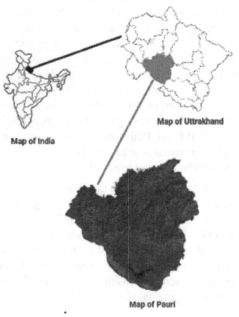

Map of Uttrakhand

Map of India

Map of Pauri

Fig. 31.1 Study area: Pauri

The study area is located at elevation of 1685.464 above, covering nearly 5319 sq km area, having a population of around 687,271. A sub-temperate to temperate climate prevails in the area and is comfortable all year long. In the higher altitudes of Dudhatoli, the temperature barely rises to 25°C in June, compared to Kotdwar's maximum temperature of 45°C. As a result, the region's average temperature ranges from 25°C to 30°C. The temperature drops to a minimum of January. Usually, rainfall begins in mid-June and lasts through mid-September, the hilly terrain's steeply wooded slopes receive enough rainfall. Winter months also occasionally record rain. The district receives 218 cm of rain on average annually, with over 90% of the rain falling during the monsoon season. Figure 31.1 represents geographical location of study area.

3. Methodology and Data

For computing change in vegetation, we mostly use normalized difference vegetation index from equation 1 & equation 2 and Enhanced vegetation index equation 3 and equation 4. Detailed methodology used in research is detailed in Fig. 31.2. We selected one image from each sensor which having no cloud cover over the study area. The Landsat 9 data sets were obtained from USGS satellite with a repetition of 16 days. NDVI uses ratio of differencing two images. Red band and Near Infrared bands.

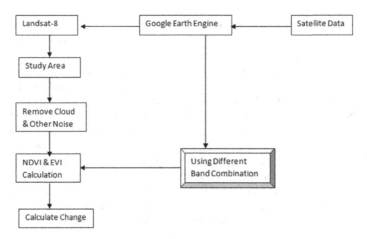

Fig. 31.2 Methodology used in research

The "Red Band" is a term commonly used in remote sensing and Earth observation to refer to a specific spectral band of electromagnetic radiation. This band is part of the visible portion of the electromagnetic spectrum and is used in various remote sensing applications, including satellite and aerial imagery, to capture information about the Earth's surface. Red Band typically covers wavelengths in the range of approximately 620 to 680 nanometers (nm) on the electromagnetic spectrum. This range includes the colors of light that humans perceive as red. In the context of remote sensing, this band is usually represented by a narrow wavelength range within this broader range. The Red Band is important in remote sensing because it is sensitive to the way objects on the Earth's surface reflect and absorb light in this wavelength range. Different materials, such as vegetation, water, soil, and built infrastructure, have varying reflectance properties in the Red Band. Healthy green vegetation absorbs a significant amount of light in the Red Band due to the presence of chlorophyll. This absorption makes vegetation appear darker in the Red Band. Red Band is a key component of remote sensing systems that capture information about the Earth's surface. It plays a crucial role in various applications, particularly in assessing vegetation health, land cover classification, and other environmental monitoring tasks.

The "Near-Infrared (NIR) Band" is another essential spectral band used in remote sensing and Earth observation. It falls within the electromagnetic spectrum but at slightly longer wavelengths than visible light. The NIR Band is particularly valuable in remote sensing applications for its ability to provide insights into various aspects of the Earth's surface and atmospheric conditions. Here's an introduction to the Near-Infrared Band. The Near-Infrared Band typically covers wavelengths in the range of approximately 750 to 900 nanometers (nm) on the electromagnetic spectrum. This range is just beyond the visible red portion of the spectrum, which is why it is called "near-infrared." While humans cannot see NIR light, it is detectable by specialized remote sensing instruments. Healthy vegetation, such as forests and crops, strongly reflects NIR light. This is because the internal structure of plant cells scatters NIR light, making vegetation appear bright in this band. Bodies of water, including lakes, rivers, and oceans, typically absorb NIR light, making them appear dark in NIR imagery. Man-made structures in urban areas, such as buildings and roads, often have moderate to high reflectance in the NIR Band. It is a crucial component for calculating the Normalized Difference Vegetation Index (NDVI), a widely used vegetation index that assesses the health and density of vegetation cover. NDVI is derived by comparing reflectance in the NIR Band to that in the Red Band. NIR data, combined with data from other spectral bands, is used to classify land cover types, including differentiating between various vegetation types, urban areas, and water bodies. NIR data is used in precision agriculture to assess crop health, detect stress, and optimize farming practices. The Near-Infrared Band's ability to capture valuable information about vegetation health and land cover makes it a critical component of remote sensing systems. It allows scientists, researchers, and analysts to monitor and understand changes in the Earth's surface and the environment.

The Normalized Difference Vegetation Index for Land Cover classification is used to easily interpret Land Resources. To perform multi-source classification, remote sensing data from Landsat TM images, as well as NDVI (Aik, Ismail, and Muharam 2020) and DEM data layers, were used. The NDVI (Srivastava and Ahmad 2016) differencing method was used for Change Detection. The NDVI method is used to determine vegetation characteristics at various NDVI threshold values. The Normalized Difference Vegetation Index (NDVI) is a measure of how green a plant is or how much photosynthetic activity it has. It's a widely used and simple-to-calculate vegetation productivity proxy based on satellite images. The NDVI is a simple numerical indicator connected to Photo- synthetically Active Radiation (PAR) that essentially assesses the capability of leaves and provides a measure of the vegetative cover on the land surface across large areas. Photosynthetic activity, vegetation cover, biomass, and the Leaf Area Score all have a positive connection with this index (LAI) The NDVI algorithm divides the total of near-infrared and red bands by the red reflectance values subtracted from the near-infrared.

$$NDVI = \frac{NIR - RED}{NIR + RED} \tag{1}$$

Where: NIR : Near Infra-Red

RED: Red Wavelength

In Landsat -8 Near Infrared Band in represented by Band- 5 and RED band is represented by Band-4 band.

$$NDVI = \frac{Band\ 5 - Band\ 4}{Band\ 5 + Band\ 4} \tag{2}$$

When it comes to bandwidth, the specific wavelength ranges used for the Red and NIR bands are crucial for accurate NDVI calculations. Narrower bandwidths within these ranges can provide more precise measurements of vegetation health, as they isolate the wavelengths that are most responsive to vegetation properties, resolution and bandwidth are essential considerations when working with NDVI data. Higher spatial resolution can capture finer details in the landscape, while the specific bandwidths of the Red and NIR bands are crucial for accurate NDVI calculations, as they represent the wavelengths where vegetation reflects and absorbs light. The combination of appropriate resolution and bandwidth helps in generating meaningful NDVI values for monitoring and analyzing vegetation health and dynamics.

EVI is an extension of NDVI that addresses some of its limitations, especially in areas with dense vegetation or high levels of aerosols. It provides a more accurate representation of vegetation health under these conditions(Srivastava and Biswas 2023)

$$EVI = \frac{G * (Band\ 5 - Band\ 4)}{Band\ 5 + C1 * Band\ 4 - C2 * Band\ 2 + L} \tag{3}$$

Where G: is the gain factor,

L: Canopy background adjustment that addresses non-linear, differential NIR, and red radiant transfer through a canopy (Here L = 1).

C1, and C2: Coefficients of the aerosol resistance , which uses the blue band to correct for aerosol influences in the red band.

For Landsat data Value of the gain factor (G) is 2.5, the Value of the aerosol resistance terms C1 and C2 are 6 and 7.5 respectively

So the EVI formula is restructured in Landsat 8 as:

$$EVI = \frac{2.5 * (Band\ 5 - Band\ 4)}{Band\ 5 + 6 * Band\ 4 - 7.5 * Band\ 2 + 1} \tag{4}$$

NDVI is a valuable and versatile tool for monitoring and assessing the state of vegetation on Earth's surface. Its ability to capture changes in vegetation health over time has applications in agriculture, ecology, forestry, and climate science, making it an essential component of environmental monitoring and research. NDVI can show how vegetation changes over time, capturing seasonal variations such as the greening of landscapes in spring and the senescence of vegetation in autumn.

4. Result and Discussion

The NDVI has been widely used to investigate the relationship between spectral variability and changes in vegetation growth rate. It is also useful for determining the production of green vegetation and detecting changes in vegetation. We have divided NDVI into five different categories. Areas that have less than zero NDVI value come in the water land cover class, and areas that have NDVI value between 0-0.2 are categorized into settlements and aquaculture land cover areas, areas that have NDVI values between 0.2 to 0.4 come to Higher density crops, areas that have NDVI values between 0.4 to 0.6 are categorized into little vegetation land cover class and areas that have NDVI value more than 0.6 are categorized into forest land cover areas.

We have divided the entire validation by calculating twice in the year first we calculate NDVI in the spring season and later we calculate NDVI in the winter season. The result obtained by NDVI analysis over the spring season is presented in Fig. 31.3 and obtained over the winter season is presented in Fig. 31.4

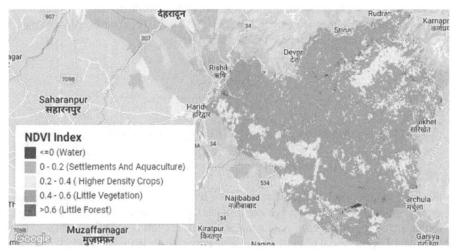

Fig. 31.3 Result obtained by NDVI and EVI analysis in spring season

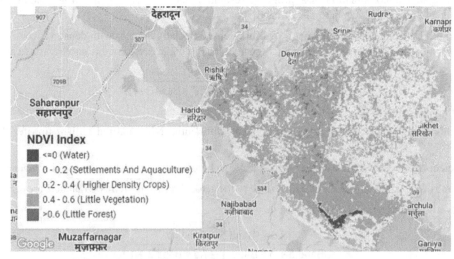

Fig. 31.4 Result obtained by NDVI and EVI analysis in winter season

The area captured in the spring and winter seasons is represented in Fig. 31.5 and results find that percentage of little Vegetation and forest is a little bit increased.

```
▼1: Object (4 properties)
     Class: 0 - 0.2 (Settlements And Aquaculture)
     Hectares: 5915.67
     Percentage: 0.94
     Pixels: 591567
▼2: Object (4 properties)
     Class: 0.2 - 0.4 ( Higher Density Crops)
     Hectares: 73354.41
     Percentage: 11.61
     Pixels: 7335441
▼3: Object (4 properties)
     Class: 0.4 - 0.6 (Little Vegetation)
     Hectares: 290547.6
     Percentage: 46
     Pixels: 29054760
▼4: Object (4 properties)
     Class: >0.6 (Little Forest)
     Hectares: 234171.33
     Percentage: 37.08
     Pixels: 23417133
```

```
▼1: Object (4 properties)
     Class: 0 - 0.2 (Settlements And Aquaculture)
     Hectares: 1840.22
     Percentage: 0.29
     Pixels: 184022
▼2: Object (4 properties)
     Class: 0.2 - 0.4 ( Higher Density Crops)
     Hectares: 20014.18
     Percentage: 3.17
     Pixels: 2001418
▼3: Object (4 properties)
     Class: 0.4 - 0.6 (Little Vegetation)
     Hectares: 173830.19
     Percentage: 27.52
     Pixels: 17383019
▼4: Object (4 properties)
     Class: >0.6 (Little Forest)
     Hectares: 421855.8
     Percentage: 66.8
     Pixels: 42185580
```

Fig. 31.5   Area captured by NDVI and EVI analysis in winter and spring season

The area captured in the spring and winter seasons is represented in figure 5 and results find that percentage of little Vegetation and forest is a little bit increased. We have calculated mean and standard deviation value of Normalize difference Vegetation Index for spring and winter season in year 2022 shown in figure 6 and for year 2010 and year 2022 in figure 7. Figure demonstrate that mean NDVI value is decreased in year 2022 compare to year 2010.

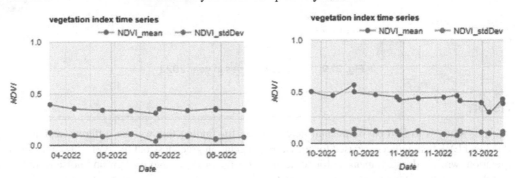

Fig. 31.6   Mean and standard deviation NDVI value in winter and spring season

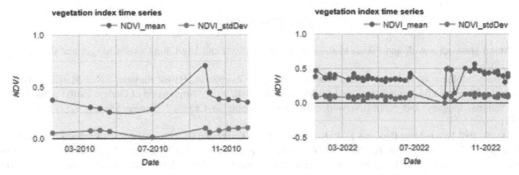

Fig. 31.7   Mean and standard deviation NDVI value in year 2010 and 2022

Later we also calculated changes in land cover areas between the years 2010 and 2022 for finding changes in the study area. For this classification, we use the classification and regression tree(CART) (Breiman et al. 2017) method with near about 848 sampling points in which 206 points belong to built-up land, 218 points belong to low vegetation area, 216 points belong to high vegetation area, and 208 points belong to water areas, after computation we find forests (high vegetation area) decreased and low vegetation area (agriculture land, park, open field) increased shown in Fig. 31.8 and Fig. 31.9 for land cover areas computed in year 2010 and Year 2022. For finding the exactness of our algorithm we compute accuracy by using a confusion matrix and find an accuracy of 89.27% in the year 2010 and 91.24% in the year 2022.

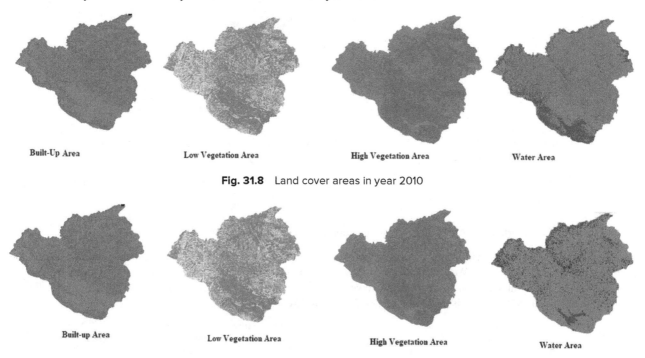

Built-Up Area   Low Vegetation Area   High Vegetation Area   Water Area

Fig. 31.8 Land cover areas in year 2010

Built-up Area   Low Vegetation Area   High Vegetation Area   Water Area

Fig. 31.9 Land cover areas in year 2022

5. Conclusion

The objective of this study is to find environmental deterioration, for finding this we use different vegetation performance indices like NDVI and EVI, both indices are used for measuring vegetation greenness but the EVI is more sensitive in locations with dense vegetation, while it does compensate for some atmospheric variables and background noise from the canopy. The result clearly validates that dense forests are decreased and low vegetation classes are increased later we justify our result with land use land cover classification.

REFERENCES

1. Aik, Jin, Mohd Hasmadi Ismail, and Farrah Melissa Muharam. 2020. "Land Use/Land Cover Changes and the Relationship." *Land* 9(372): 1–23.
2. Amani, Meisam, Mohammad Kakooei, Armin Moghimi, Arsalan Ghorbanian, Babak Ranjgar, Sahel Mahdavi, Andrew Davidson, Thierry Fisette, Patrick Rollin, Brian Brisco, and Ali Mohammadzadeh. 2020. "Application of Google Earth Engine Cloud Computing Platform, Sentinel Imagery, and Neural Networks for Crop Mapping in Canada." *Remote Sensing* 12(21): 1–18. doi: 10.3390/rs12213561.
3. Ayyangar, R. S., P. P. Nagaeshwar Rao, and K. R. Rao. 1980. "Crop Cover and Crop Phenological Information from Red and Infrared Spectral Responses." *Journal of the Indian Society of Photo-Interpretation and Remote Sensing* 8(1): 23–29. doi: 10.1007/BF02990665.
4. Bhandari, A. K., A. Kumar, and G. K. Singh. 2012. "Feature Extraction Using Normalized Difference Vegetation Index (NDVI): A Case Study of Jabalpur City." *Procedia Technology* 6: 612–21. doi: 10.1016/j.protcy.2012.10.074.
5. Breiman, Leo, Jerome H. Friedman, Richard A. Olshen, and Charles J. Stone. 2017. *Classification and Regression Trees*. Vol. 2.

6. Gandhi, G. Meera, S. Parthiban, Nagaraj Thummalu, and A. Christy. 2015. "Ndvi: Vegetation Change Detection Using Remote Sensing and Gis - A Case Study of Vellore District." *Procedia Computer Science* 57(December): 1199–1210. doi: 10.1016/j.procs.2015.07.415.

7. Gorelick, Noel, Matt Hancher, Mike Dixon, Simon Ilyushchenko, David Thau, and Rebecca Moore. 2017. "Google Earth Engine: Planetary-Scale Geospatial Analysis for Everyone." *Remote Sensing of Environment* 202: 18–27. doi: 10.1016/j.rse.2017.06.031.

8. Kogan, Felix N. 1997. "Global Drought Watch from Space." *Bulletin of the American Meteorological Society* 78(4):621–36. doi: 10.1175/1520-0477(1997)078<0621:GDWFS>2.0.CO;2.

9. Nageswara Rao, P. P., and V. R. Rao. 1984. "An Approach for Agricultural Drought Monitoring Using NOAA/AVHRR and Landsat Imagery." *Proc. IGARSS '84 Symposium, Strasbourg, 1984. Vol. 1, (ESA SP-215; Distributed ESTEC, Noordwijk)* (January 1984): 225–29.

10. Ozyavuz, M., B. C. Bilgili, and A. Salici. 2015. "Determination of Vegetation Changes with NDVI Method." *Journal of Environmental Protection and Ecology* 16(1): 264–73.

11. Srivastava, Anubhava, and Parvez Ahmad. 2016. "A Probabilistic Gossip-Based Secure Protocol for Unstructured P2P Networks." *Physics Procedia* 78(December 2015):595–602. doi: 10.1016/j.procs.2016.02.122.

12. Srivastava, Anubhava, Shruti Bharadwaj, Rakesh Dubey, and Vinamra Bhushan Sharma. 2022. "Mapping Vegetation and Measuring The Performance of Machine Learning Algorithm in LULC Classification in The Large Area Using Sentinel-2 and Landsat-8 Datasets of Dehradun As A .... Mapping Vegetation and Measuring the Performance of Machine Sentinel-2 An." (May). doi: 10.5194/isprs-archives-XLIII-B3-2022-529-2022.

13. Srivastava, Anubhava, and Susham Biswas. 2023. "Analyzing Land Cover Changes over Landsat-7 Data Using Google Earth Engine." *Proceedings of the 3rd International Conference on Artificial Intelligence and Smart Energy, ICAIS 2023* 1228–33. doi: 10.1109/ICAIS56108.2023.10073795.

14. Srivastava, Anubhava, Sandhya Umrao, and Susham Biswas. 2023. "Exploring Forest Transformation by Analyzing Spatial-Temporal Attributes of Vegetation Using Vegetation Indices." International Journal of Advanced Computer Science and Applications 14(5):1110–17. doi: 10.14569/IJACSA.2023.01405114

15. Srivastava, Anubhava, Sandhya Umrao, Susham Biswas, Rakesh dubey, and Md Iltaf Zafar. 2023. "FCCC: Forest Cover Change Calculator User Interface for Identifying Fire Incidents in Forest Region Using Satellite Data." International Journal of Advanced Computer Science and Applications 14(7):948–59. doi: 10.14569/IJACSA.2023.01407103.

16. Thenkabail, Prasad S., Pardhasaradhi G. Teluguntla, Jun Xiong, Adam Oliphant, Russell G. Congalton, Mutlu Ozdogan, Murali Krishna Gumma, James C. Tilton, Chandra Giri, Cristina Milesi, Aparna Phalke, Richard Massey, Kamini Yadav, Temuulen Sankey, Ying Zhong, Itiya Aneece, and Daniel Foley. 2021. "Global Cropland-Extent Product at 30-m Resolution (GCEP30) Derived from Landsat Satellite Time-Series Data for the Year 2015 Using Multiple Machine-Learning Algorithms on Google Earth Engine Cloud." *US Geological Survey Professional Paper* 2021(1868): 1–63. doi: 10.3133/pp1868.

17. Yang, Zhengwei, Liping Di, Genong Yu, and Zeqiang Chen. 2011. "Vegetation Condition Indices for Crop Vegetation Condition Monitoring." *International Geoscience and Remote Sensing Symposium (IGARSS)* (July): 3534–37. doi: 10.1109/IGARSS.2011.6049984.

Note: All the figures in this chapter were made by the author.

Advances in Computational Intelligence and its Applications (ICACIA-2023) – Dr. Sheikh Fahad Ahmad et al. (eds)
© 2024 Taylor & Francis Group, London, ISBN 978-1-032-78612-4

Comparative Analysis of Deep Learning Techniques for Fast Detection of COVID-19 Using CXR Images

32

**Shahid Kamal[1], Mohammad Sarfraz[2], Sumaiya Fatma,
Ifat Al Fatma, Shagufta Parween**
Electrical Engineering Department, Aligarh Muslim University, Aligarh, India

Muhammad Al Maathidi
Computer Science Department, Bahrain University, Bahrain

ABSTRACT—The COVID-19 pandemic has led to significant public health impacts and overwhelmed healthcare systems, necessitating widespread testing to control its spread. The current best practice for diagnosing COVID-19 is the Reverse Transcription Polymerase Chain Reaction (RT-PCR) test recommended by the World Health Organization, which uses a nasal swab sample from the suspected individual. However, this method is resource-intensive and has limited accuracy, with results taking several hours to obtain at a substantial cost. Therefore, alternative methods of rapid detection and diagnosis of COVID-19 are needed. Chest X-Ray (CXR) images, widely accessible through computed tomography (CT) scans and chest x-rays, present an opportunity for early COVID-19 diagnosis. This research uses the COVID-QU-Ex dataset, consisting of 33,920 CXR images, including 11,956 COVID-19 positive, 10,701 normal, and 11,263 infected samples. Seven deep learning models were employed to detect COVID-19 from CXR pictures: AlexNet, MobileNet, ResNet, DenseNet, ShuffleNet, InceptionV1, and XceptionNet. Each model's performance was assessed using five parameters: accuracy, sensitivity, precision, specificity, and F1-Score. Our experimental results demonstrate that the XceptionNet model had the highest accuracy of 98.86% in detecting COVID-19 from CXR images. This model can potentially aid radiologists in the early detection of COVID-19 cases.

KEYWORDS—Deep learning, COVID-19, CXR imaging, Convolutional neural networks

1. Introduction

The novel coronavirus emerged as a tragic disease in Wuhan, a city in china, at the end of 2019. It was a severe acute respiratory syndrome. As per a recent record by WHO[1], it has caused 631 million causalities and 6.58 million deaths. Due to this pandemic, the whole world suffered socially, mentally, and economically. The transmission rate of the virus was very high, which led to the government's strict lockdowns in several countries to reduce the infection rate[2]. Mass vaccination was helpful in some countries, but on the other hand, several countries entered second and third waves. Fever, pneumonia, cough, shortness of breath, and muscular pain are the primary symptoms of an infected person. Previously, Reverse Transcription-Polymerase Chain Reaction (RT-PCR) was used to diagnose COVID-19, which was costly, time-consuming, and required professionals[3].

RT-PCR kits are commonly available in high-income countries, however in low-income countries such as Bangladesh, the cost of an X-ray ranges from 450 BDT to 1200 BDT, whereas the cost of RT-PCR is 3000 BDT.

In India cost of an X-Ray varies from Rs.183 to Rs.1370, whereas the cost of RT-PCR varies from Rs.980 to Rs.1800. Due to the lack of healthcare facilities, medical professionals, and adequate supplies, RT- PCR kits need to be readily available[4]. Besides,

---

Corresponding Authors: [1]kamalshahid20@gmail.com, [2]msarfraz@zhcet.ac.in

DOI: 10.1201/9781003488682-32

these patients must travel to laboratories to get themselves tested, affecting people on the way. As it was time-consuming, many countries started using rapid antigen detection tests, but they gave less accurate results.

As a result, researchers have begun utilizing Deep Learning to automatically detect the virus using computed tomography (CT) scans and chest x-ray (CXR) images. [2]. CXR imaging tools are inexpensive and widely accessible in medical centers. Also, CXRs are handy, making them easier to use in homes, thereby reducing transmission risk. Reliable coronavirus detection is crucial; therefore, a fully automated classification technique is needed[1]. When the dataset was rare, the researchers used image augmentation techniques for deep learning models[3].

Large datasets enhance performance and eradicate overfitting problems [4]. This paper is organized into different sections. Sections 1 and 2 present a brief overview and related work respectively. In section 3, we analyze the model's performance. Sections 4 and 5 cover the deep learning architecture and performance metrics, respectively. Results and discussions are covered in section 6. Section 7 contains the conclusion and future work.

2. Literature Review

2.1 Related Work

The COVID x-ray dataset, created by A.M. Tahir et al.[1] is the largest CXR dataset and comprises 11,956 COVID-19 and 10,701 Normal CXR images. Its performance accuracy is 96.11%, and its sensitivity is higher than 99%. They showed sensitivity as the primary parameter to detect COVID-19.

Aysen Degerli et al.[5] experimented on the QaTa-COVID-19 dataset on the OsegNet model, with a precision of 98.09% for COVID-19 detection. Agata Gielczyk et al.[6] published an article on a new, lightweight, and supportive approach to diagnosing COVID-19 based on X-ray images.. This approach was fast and efficient, with an accuracy of 1.00 and a precision of 1.00.

Tawsifur Rahman et al.[2] presented a paper in which CNN models were used to identify COVID-19 in two symptomatic and asymptomatic suspects using cough and breath sound spectrogram images.. Karen Simonian et al.[7] presented a paper in which they demonstrated that their models could be used for various tasks and datasets. To overcome the problem of the traditional method of detecting COVID-19, Mei-Ling Huang et al.[8] employed CNN to detect COVID-19 from CXR and CT pictures in an efficient and accurate manner. They used seven convolutional neural networks: InceptionV3, DenseNet121, EfficientNet-130, Efficient Net V2, MobileNet V2, XceptionNet, and ResNet50. They have found that InceptionV3 gives the highest accuracy of 96.50% before fine-tuning, and EfficientNet V2 gives the highest accuracy of 97.73% after fine-tuning.

Shah Siddiqui et al.[4] compare deep learning algorithms for COVID-19 detection in CXR images, but they compared it on a very small dataset. This dataset is divided into COVID and Normal, with 579 CXR images belonging to the COVID class and 1773 CXR images belonging to the Normal class. They have taken three deep learning models, VGG 16, VGG-19, and InceptionV3, for comparison. VGG 16 performed best among all three models with an accuracy of 90%.

Our work aims to effectively detect COVID-19 cases from CXR images and acompare different deep-learning models for detecting COVID-19 from CXR images.

Furthermore, to achieve the highest accuracy in classifying COVID-19 from CXR image than the existing deep learning model. To train deep learning models to detect COVID-19 using the largest available dataset, as earlier researchers had trained neural network models on a minimal dataset.

3. Methodology

3.1 Dataset

At the time of this work, the COVID QU Ex dataset, created by academics at Qatar University, is the largest available dataset.

This dataset contains 33,920 CXR images, of which 11,956 are COVID-19, 11,263 are non-COVID, and 10,701 are normal (healthy) CXR images[1]. The quantity of image samples utilized for training set, validation set, and test set is displayed in Table 32.1.

Table 32.1 Covid QU Ex dataset images in each category [1]

Split Data	COVID-19	Normal
Training Set	7658	6849
Validation Set	1903	1712
Test Set	2395	2140

This dataset was compiled from various publicly available datasets such as the COVID-19 Chest X-Ray dataset, Chest X-Ray pneumonia dataset, Padchest dataset, and Montgomery and Shenzhen CXR lung mask.

3.2 Data Pre-processing

Before training the model, data pre-processing was carried out to increase the performance of the models. All the images were resized to 256×256 before being used as input to the algorithm. The images were shuffled during training, which ensures that the model does not memorize the incoming data sequence.

3.3 Deep Learning Models

In this study, seven deep-learning models have been re-implemented and trained for our analysis. The models used are AlexNet, MobileNet, ResNet, DenseNet, InceptionV1, ShuffleNet, and XceptionNet. These models are based on convolutional neural networks[9], which work on images to detect the features in the images. Convolutional Neural Networks started with LeNet-5, simply a stack of convolution for feature extraction and max pooling operation for spatial sampling.

AlexNet: AlexNet was first introduced in 2012 in the ImageNet large-scale visual recognition challenge (ILSVRC)[10]. It won the ImageNet competition by beating the previous best models with 10 % accuracy. AlexNet was trained on a subset of the ImageNet dataset comprising 1.2 million images of 1000 classes. AlexNet has eight layers (5 convolutional and the remaining fully connected layers) with learnable parameters. The activation function being used is ReLU. To avoid overfitting, it also makes use of dropout regularisation. For our needs, the last layer has only two dense units instead of 1000.

InceptionV1: InceptionV1 was first introduced in the 2014 ILSVRC ImageNet competition[11]. It has a total of 22 deep-layer networks. This Network uses multiple sets of InceptionV1 modules, which use a network-in-network approach. The InceptionV1 modules heavily use 1×1 convolutions. It serves the purpose of a dimensionality reduction module to remove the computational bottlenecks and helps the model get an enormous depth and width without sacrificing performance. A 1×1 convolution is applied before every 3×3 and 5×5 convolutions. InceptionV1 is an architecture consisting of InceptionV1 modules stacked upon each other. The basic idea of InceptionV1 is that instead of us selecting the filter sizes or pooling layers, it lets the Network decide what parameters it wants to learn. In our case, we have used InceptionV1, which has 28 convolutional layers.

ResNet: He et al. introduced ResNet in the 2015 Large Scale Visual Recognition Challenge (ILSVRC) ImageNet competition. Deep neural networks often suffer from vanishing gradient problems as the gradients are back-propagated to earlier layers, and the gradients become infinitely smaller due to repeated multiplications. He et al.[12] proposed a deep residual learning framework for training deeper networks, incorporating the main idea of an "Identity shortcut connection "that skips one or more layers. They compared three different models, which are VGG-19, plain Network (34 parameter layer), and ResNet network with 34 layers; they showed that training error reduces with the residual connection. The models were trained on 1.28 million training images. In our case, we use ResNet50, which has a 50 convolution layer.

MobileNet: MobileNet was introduced in the 2017 Large Scale Visual Recognition Challenge (ILSVRC) ImageNet competition[13].MobileNet is the most computationally efficient Network for mobile and embedded devices. MobileNet is most widely used in real-world object detection and image classification applications since it is very lightweight and takes much less memory. MobileNet uses depth-wise separable convolutions instead of the normal convolution operation. Depth-wise separable convolutions involve two operations: A depth-wise convolution subsequently followed by a pointwise convolution. Each filter in depth-wise convolution is applied to each and every input channel. The depth-wise convolution result must then be mapped to the desired number of output channels using pointwise convolution. We have used MobileNet V1 in our paper, which contains 28 layers consisting of depthwise and pointwise convolutions.

DenseNet: Huang et al.[14] proposed DenseNet in computer vision and pattern recognition(CVPR) in 2017.DenseNet alleviates the problem of vanishing gradients and promotes feature reusability and parameter reduction. DenseNet uses dense connections for the information flow between layers. Every layer receives feature maps from all previous layers as input in DenseNet and passes its feature maps to the next successive layers. The DenseNet architecture is split into dense blocks, which are then followed by a transition block. A transition block is used for down-sampling, consisting of batch normalization operation followed by a 1×1 convolution layer, and a 2×2 average pooling layer. We have used DenseNet-121 in this paper, which has 121 convolutional layers.

XceptionNet: Xception was first introduced by F. Chollet et al.[15] in Computer Vision and Pattern Recognition (CVPR). XceptionNet stands for Extreme InceptionV1. XceptionNet has outperformed InceptionV3 on the ImageNet dataset. It has the same number of trainable parameters as Inception V3. XceptionNet excessively uses Depth wise separable convolutions. In XceptionNet, channel-wise spatial convolutions are first applied, and then the channel compression is achieved using a 1×1 convolution, whereas the InceptionV1 does the Reverse of this operation. InceptionV1[11] uses ReLU(non-linearity) activation function after each convolution operation, while XceptionNet does not use non-linearity. XceptionNet has 36 convolutional layers that serve as feature extraction, and uses a linear residual connection. The number of learnable layers in XceptionNet is 71.

ShuffleNet: Zhang et al.[12] first introduced ShuffleNet in Computer Vision and Pattern Recognition (CVPR) in 2018. ShuffleNet is a highly efficient network for low computational power devices like drones, robots, and smartphones. ShuffleNet outperforms MobileNet on ImageNet and MS COCO Object detection tasks. It also achieves 13 × actual speed up over AlexNet. ShuffleNet is basically inspired from InceptionV1, Xception, and ResNet. Zhang et al. proposed a pointwise group convolution along with a residual connection to reduce the computational complexity while maintaining accuracy. ShuffleNet also performs channel shuffling for group convolutions. Channel shuffling leads to improved classification scores. ShuffleNet architecture contains a total of 50 convolutional layers.

The sample of COVID-19 and Normal images of the CXR dataset are shown in Fig. 32.1.

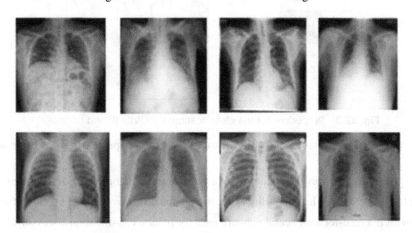

Fig. 32.1 Chest X-Ray sample images [1]

Source: https://www.kaggle.com/datasets/cf77495622971312010dd5934ee91f07ccbcfdea8e2f7778977ea8485c1914df?resource=download

4. Deep Learning Architecture

In recent years, deep learning approaches have produced outstanding achievements in image classification, object detection, image segmentation, and neural style transfer. The neural Network which is used in image classification is a Convolutional Neural Network (CNN). CNN transforms input images into matrix format, detecting useful features to classify any image. We often use multiple sets of CNN layers to detect the rich set of hierarchical features. CNN layers are used in conjunction with fully connected layers. The general procedure followed for the classification task of COVID-19 and Normal cases in this study is shown in Fig. 32.2.

A brief description of CNN models are described below:

Input Layer: In this layer, pre-processed input images are fed, and all the images are resized (in our case) 256×256×3 (width, height, and channels).

Convolutional Layers: The primary layer in CNNs extracts features from input images; in this layer, a kernel (filter) performs a convolution operation by maintaining a spatial relationship.

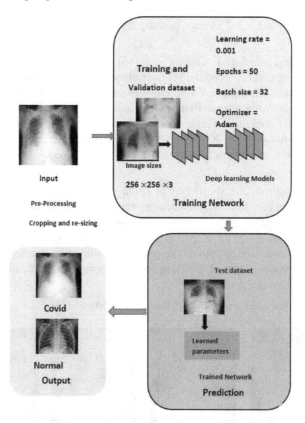

Fig. 32.2 Procedure for the classification of COVID-19 and normal[3]

Max-Pooling Layer: Max-pooling layers are applied to shrink the feature maps of CNN layers by achieving translational invariance.

Batch Normalisation Layer: It normalizes the features and provides training stability, making the training process faster.

Rectified Linear Unit (ReLU): Neurons learn non-linear decision boundaries through the activation function.

Fully Connected Layer: It is a feed-forward neural network used for feature classification after convolutional operations.

Output Layer: The final layer of the CNN has neurons equal to the number of classes. This layer is responsible for the final prediction of the classification task. In our case, the number of neurons in the output layers is two.

5. Performance Metrics

To evaluate and compare the models on the test dataset, we used five metrics: accuracy, precision, recall, specificity, and F1 score. They are determined by calculating true positive (TP), false positive (FP), true negative (TN), and false negative (FN).

1. Accuracy is defined as the ratio of correct predictions out of total predictions.

$$\text{Accuracy } (\%) = \frac{TP + TN}{TP + TN + FP + FN} \times 100\% \tag{1}$$

2. Precision is the percentage of positive class Chest X-Ray samples correctly identified out of all the samples.

$$\text{Precision } (\%) = \frac{TP}{TP + FP} \times 100\% \tag{2}$$

3. Recall (Sensitivity) is the percentage of correctly categorized positive class chest X-Ray samples among all categorized positive samples.

$$\text{Sensitivity}\,(\%) = \frac{TP}{TP + FN} \times 100\% \tag{3}$$

4. *Specificity* is defined as the sensitivity of a negative class sample.

$$\text{Specificity}\,(\%) = \frac{TN}{TN + FP} \times 100\% \tag{4}$$

5. F1 score is the harmonic mean of sensitivity and precision

$$F1 = 2\frac{\text{Precision} \times \text{Sensitivity}}{\text{Precision} + \text{Sensitivity}} \tag{5}$$

6. Results and Discussion

In this work, we trained deep learning models on the COVID X-ray dataset [1] for binary class prediction, whether COVID-19 positive or negative. Initially, a subset of 2913 images of x-rays from the dataset showed poor performance on the test dataset. To enhance the results, we trained the model on the entire dataset. To avoid overfitting, we applied dropout regularisation, randomly turning off 20% of neurons during training. We implemented the models in TensorFlow, a highly efficient deep-learning library in Python. The softmax function served as the activation function in the output layer, and we used the categorical cross-entropy loss as the loss function. We employed the Adaptive Moment Estimation (Adam) optimizer with a starting learning rate (α) of 0.001 and gradually decreased it until reaching the maximum number of epochs. We kept the default momentum values, $\beta1$ to 0.9, and $\beta2$ to 0.999. The maximum number of epochs was set to 50 for training – a batch size of 32 for both training set, and test set. We randomly shuffled training images to prevent the model from learning the training order and minimize bias.

Table 32.2 displays the model's complexity in terms of trainable parameters. AlexNet has the highest parameters of 71.99 million, while ShuffleNet has the least at 0.92 million paramters. The accuracy of the models heavily relies on the quality of the training dataset. This study used the COVID-19 X-ray dataset [1] consisting of high-quality X-ray images with distinct features. Together with utilizing suitable regularisation techniques, optimizers, and loss functions, the models accurately classified X-ray images as COVID-19 positive or normal.

Table 32.2   Model complexity and computational time [12]

Model	Parameters (Million)	Epochs	Training Time(Minute)
AlexNet	71.99	46	174.56
MobileNet	3.24	43	197.43
ResNet	23.54	43	216.88
DenseNet	6.96	47	280.88
XceptionNet	20.86	33	309.61
InceptionNet	3.22	29	188.38
ShuffleNet	0.92	50	210.6

XceptionNet performs better because of the efficient implementation rather than because of the Network's capacity. All the Models were evaluated on the test dataset, and the evaluated metrics are presented in Table 32.3. The loss and accuracy plots of XceptionNet and ResNet are shown in Fig. 32.3 and Fig. 32.4, respectively. Table 32.3 shows that the XceptionNet and ResNet have achieved the highest accuracy, 98.86%, and 98.35%, respectively.

The following two models whose accuracy is better after XceptionNet and ResNet are InceptionV1Net and MobileNet, having 98.26 % each. On the other hand, ShuffleNet and AlexNet have an accuracy of 97.21% and 97.54%, slightly less than MobileNet and ResNet. DenseNet has abysmal performance among all the models, with an accuracy of 92.92%. The test set contains 4545 images of both COVID-19, and Normal cases. The confusion matrix of XceptionNet and ResNet is shown in Fig. 32.5, and the confusion matrix of InceptionV1 and MobileNet is shown in Fig. 32.6.

Table 32.3 Performance metrics of deep learning models [1]

Model	Accuracy (%)	Recall (%)	Precision (%)	Specificity (%)	F1 Score
AlexNet	97.54	97.86	96.96	97.24	0.974
MobileNet	98.26	98.43	97.88	98.11	0.982
ResNet	98.35	98.36	98.14	98.33	0.983
DenseNet	92.92	87.30	97.46	97.95	0.921
ShuffleNet	97.21	97.53	96.59	96.91	0.971
InceptionNet	98.26	98.84	97.52	97.75	0.982
XceptionNet	98.86	98.93	98.65	98.79	0.988

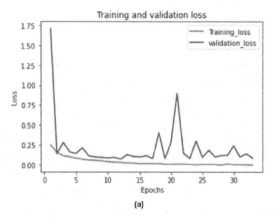
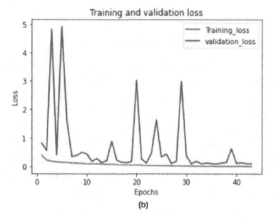

Fig. 32.3   (a) XceptionNet loss and (b) ResNet loss [1]

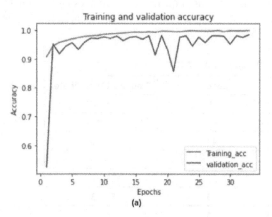
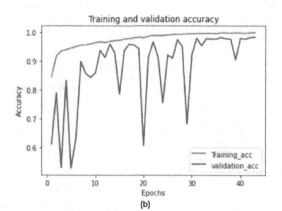

Fig. 32.4   (a) XceptionNet accuracy and (b) ResNet accuracy [1]

In a disease detection task, we should prioritize increasing the recall or reducing the number of false negatives since we do not want a patient to be misclassified as negative. In reality, the patient is positive that is having the disease. The confusion matrix of XceptionNet shows that it has the highest recall of 98.93%. It only misclassified 23 images as Normal cases and 29 as COVID-19 cases on the test dataset. While the second highest accurate model, ResNet, misclassified 35 images as Normal and 40 as COVID-19, shown in Fig. 32.5 (b). Even though InceptionV1 has slightly lesser accuracy than ResNet, it wrongly predicted only 25 images as Normal cases. Inception and MobileNet achieved the same accuracy, which is 98.26%. MobileNet's recall is only 98.43%, while InceptionV1 has 98.84%. XceptionNet has the highest F1 score of 0.988, which suggests choosing this model for the covid-19.

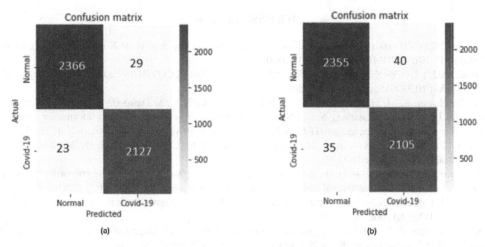

Fig. 32.5   Confusion matrix plot of (a) XceptionNet and (b) ResNet [1]

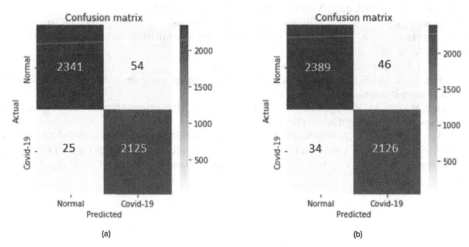

Fig. 32.6   Confusion matrix plot of (a) InceptionV1Net and (b) MobileNet [1]

The only limitation of our work is that binary classification has been used to detect COVID-19 from Chest X-Ray images. However, we plan to work on the multiclass classification in future work.

7. Conclusion

In this study, seven deep-learning models were tested for COVID-19 diagnosis using the widely available Chest X-Ray dataset (COVID QU Ex). The evaluation of the models were done on five performance metrics: Accuracy, Precision, Sensitivity, Specificity, and F1 score. The best-performing model was XceptionNet having an accuracy of 98.86%. Deep learning models often get overfitting problems when trained with fewer datasets. Most deep learning models were examined on datasets containing only a few hundred samples of Chest X-Ray in all the previous work. Therefore, they were more prone to overfitting.

We have found that the model predictions on the test dataset have improved due to training on a large dataset. The accuracy would have been further improved if the dataset had been more extensive than COVID QU Ex. In our future work, we plan to improve the accuracy further by hyperparameter tuning and extending it to a multi-class classification.

REFERENCES

1. Tahir, A. M., et al. (2021). COVID-19 infection localisation and severity grading from chest X-ray images. Computers in Biology and Medicine, 139, doi: 10.1016/J.COMPBIOMED.2021.105002.

2. Rahman, T., et al. (2022). QUCoughScope: An Intelligent Application to Detect COVID-19 Patients Using Cough and Breath Sounds. Diagnostics, 12(4), doi: 10.3390/diagnostics12040920.

3. Majeed, S. A., Darghaoth, A. M. H., Hamed, N. M. Z., Yahya, Y. A., Raed, S., & Dawood, Y. S. (2021). Detection of COVID-19 from X-Ray Images Using Transfer Learning Neural Networks. In Proceedings of the 2021 2nd Information Technology to Enhance E-Learning and other Applications Conference (IT-ELA 2021), 58–63. doi: 10.1109/IT-ELA52201.2021.9773657.

4. Siddiqui, S., et al. (2022). A Comparative Study of Deep Learning Models for COVID-19 Diagnosis Based on X-Ray Images. In (pp. 163–174). doi: 10.1007/978-981-16-9101-0_12.

5. Degerli, A., Kiranyaz, S., Chowdhury, M. E. H., & Gabbouj, M. (2022). OSegNet: Operational Segmentation Network for COVID-19 Detection using Chest X-ray Images. arXiv, vol. abs/2202.1, no. Cvdi, 5–9. [Online]. Available: http://arxiv.org/abs/2202.10185

6. Piorkowski, A., et al. (2022). A Novel Lightweight Approach to COVID-19 Diagnostics Based on Chest X-ray Images. Journal of Clinical Medicine, 11(19), 5501, doi: 10.3390/JCM11195501.

7. Simonyan, K., & Zisserman, A. (2015). Very deep convolutional networks for large-scale image recognition. 3rd International Conference on Learning Representations (ICLR 2015) - Conference Track Proceedings, 1–14.

8. Huang, M. L., & Liao, Y. C. (2022). A lightweight CNN-based network on COVID-19 detection using X-ray and CT images. Computers in Biology and Medicine, 146, 105604, doi: 10.1016/J.COMPBIOMED.2022.105604.

9. L., Y. et al. (1998). Learning algorithms for classification: a comparison on handwritten digit recognition. (pp. 261–276).

10. Krizhevsky, B. A., Sutskever, I., & Hinton, G. E. (2012). ImageNet classification with deep convolutional neural networks. Communications of the ACM, 60(6), 84–90.

11. Szegedy, C., et al. (2015). Going Deeper With Convolutions. (pp. 1–9).

12. He, K., Zhang, X., Ren, S., & Sun, J. (2016). Deep residual learning for image recognition. Proceedings of the IEEE Conference on Computer Vision and Pattern Recognition, (pp. 770-778).

13. Howard, A. G., Sandler, M., Zhu, M., Zhmoginov, A., & Chen, L. C. (2017). MobileNets: Efficient Convolutional Neural Networks for Mobile Vision Applications. arXiv preprint arXiv:1704.04861.

14. Huang, G., Liu, Z., Van Der Maaten, L., & Weinberger, K. Q. (2017). Densely Connected Convolutional Networks. In Proceedings of the 30th IEEE Conference on Computer Vision and Pattern Recognition (CVPR) (pp. 2261–2269). doi:10.1109/CVPR.2017.243

15. Chollet, F. (2017). Xception: Deep Learning with Computer Vision and Pattern Recognition (CVPR) (pp. 1800–1807). doi:10.1109/CVPR.2017.195

Advances in Computational Intelligence and its Applications (ICACIA-2023) – Dr. Sheikh Fahad Ahmad et al. (eds)
© 2024 Taylor & Francis Group, London, ISBN 978-1-032-78612-4

Accident Evasion and Warning System

33

Pramilarani K.[1], V. Reddy Dheeraj[2], B. Meenakshi Sundaram[3],
Maneesh Reddy Duddukunta[4], Vamshika Sushma Appaji[5]
Department of CSE, New Horizon College of Engineering, Bengaluru, India

ABSTRACT—The accident detection methods and potential future improvements are summarised in this publication. Highway accidents are becoming increasingly common due to increased traffic and careless driving on the part of drivers. Family members, medical staff, and law enforcement officials are frequently not informed in time. Helping the hurt accident victim therefore requires extra time. Traffic collisions are the main reason for accidents. The project's goal is to locate and identify the car by using technology that has been put inside of it to send a message through the car's system. Finding the precise location of the accident may be difficult since we can never predict where an event will take place. These situations are what our Real Time Vehicle Safety and Accident Detection Using GSM application attempts to prevent.

KEYWORDS—Vehicle tracking, Accident, Detection, SMS notification, GPS, GSM

1. Introduction

Together with the rise in automotive demand, traffic risks and accidents have increased. People's lives are at grave danger. The lack of emergency services in our country is to blame for this. This suggestion is for a system that can identify accidents far more quickly and transmit essential details to a first aid facility in seconds, such location, timing, and impact angle. The quick transmission of this warning signal to the rescue team helps to save lives. The police station and emergency workers are alerted right away after an accident. The GSM module broadcasts the message while the GPS module detects the accident's location. The accident may be accurately identified by both Micro electro mechanical systems (MEMS) sensors. You might be able to estimate the angle of the car's rollover using the information from the MEMS sensor. The easiest strategy to handle a slow emergency response to a traffic collision is to follow this procedure.

Providing victims with prompt aid as soon as feasible is the suggested course of action. Several organisations must deal with the time and money costs of unlawful drivers. The technology may also be used to sell cars, manage fleets, monitor stolen cars and luggage, among other things. A single-board embedded system with GPS and GSM modems connected to a microcontroller is part of the system. The car's electronics are now completely functional. It utilises a Mems sensor. It detects vibrations in the area where it is anchored. The acceleration level can be used to detect vehicle crashes, needless equipment stress or vibration, and vehicle tilt with respect to the earth's axis by comparing it to the baseline values. The position of the vehicle is ascertained using the Global Positioning System (GPS). The aforementioned values are given access to the car's precise position through GSM. Coordinates for longitude and latitude will be provided in the message. It is possible to determine the precise site of the accident using these factors. A SIM card is used by a GSM modem to facilitate two-way communication. This kind of module

[1]pramilaranik@newhorizonindia.edu, [2]vreddydheeraj@gmail.com, [3]dr.meenakshis@newhorizonindia.edu, [4]maneeshsreenu2001@gmail.com, [5]vamshika.appaji@gmail.com

DOI: 10.1201/9781003488682-33

operates in a manner similar to that of a typical phone. The project's goal is to create an adaptable safety and security system that is aware of its surroundings.

2. Objectives

- By employing the accelerometer to detect falls and keep track of changes in vehicle speed, accidents can be prevented.
- The Arduino serves as the main control system, detecting accidents and warning the user. The findings are shown using information from the GPS, GSM, and accelerometer systems.
- They'll get there in time to help save lives.

3. Requirements

3.1 System Hardware

A hardware platform is necessary for an embedded system to operate, just like any other electronic system. Hardware for embedded systems is produced by a microprocessor or a microcontroller. Input/output (I/O) interfaces, a user interface, memory, and a display are all components of embedded system hardware. Embedded systems frequently include the following components:

- Power Supply
- Processor
- Memory
- Timers
- Serial communication ports
- Output/Output circuits
- System application specific circuits

Embedded systems, which employ a range of CPUs, carry out the given duty. The processors that are utilised include

1. Microprocessor
2. Microcontroller
3. Digital signal processor

3.2 System Software

The software for embedded systems serves a specific function. High-level code is often written, compiled, and then installed in hardware's nonvolatile memory. While creating embedded system software, developers take into account three limitations:

- Availability of system memory
- Availability of processor's speed
- The power consumed by the stop, run, and wake up activities must be kept to a minimal minimum even if the system runs indefinitely.

4. Literature Survey

Li Jie, Li Guang-Hui, Hu Jian-ming, and others reported on a method for recovering stolen cars. Technology has increased dependability and safety. The C8051F120 Processor and a vibration sensor were utilised. Using GSM, the position of the car is sent to its owner.

The importance of a low-cost system with current internet networking capabilities was emphasised by T. Krishna Kishore et al. The Generic Packet Radio Service and the Linux operating system were combined (GPRS). Among the improvements are improved software monitoring independence, ease of data sharing, and improved identification of the vehicle's location at all times.

An automated system for detecting car accidents was shown by Nirav Thakor and colleagues using ARM and GPS. The system uses a vibration sensor or a MEMS sensor to detect car accidents. The GPS module found the location of the collision and used a GSM modem to send a message containing the coordinate information. There are more services that could be helpful in an emergency. If someone need help due to another reason, like a heart attack. He merely needs to touch one button on the device in this situation. By pushing this button, the GSM module sends a message containing the user's information and the vehicle's GPS location to the support centre.

5. Why IOT?

"Internet of Things" (IoT) encompasses physical objects or collections thereof that integrate sensors, computational capabilities, software, and other technological components. These interconnected devices and systems have the capacity to communicate with each other through the Internet or other communication networks. The rapid progress in IoT can be attributed to the convergence of various technologies, including ubiquitous computing, cost-effective sensor technology, intelligent embedded systems, and machine learning. Established domains such as embedded systems, wireless sensor networks, control systems, and automation play pivotal roles in enabling IoT applications, including those in home and building automation.

Fig. 33.1 IOT

The Internet of Things (IoT) ecosystems comprise a network of internet-connected smart devices equipped with embedded systems, encompassing processors, sensors, and communication capabilities. These devices are designed to gather, exchange, and act upon environmental data. To facilitate the sharing of sensor data, IoT devices establish connections with IoT gateways or other edge devices. Subsequently, cloud infrastructure is employed to analyse the collected data. These devices intermittently communicate data and execute commands. While these devices generally operate autonomously, users have the option to interact with them for configuration, placing orders, or data examination.

6. Methodology

With this technology, our first focus was on preventing vehicle accidents, but even after all precautions have been taken, the system may still detect situations where accidents still happen. The person is prevented from passing away as a result of a delay in seeking medical attention when the technology detects an automobile collision and immediately notifies the ambulance service and police station. The in-vehicle recording system uses GPS, GSM, and accelerometers to record auto accidents. Also, as precautionary precautions, a buzzer, led lights, and other warning devices are employed, and a motor drives the engine (control switch). These parts are all connected to the main microcontroller (Arduino Uno). The microcontroller receives a signal from the accelerometer in the event of an accident, which is then analysed. The GPS module provides real-time information on the location, speed, time, and date of the automobile in a specific area. The accelerometer recognises an accident as it happens, uses GPS to pinpoint its location, and then uses a GSM module to send a message to emergency and law enforcement organisations. A Google Map link to the accident's location is also included in the phone message, which will help first responders including ambulance services and police departments locate the victim and save lives.

- The Arduino setup is incorporated inside the crash protection or bumpers on either side of a car.
- The push button activates in the event of a collision, alerting the Arduino Board.
- For usage with the SIM808, Arduino will convert this input.
- Coordinates are sent through GSM.
- The notification is sent through GSM to the saved mobile number.
- Its GPS position is precise.
- To choose the path and location, use the software.
- After the buzzer is turned off, the device resumes normal operation if the accident was mild.

7. Proposed System

The combination of GSM and GPS technology in the accident detection and messaging system makes deployment easier. The location of the accident is determined using GPS, and GSM is utilised to send that information to the phone. Latitude and longitude information are shown on the LCD, and the Arduino manages the complete system. The blockage is discovered using an ultrasonic sensor (vehicle which is near to vehicle). If an automobile gets too close, the buzzer will sound.

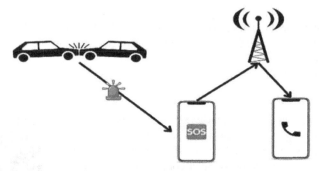

Fig. 33.2 Proposed system

8. Working

8.1 Arduino

The Arduino UNO is a widely recognized open-source microcontroller board that utilizes the ATmega328P processor and is manufactured by Arduino.cc. It functions as the central control system, responsible for accident detection and alerting the user. The system collects data from various sensors, including those for vibration, GSM, and GPRS. This data is then presented through messages or displayed on a user interface. The vibration sensor plays a crucial role in this setup, serving as both a vehicle vibration detector and an accident detection module. Information from all these modules is gathered and transmitted to a recipient using the GSM module integrated into the Arduino.

8.2 GPS Module

To simplify the process of pinpointing a specific location on Earth using a GPS module, we utilize the SIM28ML GPS module. This GPS device is capable of tracking the location of a vehicle. It functions by receiving coordinates from the GPS receiver, which are then relayed to an Arduino. The Arduino, in turn, transmits these coordinates to a designated contact via a GSM module. The output data from the GPS module is provided in the NMEA format and includes essential information such as the current position and the frequency of 1575.42 MHz.

8.3 GSM Module

To establish communication between the GPS system, GSM network, and a designated mobile number, the implementation utilizes a GSM SIM900 module. The SIM900 module operates as a triband system, functioning within the frequency ranges of EGSM900 MHz, PCS 1900 MHz, and DSC 100 MHz, spanning from 900 MHz to 1900 MHz. The connection is established by interconnecting the transmission pin of the GPS module with the reception pin of the GSM module.

8.4 Accelerometer

The primary functioning mechanism of an accelerometer involves a mass placed onto a spring. Commonly employed elements for translating the mechanical movement of an accelerometer into an electrical signal encompass piezoelectric, piezo resistive, and capacitive components. Notably, piezoelectric accelerometers are constructed from single crystals.

8.5 Vibration Sensor

A piezoelectric sensor, also known as a vibration sensor, serves as a versatile instrument capable of measuring various phenomena. It operates by converting acceleration, pressure, temperature, force, or strain into an electrical charge, enabling it to detect and quantify these factors. Additionally, this sensor continuously monitors changes in capacitance and impedance to detect the presence of airborne odors.

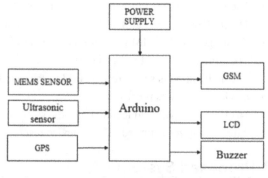

Fig. 33.3 Circuit diagram

9. Conclusion

In this project, we developed an accident detection and smart rescue system that, in the event of an emergency, not only recognises accidents, generates emergency alerts, and transmits them to the closest emergency responders, but also sends an SMS to a contact with the accident's location information. By giving emergency help as quickly as feasible, the system's real-time position tracking for the responder and the victim will significantly increase an accident victim's odds of survival.

REFERENCES

1. FSaad Masood Butt31 May 2016The International Institute for Science, Technology and Education (IISTE).
2. Bergonda, S., et. al. (2017, April). "IoT Based Vehicle Accident Detection and Tracking System Using GPS Modem", International Journal of Innovative Science and Research Technology(IJISRT) ISSN No: 2456–2165, Volume 2, Issue 4
3. T. Anitha and T. Uppalaigh focused on "Android based home automation using Raspberry pi", Proc-IEEE, vol.04, no.01, pp-2351-8665 2016
4. Md. Shaad Mahmud, Honggang Wang, A.M.Esfar-EAlam and Hua Fang has focused on "A Wireless Health Monitoring System Using Mobile Phone Accessories", Proc-IEEE,vol. 1, no. 99, pp. 2327–4662 2016
5. Hyung-Sin Kim, Hongchan Kim, jeongyeuo Paek and Saewoong Bahk has discussed on "Load Balancing Under Heavy Traffic in RPL Routing Protocol for Low Power and Lossy Networks", Proc-IEEE,vol.16, no.4, pp. 1536–1233 2017
6. R. L. Paulraj, S. K. B V, G. V. Vardhan, K. S. Pradeep, K. Hemanth and G. B. Reddy, "A Detailed Approach on Vehicle Accident Recognition and Remote Alarm Device," 2022 International Conference on Advanced Computing Technologies and Applications (ICACTA), 2022, pp. 1–5, doi: 10.1109/ICACTA54488.2022.9753270.
7. S. K. B V, S. Sharma, K. S. Swathi, K. R. Yamini, C. P. Kiran and K. Chandrika, "Review on IoT based Healthcare systems," 2022 International Conference on Advanced Computing Technologies and Applications (ICACTA), 2022, pp. 1–5, doi: 10.1109/ICACTA54488.2022.9753547.

Note: All the figures in this chapter were made by the author.

Advances in Computational Intelligence and its Applications (ICACIA-2023) – Dr. Sheikh Fahad Ahmad et al. (eds)
© 2024 Taylor & Francis Group, London, ISBN 978-1-032-78612-4

Crowd Counting for Risk Management Using Deep Learning

34

Sanjay Raghavendra[1], Sri Tanmayi Ch[2], Srishti Hiremath[3], M. Dhanalakshmi[4], Rajalaksmi[5]

Computer Science and Engineering Department,
New Horizon College of Engineering, Bangalore, India

ABSTRACT—Currently, automated crowd-counting systems are being replaced with intelligent ones using machine learning and artificial intelligence approaches. This paradigm change offers a variety of cutting-edge features for adaptive monitoring and the control of effervescent crowd gatherings. Numerous crowd-management-related jobs can be made more effective, capable, and dependable for various crowd gatherings. Despite several challenges, such as occlusion, clutter, uneven item distribution, and nonuniform object scale, convolutional neural networks offer a practical method for intelligent photo crowd analysis.[4]

KEYWORDS—Machine learning, Artificial intelligence, Crowd analysis, Technology

1. Introduction

Counting the crowd is the process of ascertaining its size. It basically aims to find the density of the crowd in a place. In real-time, crowd counting is used in many applications such as security, resource management, traffic management, disaster management, urban surveillance, etc. In the current digital era, crowd counting is used in many scenarios where it has become mandatory. Many real-world uses for crowd counting and analysis include preparing emergency evacuations in the event of fire outbreaks, catastrophic occurrences, etc., and making defensible judgments based on the population, such as arranging for water and food, spotting congestion, etc.[1] Due to this very reason crowd counting has become a very active topic to research.

Although there has been so much research based on crowd counting, it remains a real-time challenge. Challenges mainly focus on changes in the lighting, camera perspective differences, or extreme occlusions. Hence it is important to build a high-level cognitive model in such cases. Nowadays crowd counting has mostly relied on CCTV video feeds.

The most recent convolutional neural network-based crowd-counting approaches are reviewed, categorized, analyzed (limitations and distinctive features), and given a thorough performance evaluation in this article. We also highlight the potential uses for crowd-counting methods based on convolutional neural networks. In order to lay a solid foundation for future research endeavours while developing convolutional neural network-based crowd- counting approaches, we finish this study by summarising our important findings.

2. Literature Review

Crowd safety has long been an important but challenging issue, especially in densely populated meeting places. Finding a clever way of crowd analysis in public areas is essential for helping with mitigation and decision-making. Hence crowd counting

[1]sanjayraghavendra369@gmail.com, [2]1nh19cs177.sritanmayich@gmail.com, [3]srishtihiremath1228@gmail.com, [4]mdhanalak72@gmail.com, [5]hod_cse@gmail.com

DOI: 10.1201/9781003488682-34

is crucial in such kind of analysis and is now an active topic. However, current crowd-monitoring systems have a number of shortcomings, like being limited by application situations or having low-precision locations.

Various techniques have been used to implement crowd-counting in real time. Some basic methods are object detection, regression, and density-based approaches. These methods have faced many challenges

2.1 Detection-based Methods

This method counts the number of persons in an image or video using a detector resembling a shaped window to identify them based on several classifiers. Using well-trained classifiers to extract low-level characteristics (including edges and blobs) is necessary. These detection-based techniques are effective at identifying faces, but they struggle to produce accurate findings when there is a large group of people in a photograph or video. In sparse regions, detection-based counting algorithms work better, but in scenarios with large densities, the counting accuracy suffers.[10]

Fig. 34.1 Detection based crowd counting

Source: Author

2.2 Regression-based Methods

When there is a large crowd and there is a lot of randomness or clutter in the backdrop, the counting by-detection method does not work well. These difficulties can be overcome by regression-based approaches since they can extract low-level information. The low-level features, such as edge values, foreground pixels, etc., are extracted from the cropped regions of a picture. The input photos can be converted directly to scalar values using regression algorithms. However, the drawback of these approaches is their inability to comprehend crowd distributions appropriately. Density-based approaches solve this issue by doing pixel-wise regressions to improve the model's performance.

2.3 Density-based Methods

The suggested approach avoids the flaws of density maps and focuses on the direct prediction of particular places rather than just counting them, which is advantageous for later practical applications.[7] The spatial information that remained in the photographs was mostly overlooked by the earlier methods. They do not concentrate on specifically identifying each person. However, this approach focuses on density by including spatial information in the process by figuring out how local characteristics and item density maps translate to one another. Tracking a group of people at once prevents learning about each person individually. Either linear or nonlinear mapping could be used. In recent years, the focus has been on creating counting-by-density algorithms, which depend on regressors trained to estimate the population density per unit area in order to acquire the total number through integration, without the need for explicit detection.[13]

2.4 Convolutional Neural Network-based Method

Deep convolutional neural networks have gained significant traction in crowd counting during the last two years.[2] Convolutional Neural Network (CNN) based computer vision techniques are currently being employed to obtain superior accuracy than the conventional techniques, leaving traditional approaches behind. Presenting loss functions, optimizing measurement metrics, updating matching rules, fine-grained noise areas, strengthening regular constraints, combining additional labels, and optimizing training procedures are the common techniques for combating noise.[11] A large group of CNNs are intended to achieve crowd density.

- Basic CNNs: These models require a basic understanding of deep learning, including kernels, pooling layers, and convolutional layers.

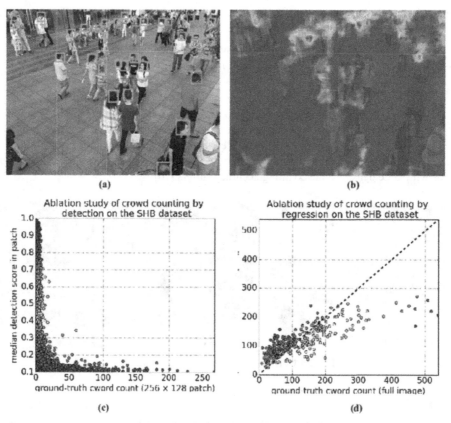

Fig. 34.2 Regression-based crowd counting

Source: Author

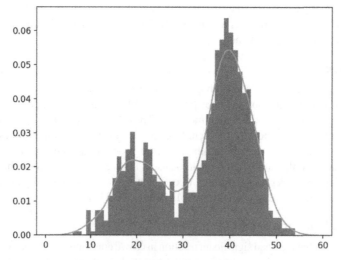

Fig. 34.3 Density-based crowd counting

Source: Author

- Scale-aware models: Where many columns or multiple resolutions are employed, these CNNs are stronger and more powerful.
- Multi-task CNN frameworks: They are able to handle tasks like a crowd-velocity estimate, foreground-background minimization, and more in addition to being able to count the number of people.

 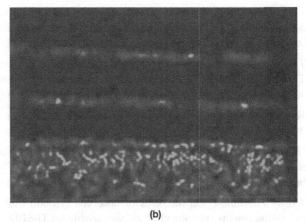

(a)   (b)

Fig. 34.4 CNN based crowd counting [paper1]

Source: Author

3. Deep Learning for Crowd Counting

One of the first researchers to use CNNs for the job of crowd density estimate was Wang et al. and Fu et al. [3]. Wang et al. proposed an end-to-end deep CNN regression model for counting people from images in extremely dense crowds [3]. They used the AlexNet network in their architecture, replacing the 4096-neuron final fully linked layer with a single neuron layer to estimate the count. Additionally, training data is supplemented with additional negative samples, whose ground truth count is set to zero, in order to eliminate erroneous responses caused by the background of the images, which include objects like buildings and trees.[3]

By spreading out the noisy background, this approach enables the model to concentrate more on the regions of interest.[12] To address significant problems such as occlusion, low visibility, and inter-and-intraobject variations due to different views, multiple CNN algorithms were presented.

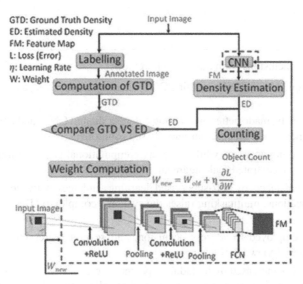

Fig. 34.5 General form of CNN algorithm[6]

Labelling: In machine learning, the process of labelling data, such as text, audio, and picture, is referred to as annotation. The annotation data are utilised by a computer or computers to find comparable patterns in previously unobserved data. Bounding-box annotation, polygonal segmentation, lines, landmarks, 3D cuboids, and dots are a few examples of the various annotation categories.

GTD computation: The data provided by direct observation rather than inference is referred to as ground truth. The GTD can be obtained in a variety of techniques, including using the Gaussian kernel, the geometry-adaptive kernel, and GANs.[6] Compared to the GTD produced by Gaussian, geometric, or body-aware approaches, the GTD from GANs is of higher quality.

GTD and ED comparison: To calculate the difference between estimated output and ground truth in crowd counting, ED and GTD are compared.[6] Different methods, including cross-entropy and MSE, were used to calculate the loss in the literature. Due to the gradient-vanishing issue, sigmoid and MSE converge substantially more slowly than sigmoid and cross-entropy.

Weight Computation: Updating the network weight to reduce loss comes next after comparing the loss between ED and GTD. Once the loss is as small as possible, this weight update procedure ends (backpropagated to CNN).

CNN: First, convolutional, reLU, pooling, and FCL are applied to the CNN that receives the input image. CNN operates by extracting picture features in the form of a feature map.[6] These characteristics are added to the regression model to estimate the crowd density map. Single, multi, and single with scale-aware networks are the three types of CNN.[6]

Density estimation: On the basis of observed (ground truth) data, it can be characterized as a method for estimating the probability density function of a random variable.[6] The ED of a crowd can be determined in a variety of approaches, including density estimate by clustering, detection, and regression. Detection and regression can be combined to improve efficiency in sparse and dense environments.

Counting: This technique counts the number of things (people, cells, automobiles, etc.) in an image or video after a density map has been computed.[6] According to image density, various popular handcrafted approaches function differently. For instance, counting by detection does well in sparse-density images because there are few overlapping objects, whereas CNN-based techniques excel in images with a wide range of densities.

4. Crowd Counting for Risk Management

Particularly in the case of large events, crowd counting and crowd density estimates are crucial components of safety monitoring and behavior analysis. They may enable early identification of problems relating to traffic or security. educating and assisting decision-makers to prevent crowd tragedies. [14] For instance, crowd counting can be used for risk management in case of an emergency evacuation. Suppose, there is an occurrence of a natural calamity in a specific area, using Crowd Counting we can find an approximate number of people present and send this information to the concerned authority so that relevant help can be provided within a short span of time.

5. Discussion

We draw the following important conclusions from our in-depth review:

- By eliminating redundant samples, basic CNN-counting CC's accuracy is improved, and multitasking raises an algorithm's total accuracy.
- Context-density CNN's map can be made better by utilizing a deeper dilated CNN, and counting accuracy can be increased by using an adaptive-density network with pose-variation-based solutions.
- Stacked pooling increases counting accuracy while lowering computational cost. Additionally, the density map's quality and accuracy are enhanced by concentrated scale aggregation modules.
- Multitask CNN accuracy is enhanced by self-supervised learning, linkages between distinct tasks, and up-and-down sampling. For real-time applications, multitasking raises the system's complexity. Deconvolution layers also improve the quality of density maps.
- Down sampling patches are employed to address occlusion, and several regression models are used to enhance the performance of the nMAE's aerial-view CNN terms.
- The PRCC's counting accuracy is increased by including a perspective-aware layer in the deconvolution network, sharing parameters across several domains, and using training scenes from all training datasets that share perspective maps with target scenes.
- Detection and regression techniques are used in conjunction with picture density and the best information transfer within CNN layers to boost the nMAE of patch-based CNN.[6] The accuracy of dense datasets is improved by combining density-level classification, a specific task-oriented regressor, and deconvolution with estimates of high-quality density maps. An approach called patch-based augmentation (changing scale) is used to deal with density datasets.

- The counting accuracy is improved by using whole-image CNN, semantic and locality-aware features, and density-level classification. These techniques are relevant in real-time applications because changing image scales can partially fix diverse-crowd density problems.
- The majority of existing models are based on the picture level, and the algorithm's real-time performance is rarely considered. The goal of crowd-counting research is to increase the real-time speed of the algorithm and decrease network complexity while maintaining counting accuracy.[9]

6. Conclusion

Intelligent crowd counting and its analysis are future advancements of manual, conventional methods. By tightly integrating machine learning and artificial intelligence technologies with the traditional crowd counting approaches, intelligent crowd counting and its analysis offer cutting-edge capabilities like adaptive control for dynamic crowd gatherings and their wide-area monitoring/surveillance. Particularly, the learned deep model is more adept at characterizing crowd situations than other hand-crafted characteristics.[5] The efficiency, capacity, dependability, and safety of many crowds' management-related jobs can be increased thanks to these cutting-edge characteristics. Uneven crowd dispersal is the main emphasis of the suggested technique. [8] Many applications that call for adaptive monitoring, identification, and management over various crowd-gathering horizons can be successfully supported by CNN approaches. In this article, we have discussed many different techniques of crowd counting. We have compared each of these techniques. We have also seen how the deep learning-based method is more efficient than any of the other techniques.

REFERENCES

1. Bhangale, U., Patil, S. S., Vishwanath, V., Thakker, P., Bansode, A., & Navandhar, D. (2020). Near Real-time Crowd Counting using Deep Learning Approach. *Procedia Computer Science, 171*, 770–779. https://doi.org/10.1016/j.procs.2020.04.084
2. Liu, L., Wang, H., Li, G., Ouyang, W., & Lin, L. (2018). Crowd Counting using Deep Recurrent Spatial-Aware Network. *International Joint Conference on Artificial Intelligence.* https://doi.org/10.24963/ijcai.2018
3. Sindagi, V. A., & Patel, V. M. (2018). A Survey of Recent Advances in CNN-based Single Image Crowd Counting and Density Estimation. *ArXiv (Cornell University).* https://doi.org/10.1016/j.patrec.2017.07.007
4. Shi, Z., Zhang, L., Liu, Y., Cao, X., Ye, Y., Cheng, M., & Zheng, G. (2018). Crowd Counting with Deep Negative Correlation Learning. *Computer Vision and Pattern Recognition.* https://doi.org/10.1109/cvpr.2018.00564
5. Zhang, C., Li, H., Wang, X., & Yang, M. (2015). Cross-scene crowd counting via deep convolutional neural networks. *Computer Vision and Pattern Recognition.* https://doi.org/10.1109/cvpr.2015.7298684
6. Ilyas, N., Shahzad, A., & Kim, K. (2019). Convolutional-Neural Network-Based Image Crowd Counting: Review, Categorization, Analysis, and Performance Evaluation. *Sensors, 20*(1), 43. https://doi.org/10.3390/s20010043
7. Song, Q., Wang, C., Jiang, Z., Wang, Y., Tai, Y., Wang, C., Li, J., Huang, F., & Wu, Y. C. (2021b). Rethinking Counting and Localization in Crowds: A Purely Point-Based Framework. *International Conference on Computer Vision.* https://doi.org/10.1109/iccv48922.2021.00335
8. Liu, Z., Chen, Y., Chen, B., Linan, Z., Wu, D. C., & Shen, G. (2019). Crowd Counting Method Based on Convolutional Neural Network with Global Density Feature. *IEEE Access.* https://doi.org/10.1109/access.2019.2926881
9. Hui Gao, Miaolei Deng, Wenjun Zhao et al. A Survey of Crowd Counting CNN-based, 15 October 2021, PREPRINT (Version 1) available at Research Square https://doi.org/10.21203/rs.3.rs-957081/v1
10. Ilyas, N., Ahmad, Z., Lee, B., & Kim, K. (2022). An effective modular approach for crowd counting in an image using convolutional neural networks. *Scientific Reports, 12*(1). https://doi.org/10.1038/s41598-022-09685-w
11. Cheng, Z., Dai, Q., Li, H., Song, J., Wu, X., & Hauptmann, A. G. (2022). Rethinking Spatial Invariance of Convolutional Networks for Object Counting. *2022 IEEE/CVF Conference on Computer Vision and Pattern Recognition (CVPR).* https://doi.org/10.1109/cvpr52688.2022.01902
12. Thanasutives, P., Fukui, K., Numao, M., & Kijsirikul, B. (2021). Encoder-Decoder Based Convolutional Neural Networks with Multi-Scale-Aware Modules for Crowd Counting. *Cornell University - ArXiv.* https://doi.org/10.1109/icpr48806.2021.9413286
13. Liu, W. E., Salzmann, M., & Fua, P. (2019). Context-Aware Crowd Counting. *Cornell University - ArXiv.* https://doi.org/10.1109/cvpr.2019.00524
14. *MRCNet: Crowd counting and density map estimation in aerial and ground imagery.* (n.d.). CORE Reader. https://core.ac.uk/reader/227532670

Advances in Computational Intelligence and its Applications (ICACIA-2023) – Dr. Sheikh Fahad Ahmad et al. (eds)
© 2024 Taylor & Francis Group, London, ISBN 978-1-032-78612-4

Tamil Character-Size Reduction Method for Storage of Large Amount of Data

35

P. Thamizhikkavi[1]
Assistant Professor [Jr. G], Department of computing Technologies,
SRMIST, Chennai

R. S. Ponmagal[2]
Associate professor, Department of computing Technologies,
SRMIST, Chennai

ABSTRACT—Tamil, an ancient language of India, has developed in different phases, and now modern Tamil script is being used in Tamil Nadu (a state in India) as the official language. The modern script has been updated over the internet with some Unicode values, and now Tamil script can be accepted by all devices which support those Unicode values. Analysing the alphabet and structure of the Tamil language, Unicode values range from 2947 to 3021. To represent the Tamil language Which requires a minimum of thirteen bits to mean a single Unicode value, technically, to represent a single character minimum of 16 bits is required. Also, composite characters need at least a set of two Unicode values to represent them. A new algorithm TC-SRM (Tamil Character-Size Reduction Method), has been proposed to cut down the size of Tamil alphabets, which helps to store more data in storage.

KEYWORDS—Tamil characters, Unicode values, Data size reduction

1. Introduction

With an estimated 76 million people using the language, which goes back over 2000 years, Tamil is one of the world's oldest ethnological groupings. Outside of India, only one of India's 22 legal languages is recognised as such, such as in Sri Lanka and Singapore[1]. Moreover, even though the vernacular differs significantly from Tamil, works in various Indian languages, including Irula, Baduga, Paniya, and Saurashtra, are written in Tamil. Alternatively, Tamil is a legal or leased language for most of the world's people. The Tamil script has one unique character, 12 vowels, 18 consonants, and 216 compound characters[2]. As a result, 247 Tamil characters have been created. Five consonants and a vowel were taken from Sanskrit's 12 vowels to make an extra 60 letters, totalling 307 alphabets.[3]

1.1 Tamil Language

Tamil is the mother language of most people in India's southern states. Small breakaway groups also speak the language in numerous shapes and countries, most notably in India's Kerala, geographical region, and Colombo[4].

Figure 35.1 depicts the 12 vowels and 18 constants, with the remaining 216 letters generated by combining vowels and consonants for 247 Tamil characters and 60 Sanskrit compound characters. The compound character ", for example, may be created by combining characters like +, as seen in figure 3[5]–[8].

[1]tp6695@srmist.edu.in, [2]ponmagas@srmist.edu.in

DOI: 10.1201/9781003488682-35

Tholkapyam consonants		Vowels											
		அ a	ஆ ā	இ i	ஈ ī	உ u	ஊ ū	எ e	ஏ ē	ஐ ai	ஒ o	ஓ ō	ஔ au
க்	k	க	கா	கி	கீ	கு	கூ	கெ	கே	கை	கொ	கோ	கௌ
ங்	ṅ	ங	ஙா	ஙி	ஙீ	ஙு	ஙூ	ஙெ	ஙே	ஙை	ஙொ	ஙோ	ஙௌ
ச்	c	ச	சா	சி	சீ	சு	சூ	செ	சே	சை	சொ	சோ	சௌ
ஞ்	ñ	ஞ	ஞா	ஞி	ஞீ	ஞு	ஞூ	ஞெ	ஞே	ஞை	ஞொ	ஞோ	ஞௌ
ட்	ṭ	ட	டா	டி	டீ	டு	டூ	டெ	டே	டை	டொ	டோ	டௌ
ண்	ṇ	ண	ணா	ணி	ணீ	ணு	ணூ	ணெ	ணே	ணை	ணொ	ணோ	ணௌ
த்	t	த	தா	தி	தீ	து	தூ	தெ	தே	தை	தொ	தோ	தௌ
ந்	n	ந	நா	நி	நீ	நு	நூ	நெ	நே	நை	நொ	நோ	நௌ
ப்	p	ப	பா	பி	பீ	பு	பூ	பெ	பே	பை	பொ	போ	பௌ
ம்	m	ம	மா	மி	மீ	மு	மூ	மெ	மே	மை	மொ	மோ	மௌ
ய்	y	ய	யா	யி	யீ	யு	யூ	யெ	யே	யை	யொ	யோ	யௌ
ர்	r	ர	ரா	ரி	ரீ	ரு	ரூ	ரெ	ரே	ரை	ரொ	ரோ	ரௌ
ல்	l	ல	லா	லி	லீ	லு	லூ	லெ	லே	லை	லொ	லோ	லௌ
வ்	v	வ	வா	வி	வீ	வு	வூ	வெ	வே	வை	வொ	வோ	வௌ
ழ்	ḻ	ழ	ழா	ழி	ழீ	ழு	ழூ	ழெ	ழே	ழை	ழொ	ழோ	ழௌ
ள்	ḷ	ள	ளா	ளி	ளீ	ளு	ளூ	ளெ	ளே	ளை	ளொ	ளோ	ளௌ
ற்	ṟ	ற	றா	றி	றீ	று	றூ	றெ	றே	றை	றொ	றோ	றௌ
ன்	ṉ	ன	னா	னி	னீ	னு	னூ	னெ	னே	னை	னொ	னோ	னௌ

Fig. 35.1 Tamil characters [1]

Source: https://unicode.org/charts/PDF/U0B80.pdf; https://www.tamilvu.org/en/Tamil-Keyboard-interfaces-fonts

Even though recognition is more difficult in Tamil, the intensity of the Kamba Ramayana and the extravagance in the content of Tirukkural, Silapathigaram, and palm leaf scripts attract researchers in this field, and those books are being digitalised and stored over the internet by the team called Project Madurai. In addition, the use of Tamil on numerous websites has expanded for communication purposes.

Some vowels need the consonant's structure to be changed straight from the vowel. Some are written by computing a vowel-related postfix to the vowel, but others are prefixes, and a few vowels are required to include both the prefix and the postfix inside the consonant. The vowel mark varies from the individual vowel letter in all circumstances. The Tamil language is written from left to right. Tamil photography, like Brahmic phonography, is said to have developed from Brahmi phonography. The earliest manuscripts used as examples of Tamil script come from the Ashokan period[9]. The text used in such manuscripts is known as Tamil-Brahmi or "Tamil script," and it differs from Ashokan Brahmi in several respects. In contrast to Ashokan Brahmi, the basic Tamil Brahmi featured a mechanism for distinguishing between pure consonants (m) and vowel consonants (v) (ma). According to Iravatham Mahadevan, the main Tamil Brahmi included a variety of punctuation marks and additional symbols to represent letters not found in Indo-Aryan and non-Tamil letters, such as harsh consonants and aspirates. Inscriptions from the second century employ the most current variant of Tamil-Brahmi, which is quite similar to the orthography described in Tolkppiyam[10], An ancient Tamil descriptive linguistics[11]–[13]. Fig. 35.2 depicts the Sanskrit consonants and their compound characters concerning vowels.

They employ pui(Dot) to cover up the natural vowel. Tamil letters eventually evolved into a circular form, and by the fifth or sixth century, they had evolved into the first kind. This text does not include any fashionable Tamil text. The Pallava clan devised a new Tamil script in the fourth century, and the letters Grantha emerged in it, along with the Vaeuttu alphabet for sounds not present in Sanskrit. Along with the Pallava script, a new script (Chola-Pallava script, which has been changed to modern Tamil phonography) re-emerged in the Chola area, with a similar glyptography development as the Pallava script, although it did not exist there. In Chola resp., new texts supplanted Vaeuttu by the seventh century. The Pallava empires dominated the Tamil-

Grantha consonants		Vowels											
		அ	ஆ	இ	FF	உ	ஊ	எ	ஏ	ஐ	ஒ	ஓ	ஒள
		a	ā	i	ī	u	ū	e	ē	ai	o	ō	au
ஸ்	ś	ஸ	ஸா	ஸி	ஸீ	ஸூ	ஸூ	ஸெ	ஸே	ஸை	ஸொ	ஸோ	ஸௌ
ஜ்	j	ஜ	ஜா	ஜி	ஜீ	ஜூ	ஜூ	ஜெ	ஜே	ஜை	ஜொ	ஜோ	ஜௌ
ஷ்	ṣ	ஷ	ஷா	ஷி	ஷீ	ஷூ	ஷூ	ஷெ	ஷே	ஷை	ஷொ	ஷோ	ஷௌ
ஸ்	s	ஸ	ஸா	ஸி	ஸீ	ஸூ	ஸூ	ஸெ	ஸே	ஸை	ஸொ	ஸோ	ஸௌ
ஹ்	h	ஹ	ஹா	ஹி	ஹீ	ஹூ	ஹூ	ஹெ	ஹே	ஹை	ஹொ	ஹோ	ஹௌ
க்ஷ்	kṣ	க்ஷ	க்ஷா	க்ஷி	க்ஷீ	க்ஷூ	க்ஷூ	க்ஷெ	க்ஷே	க்ஷை	க்ஷொ	க்ஷோ	க்ஷௌ

Fig. 35.2   Sanskrit characters [1]

Source: https://unicode.org/charts/PDF/U0B80.pdf; https://www.tamilvu.org/en/Tamil-Keyboard-interfaces-fonts

speaking area in the north. Vaeuttu, on the other hand, was used in the southern portion of the Tamil-speaking area, inside the kingdoms of Chera and Pandyan, until the Cholas conquered the Pandyan empire in the eleventh century. The Chola kinfolk presented the Chola-Pallava book as a real document after the Pallava kingdom fell apart. The Chola-Pallava literature evolved into a current Tamil text during the next several centuries. Grantha and her parent text have had a significant effect on Tamil literature. The use of palm leaves as a starting point for writing semiconductor diode to phonography changes. Because a leaf with a hole in it would split and deteriorate quickly, the author had to be careful not to puncture the leaves with a pen while writing. Consequently, distinguishing pure consonants became uncommon, and pure consonants were often written as if there had been a natural vowel. Similarly, the kuiyal ukaram vowel marking, a circular circle that appears at the top of bound words and inside the region between bound words combined, has been phased out in favour of a simple u-mark. Figure 35.3 depicts the procedure for producing compound characters concerning 12 vowels for a single consonant. The same is true for all 18 consonants and five Sanskrit consonants. [14]–[17]

The pui (Dot) did not return until the beginning of the print, but the mark kualiyal Karam was never used again, even though the sound remains and is important in Tamil measurements. In the nineteenth century, several characters were created to make typing simpler. In the twentieth century, photography was clarified further by adjustments that removed unique markers and strange forms from vowel hints utilised by consonants.[18]–[21]

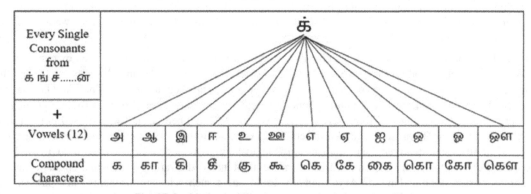

Fig. 35.3   Method of forming compound characters [1]

Source: https://unicode.org/charts/PDF/U0B80.pdf; https://www.tamilvu.org/en/Tamil-Keyboard-interfaces-fonts

Apart from its many languages, Tamil also has a small glossary of official and musical genres, known as centamil, colloquial form, koduntamil, and the word ta toth the period spent in the remarkable era was extremely distinct from a technical standpoint. As a result, the standard centamil was still in adolescence at the time of enrolment, and it was thought they had aided in the registration procedure. Centamil is often used in formal writing and speaking nowadays. It is the language of textbooks, much Tamil literature, and public speaking and debate, for example. However, koduntamil has been conquering inroads inside the Centamilian province in recent years. For example, most film series, theatres, and other forms of entertainment on television and radio are in kdduntamil, and many politicians utilise it to draw slow to them.

1.2 Tamil Scripts Unicode

Finally, given the sensitivity, it was determined that the two sentences should be categorised separately, with numerals excluded. Suggestions for coding utilised values from conventional procedures are taken into account. Despite ICTA Sri Lanka's displeasure, the proposal was approved by the Government of Tamil Nadu and included in Unicode Standard version 12.0 in March 2019. Figure 35.4 shows the Unicode Block of Tamil Supplemented with U + 11FC0 - U + 11FFF. Tamil encoding, like other South Asian Unicode publications, was initially based on ISCII standards. Tamil is encoded as abugida in both ISCII and Unicode. Each fundamental letter in abugida represents a consonant and a default vowel. The morphing letter is added to the primary character to indicate consonants with different vowels or blank consonants.[22]–[25]

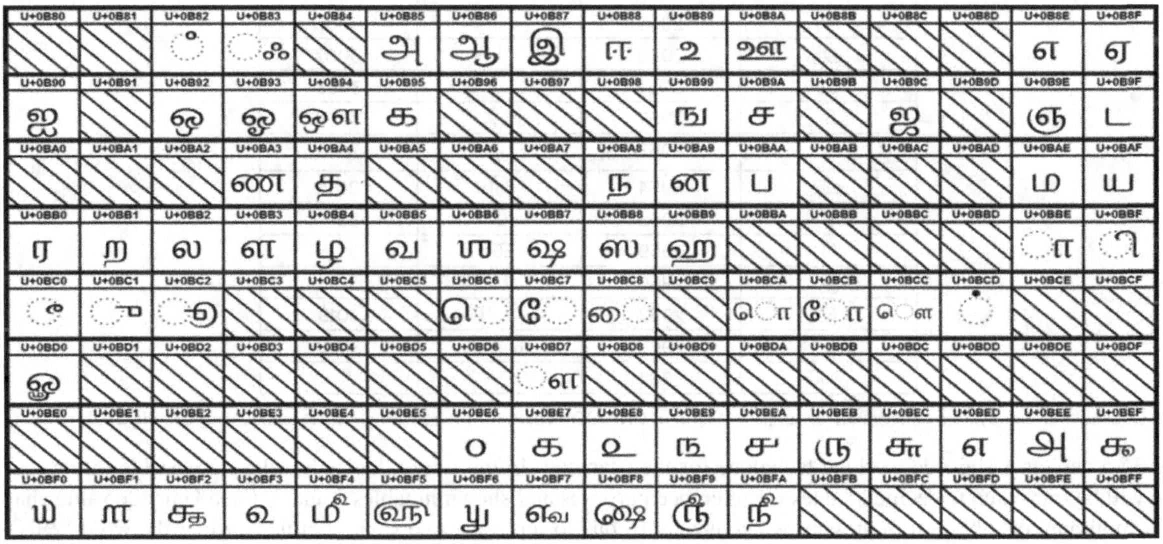

U+0B80	U+0B81	U+0B82	U+0B83	U+0B84	U+0B85	U+0B86	U+0B87	U+0B88	U+0B89	U+0B8A	U+0B8B	U+0B8C	U+0B8D	U+0B8E	U+0B8F
		◌ஂ	◌ஃ		அ	ஆ	இ	ஈ	உ	ஊ				எ	ஏ
U+0B90	U+0B91	U+0B92	U+0B93	U+0B94	U+0B95	U+0B96	U+0B97	U+0B98	U+0B99	U+0B9A	U+0B9B	U+0B9C	U+0B9D	U+0B9E	U+0B9F
ஐ		ஒ	ஓ	ஔ	க				ங	ச		ஜ		ஞ	ட
U+0BA0	U+0BA1	U+0BA2	U+0BA3	U+0BA4	U+0BA5	U+0BA6	U+0BA7	U+0BA8	U+0BA9	U+0BAA	U+0BAB	U+0BAC	U+0BAD	U+0BAE	U+0BAF
			ண	த				ந	ன	ப				ம	ய
U+0BB0	U+0BB1	U+0BB2	U+0BB3	U+0BB4	U+0BB5	U+0BB6	U+0BB7	U+0BB8	U+0BB9	U+0BBA	U+0BBB	U+0BBC	U+0BBD	U+0BBE	U+0BBF
ர	ற	ல	ள	ழ	வ	ஶ	ஷ	ஸ	ஹ					◌ா	◌ி
U+0BC0	U+0BC1	U+0BC2	U+0BC3	U+0BC4	U+0BC5	U+0BC6	U+0BC7	U+0BC8	U+0BC9	U+0BCA	U+0BCB	U+0BCC	U+0BCD	U+0BCE	U+0BCF
◌ீ	◌ு	◌ூ				ெ◌	ே◌	ை◌		ொ◌	ோ◌	ௌ◌	◌்		
U+0BD0	U+0BD1	U+0BD2	U+0BD3	U+0BD4	U+0BD5	U+0BD6	U+0BD7	U+0BD8	U+0BD9	U+0BDA	U+0BDB	U+0BDC	U+0BDD	U+0BDE	U+0BDF
ௐ							◌ௗ								
U+0BE0	U+0BE1	U+0BE2	U+0BE3	U+0BE4	U+0BE5	U+0BE6	U+0BE7	U+0BE8	U+0BE9	U+0BEA	U+0BEB	U+0BEC	U+0BED	U+0BEE	U+0BEF
						௦	௧	௨	௩	௪	௫	௬	௭	௮	௯
U+0BF0	U+0BF1	U+0BF2	U+0BF3	U+0BF4	U+0BF5	U+0BF6	U+0BF7	U+0BF8	U+0BF9	U+0BFA	U+0BFB	U+0BFC	U+0BFD	U+0BFE	U+0BFF
௰	௱	௲	௳	௴	௵	௶	௷	௸	௹	௺					

Fig. 35.4 Unicode value for Tamil character

Source: https://unicode.org/charts/PDF/U0B80.pdf; https://www.tamilvu.org/en/Tamil-Keyboard-interfaces-fonts

Eventually, because of the sensitivity, it was determined that the two texts should be classified separately, except for numerals. Suggestions for coding utilised values from conventional procedures are taken into account. Despite ICTA Sri Lanka's displeasure, the proposal was approved by the Government of Tamil Nadu and included in Unicode Standard version 12.0 in March 2019. Figure 35.4 shows the Unicode Block of Tamil Supplemented with U + 11FC0 - U + 11FFF: Tamil encoding, like other South Asian Unicode publications, was initially based on ISCII standards. Tamil is encoded as abugida in both ISCII and Unicode. Each fundamental letter in abugida represents a consonant and a default vowel. The morphing letter is added to the primary character to indicate consonants with different vowels or blank consonants.

Consonants	Vowels											
	அ 0B85	ஆ 0B86	இ 0B87	FF 0B88	உ 0B89	ஊ 0B8A	எ 0B8E	ஏ 0B8F	ஐ 0B90	ஒ 0B92	ஓ 0B93	ஔ 0B94
க் 0B95 0BCD	க 0B95	கா 0B95 0BBE	கி 0B95 0BBF	கீ 0B95 0BC0	கு 0B95 0BC1	கூ 0B95 0BC2	கெ 0B95 0BC6	கே 0B95 0BC7	கை 0B95 0BC8	கொ 0B95 0BCA	கோ 0B95 0BCB	கௌ 0B95 0BCC
ங் 0B99 0BCD	ங 0B99	ஙா 0B99 0BBE	ஙி 0B99 0BBF	ஙீ 0B99 0BC0	ஙு 0B99 0BC1	ஙூ 0B99 0BC2	ஙெ 0B99 0BC6	ஙே 0B99 0BC7	ஙை 0B99 0BC8	ஙொ 0B99 0BCA	ஙோ 0B99 0BCB	ஙௌ 0B99 0BCC

Fig. 35.5 Unicode mapping sample

Source: https://unicode.org/charts/PDF/U0B80.pdf; https://www.tamilvu.org/en/Tamil-Keyboard-interfaces-fonts

On each South Asian Unicode block, including Tamil, each point of the code representing the same phoneme is put in the same relative location. All pure consonants (consonants without matching vowels) and Tamil symbols may be rendered by mixing numerous Unicode code points, as seen in the Unicode Tamil Syllabary below. All consonants and pure Tamil letters now have word order in Unicode 5.1. Tamil ligature SRI is also included in Unicode 5.1. TAMIL SYLLABLE SHRII is the name of this sequence, which is made up of the Unicode U + 0BB6 U + 0BCD U + 0BB0 U + 0BC0 sequence.[26]–[28]

Table 35.1   Unicode in decimal numbers

Character	Unicode	Character	Unicode
ஃ	2947	்	3021
அ	2949	ா	3006
ஆ	2950	ி	3007
இ	2951	ீ	3008
ஈ	2952	ு	3009
உ	2953	ூ	3010
ஊ	2954	ெ	3014
எ	2958	ே	3015
ஏ	2959	ை	3016
ஐ	2960	ொ	3018
ஒ	2962	ோ	3019
ஓ	2963	ௌ	3020
ஔ	2964		

Source: Decimal number system conversion for representation of UNICODE value for the required characters available in Fig 35.4

Figure 35.5 depicts a Unicode working technique for the character. In the future, Unicode values accessible in hexadecimal format will be translated to decimal values for reference purposes and shown in tables 1 and 2. Each Unicode value character needs a minimum of 2 bytes to represent, which means 16 bits to represent one value. Let us consider the word "தமிழ்"; it may be viewed as just three characters, but it is in the combination of three vowels and two-character values. Lets split the word "தமிழ்" into Unicode values – த, (ம +ி),(ழ + ்). Each value needs 16 bits, so the total number of words required to represent Tamil is 5*16 = 80 bits. In contrast, translating compound characters to Sanskrit requires at least three unicode values, implying that each Unicode is 16 bits and the total size is 48 bits to represent a single Sanskrit compound letter. In the case of a composite character in Sanskrit, at least four Unicode values are required, with a minimum size of 64 bits.[29]

2. Research Gap

The standard procedure to represent the size of one Unicode is 16-bit. Let us consider an example of storing data in Unicode 16 bits format into a 1 TB hard disk; calculating the values into the number of bytes gives the calculation of 1,099,511,627,776(approximately 1 trillion). A minimum of two bytes are required to represent one Unicode 16 bits character. So, at max, only half a trillion characters can be stored inside a 1 TB hard disk. This will get more than a quarter trillion number of character if it uses the Unicode 32-bit. Discussing the best case and worst case in storing the data on the hard disk by using the Unicode-16-bit characters, the best case will be if only Tamil characters that are vowels and components are available, half a trillion characters can be represented. Illustration the worst case is if there are more Sanskrit characters and composite characters, then the storage capacity will be reduced to a quarter trillion or even more than that. The number of characters stored in a particular hard disk will be reduced by up to fifty percent on storing as Unicode-16 bit; it will again reduce yet another fifty percent while using a Unicode-32 bit.

Table 35.2   Rough calculated number of characters with respect to different Unicode style and data size

Storage size/style	Unicode-8	Unicode - 16	Unicode-32
1 KB	1024	512	256
1 MB	1 million	0.5 million	0.25 million
1 GB	1 billion	0.5 billion	0.25 billion
1 TB	1 trillion	0.5 trillion	0.25 trillion

Source: Book: File System Forensics Analysis - Brain Carrier

Table 35.2 represents the number of characters which can be described inside each data size, and the calculation increases as the data size in the real-time environment rises [30]-[34]. Thus proposing a concept or methodology to reduce the size of data concerning its Unicode-16 to a substitutional 8-bit value for the Tamil language alone. This, in turn, increases the number of characters stored in the disk space; the more the number of characters, the more the data is stored inside.

3. Tamil Character—Size Reduction Method

As discussed above, a greater number of bits is used to represent a small character. In other words, the more the character size, the less the data stored. So, to reduce the size of the character, a new algorithm TC-SRM(Tamil Character - Size Reduction Method), is being proposed, which will reduce the size of each character by more than half of its size when compared with the bit value. Let us consider that there is a separate file which consists of Tamil characters alone but has numbers, and few English characters cannot be avoided; say, for example, if the file consists of a name, the name can be written in Tamil. Still, the initiative has to be written in English only. Because if the initial in been translated into Tamil, then if it has been retranslated back to English, there is a chance it is mistranslated.

Table 35.3 Unicode in decimal numbers

Character	Unicode	Character	Unicode	Character	Unicode	Character	Unicode
க	2965	த	2980	ல	2994	ற	2998
ங	2969	ந	2984	வ	2997	ஜ	2972
ச	2970	ப	2986	ழ	2996	ஷ	2999
ஞ	2974	ம	2990	ள	2995	ஸ	3000
ட	2975	ய	2991	ன	2993	ஹ	3001
ண	2979	ர	2992	ற	2985		

Source: Decimal number system conversion for representation of UNICODE value for the required characters available in Fig 35.4

For example, the character 'த' can be mapped with both D and T. Concentrating on the Tamil meaningful words and reducing their size, an algorithm is being designed. Taking the whole Tamil character into account, along with the Sanskrit characters, there are a total of 247 (12 vowels, 18 consonants, 216 compounds, one special) and five Sanskrit characters total of 252 characters. We have not taken the count of compound characters with respect to Sanskrit for a reason which will be discussed below. Knowing the fact that bits can be represented in the count of 2,4,8,16 etc., the next near highest value of 252 (Total character) is 256(i.e. $2^8 = 256$)

So that all the 252 characters can be numbered from 0 to 251, starting with the special character, the value of decimal 0 (Binary 0000 0000), as represented in Table 35.4. Then followed by the special character vowel words are arranged as shown in Table 35.5, which follows the value from 1 to 12. After the vowel, consonants are followed, carrying the number from 13 to 30, as shown in Table 35.6; for the compound characters (216) placed from the number 31 to 246 as shown in Table 35.7, both start value and end value. Each compound character followed the order of vowel characters.

Table 35.4 Proposed TC-SRM value for special character

DEC	HEX	BIN	Character
0	00	00000000	ஂ

After the completion of all the Tamil characters, the next Sanskrit character (5) is arranged after the number 246, which will reach up to 251, as shown in Table 35.8. If the compound characters concerning Sanskrit are added, they cannot be compressed within 255. That's the reason why the Sanskrit compound character is not taken into account.

But the Sanskrit compound characters are also considered for size compression. So, the last four numbers in the list are kept as reserved for the following actions 252-Exception one, 253-Exception two, 254-Others, and 255-End. These cases will be explained when the flow chart is described, as shown in Fig. 35.6.

Before a file is transmitted, it is prefixed by a flag stating that the next upcoming characters are only Tamil characters with some exceptional cases until it gives the signal 255 (Binary 1111 1111). The original value for 255 in Unicode is "Small Latin letter y with diaeresis", which will never be used during the representation of Tamil words. The flag is set, the first character

Table 35.5 Proposed TC-SRM value for vowel

DEC	HEX	BIN	Character
1	01	00000001	அ
2	02	00000010	ஆ
3	03	00000011	இ
4	04	00000100	ஈ
5	05	00000101	உ
6	06	00000110	ஊ
7	07	00000111	எ
8	08	00001000	ஏ
9	09	00001001	ஐ
10	0A	00001010	ஒ
11	0B	00001011	ஓ
12	0C	00001100	ஒள

Table 35.6 Proposed TC-SRM value for consonant

DEC	HEX	BIN	Character
13	0D	00001101	க
14	0E	00001110	ங
15	0F	00001111	ச
16	10	00010000	ஞ
17	11	00010001	ட
18	12	00010010	ண
19	13	00010011	த
20	14	00010100	ந
21	15	00010101	ப
22	16	00010110	ம
23	17	00010111	ய
24	18	00011000	ர
25	19	00011001	ல
26	1A	00011010	வ
27	1B	00011011	ழ
28	1C	00011100	ள
29	1D	00011101	ற
30	1E	00011110	ன

Table 35.7 Proposed TC-SRM value for compound (Start value)

DEC	HEX	BIN	Character
31	IF	00011111	க்
32	20	00100000	ங்
33	21	00100001	ச்
34	22	00100010	ஞ்
35	23	00100011	ட்
36	24	00100100	ண்
37	25	00100101	த்
38	26	00100110	ந்
39	27	00100111	ப்
40	28	00101000	ம்
41	29	00101001	ய்
42	2A	00101010	ர்
43	2B	00101011	ல்
44	2C	00101100	வ்
45	2D	00101101	ழ்
46	2E	00101110	ள்
47	2F	00101111	ற்
48	30	00110000	ன்

Table 35.8 Proposed TC-SRM value for compound (End value)

DEC	HEX	BIN	Character
229	E5	11100101	கௌ
230	E6	11100110	ஙௌ
231	E7	11100111	சௌ
232	E8	11101000	ஞௌ
233	E9	11101001	டௌ
234	EA	11101010	ணௌ
235	EB	11101011	தௌ
236	EC	11101100	நௌ
237	ED	11101101	பௌ
238	EE	11101110	மௌ
239	EF	11101111	யௌ
240	FO	11110000	ரௌ
241	F1	11110001	லௌ
242	F2	11110010	வௌ
243	F3	11110011	ழௌ
244	F4	11110100	ளௌ
245	F5	11110101	றௌ
246	F6	11110110	னௌ

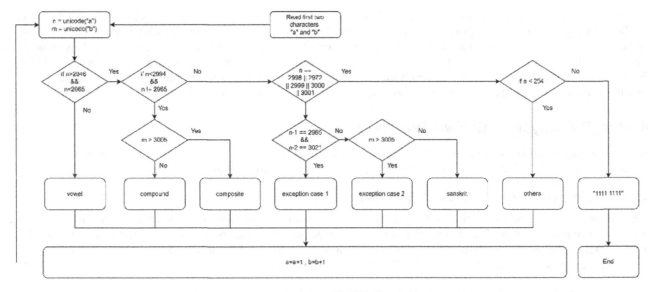

Fig. 35.6 Flowchart for the proposed algorithm TC-SRM (Tamil character – Size reduction method)

Unicode value is assigned as 'n', and the next Unicode value is taken as 'm'. Check that 'n' belongs to which major type, either vowel, consonant, or special character. If the character in 'n' is a vowel or special character, there is no postfix available to it. Table 35.9 is called, and the respective character value is selected. Then the position of 'n' and 'm' is changed to 'n + 1' and 'm + 1'.

Table 35.9 Proposed TC-SRM value for Sanskrit and exception cases

DEC	HEX	BIN	Character
247	F7	11110111	ய
248	F8	11111000	ஜ
249	F9	11111001	வ
250	FA	11111010	ஸ
251	FB	11111011	ஷ
252	FC	11111100	Exception 1
253	FD	11111101	Exception 2
254	FE	11111110	Others
255	FF	11111111	End

Suppose the Unicode value of 'n' belongs to a consonant. In that case, there comes a condition either it is postfixed or not, so to check that the value of 'm' is evaluated in case the 'm' is not a component symbol, then the respective consonant value has selected the position of 'n' and 'm' is changed to 'n+1' and 'm+1', but if 'm' is a compound symbol then the respective character is mapped from the consonant and postfix of vowel then checked in the proposed algorithm table and selected the respective value. Then the position of 'n' and 'm' is changed to 'n+2' and 'm+2'So far have just explained about the Tamil characters only, now the Sanskrit characters are considered; when the Sanskrit character does not come with any postfix, then the same if referred in the proposed table and selected, the position of 'n' and 'm' is changed to 'n+1' and 'm+1'.

When the Sanskrit words are having postfix of vowels, then comes the exceptional part. If the Sanskrit character is with postfix but without the prefix, then exception one is followed, which is the 252 signal is selected, and the next 36-bit binary value is considered as Unicode value, and after the 36 bit the value of the proposed algorithm will be considered, then the position of 'n' and 'm' is changed to 'n+2' and 'm+2'. If there is a prefix and a postfix, then the positions of 'n' and 'm' change. Initially, the position of 'n' and 'm' will be changed to 'n-2' and 'm-2' then the exception two data will be sent, which is 253. The last stored value will be removed and replaced with 253 mostly; the last detected value will be '31'. Once the 253 signal is received, the next 48 bits are the original Unicode value, followed by the proposed value.

Now the position of 'n' and 'm' is changed to 'n + 4' and 'm + 4'. Others are a case where characters who do not belong to the Tamil language are mostly symbols like ?,{,},@,%,(,), etc. English alphabets or numbers which fall in the Unicode value range 0 to 255, which is 8 bits in binary. When signal 254 is received, the next 8 bits will be the Unicode value. This proposed algorithm will end only if the position of 'n or 'm' reaches the document's end and sends the signal as 255 (binary 1111 1111). To reverse the received data back to the original Unicode values, the same process is repeated in a vice-versa manner; that is, with the received character, the corresponding vowels and consonants are formed and printed on the screen.

4. Result Analysis with Two Examples

The proposed algorithm TC-SRM is compared with the normal Unicode value size with two examples. On comparing the whole Tamil characters along with the Sanskrit character and then is to compare with just Tamil characters.

4.1 Example 1: (Tamil Characters with Sanskrit)

Considering the whole character in the Tamil language, both Tamil characters and Sanskrit characters are taken into account. In that case, there is a total of 260 Tamil characters along with 216 additional characters s, which range from the Unicode value 3006 to 3021, as the same 78 Sanskrit characters are used along with the special characters of 85. Thus the total number of bits required to represent the whole set is about 10224 bits (9.98Kb), as shown in Table 35.10.

Table 35.10 Bit size evaluation for whole alphabets

Unicode bit representation(Whole alphabets)			
	Total character	Bit for each	Minimum bit
uir & mei	260	16	4160
uirmei(tamil)	216	16	3456
sanscrit	78	16	1248
uirmei(sanscrit)	85	16	1360
Total			**10224**
Proposed TC-SRM bit representation(Whole alphabets)			
	Total character	Bit for each	Minimum bit
uir & mei	247	8	1976
sanscrit	91	16	1456
uirmei(sanscrit)	85	16	1360
Total			**4792**

When the same set of characters is represented in the proposed algorithm, the minimum number of bits required to represent is 4792 bits (4.43Kb). Size reduction is made up to 53.12percentage, as shown in Table 35.11.

Table 35.11 Size compressed for whole alphabets

Type	Bits	Size
Unicode representation	10224	53.12% reduced
TC-SRM representation	4792	

4.2 Example 2: (Tamil Characters Only)

In this example, we consider only the Tamil characters alone, just the 247 characters alone. To represent those 247 characters with the help of Unicode values, it needs 260 Tamil characters and 216 additional characters, so the minimum size required to represent the character is 7616 bits (7.43 Kb). Representing the same above 247 Tamil characters in the proposed algorithm is 1976 bits (1.92Kb); thus, the data size is reduced up to 74 percent, which is nearly just a quarter size of the original data as shown in Table 35.12 and Table 35.13.

Table 35.12 Bit size evaluation for tamil alphabet alone

Unicode bit representation (Tamil alone)			
	Total character	Bit for each	Minimum bit
uir & mei	260	16	4160
uirmei(tamil)	216	16	3456
Total			7616
Proposed TC-SRM bit representation (Tamil alone)			
	Total character	Bit for each	Minimum bit
uir & mei	247	8	1976
Total			1976

Table 35.13 Size compressed for whole alphabets

Type	Bits	Size
Unicode representation	7616	74.05% reduced
TC-SRM representation	1976	

The proposed algorithm will help reduce the file's size to more than half its original size, so it will surely increase the number of data stored in the storage.

5. Conclusion

Using this Tamil Character—size reduction method, the Unicode 16-bit is converted into an 8-bit representation. Using this method, the size of the data is reduced with the best case of seventy-four percent and the worst chance of up to fifty percent. This comparison shows that when the character's size is reduced, the left-out space can be used for a more significant number of storage. As discussed above, the entire storage potential is effectively used up to its hundred percent. This method is now only proposed for storage purposes since, in the automation world, all hand-written documents are converted into digital format. To store the data in the proposed method, massive data is located in a single disk space which will also be useful for administrative controls. TC-SRM mainly focus on the regional language Tamil, as it is one of the Unicode 16-bit representation characters. This research on size reduction can be carried out in any language which falls under the Unicode 16-bit or even for Unicode 32-bit.

REFERENCES

1. N. Shaffi and F. Hajamohideen, "UTHCD: A New Benchmarking for Tamil Handwritten OCR," *IEEE Access*, vol. 9, pp. 101469–101493, 2021, doi: 10.1109/ACCESS.2021.3096823.
2. T. RUDRAPATHY, C. S. RUDRAPATHY, and D. KUMAR, "TAMIL EḶUTTU VARIVAṬIVA CĪRAMAIPPU [TAMIL SCRIPT REFORM]," *Muallim Journal of Social Science and Humanities*, pp. 126–133, Jul. 2021, doi: 10.33306/mjssh/144.
3. "AN ANALYSIS ABOUT SYMBOLS IN TAMIL BRAHMI INSCRIPTIONS," 2020. [Online]. Available: https://www.researchgate.net/publication/343345473
4. A. C, "Tamil Literary dictionaries - the need and uses of Encyclopedia," *International Research Journal of Tamil*, vol. 2, no. 3, pp. 39–51, May 2020, doi: 10.34256/irjt2034.
5. M. Munivel and V. S. Felix Enigo, "Optical Character Recognition for Printed Tamizhi Documents using Deep Neural Networks," *DESIDOC Journal of Library and Information Technology*, vol. 42, no. 4, pp. 227–233, Jul. 2022, doi: 10.14429/djlit.42.4.17742.
6. S. Athisayamani, A. R. Singh, and T. Athithan, "Recognition of Ancient Tamil Palm Leaf Vowel Characters in Historical Documents using B-spline Curve Recognition," in *Procedia Computer Science*, 2020, vol. 171, pp. 2302–2309. doi: 10.1016/j.procs.2020.04.249.
7. A. V and S. G. S, "Lexical Theoretical Development in Applied Tamil Grammar Texts," *International Research Journal of Tamil*, vol. 4, no. S-18, pp. 7–19, Dec. 2022, doi: 10.34256/irjt224s182.
8. P. T and S. L, "Guidance to Transcription in Tamil Language with Reference to Tamil Grammar Texts," *International Research Journal of Tamil*, vol. 4, no. S-8, pp. 28–47, Jun. 2022, doi: 10.34256/irjt22s85.
9. N. M, "Language changes in Tamil due to Dravidianism," *International Research Journal of Tamil*, vol. 4, no. S-5, pp. 201–206, Aug. 2022, doi: 10.34256/irjt22s531.

10. S. THIRUNAVUKKARASU, "TAMIL ILAKKANAC CIRAPPUKAL [SPECIALTY IN TAMIL GRAMMAR]," *Muallim Journal of Social Science and Humanities*, pp. 10–16, Oct. 2021, doi: 10.33306/mjssh/155.

11. A. Radha and P. Gp, "International Journal of Tamil Language and Literary Studies History View project Archaeology and History View project", doi: 10.5281/zenodo.3628534.

12. A. Prof, Thivaharan S, and Srivatsun G, "A PROCEDURAL STUDY ON MORPHOLOGICAL ANALYZERS FOR TAMIL LANGUAGE USING THE LEXICAL-SURFACE RULE BASED CORRESPONDENCES," *Article in International Journal of Scientific Research*, 2021, doi: 10.24327/ijrsr.2020.1108.4595.

13. R. Niels and L. Vuurpijl, "Dynamic time warping applied to tamil character recognition," in *Proceedings of the International Conference on Document Analysis and Recognition, ICDAR*, 2005, vol. 2005, pp. 730–734. doi: 10.1109/ICDAR.2005.96.

14. N. M, "Language changes in Tamil due to Dravidianism," *International Research Journal of Tamil*, vol. 4, no. S-5, pp. 201–206, Aug. 2022, doi: 10.34256/irjt22s531.

15. S. Athisayamani, A. R. Singh, and T. Athithan, "Recognition of Ancient Tamil Palm Leaf Vowel Characters in Historical Documents using B-spline Curve Recognition," in *Procedia Computer Science*, 2020, vol. 171, pp. 2302–2309. doi: 10.1016/j.procs.2020.04.249.

16. S. R. R and M. S. M, "Tamil Character Recognition in Palm Leaf Manuscripts," *International Research Journal of Tamil*, vol. 3, no. 2, pp. 70–77, Apr. 2021, doi: 10.34256/irjt21210.

17. A. Professor, "Performance Analysis of Text To Speech Synthesis System Using HMM And Prosody Features With Parsing For Tamil Language," *International Research Journal of Engineering and Technology*, 2016, [Online]. Available: https://www.researchgate.net/publication/331801601

18. T. Thendral, M. S. Vijaya, and S. Karpagavalli, "Analysis of Tamil character writings and identification of writer using Support Vector Machine," in *Proceedings of 2014 IEEE International Conference on Advanced Communication, Control and Computing Technologies, ICACCCT 2014*, Jan. 2015, pp. 1407–1411. doi: 10.1109/ICACCCT.2014.7019332.

19. B. R. Kavitha and C. Srimathi, "Benchmarking on offline Handwritten Tamil Character Recognition using convolutional neural networks," *Journal of King Saud University - Computer and Information Sciences*, vol. 34, no. 4, pp. 1183–1190, Apr. 2022, doi: 10.1016/j.jksuci.2019.06.004.

20. Mrs. R. Iyswarya, S. Deepak, P. Jagathratchagan, and J. Kailash, "Handwritten Tamil Character Recognition Using Convolution Neural Network by Adam Optimizer," *International Journal of Advanced Research in Science, Communication and Technology*, pp. 40–45, Jun. 2021, doi: 10.48175/ijarsct-1356.

21. G. Devi S, S. Vairavasundaram, Y. Teekaraman, R. Kuppusamy, and A. Radhakrishnan, "A Deep Learning Approach for Recognizing the Cursive Tamil Characters in Palm Leaf Manuscripts," *Comput Intell Neurosci*, vol. 2022, 2022, doi: 10.1155/2022/3432330.

22. M. H. Changrampadi, A. Shahina, M. Badri Narayanan, and A. Nayeemulla Khan, "End-to-end speech recognition of tamil language," *Intelligent Automation and Soft Computing*, vol. 32, no. 2, pp. 1309–1323, 2022, doi: 10.32604/iasc.2022.022021.

23. K. Sarveswaran, G. Dias, and M. Butt, "ThamizhiMorph: A morphological parser for the Tamil language," *Machine Translation*, vol. 35, no. 1, pp. 37–70, Apr. 2021, doi: 10.1007/s10590-021-09261-5.

24. T. FERNANDAZ SELVAMANY, "TAMILMOLIK KARRAL KARPITTAL [TAMIL LANGUAGE TEACHING AND LEARNING]," *Muallim Journal of Social Science and Humanities*, pp. 69–73, Jan. 2022, doi: 10.33306/mjssh/178.

25. A. G. Ramakrishnan, "Why script reform in Tamil is not desirable Medical Signal Processing View project Speaker and background change detection View project," 2016. [Online]. Available: https://www.researchgate.net/publication/346646667

26. A. Professor, "Performance Analysis of Text To Speech Synthesis System Using HMM And Prosody Features With Parsing For Tamil Language," *International Research Journal of Engineering and Technology*, 2016, [Online]. Available: https://www.researchgate.net/publication/331801601

27. S. N, "Effect of Regional Dialects in Learning Tamil Language," *International Research Journal of Tamil*, vol. 4, no. S-9, pp. 1–6, Jul. 2022, doi: 10.34256/irjt22s91.

28. N. Zaynalov, Uk. Narzullaev, A. Muhamadieva, I. Rahmatullaev, and R. Buranova, "Combining Invisible Unicode Characters to Hide Information in a Text Document."

29. B. S. Castro and J. J. Jose, "Modified Vigenere Cipher Employing Unicode Tamil Characters," 2019. [Online]. Available: www.iosrjen.org

Advances in Computational Intelligence and its Applications (ICACIA-2023) – Dr. Sheikh Fahad Ahmad et al. (eds)
© 2024 Taylor & Francis Group, London, ISBN 978-1-032-78612-4

Stochastic Modelling and Real Time Solution for SCPP Problem for the Internet of Vehicles (IoV)

36

Divya Lanka[1]

Research Scholar,
Puducherry Technological University

Selvaradjou Kandasamy[2]

Professor,
Puducherry Technological University

ABSTRACT—The SDN controller placement problem is a crucial part of the SDN Controllers for provisioning the bandwidth, resources to the requesting nodes. In addition, the Internet of Vehicles is too dynamic where the vehicles exchange information between them and with the Road Side Units (RSU) rapidly and hence they need fast, secure and best bandwidth utilization which are provisioned by the SDN Controllers. Such controllers need to be placed in correct location so all vehicles in the network can be provisioned by the controllers. This paper provides a comprehensive review of various SDN controller placement problems (SCPP) and the strategies followed for controller placement. This study also surveys various performance metrics used for the controller placement problem for the internet of vehicles. In this paper we propose a stochastic modelling technique using reinforcement learning for bandwidth provisioning and to apply real time algorithms to handle dynamic vehicular traffic. This study has a learning state where best bandwidth management was obtained compared to other policies.

KEYWORDS—Internet of vehicles, software defined networks, controller placement problem, reinforcement learning.

1. Introduction

The technical revolution in the present days has a wide spread across all activities. Devices that are smart and connected are proliferating day by day. By 2025, Internet of Things (IoT) devices may reach to 70 billion. Industries and cities are fetching many advantages with smart-connected things. Smart Intelligent Transportation Systems (SITS) are paving ways many new applications. SITS enables citizens with innovative applications for better traffic management, logistics, low cost and safe transport with intelligent, coordinated IoT devices and faster communication technologies like 5G, 6G. Internet of Vehicles (IoV) is derived from Internet of Things (IoT) and Vehicular Adhoc Networks (VANET). IoV eases the communication between autonomous vehicles and Road Side Units (RSU) over the internet. The communication in IoV should be dynamic as the vehicles mi-grates with a fast pace. Centralized management of IoV is a hectic job that needs a strict attention to make communication feasible.

Managing vast networks with centralized network control becomes difficult with the growth of IoT networks. Software Defined Network (SDN) provides a soft-ware control, Application Programming Interfaces (API), decentralized network control for the underlying IoT network. SDN controls the network by removing dedicated switches, routers and controls network through software. SDN sepa-rates the data layer and control layer that provides more control, flexibility and high network throughput [1],

[1]divya44@ptuniv.edu.in, [2]selvaraj@ptuniv.edu.in

DOI: 10.1201/9781003488682-36

[2], [3]. Data plane is responsible for data forwarding, multicasting, and segmentation of data. Control plane is responsible for generating routes, framing rules, flow table formation and data forwarding policies. The data is sent from nodes to switches, then the switch will forward packets based on flow table information given by controller. In the view of autonomous communication and connectivity in IoV, SDN can serve better to cater the needs of IoV. Adopting SDN technology in IoV handles varying data traffic and mobility of vehicles well. SDN decouples control and data planes and supports communication between the planes using north bound, south bound Application Programming Interfaces (API) as shown in Fig. 36.1. In SDN, controllers plays a prominent role to real time communication between the vehicles, RSUs, cloud and infrastructure.

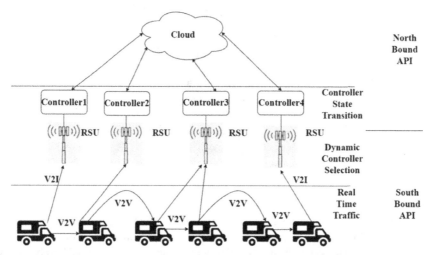

Fig. 36.1 Internet of vehicles coupled with software defined network [9]

The IoV control and management were handled by SDN controller. SDN controller provides bandwidth to IoV and faster communication to IoV when placed properly. The control plane in SDN handle all the packets arriving from the data plane. The controller determines the flow rules for devices in data plane. Hence, efficient load balancing, proper placement of SDN controllers and finding optimal number of controllers triggers the working of SDN controllers. The main attention in the recent days is finding the optimal placement the controllers, how the controllers provision the bandwidth to the vehicles and how securely the controllers perform the communication. This paper gives an elaborate view on SDN Controller Placement Problem (SCPP), various methodologies proposed to handle SCPP and what metrics are required to optimize the SDN controller utilization. SCPP is considered as a NP Hard problem that requires at most optimization to get the exact location to place the controllers. Energy cost, reliability, path sustainability, link failures, load of SDN controllers, reliability, latency and high utilization of controller functionalities are various quality of service issues for SCPP problem. SCPP is a recent thrust area, where the networks are moving towards distributed control management. SDN controller plays a prominent role in SDN to handle the data volumes from the data plane and then transmit to cloud and applications. Earlier the researchers had worked upon SCPP and proposed various SCPP solutions to locate exact controller positions, to find number of controllers required and link quality between controllers and switches.

In software defined IoV, the vehicles join the network at any time and leave the network at any time. To manage huge volumes of vehicular data, vehicles (switches) in data plane should connect through reliable links to the controller. A single controller cannot manage the mobile nodes, IoV environment requires multiple controllers. Assigning the switches carefully to controllers, designing flow rules for data switches, link quality, path reliability, controller load and proper bandwidth utilization are the factors that impact the performance of SDN for IoV. Most of the existing works were performed on latency and capacity of SDN controller. To maintain all the SDN Key Performance Indicators (KPI) like bandwidth provisioning, load balancing, latency, energy cost, delay, jitter, reliability: placement of controllers and determining the locations of controllers are directly proportional to the controller's performance. It is also observed that only few existing works experimented with multiple objectives in SCPP [4], [5], [20].

Considering a network with n number of nodes and m number of SDN controllers where (m<n) requires multi objectives to find the optimal number of controllers and location of controllers. Solving SCPP problem with a single objective may not give the optimal location of controllers. At the same time, single controller cannot handle high density networks and the dynamic

traffic in real-time. Probability and conditional probability based mathematical models were not ideal solutions for estimating the failure probability for multiple controllers. The authors in [25] mentioned that betweenness centrality principle and decision making methods were best suitable for SCPP in finding SCPP problems. The betweenness centrality principle detects the switch influence in the traffic flow towards SDN controller.

The contributions of the work are

1. A comprehensive survey and various metrics studied on SCPP problems were reviewed in this work.
2. We modelled the SDN controller based on reinforcement learning for bandwidth management.
3. To handle dynamic data, real time algorithms were implemented to select the controllers depending upon their load.
4. Simulations are carried out such that SDN controllers objectives like latency, load balance, link quality, bandwidth provisioning were converged.

The rest of the paper is as follows. We presented the related research in section-2, proposed methodology in section-3 and conclusion in section-4.

2. Literature Review

Solutions to SCPP in literature relates SCPP as a NP hard problem that includes methodologies like involving multi SDN controllers to overcome single point failures and to cover large networks, partitioning the network, bio inspired solutions, and simulated annealing. Most of the works were done on SDN wide area networks, IoV and IoT. Various methods were proposed in the existing research using network partitions, thermo dynamic theories, game theory optimizations.

2.1 Clustering Methods and Genetic Algorithms

The authors Chen et al. [1] divided the networks into partitions based on the den-sity and then placed the controllers by examining the propagation delay but they did not consider the load on the controllers that might cause congestion on the links between switches and controllers. Qi et al. also partitioned the network based on density that focused on reducing the latency. The authors formed the sub networks by finding the centrality of closeness between switches and controllers in sub network. This work had outperformed compared to k-means by 35 % and k-means optimized version by 10% [28]. Sminesh et al. explored about non parametric clustering because normal clustering algorithms need a lot of controllers up on partitioning the network. The work focused on minimizing latency and load balancing through reformed density peak clustering algorithm. The drawback of the work is to consider real time controllers load, resilience and congestion at switch to controller links [30].

Angelo et al. [2] implemented genetic evolutionary algorithm for controller placement. Instead of replacement of SDN controller, the authors has taken reassignment of SDN controllers by including interactions with controllers and link failures. Amin et al. [3] concerned that SCPP as a NP hard problem and solved it using garter snake optimization method and controller statistics to find the number of controllers required in the network. The authors performed multi linear regression and statistical analysis to predict the delays from switch to controllers and controllers to switch. To map the garter snakes to controllers the authors used the controller features like load and ports supported. Variable traffic and dynamic nature of IoT are not considered. Amin et al., Saeed et al. and Alouache et al. [4] [5] [6] examined multiple objectives using genetic algorithms to handle SCPP for in-band mode of communication. Objectives like hop count, latency, controller load, reliability of routes between switch to controller and controller to controller were taken into account to find the location of controller. Adekoya et al. [6] proposed genetic algorithm and particle swarm optimization technique for multi objective controller placement in SDN. The authors worked on scalability by hyper volume measure that includes diversity, convergence with pareto search. Another work that worked on pareto search was given in [27] implemented in MATlab that says that time and accuracy are reciprocal to each other. The proposed method has faster execution times and low accuracy in regard to memory need and cost. This work achieved improved result with fast execution times in huge and dynamic networks.

2.2 Fog and Mobile Computing in SDN

Herrera et al. worked for fog nodes placement in SDN. The authors used unsupervised clustering techniques to reduce latency and time in Industrial IoT and SDN networks. The authors found the initial medoids first and later medoids were modified using random selection, cluster head selection and centrality points. After cluster formulation, the hosts can select the minimal latency fog node for transmission by assigning priorities for host (traffic flow). This work is not multi objective and did not considered reliability, fault tolerance [18].

Pokhrel et al. proposed to introduce mobile base stations with SDN features for IoV. This proposal can provide security, increase scalability of network and flexibility. The authors used intent based methods and mathematics to integrate SDN and IoV. The authors developed security mechanism with policies to get controller services for the vehicles. With this security mechanism the nodes were separated as guest and authenticated nodes. Guest nodes can only access the internal resources but authenticated services can access internal resources, controller services and the internet. For every incoming flow, it matches with policy framework and then only a data flow is accepted or rejected [17]. The developed algorithm is not executed across multiple SDN controllers in machine learning.

Zhai et al. offloaded some tasks in IoV to fog nodes considering energy consumption. The battery power is taken as weight factor to achieve energy optimization. The authors developed a heuristic algorithm to fing the optimal node for task offloading but may give optimal solution all the times. This work also incur some overload when migrating between the applications and was not experimented on real time fog environment [18]. Xu et al. mentioned that using edge computing services in IoV may reveal the sensitive information like location information, driver information and vehicle parameters. Hence, the authors developed a secure service mechanism in edge computing based SDN-IoV scenarios. The authors focused on energy utilization, latency and load balancing with privacy preserving. The authors developed a location-privacy based service model with hashing to attain Quality of Experience (QoE) metrics. The developed model is not tested under real data traffic [19].

2.3 Game Theory and Reinforcement Learning

Placing the controllers at farther distances from data plane introduce the communications delay. Placing the controllers close to the data plane reduce the delay. Controller placement in hierarchical way at internet and at RSU's reduce the delay better when compared to centralized placement of controllers [7]. Placing controller for subset of switches with energy aware and considering dynamic IoT traffic is specified in [8]. The authors considered in band SDN control plane and link activation considering IoV data to control SDN controller congestion and overload. The authors partitioned the network using coalition game theory and then routed the data to controller by selecting links with less energy consumption. The links were activated and deactivated upon the usage and the data traffic. The authors assigned ranks for placing the switches in the data plane. The main limitation with the work is the authors did-not considered the mobility of nodes in IoT that might have a serious effect on the membership in coalition game theory. Implementing mobile edge computing along with SDN suits best for IoV environment given by Li et al. [9]. In this work the authors observed the delay, balancing load of controller and route reliability. The authors used Q learning to specify the states and actions for edge controllers and domain controllers to know the position of root SDN controller. The switches (agents) select the controllers depending on the controllers load. The main limitation is that energy aware link selection is not considered.

Software defined IoV is also used for controlling accidents in vehicular environment by detecting drivers who feel drowsy while driving. Saleh et al. pro-posed that using edge computing in IoV can detect sleepy drivers within less period of time when comparing with standard computing methods. The authors considered the features like behavioral, biological and automobile for drowsiness assessment. Acceleration of pedals, heartbeat, working of brain, expressions and steering direction are parameters involved to detect exact driver drowsiness. This work worked well using mobile edge computing and machine learning techniques than the other works. The drawback of work is a single controller cannot handle huge volumes of data and requires multi-level controllers to handle IoV traffic [17]. Petale et al. used decision making techniques for problems with uncertainty like MAXIMAX, Betweenness principality, Horwicz criterion for finding optimal controller locations that have minimum latency in dynamic traffic conditions. The authors stated that installing multi controllers can reduce link failures with low latency and also mentioned that probabilistic methods were not suitable for SCPP problem to find the failure rate of controllers. The authors proved that decision making techniques were good at allocating the switches to the controllers examining the capacity at the controllers. The authors also tested their proposed method in MININET to test the scalability under various topologies like dense and sparse topologies. The authors achieved better controller placement in terms of resource optimization, less memory usage and latency. The authors determined that a single solution is not feasible in all situations as network size, density vary for all networks that effects the network management [25].

2.4 Meta Heuristic and Bio Inspired Algorithms

Bio inspired techniques are derived from biological creatures like ants, birds and fish etc. These features suite for dense networks for routing optimizations and SDN controller placement. Ant colony, particle swarm and genetic algorithms are various algorithms used in literature for SCPP problem. Simulated annealing is a heuristic approach that helps to find an optimal solution when there is discrete search space. Neamah et al. [10] pro-posed simulated annealing method to enhance the efficiency with multiple SDN controllers. The authors considered the distance from switch to controller and transmission time for transmissions. The authors did not con-sider the mobility of nodes and dynamic traffic. Another effort in the direction of simulated annealing was given in [26] using network function virtualization. This work has taken controller resilience as SCPP, then applied simulated annealing and then discovers optimal controller location. In this attempt the authors assumed that controller, switches and network functions were executed on same machine. At a time only one functionality will be active and a switch can be converted into controller upon the requirement. The calculations were distributed to both switches and controllers to reduce the cost and enhance the reliability. This work employs Dijkstra's and Floyd warshall algorithms to route the data to the controller from switches. This work has achieved minimum latency, cost and high reliability. This work was restricted for single controller resilience and need to be tested on different topologies.

Soleymanifar et al. worked on placement of controller in real time depending upon the traffic from the data plane [21]. Firouz et al. implemented swarm optimization technique for SCPP to achieve more convergence and reduced propagation delay. The authors implemented manta ray foraging techniques for finding best cluster heads after forming the SDN nodes to clusters. Then the data is forwarded using dijkstras's routing algorithm. This investigation needs more processor time and memory [22]. Tahmasebi et al. presented that controller placement using CUCKOO optimization method is a meta heuristic approach which was bio inspired by nature. The authors aimed to minimize latency with optimal controller placement. They proved that the method had performed well compared with linear programming and annealing techniques. The limitation of the work is that they did not consider multiple objectives and did not focused on increasing network performance, cost and overhead for controller to controller coordination [29].

2.5 Summary of Existing Works

The literature review is compared and summarized in Table 36.1 that was built considering the existing works.

Table 36.1   Comparison of literature work [9]

References		[1]	[2]	[3]	[4]	[5]	[6]	[7]	[10]	[19]	[20]	[21]	[22]
SCPP		✓	✓	✓	✓	✓	✓	✓	✓		✓		✓
Dynamic Traffic			✓		✓			✓	✓	✓	✓		
Multi Objective					✓	✓	✓		✓		✓		
Multiple controllers					✓	✓	✓	✓	✓	✓	✓		✓
Real-time SCPP												✓	
Integrated Technologies with SDN	Edge /Fog Computing									✓	✓		
	Bio Inspired			✓			✓		✓				✓
	Intent Based						✓						
	Quadratic Programming							✓					
	Clustering	✓										✓	
	Evolutionary		✓		✓	✓	✓						
Key Quality metrics	Latency	✓				✓		✓					
	Reliability		✓		✓				✓				
	Load balance		✓			✓		✓			✓		✓
	Bandwidth provisioning												
	Energy cost							✓			✓	✓	
	Delay	✓			✓		✓						✓
	Scalability									✓			
	Cost									✓	✓	✓	
	Time			✓	✓		✓			✓	✓		
	Hop count				✓								
	Availability				✓								
	Throughput									✓			

3. Proposed Methodology

SCPP can be handled carefully by implementing reinforcement learning. With reinforcement learning the SDN controller can be carefully designed in such a way to connect to a subset of vehicles on a specific path. The controller can transit between the various states to provide services with careful bandwidth provisioning and minimum latency. Limiting the bandwidth utilization can cut off energy price and energy consumption.

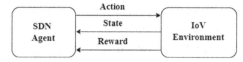

Fig. 36.2 Reinforcement learning in SDN [31]

In software defined IoV, reinforcement learning helps SDN controller how to perform actions in an IoV environment as shown in Fig. 36.2. This enables the SDN controller how to handle the variable requests coming from the vehicles from data plane by state transitions. Semi Markov Decision Process is used in our proposed work to best suite with IoV scenarios as they are of discrete time and achieves optimized learning. The SDN controller transits between the initial, active and learning states. The main objectives of the research are:

1. Designing state transitions using SMDP for SDN controllers
2. Implementing reinforcement learning to solve SMDP problem
3. Framing data flow rules and policies for controller
4. Then finding the optimal locations and count of controllers to solve SCPP.

The flow chart in Fig. 36.3. Specifies the controller learning process using Q learning. Firstly, initialize the Q factor table with random values. Then the learning process starts, for every action, there is a state transition and a reward is associated with it. Select the action with highest reward. Then apply the Q-function to adjust the reward. Then transit to the next state. If the terminate state is not reached then again select the action with highest reward. If the controller reaches terminate state and learning process is completed then form the Q-table with optimal values. If terminate state is met and learning process is not met then again choose the start the learning process.

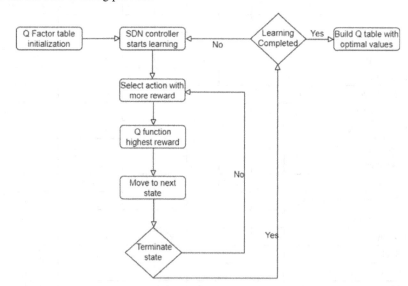

Fig. 36.3 Flow chart for SDN controller learning process using Q learning [32]

After the Q-factor table formulation, the best SDN controller states are related to the controller bandwidth allocation policies. Three polices may handle various bandwidth requests like first policy serves normal incoming traffic, second policy allocates bandwidth on the request and third policy allocates the bandwidth dynamically depending upon the application. Hence with

Q-learning the SDN controller is modelled to carefully handle the incoming requests from vehicles. A single controller cannot handle all the incoming requests from the vehicles in IoV scenarios. So, we propose to use multiple controllers to satisfy the re-quests from the data plane. But, a proper placement of controller plays utmost importance in SCPP. So as to balance the load between controllers, to minimize the request processing latency the location of controllers is also important. Determining the number of controllers and allocating controllers dynamically to the data plane nodes play a prominent role to solve the SCPP problem. In IoV the data requests servicing time is stringent and requests are raised dynamically. Hence they need real time scheduling algorithms for IoV.

For multi SDN controllers IoV task allocation, we propose to implement RMA (Next-Fit) algorithm and EDF (Bin packing) for static task allocation and FAB algorithm for dynamic allocation. To allocate real-time vehicle request to multiple SDN controllers, the vehicles first register with the RSU's, then the controller allocation is made before processing the request by the controller. In RMA (Next fit) the vehicle requests are processed based the controller utilization by the tasks. Then each request is assigned to the controller with less utilization. If the number of SDN controllers are fixed then this algorithm works well. In RMA (next fit) all the vehicle requests are grouped to classes based on the vehicle re-quest controller utilization and the partitions are assigned to each SDN controller. The algorithm executes the requests with similar controller utilization are processed by the same controller. The vehicle requests are grouped based on equation 1. If requests are to be divided to various n classes, a request r belongs to class i, 0<=m<=n.

$$\left(2^{\frac{1}{m}+1} - 1\right) < \frac{ei}{pi} \le \left(2^{\frac{1}{m}} - 1\right) \tag{1}$$

Taking 'x' as number of incoming requests from vehicles. The factor of utilization is derived by UF given in equation 2.

$$Ux = x(2^{\frac{1}{x}} - 1) < 1 \tag{2}$$

EDF (Bin packing) is a Np-complete problem that allocate the requests to the controller such that the requests at a controller can be successfully executed by EDF. In this algorithm the SDN controller utilization should not exceed 100%. The controller utilization is given in equation 3.

$$Cu = \sum_{0}^{Cu} ui < U < 1 \tag{3}$$

In IoV, any SDN controller should execute any dynamic requests coming from the vehicles. So, focused and addressing algorithm can well execute the real time requests from vehicles. The SDN controller maintains the information of all vehicles ID's that it has committed to process, their processing time and their periods. SDN controllers also maintain other controller's current statistics. Whenever an SDN controller receives a request from the vehicles and if the controller is over-loaded, then it selects one controller (focused controller) with minimum load to process the request. But directly sending the request to focused controller leads to obsolete information, so the controller send bidding request to other controllers. Then the controller is selected based on the controller load and proximity to the vehicle. But this algorithm may have more communication overhead.

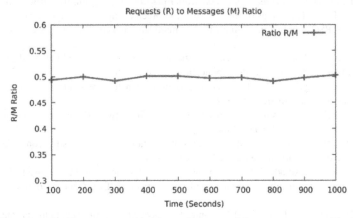

Fig. 36.4   Ratio between the Requests sent by the switches and the messages sent by the controller [33]

For better placement algorithms, the ratio between the requests and messages is plotted in Fig. 36.4. It shows on an average of 0.5 which indicates that irrespective of the time the SDN controllers are used, the ratio is almost the same. This indicates that all the messages sent by the switches are satisfied by the controllers or the controllers send the messages to the switches whenever it is requested. As per the SDN controller modelling portrayed in Fig. 36.5. With the learning state bandwidth management is better managed when compared to listen and hard states of SDN controller. In the overall design, this is the way how we improved our bandwidth management.

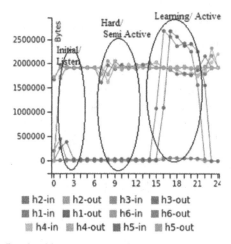

Fig. 36.5   Bandwidth management by various SDN controller states

Source: Result taken from mininet emulation tool

4. Conclusion

In this work, we did an extensive review on SCPP and bandwidth provision at SDN controller for IoV and proposed a solution using Q factor in reinforcement learning for better bandwidth management. To achieve this, we have designed various states for SDN controller and observed that learning state of SDN controller achieved noble bandwidth management compared to other state policies. Once the controller states are designed, the varying IoV traffic can be separated based on the requests from vehicles. We propose that by applying real time algorithms at SDN controller can help to find the optimal number of controllers required and to optimally find the location of controllers. As an extension and implementation, this idea will be evaluated over open flow switches in NS3.

REFERENCES

1. Chen, J., Xiong, Y., and He, D. (2022). A density-based controller placement algorithm for software defined networks. In 2022 IEEE International Conferences on Internet of Things (iThings) and IEEE Green Computing Communications (GreenCom) and IEEE Cyber, Physical Social Computing (CPSCom) and IEEE Smart Data (SmartData) and IEEE Congress on Cybermatics (Cybermatics), pages 287–291.
2. D'Angelo, G. and Palmieri, F. (2023). A co-evolutionary genetic algorithm for robust and balanced controller placement in software-defined networks. Journal of Network and Computer Applications, page 103583.
3. Amin, A., Jahanshahi, M., and Meybodi, M. (2023). Gsocpp optimization for predicting the proper number of controllers in sdn. International Journal of Industrial Mathematics, 15(1): 27–38.
4. Saeed, K. and Ullah, M. O. (2022). Toward reliable controller placements in software-defined network using constrained multi-objective optimization technique. IEEE Access, 10:129865–129883.
5. Alouache, L., Yassa, S., and Ahfir, A. (2022). A multi-objective optimization approach for sdvn controllers placement problem. In 2022 13th International Conference on Network of the Future (NoF), pages 1–9.
6. Adekoya, O. and Aneiba, A. (2022). An adapted nondominated sorting genetic algorithm iii (nsga-iii) with repair-based operator for solving controller placement problem in software-defined wide area networks. IEEE Open Journal of the Communications Society, 3: 888–901. 4
7. Liyanage, K. S. K., Ma, M., and Chong, P. H. J. (2018). Controller placement optimization in hierarchical distributed software defined vehicular networks. Computer Networks, 135: 226–239.

8. Maity, I., Misra, S., and Mandal, C. (2022). Scope: Cost-efficient qos-aware switch and controller placement in hybrid sdn. IEEE Systems Journal, 16(3): 4873–4880.

9. Li, B., Deng, X., Chen, X., Deng, Y., and Yin, J. (2022). Mec-based dynamic controller placement in sd-iov: A deep reinforcement learning approach. IEEE Transactions on Vehicular Technology, 71(9): 10044–10058.

10. Radam, N. S., Al-Janabi, S. T. F., and Jasim, K. S. (2023). Using metaheuristics (sa-mcsdn) optimized for multi-controller placement in software-defined networking. Future Internet, 15(1): 39.

11. Deng, D.-J., Lien, S.-Y., Lin, C.-C., Hung, S.-C., and Chen, W.-B. (2017). Latency control in software-defined mobile-edge vehicular networking. IEEE Communications Magazine, 55(8): 87–93.

12. Amin, R., Pali, I., and Sureshkumar, V. (2021). Software-defined network enabled vehicle to vehicle secured data transmission protocol in vanets. Journal of Information Security and Applications, 58: 102729.

13. Cui, X., Gao, X., Ma, Y., and Wang, W. (2020). A controller deployment scheme in 5g-iot network based on sdn. EURASIP Journal on Wireless Communications and Networking, 2020(1): 1–19.

14. Barış, K. and ÖZG ÖVDE, B. A. (2020). Effect of rsu placement on autonomous vehicle v2i scenarios. Balkan Journal of Electrical and Computer Engineering, 8(3): 272–284.

15. Lin, N., Zhao, Q., Zhao, L., Hawbani, A., Liu, L., and Min, G. (2021). A novel cost effective controller placement scheme for software-defined vehicular networks. IEEE Internet of Things Journal, 8(18): 14080–14093.

16. Saleh SN, Fathy C. A Novel Deep-Learning Model for Remote Driver Monitoring in SDN-Based Internet of Autonomous Vehicles Using 5G Technologies. Applied Sciences. 2023; 13(2) :875.

17. Pokhrel, S.R., 2021. Software defined internet of vehicles for automation and orchestration. IEEE Transactions on Intelligent Transportation Systems, 22(6), pp. 3890–3899.

18. Zhai, Y., Sun, W., Wu, J., Zhu, L., Shen, J., Du, X. and Guizani, M., 2020. An energy aware offloading scheme for interdependent applications in software-defined IoV with fog computing architecture. IEEE Transactions on Intelligent Transportation Systems, 22(6), pp. 3813–3823.

19. Xu, X., Huang, Q., Zhu, H., Sharma, S., Zhang, X., Qi, L. and Bhuiyan, M.Z.A., 2020. Secure service offloading for internet of vehicles in SDN-enabled mobile edge computing. IEEE Transactions on Intelligent Transportation Systems, 22(6), pp. 3720–3729.

20. Liu, W.L., Yen, L.H. and Wang, T.P., 2022, May. Distributed Approach to Adaptive SDN Controller Placement Problem. In ICC 2022-IEEE International Conference on Communications (pp. 2744–2749). IEEE.

21. Soleymanifar, R. and Beck, C., 2022, June. RCP: A Temporal Clustering Algorithm for Real-time Controller Placement in Mobile SDN Systems. In 2022 American Control Conference (ACC) (pp. 2767-2772). IEEE.

22. Firouz, N., Masdari, M., Sangar, A.B. and Majidzadeh, K., 2021. A novel controller placement algorithm based on network portioning concept and a hybrid discrete optimization algorithm for multi-controller software-defined networks. Cluster Computing, 24, pp. 2511–2544.

23. Rath, Hemant Kumar, Vishvesh Revoori, Shameemraj M. Nadaf, and Anantha Simha. "Optimal controller placement in Software Defined Networks (SDN) using a non-zero-sum game." In Proceeding of IEEE International Symposium on a World of Wireless, Mobile and Multimedia Networks 2014, pp. 1–6. IEEE, 2014.

24. N. Lin, Q. Zhao, L. Zhao, A. Hawbani, L. Liu and G. Min, "A Novel Cost-Effective Controller Placement Scheme for Software-Defined Vehicular Networks," in IEEE Internet of Things Journal, vol. 8, no. 18, pp. 14080-14093, 15 Sept.15, 2021, doi: 10.1109/JIOT.2021.3069878.

25. Petale, S. and Thangaraj, J., 2019. Failure-based controller placement in software defined networks. IEEE Transactions on Network and Service Management, 17(1), pp. 503–516.

26. Li, H., De Grande, R. E., & Boukerche, A. (2017, May). An efficient CPP solution for resilience-oriented SDN controller deployment. In 2017 IEEE International Parallel and Distributed Processing Symposium Workshops (IPDPSW) (pp. 540–549). IEEE.

27. Lange, S., Gebert, S., Zinner, T., Tran-Gia, P., Hock, D., Jarschel, M., & Hoffmann, M. (2015). Heuristic approaches to the controller placement problem in large scale SDN networks. IEEE Transactions on Network and Service Management, 12(1), 4–17.

28. Qi, Yuezhen, Dongbin Wang, Wenbin Yao, Haifeng Li, and Yuhua Cao. "Towards multi-controller placement for SDN based on density peaks clustering." In ICC 2019-2019 IEEE international conference on communications (ICC), pp. 1-6. IEEE, 2019.

29. Tahmasebi, S., Safi, M., Zolfi, S., Maghsoudi, M. R., Faragardi, H. R., & Fotouhi, H. (2020). Cuckoo-PC: an evolutionary synchronization-aware placement of SDN controllers for optimizing the network performance in WSNs. Sensors, 20(11), 3231.

30. Sminesh, C. N., Kanaga, E. G. M., & Roy, A. (2019). Optimal multi-controller placement strategy in SD-WAN using modified density peak clustering. IET Communications, 13(20), 3509–3518.

31. Wang D, Song B, Lin P, Yu FR, Du X, Guizani M. Resource management for edge intelligence (EI)-assisted IoV using quantum-inspired reinforcement learning. IEEE Internet of Things Journal. 2021 Dec 23;9(14):12588-600.

32. Chin YK, Lee LK, Bolong N, Yang SS, Teo KT. Exploring Q-learning optimization in traffic signal timing plan management. In2011 third international conference on computational intelligence, communication systems and networks 2011 Jul 26 (pp. 269–274). IEEE.

33. Chen Y, Berkhin P, Anderson B, Devanur NR. Real-time bidding algorithms for performance-based display ad allocation. InProceedings of the 17th ACM SIGKDD international conference on Knowledge discovery and data mining 2011 Aug 21 (pp. 1307-1315).

Advances in Computational Intelligence and its Applications (ICACIA-2023) – Dr. Sheikh Fahad Ahmad et al. (eds)
© 2024 Taylor & Francis Group, London, ISBN 978-1-032-78612-4

Security Level Detection of Cryptosystems Using Machine Learning

37

Srividhya Ganesan[1]

Sr Assistant Professor, Department of CSE,
New Horizon College of Engineering Bangalore, India

Rachana P.[2]

Associate Professor, Department of CSE,
New Horizon College of Engineering Bangalore, India

Pokala Keerthana[3], N. Karthik Reddy[4], Niharika Reddy R.[5]

Department of CSE, New Horizon College of
Engineering Bangalore, India

ABSTRACT—With new enhancements of digital media technologies, privacy and security of the digital data is now an important concern. Researchers concentrate their work on enhancing the current algorithms to address security flaws. Many encryption methods that have been developed over the past few decades have been shown to be insecure, posing serious risks to sensitive data. Selecting the right encryption method is crucial for preventing these attacks, but the algorithm to use in any given circumstance relies on the type of data that has to be safeguarded. However, it takes longer to process each cryptosystem individually. With the aid of Support Vector Machines(SVM), By indicating the accuracy level of each encryption algorithm, we have proposed a security level identification approach for image encryption techniques that enables rapid and accurate selection of the best encryption algorithms.

KEYWORDS—Support vector machine (SVM), Image encryption,Cryptosystems

1. Introduction

Security and protection of data has become most important topic of research because of rapid increase in transferring data across many insecure channels. Many researchers have developed several encryption techniques to secure the data from unauthorized users[1]-[5].

Diffusion and confusion (which is also known as scrambling) are two aspects which plays major role while encrypting digital images. According to Claud Shannon's theory in [6], a safe cryptosystem has mechanisms for confusion and diffusion. In digital pictures, the The scrambling procedure is applicable to either the rows and columns or the pixels, changing the original pixel values by diffusion. To put it in other way, Every unique pixel value is swapped out for an S-box unique value throughout the substitution procedure.

However, merely sending data in a format which is encrypted is inadequate to ensure its privacy. Suppose, if a single substitution box is utilized (S-box) to encrypt a picture, substituted or encrypted image may nevertheless contain information that can be seen. This indicates that the original image cannot be adequately hidden using a single S-box for encryption. Due to the

[1]v.vidhya8@gmail.com, [2]2000.rachana@gmail.com, [3]1nh19cs125.keerthana@gmail.com, [4]1nh19cs106.karthik@gmail.com,
[5]1nh19cs113niharika@gmail.com

DOI: 10.1201/9781003488682-37

encryption techniques lack of security, even when the data is encrypted during transmission, unauthorised people can still access it., which we can see in Fig. 37.1(b). Therefore, to be able to increase encryption security,strong encryption algorithm must be used.

 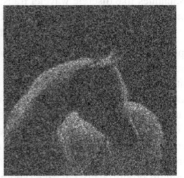

(a) Plain horse image   (b) Image encrypted using single S-box

Fig. 37.1   Single S-box encryption

Source: Adapter from the paper "Image Encryption Using Dynamic S-Box Substitution in the Wavelet Domain"

The encryption algorithm's level of security, the strength of the picture is significantly influenced by the algorithm, which was used to encrypt it. An extremely powerful encryption method will be used to completely encrypt a plain picture, protecting it against assaults on its availability, secrecy, and integrity.

In addition to security, time complexity is a crucial consideration when choosing the right encryption method. Which cryptosystem you employ will depend on the type of application being encrypted since various types of data need different degrees of security. The most secure encryption technique now in use, for instance, is the Advanced Encryption Standard (AES) [7]. However, because AES needs extra rounds, which prolongs the time it takes to encrypt the original data, it is not appropriate for applications that need for speedy encryption. Additionally, the time complexity is influenced by how many pixels are present in the source image overall. The more pixels there are in the raw image, the longer it will take to encrypt it [8]. The processing time, on the other hand, might not need to be as carefully taken into account if main goal is just to encrypt a plain image which has high security. Strong encryption improves security, but it is not always a property of quick encryption, which is sometimes chosen [9].

An entropy, correlation, energy, or homogeneity statistical study should be conducted on an encryption algorithm to determine its level of security. These tasks can be accomplished by analyzing the statistics of each encryption algorithm's security settings and testing each encryption algorithm. We can select the best and strongest alternative from those examined after conducting such security studies on various encryption algorithms one by one. However, this procedure frequently consumes too much time, delaying completion of the intended task. Instead, we suggest that a Machine Learning model can take the place of this manual testing and quickly, conveniently, and precisely choose the strongest encryption technique.

Based on the encryption algorithms typical security criteria, we have categorized the three tiers of encryption algorithm security (strong, acceptable, and weak). We the values of the security parameters various enciphered images produced by various encryption techniques in order to support the aforementioned claim. The images cannot be successfully encrypted using weak or moderate encryption techniques. Figure 3 displays the images that were encrypted using weak and medium encryption techniques.

Principles for classification: The suggested model must abide by the following rules in order to categorize encryption algorithms into three groups (strong, acceptable, and weak).

- The decision regarding each category's classification will be made based on the security parameter's values.
- For weak, acceptable, and good security, we separated the parameters respective ranges into three intervals. Below 50% of the feature values must fall inside the permitted interval values for weak security level.
- At least 65 percent of feature values must fall inside the permitted interval values for acceptable security.
- More than 80% of the feature values must fall inside the allowable interval ranges for good security.

To evaluate the level of security of various cryptosystems, we have created a unique model employing a Support Vector Machine (SVM).

2. Literature Review

There are several encryption techniques that have been suggested as ways to protect photos before transmission. Chaos theory or transformation techniques like discrete wavelet transformation, discrete cosine transformation, and discrete Fourier transformation [11]–[16] may be used to design encryption algorithms. These, however, are just a handful of the several image encryption methods that have been published recently. Additional information on each category is given below:

A method of image encryption based on chaos and cosine transformation was suggested in [17]. Instead of using a single chaotic system, three separate chaotic maps were used in this study. The idea behind employing many chaotic maps was to increase the total complexity of the algorithm and allow it to behave in a more complex and dynamic way. Using a piece-wise linear chaotic map, Kaur et al. proposed a novel optical image encryption method in [18] that demonstrated its ability to generate vectors of various orders (PWLCM) [19]. This was done to increase the encryption algorithm's level of security. Khan et al. in [20] developed a chaos-based selective picture encryption system for quick image encryption. Although selective encryption systems are effective for real-time applications that need quick encryption, They are ineffective for text encryption because text encryption demands that every bit be encrypted in order for the data to be sufficiently obscured. The statistical study proved that these algorithms produced effective encryption, however these results were insufficient to verify the proposed work's level of security. To give a more accurate evaluation of that particular encryption technique, more research would be required. Although chaos is capable of producing random numbers, Nardo et al. described restrictions of chaos-based encryption techniques in [21], contending that because, These methods are used in computers with finite precision, dynamic deterioration results, rendering chaos-based encryption insecure. The authors implemented chaos-based systems employing various interval delays to produce a finite accuracy mistake, which was then used to encrypt plain images. In[22] authors claimed that the reliance on initial values in chaos-based communication systems makes them insufficiently safe, implying their security might be compromised by knowing these early values. This is one of the constraints of chaos that they explained. In our earlier work, a bit-plane extraction method is included to suggest a novel image encryption approach based on multiple chaotic systems, enhancing the security of the chaos-based cryptosystem [23]. The primary goal of the suggested method was to shorten required processing time while simultaneously extending the amount of how much is hidden. [10] proposes an image encryption technique based on the chaotic logistic map (CLM) [24]. Given their potent, nonlinear offering of a diffusion source, S-boxes are frequently used in chaos-based picture encryption. By using multiple substitution box (S-box) image encryption, where the choice of a specific S-box is determined by the random values generated by the CLM, the author of this study was able to overcome the shortcomings of single substitution box (S-box) encryption. To withstand statistical attacks, the S-box must be robust because the effectiveness of chaos-based encryption methods depends on it. For security experts, the creation of powerful S-boxes is a crucial research field.

Previously, we created a CLM-based methodology that could create a new S-box in [25] to address problems associated with employing weak S-boxes. A small difference in the starting values of CLM may have an impact on the values of the S-box that is thus formed. A colour image presents an even greater encryption challenge than a grayscale image, aside from the grayscale image itself. This is due to the requirement that all three channels—R, G, and B—be encrypted when using colour image encryption. [26] proposes a colour image encryption method that makes use a chaotic hybrid system. The authors initially dispersed the jumbled components using a mitochondrial DNA sequence after encrypting each R, G, and B component separately using the phenomena of confusion.

The security of each of the encryption techniques discussed above varies; few are strong, few are acceptable, and others are weak. The complexity of an algorithm's mathematical structure determines which category it belongs to.

3. Support Vector Machine for Classification

Support Vector Machine (SVM), in comparison to other data classification algorithms, typically perform better in terms of classification accuracy. One of the most well-known methods for enhancing the anticipated outcome is SVM. SVMs and other approaches differ much in categorisation, especially when there are few input data points. SVMs are effective tools used in data categorization and regression analysis. SVMs have a clear benefit since they train using a smaller subset of support vectors—often just a small percentage of the initial data set. Using this small amount of data, a set of support vectors reflecting a particular classification issue is created. Getting a model that increases performance for the training data is the main goal of pattern classification. SVM's primary goal is to partition the training set's classes into as many distinct groups as possible using a surface that increases the distance between them. Alternatively, The Generalisation capability of a model can be increased using SVM[33].

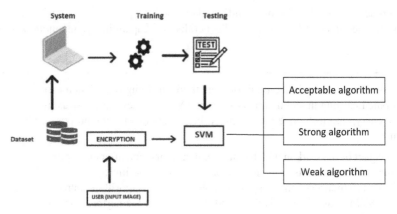

Fig. 37.2 Block diagram for proposed work

Source: Author

The SVM technique is frequently used for classification tasks, especially those like classifying objects from samples of unobserved data [27]. SVM is employed in this case to assess the degree of security of various algorithms, classifying them as strong, acceptable, or weak.

4. Proposed Model for Cryptosystem Security Level Detection

Numerous encryption methods, such as chaos and transformation-based, have been presented during the past few years. Some of the encryption techniques in use today are discovered as weak and, after statistical examination of their data, to not provide very solid security. Analyzing the statistics of a security parameter's encryption algorithm is one technique for figuring out how secure it is.

A particular algorithm's security level can be determined by:

- • Consider a set of information drawn from several cypher images generated by a range of encryption methods [10], [20], [28]– [32]. In Fig. 37.3, the cypher pictures are displayed.
- Identify characteristics in the cypher images.

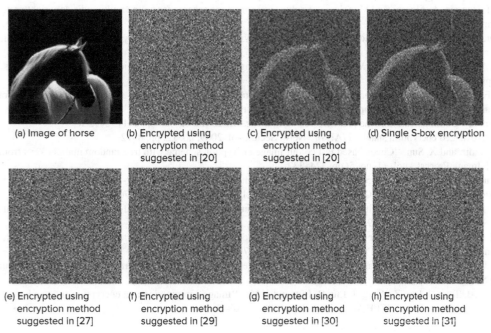

(a) Image of horse   (b) Encrypted using encryption method suggested in [20]   (c) Encrypted using encryption method suggested in [20]   (d) Single S-box encryption

(e) Encrypted using encryption method suggested in [27]   (f) Encrypted using encryption method suggested in [29]   (g) Encrypted using encryption method suggested in [30]   (h) Encrypted using encryption method suggested in [31]

Fig. 37.3 Encrypted images using existing algorithms

Source: Author

SVMs have a relatively simple theoretical background and are likely the most popular machine learning paradigm for supervised learning. They are famous for their dependability, excellent generalisation capabilities, and unique worldwide optimal solutions.

5. Flowchart

Drawing these comparisons one at a time is the traditional method for doing this, which can take a lot of time. A Machine Learning model that makes use of SVM was developed by us in order to choose a suitable encryption technique more rapidly. Fig. 37.2 contains the proposed work's schematic diagram.

Figure 37.4, shows the flowchart of the work in which data is gathered first and after encrypting the image securely, features of the image is extracted by preprocessing the image and SVM classifies the image and predicts which algorithm is most suitable and which algorithm is strong, weak and acceptable. With SVM, classification is done and it maximizes the performance of the data.

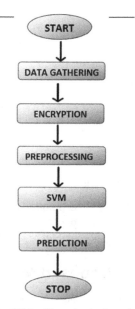

6. Conclusion

In this study, we developed and proposed a methodology which can quickly, precisely assess level of security of several encryption schemes. Building a dataset and adding characteristics was the first step which represents the security parameters shared by different encryption techniques. We have separated the values of all attributes into three intervals—strong, acceptable, and weak—that represent the resulting levels of security in order to generate a dataset. The various encryption techniques are then evaluated on our suggested model to gauge the level of security each one delivers. Using traditional testing methods, the operation traditionally takes a considerable time to complete, using our technique might result in testing being finished quickly, which would save a lot of time.

Fig. 37.4 Flowchart of work

Source: Author

REFERENCES

1. I. Hussain, A. Anees, A. H. Alkhaldi, M. Aslam, N. Siddiqui, and R. Ahmed, "Image encryption based on Chebyshev chaotic map and S8 S-boxes," Optica Applicata, vol. 49, no. 2, pp. 317–330, 2019.
2. A. Anees, I. Hussain, A. Algarni, and M. Aslam, "A robust watermarking scheme for online multimedia copyright protection using new chaotic map," Secur. Commun. Netw., vol. 2018, pp. 1–20
3. A. Shafique and J. Ahmed, "Dynamic substitution based encryption algorithm for highly correlated data," Multidimensional Syst. Signal Process., May 2020.
4. F. Ahmed, A. Anees, V. U. Abbas, and M. Y. Siyal, "A noisy channel tolerant image encryption scheme," Wireless Pers. Commun., vol. 77, no. 4, pp. 2771–2791.
5. M. A. B. Farah, R. Guesmi, A. Kachouri, and M. Samet, "A novel chaos based optical image encryption using fractional Fourier transform and DNA sequence operation," Opt. Laser Technol., vol. 121, Jan. 2020, Art. no. 105777.
6. C. E. Shannon, "Communication in the presence of noise," Proc. IEEE, vol. 72, no. 9, pp. 1192–1201.
7. S. Heron, "Advanced encryption standard (AES)," Netw. Secur., vol. 2009, no. 12, pp. 8–12.
8. H. Liu, A. Kadir, and X. Sun, "Chaos-based fast colour image encryption scheme with true random number keys from environmental noise," IET Image Process., vol. 11, no. 5, pp. 324–332.
9. Y.-L. Lee and W.-H. Tsai, "A new secure image transmission technique via secret-fragment-visible mosaic images by nearly reversible color transformations," IEEE Trans. Circuits Syst. Video Technol., vol. 24, no. 4, pp. 695–703
10. A. Anees, A. M. Siddiqui, and F. Ahmed, "Chaotic substitution for highly autocorrelated data in encryption algorithm," Commun. Nonlinear Sci. Numer. Simul., vol. 19, no. 9, pp. 3106–3118.
11. M. Khalili and D. Asatryan, "Colour spaces effects on improved discrete wavelet transform-based digital image watermarking using Arnold transform map," IET Signal Process., vol. 7, no. 3, pp. 177–187.
12. L. Zhang, J. Wu, and N. Zhou, "Image encryption with discrete fractional cosine transform and chaos," in Proc. 5th Int. Conf. Inf. Assurance Secur., vol. 2, pp. 61–64
13. M. Zhang, X.-J. Tong, J. Liu, Z. Wang, J. Liu, B. Liu, and J. Ma, "Image compression and encryption scheme based on compressive sensing and Fourier transform," IEEE Access, vol. 8, pp. 40838–40849.

14. J. S. Khan, W. Boulila, J. Ahmad, S. Rubaiee, A. U. Rehman, R. Alroobaea, and W. J. Buchanan, "DNA and plaintext dependent chaotic visual selective image encryption," IEEE Access, vol. 8, pp. 159732–159744.

15. A. Qayyum, J. Ahmad, W. Boulila, S. Rubaiee, Arshad, F. Masood, F. Khan, and W. J. Buchanan, "Chaos-based confusion and diffusion of image pixels using dynamic substitution," IEEE Access, vol. 8, pp. 140876–140895, 2020.

16. F. Masood, W. Boulila, J. Ahmad, Arshad, S. Sankar, S. Rubaiee, and W. J. Buchanan, "A novel privacy approach of digital aerial images based on mersenne twister method with DNA genetic encoding and chaos," Remote Sens., vol. 12, no. 11, p. 1893, Jun. 2020.

17. Z. Hua, Y. Zhou, and H. Huang, "Cosine-transform-based chaotic system for image encryption," Inf. Sci., vol. 480, pp. 403–419, Apr. 2019.

18. G. Kaur, R. Agarwal, and V. Patidar, "Chaos based multiple order optical transform for 2D image encryption," Eng. Sci. Technol., Int. J., vol. 23, no. 5, pp. 998–1014, Oct. 2020.

19. Abhishek, S. N. George, and P. P. Deepthi, "PWLCM based image encryption through compressive sensing," in Proc. IEEE Recent Adv. Intell. Comput. Syst. (RAICS), pp. 48–52.

20. J. S. Khan and J. Ahmad, "Chaos based efficient selective image encryption," Multidimensional Syst. Signal Process., vol. 30, no. 2, pp. 943–961, Apr. 2019.

21. L. G. Nardo, E. G. Nepomuceno, J. Arias-Garcia, and D. N. Butusov, "Image encryption using finite-precision error," Chaos, Solitons Fractals, vol. 123, pp. 69–78, Jun. 2019.

22. A. Anees and I. Hussain, "A novel method to identify initial values of chaotic maps in cybersecurity," Symmetry, vol. 11, no. 2, p. 140, Jan. 2019.

23. A. Shafique and J. Shahid, "Novel image encryption cryptosystem based on binary bit planes extraction and multiple chaotic maps," Eur. Phys. J. Plus, vol. 133, no. 8, p. 331.

24. N. K. Pareek, V. Patidar, and K. K. Sud, "Image encryption using chaotic logistic map," Image Vis. Comput., vol. 24, no. 9, pp. 926–934.

25. A. Shafique, "A new algorithm for the construction of substitution box by using chaotic map," Eur. Phys. J. Plus, vol. 135, no. 2, pp. 1–13, Feb. 2020.

26. H. G. Mohamed, D. H. ElKamchouchi, and K. H. Moussa, "A novel color image encryption algorithm based on hyperchaotic maps and mitochondrial DNA sequences," Entropy, vol. 22

27. H. G. Mohamed, D. H. ElKamchouchi, and K. H. Moussa, "A novel color image encryption algorithm based on hyperchaotic maps and mitochondrial DNA sequences," Entropy, vol. 22

28. R. Guesmi, M. A. B. Farah, A. Kachouri, and M. Samet, "A novel chaos-based image encryption using DNA sequence operation and secure hash algorithm SHA-2," Nonlinear Dyn., vol. 83, no. 3, pp. 1123–1136.

29. Y. Li, C. Wang, and H. Chen, "A hyper-chaos-based image encryption algorithm using pixel-level permutation and bit-level permutation," Opt. Lasers Eng., vol. 90, pp. 238–246.

30. R. Ge, G. Yang, J. Wu, Y. Chen, G. Coatrieux, and L. Luo, "A novel chaosbased symmetric image encryption using bit-pair level process," IEEE Access, vol. 7, pp. 99470–99480, 2019.

31. P. R. Krishna, C. V. M. S. Teja, S. R. Devi, and V. Thanikaiselvan, "A chaos based image encryption using tinkerbell map functions," in Proc. 2nd Int. Conf. Electron., Commun. Aerosp. Technol. (ICECA), pp. 578–582.

32. A. Roy, A. P. Misra, and S. Banerjee, "Chaos-based image encryption using vertical-cavity surface-emitting lasers," Optik, vol. 176, pp. 119–131, Jan. 2019.

33. A comprehensive survey on support vector machine classification: Applications, challenges and trends Jair Cervantes a, Farid Garcia-Lamont a, Lisbeth Rodríguez-Mazahua b, Asdrubal Lopez c.

Advances in Computational Intelligence and its Applications (ICACIA-2023) – Dr. Sheikh Fahad Ahmad et al. (eds)
© 2024 Taylor & Francis Group, London, ISBN 978-1-032-78612-4

Colorization of Black and White Image and Video Using CNN

38

K. Tejashwini[1], M. Soumya[2], P. Kalyani[3],
G. Deepika[4], C. N. Sujatha[5]
Sreenidhi Institute of Science and Technology,
Department of Electronics and Communication Engineering

ABSTRACT—This paper addresses the challenge of effectively generating a colour version of a gray-scale image. Past approaches either demanded substantial user intervention or resulted in colorizations with muted tones due to the inherent limitations of the task. We introduce a fully automated method for creating vibrant and precise colorizations. By reframing the problem as a classification task, we aim to diversify the colour palette in the final result. To achieve this, we implement class-rebalancing techniques during the training phase while acknowledging and working with the inherent uncertainty of the task. During the testing phase, our system, which has been trained on a dataset consisting of over a million colour images, is implemented as a feed-forward pass in a Convolutional Neural Network (CNN). To assess the effectiveness of our approach, we employ a "colorization Turing test" where humans are presented with a choice between a colour image generated by our system and a ground truth colour image. In 32% of these tests, our technology successfully deceives human evaluators, representing a significant improvement compared to earlier methods. Additionally, we demonstrate how colorization, functioning as a cross-channel encoder, can be used as a valuable pre-training task for self-supervised learning. Across a range of feature learning benchmarks, this approach consistently delivers satisfactory results.

KEYWORDS—De-saturation, Colorization, CNN, Vision for graphics, Self-supervised learning

1. Introduction

Colorization is the procedure of adding colours to the gray scale images, monochromatic videos, and certain other dynamic visuals. It also has the capability to restore and bring a modern touch to black-and-white films. With the advancement of Image Processing technology, it has become more common. It has become the crucial part of aesthetic and archival photography over the years. Because of technological limitations, there were only black-and-white images available when photography was invented. These issues are no longer the result of technological advancements that have become a part of our daily lives. Image colorization stands as an interdisciplinary domain, encompassing elements such as computer vision, computer-generated graphics, computer-based pattern recognition, and human-computer interaction. widely used colorization methods have been widely used in a variety of industries, encompassing tasks such as automatically adding color to cartoons, restoring color in old films, and infusing color into grayscale photos. These methods can be classified into two primary categories, depending on the type of input being colorized. The first category deals with imbuing color into black and white images and videos, which are essentially regular visuals devoid of any color content. The second category focuses on the colorization of black-and-white artwork, including sketches, manga, and cartoons rendered in black-and-white or line-art style.

[1]tejashwini.kashireddy@gmail.com, [2]soumyamekiri2001@gmail.com, [3]kalyanipadala2002@gmail.com, [4]deepikag@sreenidhi.edu.in, [5]cnsujatha@gmail.com

DOI: 10.1201/9781003488682-38

Grayscale-based colorization methods struggle due to the lack of texture details in sketch images. To improve performance, new techniques for line feature extraction and boundary determination, considering temporal and semantic links between lines, are necessary. Traditional colorization methods are labor-intensive, with critical parameter selection, making manual interaction and parameter optimization time-consuming. This method that is Colorization is frequently used in short films, particularly in cartoons and grayscale videos.

Video colorization is the method of adding color to videos which are in black and white , considering individual frames. By applying this image colorization techniques to videos, there can be discontinuities. Lei and Chen (2019) introduced an automated model for black-and-white video colorization that doesn't require user input or reference images. A self-regularization and diversity loss function is used by them to ensure consistency and diversity in grayscale video colorization. This self-regularization loss includes bilateral and temporal terms that enforce color consistency between adjacent pixels and frames. A Diversity Loss is used to align multiple results with real color images. However, the method may not consistently produce rich colorization results despite generating multiple outcomes.

2. Literature Survey

Colorization results by applying colours to the black and white images. The techniques like Convolutional Neural Networks are designed specifically to process and handle the images data. Most writers contributed significantly to the development of this concept. Richard Zhang proposed an optimised solution in Convolutional Neural Network using a large dataset and a single feed-forward pass. Their main motivation is to train. Human subjects were used to test the output, which was able to deceive 32% of them and had a large number of neurons. Various architectures were used in the numerous attempts. Domonkos Varga suggested the goal of automated colouring of images of cartoon because, unlike natural images, their colours vary from animator to animator. The large set of data was used to train the cartoon images, 30% of which were used for documentation and the remainder for training. However, without any prediction the cartoons are produced with greater colour than the original image and consideration is personalised and moderate. Shweta Slave put forward the same viewpoint, utilising image classifier of google ,There are four different components the system model which are Inception ResNet V2.Encoder, Feature Extractor, Fusion Layer, and Decoder

The system is capable of producing acceptable results when given adequate resources like Central Processing Unit, Memory unit and adequate data set. The above system is usually used as a proof of implementation of the concept. Yu Chen proposed a solution to the problem of colouring Chinese films from the past. They are used as the existing dataset for the Chinese pictures so as to tune the complete system model. This method of network employs multiscale convolution kernels and combines low and middle VGG-16 features. V.K. Putri produced a technique for converting simple images into colourful pictures. It employs colour prediction in the CIELab colour space as well as the sketch inversion model. This viewpoint can process the plots which are drawn by the hand as well as different types of geometric transformations. The disadvantage discovered was the dataset was bounded, but it performs well in uncontrolled situations. Several papers have employed the same quantity of neurons as the dimension of the feature descriptor extracted from every pixel coordinate in a grayscale image.

In 2018, Vondrick et al. introduced a self-supervised learning technique for video colorization with a focus on visual tracking. This approach involves transferring colors from a reference frame, necessitating the model's ability to correctly identify and apply the appropriate colors to specific regions. It also has the capability to track individuals' movements within videos. To address the challenge of maintaining color consistency across video frames while ensuring frame-level color stability, this model employs a pointing mechanism. However, it's important to note that this pointing mechanism may still exhibit some imprecision, and the color boundaries in the resulting colorized frames may at times appear ambiguous.

In 2019, Iizuka and Simo-Serra introduced an all-in-one framework for enhancing the black-and-white films. They utilized source-reference attention to adjust the color of the reference image within the targeted particular image. This attention mechanism involves operations done to the matrix on features from both images to capture non-local similarities, a technique gaining popularity in recent years, as seen in works by He et al. (2018), Zhang et al. (2019), Shi et al. (2022), Lee et al. (2020), and Siyao et al. (2021).

3. Methodologies and Actual Work

In this approach, we construct a deep convolutional neural network that transforms grayscale images into colorized versions. Initially, we resize our black-and-white image to 256 x 256 pixels, which serves as input for our neural network. To generate images with lifelike colors, our model is trained on diverse, colorful images. These generated images have the potential to convincingly deceive observers. While the RGB color space has three channels, the CIE Lab color space, similar to RGB, uses only the "a" and "b" channels for color information. We use the "L" (lightness) channel as the neural network's grayscale input since it represents intensity alone. The resulting "a" and "b" channels are then combined with the "L" channel. The trained network predicts the "a" and "b" channels, and finally, the "Lab" image is converted back to the RGB color space.

Larsson and Iizuka have developed systems akin to ours, harnessing extensive data through Convolutional Neural Networks (CNNs). Nevertheless, their approaches diverge in terms of loss functions and CNN architectures. Specifically, Iizuka et al. utilize a regression loss, while Larsson et al. employ an unrebalanced classification loss, albeit with rebalanced rare classes. We investigate how each of these loss functions interacts with our approach.

In the context of CNN architectures, Larsson et al. implement hyper columns on a VGG network, whereas Iizuka and their collaborators utilize a two-stream architecture. This architecture combines both local and global features, merging them into a unified stream. They employ a VGG-styled network equipped with dilated convolutions. Notably, unlike Larsson et al. and our work, Iizuka et al. train their model using the Places dataset.

Our primary aim is to map the function Yb = F(X) with the associated two channels of colour Y∈R(H*W*2) when inputted a brightness channel X∈ℝ^(H*W*1), where W & H are the photo parameters.

This task is completed using the CIE Lab color space, since distances within this space correlated to how colors are perceived by colors, we compute the Euclidean loss (L2 distance) with in the actual colors and predicted colors.

$$L_2(\hat{\mathbf{Y}}, \mathbf{Y}) = \frac{1}{2} \sum_{h,w} \|\mathbf{Y}_{h,w} - \hat{\mathbf{Y}}_{h,w}\|_2^2$$

Nonetheless, the Euclidean loss function was vulnerable to the inherent uncertainty and multiple possible outcomes in the colorization task. When an object exhibits a range of distinct AB values, the best Euclidean loss solution is typically the mean value from that range. In the context of color prediction, this averaging tendency tends to favor producing colorizations that appear more grayish and desaturated. Additionally, if the set of potential colorizations is not convex, the solution may fall outside of the set, leading to implausible results.

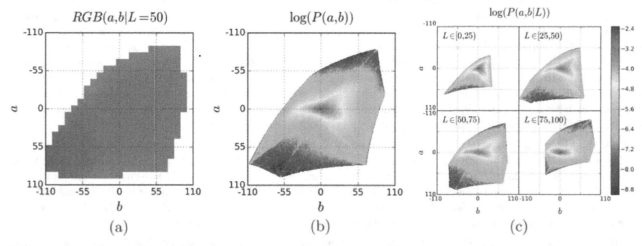

Fig. 38.1 (a) Displays the AB color space that has been divided into a grid with a size of 10, resulting in a total of 313 AB pairs. (b) Illustrates the empirical probability distribution of AB values using a logarithmic scale, while the empirical logarithmic scale probability distribution of AB values based on the L channel is represented by (c). [1]

The problem is chosen by us as a multinomial classification problem. As portrayed in Figure 6, we discretize the AB output space into 10 bins while maintaining a total of Q = 313 in-gamut values (a). For a given input X, we establish a mapping Zb = G(X) to create a probability distribution over potential colors, where Zb∈ 0, 1, and Q represents the number of quantized AB values. To compare the predicted Zb with the ground truth, we introduce the function Z = H (-1) gt (Y), which transforms the ground truth color Y into a vector Z using a soft-encoding approach2.

Next, we apply the multinomial cross-entropy loss, denoted as Lcl(,), which is defined as follows:

$$L_{cl}(\hat{\mathbf{Z}}, \mathbf{Z}) = -\sum_{h,w} v(\mathbf{Y}_{h,w}) \sum_q \mathbf{Z}_{h,w,q} \log(\hat{\mathbf{Z}}_{h,w,q})$$

where, as stated in Section 2.2 below, v(.) is a weighting factor used to readjust the loss according to the rarity of colour classes.

Lastly, we transfer the probability distribution Zb to the colour values Yb and Zb using the equation Yb = H(Zb) (Zb).

3.1 Class Re-balancing

The range of AB values in naturally occurring photos is strongly skewed towards low AB values due to the existence of backdrops like clouds, pavement, dirt, and walls. 1.3M Image Net pictures to be trained with empirical pixel distribution in A&B space. Notably, nature pictures have orders of magnitude more pixels at de-saturated values than at saturated ones. Without accounting for this, de-saturated AB values predominate in the loss function. The loss of each pixel is reweighed based on the rarity of its colour at train time, we take into consideration class imbalance. Similar to asymptotically resampling the training space, this is a frequent practice. Each pixel is given a weight w RQ based on the closest AB bin.

We start with the ImageNet training set and analyze the likelihood of colors within a specific quantized color space called ABPB, represented as pb €(Q). To make this distribution smoother, we apply a Gaussian kernel called G. The result is a smoothed empirical distribution, denoted as p €(Q). We then combine this distribution with a uniform one, giving each a weight between 0 and 1. Afterward, we calculate the reciprocal of these weights and normalize them so that they add up to 1. Our experiments revealed that the values 1, 2, and 5 worked well for this process.

3.2 Class Probabilities to Point the Estimates

In the final definition, H is a function that converts the projected distribution from Zb to a rough estimate associated with Yb in the AB region. When working with two sample images in the rightmost column, one option is to use the most common prediction for each pixel. This approach produces vivid but occasionally erratic spatial results, as seen in the irregular red patches on the bus. On the other hand, averaging the predicted distribution yields consistent spatial outcomes but lacks color saturation and appears unnaturally sepia-toned. This isn't surprising since optimizing for a Euclidean loss in a regression framework faces similar issues to averaging after classification. By adjusting the temperature (T) of the softmax distributions and averaging the results, we can combine the strengths of both methods. This process is often referred to as obtaining the annealed mean of the distribution using simulated annealing.

$$H(\mathbf{Z}_{h,w}) = E[f_T(\mathbf{Z}_{h,w})], \ f_T(\mathbf{z}) = \frac{\exp(\log(\mathbf{z})/T)}{\sum_q \exp(\log(\mathbf{z}_p)/T)}$$

The annealed mean process H generates a final prediction, while the CNN G produces a predicted distribution for all pixels in our overall system F. It's worth noting that H can function as a feed-forward step within the CNN and operate individually on each pixel using a single parameter, even though the entire system is not entirely trainable from start to finish.

When T is set to 1, the distribution remains unchanged. Decreasing T leads to a distribution with sharper peaks and edges, and when T is set to 0, the distribution's mode becomes a 1-hot encoding. We found that using a temperature parameter of T = 0.38 in the annealed-mean process preserves the spatial consistency of the mean and maintains the vividness of the mode in the output. While the photos on the right illustrate respective modes, the ones on the left represent the expected colour distribution means. T is programmed in our system to be 0.38.

3.3 Evaluation of the Quality of Colorization

Our network was trained on a dataset consisting of 1.3 million images from the ImageNet training set. We validated the model's performance using the first 10000 images from the validation set and conducted testing on an additional ten thousand images from the same validation set. Table 38.1 presents the numerical output for three different metrics, and in Fig. 38.1, we analyze specific cases of success and failure.

To investigate the impact of different loss functions, we trained our Convolutional Neural Network (CNN) and compared it to previous and contemporary methods. These approaches all utilized CNNs trained on the ImageNet dataset, and we also included basic baseline comparisons in our assessment.

1. **Ours (full)** The entire process, as described in Equation 2, incorporating classification loss and class re-balancing, was explained and supported in Section 2.2. Using the ADAM solver, the neural network was taught from inception using k-means initialization over roughly 450,000 iterations.

2. **Ours (class)** The system is equipped with a classification loss function, but it does not incorporate any form of class rebalancing.

Table 38.1 Colorizarion results on ImageNet [1]

Colorization Results on ImageNet							
Method	**Model**			**AuC**		**VGG Top-1 Class Acc (%)**	**AMT Labeled Real (%)**
	Params (MB)	**Feats (MB)**	**Runtime (ms)**	**non-rebal (%)**	**rebal (%)**		
Ground Truth	—	—	—	100	100	68.3	50
Gray	—	—	—	89.1	58.0	52.7	—
Random	—	—	—	84.2	57.3	41.0	13.0 ± 4.4
Dahl [2]	—	—	—	90.4	58.9	48.7	18.3 ± 2.8
Larsson et al. [23]	588	495	122.1	91.7	65.9	59.4	27.2 ± 2.7
Ours (L2)	129	127	17.8	91.2	64.4	54.9	21.2 ± 2.5
Ours (L2, ft)	129	127	17.8	91.5	66.2	56.5	23.9 ± 2.8
Ours (class)	129	142	22.1	91.6	65.1	56.6	25.2 ± 2.7
Ours (full)	129	142	22.1	89.5	67.3	56.0	32.3 ± 2.2

Table 38.1 shows AUC, or the region beneath the curve in a continuous error distribution for the AB color space represents the colorization results obtained from the analysis of the ImageNet testing dataset. The second column in the results displays this statistic when class balancing is taken into account.

In Column 4, we present the results of our original vs. fake test conducted using Amazon Mechanical Turk (AMT), along with the indicated mean, standard deviation, and bootstrap estimation. It's worth highlighting that an image-generating algorithm with perfect accuracy would perform 50% better than what we observed. In all cases, higher values indicate better performance for the metrics. Each row corresponds to different algorithms, and you can find descriptions for each of them in the accompanying text. We used Caffe to measure parameters, feature memory, and runtime on a Titan X GPU.

Figure 38.2 shows the examples of the outcomes from our Image Net test dataset which are used in colorization of black and white image using the convolutional neural network model.

When comparing a classification loss without the incorporation of regression loss rebalancing to our categorization loss with rebalancing, we observe that the latter yields more precise and vibrant outcomes. Successful colorizations are those that exceed the dotted threshold. Here are some common mistakes frequently encountered: In complex indoor scenes, a sepia tone is often applied as the default choice, and maintaining consistency over long distances is frequently overlooked.

3. **Ours (L2)** Following the same training procedure, we trained our network entirely anew, incorporating the L2 regression loss as defined in Equation 1.

4. **Ours (L2, ft)** Our network was optimised with a rebalancing network that utilised our complete classification after having been taught using L2 regression loss.

5. **Larsson et al. [23]** In these sessions, a Convolutional Neural Network methodology may be shown.as well.

6. **Dahl [2]** Based on our complete classification, a rebalancing network was used to fine-tune our network after it had been trained using L2 regression loss.

7. **Gray** Colour pixel turn to grey when (a,b)=0

8. At **random** The random image in the learning data set is used to get the colors.

RMS error on pixel values and other simple quantitative indicators generally fall short of portraying visual authenticity, giving evaluation of the image's quality challenging. To solve the weaknesses of any evaluation, we tested with 3 different quality criteria, as indicated in Table 38.1.

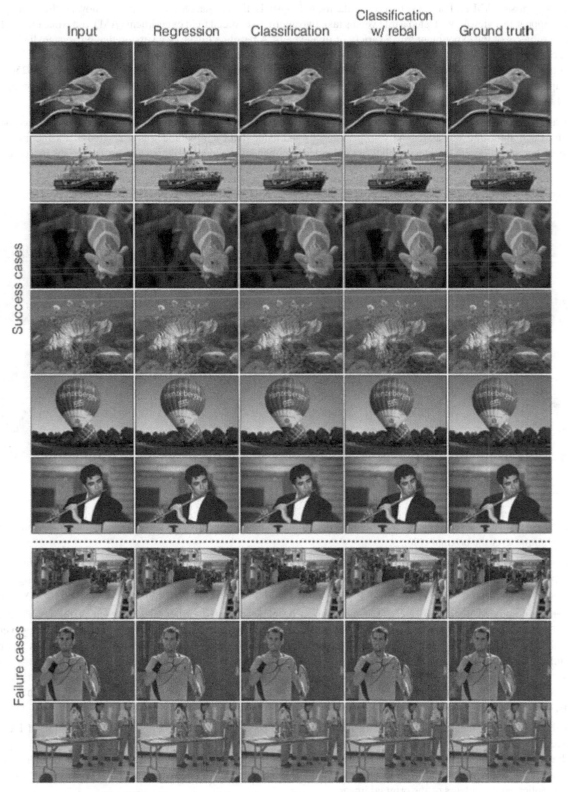

Fig. 38.2   Examples of the outcomes from our Image Net test dataset [1]

Perceptual realism (AMT): For many purposes, like those in visuals, the ultimate test of coloring is how aesthetically pleasing the colors appear to a viewer. We tested a true versus fake two alternative forced field experiment (AMT) on Amazon Mechanical Turk. The subjects of the experiment saw a variety of image pairs. A baseline image or a version that our system had recolored were placed next to a color image. On a picture they thought had been edited by a computer programme, the participants were told to click on it. Following each pair, participants had an unlimited amount of time to respond to one of 256256 distinct photographs.40 test pairings were followed by 10 practise trials (which were excluded from the analysis that followed). Users obtained feedback on how accurate their response was during the practise trials.

There was no feedback for the 40 trial pairs. Users were able to finish one session at once, and each session tested only one algorithm. Each algorithm was assessed by 40 persons. To guarantee that each method was evaluated in a same manner (like the time of day, statistics, etc.), all test periods are uploaded simultaneously and distributed among Turkerians in a certain way.

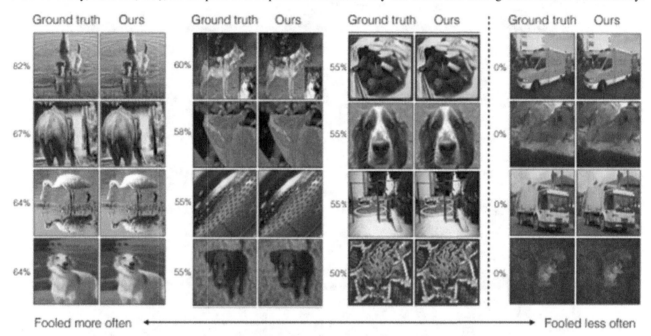

Fig. 38.3   images ranked by frequency [1]

The photos are shown in descending order in Figure 3 according on how frequently AMT users favored the colorization created by our technique over the original color.

Users thought the colorizations to the left of the actual fact, shown by the dashed lines in all pairs, were more realistic in 50% of the experiments. Sometimes, this can be attributed to the actual image's weak white adjusting, which our technology corrects and predicts will have a more typical aspect. In the cases to the correct side of the dotted line, participants were never duped.

This exercise compared the real image to the randomized baseline indicated earlier 87% of each of the people correctly identified the difference. This was done to ensure that consumers could complete 10% of the trials. The fact that they were able to recognize the artificial nature of these seemingly random colorizations shows that they were aware of their task and paying attention.Detection skills of the participants We had a few minor issues with our algorithm. The far right column contains instances of pairs in which users consistently recognized the fake image. Each pair was assessed by a minimum of ten testers. In spite of apparently great findings, close examination indicates that our colorizations for these photographs have glaring artefacts, such as the yellow spots on both of the automobiles.

Nevertheless, Table 1 demonstrates that 32% of buyers were fooled by our entire system. With the exception of Larsson et al., where the variation was irrelevant (when p=0.10; all stats obtained using boot-strap), this figure is significantly higher than other examined approaches. (In each example, p 0.05).These results demonstrate the effectiveness of using both the categorization and class rebalancing. The customers would only have a choice among two comparable images if our programme faithfully replicated the colours of the original image.

On 50% of their occasions, they scammed me based on my expectations. We were surprised to uncover situations when customers were deceived more frequently than 50% of the time, proving the accuracy of our findings. were regarded to be more trustworthy than the facts. Some illustrations are provided. In many cases where the original image is off-balance or has odd colors, our method yields a more typical appearance.

Raw accuracy (AUC): We calculate the proportion of predicted pixel colors in AB color space that are near the ground truth by less than a thresholded L2 length as the test of low level. Next, we create Using a cumulative weight function , the surface underneath the plot (AUC) was integrated, then normalization was performed using thresholds ranging from 0 to 150. It should be highlighted that while our method looks for plausibility, the AUC metric assesses raw prediction accuracy.

When trained on classification without rebalancing (when learned from scratch), our network outperforms our L2 counterpart. The performance of the L2 net is identical to that of the colour classification network when it is fine-tuned from it. This shows that while the L2 measure can generate precise colorizations, it is challenging to improve from scratch. The method developed by Larsson reaches a somewhat higher accuracy. Because of the AB value distribution in real-world photographs, this metric is dominated by de-saturated pixels. Because of this, even trying to predict grey for each individual pixel performs excellently, and our complete method with category rebalancing produces results that are somewhat comparable.

On the other hand, image regions that are perceptually interesting have an allocation of ab values with better absorption values. Hence, using Equation 4, setting = 0, we reweight the pixels inversely using colour class probability to calculate a class-balanced AUC metric. On this indicator, our complete solution beats all variations and comparing methods, showing that the training objective's class-rebalancing produced the expected outcome.

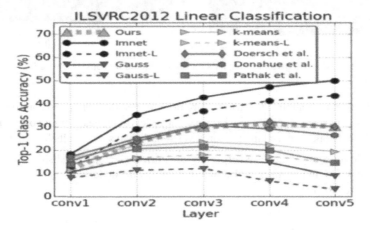

Fig. 38.4 ImageNet linear classification [1]

Figure 38.4 depicts an extension of the Image Net classification challenge. Internal layer linear classifiers are taught, while pre-trained networks are frozen. The characteristics are average-pooled using the same kernel and stride sizes as long as the feature dimensions are less than 10 k. Gaussian initializations and Image Net's k-means, respectively, were enact using grayscale (dotted) and color (solid) inputs.

3.4 Self-Supervised Feature Learning via Cross-Channel Encoding

Additionally, we consider how colorization might be used to communicate learning more effectively while simultaneously improving the colorization's visual appeal. Because both the input and output image channels differ, our idea is comparable to an auto-encoder, which is why the acronym cross-channel encoder was suggested.

We do 2 pairs of tests on our system to evaluate the extraction of features learned using this type of cross-channel encoding. By modifying the trained linear classifiers and the learned representation to classify objects in previously viewed data,, we first assess the features' ability to generalise to new tasks. Second, we use the PASCAL dataset to train the network   perform classification, detection, and segmentation tasks. This series of tests evaluates the acquired representation of data generalisation as well as holding-out difficulties. To compare favorably to past feature learning algorithms, we used our entire approach to retrain an Alex Net model on the colorization problem for 450k iterations. We discover that the resulting learnt representation performs better on item categorization and segmentation tasks than earlier approaches.

4. Results and Discussion

After the model had been trained, it was given images from the test dataset. Some photos produced results that appeared promising, delivering remarkably lifelike visuals. Some photographs may have performed poorly because to the short amount of data and lack of variability in the training set. The color of the dynasty attire, for example, was not recognized by the model. The result was bad coloration.

(a)   (b)

Fig. 38.5 (a) is the input image which is given to the CNN model and (b) is the output of the (a) which is colorized version

Source: Author

The algorithm performs better when certain image attributes are present. People seem to be comfortable with things found in nature, including the sky, trees, and rivers, for instance. However, not everything has vibrant colors. The dataset included 150 coloredotos. Figure, where the network produced their colored version, displays the results for a few test examples

Figure 38.6 shows the examples of some of the most perplexing categories. The top rows display the true image. The images in the bottom rows have been recolored. In parentheses, the rank of common misunderstanding. After re-colorization, the ground truth and confused categories are labelled.

4.1 Colorization in video

The only colorization outcomes that have been discussed thus far are those for individual photographs. The initial material was obtained from video sequences, despite the fact that it is clear from that the ultimate objective was to successfully colourize an entire image series.

However, many problems are not visible until the photographs are put together into an order. For instance, most things have a propensity to change colour with size or rotation; translation is less influenced by this since layers of convolution are translationally invariant and tiny filter sizes are used to counteract it. Similar results can be obtained using occlusion, but they are not as noticeable. These problems imply that the models still lack sufficient rotational or scale invariance.

There are no glaring improvements or losses between the variants, and the majority of these problems are shared by all model versions. As a result, there are strange-looking instances where objects' hues shift as they move erratically to the right or left to the camera or up or down in relation to it. Patterns seem better when they are made from photos that have undergone refining. Although colored consume enrichment results in significantly more appealing colorizations for single photos, it produces annoying color fluctuation between images when group size change and are arranged in sequences (when too much inconsistent coloring occurs). With the exception of objects that were fairly prevalent in the dataset (hats, faces, grass), the results are more consistent when using ensemble mean photos, with minimal flashing and evenly colored items. However, the colors appear darker and are generally less bright overall. Despite this flaw, in our opinion, the best-looking films are produced when average snapshots of the subdivided and colored images are combined with videos.

Finally, this is where the method fails; possibly because of the challenging nature of the set used for training (or rather, because of its small size), minor changes in an object's size, tilt, or even the location in relation to another object could end up resulting

Fig. 38.6 Examples of perplexing category images [1]

in substantial variations in colorization, resulting in chronological colour shifts that are audible. Even if the issues could be overcome by periodic filtering, picking important images still needs human intervention and aesthetic colorization adjustments.

5. Conclusion

Image colorization, a specialised area of computer graphics, is an illustration of a difficult pixel prediction problem. Here, we show how colouring an image with a deep CNN and a well selected performance metric may be even more effective at producing results and being accurate to actual colour images.

Our method works well as a visual output and as an incentive job for learning representations. Our network builds an extremely useful representation for object classification, detection, and segmentation despite only having been taught to recognize colors. This network performs better than current self-supervised previous training methods.

With the use of cutting-edge CNN techniques and authentic greyscale images, we have offered a fully automatic colorization solution. We have shown that the method can colorize certain areas of photos in a convincing and bright way, and that it has properties that could applied to sequences of video as well when employing the right loss function and color representation. Our algorithm excels with animals like cats and dogs since the dataset we chose, ImageNet, contains a large amount of photos of these animals. Even outdoor scenarios get good results with our methodology. The model also features an orange sunset. The model produces realistic images even with the sketches.

In this experiment, we have shown that Deep CNN can be used to effectively color photographs, as opposed to the more conventional human procedure. The objective of this study is to produce an output image that, although not necessarily being identical to the input, is realistically comparable to it. Other adjustments, such as image zooming and flipping, were made in order to prevent overfitting. High-level features are extracted using the model. This picture colorization technique makes use of deep neural networks to offer a successful, completely computerized the coloring answer, avoiding user tries and the dependency on the sample color image. The neuronal community receives and inputs a variety of informative yet discriminative functions, including are Patch, DAISY, and a brand-new semantic function. When utilizing combined bilateral filtering to ensure that the colorization is of high quality and artifact-free, the result color values are sensitive.

REFERENCES

1. Richard Zhang, Phillip Isola Alexei A. Efros, (2016). Colorful image colorization; (pp. 649–666)
2. Kim, H. I. and Yoo, S. B. (2020).Trends in Super-High-Definition Imaging Techniques Based on Deep Neural Networks.
3. Huang, Y. C., Tung, Y. S., Chen, J. C., Wang, S. W. and Wu, J. L. (2005). An adaptive edge detection based colorization algorithm and its applications.(pp. 351– 354).
4. Yatziv L. and Sapiro, G. (2006).Fast image and video colorization using chrominance blending. IEEE Trans. Image Process. (pp.112– 129).
5. Larsson. G., Maire. M., Shakhnarovich. G, (2016).Learning representations for automatic colorization. European Conference on Computer Vision.
6. F. Yu and V. Koltun,(2015). Multi-scale context aggregation by dilated convolutions, vol. abs/1511.07122, (pp. 3–20). IEEE.
7. Federico Baldassare, Diego Gonzalez Morn and Lucas Rodes-Guirao,(2017)Deep Koalarization: Image Colorization using CNNs and Inception-Resnet-v2, arXiv: 1712.03400.
8. Kreahenbuhl P, Doersch C, Donahue, J, Darrell,(2016) Data-dependent initializations of convolutional neural networks. ICOLR.
9. Varga, D., Szabo, C. A. and Sziranyi, T.(2017) Automatic cartoon colorization based on convolutional neural network(pp. 1–6).
10. Martínez B., Casas S., Vidal-González M., Vera L. and García-Pereira I. (2018) An edutainment augmented reality mirror for the dissemination and reinterpretation of cultural heritage.

Advances in Computational Intelligence and its Applications (ICACIA-2023) – Dr. Sheikh Fahad Ahmad et al. (eds)
© 2024 Taylor & Francis Group, London, ISBN 978-1-032-78612-4

Detection Mechanism for the Analysis of Malicious Script to Safeguard the Networked Systems

39

Md Nahidul Alam[1], Mayuri Kumari, Abishek Singh, Preeti Dubey, Avinash Kumar[2], Saptadeepa Kalita

Department of Computer Science and Engineering,
School of Engineering and Technology (SET), Sharda University, India

ABSTRACT—The world has seen footprints of cyber criminals for various years. The harmful code journey started from viruses and has reached tore powerful malicious code such as malware and ransomware. The ransomware and viruses have become one of the vital threats in the digital era. Now every person is connected with digital devices in the form of laptops, desktops, smart watches, tablets and many others. These devices highly rely on internet for its working at full potential, and hereby these devices provide gateway to malware and ransomware via internet. These may enter in the form of phishing mails, URL links, plug-in updates, and various other means. Therefore, it is important to understand the philosophy of malware and ransomware in order to understand its working properly and safeguard the system from malware and ransomware based cyber-attacks. The paper here explicitly discusses the detection mechanisms. Also, the work here depicts the most vital state-of-art concepts in order to demonstrate the penetrating mechanism of harmful and malicious scripts. The work also focuses on various recent approaches that could make the detection of these harmful scripts more efficient.

KEYWORDS—Malware, Ransomware, Machine learning, Deep learning, Feature extraction

1. Introduction

Virus (vital information under siege) A computer virus is a malicious software program that silently installs itself on a user's computer and performs malicious acts. It is capable of self-replication, attaching to other files or programs, and infecting them as a result.

In 1983, Fred Cohen provided the first official definition of the phrase "computer virus." No one ever gets a computer virus naturally. They are usually brought on by humans. However, since they are produced and dispersed, no one has direct control over how they diffuse. A virus that has infected a computer attaches itself to another software so that when the host program runs, the virus's actions are also activated. It has the ability to replicate itself, attaching to other files or programs and infecting them in the process. However, not all computer infections are harmful.

Malware is "software intended to damage or partially control the operation of a computer, mobile device, computer system, or computer network." The malware subcategory of software includes things like viruses, worms, Trojan horses, and bots. Malware and malicious code are common names for malicious software (malcode). It is computer code or application designed specifically to damage, interferes with, steals from, or otherwise violate the rights of hosts, networks, or data. Malware is also software developed with the purpose of damaging a computer, mobile device, computer system, or computer network or of taking over some of its functions. One of the most common types of cybercrime and one of the biggest issues with internet

[1]2019000321.md@ug.sharda.ac.in, [2]avinashkr338@gmail.com

DOI: 10.1201/9781003488682-39

cybersecurity that businesses are currently facing is ransomware. A type of malware known as ransomware starts by encrypting files and data on a single PC before spreading to servers and vast networks. There are just a few options left for victims: either they pay the cybercriminals behind the ransomware attack to gain access to their network's encryption, recover their data from backups, or hope that a decryption key will ultimately become accessible to the general public or else they start over from scratch.

The goal of Machine Learning (ML), a subfield of Artificial Intelligence (AI) in computer science, enables learning, reasoning, and decision-making without the need for Human Intervention (HI). Machine learning, to put it simply, allows people to enter enormous volumes of data into computer algorithms, which analyze, recommend, and make decisions solely based on the supplied data. If any adjustments are discovered, the algorithm will be able to use the data to enhance future assessments.

Data is the foundation of every business. Data-driven decisions are becoming increasingly crucial for staying competitive or falling further behind. With the aid of machine learning, it may be feasible to unlock the value of corporate and consumer data and make decisions that keep a corporation ahead of the competition.

For the purpose of securing IoT systems and devices, several studies have been conducted. To the best of our knowledge, no previous research has been done to compile the essential aspects that may protect the IoT system from cyber-attacks. This article provides cutting-edge solutions and bridges the gap between leveraging several critical technologies to protect IoT The main contributions of this paper are in brief, listed below.

- The different attack vectors that are developing in IoT and were previously available on a typical client-server system are presented in this paper.
- The most important IoT attack model that might be used to study the IoT system and its surroundings is presented in this paper.
- This study examines numerous measures that might improve consumer trust in IT-based systems.
- This paper offers some strategies that might be used to IoT to strengthen its defences against cyberattacks.

2. Literature Review

2.1 Virus Detection Mechanism for Android Platforms

H. K. Sk et al. (2022) depicts how AI plays a major role is reducing the time or space complexity of a give set of rules. Artificial intelligence more focus in finding the optimal solution without searching the whole solution space S. Jalali et al. (2012). Machine learning is a part of artificial intelligence in which machine learns and soft coded to solve any specific set of problems in minimum possible time without traversing the whole space.

There are various techniques that are used to make a proper pipeline of the workflow of model training. The first thing which comes is to understand the problem. There are two major things in machine learning before continuing in making of pipeline X. Q. Wang et al. (2014).

2.2 Detection of Virus using Genetic algorithm

Javaher et al. (2021) detects the rare and obfuscated classes of virus and possible potential future mutations of these virus that are caused by some metamorphic engines. For this purpose, seven different kinds of virus are randomly chosen that includes stealth, spywares, kernel root-kit, injector, blocker, boot kit, evader, and file less. The behavioral features of these seven types of viruses are extracted by unpacking them dynamically and therefore, by tracking their API calls at Windows Kernel level. A series of the system API calls with the help of the tracker-filter-drivers has been extracted in a sandbox environment. The elite selection method used to select the most obfuscated and metamorphic virus from the primary population. Elite Selection is done by maximization of the Malignancy Rate (MR) and minimization of the Tracking Rate (TR). The MR component is the malignity if the sampled virus behavior and the TR is the rate of detection of the scanners that shows the correctly classified malware's percentage. The behavioral chromosomes are the formation of the mapping extracted APIs to genes with the help of linear regression. The analysis system consists of an Inside simulator along with a human emulator for deceiving the intelligent classes of virus to successfully execute by them-selves and thus avoid machine halting. The evolution method is carried out by means of cross over and permutation of the genes that are encoded on basis on the location of the kernel-level machine functions. In order to make optimization of the important indicators of malignancy as well as tracking percentage with a linear time complexity, an objective function has been introduced. This confirms that the new generations created from parents' mutations can lead to more destruction and are stealthier as compared to their parents. Two popular models J48 and deep neural network models were implemented for classification in the domain of behavioral virus detection.

2.3 Virus Detection Using Deep Learning

X. Xing et al. (2020) processes the first step of this detection process is to transform the benign files and the virus samples to their corresponding grey-scale images by the process of decomplication of the APK files. This primary preprocessing step is required in order to proper input data for the ML Neural Network model. The extraction of the binary codes from the benign files and virus samples are performed from methods in software. Further, it is converted to decimal data bytes by bytes that are then fill up with the pixel values. And some information is converted to byte code for completion of the generation of grey scale images and then fill up the blank spaces with zeros.

Thus, after this preprocessing step, the grey-scale images had to passed two deep learning-based models for completing two tasks. The first model is termed as Automatic Encoder Network-1 (AE-1) and the second is known as Automatic Encoder Network-2 (AE-2). Autoencoders comprises of both encoding as well as decoding network. The purpose of the encoding network is for achieving dimensionality reduction. The purpose of decoding network is reconstruction of the input of the model. AE-1 is used for analyzing the feasibility, the features that corresponds to the software usage of the grey-scale images to represent. It is observed that using on one autoencoder AE-1 leads to less stability for the classification purpose, therefore AE-2 is also integrated with AE-1. AE-1 is unsupervised deep learning network where the input software samples are unlabeled. The AE-2 is supervised deep learning network. AE-2 classifying the input samples into two classifications i.e., malicious software and benign software's

The AE-1 autoencoder comprises of convolutional layers and lastly the up-sampling layers. Rule activation function is used in this network. AE-1 makes analysis if there is possibility of reconstructing the virus feature image based by taking in consideration of the numerical magnitude of the similarity of the actual sample and reconstructed sample. The structure of the second autoencoder AE-2 is like that of AE-1. The only difference is the additional external multi-layer perceptron. This facilitates for classification and evaluation of the network model. The output of AE-1 i.e., the high dimensionality features like virus as well as benign software is used for training the perceptron layer. This layer gives two-dimension vectors as output to detect the malware and benign software.

2.3 The Detection of Viral Variations Using Sequential Deep Learning and Drift Detection

A. A. Darem et al. (2021) mentioned the fundamental premise of drift detection is that the statistical characteristics of the dependent variable tend to change over time. The use of code obfuscation techniques by the creators of these infections is what causes these variations in representative features over time. As a result, it is advised to employ the statistical process control (SPC) technique for both drift detection and activating incremental learners. In binary classification, there are only two possible class levels: one or zero. One can assume that the sample will begin when the value approaches zero. If the result gets close to 1, the sample has a virus. The discrepancy between the actual class label and the expected class label acts as a warning indication when a prediction is off.

Three states—the control state, the warning level state, and the third, the out-of-control state—are constructed based on the categorization error distribution. When the average error rate stays within the parameters of the known error distribution, it is referred to as the in-control state or control level state. The distribution error threshold is crossed by the mean value of the anticipated error, which enters the warning level state. For future usage by incremental learners, virus samples are collected and stored in manageable buffer sizes in this scenario. Small windows and rapid batches are subject to the incremental learner until the error is minimized and reaches the control threshold. An "out-of-control state" is one in which the mean error rate tends to diverge substantially more than the reference error that is determined prior to the alert level. In this case, batch incremental modelling calls for a very big batch size. The batch consists of samples that have been incorrectly categorized from the warning state through this specific instance of the out-of-control condition. Since a smaller batch can cause bias issues in incremental learning, a large batch is necessary for incrementing. The terrible amnesia that results from this modelling is another issue.

2.4 Machine-Based Detection for Malware Images

A Cohen. El.al (2020) gives detailed about an increase in malware attacks with popular JPEG Image formats in recent time. Attackers hide the malware inside this kind of image in JPG format to look legit and attack the system as the image is downloaded into the system. In this research, concentrates on how machine-based detection can help in finding the malware image used by hackers to enter the victim's system.

The most common image format is joint photographic expert group, primarily due to lossy compression. Almost everyone uses it, from little businesses to major organizations and institutions. It is almost found everywhere from a single user to cyberspace. Due to its harmless reputation and large use cyber attackers use it to deliver a malicious payload to their victims.

2.5 Static Analysis for Malware Detection

Yan pan el. al (2020) describes that in recent times there is been an increase in android malware due to the pervasiveness of android software. As the attackers take the advantage of the vulnerabilities of the android software and enter the system of a user, it is a major concern to users because they steal and used victims' information for their benefit.

Static analysis can be utilized to efficiently counter Android Malware (AM). Static analysis still has a lot of difficulties, though. Therefore, depending on the present research community, it's essential to create some unique strategies for boosting AM detection. Additionally, it is crucial to have a uniform platform that is utilized to assess performance. There are several methods for effective Android malware detection. Android has grown to be one of the most popular internet operating systems thanks to the rapid expansion of the mobile market over the past two decades. So far 80% of the digital markets are captured by android, here it becomes the main target to be attacked.

Following the identification of closely related works, in this paper performed this systematic literature research to gain a complete understanding static analysis using Android Malware (AM) detection during the last few years (SLR). The following is a list of this SLR's key contributions.

- This SLR is conducted based on the salient features of the detection of android-based Malware using static analysis.
- Static analysis is efficient in detecting Android Malware (AM), and neural network models outperform non-neural network models, according to empirical evidence.
- Finally, we discuss it and present the upcoming work on Android Malware (AM) detection via static analysis.

This SLR's remaining sections are organized as follows. The general overall review and the research questions processes are presented in these Sections.

2.6 Static Techniques: Android-based Malware

One sort of code analysis is static techniques, which accepts input in the form of code, and then analyses the code without running it to verify the specification of the program. Compared to dynamic analysis static analysis does not need to run or execute a program to analyze it. Due to this advantage, static malware analysis has an upper hand in android-based detection over dynamic malware analysis.

Android characteristic for detection

This category primarily collects data about Android characteristics, which may be done using both configuration files and binary files with byte code programs. After that, other features like hardware components, approvals, API calls, and intentions can be gathered. These qualities are thought of as features, vectors that are used in predictive techniques or picked up by machine learning algorithms to identify malware on Android.

OP code-based method

The binary files of the APK are from where the opcode is taken. A large number of loosely packed files that each represent a class file for this program and are built up of a string of opcode sequences make up the binary files, which are composed of these files. In order to identify malware, this method focuses on combining deep learning or natural language processing models with opcode sequences as text.

Program graph-based method

The binary APK files are used to extract the program graph. In comparison to the two methods above, primary research indicates that more syntactic or semantic data can be gathered by the program graph. Program graph-based methods are therefore frequently used in research to evaluate and categorize malware.

Symbolic execution-based method

By substituting concrete variables for abstract symbols, symbolic execution simulates the execution of applications with high accuracy. In order to create expressions and limitations, these abstract symbols are used, solver could utilize them based on the conditional branches of the application's provided paths. Expressions and restrictions from malicious programs are then compiled into a rule library. Applications will be categorized as dangerous if their expressions and constraints match those in this rule library.

2.7 Ransomware Threat-hunting Technology

In this study work, F. Aldauiji et al. (2022) discusses cyber security intelligence and threat detection. Data analysis and Cyber Threat Intelligence (CTI) methods are used in cyber threat hunting, a cutting-edge proactive malware detection strategy. In order to identify strange behaviors, CTH systems mainly rely on internal data sources and proactive techniques. To boost the searching ability, an accurate CTI approach is needed to collect information from external data sets and integrate this with statistics from internal sources. The most efficient data analysis method must then be employed by the CTH methodology to unearth vital details regarding anomalous models in the early running activities.

Finding trustworthy information about cyber risks might help you proactively defend against current attacks M.F. Haque et al. (2021). Several CTI methods have been suggested for acquiring reliable information in a timely manner. CTI can offer comprehensive information about potential cyberattacks. For example, a phishing e-mail attack could contain number of crucial components, including the attack strategy, such offender or target data, as well as the equipment and software used to conduct the attack T. N Jagatic et al. (2007).

Numerous capabilities are required in order to supply complete CTI to unearth information. In-depth data analysis, experience with web crawling and anti-crawling programs, language competency, awareness of cyberspace conditions, and appreciation of the intricate designs of hazardous resources are all necessary for finding sources online S. Samtani et al. (2017). Repositories, IRC channels, and developer forums are just a few of the online spaces where material and information are shared. web crawling program, which frequently analyses web sources to find web content E. Uzun et al. (2014). A web crawler can be employed for a variety of tasks, including information discovery and extraction as well as the organization of web material.

The concept of CTH suggests combining a strong data analysis method with an efficient CTI method to identify cyber risks. A remarkable majority of the current foundation of CTH methods is the application of machine learning methodologies. The sections that follow provide descriptions of the CTH's main advancement patterns. Following are the approaches for hunting out ransomware and preventing it from getting into the system

2.8 Multi-classifier Network-based Ransomware Detection System

A. O. Almashhadani et al. (2017) have centered their attention on topics connected to Locky Ransomware. The Locky (Ransom Locky) family of ransomware, which was first released in February 2016, employs a hybrid cryptosystem and was recognized by Symantec as one of the biggest dangers from ransomware in 2017 Bleeping Computer et al. (2016). It is primarily spread through spam campaigns, although it can also spread with exploit kits like Neutrino and Rig. It searches for specific file types after infection and monitors the victim's devices, including network drives, for them before encrypting them with the AES and RSA algorithms K. Cabaj et al. (2017). PDF, DOC, and JPG are some of these file kinds.

One of Locky's distinguishing characteristics is the way it locates its C&C server using the Domain Generation Algorithm (DGA) D. K. Vishwakarma et al. (2017). Occasionally, malicious Office documents with macro capabilities seen in spam emails spread Locky. This attachment launches a downloader script that connects to a URL on the victim's computer, downloads Locky's executable file, and installs it. After being fully installed, Locky will attempt to locate and contact one or more of the following command-and-control servers in order to exchange encryption keys and do the harmful operations it was designed to do:

- It employs an encrypted list of hardcoded IP addresses to create a TCP session with its (C&C) Command and Control server (s).
- Locky tries to locate its Command and Control (C&C) server(s) via the Domain Generation Algorithm (DGA), which frequently produces many pseudo-random host names,
- If these hard-coded addresses are unreachable, that is, blocked, or the connection was interrupted.
- Locky keeps requesting the Domain Name System (DNS) for these names until the Command and Control (C&C) server(s) are located.
- Locky uses the NetBIOS Name Service (NBNS) protocol to search the local network for an earlier infected system that has proactively established the C&C server name if the DGA method also fails.

3. Conclusion

The paper has discussed most vital aspects of harmful scripts. It also explains the most important methodologies that could be best used for their detection in all set of computational system. The work will provide platform for future research work that could lead to more refinement in detection approach in order to avoid the catastrophic situation in normal working of system due to harmful and malicious code attack in the form of viruses, malware and ransomware.

REFERENCES

1. A. A. Darem, F. A. Ghaleb, A. A. Al-Hashmi, J. H. Abawajy, S. M. Alanazi and A. Y. Al-Rezami, "An Adaptive Behavioral-Based Incremental Batch Learning Malware Variants Detection Model Using Concept Drift Detection and Sequential Deep Learning," in IEEE Access, vol. 9, pp. 97180–97196, 2021, doi: 10.1109/ACCESS.2021.3093366.

2. A. Cohen, N. Nissim and Y. Elovici, "MalJPEG: Machine Learning Based Solution for the Detection of Malicious JPEG Images," in IEEE Access, vol. 8, pp. 19997–20011, 2020, doi: 10.1109/ACCESS.2020.2969022.

3. Bleeping computer, (2016). Locky Ransomware Information, Help Guide, and FAQ. [Online]. Available: https://www.bleepingcomputer.com/virusremoval/locky-ransomware-information-help

4. D. Javaheri, P. Lalbakhsh and M. Hosseinzadeh, "A Novel Method for Detecting Future Generations of Targeted and Metamorphic Malware Based on Genetic Algorithm," in IEEE Access, vol. 9, pp. 69951–69970, 2021, doi: 10.1109/ACCESS.2021.3077295.

5. D. O'Brien, "Internet security threat report ransomware 2017," Symantec Corp., Mountain View, CA, USA, 2017, p. 35. [Online]. Available: www.symantec.com

6. E. Uzun, E. Serdar Güner, Y. Kiliçaslan, T. Yerlikaya, and H. V. Agun, "An effective and efficient web content extractor for optimizing the crawling process," Softw., Pract. Exper., vol. 44, no. 10, pp. 1181–1199, Oct. 2014, doi: 10.1002/spe.2195.

7. F. Aldauiji, O. Batarfi and M. Bayousef, "Utilizing Cyber Threat Hunting Techniques to Find Ransomware Attacks: A Survey of the State of the Art," in IEEE Access, vol. 10, pp. 61695–61706, 2022, doi: 10.1109/ACCESS.2022.3181278.

8. H. K. Sk and M. A. V, "A Literature Review on Android Mobile Malware Detection using Machine Learning Techniques," 2022 6th International Conference on Computing Methodologies and Communication (ICCMC), 2022, pp. 986–991, doi: 10.1109/ICCMC53470.2022.9753746.

9. K. Cabaj, P. Gawkowski, K. Grochowski, A. Nowikowski, and P. Zórawski, "The impact of malware evolution on the analysis methods and infrastructure," in Proc. Federated Conf. Comput. Sci. Inf. Syst. (FedCSIS), Sep. 2017, pp. 549–553.

10. M. F. Haque and R. Krishnan, "Toward automated cyber defense with secure sharing of structured cyber threat intelligence," Inf. Syst. Frontiers, vol. 23, no. 4, pp. 883–896, Aug. 2021, doi: 10.1007/s10796-020-10103-7.

11. S. Jalali and C. Wohlin, "Systematic literature studies: Database searches vs. backward snowballing," in Proc. ACM-IEEE Int. Symp. Empirical Softw. Eng. Meas., Lund, Sweden, Sep. 2012, pp. 29–38.

12. S. Samtani, R. Chinn, H. Chen, and J. F. Nunamaker, "Exploring emerging hacker assets and key hackers for proactive cyber threat intelligence," J. Manage. Inf. Syst., vol. 34, no. 4, pp. 1023–1053, Oct. 2017, doi: 10.1080/07421222.2017.1394049.

13. T. N. Jagatic, N. A. Johnson, M. Jakobsson, and F. Menczer, "Social phishing," Commun. ACM, vol. 50, no. 10, pp. 94–100, 2007, doi: 10.1145/1290958.1290968.

14. X. Jin, X. Xing, H. Elahi, G. Wang and H. Jiang, "A Malware Detection Approach Using Malware Images and Autoencoders," 2020 IEEE 17th International Conference on Mobile Ad Hoc and Sensor Systems (MASS), 2020, pp. 1–6, doi: 10.1109/MASS50613.2020.00009.

15. X. Q. Wang, Y. W. Wang, L. M. Liu, L. G. Lei, and J. W. Jing, "WrapDroid: Flexible and fine-grained scheme towards regulating behaviors of Android apps," in Proc. Int. Conf. Inf. Secur. Cryptol. (ICISC), Seoul, South Korea, 2014, pp. 255–268.

16. Y. Pan, X. Ge, C. Fang and Y. Fan, "A Systematic Literature Review of Android Malware Detection Using Static Analysis," in IEEE Access, vol. 8, pp. 116363–116379, 2020, doi: 10.1109/ACCESS.2020.3002842.

Advances in Computational Intelligence and its Applications (ICACIA-2023) – Dr. Sheikh Fahad Ahmad et al. (eds)
© 2024 Taylor & Francis Group, London, ISBN 978-1-032-78612-4

An Electromyography Based System for Sitting and Walking Postures

40

Piyush Deshpande[1], Viraj Deshpande[2]

Department of Electronics and Telecommunication,
Vishwakarma Institute of Technology, Pune, India

ABSTRACT—An Electromyography (EMG) based classification of sitting and walking posture method is presented in this paper. This system is one of the models of lower limb prosthesis. Total 8 subjects participated to emulate sitting and walking postures. Bandpass filter of frequency of 10-200 Hz with sampling rate of 512Hz is applied. Zero Crossing time domain feature is effective to differentiate activities. Decision Tree, SVM, KNN and Random Forest classifiers are used for classification and recognition. Random Forest yielded maximum accuracy of 99.19%.

KEYWORDS—Electromyography (EMG), Machine learning, Detection of sitting activities, Detection of walking activities

1. Introduction

The Census of India 2011[1] disclosed that 20% of the handicapped people have disability in movement. Biological signals captured from electromyography (EMG) [2] devices can be used to solve problems related to motor disabilities. EMG signal measures electric current generated in muscles. These signals contain information of targeted muscle activity. Prosthetic/ Artificial limbs [3] can be operated by acquiring detected signals from impulses within skeletal muscles. EMG signals are of great importance to control various assistive aids.

2. Literature Review

2.1 Ownership Concentration And Stock Return

Acquisition of EMG signals is followed by removal of noise. As mentioned in [4]-[6], noise is generated due movement of muscle underneath the skin and thermal noise. Noise can be removed using various filters. Butterworth filter was selected in [7]. The reason included less overshoot time and quicker settling time in response to signal transients.

The classification explained in [8] was used to classify walking over flat ground, upstairs, downstairs, uphill and downhill. EMG signals of 27 participants were taken into consideration. Waveplus wireless EMG machine was used for acquiring of signals. The muscles of interest were rectus femoris, semitendinosus, soleus, flexor hallucis longus, extensor digitizing longus, vastus medialis, tibialis anterior, vastus lateralis and gastrocnemius. The experiment was performed with sampling rate of 1200 Hz.

Time Domain features were extracted in [9]. The extracted features were reduced using Principal Component Analysis. The reduced features were classified using Linear Discriminant Analysis. Upper extremity prostheses [10] are controlled by eight features. Activation of muscles [11] is computed through the energy kernel method. A group of time-frequency-based representations to improve the classification of myoelectric signal patterns is discussed in [12]. Auto regressive model (AR) is

[1]piyush.deshpande19@vit.edu, [2]viraj.deshpande19@vit.edu

DOI: 10.1201/9781003488682-40

a stationary model. This makes extracting features of non-stationary EMG signals difficult Adaptive model is non stationary and can be used to extract features. Individuals use muscles differently to perform the same tasks. The paper [13] exploited a control system for movement of EMG based shoulder movement using Mixed Reality (MR) device. Butterworth filter with frequency from 10-400Hz was applied. The obtained signals were classified using SVM and KNN. The results of this system were divided into reaching movements and reach to grasp movements. The reaching movements gave an accuracy of 32% higher than the conventional methods and reach to grasp gave an accuracy of 69% higher than conventional methods. EMG based prosthetic hand [14] was used to compute pattern recognition methods. Pattern recognition methods were calculated for 6 hand motions collected from 10 subjects and 2 transradial amputees. Features were extracted using 6 classifiers. Random Forest generated best results. Simple logistic regression gave the best results. The method [15] for improving the performance of EMG decoder in rehabilitation robots was discussed. The suggested mechanism offered bumpless switching mechanism (BSM). This produced smoother results as compared to decoder without BSM. An EMG based Musculoskeletal model [16] estimated continuous wrist motion. The mean R^2 value for all motion trials is 0.9. Prediction Compensation scheme for knee joint was employed in [17]. Variance, Mean and Absolute Deviation were extracted from PCA. Focussed time delayed neural network is applied on EMG signals to develop a controller. Activation of muscle is computed through the energy kernel method. A new method used rehabilitation robots [18] to assist joint motions was exploited to predict intentions of voluntary motions. Decision tree-based classifier was built in the system. A simple motion is divided into linear 6 inputs for activation of 6 arm muscles. Outputs include 3 outputs of voluntary forces of participants. The classification of finger movements and hand grips [19] was performed using EMG data from intrinsic and extrinsic hand muscles. The accuracy of the SVM classifier was determined to be 89.93%. Accuracy of 96% for nonamputees was observed. EMG pattern was classified using adaptive and block processing [20].

3. Methodology and Model Specifications

A system for classification of sitting and walking movements is proposed in this paper. An overview of the system is depicted in Fig. 40.1.

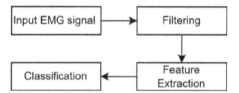

Fig. 40.1 Overview for classification of walking and sitting movements

Source: Author

3.1 Experimental Setup

The acquisition of EMG signals was carried out using Clarity Medical's EMG Machine. It is a 4 channel device having 2 electrodes per channel. EMG signals of 8healthy subjects were acquired. Movements of walking and sitting were recorded as depicted in Fig. 40.1. The system was used to record muscle activation data from participant's biceps femoris (BF), rectus femoris (RF), vastus medialis (VM) and semitendinosus (ST) at a sampling rate of 512 Hz, as shown in Fig. 40.2.

The subjects were told to sit in a relaxed position for 20-25 seconds as shown in Fig. 403(b). The subjects were then made to walk without altering displacement for 20-25 seconds. This process was carried out for all the participants.

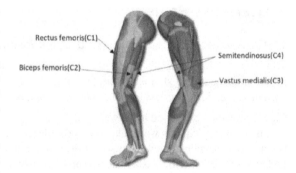

Fig. 40.2 Electrode positions for data acquisition [5]

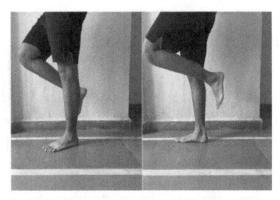

Fig. 40.3 Movements involving (a) Walking, (b) Sitting

Source: Author

3.2 Dataset Description

The recorded EMG signal data consists of 5 columns where the first column contains the time stamp and the remaining contains the data corresponding to each channel. The matrix for each activity has 8000 rows. The data is further divided into training and testing sets. EMG data acquired from 6 subjects makes the training set and rest of 2 subject's data builds the testing set.

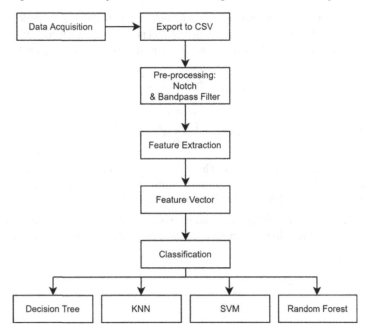

Fig. 40.4 Workflow for detecting lower limb movement using electromyography

Source: Author

The raw EMG data is collected from the EMG machine and the features were extracted to generate feature vector as shown in Fig. 40.4.

3.3 Preprocessing

The bandpass filter and the notch filter are used for preprocessing. The corresponding waveform for walking is as shown in Fig. 40.5. A notch filter with lower cutoff frequency of 49 Hz and higher cutoff frequency of 51 Hz is used to remove the noise of supply frequency of 50 Hz. A bandpass filter is used to filter the signal and contain frequencies within range of 10-200 Hz. This frequency range is selected as it is found that the surface EMG signal contributing towards class identification lie in this range.

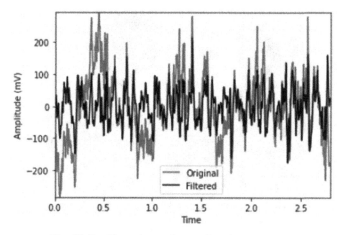

Fig. 40.5 Filtered signal using bandpass filtering

Source: Author

The comparison of filtered and original signal after applying bandpass filter is shown in Fig. 40.5.

3.4 Feature Extraction

The time and frequency domain features were extracted to form feature vector. In the frequency domain, features like frequency ratio, mean power, total power, mean frequency, median frequency, and peak frequency were retrieved. Root mean square, zero crossing, mean absolute value, average amplitude change, and absolute standard deviation were time domain characteristics.

$$\text{Variance} = \frac{\sum_1^m (y_p - u)^2}{m - 1} \tag{1}$$

$$RMS = \sqrt{\frac{1}{m} \sum_1^m u^2} \tag{2}$$

The variance in EMG signal was calculated using eq. 1. The average of the square of difference (y_p) and mean of data (u) is computed for finding the variance. Mean of the data (u) is used further to calculate root mean square (RMS) value. The total number of zero amplitude levels crossed by EMG signal is shown in Fig. 40.6.

Considerable difference between walking and sitting activities are visible in the boxplot as conveyed in Fig. 40.6. The box plots represent the distribution of data with the help of lower quartile, median, and upper quartile. The red line shows the median of the feature.

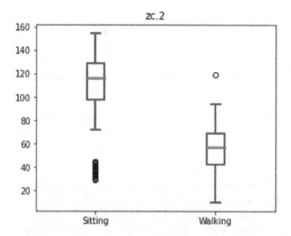

Fig. 40.6 Boxplot of zero crossing for sitting and walking activities

Source: Author

Algorithm 1: Zero Crossing Feature Extraction
Input: Time-series signal **Output**: Zero Crossing estimation **Initialize**: zero_crossing

1: count = 0
2: normal = mean + 3*standard_deviation
2: **for** dp in signal
3: mul = signal[dp] * signal[dp+1]
   diff = abs(signal[dp] – signal[dp+1])
   ifmul < 0 **and** diff > normal
   count++
   end if
4: zero_crossing.append(count)

Algorithm 1 depicts time series zero crossing feature extraction of signal. Overlapping windowing technique is used to generate features and values corresponding to 3 domains are calculated.

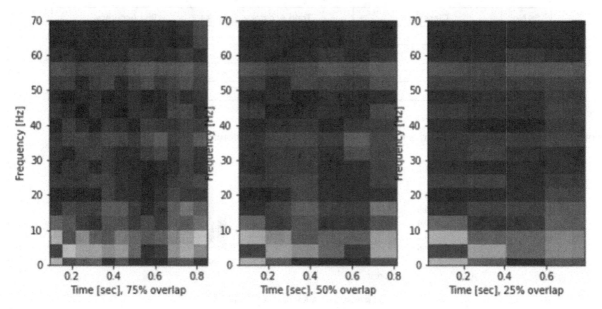

Fig. 40.7   Windowing of the signal with overlap of 25%, 50% and 75%

Source: Author

These values are appended in final feature vector. 50% overlapping is chosen for further analysis. The frequency distribution in 3 windows of different sizes is shown in Fig. 40.7.

3.5 Classification of Activities

The classifiers were provided with labelled data. Value of '1' was labelled for walking activity and '0' for sitting activity.

Classification is performed using 4 classifiers. Random Forest classifier combines the number of decision trees and takes the average to improve the accuracy. This combines the estimate from each tree, rather than depending on a single decision tree to estimate the final outcome which is based on majority of votes. The accuracy obtained in this work is 99.19%. The predictions Z of n trees each with weight function Ni, averaged in a random forest is given in eq. 3.

$$Z = \frac{1}{n}[\sum_{i=1}^{n} \cdot \sum_{j=1}^{m} N_i \left(x_j, x' \right) y_j] \tag{3}$$

A decision tree is a tree-structured classifier in which the internal node reflects the dataset's features, the branch represents the decision rule, and the leaf node represents the results. Decision tree gave a training accuracy of 90.32%. Support Vector machine (SVM) is used to find the optimum decision boundary for classifying n-dimensional space into classes so the next data points can be placed in the proper group. The accuracy of SVM turned out to be 50%. KNN technique is used to swiftly sort new data into well defined categories. The accuracy obtained was 77%. This is a method to classify a data point 'q', its k closest neighbors are retrieved by finding Euclidean distance D given by the eq. 4, resulting in a 'q' neighborhood Euclidean distance between $q(j_1, k_1)$ and the k-neighbors.

$$D = \sqrt{(j_2 - j_1)^2 + (k_2 - k_1)^2} \tag{4}$$

4. Empirical Results

The accuracies for the classifiers Decision Tree, Random Forest, SVM and KNN are achieved. Training and testing accuracies of various classifiers is represented in Table 40.1. For KNN classifier, value of K is chosen as 5. It has an accuracy that could give considerable predictions as compared to previously mentioned classifiers. But decision trees tend to overfit thus not suitable to give accurate results. Finally, the Random Forest classifier shows the maximum result in terms of testing accuracy.99.19% testing accuracy score is observed.

Table 40.1 Training and testing accuracies

Sr. No	Classifier	Train Accuracy	Test Accuracy
1	Random Forest	98.11%	99.19%
2	KNN	84.13%	77.41%
3	Decision Tree	90.32%	74.19%
4	SVM	100%	50%

Source: Author

The other performance evaluation metrics used are precision,recall and F1 scoreas shown

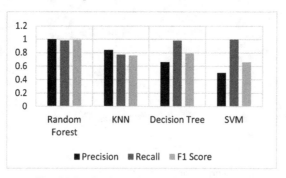

Fig. 40.8 Performance evaluation metrics

Source: Author

5. Conclusion

The system presented EMG based classification of sitting and walking postures. Acquisition of EMG signals was performed using Clarity Medical's four channeled EMG Machine. Electrodes were placed at RF, BF, VM and ST muscles as explained in Experimental Setup. The subjects emulated walking and sitting postures for 20-25 seconds per activity. The correctness of the data while recording was ensured. Time Domain, frequency domain and time frequency domain features were extracted using windowing technique. An array of five classifiers was used for classification. Random Forest provided highest testing accuracy of 99.19%. Authors will be using this system to develop lower limb prosthesis.

REFERENCES

1. Sample Registration System: Registrar General and Census Commissioner of India, Ministry of Home Affairs. (2011). [Online]. Available:https://censusindia.gov.in/census.website/

2. Y. Zhao, Z. Zhang, Z. Li, Z. Yang, A. A. Dehghani-Sanij and S. Xie, "An EMG-Driven Musculoskeletal Model for Estimating Continuous Wrist Motion," in IEEE Transactions on Neural Systems and Rehabilitation Engineering, pp. 3113–3120, Dec. 2020.

3. T. Sugiarto, C. -L. Hsu, C. -T. Sun, W. -C. Hsu, S. -H. Ye and K. -T. Lu, "Surface EMG vs. High-Density EMG: Tradeoff Between Performance and Usability for Head Orientation Prediction in VR Application," in IEEE Access, pp. 45418–45427, 2021.

4. Y. Huang, R. Song, A. Argha, A. V. Savkin, B. G. Celler and S. W. Su, "Continuous Description of Human 3D Motion Intent Through Switching Mechanism," in IEEE Transactions on Neural Systems and Rehabilitation Engineering, pp. 277–286, Jan. 2020.

5. U. Côté-Allard et al., "A Transferable Adaptive Domain Adversarial Neural Network for Virtual Reality Augmented EMG-Based Gesture Recognition," in IEEE Transactions on Neural Systems and Rehabilitation Engineering, pp. 546–555, 2021.

6. X. Chen, Y. Zeng and Y. Yin, "Improving the Transparency of an Exoskeleton Knee Joint Based on the Understanding of Motor Intent Using Energy Kernel Method of EMG," in IEEE Transactions on Neural Systems and Rehabilitation Engineering, pp. 577–588, June 2017.

7. J. Tryon and A. L. Trejos, "Classification of Task Weight During Dynamic Motion Using EEG–EMG Fusion," in IEEE Sensors Journal, pp. 5012–5021, 15 Feb.15, 2021.

8. A. A. Adewuyi, L. J. Hargrove and T. A. Kuiken, "An Analysis of Intrinsic and Extrinsic Hand Muscle EMG for Improved Pattern Recognition Control," in IEEE Transactions on Neural Systems and Rehabilitation Engineering, pp. 485–494, April 2016.

9. K. Kiguchi and Y. Hayashi, "An EMG-Based Control for an Upper-Limb Power-Assist Exoskeleton Robot," in IEEE Transactions on Systems, Man, and Cybernetics, Part B (Cybernetics), pp. 1064–1071, Aug.2012.

10. Y. Huang, R. Song, A. Argha, B. G. Celler, A. V. Savkin and S. W. Su, "Human Motion Intent Description Based on Bumpless Switching Mechanism for Rehabilitation Robot," in IEEE Transactions on Neural Systems and Rehabilitation Engineering, pp. 673–682, 2021.

11. M. K. Jung et al., "Intramuscular EMG-Driven Musculoskeletal Modelling: Towards Implanted Muscle Interfacing in Spinal Cord Injury Patients," in IEEE Transactions on Biomedical Engineering, pp. 63–74, Jan. 2022.

12. Seok-pil Lee, Jung-sub Kim and Sang-hui Park, "An enhanced feature extraction algorithm for EMG pattern classification," in IEEE Transactions on Rehabilitation Engineering, pp. 439–443, Dec. 1996,

13. E. A. Clancy and N. Hogan, "Influence of joint angle on the calibration and performance of EMG amplitude estimators," in IEEE Transactions on Biomedical Engineering, pp. 664–668, May 1998.

14. P. Geethanjali and K. K. Ray, "A Low-Cost Real-Time Research Platform for EMG Pattern Recognition-Based Prosthetic Hand," in IEEE/ASME Transactions on Mechatronics, pp. 1948–1955, Aug. 2015

15. M. K. Jung et al., "Intramuscular EMG-Driven Musculoskeletal Modelling: Towards Implanted Muscle Interfacing in Spinal Cord Injury Patients," in IEEE Transactions on Biomedical Engineering, pp. 63–74, Jan. 2022.

16. S. Togo, K. Matsumoto, S. Kimizuka, Y. Jiang and H. Yokoi, "Semi-Automated Control System for Reaching Movements in EMG Shoulder Disarticulation Prosthesis Based on Mixed Reality Device," in IEEE Open Journal of Engineering in Medicine and Biology, pp. 55–64, 2021

17. A. Dwivedi, Y. Kwon, A. J. McDaid and M. Liarokapis, "A Learning Scheme for EMG Based Decoding of Dexterous, In-Hand Manipulation Motions," in IEEE Transactions on Neural Systems and Rehabilitation Engineering, pp. 2205–2215, Oct.2019.

18. J. Ryu, B. Lee and D. Kim, "sEMG Signal-Based Lower Limb Human Motion Detection Using a Top and Slope Feature Extraction Algorithm," in IEEE Signal Processing Letters, pp. 929–932, July 2017.

19. Nyhof, Luke, Imali Hettiarachchi, Shady Mohammed, and Saeid Nahavandi. "Adaptive-multi-reference least means squares filter." In International Conference on Neural Information Processing, 2014. pp. 527–534.

20. Rechy-Ramirez, E. J., and H. Hu. "Bio-signal based control in assistive robots: A survey. Digital Communications and Networks, 1 (2): 85–101." 2015.

Advances in Computational Intelligence and its Applications (ICACIA-2023) – Dr. Sheikh Fahad Ahmad et al. (eds)
© 2024 Taylor & Francis Group, London, ISBN 978-1-032-78612-4

Comparison of Latency Minimisation Techniques and Performance Evaluation for Application Mapping in RTNoC (Real Time Network on Chip)

41

Shweta Ashtekar[1]

Assistant Professor, Department of Electronics Engineering,
Ramrao Adik Institute of Technology Y Patil deemed to be University, Navi Mumbai, India

Kushal Tuckley

Adjunct Professor, Department of Electrical Engineering,
IIT Bombay, India

ABSTRACT—In the last decade, to accomplish the High performance in Real time Embedded applications, the dependency on Multi core processor systems has been increased. A Network on Chip (NoC) provides a packet switched fabric for on chip communication and has proved real many core interconnect solution compared to shared bus approach SoC (System on Chip). One of the major challenge in Hard Real Time NoC systems is the Latency. This paper presents various approaches implemented for minimizing Communication Latency(End to End Transport Latency) as well as Computational Latency(Task allocation & Inter task Synchronisation).Efficient Mapping of application tasks on various cores contribute to Latency minimization. This paper also shows the experimental results of various mapping algorithms on Embedded applications.

KEYWORDS—Real time NOC, Communication latency minimization, Application mapping

1. Introduction

In today's era, for various high performance complex applications such as real time multimedia, Robotics, Communication, Aunomous driving, IoT (Internet of Things), Industrial etc, there is immense need of more scalable and powerful systems which supports parallel computations. The traditional bus based approach of MPSoC (Multiprocessor System on Chip) is less suitable to satisfy these huge demands of the mentioned applications because as the number of cores are increased the issues like power, QoS (Quality of Service), contention on communication leads to degraded performance, To overcome these limitations, NoC (Network on Chip) is an efficient as well as highly scalable interconnect solution or Communication architecture.

NoC an interconnect architecture incorporates multiple Processing Elements (PEs) which are connected with each other using routers. A PE is a node or core such as CPU, GPU, ASIC (Application Specific Integrated Circuit),memory controller or DSP processor. The Data generated by PE is converted into packets by NI (Network Interface) and then communication takes place between given source and destination using network fabric consisting of routers and interconnection links as shown in Fig. 41.1.

Realtime applications are most important part of the embedded systems field. But while using network on chips in real-time systems, there exists number of complex problems or constraints. In real time embedded systems having Multi core processors the processing time of any task depends on two components as the task execution time (time required for code in the specific core) and end to end transmission time required for sending data between number of cores and with memory. To provide reliable estimate of processing times, the predictability of mentioned components is essential. Transportation delays

---

[1]shweta.ashtekar@rait.ac.in, [2]kushal_tuckley@rediffmail.com

DOI: 10.1201/9781003488682-41

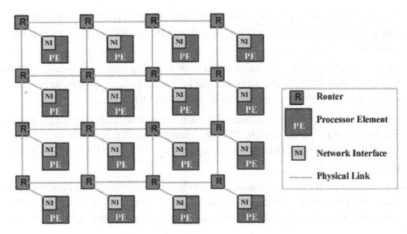

Fig. 41.1 Structure of 2 D Mesh (4 *4) NoC [24]

in between the NoC routers should be predictable so as to guarantee source to destination latency that should not exceed the assigned deadline for task execution. For NoCs in Real time systems (RTNOC) various complexities or limitations arises such as Latency, guaranteed, adaptivity, application mapping, scheduling, QoS (Quality of Service).

The real time tasks can be implemented using various models. One of the most preferred model is using Directed acyclic graphs (DAGs). In this model, each of the tasks is represented through different nodes with edges in between nodes which shows the data transfer which has to be carried out between the tasks.

The elaborate details of the paper are organized as: section II explains motivation for the implementation. Section III mentions about the survey of Latency minimization techniques. Section IV gives the results of experiments. Section V provides the future scope and conclusion.

2. Motivation

For implementing any real time application using NoC architecture, different complex constraints arises since the communication performance of real time system is dependent on getting correct results as well as following the execution and completion deadline. To behave the system correctly, both the communication & Computation between the different units must be completed within assigned strict deadlines. So Latency minimization is one of the major issue that needs to be focused in order to have guaranteed performance of the real time system. For each packet, the network latency should not exceeds the deadline assigned to it. The set of real time tasks transmitted over the NoC network are referred as scheduled if all packets of that set of tasks will meet the individual deadline.

The total Latency includes mainly two factors as Communication(Network or transport or end to end) Latency and Computational Latency. Communication Latency is determined by the size of packet, Bandwidth of the link, source/destination routing distance, delay for packetization/depacketization, delay at NI, Router delay, Network congestion delay, overhead as well as network traffic whereas Computational Latency depends on Execution time, Task Deadline and Inter task communication. Latency is a very crucial factor while working with Hard real time systems and reducing the latency can prevent catastrophic consequences resulting due to this latency.

3. Literature Review

This Literature survey provides detailed Study of current research approaches on Latency minimisation in Real Time NOC considering both Communication Latencies and Computational latencies.

3.1 Communication Latency

In paper[22],in order to get 2 to 3 times better performance than CONNECT which is an open source low latency NoC design targeted for field-programmable gate array (FPGA),a two clock cycle microarchitecture has been proposed in which an efficient request masking technique is proposed that will combine VC allocation with switch allocation The proposed technique is optimised considering area overhead and operating frequency. The research paper [23] summarises how to minimise the expected network transmission latency and reduce the resource consumption as well as power consumption by using optimised particle swarm optimization (PSO).

The paper[21]discusses an improved algorithm for application task mapping and scheduling on multi core platform. This dynamic algorithm is energy aware and for real-time situations an efficient resource allocation is carried out that will improve the deadline achievement. This algorithm also incorporates task migration technique.

Paper [20] has presented a micro architecture for NoC router for achieving low latency or single cycle latency for all packets transmitted in the same direction using a static straight VC/SW allocator (SSA). In order to achieve single cycle latency in existing methods a complex VC allocator or crossbar switch is required The proposed SSA is having simple architecture as well as works in parallel with earlier VC allocator.

A novel slot based scheduling algorithm for acyclic transaction sets in NoC is proposed in Paper [19]. The proposed algorithm has introduced a competitive sufficient schedulability utilization bound. The algorithm performs better while comparing with existing fixed priority techniques and also has less overhead by introducing parallelism between overlapped transmissions.

In paper [18] a more efficient algorithm is proposed in which task scheduling and core mapping is done separately. An Optimized particle swarm optimization (PSO) is employed in order to achieve the first stage with less task running as well as least task execution time the second stage is carried with the minimum expected network transportation delay and less resource & power consumption In order to optimise the system performance, along with total time spent, resource cost is also taken into consideration.

By introducing non pre-emptive regions to NoCs packets, and selecting a suitable length of such regions, Paper [1]has improved overall schedulability by reducing response times of some of the tasks. This will in turn improved the NoC core utilization by admitting more real time tasks or traffic whereas existing methods support static priorities. By using this technique the task pre-emption occurs in between transmission of consecutive flits.

An enhanced fault tolerant run time resource allocation strategy is presented in paper[2]. The proposed design algorithm provided an integrated scheduling with mapping method that considers effect of failure susceptible PEs during execution of application as well as application deadline and transportation energy failure-prone PEs on application execution. Application reliability can be improved effectively that selects a task using policy for task replication.

In paper [3] a Response time analysis (RTA) approach is used to check the schedulability of tasks & parameter of pre-emption threshold is used to schedule the release of invalid pre emption.In this the dynamic scheduling technique named DSPT (Dynamic Scheduling with Pre emption Threshold) implies improved success rate and reduces delay time.

In Paper [4] clustering of tasks as per the requirement of level of guaranteed services in various groups is done where using scheduling algorithm, each task will be assigned a priority. In case of congestion scenario, the highest priority tasks are allowed to go depending on priority aware arbitration policy. Both scheduling policy and arbitration policy limits the interference as well as simplify the worst case analysis and guarantees each of the service level.

The DHARA approach give in paper [5],based on checking packet's timing requirement the priority is changed dynamically to improve the latency. The latency improvement and count of late packets against increased latency for high priority packets.

The paper [6] focus on energy minimization by allocating task by proposed MOGA (Multi Objective Genetic Optimisation) algorithm which is capable of assigning fixed priority task allocation. The energy macro models along with real time schedulabilty are integrated into a multi objective fitness algorithm in order to meet timing constraints and energy is minimised. In case of dynamic situations, to guarantee schedulability, an algorithm by combining GESA and DEAMS(Deadline and Energy Aware Dynamic Mapping and Scheduling) is proposed. Task mapping of incoming tasks is done by DEAMS algorithm whereas priority assignment in set of tasks is done using modified GESA [7].

The paper[8] considers the scheduling problem aging-aware under the NBTI aging effect on the NoC system with the goal of optimal total completion time. This problem is formulated as a 0-1 planning problem. The article proposes to use the BPSO algorithm to solve this problem and compare it with the scheduling results obtained without considering the NBTI aging effect. The algorithmic results and HNOCS simulation experiments show that the scheduling aging-aware under the NBTI aging effect has lower make span and higher throughput rate, it also can adapt to different scale networks and it will be more reliable.

In this paper[9],to avoid the congestion, both spatial as well as temporal characteristics of communication are taken into consideration. While considering spatial feature, by utilising paths which are overlapped will estimate level of contention so that can be minimised during mapping stage only. Where as in temporal aspect, by adding additional latency, and sequential data transfer. An efficient algorithm that integrates local searching with genetic algorithm by applying different initialization and evolution process is proposed to optimise the design concerns and constraints..

In order to improve schedulability, a segmentation based RRA approach in real time systems [10]. The algorithm focuses on address transmission of both real time and Best effort traffic flows in same NoC. This solution provides low latency for best effort tasks and guarantees schedulability of real time traffic This proposed segmentation based approach efficiently improves schedulability of entire network after the result evaluation.

As shown in paper[11], based on various characteristics of NoC architectures and applications latency prediction will be decided. Various AI techniques are implemented to predict the latencies with approximate 99% of accuracy. Specifically for nine attributes, a Random Tree proved as latency Predictor.

By taking into consideration the multitasking ability of the processors, cost of communication as well as timing of tasks, various task allocation strategies are decided at design time. It has been observed from experimental results of proposed algorithm that there is reduction in network latency by 34.2% and communication cost by 26 %. The deadline is satisfied by 42.1% Also overhead of allocation time reduction is by 32% when compared with existing methods. [12].

3.2 Computational Latency

In this work of paper [13], a Petri net based modelling strategy is discussed that will provide an accurate prediction of the application. By considering core as well as path exclusions along with parallelisms were automatically considered in the simulation. The experimental results for the communication intensive mapping solutions achieved increased accuracy when application runtime is estimated. As there are limited number of processing elements in an NoC system, application mapping is key issue. As in paper [14], a hierarchical and dependency-aware (HDA) task mapping algorithm is proposed which covers the aspects of spatial mapping and inter-task dependency (temporal)in order to enhance the process of task mapping. From experiments results it has been observed that the HDA method can reduce the total processing time by up to 40.79% and 25.5%, respectively.

Shao et al. [15] has proposed a near convex region task mapping to support heterogeneous NoC platform. In such cases a dispersion factor, a centralization factor, and a natural strategy are utilised in order to select a convex region for deciding how many accelerating PEs should be used.

In [16], a PN model is provided for mapping of applications A stagewise process is elaborated so as to demonstrate how to represent a task using PN model and how to rearrange it to mapped model in order to utilise it. The mentioned technique supports task parallelism in two aspects as fully parallelism and pipelining.

Following are some of the factors affecting the Latency issues in Real Time NOC systems

- *Task Scheduling:* Task scheduling is important for defining the efficiency and performance of entire NOC system. Although there are numerous static or Dynamic scheduling algorithms exits still there is need for very efficient Hybrid scheduling techniques to be implemented.

- *Application Mapping:* After the communication infrastructure is selected, the next step is to allocate the processor cores that are executing the application tasks with routers is challenging in the overall system design The application mapping problem is critical since it directly affects the communication time, Bandwidth requirement and delay in the routers.

- *Resource Wastage to meet Stimulability:* Many real time systems are designed with extra resources to guaranty the completion of timing requirement or achieve schedulability of various tasks but that can lead to wastage of many resources.

- *Low latency NoC router Design:* Usually a latency of one clock cycle is ideal for NoC router to forward a packet or flit to the destination port when there is no issue of congestion or contention. For achieving this condition a newly came flit must go through every routers pipeline. There is need of NoC router which has low latency.

- *Congestion Avoidance:* One of the major contributing factor or reason for transmission performance degradation is network congestion in NoC systems. Various mechanisms still need to be designed so as to decrease the packet transportation delay and improve the overall network performance.

- *Overhead Reduction:* Overhead caused during the remapping for each task in case of Run time scheduling and mapping will affect the overall timing constraints. By proposing different hybrid approaches in order to reduce overhead that combines advantages of both design time and run time strategies.

- *Accurate Predictability by applying Machine learning techniques:* Various performance affecting factors such as overall latency of network, flit latency & hop count has to be considered since they are affecting the overall execution and architectural performance. Different machine learning or AI based algorithms needs to be incorporated so as to provide accurate measurements as well as predictions required for efficient framework.

- *Hardware Evaluation:* For actual realisation and synthesis of the system or application, hardware implementation on platforms like FPGA or Xilinx tools is required in many cases to get efficient processing systems and initiate a performance analysis between different designs and methodologies.

4. Experimental Results

An efficient Application mapping Technique helps to minimise the Communication and Computational Latency. Application mapping process involves mapping of tasks onto various cores or PEs in Network on chip systems.

To evaluate performance, the systemC /C++ based NoCTweak Simulator [17] has been utilised. The results are carried on (8 by 8) 2D Mesh Topology

For implementation following four Embedded Real Time applications are used for evaluating performance using Application mapping.

(a) MWD-Multi Window Display (with 12 Tasks)
(b) VOPD-Video Object Plan Decoder(with 16 Tasks)
(c) MMS-Multi Media System (with 25 Tasks)
(d) Telecom-E3S Telecom Benchmark(with 30 Tasks)

Platform description of Simulation Environment is shown in Table 41.1.

Table 41.1 Platform description of simulation environment

Parameter	Value
Router type:	Wormhole-pipeline
Routing algorithm:	XY Dimension-ordered
Pipeline stages :	3
Pipeline Type:	5
Input clock frequency:	2000 (MHz)
Operating clock frequency	2000 (MHz)
Flit Injection Rate (fir)	0.2,0.4.0.6,0.8.1.0
Buffer Depth (Flits)	2,4,8.16

Source: Author

The Two mapping algorithms in NocTweak Simulator as Random and NMAP are used to perform the following operations.

(a) By changing Flit Injection Rate (Fir) for the 4 embedded traffics and executing both the algorithms the Latency performance (Normalized Average Network Latency) has been evaluated as shown in Table 41.2 and 41.3 as well as in Fig. 41.2 and 41.3.

Table 41.2 Average network latency (cycles) using NMAP algorithm

Flit Injection Rate(Fir) (Flits/cycle)	Average Network Latency (Cycles) for Embedded Application			
	MWD (12 tasks)	VOPD (16 tasks)	MMS (25 tasks)	TELECOM (30 tasks)
0.2	12.28	12.084	11.822	11.97
0.4	14.05	13.579	14.1	12.71
0.6	27.65	426.076	1778.51	14.04
0.8	4117.32	2481.738	4466.761	18.03
1	7648.38	3473.406	5055.677	1145.013

Source: Author

Table 41.3 Average network latency (cycles) using embedded application

Flit Injection Rate(Fir) (Flits/cycle)	Average Network Latency (Cycles) for Embedded Application			
	MWD (12 tasks)	VOPD (16 tasks)	MMS (25 tasks)	TELECOM (30 tasks)
0.2	16.96	16.98	17.13	20.97
0.4	30.56	19.12	20.81	21.44
0.6	4246	288	3125	27
0.8	8896	5548	4942	2207
1	11800	9942	6697	4416

Source: Author's compilation

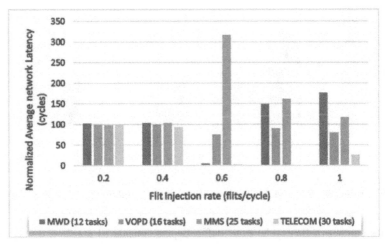

Fig. 41.2 Performance of average latency vs fir using NMAP algorithm

Source: Author

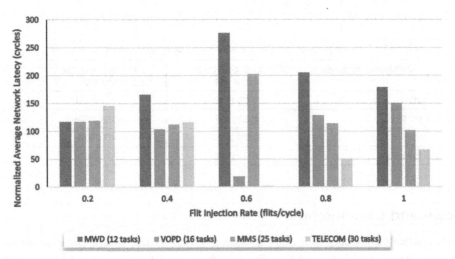

Fig. 41.3 Performance average latency vs fir using random algorithm

Source: Author

It has been observed that For each run, we change the value of "fir" so that we can get the results of network latency for comparison. Fir specifies the rate that packets or flits are injected into the router. The delay is sensitive to Fir and affecting overall network performance. At some point saturation occurs and due to congestion, the average latency gets reduced.

(b) By changing the Buffer size for different applications as shown in Fig. 41.4.

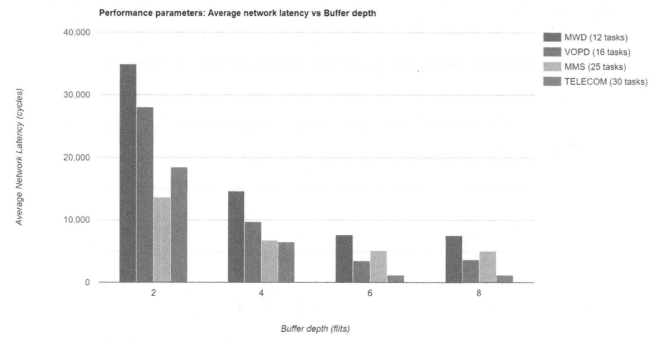

Fig. 41.4 Performance average latency vs buffer depth using random and NMAP algorithm

Source: Author

Buffer depth specifies number of flits/cycle. Four buffer depths considered are 2, 4, 8 and 16 flits per buffer queue. Clearly, increasing buffer depth improves network performance as shown in the Fig. 41.4. By increasing buffer depth from 2 to 4 and 8 reduces latency by almost 34.09% and 12.2% respectively.

(c) By changing the network size for the 4 embedded traffics as well as changing Fir and executing both the algorithms the Latency performance (Average Network Latency) has been evaluated using NMAP algorithm as shown in Table 41.4.

Table 41.4 Average network latency (cycles) by changing network size and fir

Embedded Application	Fir = 0.2 N/w size 8*8 6*6	Fir =0.8 N/w size 8*8 6*6
VOPD	12.08 17.73	2481 2633
MMS	11.82 17.51	4466 4579
MWD	12.28 18.04	4117 3924
Telecom	11.97 17.41	18.03 28.26

Source: Author

5. Future scope and Conclusion

NoC-based multicore platforms are emerging in implementation of various real time application domains such as cloud computing, automotive, avionic applications, and multimedia applications. The complexity of Latency problem increases in multicore systems when multiple real time applications are executed in parallel to maximize the use of system resources. By optimizing Latency (Computational & Communication), a better performance can be guaranteed for implementing various real time NoC systems. As a future scope, a hybrid approach for application mapping will be proposed and compared with the existing mapping methods for Latency Minimization or Optimization.

REFERENCES

1. Meng Liu, Matthias Becker, Moris Behnam, Thomas Nolte, "Scheduling Real-Time Packets with Non-Preemptive Regions on Priority-based NoCs", 22nd International Conference on Embedded and Real-Time Computing Systems and Applications, 2016 IEEE.

2. Navonil Chatterjee, Suraj Paul, and Santanu Chattopadhyay, "Fault-Tolerant Dynamic Task Mapping and Scheduling for Network-on-Chip-Based Multicore Platform", ACM Trans. Embed. Comput. Syst. 16, 4, Article 108 (May 2017), 24 page.

3. Wenle Wang, Yuan Wang, JiangYan Dai, Zhonghua Cao, "Dynamic Soft Real-Time Scheduling with Preemption Threshold for Streaming Media", Hindawi International Journal of Digital Multimedia Broadcasting Volume 2019, Article ID 5284968, 7 pages.

4. Z. Shi and A. Burns, "Real-time communication analysis for onchip networks with wormhole switching," in Proc. 2nd ACM/ IEEE Int. Symp. Netw.-on-Chip, 2008, pp. 161–170.

5. B. Sudev, L. S. Indrusiak, and J. Harbin, "Network-on-chip packet prioritisation based on instantaneous slack awareness," in Proc. IEEE 13th Int. Conf. Ind. Informat., 2015, pp. 227–232.

6. M. N. S. M. Sayuti and L. S. Indrusiak, "Real-time low power task mapping in networks-on-chip," in Proc. IEEE Comput. Soc. Annu. Symp. VLSI, Aug. 2013, pp. 14–19.

7. Khare, A., Nallamalli, M., Patil, C., & Chattopadhayay, S. (2018). Mapping and Priority Assignment for Real-Time Network-on-chip with Static and Dynamic Applications. 2018 4th International Conference for Convergence in Technology (I2CT).

8. Tu, J., Yang, T., Yin, L., Xie, S., Xu, R., & Sun, J. (2018). "Aging-Aware Task Scheduling for Mesh-Based Network-on-Chips Under Aging Effect. "Journal of Circuits,Systems and Computers. doi:10.1142/s0218126619501469.

9. Rongjie Yan, Yupeng Zhou, Anyu Cai, Changwen Li," Contention-Aware Mapping and Scheduling Optimization for NoC-Based MPSoCs", Vol. 30, 2020, Proceedings of the Thirtieth International Conference on Automated Planning and Scheduling.

10. Liu, M., Becker, M., Behnam, M., & Nolte, T. (2017). "Using segmentation to improve schedulability of RRA-based NoCs with mixed traffic." 2017, 22nd Asia and South Pacific Design Automation Conference (ASP-DAC).

11. Jeferson Silva, Márcio Kreutz,Monica Pereira, Marjory Da Costa-Abreu, "An investigation of latency prediction for NoC-based communication architectures using machine learning techniques", The Journal of Supercomputing (2019) 75:7573–7591

12. Suraj Pau, Navonil Chatterjee, Prasun Ghosal, Jean-Philippe Diguet, "A Hybrid Adaptive Strategy for Task Allocation and Scheduling for Multi-applications on NoCbased Multicore Systems with Resource Sharing" Conference 2021: The Design, Automation, and Test in Europe (DATE) Conference and ExhibitionAt: Virtual Event Grenoble, France.

13. MostafaRaeisi-Varzaneh,Hossein Sabaghian-Bidgoli, "A Petri-net-basedcommunication-aware modeling for performance evaluation of NOC application mapping",The Journal of Supercomputing, Springer Science+Business Media, LLC, part of Springer Nature 2020.

14. Hierarchical and dependency-aware task mapping for NoCbased systems. In: 2018 11th International Workshop on Network on Chip Architectures (NoCArc), Fukuoka, pp 1–6.

15. J. Shao, T.-Z. Chen, and L. Liu, "Incremental run-time application mapping for heterogeneous network on chip," in Proc. Int. Conf. High Performance Computing and Communication. IEEE, Jun. 2012, pp.485–492.

16. Sabaghian-Bidgoli H, Shahabi SA, Navabi Z (2014) A novel modeling approach for system-level application mapping targeted for confgurable architecture. Can J Electr Comput Eng. https://doi.org/10.1109/CJECE.2014.232605.

17. Anh T. Tran, Bevan M. Baas, "NoCTweak: A Highly Parameterizable Simulator for Early Exploration of Performance and Energy of Networks On-Chip," in Technical Report, VLSI Computation Lab, ECE Department,UC Davis, 2012.

18. Peng-Fei Yang and Quan Wang "Effective Task Scheduling and IP Mapping Algorithm for Heterogeneous NoC-Based MPSoC", Hindawi Publishing Corporation, Mathematical Problems in Engineering,Volume 2014, Article ID 202748, 8 pages.

19. Bach D. Bui1, Marco Caccamo2, Rodolfo Pellizzoni3,"A Slot-based Real-time Scheduling Algorithm for Concurrent Transactions in NoC", 17th IEEE International Conference on Embedded and Real-Time Computing Systems and Applications,2011.

20. Monemi, A., Ooi, C. Y., Palesi, M., & Marsono, M. N. (2016). Low latency networkon-chip router using static straight allocator. 2016 3rd International Conference on Information Technology, Computer, and Electrical Engineering (ICITACEE).

21. Monemi, A., Ooi, C. Y., Palesi, M., & Marsono, M. N. (2016). Low latency networkon-chip router using static straight allocator. 2016 3rd International Conference on Information Technology, Computer, and Electrical Engineering (ICITACEE).

22. Alireza Monemi, Chia Yee Ooi, and Muhammad Nadzir Marsono, "Low Latency Network-on-Chip Router Microarchitecture Using Request Masking Technique", Hindawi Publishing Corporation International Journal of Reconfigurable Computing Volume 2015, Article ID 570836, 13 pages.

23. Peng-Fei Yang and Quan Wang.,"Effective Task Scheduling and IP Mapping Algorithm for Heterogeneous NoC-Based MPSoC", Hindawi Publishing Corporation, Mathematical Problems in Engineering,Volume 2014, Article ID 202748, 8 pages.

24. Mohammed Amine Meghabber1, Abdelkader Aroui, Lakhdar Loukil, Abou El Hassan Benyamina, Kamel Benhaoua, Toufik Djeradi,"A Flexible Network on-Chip Router for Data-Flow Monitoring", The 5th International Conference on Electrical Engineering Boumerdes (ICEE-B) October 29-31, 2017, Boumerdes, Algeria.

Advances in Computational Intelligence and its Applications (ICACIA-2023) – Dr. Sheikh Fahad Ahmad et al. (eds)
© 2024 Taylor & Francis Group, London, ISBN 978-1-032-78612-4

Classification of Customers Using Machine Learning

42

**S. Vaishnavi[1], C. N. Sujatha[2], P. Archana[3],
P. Naveen Kumar[4], G. Akanksha[5]**

Sreenidhi institute of science and technology,
Department of Electronics and communication engineering

ABSTRACT—The most typical method of separating one customer from another in software's is to advertise a set of visitors as decoration and the remainder guests as standard. Client segmentation is crucial in both client service operation literature and software's. In this study, client data that has been manually segregated for a corporation is anatomized. Using actual data from payments made by the company's visitors, the research tries to solve the data segmentation issue. The result is searched inside machine literacy styles since they might be used to decipher issues with data operation. Different bracket designs that are used to differentiate between extras and regular customers in a client database are contrasted. Guest payment data in two dimensions is utilised as input variables (features), and the separation performances of the various approaches are contrasted. The k- means grouping technique is employed in this design to achieve this. Additionally, a two-factor dataset of certain patterns discovered in the retail industry is used to train the software.

KEYWORDS—Supervised learning, Machine learning, Advanced analytics, Fraud detection, Marketing communications Systems, Fraudsters

1. Introduction

Simply put, customer segmentation is the process of categorizing your visitors into different categories (for instance, by descriptive criteria like age). Associations can use it to better understand their visitors. It is simpler to form strategic judgments about product growth and marketing when you are aware of the distinctions across client groups. The possibilities for becoming a member are limitless and heavily depend on the value of the customer data you have available. There are various methods for segmenting clients, and they are based on four major categories of parameters. a geographical term The position of the stoner is the key to truly simple client categorization. Colorful methods can be used to emphasize this. By megacity, state, country, or zip code, for example. The structure, dimensions, and movements of visitors over time and space are taken into account in demographic segmentation. Gender disparities are often used by businesses to manufacture and sell products. Based on previously seen visitor behaviors that can be used to predict future behavior, behavioral segmentation was developed. As an example, popular brands or times when guests make the most purchases. Psychographic segmentation is a procedure that involves gathering information about consumers and classifying them into groups according to psychological characteristics like personality, way of life, social position, activities, interests, opinions, and attitudes.

Machine literacy techniques are great for understanding perception, spotting trends, and examining customer data. Intelligently intuitive models are essential tools for decision-makers. They can precisely identify client components, making it more

---

[1]vaishnavivaishuvaishu67@gmail.com, [2]cnsujatha@gmail.com, [3]archanap@sreenidhi.edu.in, [4]pochampallyn aveenkumar@gmail.com,
[5]akankshagujja23@gmail.com

DOI: 10.1201/9781003488682-42

challenging to carry out the task manually or using conventional logical methods. There are numerous types of problems, and each machine learning technique is best suited for a particular class of problems. A very well-liked machine literacy strategy for client segmentation is the k-means clustering procedure. There are more comparable clustering methods in addition to DBSCAN, Agglomerative Clustering, and Birches.

The purpose of client segmentation is to assist you in tailoring your marketing strategies to satisfy the unique needs of each consumer group. You also have a better opportunity to engage with your visitors thanks to this marketing strategy. Those are the reasons why customer segmentation enables profitable business with your visitors. Customer segmentation is the process of classifying a company's clients based on the characteristics they share. To maximize each client's contribution to the business, it is vital to decide how to connect with visitors within each segment. Today's firms face fierce competition, therefore every firm searches for strategies to boost sales. Statistics are the most important factor in every business decision. We are able to run a few processes to determine consumer interests using grouped or ungrouped facts. To extract database statistics in a form that is human understandable, data mining is helpful. However, we might not be able to extract the factual heirs from the complete dataset. Customer segmentation is heavily based on factors like age, gender, spend score, income, and demographics. By doing so, we are in a position to capture outcomes such as which products generate significant profits for the business or which age group shops the most, etc. Therefore, the company places a lot of emphasis on those demographic groups and goods that are less likely to result in increased profits for the business.

2. Literature Survey

Sausen, K., Tomczak, T., & Herrmann, A. (2005) proposed that the most recent findings in the field of CRM (Customer relationship Management) integration. It claims that CRM connection is essential to business success at the initiative or enterprise level after introducing the notions of relationship management with customers (CRM) and integration. It is evident that research has mostly focused on the particulars of those fields based on the findings of both internal and external market studies as well as a systematic evaluation of the literature of chosen papers in top journals across five disciplines. It's interesting to note that few people use suitable firm theories as a basis for their explanations of CRM integration. This report identifies areas for further study that are currently unexplored by researchers and practitioners alike.

Guozheng Zhang in oct 2017, he said that In today's overly competitive commercial environment, customer segmentation is a problem that is becoming more and more urgent. Research on the use of data mining technology in consumer segmentation has become more and more prevalent in the literature, with good results. But instead of working from a logical framework, the majority of them just segment customers using a particular data mining tool from a certain point. Consumer retention is another important goal of customer segmentation. Although earlier segmentation techniques could tell which group requires more attention, they couldn't tell which action to take based on the rate of customer churn. In this study, we design a new customer segmentation approach based on customer survival character and propose a framework for customer segmentation based on data mining. There were two steps in the new consumer segmentation process. First, customers are divided into various segments using the K-means clustering algorithm that have the same internal churn tendency (survival function). The second step of the procedure tests the accuracy of clustering and identifies a customer turnover trend by predicting each cluster's survival/hazard function using survival analysis. A dataset from China Telecommunications Company was subjected to the aforementioned methodology, and the results include some helpful management recommendations.

In July 2021, Dhiraj Kumar came to the conclusion that it was not a good idea to use the same modeling technique, email, text message, or advertisement to reach every customer. The needs of the client may change. A one-size-fits-all approach to business typically results in lesser levels of engagement, click-through rates, and ultimately, revenue. Customer segmentation will aid in resolving this problem. By selecting the right number of various consumer groups, you can better understand the variations between the various groups of your clients and meet their needs. Customer segmentation improves customer experience while boosting business earnings. As a result, segmentation is crucial if you want to beat your competitors and draw in more customers. Machine learning is unquestionably the most effective strategy.

It is better if there is was between the data and its cluster centroid. K-Means method is used to do this. The analysis of various approaches, results, and shortcomings of various authors is provided here. A technique for grouping products was suggested by Vladim'ir Holy et al. [1]. With the help of a genetic algorithm applied to both real and simulated data, the author posed an optimization issue. The pa parameter is the number of clusters. The method yields the opposite outcomes, the author demonstrated and proposed, if the number of clusters exceeds the number of categories. A categorization method was presented by Elham Photoohi Bafghi [2]. Customers are categorised according to their shopping and financial circumstances applied genetic algorithm, and precision is assessed. Customers with similar purchasing habits were grouped together. Customers are segmented, according to Jayant Tikmani et al [3],The K-Means clustering algorithm is used on subscribers of television companies. The study's main finding is that, out of 80 customers, 13 strongly agreed that television was essential. Only 16 consumers were in agreement, and 18 customers were firmly opposed. In spss, four clusters are created and put into use. K-Means algorithm was implemented by Yen-Chung Liu et al. on data in sequence. Based on their purchasing habits, the clients are divided into groups. The same customer may therefore be in different clusters, numerous clusters, or not in any clusters at all. It was carried out in MATLAB. An approach for a decision assistance system was put forth by Krzysztof Maecki [5]. Based on the website online users are viewing, the author designed a topology for them. Customers are divided into three categories: information seekers, online store visitors, and opportunity seekers. These four different client types differ by 95.9%.

3. Proposed Methodology

The terms "system analysis" and "requirements analysis" are synonymous. Additionally, the decision-maker may use it to reach a more knowledgeable judgment than he otherwise would have being able to in order to investigate the scenario, evaluate the project objectives, and break down what needs to be constructed and used to involve people in order to establish clear requirements, this approach comprises brainstorming and breaking the system down into its component elements.

3.1 Software Requirements

- Operating System: Microsoft Windows/Linux/MacOS
- Technology: Machine Learning
- Tools: Jupyter Notebook or Spyder
- Platform: Anaconda Distribution or Google Collab

3.2 Hardware Requirements

Processor:

- Any Intel or AMD x86 - 64bit processor is required as a minimum.
- Any Intel or AMD CPU with at least 4 logical cores and hyperthreading support is recommended. Intel i5 8th generation equivalent or higher is preferred.
- RAM: Minimum: 8 GB DDR4 RAM, Recommended: 8 - 16 GB DDR4 RAM or 8 GB DDR5 RAM.

In order to meet particular criteria, a service's architecture, components, subsystems, interactions, and data must be chosen. This process is known as system design. In a word, the implementation of system thinking to product creation is what it is all about. The methods for designing and analyzing computer systems that are object-oriented are fast taking the lead in terms of popularity

3.3 Architecture

Figure 42.1 shows the data flow model which describes the overall how the data related to customers are divided based on the parameters.

3.4 UML Diagrams

Classes that implement one or more interface classes are the most crucial components of any objects-oriented system.

A class is a group of objects with related attributes, methods, relationships, and meanings, as shown in the class diagram in Fig. 42.2 of this article. The sequence diagram draws attention to how the messages are time-ordered. With a focus on message time ordering, it mainly shows a collection of objects and the messages

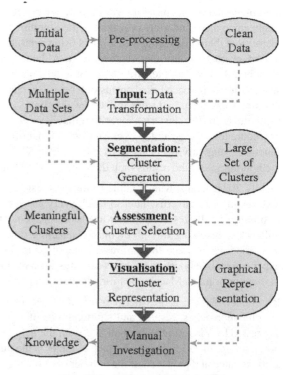

Fig. 42.1 Data flow of modal [14]

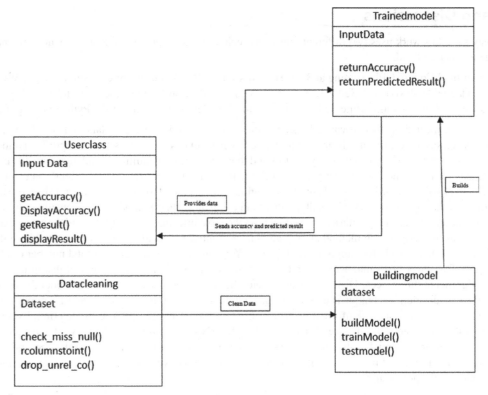

Fig. 42.2 Class diagram

Source: Author

sent and received by those objects. The sequence in which the elements of the interaction take place is demonstrated. Vertical (time) and horizontal (space), which are made up of distinct items, are the two dimensions that make up this. A named element that depicts a specific participant is called a lifeline in a sequence diagram. For each instance in a sequence diagram, a lifeline is utilized as a symbol. Lifeline components are found at the top of a sequence diagram.

3.5 Modules

Data Gathering module: This topic covers dataset gathering in order to build a machine learning model. This page contains the data that Wholesale customers gave. The dataset given to the wholesale client is fictitious and made available on Kaggle..

Cleaning the Dataset: The dataset provided by the wholesale customer will be cleaned in this module. The overall process for cleaning a dataset involves eliminating any redundant or superfluous observations, handling missing data, handling null values, etc. There are some categorical data as well as four useless columns in our dataset, which we will eliminate. In this case, we will use the Label Encoder from Scikit Learn to convert the categorical data to numerical (integer) data.

Training the Model: We will split the data into training and test sets using the two techniques discussed in the previous session, and then perform the simulation using the training dataset. K-means and DBSCAN implementations of two distinct algorithms will be employed in this project to train our model. On our dataset, we will train our algorithm in order to compare accuracy and choose the most accurate model for our predictions.

Testing the Model: After the model has been trained, we will test it using test data to see how accurate it is. Since then, we have created a vast array of modeling methodologies. We can select the model that most closely predicts client behavior out of all those under consideration.

Predicting using the model: We will make predictions about customer attrition using the most precise model from the aforementioned module for each input detail of the clients.

4. Result and Discussions

As was previously said, this work uses two different clustering techniques to implement client segmentation, and the crime is committed in the manner outlined.

External setup: An Intel Core i5 CPU running at 3.2 GHz and 4 GB of RAM is used for execution. We use WEKA (Waikato Platform for Knowledge Analysis) and Scikit-Learn. WEKA is a collection of machine learning tools developed by the University of Waikato in New Zealand, while Scikit-Learn is a machine learning toolkit for the Python programming language.

Data set: for client segmentation, this research leverages the Noncommercial visitor's dataset from the machine literacy repository at the University of California, Irvine. This dataset, which relates to visitors to a nonprofit distributor, includes information on the consumption of various items by visitors and their recurring expenditure. In all, there are 440 examples and 8 qualities. While each instance in the collection represents a client, the characteristics reveal each client's recurring purchases of various commodities. Two dataset attributes—Channel and Region—are excluded to facilitate the crime because they have little bearing on visitors' purchasing patterns. Additionally, rather than using any other method for segmentation, this article is more interested in taking visitors' purchasing patterns into account. As the most often used bone of its kind, k- means has indeed been selected in this study as the perpetration method among all cluster grounded algorithms. Kmeans must choose the value for k and the separation metric to utilise before applying to a dataset. You can estimate the relevant total number of clusters, k, in a variety of ways (18). This study takes into account up to five visitor clusters. Then, despite the fact that ultimately, they don't reveal that many significant differences, Distance measure and Distance measure are utilised as model for measuring for k-means. The "point Normalization" technique is used to evaluate all the values falling between -1 and 1. For our project, we used a dataset of mall customers that contained information such as Customer ID, Gender, and Age. To determine whether algorithm is more effective for the aforementioned data set, k-means and DBSCAN were compared. The very effective clusters produced by the K-means algorithm are essential to its effectiveness. But it can be challenging to figure out the appropriate cluster size. In this post, we focus on the optimal method, albeit there are a few additional ways to figure out the ideal amount of clusters. Below is a description of the procedure:

Elbow Method: One of the approaches most frequently used to determine the ideal number of clusters is the elbow technique. The WCSS value idea is used in this technique. "WCSS" stands for Within Cluster the Sum of Squares and refers to the term "total variations inside a cluster."

Table 42.1 Example of sample dataset used

	Customer ID	Gender	Age	Annual Income(k$)	Spending Score(0-100)
0	1	male	19	15	39
1	2	male	21	15	81
2	3	male	20	16	6
3	4	male	16	17	77

Source: Author

Table 42.1 represents Sample dataset it has customer Id which is unique for each customer, and Gender for distinguish between the male and female customer's Age, Annual income is the total income of individuals per year, spending score is nothing but amount they spent.

Customer segmentation is crucial in both literature and software on customer relationship management. Promoting a group of consumers as premium and the remainder customers as standard is the most popular method of differentiating one client from another. This research examines a company's manually segregated consumer data. By utilizing the company's actual data regarding the payments of its clients, the study seeks to resolve the data segmentation challenge. Since machine learning techniques are helpful in resolving data management issues, these techniques are searched for a solution. Comparing several classification techniques that are used to separate premium and standard clients from a company's database. The methods are contrasted based on how well they separate two-dimensional customer payment information (features) from other methods. For this, the k-means clustering technique is employed in this project. Additionally, the software is trained using a two-factor dataset comprising a few patterns gleaned from the retail industry.

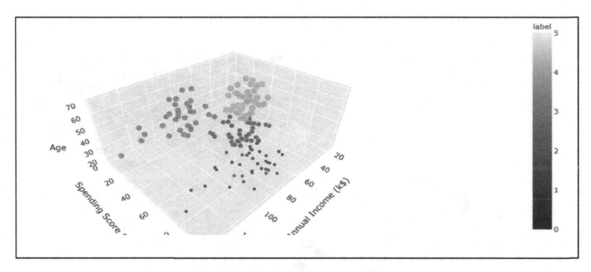

Fig. 42.3 3D plot for K-means algorithm

Source: Author

Figure 42.3 displays a 3D plot to represent the customers' spending score in relation to their yearly income. The five classes into which the data points are divided are each represented by a distinct color.

Elbow Plot

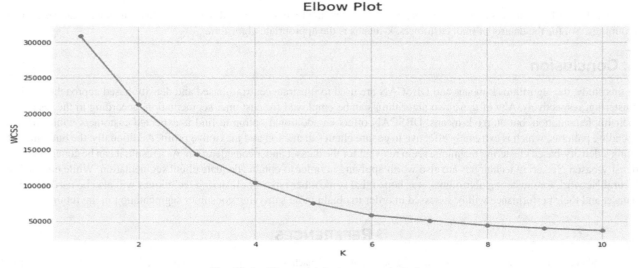

Fig. 42.4 Elbow plot for k-means clustering

Source: Author

Figure 42.4 shows using elbow plot for elbow plot Then, at the moment where it starts to drop, the Within Cluster Sum of Squared Errors (WSS) is computed for each of those k values. This appears as an elbow in the WSS-versus-k plot. The summary is contained in the list of actions that follows. When utilizing K-Means clustering, K can range from 1 to 10 clusters, WCSS can be calculated for each cluster, and K clusters can be plotted against the WCSS curve. In general, it is believed that the right number of clusters depends on where the bend (knee) in the plot is located. The best K is attained using the elbow technique, and K is shown to have a value of 5.

Figure 42.5 displays DBSCAN, or Density-Based Spatially Clustering of Programs with Noise. This approach, one of the most used clustering methods, operates based on item density. The epsilon and midpoint choices have a significant impact on DBSCAN. It is essential to understand how to select the epsilon and midpoint values. By making a small adjustment to these settings, the DBSCAN algorithm's results can be significantly changed. DBSCAN obviously failed to produce logical clusters. It is most probable because DBCSAN seeks clusters based on point density. DBSCAN won't recognize the least dense group as

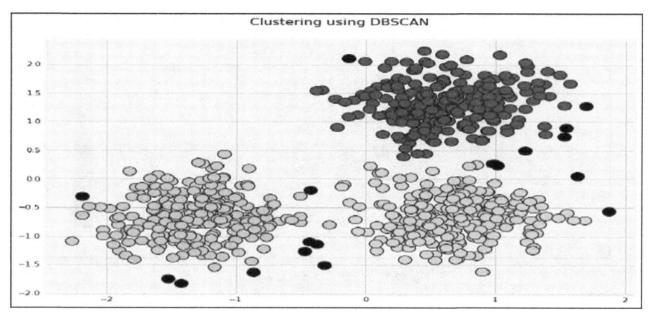

Fig. 42.5 2D plot for DBSCAN algorithm

Source: Author

a cluster if one of our clusters is less dense than the others, leading to less-than-ideal results. K-Means then generated plausible groupings. So, for the dataset of mall customers, k-means is the appropriate algorithm.

5. Conclusion

In this study, the algorithms k-means and DBSCAN are used to illustrate centroid-based and density-based approaches to data clustering, respectively. Any of these two algorithms can be employed for customer segmentation, according to the results of their implementation, but unlike k-means, DBSCAN offers an additional option to find unexpected customers with different spending patterns, which is extremely effective to ensure client satisfaction and maximize profit. Additionally, the outcomes of using a density-based clustering technique seem relevant for the dataset under consideration. As a result, it can be concluded that density-based clustering techniques are also worth applying in order to obtain adequate client segmentation. While employing Neural Network for clustering algorithms, it is hoped that some other types of clustering techniques will also be used on other dataset and their performance will be assessed in order to obtain more satisfying consumer segmentation in the future.

REFERENCES

1. Banduni, A. Ilavendhan,(2020) "Customer segmentation using machine learning", International journal of innovative research in technology, Volume **7**, Issue 2, ISSN: 2349-6002, July (2020).
2. "Customer segmentation based on survival character," IEEE, Jul.2003.
3. "Customer Segmentation Using K Means Clustering," Towards Data Science, Apr. 2019.
4. V. Vijilesh,(2021) "CUSTOMER SEGMENTATION USING MACHINE LEARNING," International Research Journal of Engineering and Technology (IRJET), vol. 08, no. 05, May 2021.
5. Expert Systems with Applications, vol. 100, Feb. 2018, "Retail Business Analytics: Customer Visit Segmentation Using Market Basket Data."
6. "CUSTOMER SEGMENTATION USING MACHINE LEARNING," IJCRT, AMAN BANDUNI and ILAVENDHAN A, vol. 05, 2018.
7. Tushar Kansal; Suraj Bahuguna; Vishal Singh; Tanupriya Choudhury, (2019) "Customer Segmentation using K-means Clustering," IEEE, Jul. 2019.
8. O. C. Kalu, E. & C (2015)"Application of the K-Means Algorithm for Efficient Customer Segmentation: A Strategy for Targeted Customer Services," vol. 4, no. 10, 2015, by Pascal Ezenkwu, International Journal of Advanced Research in Artificial Intelligence.
9. Dhiraj Kumar,(2021) "Implementing Customer Segmentation Using Machine Learning [Beginners Guide]," neptuneblog, Dec. 13, 2021.

10. K. Maheswari, (2019) "Finding Best Possible Number of Clusters using K- Means Algorithm," International Journal of Engineering and Advanced Technology (IJEAT), vol. 9, no. 1S4, Dec. 2019.

11. Dhiraj Kumar, (2021) "Implementing Customer Segmentation Using Machine Learning", July 10th 2021. Ashutosh Bhardwaj,(2020) "Silhouette Coefficient Validating clustering techniques," Towards DataScience, May 26, 2020

12. Sausen, K., Tomczak, T., & Herrmann, A. (2005). Development of a taxonomy of strategic market segmentation: a framework for bridging the implementation gap between normative segmentation and business practice. Journal of Strategic Marketing, 13(3), 151–173.

13. Kashwan, K. R., & Velu, C. M. (2013). Customer segmentation using clustering and data mining techniques. International Journal of Computer Theory and Engineering, 5(6), 856.

14. G. Lefait and T. Kechadi, "Customer Segmentation Architecture Based on Clustering Techniques, 2010 Fourth International Conference on Digital Society, Electronic ISBN:978-1-4244-5806-6. Print ISBN:978-1-4244-5805-9, DOI: 10.1109/ICDS.2010.47, Held on 10-16 February 2010, Saint Maarten, Netherlands Antilles. It is updated in the pdf file with name 42_ICACIA_KLH.pdf

Phishing Website Detection Using Machine Learning

43

Shaik Salman[1]

Computer Science and Engineering,
Kalasalingam Academy of Research and Education, Anandnagar, Krishnankoil

PonSuresh Manoharan[2]

Assistant professor, Computer Science and Engineering,
Kalasalingam Academy of Research and Education, Anandnagar, Krishnankoil

Sirgapuram Siddartha[3], Puttakokkula Bhanu Teja[4], Utsav Garg[5]

Computer Science and Engineering,
Kalasalingam Academy of Research and Education, Anandnagar, Krishnankoil

ABSTRACT—Despite the many protective measures available, phishing still represents a significant risk. Reactive blacklisting of URLs is still the main mitigation method. Because phishing sites are only active for a short while, this strategy is worthless. Because of this, more current techniques concentrate on proactive or real-time phishing URL detection techniques. PhishStorm, a system for automatically detecting phishing attacks, is introduced in this project. potential phishing websites. PhishStorm is capable of interacting frequently claim that the URL's top-level domain, path, and query have little to no link to the low-level domain, which needs to be registered. The use of experimental data is illustrated in this article. It can be utilised to support this observation. In order to achieve this, we define a brandnew notion of intra-URL relevance and assess it based on attributes gleaned from the words used to construct the URL and queries from the Google and Yahoo search engines. In order to identify phishing URLs from real-world data sets, these attributes are subsequently used in machine learning-based classification. Our system was tested against 96,018 authentic and phishing URLs, and it correctly classified 94.91% of them with only 1.44% of false positives. It has been suggested to expand an effective (>99%) URL phishing scoring system. Using large data architectures like STORM and sophisticated Bloom filter data structures

KEYWORDS—PhishStorm, HTTP, URL, Bloom filter, Big data, Phishing and legitimate

1. Introduction

Developing nations actively use the Internet to facilitate communication and access to information, and more recently, Internet applications have increased their user base. Because of this, communication and information transfer through social networks like banking, ecommerce, email, and social media applications like Instagram have significantly risen owing to the Internet and have a significant positive impact on our lives increase. On the other hand, security measures are disorganised, fall short in stopping a variety of online dangers, and do not shield users. Even for knowledgeable and experienced users, this is a serious security risk, and phishing assaults and other cyberthreats can result in substantial financial losses. Phishing is a deceptive online attack when fraudsters send messages to user accounts in an effort to get sensitive data, such as financial and personal

[1]salmanurscool@gmail.com, [2]Ponsuresh.techie@gmail.com, [3]siddarthasid1143@gmail.com, [4]bhanumudhiraj001@gmail.com, [5]utsavgarg439@gmail.com

DOI: 10.1201/9781003488682-43

information. Phishing attempts typically target official websites, credit card firms, or emails in an effort to steal financial data. There is a URL link that may be utilised to take the user to another page on her website after completing these tasks. Your connection is being made to what appears to be a false girlfriend website, and any data you share with it is being transmitted to phishers. In Q1, Q2, and Q3 of 2020, there were 165,772,146,994 and 571,764 phishing websites, respectively year, phishing websites totaling 884,530 different variations were found.

We found 180,768,182,465 and 266,378 websites in 2019 when we looked at it in the same order, for a total of 629,611 websites. This translates to an annual increase in phishing sites of almost 40%. Usually, in phishing assaults, phishers recommend fake websites. This website resembles his primary website in many ways, yet it has a misleadingly similar URL.This allows access to your identifying details The fraudulent URL's affiliation with phishing can be identified by a vigilant user. However, phishers cover up their con games by employing social engineering strategies and exploiting human weaknesses. As part of their misleading phishing scheme, phishers send emails that impersonate the legitimate email addresses of institutions and organisations. Users who open these emails are taken to dangerous websites when they click on them. These credentials were supplied by users of this website. An additional server is where this data is kept. In order to commit online crimes, phishers employ them. Different phishing strategies and tactics have been created as technology advances to acquire sensitive user data.

2. Literature Review

Literature research is the stage of the software development process that requires the highest importance. The time factor, profitability, and company strengths should all be considered when developing a tool. Following the completion of these, you must choose which programming languages and operating systems you can utilize to create your tools in the following ten steps. Once they begin creating tools, programmers require a lot of assistance from other sources. Dedicated programmers, books, and websites can all provide this support. Prior to the planned system being built, the aforementioned evaluations will be taken into account.

2.1 Phishing Website Classification and Detection Using Machine Learning

this article, we create a smart system that can recognize phishing websites. Machine learning models are the foundation of this intelligent system. This article's goals are to investigate the characteristics of phishing sites, choose the best systems to combine, and train a classifier using a classifier that performs better.

2.2 Phishing Detection using URLs and Hyperlinks Information by Machine Learning Approach

This article has detailed a variety of hyperlink detection algorithms and properties of URLs that can be used to tell harmful websites from good ones. There are six basic methods: fuzzy rules, machine learning, image processing, heuristics, and CANTINA-based methods.

2.3 Phishing Evolves: Analyzing the Enduring Cybercrime

The aim of this study is to summarize the condition of phishing at the moment, anticipated technological developments and short-term trends, and the best enforcement and preventative methods. About 60 IT security experts, "hackers," and academic researchers were interviewed for these statistics. An operational framework was supplied by routine activity theory. It's not a good enough excuse for most crimes, but it works for cyber crime. Despite the abundance of preventative methods, phishing is still a serious concern because the principal countermeasure still relies on reactive blacklisting of URL.

Lifespan of phishing sites, this technique is ineffective. As such, newer approaches rely on real-time or proactive phishing URL detection techniques. This project presents, an automatic phishing detection system that can analyze arbitrary URLs in real time to identify potential phishing sites. PhishStorm can communicate with any email server or HTTP proxy. Phishing URLs typically claim that there is little relationship between the part of the URL that requires registration and the rest of the URL.

3. Data and variables

3.1 Phishing Dataset

I made a phishing record with PhishTank. People can send phishing emails and websites using the community project PhishTank. Before being confirmed as malicious and blacklisted, suspicious phishing URLs are reviewed again by a number of individuals.

A list of legitimate and functioning phishing URLs is provided by PhishTank. Deprecated or URLs with simply and . b.REMurl = Additionally, we have already covered how to recognize such phishing domains. Following this decision, the phishing records contained 48,009 advanced phishing URLs. This indicates that fewer of url were blocked.

3.2 Legitimate Dataset

To provide further tutorial examples of legal URLs, we have selected URLs from the Open Directory Project A DMOZ is an online directory with more content than just phishing records with the, such previously defunct URLs. 48,009 valid URLs were kept out of the remaining group after uniform random selection. We constructed that is balanced (half are malicious, half are valid). We acknowledge that the mix of phishing and canonical URLs is not quite 50/50. But utilizing 10-fold cross-validation, is utilized evaluate efficency derived attributes in identifying phishing and genuine URLs. As was discussed in, cross-validating with unbalanced data sets can produce false results. These are feature-extracted URLs is Publicly available for research purposes.

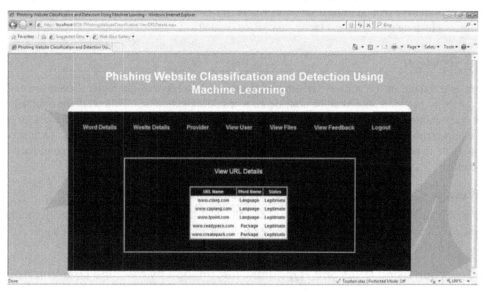

Fig. 43.1 URL details

Source: Author

3.3 URL Classification

Given the variety of supervised classification algorithms, a number of classifiers were applied to evaluate the dataset. We evaluated seven classifiers, including rules, functions, and trees. 10-fold cross-validation was used as a preliminary step to choose the most promising techniques before classifying without parameter optimization. True positive, true negative, and accuracy results for each classifier. For ease of definition, consider this URL:We define for URLs:

* Phishing classified as phishing: true positives (TP) and

$$TPrate = TP/(TP + FN)$$

* Legitimate classified as phishing: false positives (FP) and

$$FPrate = FP/(TN + FP)$$

* Legitimate classified as legitimate: true negatives (TN) and

$$TNrate = TN/(TN + FP)$$

* Phishing classified as legitimate: false negatives (FN) and

$$FNrate = FN/(TP + FN)$$

and the accuracy:

$$Accuracy = (TP + TN)/(TP + TN + FP + FN)$$

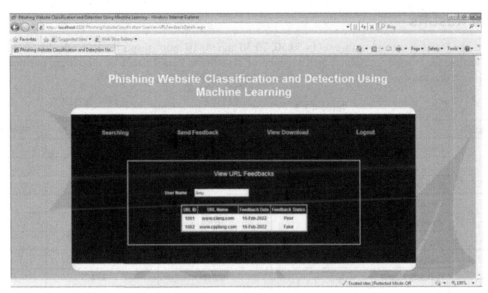

Fig. 43.2 URL classification

Source: Author

Table 43.1 URL classification based on phishing and legitimate

	Classified as phishing	**Classified as legitimate**
Phishing website	True Positive (TP)	False Negative (FN)
Legitimate website	False Positive (FP)	True Negative (TN)

Source: Author

3.4 URL Rating

Random Forest provides soft prediction values in the [0; 0] and [1] ranges. The identification threshold was established in the part before to assess a URL's phishing risk. However, it may be more effective to use soft prediction values in the [0; 1] range and some of their subranges to make judgements on URL phishing. Therefore, we looked at how often weak predictions about legitimate or phishing URLs occur.

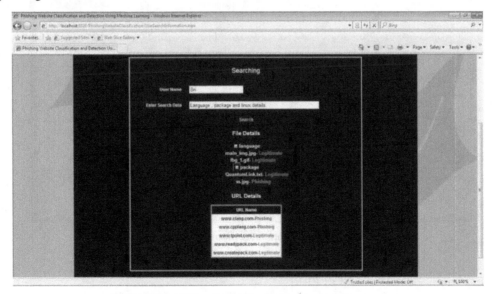

Fig. 43.3 URL rating with phishing and legitimate

Source: Author

4. Empirical Results

Dataset is divided into training set and testing set in 50:50, 70:30 and 90:10 ratios respectively. Each classifier is trained using training set and testing set is used to evaluate performance of classifiers. Performance of classifiers has been evaluated by calculating classifier's accuracy score, false negative rate and false positive rate.

Table 43.2 Classfiers permance table

Dataset split ratio	Classifiers	Accuracy score	False negative rate	False positive rate
50:50	Decision tree	96.71	3.69	2.93
	Random forest	96.72	3.69	2.91
	Support vector machine	96.40	5.26	2.08
70:30	Decision tree	96.80	3.43	2.99
	Random forest	96.84	3.35	2.98
	Support vector machine	96.40	5.13	2.17
90:10	Decision tree	97.11	3.18	2.66
	Random forest	**97.14**	**3.14**	2.61
	Support vector machine	96.51	4.73	2.34

Source: Author

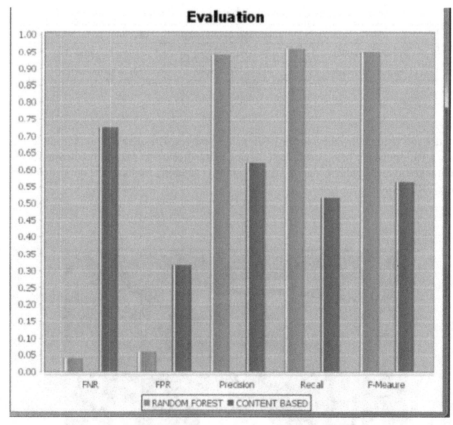

Fig. 43.4 Performance metric comparison

Source: Author

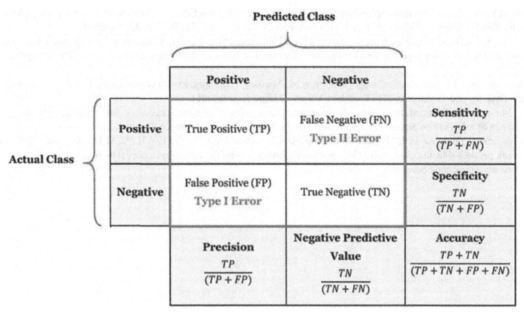

Fig. 43.5 Confustion matrix to URL classifier

Source: Author

5. Conclusion

With the use of lexical URL analysis, this project introduces PhishStorm, a powerful phishing URL detection system. On affinities in the URL, this strategy is built. This affinity represents how the words in the URL, particularly the freely definable portion of the URL, relate to the registered domain. We identify 12 factors that define internal relevance and popularity in URLs data set consisting phishing and legal URLs was supervisely classified using the suggested feature. The classification accuracy in this trial was 94.91%, while the false positive rate was a respectably low 1.44%. By adding a URL scoring system called PhishStorm that determines a URL's risk score on the fly, this experiment was made more extensive. Risk analysis of the test dataset is 84.97% of the dataset's phishing URLs and 99.22% of the canonical URLs can be recognised accurately. By using contemporary big data streaming architectures and patterns based on STORM and Bloom filters, we expanded the original approach to real-time analytics.

REFERENCES

1. Samuel Marchal, Jérôme François, Radu State, and Thomas Engel, "PhishStorm: Detecting Phishing With Streaming Analytics," IEEE Transactions on Network and Service Management, vol. 11, issue: 4, pp. 458–471, December 2014

2. Mohammed Nazim Feroz, Susan Mengel, "Phishing URL Detection Using URL Ranking," IEEE International Congress on Big Data, July 2015.

3. Mahdieh Zabihimayvan, Derek Doran, "Fuzzy Rough Set Feature Selection to Enhance Phishing Attack Detection," International Conference on Fuzzy Systems (FUZZ-IEEE), New Orleans, LA, USA, June 2019

4. Moitrayee Chatterjee, Akbar-Siami Namin, "Detecting Phishing Websites through Deep Reinforcement Learning," IEEE 43rd Annual Computer Software and Applications Conference (COMPSAC), July 2019.

5. Chun-Ying Huang, Shang-Pin Ma, WeiLin Yeh, Chia-Yi Lin, Chien Tsung Liu, "Mitigate web phishing using site signatures," TENCON 20102010 IEEE Region 10 Conference, January 2011.

6. Aaron Blum, Brad Wardman, Thamar Solorio, Gary Warner, "Lexical feature based phishing URL detection using online learning," 3rd ACM workshop on Artificial intelligence and security, Chicago, Illinois, USA, pp. 54–60, August 2010 [7] Mohammed Al-Janabi,Ed de Quincey, PeterAndras, "Using supervised machine learning algorithms to detect suspicious URLs in online social networks," IEEE/ACM International Conference on Advances in Social Networks Analysis and Mining 2017, Sydney, Australia, pp. 1104–1111, July 2010

8. Erzhou Zhu, Yuyang Chen, Chengcheng Ye, Xuejun Li, Feng Liu, "OFSNN: An Effective Phishing Websites Detection Model Based on Optimal Feature Selection and Neural Network," IEEE Access (Volume:7), pp. 73271–73284, June 2019.

9. Ankesh Anand, Kshitij Gorde, Joel Ruben, Antony Moniz, Noseong Park, Tanmoy Chakraborty, Bei Tseng Chu, "Phishing URL Detection with Oversampling based on Text Generative Adversarial Networks," IEEE International Conference on Big Data (Big Data), December 2018.

10. Justin Ma,Lawrence K. Saul, StefanSavage, Geoffrey M. Voelker, "Learning to detect malicious URLs," ACM Transactions on Intelligent Systems and Technology (TIST) archive Volume 2 Issue 3, April 2011.

11. Youness Mourtaji, Mohammed Bouhorma, Alghazzawi, "Perception of a new framework for detecting phishing web pages," Mediterranean Symposium on Smart City Application Article No. 11, Tangier, Morocco, October 2017.

12. Akihito Nakamura, FumaDobashi, "Proactive Phishing Sites Detection," WI '19 IEEE/WIC/ACM International Conference on Web Intelligence), pp. 443–448, October 2019 [13]https://www.phishtank.com/ developer_info.php, [Online].

13. https://www.phishtank.com/ developer_info.php, [Online].

Advances in Computational Intelligence and its Applications (ICACIA-2023) – Dr. Sheikh Fahad Ahmad et al. (eds)
© 2024 Taylor & Francis Group, London, ISBN 978-1-032-78612-4

VANET Routing Protocol Using Particle Swarm Optimization

44

Pallavi Golla, D. V. S. Akash,
S. Pranay Sai, Y. Sarada Devi

V. R. Siddhartha Engineering College,
Vijayawada, Andhra Pradesh

Ramasamy Mariappan*

School of Computer Science and Engineering,
VIT Vellore, Vellore, India

ABSTRACT—Vehicular Ad hoc networks (VANETs) are becoming quite popular, and new technologies are being developed within them. VANETs are used for a host of factors, including information transfer, delay reduction, and on a variety of parameters like delay, throughput, packet delivery ratio. VANETs employ a variety of protocols for service delivery. Ad Hoc On-Demand Distance Vector Routing (AODV), Dynamic supply Routing (DSR), Destination-Sequenced Distance-Vector (DSDV) and other routing protocols are reviewed from the current literature. This paper proposes a VANET routing protocol using a stable clustering-based approach called Particle Swarm Optimization (PSO) and framed up a methodology. Further to this PSO, Evolving Data Clustering Algorithm (EDCA), Grasshopper Optimization, Affinity Propagation clustering technique were the focus of this study.

KEYWORDS—Vehicular Ad hoc network (VANET), Ad Hoc on-demand distance vector routing (AODV), Dynamic supply routing (DSR), Destination-sequenced distance-vector (DSDV), Particle swarm optimization (PSO)

1. Introduction

A novel expertise is anticipated to deliver amenities for the passengers, such as security applications, driver support, crisis warning, etc., with the rapid increase in the number of vehicles on the road. As shown in Fig. 44.1, the concept of "ad hoc network refers to a certain type of wireless communication network that is created employing a collection of mobile nodes equipped with wireless transcription tools. Among the variants of MANET, the vehicular ad hoc network (VANET) has some special characteristics. These days, VANETs are becoming more common as a consequence of the requirement to care for the rising number of wireless devices which can be used in automobiles. VANETs provide a broad range of services, including information transfer, delay reduction, security, routing, and others [2]. For delivering those services and enhancing those performances, it employs various protocols. In this study, we focused on protocols for increasing the performance of the output parameters and for routing. Among them are the algorithms AODV, DSR, and Clustering.

As per their location claim and route updating technique, routing protocols for VANETs are primarily split into following groups:

(i) Position Based Routing Protocol
(ii) Topology Based Routing Protocol

*Corresponding author: prof.mariappan.r@gmail.com

DOI: 10.1201/9781003488682-44

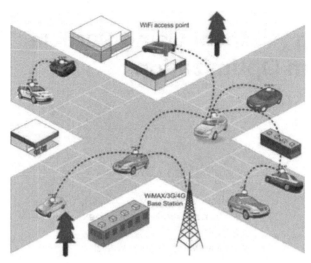

Fig. 44.1 Architecture of VANET routing [16]

(iii) Broadcast Based Routing Protocol

(iv) Cluster Based Routing Protocol

Focus is done on the topology-based protocol out of the protocols. It forwards the packet from the source node to the destination node using the information that is currently available about the network's links. There are several benefits and drawbacks to this approach.

Benefits:

The habit of a smaller amount of resources, they use minimal bandwidth and it is beaconless

Drawbacks:

Because of the rapidly shifting vehicles, it can possibly fail to detect a complete path and produce unwanted flooding. These can be broken down into three categories in general. They are:

(i) Proactive routing

(ii) Reactive routing

(iii) Hybrid routing

1.1 Proactive Routing Protocol

The shortest path algorithms are used to select direction path, and routine route updates are performed. The drawback of adopting this protocol is that maintaining unused route pathways takes up a significant portion of the available bandwidth. Proactive routing methods are inappropriate for vehicle networks because they are dynamic. OLSR (Optimized Link State Routing) and DSDV (Destination-Sequenced Distance-Vector) are the most often used proactive routing techniques [3].

1.2 Reactive Routing Protocol

When there were formerly accessible routes, at present in use at slightly given moment, reactive routing systems identify the path for routing based on necessity & preserve only the routing paths that are currently in use, thereby reducing network overhead. Many different reactive routing systems, like as DSR (Dynamic supply Routing), TORA (Temporally Ordered Routing Protocol), and AODV (Ad Hoc On-Demand Distance Vector Routing), have been implemented. Because there are no beacons, it consumes less bandwidth and therefore less memory [3].

1.3 Hybrid Routing Protocol

The system is fragmented to 2 areas by this protocol: local and global. Zone Routing Protocol (ZRP) reduces routing overhead and latency caused by the route discovery process by merging local and global reactive routing protocols to achieve greater efficiency with scalability. Although these protocols are still in use, cluster-based routing protocols have emerged as a result of technological advancements [2].

1.4 Cluster Based Routing Protocol

Vehicles that share alike features, like speed, route etc. are grouped to form a cluster. A cluster head is required to oversee the communication between various cluster nodes or with other clusters. It is capable of scaling well in huge networks. We reviewed a few clustering- based techniques in this work [2].

2. Literature Review

Several studies try to understand the impact of urban environment congestion on VANET routing using clustering technique. There have been tasks involved that rely on different approaches, yet smart approaches are suggested [1]. The works emphasize on clustering techniques and processes. The position, velocity, communication, data rate and neighbour list were taken into consideration by the researchers while using the affinity propagation clustering technique [5].

They used MATLAB software to simulate a real-world scenario including cluster maintenance. The average throughput of nodes, number of CHs, packet loss rate, packet delay, duration of CMs, duration of CHs, rate of CHs were the parameters considered. The GAPC algorithm uses the beacon signals to identify the out-of-the-ordinary vehicles that are within one hop of each other and creates a standard list of neighbours for each one of them. Utilizing the parameters of position and speed, the authors applied the affinity propagation clustering technique [6].

For real-time simulations without cluster upkeep, they employed MATLAB simulation software. Iterations and clusters were kept to a minimum, which is how well they performed. For adequate clustering information, the velocity component is the primary term needed. Grasshopper optimization technique considered the parameters like direction, location & velocity. MATLAB software was used to simulate a real-time scenario without the need for cluster maintenance. The number of clusters they used determined their performance [7].

The authors who employed the particle swarm optimization technique took into account the fitness function, velocity coding rules, and route particle. For simulation with cluster maintenance and a real-world scenario, they employed software NS3 and SUMO. Packet Delivery Ratio (PDR) and delay were the parameters studied [8]. The node density, transmission range, speed, direction were considered to understand the WO method by the investigators. Real-time scenarios and cluster maintenance were not employed, and the software used was not specified. The load balance factor and cluster count are the results they acquired [9]. The location and velocity parameters were taken into consideration when the authors applied the Spectral clustering algorithm [10], Force-directed algorithm, and Whole cluster stability algorithm.

For simulations with no cluster upkeep and real-time scenarios, they employed the SUMO and MOVE applications. In order to achieve system stability, the optimization target is the average lifetime of all clusters. They were successful in achieving average cluster lifetime and cluster size. Our approach is not sensitive to initial parameter values, according to the clustering size initialization value. Virtual location, comparative speed, and period of link established were taken into consideration by the authors when the Unified framework of clustering algorithm is used [11]. For simulation with cluster preservation but no real-world scenario, the software packages NS2 and SUMO were used. CH length, duration of CM, count of clusters, efficiency of clustering, initial cluster heads (CHs), CM disconnection rate, average role change rate, CM re-clustering latency, and re-clustering success ratio of CM were the parameters studied to understand the performance of the proposed system.

Compared to lower ID and one-hop VMaSC, UFC performed better in terms of cluster stability. The information of the route established was studied by authors by means of the path- based clustering technique. For simulations with real-time scenarios and no cluster maintenance, they employed the OMNeT++ and SUMO software. The results they acquired include the rate of cumulative cluster members, overhead total, collective data, and data rate [12]. Considering partitioning of grid and mobility of vehicle, the authors employed a center-based stable evolving clustering algorithm. With cluster maintenance and no real-time scenario, they employed the MATLAB simulation software. They measured clustering effectiveness, avg cluster head (CH) duration, avg cluster member duration, and counts. By 65% and 394%, respectively [13], it increased the efficiency of the evolving data clustering algorithm (EDCA) and the center-based grid partitioning (CEC-GP).

The authors took into account the vehicles velocity, position, direction, and traffic regularity while using the stable clustering approach [14]. For simulation with cluster maintenance and real-world scenario, they employed NS3 and SUMO software. Cluster head alterations are how they got their performance. The position, node density, link reliability and velocity were considered by PSO algorithm and the concentration of nodes points clustering technique. For simulations including cluster maintenance and real-world scenarios, MATLAB software was used. They achieved the following performances: CH lifespan, CM lifetime, average cluster size, Clustering efficiency, PDR, and delay [1]. A proactive routing system called Destination

Sequenced Distance-vector Routing (DSDV) is a variation of the traditional Bellman-Ford routing method. Each node in DSDV maintains a copy of a database that contains the location identification of a destination, the shortest separation metric to that route measured in bounce counts, and the position identifier of the hub that serves as the primary hop on the shortest route to the destination. The DSDV protocol has the drawback that it needs to update its routing table on a frequent basis, which drains more battery life and uses up little bandwidth [15]. DSR is an on-demand or reactive routing protocol. It is an easy-to-use routing protocol that is both effective and efficient that was created especially for use in multi-hop wireless ad hoc networks. The network completely self-sorts and designs itself; it does not depend on an existing system foundation or uniform structure. Course maintenance and course disclosure, the two key elements, work together to make it possible for source courses to be supported and revealed in this network. DSR protocol has a higher delay than table driven protocols [15], and the route maintenance mechanism does not fix a broken link locally.

A reactive routing protocol is the AODV protocol. It is designed to operate in ad-hoc networks where network act as routers and get their routes when they need to convey data. Updated routing table is used by AODV at each destination. The main benefit of AODV is that it tries to reduce overhead and efficiently use bandwidth by reducing the use of control messages. The main disadvantages of AODV are that it consumes extra bandwidth due to periodic beaconing, requires more time for connection setup, and takes longer to establish a route than other approaches [4].

3. Methodology

We mainly focused on cluster-based protocols and used PSO algorithm in this study because topology-based protocols have various limitations. The PSO approach is a member of swarm intelligence techniques family [1]. This approach is usually used to address optimization issues. The social behaviour of birds in a flock served as the model for the population-based search algorithm known as the PSO. Each entity serves as a particle representation & is regarded as predictable solution. The particles move at variable speeds in a hyper-dimensional search space. Each particle's position and speed are dynamically changing according to its own flying history and the individuals' socio- psychological tendencies, within the swarm.

The Particle Swarm Optimization (PSO) algorithm is a metaheuristic optimization technique that is inspired by the collective behavior of bird flocks or fish schools. The algorithm consists of a swarm of particles moving through a search space, where each particle represents a potential solution. The particles move toward the optimal solution by adjusting their positions based on their own experience and the experience of the swarm. Here is a methodology for implementing the PSO algorithm:

1. *Define the problem:* Clearly define the problem to be solved, including the objective function to be optimized and any constraints that must be considered.

2. *Initialize the swarm:* Define the number of particles in the swarm and randomly initialize their positions and velocities within the search space.

3. *Evaluate the fitness:* Evaluate the fitness of each particle by calculating the value of the objective function for its current position.

4. *Update the personal best:* Update the personal best position of each particle based on its best fitness value.

5. *Update the global best:* Update the global best position of the swarm based on the best personal best positions of all the particles.

6. *Update the velocity and position:* Update the velocity and position of each particle using the following equations:

   velocity = inertia_weight * velocity + cognitive_factor * random_uniform() * (personal_best_position - current_ position) + social_factor * random_uniform() * (global_best_position - current_position)

   position = current_position + velocity

   where, inertia_weight: controls the momentum of the particle and is typically decreased over time. cognitive_factor: controls the tendency of the particle to move toward its personal best position. social_factor: controls the tendency of the particle to move toward the global best position. random_uniform(): generates a random number between 0 and 1.

7. *Repeat:* Repeat steps 3-6 for a specified number of iterations or until a stopping criterion is met (e.g., the objective function value reaches a threshold or the maximum no. of iterations is reached).

8. *Output the result:* Output the best solution found by the algorithm, which corresponds to the global best position of the swarm.

9. *Parameter tuning:* Tune the parameters of the algorithm, including the number of particles, the values of the cognitive and social factors, and the inertia weight, to obtain the best performance for the problem at hand.

The presence of a memory enables each particle to remember its ideal location inside the search space. Experience or expertise have an impact on this change. By using this approach, the search solution is discovered in order to goback to the search space's top positions.

The PSO approach provides a number of benefits, including:

 (i) The strategy is straightforward to comprehend and use.
 (ii) There are not many parameters that need changing.
 (iii) The computing time needed by the approach is insufficient.
 (iv) The method is based not just on position but also on velocity.
 (v) It can swiftly condense.

The flow of the PSO algorithm is shown in Fig. 44.2.

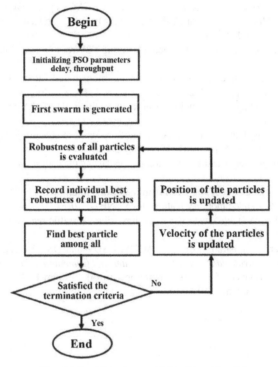

Fig. 44.2 Flowchart of PSO Algorithm [1]

The PSO procedure generates a people of evenly distributed elements in the search area and determines where each particle should be placed. Based on their discrete endpoints & the preceding ideal location, particles then update their positions and velocities. The algorithm then uses information sharing between the particles to identify the best answer. The method is iteratively executed, which means that it recurred until the criteria are met. This supports the algorithm's convergence completely.

4. Conclusion

In this work, we looked at a few VANET routing protocols and how they performed in terms of various metrics like delay, throughput, packet delivery ratio. We focused on cluster-based approaches because we noted that topology-based protocols had some limitations like more delay, average packet delivery ratio [1]. The major shortcoming with VANET routing is maintaining information transfer while a high vehicle density and mobility. Machine learning approaches can help with this. Additionally, machine learning can be applied into the maintenance stage to account in intricate models of traffic.

REFERENCES

1. K. Kandali, L. Bennis, O. E. Bannay and H. Bennis, "An Intelligent Machine Learning Based Routing Scheme for VANET," in IEEE Access, vol. 10, pp. 74318–74333, 2022, doi: 10.1109/ACCESS.2022.3190964.

2. Singh, S., & Agrawal, S. (2014). VANET routing protocols: Issues and challenges. 2014 Recent Advances in Engineering and Computational Sciences (RAECS). doi:10.1109/raecs.2014.6799625

3. S. Zeadally, R. Hunt, Y.S. Chen, A. Irwin & A. Hassan, "Vehicular ad hoc networks (VANETS): status, results and challenges," © Springer Science+ Business Media, LLC 2010.

4. Ding, B., Chen, Z., Wang, Y., & Yu, H. (2011). An improved AODV routing protocol forVANETs. 2011 International Conference on Wireless Communications and Signal Processing(WCSP). doi:10.1109/wcsp.2011.6096736

5. X. Bi, B. Guo, L. Shi, Y. Lu, L. Feng and Z. Lyu, "A new affinity propagation clustering algorithm for V2V-supported VANETs", *IEEE Access*, vol. 8, pp. 71405–71421, 2020.

6. T. Koshimizu, H. Wang, Z. Pan, J. Liu and S. Shimamoto, "Normalized multi-dimensionalparameter-based affinity propagation clustering for cellular V2X", *Proc. IEEE Wireless Commun. Netw. Conf. (WCNC)*, pp. 1–6, Apr. 2018.

7. W. Ahsan, M. F. Khan, F. Aadil, M. Maqsood, S. Ashraf, Y. Nam, et al., "Optimized nodeclustering in VANETs by using meta-heuristic algorithms", *Electronics*, vol. 9, no. 3, pp. 1–14, 2020.

8. X. Bao, H. Li, G. Zhao, L. Chang, J. Zhou and Y. Li, "Efficient clustering V2V routing based on PSO in VANETs", *Measurement*, vol. 152, Feb. 2020.

9. G. Husnain and S. Anwar, "An intelligent cluster optimization algorithm based on whale optimization algorithm for VANETs (WOACNET)", *PLoS ONE*, vol. 16, no. 3, pp. 1–22, 2021.

10. G. Liu, N. Qi, J. Chen, C. Dong and Z. Huang, "Enhancing clustering stability in VANET:A spectral clustering based approach", *China Commun.*, vol. 17, no. 4, pp. 140–151, Apr. 2020.

11. M. Ren, J. Zhang, L. Khoukhi, H. Labiod and V. Vèque, "A unified framework of clustering approach in vehicular ad hoc networks", *IEEE Trans. Intell. Transp. Syst.*, vol. 19, no. 5, pp. 1401–1414, May 2018.

12. M. Seo, S. Lee and S. Lee, "Clustering-based data dissemination protocol using the path similarity for autonomous vehicles", *Symmetry*, vol. 11, no. 2, pp. 260, Feb. 2019.

13. M. S. Talib, A. Hassan, T. Alamery, Z. A. Abas, A. A.-J. Mohammed, A. J. Ibrahim, et al., "A center-based stable evolving clustering algorithm with grid partitioning and extended mobility features for VANETs", *IEEE Access*, vol. 8, pp. 169908–169921, 2020.

14. H. W. Tseng, R. Y. Wu and C. W. Lo, "A stable clustering algorithm using the traffic regularity of buses in urban VANET scenarios", *Wireless Netw.*, vol. 1, pp. 1–15, May 2019.

15. Rajeshkumar, V., and P. Sivakumar. "Comparative study of AODV, DSDV and DSR routing protocols in MANET using network simulator-2." *International Journal of Advanced Research in Computer and Communication Engineering* 2.12 (2013): 2319–5940.

16. Modeling tools to evaluate the performance of wireless multi-hop networks Hakim Badis, Abderrezak Rachedi, in Modeling and Simulation of Computer Networks and Systems, 2015.

Printed in the United States
by Baker & Taylor Publisher Services